DISCARD

BETHANY COLLEGE LIBRARY

Quiet Revolution

QUIET
REVOLUTION

The Struggle for the
Democratic Party
and the Shaping
of Post-Reform Politics

BYRON E. SHAFER

Russell Sage Foundation   *New York*

The Russell Sage Foundation

The Russell Sage Foundation, one of the oldest of America's general purpose foundations, was established in 1907 by Mrs. Margaret Olivia Sage for "the improvement of social and living conditions in the United States." The Foundation seeks to fulfill this mandate by fostering the development and dissemination of knowledge about the political, social, and economic problems of America. It conducts research in the social sciences and public policy, and publishes books and pamphlets that derive from this research.

The Foundation provides support for individual scholars and collaborates with other granting agencies and academic institutions in studies of social problems. It maintains a professional staff of social scientists who engage in their own research as well as advise on Foundation programs and projects. The Foundation also conducts a Visiting Scholar Program, under which established scholars working in areas of current interest to the Foundation join the staff for a year to consult and to continue their own research and writing. Finally, a Postdoctoral Fellowship Program enables promising young scholars to devote full time to their research while in residence for a year at the Foundation.

The Board of Trustees is responsible for the general policies and oversight of the Foundation, while the immediate administrative direction of the program and staff is vested in the President, assisted by the officers and staff. The President bears final responsibility for the decision to publish a manuscript as a Russell Sage Foundation book. In reaching a judgment on the competence, accuracy, and objectivity of each study, the President is advised by the staff and a panel of special readers.

The conclusions and interpretations in Russell Sage Foundation publications are those of the authors and not of the Foundation, its Trustees, or its staff. Publication by the Foundation, therefore, does not imply endorsement of the contents of the study. It does signify that the manuscript has been reviewed by competent scholars in the field and that the Foundation finds it worthy of public consideration.

Library of Congress Catalog Number: 83–61130
Standard Book Number: 0–87154–765–1

For the Fathers

Edmond F. Dwyer
Robert K. Merton
B. Henry Shafer

Who Waited Patiently

CONTENTS

PART II

The Politics of Implementation

CONTENTS

Appendices, Acknowledgments, and Notes

Quiet Revolution

INTRODUCTION

The Hidden Struggle: Reform Politics, Institutional Change, and the Circulation of Elites, 1968–1972

IN WHICH, the extent of the change in the mechanics of presidential selection as a result of reform politics is highlighted; the implications of this institutional change for the dominant groups within the dominant party in American national politics are emphasized; and the continuing consequences of what began as a conflict between opposing coalitions of Democratic elites are suggested. AND IN WHICH, the major chronological divisions within the historical narrative are outlined; the themes of the book—reform politics, institutional change, and the circulation of elites—are introduced; and the architecture of the chapters developing both this historical account and these basic themes is presented.

ON JANUARY 24, 1972, Iowa Democrats assembled in local precinct meetings to begin selecting a state delegation to the 1972 Democratic National Convention. In doing so, they inaugurated a new era in American presidential politics. The handful among the eligibles who turned out in a gradually intensifying snowstorm are not likely to enter the history books for their political clairvoyance. Their favorite, Senator Edmund S. Muskie of Maine, was to be knocked from the nomination race almost exactly three months after they offered him his initial delegate support. But by virtue of their January date for delegate selection, Iowa Democrats did become the first participants in a revamped process of presidential nomination, a process which had undergone a collection of reforms so extensive as to be effectively unprecedented in American history.

The sheer amount of formal change in the mechanics of delegate selection between 1968 and 1972, quite apart from its practical impact on presidential politics and on a crucial, continuing group of national political actors, marked this period as noteworthy. Not surprisingly, structural change of this magnitude did not progress in an orderly and methodical manner, with opponents bowing to a superior virtue and then rushing to join the cause. Instead, it had a politics all its own. This book is the story of that other politics, the politics of Democratic party reform.

The reform narrative which constitutes the largest single element of the book attempts a careful reconstruction of internal party politics between 1968 and 1972. But this chronicle is presented to explain the arrival of a revolutionary change in the mechanics of presidential selection, the greatest systematically planned and centrally imposed shift in the institutions of delegate selection in all of American history. This institutional change, in turn, is linked continually to the rise of a new coalition of Democratic elites and to the possibility that this aspiring coalition has replaced an older, established version as the dominant force in the majority party in American national politics. As a result, the book, at its maximum extension, is an effort to portray the reshaping of political life in modern America, the rise of the institutional arrangements and specialized actors which differentiate this politics from its predecessors and which characterize it into the foreseeable future.

The underlying chronicle divides almost naturally into a politics of recommendation, where the substance of party reform was at issue, and a politics of implementation, where the fate of recommended reforms was determined. The book, of course, follows this division. The bruising National Convention of 1968 confronted the Democrats with a crisis, to which a national reform commission was a plausible response (chapter 1). During what became the politics of recommendation, this commission provided a forum within which diverse individuals and organizations could contend over the proper definition of party reform (chapters 2–8). The framing of an aggressive reform document by the victors in this struggle then contributed an extended, intricate, and far more consequential politics of implementation—where these recommendations were successfully converted into real institutions of delegate selection, with the potential for altering not just presidential politics but national politics more generally (chapters 9–18).

The reconstruction of these developments proceeds month by month, week by week, and sometimes almost minute by minute. Several considerations prompted this approach. At bottom, the change itself—the shift in the institutions of presidential selection and in the associated circle of specialized actors for national politics—was so quiet, so nearly invisible, that most observers missed it as it arrived. In the absence of a detailed account, they can—perhaps—be excused for having overlooked its revolutionary character, although the absence of such an account also made it difficult to perceive the immediate implications of this change, which were rooted in the politics producing it. Beyond that, elite activities—conversations, memoranda, understandings, "deals"—necessarily constitute the facts of the case, and the accuracy of their interpretation can be judged only when they are presented in careful detail. The claims to be made for the impact of these (essentially elite) events are substantial, both theoretically and practically. The account supporting these claims must be dense enough, rich enough, and tightly enough organized to bear them out.

For many, this reform narrative itself will be of primary interest. For them, it is structured as a contemporary historical record, following important developments in recent American history and the forces and agents, publicized and obscure, which contributed to them. At the same time, this organized factual account—and numerous subaccounts—can surely be applied to the intellectual concerns of individual readers, over and above the applications suggested by the author. Finally, the central narrative attempts to share the inherent fascination of political maneuvers closely observed and the intermittent high drama of momentous events unfolding.

The book, however, aspires to more than that. For the narrative is developed not just around the stages of reform politics but around two other organizing concepts. The first is institutional change. The second is the circulation of elites. Both are elaborated, in part, to make the narrative more comprehensible and to emphasize the importance of the events which compose it. Even here, the near-invisibility of many of these events probably adds to the value of these two central concepts. But the two notions are utilized primarily to comment upon events as they unfold and to place their cumulative impact—this particular set of institutional changes, this particular example of elite circulation—in the context of similar grand shifts in the political lives of other societies.

The formal changes in the structure, rules, and procedures of delegate selection, and hence presidential nomination, resulting from reform politics within the Democratic party between 1968 and 1972 were themselves hidden from many observers. Yet they could be objectively cataloged, and the catalog possesses an undeniable—a historic—sweep. In turn, these formal changes promised to elicit extensively altered practical responses from major political actors. As a result, they constitute a rare case of concentrated, comprehensive, institutional change.

A student of the mechanics of major-party presidential nominations must look as far back as the early 1900s, when presidential primaries were introduced, to find procedural innovations that were at all comparable. Nothing in the interim rivals the main institutional creations of either period. Nevertheless, the raw number of new rules for delegate selection devised between 1968 and 1972 easily surpassed the counterpart number for 1908 to 1912, the last great burst of nomination reform.[1] Accordingly, that same student must really look as far back as the 1830s, when national party conventions were themselves invented, to find changes of a comparable intensity, of a comparable institutional reach.

In preparation for the Democratic National Convention of 1831, every state needed to design a procedure for delegate selection, and most such designs differed sharply from previous state practice.[2] In preparation for the Democratic National Convention of 1972, every state was forced to amend the rules governing its delegate selection, and most did so in fundamental ways, to the point where half abandoned the basic institutional device which they had used only four years before.[3] No national convention in the interim, from 1831 to 1972, could have met these same standards for the scope of change in the matrix of institutions for delegate selection. No national convention, ever, could have met these standards for the scope of centrally planned, centrally initiated change, much less of self-conscious, deliberate "reform."

The general public perception of this change—that there were significantly more presidential primaries in 1972 than there had been in 1968—was accurate, but notably incomplete. The balance between primary and convention systems for selecting delegates had indeed shifted, but so had the types of primaries which were permitted or proscribed, the types of party conventions which were condoned or banned, the strictures under which presidential contenders could obtain delegates from either primaries or conventions, and even the desired characteristics of these delegates themselves. Along the way, and perhaps most crucially, the official party had been *erased* from what was still nominally the party's nomination process.

The successful implementation of a sweeping reform package—centrally planned and imposed, institutionally comprehensive and consistent, geographically comprehensive as well—almost guaranteed that the nomination process would *operate* differently afterward. The magnitude of this difference could not be described with certainty at the time these reforms were implemented. Actual political tests, subsequent and varied, would determine that. Nevertheless, the general areas where this new presidential politics would differ from the old were discernible by the time these structural reforms had been put into place; they were, indeed, inherent in the organizational character, as well as the breadth and depth, of these changes.

The critical resources for nomination politicking, for example, were sure to be revalued by reform rules with this much institutional reach. In consequence, the identity of those who held these resources, the key participants,

6

would predictably be affected. The character of the public issues which could be useful to a nomination campaign was presumably responsive to the mechanics of the nomination process, and not just to the tenor of the times. The type of candidate who would emerge and prosper in this new environment would likely differ, too. In short, the entire fabric of presidential politics seemed fated, or doomed, to be reshaped in tandem with these more formal alterations.[4]

Yet even before these practical effects had been realized, the undeniable result—the irreducible core of this institutional change—was the imposition of extensive, externally generated, theoretically consistent reforms, inimical to the process of delegate selection and presidential nomination as it had previously been conducted by the official party. Moreover, what was thus a critical specific event in the history of American politics was also, in a more abstract sense, only one more example of a critical, recurring event in the lives of political societies generally: the circulation of elites, the replacement of one group of specialized political actors with another of noticeably different origins, values, and ways of pursuing politics.[5]

The period from 1968 to 1972 saw the rise of an alternative coalition of Democratic elites, different in social background, political experience, and policy preference from the coalition which had previously dominated the national Democratic party. The ability of this aspiring, alternative, Democratic coalition to use reform politics and institutional change to unseat and replace the traditional, established coalition, and the possibility that this substitution was a permanent feature of the political landscape, would, by themselves, have marked this period as worthy of investigation. Serious attempts at comprehensive replacement of political elites are rare. Successful attempts are rarer still. Realized, they constitute a special opportunity to examine the process of elite circulation.

Ranged on one side in this dispute was the orthodox Democratic coalition, composed of the regular party and its associated interests. The heart of the regular party was actually those state parties which still possessed old-fashioned party organization, but the regular coalition extended to the dominant faction within party officialdom in most states across the nation. The core of its associated interests was organized labor, although the coalition also included, more ambivalently, the major civil rights organizations.

Ranged on the other side was an alternative Democratic coalition, composed of party reformers old and new, and *their* associated interests. The heart of this reform movement was the new wave of party insurgents who had surfaced in the losing nomination campaigns of 1968, but its troops were the organized reform factions which existed within many regular parties across the country, and the movement drew some significant support from the official party leadership in states with a more volunteer-based politics. The core of its associated interests were the liberal interest groups and the explicit reform organizations, although the alternative coalition came to include the major feminist organizations, too.

The triumph of this alternative coalition of Democratic elites over its orthodox, established counterpart—aided by the character of reform politics and by the institutional change which followed from it—was a major event in its own right. That triumph was clear and uncompromised; it occurred within the dominant party in American national politics; it resulted in part from a major change in political institutions and was in part "institutionalized" by it.

Yet there was reason to believe that this immediate and concrete victory would yield even broader consequences over the long run. For besides the specific social backgrounds, formative political experiences, and policy goals which separated the orthodox Democratic coalition from its aspiring replacement, there were additional differences of a still more fundamental sort, and these threatened to remain as long as the institutions which had arrived with them survived, that is, even if the alternative Democratic coalition, as constituted in the year of 1972, did not.

These differences could be summarized with the observation that the old coalition was based in blue-collar constituencies, while the newer version was white-collar from top to bottom. But that difference implied not just a different set of social attachments but a different set of practical skills, skills now necessary to succeed in politics. This meant, most fundamentally, that the elite replacement associated with this sweeping institutional change might not end with the triumph of this particular reform coalition but might go on to alter the continuing character of national Democratic elites and perhaps, if the institutions of reform spread, the character of national elites within the Republican party as well.

Even if these grand changes did not come to pass, the success of a sweeping movement for Democratic party reform in the period from 1968 to 1972, as consolidated over the succeeding decade, was both evidence that one cadre of party figures had been defeated by another *and* impetus for an extended replacement along the same lines. And because convention delegates and campaign staff are integral to the selection of American presidents and because presidents are able to influence the nature of the elites in the larger institutionalized presidency, in the federal executive branch, and even in the federal judiciary, the ramifications of this triumph were likely, in short order, to be felt throughout American government.

INTRODUCTION

Wide-ranging shifts in the practical character of presidential politics, and attendant shifts in critical elite strata, do not occur often in the life of any nation, and American political life proves no exception. But then, neither do formal changes of the magnitude occurring between 1968 and 1972 within the national Democratic party. Perhaps those facts alone are sufficient to justify a detailed chronicle of the reform politics behind them.

Almost all of this chronicle has been developed from extended interviews with the principal participants and from associated archival materials—memoranda, correspondence, drafts and counterdrafts. The participants were remarkably ready to talk, easily and at length; more than 120 of them contributed personal interviews. Their archival traces were unusually rich, thanks in part to their own concern with history and in part to serendipitous historical events. Whenever possible—and this proved feasible to a surprising extent—the principal actors, or at least their personal records, are permitted to speak for themselves. This is intended to provide a sense of their actions from the perspective of the participants, to contribute an additional basis for evaluating the outcome of those actions, and to conjure up the flavor, the emotional and contextual richness, of these events as they happened.

This account has, of course, been focused on the politics producing a revolutionary set of reform recommendations and on the politics leading to the concrete implementation of these abstract standards. Yet along the way, the story touches on matters as diverse as the means by which practical persons interpret abstract change, the way in which ideologies and even slogans can acquire concrete political influence, the reasons why the news media present an organizationally biased view of party politics, the role that social groups and social ties play in constructing political reality, and the possibility that differential patterns of attention to political affairs, almost alone, can produce a changed political world with changed prospects for most participants.

Such a book, combining the "report of record" for reform politics with an examination of larger concepts like institutional change and elite circulation, presents obvious problems of exposition. Too slight a concentration on the facts of the case diminishes the record and leaves the analysis undefended. Too great a concentration makes the record unapproachable and buries the analysis. The solution adopted here is architectural, with a parallel construction for each chapter. Each begins with an overview of narrative developments and major theoretical points. The narrative itself then follows in historical detail, in two or three titled subsections. A concluding section on implications summarizes narrative and extends analysis.

As a result, readers whose primary interest is these larger speculations can concentrate on the beginning and end of each chapter, dipping into the middle as mood or necessity dictates. Readers who are interested in the political history of this period for its particular actors, organizations, or events can delve into the broad middle parts of relevant chapters, skipping the larger framework. And readers who are interested in the chronicle *and* its implications—as well as that continued practical fascination and intermittent high drama—can simply turn the page.

PART I

The Politics
of Recommendation

CHAPTER

1

The Idea of a Reform Commission:

The McCarthy Campaign and the "Mandate"

IN WHICH, an independent reform commission is established as part of the nomination campaign of Eugene McCarthy; the focus of this commission shifts from the nomination of an insurgent to the pursuit of party reform; and commission principals succeed in extracting a set of prospective reform resolutions from the Democratic National Convention. AND IN WHICH, reform politics emerges as a central activity in Democratic party affairs, with its own substantive issues, its own specialized actors, and its own attentive public; sweeping institutional change becomes the continuing goal of party insurgents; and an alternative coalition of Democratic elites, bent on achieving that goal and likely to benefit from it, begins to take shape.

THERE IS no shortage of major events, or even of grand historical trends, which surely helped to shape the environment for conflict over party reform in the period from 1968 to 1972. But if political analysts are content to start at the point where specific recommendations for reform, which became the direct antecedents of sweeping institutional change, began to acquire organized elite support, their task becomes considerably easier. Under those conditions, the presidential nominating reforms which bore their first fruit when Iowa Democrats boosted Edmund Muskie at their local precinct caucuses in January of 1972 had their roots in a meeting of the Connecticut steering committee of the McCarthy for President campaign, on the evening of June 23, 1968, in West Hartford, Connecticut.

That meeting produced an unofficial study commission, ostensibly neutral in presidential preference and charged with commenting on existing arrangements for delegate selection. Thereafter, this commission, its report, and, espe-

13

cially, its associated personnel played a crucial catalytic role in the politics of party reform. The commission produced a document calling for sweeping change in the institutions of delegate selection. That document became a tactical device in maneuvers at the 1968 Convention *and* a long-run influence on the thinking of reformers in general. Those associated with its progress became critical actors in reform battles at the 1968 Convention *and* the nucleus of a more critical, long-run coalition of self-conscious party reformers.

The commission itself—formally the Commission on the Democratic Selection of Presidential Nominees, informally the Hughes Commission—was an evanescent entity. Its members were hastily, almost frantically, recruited. Its lone meeting was hardly enough to permit them to make each other's acquaintance. All traces of its organizational existence were gone within eight months of its creation.

Nevertheless, the simple fact that the commission had a report and supporting personnel in place at the Democratic Convention was to have substantial consequences, when combined with autonomous developments at the convention itself. These developments ranged from civil disturbances outside the convention hall through tactical machinations by contending candidates inside to procedural confusion on what became the crucial reform vote. The commission operation, for all its evanescence, was sufficient to take advantage of these events and bend them to the cause of party reform.

The most concrete and immediate upshot was a set of convention resolutions addressing various reform issues. The implementation of these resolutions—the subsequent struggle over appointment of the commissions which they authorized—provided the context for reform politics in the six months following the National Convention. The interpretation of these resolutions—the ensuing struggle over the framing of specific recommendations by these newly appointed commissions—was at the center of reform politics through 1969 and into 1970. But the most important outcome of the effort to extract reform resolutions from the 1968 Convention was the creation of a nucleus of reform actors: More than the reform resolutions themselves, these individuals became central to the politics of party reform in the months—indeed the years—to follow.

The Creation of the Hughes Commission

This portentous chain of events began inauspiciously on the morning of June 23, 1968, when the Democratic state convention in Hartford, Connecticut, selected nine McCarthy partisans and thirty-five others to go on to the national convention.[1] These "others," while publicly independent, were either privately committed to Vice President Humphrey or predictably inclined to shift in his direction once the balloting began. The McCarthyites, along with their campaign leadership, met in West Hartford on the evening of June 23 to discuss a response to what they viewed as not just an unfortunate but an inequitable situation.

Those who gathered in West Hartford were united in the belief that nine forty-fourths was a wholly inadequate fraction to express the real strength of their candidate in Connecticut and that a credentials challenge was consequently required. This ethical consensus, however, ran up against an immediate strategic problem: There had been nothing explicitly illegal in the outcome of the state convention, and, indeed, the 35-to-9 split had accurately mirrored the 760-to-200 division among convention delegates. If the result, then, seemed both disappointing and misleading, it was still procedurally lawful.

The West Hartford conferees gradually moved toward agreement on a strategic response. They proposed to establish a formally neutral investigative commission, to study the issue of fair party rules. The findings and recommendations of this commission could then become the formally disinterested support for a challenge to the Connecticut outcome and could be marshaled against the inevitable assertion by the other Connecticut delegates that they, after all, were legally chosen. Geoffrey Cowan, McCarthy coordinator for Connecticut, pushed for the creation of this new body as the best alternative in a bad situation:

> The outcome of that meeting was the Hughes Commission. It grew out of my own frustration at delegate-hunting in Connecticut. We got only nine of forty-four. We were denied a fair proportion on any basis of counting. Our problem was, we could get plenty of "fancy" people. We had Arthur Miller [the playwright] as an alternate delegate. Louis Pollak [dean of the Yale Law School] had agreed to handle the case before the Credentials Committee. Miller could plead our case eloquently, and Pollak had prestige and skill, but the problem was that there was no *law* to go on. We needed some way to document delegate selection. We needed some written document to back the challenge.[2]

The new group, in its original conception, was to be modeled on the National Advisory Commission on Civil Disorders, better known as the Kerner Commission.[3] On that analogy, its report would begin with an abstract argument about the prerequisites of internal party democracy, follow with a collection of recommendations for bringing the Democratic party into conformity with those prerequisites, and close with a series of appendices on the reality of delegate selection in the individual states.

This idea had already received some consideration from various elements in the McCarthy camp. The West Hartford meeting, at the suggestion of Geoff Cowan, decided to pull the idea out of the air and see if it could be turned to McCarthy's advantage. The proposed body was christened the Commission on the Democratic Selection of Presidential Nominees, and the assembled McCarthy partisans, after discussing possible staff, commissioners, and funding, nominated Cowan for the job of pulling all three together.

While it was impossible, at that time, to envision the trail of events which would follow, it was not difficult to see the immediate needs of this commission and the severe time pressures under which these needs had to be met. First, there had to be a staff. Then, there had to be commissioners—arguably a diverse and respectable lot. After that, there had to be a report urging extensive reforms. Behind it, there had to be an organized lobbying effort, to allow that report to contribute to a McCarthy nomination. Underneath all this, there had to be some minimal financing, to permit the whole operation to go forward.

Cowan began a simultaneous attack on all these fronts. To secure the basic wherewithal for his commission, he struck a bargain with William M. Johnson II, a McCarthy sympathizer from Connecticut with a small publishing house in New York. Johnson put up $10,000 for expenses and agreed to print the commission report. If nothing came of the venture, his costs would become a contribution to the McCarthy campaign. If a major book on party democracy resulted, Johnson would have first refusal rights for publication.[4]

The West Hartford discussants had agreed that Cowan should not take the top staff slot, since he already held such an evident, campaign-related stake in the report of his commission. He adopted the title of associate director. For director, he tapped Thomas P. Alder, an old friend from civil rights battles of the early 1960s. During the spring nomination campaigns, Alder had been involved in an attempt to nurture a fourth major party, to the left of the Democrats, but by the time the Commission on the Democratic Selection of Presidential Nominees became active, he was disenchanted with that effort:

> I had helped Marcus Raskin launch the "New Party" in Washington, D.C. Dick Gregory and then [Benjamin] Spock got tacked on more or less accidentally. In late spring and early summer, the New Party actually had position papers on the issues. These white papers, this subterranean flow of white papers were an amalgam of "the government is illegitimate," plus "neighborhood control is good." Much of this was Institute of Policy Studies [IPS]–based. I had to make a small break with the New Party people in order to do the Hughes Commission work.
>
> By the time of the plenary sessions of the New Party in Chicago, it began to have a different orientation. It was just to be a fourth-party ballot slot, beyond

Republicans, Democrats, and the American Independent Party. There were very few seasoned tacticians in the New Party at that time; it was a media event of Spock, Gregory, and Raskin. This was splitting the IPS people, many of whom felt that it was bootless and off the point. The fourth party didn't get McCarthy. It didn't become a service party after the convention. It became instead a party of example and personal drama.

Ten young lawyers, most with a background in either civil rights or poverty law, were easily recruited to flesh out the staff. In partisan terms, these ten plus Alder and Cowan comprised five supporters of Eugene McCarthy, one (former) partisan of Robert Kennedy, and six previous inactives. Eli J. Segal, convention-states coordinator for McCarthy, was added as liaison with the McCarthy campaign proper, and the staff was judged complete. The group acquired a donated apartment-office at 218 West Tenth Street in New York's Greenwich Village and began to research their report.[5]

Locating a dozen young lawyers who would sacrifice their summer vacations proved much less difficult than finding a half dozen prestigious public figures who would invest in the commission idea. The problem lay not in any staff ambivalence about the characteristics of their ideal commissioners. The chairman should be someone of national stature, who would endorse proposals for structural change and who was an active McCarthy supporter. The vice chairman should share the first two attributes but be a known Humphrey backer. The other commissioners should have some logical connection with reform as an issue and be arguably "representative." Cowan set to work with these criteria:

> We wanted some sort of balance on the thing. We needed someone from each of the major candidate's supporters, but someone who would reliably be for reform. We needed a black, of course, and a woman. We didn't worry about a young person, maybe because we were all young ourselves.

Alder and Cowan quickly settled on their candidate for chairman: Bronson C. LaFollette, Democratic nominee and, they felt, soon-to-be-governor of Wisconsin. The Badger State was a stronghold of independent politics; LaFollette was a McCarthy backer; "the LaFollette Commission" had the ring of continuity with generations of American reform. But despite indications that the principal was interested, he could not be pinned down. When the delay began to threaten the entire project, the two staffers gave up on LaFollette.

By the time their next several choices had turned them down more directly, the last week in July was at hand. In some desperation, they contacted Harold E. Hughes, governor of Iowa. Hughes lacked national stature and was not personally connected to any commission operatives. On the other hand, he was a McCarthy supporter, and he was reputed to be interested in the reform issue—and in playing an immediate role in national politics. Hughes accepted their offer in writing, and the commission had a chairman.

If the search for a chairman was difficult, the search for a vice chairman was more so. Again, the staff had an early favorite, Adlai E. Stevenson III, state treasurer of Illinois. Again, however, their first choice turned them down, as did the next several possibilities. They eventually queried Representative Donald M. Fraser of Minnesota. While hardly a household word, Fraser was at least chairman of the Democratic Study Group in the U.S. House; he was an early endorser of the vice president; he was an outspoken critic of the Vietnam War. Like Hughes, he was not put off by the initial preference of the staff for someone else, and he even declined to name a staff co-director.

The recruitment of the other commissioners was less nerve-racking, since they did not have to meet as strict criteria. Frederick G. Dutton, a long-time activist in California politics and a confidant of the late Senator Robert Kennedy, came aboard without hesitation.[6] H. Julian Bond, state representative from Georgia, was leading a major credentials challenge involving racial discrimination and saw this as a logical extension. Doris Fleeson Kimball, former political columnist for the *Washington Star,* was glad to fill the "woman's slot" on the commission. Harry Ashmore, director of the Center for the Study of Democratic Institutions, was a "natural" for appointment as one of the commission's professional experts and expressed immediate interest. Finally, Alexander M. Bickel, professor of law at Yale University, brought true, blue-ribbon, intellectual credentials to the undertaking.

The scramble to amass these commissioners prevented second thoughts about their probable behavior, although Bond and Bickel did worry the commission staff. Despite his challenge to discrimination in party affairs, Bond was believed to place both civil rights and social welfare above party reform in his personal canon. Despite *that,* major black spokesmen of any stripe, after party regulars and active Humphreyites were eliminated, remained in too short a supply to justify exlusion. Alder and Cowan, along with several other staffers, had been students of Bickel. While they worried about his independent turn of mind, they appreciated his value in their quest for a neutral public profile, and they invited him to join anyway.

Alder and Cowan had intended to add a white southerner to this group and had offered a seat to Richmond Flowers, the former attorney general of Alabama. Like LaFollette, Flowers had indicated an interest when reached by telephone, but he, too, had failed to confirm in writing and had then dropped out of touch. His name was deleted from the list, leaving Ashmore, an ex-Arkansan, to represent "the new South."

Although this roster, when it finally assembled as a commission, was to prove quite satisfactory to its recruiters, they remained anxious about its very existence almost to the day it met. Part of their discomfort stemmed from the difficulty in attracting, or in nailing down, their commissioners. By July 25, Staff Director Alder was confident of only three members, and one of these was Richmond Flowers. At that point, Alder still lacked both a chairman and a vice chairman.[7]

This uncertainty was intensified by the fact that everything in the operation had to be done simultaneously. Commissioners had to be recruited, a report had to be researched, the political groundwork for its reception had to be laid—and ineffectiveness in any one of these links might threaten the entire project. Thus, while the membership would later be defended as a coherent whole, with each commissioner embodying various external interests, the recruitment process always appeared as much more of a jumble to staffers like Cowan at commission headquarters:

> We had only six weeks to put the whole thing out. First we couldn't get our chairman, and we couldn't get *any* Humphrey people at all. Stevenson wouldn't help. Tom and I knew Don Fraser, so we knew he would be decent. Hughes became chairman, and Fraser vice chairman. Dutton was a Kennedy person, and he had written those books. Bond at least was leading one of the major challenges, although he always had other irons in the fire. Ashmore never showed. Doris Fleeson Kimball had been a New Deal reporter and columnist for the *Washington Star*. Kimball's daughter was Blair Clark's secretary, and he was a friend of ours. Sometimes we'd call someone, and he'd turn us down, but suggest someone else.

While the staff was assembling the commission under whose direction they would theoretically operate, they were also pursuing the political end of commission business, along two related tracks. On the more narrowly administrative side, research and development on a commission report proceeded apace. On the more explicitly political track, efforts to increase the impact of that report were likewise under way.

The time for these activities was further compressed by the fact that Connecticut McCarthy supporters had actually walked out of the state convention on June 23, to protest their nine-delegate allotment. As a result, it was not until a new compromise was reached with the state party leadership on July 2 that Cowan went to work full-time on the commission idea.[8] Within three weeks, he had his entire staff, but it needed fifty state reports by the end of the first week in August, a draft report for a full commission meeting at the end of the second week, and a published booklet for the convention in Chicago by the end of the third.

When the paucity of reference materials on state delegate selection was added to these scheduling constraints—a few bureaucratic compilations, a little academic research, the newspaper room at the New York Public Library, and the practical experience of McCarthy delegate-hunters were all that was available—the staff was forced to change plans. Instead of fifty chapters for fifty states, they shifted to summary tables, with more detailed investigations of eight or ten key examples. Political considerations reinforced this strategy, since the central goal was to document a number of dramatic abuses and to document them so persuasively that the commissioners and then the members of convention committees could not wish away the associated recommendations for reform.

In order to increase the likelihood that this report would influence convention decisions, the staff developed an external strategy as well. Anne Wexler, a McCarthy delegate from Connecticut and a participant in the West Hartford meeting, suggested that they identify two members on the Rules and Credentials committees who would be willing to call for the creation of an impartial study commission to look into issues facing these committees. The group which Alder was recruiting would, of course, be that commission.

Wexler already possessed a seat on Rules, one which John M. Bailey, Connecticut state *and* Democratic national chairman, had conceded as part of the July 2 deal in Connecticut.[9] Wexler and Alder then jointly sought a colleague on Rules and two sympathizers on Credentials. William F. Sueppel, Iowa delegate and Rules member, was their first convert, and he represented a double success: It was Sueppel who suggested Harold Hughes for commission chairman, at the point when that search was becoming desperate. Subsequently, Howard Morgan of Oregon and Arie P. Taylor of Colorado agreed to join the ranks of Hughes Commission "sponsors" on the Credentials side.

By August 4, the commission had its full seven members, its research agenda, and its political strategy. On that day, Hughes and Wexler flew to Chicago to hold a preliminary press conference and to reveal the existence of their commission. The press release advertising the event offered the authorized rationale for the creation of that body:

> A group of delegates to the Democratic National Convention today announced the appointment of Governor Harold Hughes of Iowa to head the seven-member Commission on the Democratic Selection of Presidential Nominees. The announcement came at a late morning press conference in the Bel-Air Room of Chicago's Conrad Hilton Hotel.
>
> The Commission "will make an immediate study and compile a report for us on the delegate selection procedures and the rules of the Democratic National Convention," according to Mrs. Anne Wexler of Connecticut, a member of the Convention's Rules Committee.

She explained that she and three other members of the Rules and Credentials Committees had formed the Commission to remedy their "lack of information in assessing the issues that will come before the committees."[10]

Two days later, a "Dear Fellow Delegate" letter, drafted by Alder and signed by the four sponsors, went out to all 220 members of the Rules and Credentials committees. The letter emphasized the complexity of the technical issues which committee members would face. It announced the report of the Commission on the Democratic Selection of Presidential Nominees as an aid to meeting this complexity. And it offered the commission as a staff resource at the convention or, in advance, by telephone from its office in New York.[11]

The commission which was thereby announced to the world held its first and only meeting on Tuesday, August 13, at the home of staffer Philip W. Moore in Winnetka, Illinois. Despite the fleeting character of this gathering—and indeed of the commission as a whole—the specific deliberations of the assembled commissioners were not inconsequential. These recommendations formed the primary substance of the commission report; when that document came to play a key role at the Democratic Convention, its contents acquired an incidental historic significance. Beyond that, these specific recommendations were destined to influence the report of the *official* reform body to follow; they thus acquired an influence on the politics of party reform which would not evaporate when the Convention—and the Hughes Commission—disappeared.

The document at the center of this discussion contained proposals for both the process of delegate selection and the operation of national conventions. In scope, this draft report ranged from the grandeur of abolishing the institutions through which a majority of all delegates to the 1968 Convention had been selected, to the minutia of guaranteeing rapid publication of National Committee transcripts. By bulk, the document centered on convention rules. But in its potential impact on presidential politics, the key sections dealt with delegate selection.

Because all of its specific proposals had been developed, researched, drafted, and typed in less than a month, the commissioners had to face them without benefit of prior study. Despite the presence of all the principals except Ashmore, discussion quickly became a five-cornered affair, featuring Bickel, Dutton, and Fraser among the commissioners, and Alder and Cowan from the staff, with occasional interrogation by Chairman Hughes.[12]

In short order, the commissioners assented to some sweeping proposals, especially in the realm of delegate selection. When they began, there were five basic institutions for selecting delegates. The commissioners agreed to the abolition of three—devices which, in combination, had created between 55 and 60 percent of all delegates to the 1968 Convention. Beyond that, they recommended that delegates be shifted extensively among the states, by changing the existing, complex, apportionment formula to one based solely on state population. Finally, they moved well down the road to racial quotas, by recommending that the National Convention place an "affirmative obligation" on state parties to encourage black participation and that any gross disparities between black presence in the delegation and in the population of a state be taken as presumptive evidence of noncompliance.

The staff was stopped only twice on its way through this part of the agenda. The first time was on a proposal for allocating delegates to presidential contenders. The staff recommended abolishing the winner-take-all rule for delegate allocation, with its provision that the plurality vote leader among presidential candidates be allotted all of a state delegation. In response, Fred Dutton of California rose to the defense of the giant winner-take-all California primary, and his manner left no doubt about the intensity of his concern.

The second deliberate halt was on a proposal to eliminate a fourth basic institution of delegate selection. In this, the staff recommended abolishing all convention systems, leaving only presidential primaries centered on national candidates as the means to nominate a president. Don Fraser of Minnesota made the lengthy counterargument here, asserting that a convention system in which any Democrat—and not just party officials—could participate was often highly responsive, and he adduced Minnesota as an example.

The first of these conflicts, over delegate allocation, created a dilemma for Chairman Hughes. If he drove the issue to a vote, he might split the commission deeply enough to impair its political efficacy. If he let the issue slide, he would have to champion a set of reforms with what he regarded as an evident, major, internal inconsistency. After some hesitation, the chairman resigned himself to the second course, and the winner-take-all primary—and thus the system of party conventions as well—escaped condemnation. Alder traced their reprieve almost solely to the haste with which the commission had been assembled:

> Hughes and I never had any understanding as to whether I would call for a division vote. We had met each other in person for the first time that morning, and you have to remember that we had never met before that. We didn't have much time before the meeting, and I took that time to acquaint him with the substance of staff recommendations, so that there wouldn't be any unpleasant surprises for him when things came up.
>
> When the winner-take-all thing blew up, I hoped that we could come up with language that would cover this over. If we drove it through to a fight, it might

create fear at the table about the whole operation. I looked down at Hughes for some guidance, for a shake of the head or something. He was glazed. His eyes had turned opalescent. He hadn't foreseen this. So I uttered the provision that they should be clear on an enormous unanimity on rules and suggestions, and that was that.

After a late lunch, the commissioners turned to the rules and procedures of the National Convention itself and continued with their aggressive recommendations for reform. In truth, they began by ratifying the traditional, limited provision on party loyalty,[13] but after that, they charged boldly ahead. The commissioners recommended that the Democratic National Committee provide per diem allowances to delegates, to combat economic discrimination. They approved mechanisms to guarantee roll-call votes. They endorsed regulations allocating time to debate committee reports. They agreed that contested delegations should not be permitted to vote on any matters until their status was resolved, although several commissioners did comment on the potential for abuse in such a resolution. They argued that only newly elected members of the National Committee should be seated as ex officio delegates and that those members should be counted against a state's delegate total even then.

By late afternoon, the staff agenda was completed, and the commissioners were free to leave commission business behind and concentrate on the dash to O'Hare International Airport. They had made their final collective contribution to the commission report. They were close to having made their final contribution to commission activity.

Hughes would pressure a reluctant John Bailey into providing the commission staff with office space and floor passes at the National Convention; he would address the Rules Committee on the subject of nomination reform; he would engage in some personal lobbying on behalf of the Rules Minority Report. Bickel would address the Credentials Committee, and Bickel and Dutton would each undertake some miscellaneous errands in the name of the commission during the months after Chicago. Otherwise, once the Winnetka meeting was over, the Hughes Commission reverted to being solely a staff operation. With hindsight, several of its commissioners, including Dutton, would allege that it had always been:

> The truth of the matter is that the Hughes Commission was really just Tom Alder and, to a lesser extent, Geoff Cowan. They had the documents ready for us. I guess in retrospect that exercise was considerably bound by naiveté. They weren't looking at what they were doing to political parties, but they were coming with what they had as preconceptions about politics, that they brought with them from the anti-War movement, or from school, or from wherever. We, for our part, weren't looking at anything, since we never had anything to look at in advance.

Staff Director Alder did not dispute this judgment about the evanescent nature of the commission, or at least of the commissioners as a functioning group:

> I don't wonder if Hughes doesn't remember many of the details of those days. You've got to remember that there was more shadow than substance to the Hughes Commission *as a Commission.* There was a product, that booklet, but otherwise it was in many ways a media event. There was only one meeting. Hughes had never met the staff before that meeting. If Anne Wexler hadn't known Bill Sueppel, who knows how much farther it could have gotten. On the other hand, we had those press conferences, and the resolutions before the committees, and it took off. On the other hand, we could have had Bronson LaFollette instead of Hughes, and Richmond Flowers, too. I don't remember the details, but LaFollette got involved in some hanky-panky during his campaign, with a secretary I think, and Flowers was indicted for something or other shortly after we had invited him to join.

In the final crush to publish an official document, the staff actually made some additional, minor contributions to the outcome of the Winnetka meeting. With the tacit support of Chairman Hughes and the more active encouragement of Alder and Cowan, and in an environment where the other commissioners were insulated from any editorial role, Simon Lazarus polished a report which hewed scrupulously in its substance to the formal actions from Winnetka, but which awarded its rhetoric to the original staff positions.

On the institutions of delegate selection, Lazarus used his examples to denigrate the convention system in general and Fraser's Minnesota in particular, and he then threw in a totally new suggestion, that the results of any state convention be contestable in a "challenge primary" like that of Connecticut. On the rules for delegate allocation, he used his examples to deride the winner-take-all rule in general, and Dutton's California in particular, and to plump for any and all allocation arrangements which would provide some form of proportional representation.[14]

Even apart from these rhetorical emendations, however, the report constituted a call for sweeping institutional change. Between Wednesday morning, August 14, and Thursday morning, August 22, Lazarus managed to write and William Johnson managed to print the resulting eighty-page booklet on party reform, *The Democratic Choice.* It began, once again, with the public rationale of the Hughes Commission for its own creation:

> This Commission was called into existence by members of the Committee on Rules and Order of Business and the Committee on Credentials of the 1968 Democratic National Convention. They asked the Commission to assemble a

staff and to make an independent study of the convention and the delegate selection process. The Commission was to present to the Committees and to the Convention itself a report on its findings, along with recommendations for bringing the nominating process more closely into harmony with essential democratic principles.

We have completed our study. Included with this preface to our report is a summary statement of our principal conclusions and recommendations.[15]

There followed, in order: a seven-page recap of commission suggestions, entitled "Findings and Recommendations"; a chapter on historical reform and change, "Democracy and the Democratic Party—1968"; a chapter on party rules in the period leading up to a convention, "Convention Delegate Selection: How States Choose"; and a chapter on rules at the quadrennial gathering itself, "Democracy at the National Convention." But the words which most accurately represented the thrust of the report and which served as the rallying cry for those who had the most hope for its impact followed immediately upon the opening two paragraphs:

> This Convention is on trial. The responsibilities of these Committees, and of all delegates to this Convention are unprecedented. To an extent not matched since the turn of the century, events in 1968 have called into question the integrity of the convention system for nominating presidential candidates. Recent developments have put the future of the two-party system itself into serious jeopardy. . . .
>
> The crisis of the Democratic Party is a genuine crisis for democracy in America and especially for the two-party system. Racial minorities, the poor, the young, members of the upper-middle class, and much of the lower-middle and working classes as well—all are seriously considering transferring their allegiance away from either of the two major parties. . . . We recommend the following principal proposals to the Convention and its principal Committees, some to validate the procedures of the 1968 Convention itself, others to be implemented prospectively, to purify—and hopefully to preserve—the power exercised by future Democratic National Conventions.[16]

The Extraction of Reform Resolutions

While Simon Lazarus III was still writing the final version of the report of the Commission on the Democratic Selection of Presidential Nominees, others connected with the commission were beginning to think about ways to maximize the impact of that report within the convention. Although the commission device had been conceived as an aid to the McCarthy campaign within the Credentials Committee, those responsible for targeting the commission's report had, in fact, begun to focus on the Rules Committee instead.

This change was largely a response to the issues and alignments which were developing in all three convention committees. In Credentials, where a record number of challenges awaited, or in Platform, where a do-or-die fight was brewing over Vietnam, additional tactical efforts had become superfluous. In both locales, the major issues had emerged for all to see, and the coalitions which might be formed around them had taken on a more precise, and limiting, character.

Only in Rules had the major issues become *less* apparent, so that the factional situation had presumably increased in fluidity. This was true primarily because the drawing card for Rules debates—the unit rule fight—had already been devalued. A unit rule was an arrangement by which a majority of a state's delegates could decide to cast the entire vote of their delegation, as a bloc. Eleven southern and border states retained the formal right to use this rule, although not all would normally do so.

Abolition of the unit rule initially promised some minor direct benefits to the McCarthy campaign, by freeing a handful of delegates who were bound by it against their will. The major advantage of abolition, however, was always indirect: An attempt at abolition promised to increase tensions within the Humphrey coalition, pitting liberal Humphrey backers against their more conservative allies. But before the Rules Committee ever assembled, the vice president moved to contain that possibility by revealing that he, too, favored an end to the rule.[17] McCarthy partisans could still counter with a more abrasive resolution on the matter, but after this they needed something extra to tax the Humphrey coalition.

The Democratic Choice had to provide it. Because mere publication could not be expected to do the job, Anne Wexler set about organizing a whip system for the Rules Committee, so that all those who might be sympathetic to the content of the commission report would at least show up. Wexler hoped to guarantee a sufficiently cohesive bloc to force debate on the numerous rules proposals contained in the commission document. To that end, a copy would be resting on the chair of every member when the Rules Committee held its initial session on Thursday morning, August 22.

No countervailing effort emerged in the two-week period before the Rules Committee was to meet. The Humphrey leadership did organize to rebut the profusion of credentials challenges emanating from the McCarthy forces and to support the views of the vice president on a platform. But they devoted little attention to party rules. The Rules Committee was an unlikely locale for developments which could influence the nomination; its chairman, Governor Samuel H. Shapiro of Illinois, was an unlikely person to cater to anti-Humphrey sentiment. The Humphrey leadership thus confined itself to designating a caucus leader, James C. Wright, Jr., congressman from Texas, and to delegating any subsequent negotiations to him.

By Wednesday, August 21, Wright had become aware of the general McCarthy strategy for Rules. He had obtained a copy of *The Democratic Choice* as well, and he went to work, through that Wednesday evening, on a printed alternative, a counterdocument to keep Humphrey partisans and genuine uncommitteds out of the McCarthy camp. His rebuttals, with the exception of one on the unit rule, eventually achieved their short-run goal, the maintenance of unity within the Humphrey coalition. Wright even found a reform issue, the question of party loyalty, with which he could tax the reformers. Otherwise, the Wright memo acquired its historical interest because it represented the first explicit counterattack by the regular party against emerging reform forces—and almost the last successful one.

Wright's opening attack on the legitimacy and neutrality of the commission enterprise set the tone for his whole document:

> An unofficial, largely self-appointed group under the chairmanship of Governor Hughes of Iowa, composed principally of McCarthy supporters, has prepared a lengthy document embodying a long series of quite radical changes in the convention rules. Some of these changes may indeed merit careful and sympathetic consideration for the future. If made applicable at this late date to the 1968 Convention, they would seem designed expressly to *alter the outcome* of the convention by disfranchising large numbers of duly elected delegates.[18]

The next morning, before the scheduled 10:00 A.M. meeting of the Rules Committee, Congressman Wright held a caucus for all committee members potentially sympathetic to Hubert Humphrey and made them a gift of his "Rules Committee Memorandum."

Whatever its general impact, one shortcoming was immediately evident: The provisions on the unit rule in the Wright memorandum were unacceptable to a majority of those present. Wright himself had been willing to consider retaining the rule, and he was pointedly opposed to altering it once delegates had been chosen. The bulk of his caucusers, however, would have none of this. Thereafter, Wright's personal efforts on the issue were all bent toward finding language on abolition which would not enrage the more conservative backers of the vice president—a matter of some delicacy, since many of them were already uncomfortable in backing a long-time liberal and might be alienated completely if he were to offend their organizational preferences as well as their ideology.

The Politics of Recommendation

The first session of the Rules Committee was gaveled to order later that morning, August 22, at 10:16 A.M.[19] For high drama at the 1968 Democratic Convention, Rules would be upstaged by Platform. The most visible public issue to be addressed by the convention, its stand on American policy on South Vietnam, was to be shaped by the Platform Committee and then resolved in a lengthy, emotion-charged debate on the convention floor. For sheer amount of conflict, Rules would be surpassed by Credentials. With seventeen separate challenges in fifteen different states, the Credentials Committee was to establish a modern record. But for long-run impact on presidential politics, Rules would have no equal. *The minority report of the Rules Committee, as augmented by developments in the Credentials Committee and in the Democratic National Committee itself, was to become the "mandate"—the hunting license, really—for the greatest systematic change in presidential nominating procedures in all of American history.*

Nothing about this initial assembly afforded any portent of a historic role. On Thursday morning, the committee adopted a hearing schedule, endured an hour-long wrangle over the proper definition of its own membership, and then adjourned for lunch. The afternoon session opened with its first and most lengthy expert testimony, from Iowa Governor Hughes. Hughes ran through the recommendations of his Commission on the Democratic Selection of Presidential Nominees and thereby sparked an internal debate which continued through the late evening of the next day.

The centerpiece in this debate was still the question of the unit rule, and both the afternoon session on Thursday and the morning session on Friday were devoted to unit rule arguments, with the exception of forty-five minutes for a resolution adding Democratic state chairmen and presidents of Young Democratic Clubs to the Democratic National Committee. Finally, on Friday afternoon, after the Rules Committee had gone into executive session to draft its report, the contents of *The Democratic Choice* began to attract attention. The committee did not recess permanently until 11:28 that night, and almost all of the intervening hours were devoted to debating the recommendations of the Hughes Commission.

Lopsided votes defeated most of these recommendations, although the committee did agree to a proposal on polling delegations and to one on early designation of convention committees. It went along, as well, with the request by McCarthy delegates for a change in the order of business, so that credentials challenges could be settled first, and it added provisions to control the length of nominating speeches, to ban demonstrations after those speeches, and to place the District of Columbia in its alphabetical spot in the roll of the states.

THE IDEA OF A REFORM COMMISSION

While the statistical bulk of suggestions from the Hughes Commission was summarily dismissed, a number of items were also discussed and then tabled "for future study." As the list of such items grew, commission partisans like Anne Wexler began to see an opportunity, if not to use their reform proposals to aid Senator McCarthy, at least to obtain an additional arena in which to fight for the proposals themselves:

> I spent my time on the Rules minority report. They debated much that was in the Hughes Commission report, nearly item by item. We got killed on most of it. But then things started getting voted on and referred to a commission, that *might* be set up, *if* one was going to get set up. We felt that more and more of the Hughes Commission Report was thus becoming implied in the Majority Report.

The committee majority did, in fact, redeem this implicit promise before the evening was over, by adopting a resolution calling for a study commission on party rules, one which would meet during the next four years, discuss these issues in greater detail, and make recommendations, through the National Committee, to the 1972 Convention:

> Therefore, be it resolved, that the Chairman of the Democratic National Committee appoint a Commission to be called the Rules Commission, and consisting of members knowledgeable in matters of parliamentary procedure and familiar with Convention procedure of the Democratic Party, and that said Commission be charged with the duty of studying and evaluating and codifying the rules of past Democratic National Conventions, and investigating the advisability of rules changes, and the Commission report its findings to the Democratic National Committee in a timely manner in order that the Democratic National Committee may submit said findings to the Rules Committee on the 1972 National Convention for acceptance, rejection, modification or amendment. It is the will of this Convention that this Commission shall give serious consideration to the establishment of:
> 1. Permanent rules for committees of the Convention both as to preconvention and convention procedures.
> 2. Permanent rules of the Convention.
> 3. Other matters that may be appropriate.[20]

Relatively little additional time was devoted to the issue of the unit rule during this final session. The dominant faction within the committee had maintained its cohesion throughout the debates of Thursday afternoon and Friday morning, and the majority wrote its own views directly into the committee report, with asides to the minority factions on either side. To the militant abolitionists, the majority gave an end to the unit rule for the future and a suspension for the present, but it insisted that this suspension apply to delegates bound against their will in primary as well as convention states. To those who favored retention, it offered language that, in 1968, would not "abolish" the unit rule, but would merely guarantee that the convention not enforce it.[21]

While the executive session of Friday evening was still under way, Cowan and Lazarus went to work on a single McCarthyite–Hughes Commission response to these proposals. On the unit rule, they continued to prefer immediate prohibition, rather than suspension, and subsequent proscription at all levels, not just the state level. For the study commission, they wanted to impart specific objectives, rather than leave that body free to do some undefined analysis:

> Be it resolved, that the Call to the 1972 Democratic National Convention shall contain the following language:
> It is understood that a state Democratic party, in selecting and certifying delegates to the National Convention, thereby undertakes to assure that such delegates have been selected through a process in which all Democratic voters have had full and timely opportunity to participate. In determining whether a state party has complied with this mandate, the convention shall require that:
> (1) The unit rule not be used in any stage of the delegate selection process; and
> (2) All feasible efforts have been made to assure that delegates are selected through party primary, convention, or committee procedures open to public participation within the calendar year of the National Convention.[22]

The major tactical innovation in this minority report was the intimate linking of a ban on the unit rule with an official condemnation of insufficiently participatory devices for delegate selection, the latter being the intended implication of "full and timely opportunity to participate." Cowan and Lazarus saw no chance that the convention would explicitly prohibit those basic *institutions* of delegate selection which, in their view, most severely impeded direct participation. They feared that the convention might even reject their guarded phrasing of that general *goal.* But they did see some slight chance that a majority would be willing to accept their tougher position on the unit rule and, in doing so, would adopt the rest of the minority report—which could be defined more specifically later.

Cowan and Lazarus were reinforced in this strategy by developments in the Credentials Committee, which was going into its fourth full day of activity by the time Rules met. The two committees, while differing in the size of their workloads, were not dissimilar factionally, although a higher turnout in Credentials had reduced the proportionate influence of the McCarthy delegates and their allies. Yet the element which most clearly differentiated the

Credentials sessions of 1968 from those of 1960 or 1964 was not a particular factional alignment, but the sheer number of challenges to be heard and the time it took to hear them.

Credentials had gone into session at 9:25 A.M. on August 19 and would recess for the last time at 3:30 P.M. on August 26. By the time he was well into this clogged calendar, Chairman Richard J. Hughes, governor of New Jersey, had publicly endorsed an attempt to see that his experience was not repeated. He suggested a study commission to establish standards for delegate selection before the next convention, standards which would presumably obviate most challenges and resolve the rest.

Hughes had just completed a term as chairman of the first such commission in Democratic party history, the Special Equal Rights Committee [SERC]. Under his direction, the SERC had developed six antidiscrimination guidelines, and Hughes had then shepherded these through the National Committee and into the Call to the 1968 Convention.[23] With that background, he was at least not predisposed against the commission device. His labors during the remainder of the week of August 19–27 convinced him of its positive features, and the last act of the Credentials Committee before it recessed on Monday afternoon was to vote out a resolution proposing a study commission on delegate selection rules.

The drafting of that resolution was entrusted to Philip M. Stern, a delegate from Washington, D.C., under the supervision of Richard Hughes. Stern was a long-time friend of Cowan and Alder and had been an active participant in their preconvention planning. Once he had been assigned to draft the Credentials majority report, his two friends possessed an opportunity to coordinate its contents with those of the Rules minority report.

At a strategy meeting before the final session of the Rules Committee on Friday, Alder, Cowan, Stern, Wexler, and several others took this opportunity. They agreed to adopt the moderate approach of the Credentials majority report as their backstop position and to try to put extra substance into it through the Rules minority report. In this way, they could take advantage of any marginal leverage which Stern's drafting rights provided in Credentials; they could couple their preferred, tougher language on delegate selection with prohibition of the unit rule in Rules; and they could avoid having two similar minority reports on the convention floor. Though guarded about the real prospects of such a strategy, Tom Alder was delighted to make the attempt:

> Although they came from a common source, it wasn't clear that the two resolutions could be gotten through. Fall-back position number two [the Credentials majority report] had to be voted on first, but it *was* a fall-back in our minds.

Stern's draft of the Credentials majority report did indeed sail through the committee in its final session on Monday afternoon, and the convention had a second resolution which would affect delegate selection in the future:

> This Committee recommends that the Chairman of the Democratic National Committee establish a Special Committee to:
>
> A.   Study the delegation selection processes in effect in the various states, in the context of the peculiar circumstances, needs, and traditions in which each state's laws and practices find their roots.
>
> B.   Recommend to the Democratic National Committee such improvements as can assure even broader citizen participation in the delegate selection process.
>
> C.   Aid the state Democratic parties in working toward relevant changes in state law and party rules.
>
> D.   Report its findings and recommendations to the Democratic National Committee and make them available to the 1972 Convention and the committees thereof.
>
> Among the matters which the Credentials Committee feels should come under the consideration of the new Committee—matters on which the Democratic Party has not in the past expressed itself clearly and directly—are the following:
>
> 1.   Timeliness. . . .
> 2.   Grass-roots participation. . . .
> 3.   Unit rule at the state and local level. . . .[24]

On the eve of the convention, then, there were three formal resolutions about the mechanics of nominating a president on the agenda for the full gathering. The first was the Credentials majority report, calling for a Special Committee to study the process of delegate selection. The second was the Rules majority report, calling for a Rules Commission to study convention regulations. And the third was the Rules minority report, directly banning certain practices in *delegate selection,* and otherwise commanding the *Special Committee* (created by the Credentials majority report) to use certain general notions about democracy in the larger analysis which it would presumably undertake.

Surprisingly, the first effective reform vote at the 1968 Convention came on none of these resolutions. Rather, it was taken in the traditional convention session of the National Committee, on Saturday afternoon, August 24. The final substantive item on the agenda at that meeting, before a series of routine resolutions, was a report from Richard Hughes and his Special Equal Rights Committee. The lengthy report, which passed easily on a voice vote, contained a suggestion for yet another study commission:

> 4) That a Commission on Party Structure should be created to study the relationship between the National Democratic Party and its constituent State Demo-

cratic Parties, in order that full participation of all Democrats without regard to race, color, creed or national origin may be facilitated by uniform standards for structure and operation.[25]

Unlike the proposed Rules Commission of the Rules majority report, which surfaced as an issue both during and after the convention, generating conflict at every appearance, the proposed Commission on Party Structure from the Special Equal Rights Committee occasioned no debate either within the National Committee or outside of it. It received no attention from the press, from insurgent delegates, or from liberal or conservative members of the Humphrey coalition. In fact, it disappeared from public notice until January of 1969.

Of the three other resolutions dealing with future party rules, the Credentials majority report went through first. At 9:25 P.M., on Tuesday evening, August 27, Richard Hughes, Credentials chairman, offered his resolution to establish a Special Committee to study delegate selection. While there had been notable divisions over the Texas, Alabama, North Carolina, and two Georgia minority reports, there were none over the majority report. Hughes spoke in its behalf for about eight minutes, no one spoke against it, and it carried on a voice vote. By 9:33 P.M., Credentials business for the 1968 Convention was finished.

A bit of Rules business had already been to the floor before this Credentials presentation, and the rest followed shortly thereafter. On Monday evening, after the introductory speeches, Rules Chairman Samuel Shapiro had introduced the temporary standards from his committee, for use until the convention adopted permanent rules the next night. His introduction had drawn two dissents, one from Tom Gordon of the Texas delegation, who wished to retain the unit rule, and one from Jesse M. Unruh of the California delegation, who wanted to postpone balloting on the Credentials minority reports. Shapiro had defeated Gordon on a voice vote and then, when Unruh had requested a roll call, had handed the Californian a two-to-one drubbing.

When he returned to the podium on Tuesday evening, the Illinois governor carried the Rules majority report with him. Joseph F. Crangle, chairman of the New York delegation, came forward with the Rules minority report, which he offered as an *amendment* to the majority report, and debate began on what was to be the only successful minority report at the 1968 Convention.

The Rules minority report had already benefited from a substantial lobbying campaign by the Hughes Commission staff, able to move about on the floor because of the official status which National Chairman Bailey had reluctantly granted. Joe Crangle was about to marshal his forces to suggest as broad a range of support as possible. Nevertheless, Alder, Cowan, and Eli Segal, their official link with the McCarthy campaign, all expected one more loss, reasoning that the strongest minority report should have been the one to seat the insurgent delegation in Georgia. That report had failed, 1,041 1/2 to 1,413, and they expected the Rules minority report to follow suit.

The first indication that the pattern might be different came just before the roll call, when Robert C. McCandless, coordinator of communications for the Humphrey forces, announced tersely to his floor operatives that "we have no position on this." Max M. Kampelman, one of the chief strategists for the vice president, saw the issue, first, as comparatively inconsequential, and, second, as well worth sidestepping in any case:

> There was not much attention to the Rules Committee reports. Our objective was to get a nominee. This was unimportant, except as it might have some effect on the nomination. We said to ourselves, if you're going to *study* it, you can control it. If you get the nomination, you'll have control of the DNC. If you have the DNC, then you'll control any *study*. A study commission could be a way of harmonizing the issue. What we were concerned about was the question of the unit rule. We didn't want to do anything to upset the main job.[26]

The roll call which followed was noteworthy for more than the fact that it produced the only insurgent victory of the convention. It was also, by a clear margin, the most confused ballot of that confused and unhappy gathering. Numerous delegations passed because they were sufficiently stirred from earlier battles to be unable to poll themselves quickly. Numerous others passed because they could not determine the precise nature of the question. This general uncertainty infected the news media as well, and reporters fed it back into the hall. John Chancellor of NBC, queried on the air about the substance of the resolution, said it was "the unit rule again," and those delegates who were watching their own activity on small portable televisions inevitably saw him say so.[27]

Any delegate who *was* confused by all this was about to be plunged into deeper uncertainty by Permanent Chairman Carl B. Albert, majority leader of the U.S. House. Having run through the roll of the states without much success, Albert moved to suspend the rules and go directly into debate on a second minority report, the one adding state chairmen and Young Democratic presidents to the Democratic National Committee. As a result, nearly half the delegates had to be polled on the first Rules minority report while simultaneously listening to arguments on a second. A minute-by-minute account of the proceedings in *Congressional Quarterly* gives some indication of their dilemma:

10:42 P.M.—Albert says nine delegations had asked for a roll call and he puts the question. Alaska asks that the question be restated before roll call begins. Roll call then resumed with many "passes."

11:16 P.M.—When delay continues because of state caucuses during the roll call, Albert says that "nothing but a point of order can interrupt a roll call under the rules of the Convention and the House of Representatives." But he says the Chair can ask for unanimous consent to suspend the rules in order to interrupt the roll call for other business. When Albert makes this request and then says "the Chair hears no objection," shouts of no are heard. Albert says he "cannot interpret that kind of sound" and states that there is no objection, cutting off mild shouts of protest.

11:18 P.M.—Signs reading "We want Kennedy" appear near the New York and California delegations, accompanied by a chant with the same sentiment. Albert says demonstrations are not in order and gavels it down, saying "we won't be able to nominate any candidate unless our business is carried out." Signs disappear and quiet is restored.

11:20 P.M.—James B. Hunt, Jr. (N.C.) says he speaks for 21 members of the Rules Committee with a minority resolution to seat presidents of state Young Democrats organizations and Democratic state chairmen as members of the Democratic National Committee. The "youth" resolution is supported by speeches from Sen. Birch Bayh (Ind.), Lt. Gov. Wendell Ford (Ky.), James M. Sprouse, nominee for Governor of West Virginia, and Sen. Joseph Tydings (Md.)

11:35 P.M.—Providence, R.I., Mayor Joseph A. Doorley, Jr., speaks against the resolution, claiming that it would enlarge the National Committee unduly.

11:38 P.M.—Albert calls for a roll call, saying he had requests from 15 states. Roll call on unit rule is completed first. Outcome is 1,350 for the unit-rule minority resolution, 1,206 against, thus winning adoption.[28]

This outcome was a genuine surprise, although the attempt by Chairman Albert to move ahead and debate the platform plank on Vietnam prevented even the deeply interested from trying to explain it at the time. Afterward, hindsight would suggest several contributing factors. The formal content of the resolution surely influenced the decision of some individual delegates, and even of some coherent factions within specific states. The developing atmosphere of the convention itself, the total convention context, clearly swayed a substantial, if even more scattered, set of voters. Finally, several noteworthy efforts at personal lobbying shifted a few large, identifiable blocs.[29]

Because the Rules minority report had come up under such confused conditions, it was possible for delegates to interpret it in two separate ways. They could focus on the toughened prohibition of the unit rule, to the effect that the rule "not be used in any stage of the delegate selection process," or they could look at the second major clause, requiring "primary, convention, or committee procedures open to public participation within the calendar year."

Presumably, most of those who were fundamentally confused leaned toward the first reading, with its more extensive proscriptions on the unit rule. The speakers on the Rules minority report all slanted their remarks that way; television newsmen reinforced the same partial misperception; Chairman Albert did likewise. To the extent that delegates shared this muddled perception, that fact surely contributed to the success of the minority report. The convention had already gone on record in opposition to the unit rule, for 1968 and forevermore; there was no clear reason not to reaffirm that sentiment. Even this predisposition, however, was not uniform in its impact. Those states which still permitted the unit rule actually contributed a greater margin against the Rules minority report than against throwing out the entire Georgia delegation, although the convention as a whole was shifting by 515 votes in the other direction. In any case, Segal, for one, was happy to accept this dividend of confusion: "Those events in that '68 Convention—no one knew what was going on. Nobody knew. It was chaos on the floor."[30]

But there was a second section to the Rules minority report, the one endorsing more public participation in delegate selection, and there must have been some delegates who saw this as the critical part. Again, the net effect of concentration on this second section was surely beneficial. But again, some of the more organizationally conservative delegates were clearly repelled by this same provision. John Bailey, for example, came down onto the floor to firm up the Connecticut delegation because he believed that this might reduce the role of the organized party in presidential politics; the Connecticut ballot went more strongly against the Rules minority report than against unseating the entire Georgia delegation. Subsequently, Wexler contrasted the insight of Bailey with the misperceptions of other state leaders:

> Bailey knew immediately what the minority report implied. Bailey laid it down hard to the Connecticut delegation. He was a smart man, and he knew. But many state chairmen didn't understand. Plus there was no organized attempt to stop it. Neither O'Brien nor Humphrey did anything about it. That was such a heated convention, with so much going on. Many people felt that this was a way to throw the liberals a bone. Plus the fact that nobody understood it.

A far different sort of influence on the outcome derived from the emotional atmosphere of the convention hall. By Tuesday, a generalized unhappiness about the course of the convention, about events both inside and out, had infected many of the delegates. In that context, it became plausible for concerned delegates to select the Rules minority report as a means for placating the dissidents, or as a means for separating themselves from more extreme reactions by the convention leadership. The Humphrey·spokesmen actually facilitated this response, by telling delegates to go with their individual preferences. On the other hand, some negative votes were surely cast by those who wanted to sustain the Chair *against* dissidents, any dissidents. This was a primary motive for Mayor Richard J. Daley, especially since Rules Chairman Shapiro was his home-state governor; Illinois was indeed more unified against the Rules minority report than it had been against the Georgia challenge.

These atmospheric effects did not reach their peak until the following evening, but they were easily strong enough by Tuesday night to sway added individual votes on both sides. Theodore H. White, in his account of the Humphrey nomination the next night, provided perhaps the most vivid sense of the visceral impact of "atmosphere":

> Slowly, his anger grew as he watched the television sets and what was to be the penultimate climax on his way to the Presidency, a milestone in the career of the "politics of joy." Alioto rose on screen to nominate him; back and forth the cameras swung from Alioto to pudgy, cigar-smoking politicians, to Daley, with his undershot, angry jaw, painting visually without words the nomination of the Warrior of Joy as a puppet of the old machines. Carl Stokes, the black mayor of Cleveland, was next—to second Humphrey's nomination—and then, at 9:55, NBC's film of the bloodshed had finally been edited, and Stokes was wiped from the nation's vision to show the violence in living color.
>
> The Humphrey staff is furious—Stokes is their signature on the Humphrey civil-rights commitment; and Stokes' dark face is being wiped from the nation's view to show blood—Hubert Humphrey being nominated in a sea of blood.[31]

Finally, the minority report benefited from several sharply focused personal contacts by Harold Hughes, Iowa governor and commission chairman. Hughes had first firmed up his own delegation. Where Iowa had supported the Georgia challenge by a vote of 32 to 12, Hughes whacked it into line behind the Rules minority report, 46 to 0. Then, in a much more impressive effort, Hughes corralled the entire *Missouri* delegation—larger than Iowa's, structurally conservative, and voting consistently in the opposite direction.

The biggest net shift in any state came in Missouri, where Governor Warren E. Hearnes led his powerful state delegation, authorized to use the unit rule, toward a unanimous vote against its retention and for the Rules minority report. Hughes simply asked Hearnes for a personal favor, since the minority report was associated with the commission which bore Hughes's name. Hearnes simply assented. Those who observed this maneuver, like Alder, were as surprised by Hearnes's response as they were by the final tally: "Hughes just asked Hearnes to go with the resolution. He walked over and gave him a great big bearhug, and then he just asked him." But if the motivations behind these votes were tangential and idiosyncratic, their impact was powerful and direct. The shifts in Iowa and Missouri, by themselves, provided almost the entire margin of victory for the Rules minority report.

Implications

Whether these developments would amount to anything was unclear when the balloting ended, and unclear when the convention adjourned. A dissident proposal had succeeded, and this Rules minority report had strengthened the instructions to the commission on delegate selection which the convention had authorized. On the other hand, most analysts concluded that little of any consequence had occurred. The insurgents had indeed won a vote, but it was to be their only win. It would have no impact on the "real business" of the convention, the nomination of a potential president.

Most major newspapers gave their lead story about the convention events of Tuesday to the uproar over the unsuccessful attempt by Chairman Albert to handle the Vietnam plank in the early hours of the morning. Most gave their second lead to the disturbances outside the convention hall. The *New York Times* did comment elsewhere on the sweeping possibilities inherent in the Rules minority report—if the study commissions were appointed, if they issued recommendations in line with the wishes of self-conscious party reformers, and if both the National Committee and the fifty-five state, district, and territorial parties accepted those recommendations and put them into effect. Yet most newspapers which even noted the passage of this minority report gave it essentially pro forma treatment, in their pieces about the various credentials challenges. And many papers did not mention the Rules minority report at all, thereby implicitly dismissing its potential.[32]

They were to be quite wrong. With the passage of the Rules minority report, at about 11:40 P.M. on Tuesday, August 27, the character of the politics of party reform changed. At an absolute minimum, passage of this report guaranteed that there would be additional stages to reform politics. Beyond that, passage created the possibility that a set of new organizational arenas for this politics would follow. Finally, passage of the Rules minority report both generated and testified to a loosely connected network of party dissidents who were—at least temporarily—both mobilized into party politics and focused upon party rules and structures.

The convention had actually produced three general statements on the subject of party reform: The Rules minority report, amending the majority report; the Credentials majority report; and the final report of the Special Equal Rights Committee. All three would inevitably acquire their meaning, and hence their impact on presidential nominating procedures, through the politics surrounding their implementation. Yet all three were, at a minimum, concrete directives which would have to be addressed by major party actors—and which could be aggressively addressed by others as well.

Moreover, these resolutions promised the creation of one, two, three, or more specialized arenas for reform politics, in the form of their authorized study commissions. Unless the regular party responded by refusing to appoint these commissions at all, they promised to become the organizational forums within which the practical meaning of reform resolutions would be determined.

Nothing guaranteed that the product of these commissions would be sweeping institutional reform. The drafters of the Rules minority report had tried to give any reform commissions a clear direction. The Hughes Commission had given them a more specific legacy. But the resolutions authorizing them remained vague and general, and the conditions of their passage had obscured this mandate even further. Moreover, the Hughes Commission itself had been a marginal operation, and no official successor was obliged to heed its product.

Instead, the product of these commissions would be shaped much more clearly by the politics of their appointment, by the character of their members—leaders, commissioners, and staff—and by the reform politics which unfolded within their boundaries. Sweeping institutional change might still result. Systematic attempts to clean up the existing system might even more plausibly follow. So might a thorough whitewash of the entire issue.

If there was an early indication that the most expansive, and not the most restrictive, scenario was likely to follow—that the eventual product would be aggressive reform commissions, framing aggressive recommendations for institutional change, on a model almost completely at variance with existing party arrangements—it probably lay in the appearance of a national nucleus of incipient party reformers, courtesy of the 1968 Convention. For these people, reform politics, not presidential politics, was of primary concern. They were not yet a full-blown alternative coalition of Democratic elites, ready to challenge the established coalition for leadership of the party and ready to reshape national politics in their own image. But they were the beginnings—the nucleus—of that coalition.

The conversion from nomination politics to reform politics had been clearest, and the resulting connections were strongest, among those who had been part of the Hughes Commission or who had been associated with its convention endeavors. Some of the more explicit commission actors, like Tom Alder, had always cared primarily for the reform aspects of the operation, and only incidentally for its contribution to the McCarthy campaign. Others from the McCarthy campaign proper, like Eli Segal and Anne Wexler, had begun by conceiving of the commission as one more appendage of the nomination effort and had only later come to value its recommendations as ends in themselves. Segal's growing attachment to the Rules minority report surprised even himself:

> Afterwards, I was exhilarated when I returned to my room that night. I couldn't say it, because we had lost on Vietnam. But I was excited as hell that we had established this thing. I went from being anti-Vietnam, to being a reform Democrat, that night.

Around these individuals, at a greater distance and with more tenuous connections, was a much larger group of potentially interested, potentially mobilizable, and potentially influential reform actors. These were the individuals who had participated in the insurgent nomination campaigns of 1968, especially the McCarthy campaign, or who were already involved with reform politics in their home areas but had been particularly exercised by developments at the ill-fated 1968 Convention. In the normal course of events, the campaigns which had united them or the incidents which had aroused them would quickly fade. Yet if their interest could be maintained, they constituted a crucial pool of recruits for a more extensive reform politics to follow.

Ultimately and ironically, then, a device—the Commission on the Democratic Selection of Presidential Nominees—which had begun as an adjunct to the credentials challenges thrown up by the McCarthy campaign, and which had been refocused to serve the McCarthy nomination effort more generally, had provided scant practical help to either. Instead, it had created much of the substance, all of the initial arenas, and many of the participants for the next stage of reform politics.

In short, if the commission device had failed in all its intended purposes, it had combined with autonomous developments at the convention to produce some far more consequential effects. It had given rise to a set of new directives for party reform. It had elicited the promise of new and specialized arenas in which reform politics might be pursued. And it had begun to form a self-aware circle of actors with whom that politics would have priority over the ensuing months and years. The number of those who shared this awareness in the fall of 1968 was still quite small. But the factors nurturing it—official resolutions which could be read to authorize nearly anything (or nothing), as well as an elite constituency which, at least temporarily, cared more about the politics of party rules than about presidential politics—were fated to convert the issue of party reform into an independent political phenomenon during the four years to follow.

CHAPTER

2

A Politics of Party Reform:

The Humphrey Campaign and

The Party Structure Commission

IN WHICH, negotiations over the appointment of official reform commissions continue through the general election and into the postelection period; one of these bodies, the Commission on Party Structure and Delegate Selection, moves to the center of these negotiations—and to the forefront of potential impact on party reform; and a new national chairman, Fred R. Harris, gets to select this commission and its leadership. AND IN WHICH, reform politics is institutionalized, for the duration of the struggle over reform recommendations, in the Party Structure Commission; the prospects for sweeping institutional change are enhanced by appointments following from the private, proreform agenda of incoming Chairman Harris; and the incipient coalition of alternative Democratic elites, while ambiguously successful on the commission proper, secures unambiguous domination of its leadership and staff.

BETWEEN AUGUST of 1968 and February of 1969, the Democratic party moved from a national convention in which the regular party had stoutly—perhaps too stoutly—defended itself against party insurgents, to an official party commission which charged surrogates for those very insurgents with reforming the regular party. During five and a half months of nearly invisible maneuvering, the entire party was propelled in a new direction, with a destination unknown even to those who helped establish this portentous new course.

The Democratic National Convention of 1968 was an eminently forgettable experience for nearly everyone. The reform resolutions which slipped through in the midst of its more dramatic and conflictual developments had

41

no inherent claim on the major actors in party politics in the period following the convention. Yet within weeks, serious negotiations about the composition—and thus the projected orientation—of the commissions authorized by these resolutions were under way, and these negotiations continued until the end of February, when the commissions themselves finally assembled to confront their charge.

The convention reports calling for one or more party reform commissions first resurfaced as bargaining counters in the general election campaign. In theory, their creation could provide the Humphrey for President operation with renewed support from McCarthy partisans, while it offered these former McCarthyites a realization of their one clear gain from the 1968 Convention. In practice, this first attempt at commission creation foundered on divisions and suspicions remaining from that convention. Nevertheless, this opening round of negotiations generated sufficient momentum to keep the issue alive. In the process, it provided a specific focus for the small group of reform activists who had come together at the convention and who were welded back together as bargaining over commission appointments proceeded.

Negotiations did indeed continue after the November election, under the direction of Lawrence F. O'Brien, the Democratic national chairman. In the manner of national party chairmen throughout history, O'Brien saw commission appointments as an opportunity to begin healing those divisions which the convention, and then the campaign, had underlined all too clearly. Yet the actual composition of these commissions was determined by the successor to O'Brien at the National Committee, Fred R. Harris, and Harris had something very different in mind. He planned to install the growing "reform wing" of the party within these commissions. He expected commissions composed in this fashion to support the brand of party reform preferred by these individuals. He hoped that these reforms would rebound to his personal credit, while the reformers rallied to his personal cause.

By the time Harris achieved the chairmanship, it was clear to most participants that the commission on delegate selection, rather than the one on convention rules, would be the central arena for practical reform politics. Accordingly, Harris labored to create a superficially indeterminate but fundamentally proreform majority within this Commission on Party Structure and Delegate Selection. Harris did not cater to the leading lights of the reform movement, a decision which eventually cost him most of his personal goals. But he certainly did not cater to hard-line—or even moderate—party regulars. Instead, he attempted to create a commission of apparently neutral, almost faceless individuals, who were nevertheless sympathetic to the reform doctrine of the moment, aimed at creating a fluid and participatory political party.

Even Harris did not foresee the extent to which the still-small cadre of reform activists would dominate this reform commission. Yet his newly appointed commission leaders, Chairman George S. McGovern and Vice Chairman Harold E. Hughes, were primarily concerned with the emerging reform constituency. In turn, these leaders recruited a staff—the individuals who would shape at least the rough agenda for party reform and perhaps its detailed substance—which took the whole operation even further toward the preferences of newly mobilized reform activists.

When all this was done, the contours for a subsequent reform politics were largely established as well. The politics of party reform moved quickly inside the boundaries of the Party Structure Commission. After that, reform politics centered on efforts to influence the content of reform recommendations emanating from that commission. This "politics of recommendation" stretched intensively through late November of 1969 and intermittently through April of 1970. It ended with the framing of a practical definition—*the* practical definition—for party reform.

As a result, the politics of empaneling the Party Structure Commission acquired, by hindsight, additional importance. At a minimum, the creation of this commission established that there would be a continuing politics of party reform within the national Democratic party. Beyond that, it determined the receptivity, or at least the inherent parameters, to the recommendations for institutional change which this commission would consider. At the same time, and finally, creation of the Party Structure Commission both continued the mobilization of the constituency for extensive party reform and transferred key actors from that constituency to the leadership and, especially, the staff of the key reform commission.

The Negotiations on Commission Appointment

In the beginning, none of these results seemed likely. Few people even departed the 1968 Convention with its resolutions on party reform uppermost in their minds. The exceptions, of course, were found among those who had come to consider convention battles over party rules as ends in themselves, rather than as tactics to derail the vice president. The top staffers at the Hughes Commission, like Tom Alder and Geoff Cowan, and some interested delegate-hunters from the McCarthy campaign, like Anne Wexler and Eli Segal, were the heart of this group. Early in September, Alder and some of these others reached a specific decision *not* to shelve the Hughes Commission:

I went, with the Cowans, Jack Newfield, and some others to the Cape after the convention, to get wet. When we started talking again, the first question was, "How are these commissions going to get appointed? *When* are they going to get appointed?"

Those who took part in these Labor Day discussions agreed that the Hughes Commission should be kept alive, at least as a letterhead and staff operation, in case it could generate some pressure for appointment of the Rules and Special committees. While prospects did not appear bright, Alder saw them getting even dimmer unless there were some immediate follow-through:

> Reformers at the time believed that Hearnes would be the chairman. They felt that Humphrey would lose, and O'Brien would leave, and that the party, instead of taking that as a lesson, would go back with someone like Hearnes, or Hearnes's National Committeeman. The party would fall into the custody of the inheritors.

Accordingly, after closing the donated office of the Hughes Commission in New York, Alder, with his own funds and a contribution from Cowan and Wexler, rented Suite 504 at 1029 Vermont Avenue, N.W., Washington, D.C., and put the Commission on the Democratic Selection of Presidential Nominees back into business.

Shortly after the transplanted Hughes Commission reopened, the first of what would be a series of false starts on the appointment of official reform commissions began. Actually, there were to be two of these efforts, one from each side of the reformer-regular split. Neither was to be directly effective; both were to contribute to the hostility and suspicion surrounding party affairs in general.

The first move sprang from developments internal to the Humphrey for President campaign. In mid-September, Stephen A. Mitchell, the (former) convention coordinator for the McCarthy forces, joined ex-Governor Terry Sanford of North Carolina as co-chairman of "Citizens for Humphrey-Muskie." Mitchell's major responsibility was to bring the McCarthy loyalists back into the national campaign. One of his first ideas was to have Hubert Humphrey call for creation of the reform commission which the convention had authorized. Humphrey snapped up the idea and put it in a letter to Larry O'Brien, his new Democratic national chairman:

> A resolution adopted by the Rules Committee of the Democratic National Committee called upon the National Chairman to appoint a Rules Study Commission to be charged with studying and evaluating and codifying the rules of past Democratic National Conventions and investigating the advisability of rules changes.

I am vitally interested in this project. I am particularly interested in developing recommendations which will maximize democracy in the nomination process and which will insure open conventions, free discussion, and logical, fair, and orderly procedures.

In view of the overriding public interest in the contemplated study, I hope that you will be able to proceed as rapidly as possible, with the formation of the Rules Study Commission. In the formation of the Commission I urge that all points of view be sought out and appropriately represented and that particular notice be taken of the report submitted to the Rules Committee by the Committee headed by the Honorable Harold Hughes, Governor of Iowa.[1]

O'Brien incorporated this letter into a press release the next day, October 8, asserting that he would "begin immediate consultation with Democratic Party leaders around the country in order to act speedily on Vice President Humphrey's request."[2] As an attention-getting device, however, the release was a failure. Few major news media even picked it up, and the staff at the National Committee quickly turned to other matters.

About the same time, there was a parallel, independent attempt among former McCarthy activists to use commission appointment as a bridge between McCarthy and Humphrey supporters. On October 7, Gerald N. Hill, chairman of the California Democratic Council, announced that "reform of the Democratic Party" was one of four points which Eugene McCarthy was asking as the price for an endorsement of the national Democratic ticket.[3] But the next day, McCarthy's senatorial office issued a statement asserting that Hill had been incorrect. Later that night, the former candidate himself appeared to crush all such possibilities, when he spoke at a fundraiser for party insurgents in New York:

The call goes up now for party unity, but this is the same thing urged on us when we first began to challenge. I see no reason why if the cry for unity then was not acceptable, it's any more acceptable today.[4]

The failure of this second initiative should have been the end of the matter, at least until after the election. The Humphrey campaign was undermanned, underfinanced, and dispirited; it had no stray resources to devote to canvassing for commissioners. McCarthy himself was more quixotic than ever; if the remaining McCarthy partisans could be swayed at all, it would have to be through something other than the endorsement of their erstwhile leader—or the announcement of a party reform commission.

Nevertheless, the mere announcement that appointment was imminent set off a chain reaction which kept the issue alive, through election day and beyond. First came a persistent rumor that the permanent chairman of the 1968 Convention, Congressman Carl D. Albert of Oklahoma, and the temporary chairman of the 1968 Convention, Senator Daniel K. Inouye of Hawaii, were in line for commission leadership. Those who had been most concerned with the membership of any official commissions found this rumored arrangement to be an unacceptable capitulation to one faction from rules battles at the convention. Alder turned to rallying outside pressures:

> They announced that they would appoint a joint commission, which would be co-chaired by Albert and Inouye. It was formally leaked. This was an abortive attempt to announce it, but it was then treated as a trial balloon.
>
> I called Gallegos in New Mexico, someone in California, had Wexler call Crangle. We did a phone network right away, playing the trial balloon game to the hilt. We let them know that people were out there watching. Very quickly, we got a call back from Kapenstein, saying that they would do it right. He wanted me to stop signaling people. I kept having people call in, so that they would have the full force of the deal.

If appointment of this commission was not sufficient to activate McCarthy partisans, any appearance of playing games with that appointment risked inciting them to further damage. The office of the national chairman accordingly insisted that Albert and Inouye had never been even a remote possibility for the top commission slots, much less the occupants of a trial balloon, and Chairman O'Brien had Ira Kapenstein, the deputy national chairman, call Alder directly to confirm that fact.

Alder, however, had found a second source of worry. The press release of October 8 had mentioned the Rules Commission, authorized by the Rules majority report, but had ignored the Special Committee, born of the union of the Credentials majority report with the Rules minority report. When Alder queried national headquarters on the matter, however, an intricate procedural exchange resulted. Harold Gordon, deputy general counsel, noted that there was as yet no official record of convention decisions, so that the issue of one commission or two was effectively moot. Alder convinced Adlai Stevenson III, Illinois state treasurer, to intervene with Governor Shapiro and produce a transcript. Gordon then replied that no action could be taken on either one or two commissions, because the resolutions themselves appeared to be inconsistent, or even mutually invalidating.

Alder again turned to his telephone network, this time to press for confirmation that there would indeed be *two* commissions and that they would be appointed *soon*. On the dissident side, he urged members of the New Democratic Coalition, the umbrella group which was being formed to give advocates of a "new politics" some organizational focus, to query the office of the national chairman about the appointment of these commissions.[5] On the regular side, he mailed every member of the National Committee a new "Memorandum: Principal Actions of the 1968 Democratic Convention," which listed the provisions of the Credentials majority, Rules majority, and Rules minority reports, though not those of the report of the National Committee's own Special Equal Rights Committee.[6] In Washington, Alder asked Fred Dutton to pay a personal call on Chairman O'Brien, and Dutton did so. In Iowa, he appealed to Governor Hughes, and Hughes agreed to have Alder draft a quasi-public letter to O'Brien which he (Hughes) would sign, a letter urging fast action on the *Special Committee.*[7]

Again, whatever the legal merits of the matter, its politics dictated a reversal at the National Committee. Martin L. Friedman, the general counsel, called a luncheon meeting with Deputy Counsel Gordon of the National Committee and Staff Director Alder of the Hughes Commission. There, Friedman underlined the judgment of Chairman O'Brien that appointments should be made to two commissions at the earliest possible opportunity. A week later, O'Brien reaffirmed this position in his quasi-public response to Governor Hughes:

> There has been some confusion about the role of the Special Committee and that of the Rules Study Commission. In my view they are to be separate entities with separate functions. I do appreciate the importance of establishing these organizations just as soon as practicable. We have had a great number of suggestions concerning the composition and organization of the Rules Study Commission but very few relating to the Special Committee. I would welcome your views.
>
> As you recognize in your letter, our overriding preoccupation at this point is with the election campaign. You may be assured, however, that we will get to the matter of the Special Committee immediately after November 15.[8]

This intricate minuet over the number, shape, and birthdate of Democratic reform commissions did establish that there were to be two such bodies, appointed "soon." Beyond that, it testified only to the level of suspicion among those with an interest in their composition. Negotiations over the membership of the two commissions were nevertheless resumed in mid-November, on the down side of a losing election, with Chairman O'Brien himself taking the lead role. O'Brien was intensely aware of the party split which had come to focus on these two promised bodies, and his general approach was to try to make a virtue of necessity. He intended to appoint major spokesmen for the various and unhappy factions within his party to both commissions and to use the commissions themselves to hammer out a modus vivendi within the party as a whole.

Yet while O'Brien was clearly moving ahead in this approach, there was a wild card in his discussions. He was known to have financial worries, to have offers in private business, and to have no commitment to stay at the National Committee past the general election. O'Brien, accordingly, might or might not remain as chairman; if he left, he might or might not make any appointments; if he did not, his successor might or might not feel constrained by any recommendations.

While he weighed his options, the chairman did set to work on two lists. He began by initiating a wide range of contacts. In short order, an even larger group of potential commissioners came looking for him. The resulting discussions rambled far and wide, but three regular lines of communication did surface. The first line ran to the entourage of the outgoing vice president, a line of declining importance at a time of defeat for Hubert Humphrey and of career disruption for his supporters.[9] The second line ran to political associates of the late Senator Robert Kennedy and, especially, of his brother, Edward M. "Ted" Kennedy of Massachusetts, who were more than happy to take up the slack from the disengagement of the vice president.[10] And the third major line of communication ran to Tom Alder at the Hughes Commission. Fred Dutton, who had a foot in both the Kennedy and the Hughes camps, marveled at the extent to which the commission group, with little more than a letterhead, an office, and a telephone, could deal themselves into these negotiations:

> I had several meetings with Geoff [Cowan] after the convention. We worked on it with Geoff and Harry [Hughes]. The thing was being discussed like it was a political science paper. Tying it to constituencies never really went on. There was very little attempt to recruit key figures. Somebody in labor, some key blacks, but that was all. This was *the* piece of paper, and we were going to run with it. Chicago gave us a sense that we could flex our muscles.

The lists which O'Brien developed were noteworthy, in light of the ultimate appointments, both for the range of party interests which they represented and for the celebrity of the representatives themselves. O'Brien was willing to name symbolic leaders of "the new politics," like the co-chairmen of the New Democratic Coalition, Paul Schrade and Donald O. Peterson. He was willing to pit them against equally symbolic products of "the old politics," like Governor Samuel H. Shapiro of Illinois and Mayor Joseph M. Barr of Pittsburgh.

Despite this, the contents of any and all such lists become irrelevant in early January, when O'Brien resigned from the national chairmanship without making any appointments. In one of his last acts of housekeeping, he put his file of recommendations in order, cleaned up his draft lists, and left both as a valedictory to his successor. After that, he exited—permanently, he thought —from the politics of party reform.

Well before O'Brien had made his resignation official, Vice President Humphrey, the titular leader of his party and the man who traditionally would nominate a successor, had tentatively settled on his candidate—the man whose first major act as chairman would be the appointment of two party reform commissions. Humphrey's basic preference was to keep O'Brien, but he recognized the pressures on the sitting chairman, and he was ready to turn to ex-Governor Sanford of North Carolina to fill O'Brien's shoes. A few of the peripheral Humphrey advisers favored Senator Fred R. Harris of Oklahoma, but most of his intimates, like Max M. Kampelman, shared the vice president's ranking:

> Humphrey would have preferred to have O'Brien stay on. Most of the Humphrey *people* would have preferred to keep him on. The Johnson people weren't happy. O'Brien didn't like the idea of being beaten up regularly. He needed money, but he wasn't getting paid. Humphrey did ask O'Brien to stay. O'Brien was not *begged;* Humphrey asked but did not beg. The Johnson people and almost all of the Humphrey people were then pushing Sanford.

When it became clear, as December wore on, that O'Brien's mind was made up, Humphrey himself entered serious discussions with Sanford. The former governor, however, was somewhat reticent, citing family concerns and a desire to return to North Carolina, and the two men agreed to talk further. As a result, the formal resignation of O'Brien occurred while Humphrey was in Norway, as official U.S. representative at the funeral of Trygve Lie, former secretary-general of the United Nations. O'Brien's departure hit the newspapers on Tuesday, January 7; Fred Harris moved immediately—and independently—to see if the chairmanship might still be available.[11]

Surprisingly, Harris was successful. Humphrey agreed to back him for the post and passed the word to his aides at home. Most, like Kampelman, were caught unaware:

> While Humphrey was in Europe, he gave it to Harris. Harris pleaded with him by phone. Humphrey's company in Europe was his physician, Edgar Berman, who lobbied for Harris. The combination of that call, with Edgar's presence, with Sanford's standoffishness. Humphrey felt a tremendous appreciation to Harris. Harris had been a close friend of Robert Kennedy and had gotten the big build-up from the Kennedy people. The fact that Harris went to Humphrey rather than Kennedy, the fact that he was prepared to assume the chairmanship and be openly identified with Humphrey, was a plus. Mondale took things away from Harris during the campaign; he pulled back because of Mondale's aggressiveness. Then Harris wanted to be vice president, and he didn't get it. Humphrey felt he owed him the National Committee.

The vice president returned from Norway late in the day of January 8. On the 9th, he met with Harris, Sanford, and James G. O'Hara, congressman from Michigan and the third man in press speculation about the national chairmanship. On the 10th, Sanford announced that he was not a candidate. And on the 11th, Humphrey made his Norwegian decision public, revealing that it would be Fred Harris for Democratic national chairman. When a press boomlet for Richard Hughes, governor of New Jersey, former Credentials chairman, and the rallying point for an unlikely coalition of opponents, fell apart a few days later, the selection of Harris as the unopposed choice was effectively assured.[12]

The Humphrey advisers, beyond having preferred Sanford, were actively dismayed at the elevation of Harris. They felt, first, that Harris was not particularly loyal to the vice president; second, that he had no real concern with the party as an organization; and third, in consequence, that he would be likely to permit changes within the party which would be harmful to the future of Hubert H. Humphrey. The checkered character of Harris's recent career in politics reinforced these fears. In a short period, Harris had moved from being the protégé of Senator Robert S. Kerr of Oklahoma, to being a premier ally of Senator Robert F. Kennedy of New York, to being campaign manager for Vice President Hubert Humphrey—to some new, unpredictable set of loyalties. Kampelman was unsettled by this possible next incarnation:

> One of the arguments against Harris was that he had his own personal goals and couldn't be trusted on the important issues of the *party*. I had a very sour feeling. I said at the time that Humphrey was making a mistake and hurting the party on Harris. I was not paying much attention to these commissions. Humphrey felt, I think, that Welsh was paying some attention. But Humphrey was emotionally very down; he had really retreated from the process, and the Humphrey operation depended on Bill Welsh.

From the other side, in the Harris camp, there were indeed plans to make the chairmanship a podium from which Harris would stake out a new, more independent, and more reformist position. Verrick O. French, who became executive assistant to the chairman at the National Committee, discussed these possibilities at some length with Harris before the Oklahoma Senator put a rush on Humphrey for the job:

> These [the commissions] seemed like the real opportunity. Fred had gotten interested in the issue of reform. He never focused on it on the operational level in 1968, since he wanted every delegate he could get. But the more he thought about it, the more he saw it from the point of view of equity, and from the point of view of a political problem. What ought to be done, the necessity of doing

it to demonstrate to a major part of the reform effort that he was their kind of guy. He thought that he could be an ideological chairman, and the ideology he would put forth would be the ideology of party reform.

But nobody knew what that meant. He didn't think of himself as a centrist; he was going to be decidedly left, i.e., rights for women, blacks, and young people, welfare rights. Somehow, you see, nobody understood this about Fred until he said it out loud. He had not been a part of the reform effort. The labor guys didn't oppose him, but in fact said he sounded good. Mary Zon was a major influence on Barkan's opinion in this regard. To the extent that there was opposition to Harris as chairman among the reformers, it was reassuring to the labor entourage.

But if Harris was in fact going to be the "chairman of reform," he managed to begin on exactly the wrong foot. In preparing for the next meeting of the National Committee on January 14, where Harris would be confirmed, he set his staff to combing the record of the 1968 Convention, to guarantee precise execution of all convention directives. What he discovered, of course, was that he was under orders to appoint not two commissions, but three—a Rules Committee, a Special Committee, and a Committee on Party Structure, the successor to the Special Equal Rights Committee. Harris's staff, however, noticed that the charge of the Party Structure Committee and that of the Special Committee were clearly overlapping. For his initial meeting of the National Committee, then, Harris asked for a resolution merging the two committees. It passed without debate.[13]

What had been done in the name of good housekeeping was to be received by those who were most concerned with these resolutions in a very different manner. Alder, for one, reacted with dismay:

> The January DNC meeting was a surprise, because Harris ran a resolution through the DNC. The DNC had run a resolution through the Convention to set up a commission to continue the work of the *Richard* Hughes Commission. I and others felt that Harris was trying to subordinate the mandate of the Convention to the DNC. We feared, in addition to Harris's secrecy, his intentions for the whole business.
>
> It looked like the January merger resolution was an effort to try to subordinate the two commissions. The tenor of the resolution so misrepresented the action of the Convention that I began to mail out the short piece on the history of these resolutions again.

If Harris's hidden agenda involved the furtherance of thorough party reform, that fact was not to gain him any immediate points with Alder's reform network. For the reformers, Harris remained the protégé of Robert Kerr who had managed the campaign of Hubert Humphrey. If he had also climbed on and off the bandwagon of Robert Kennedy, that seemed more a sign of opportunism than a commitment to reform. When Harris introduced Resolution No. 12, the merger resolution which created the newly titled Commission on Party Structure and Delegate Selection, he appeared to be living up to all these fears.

In response, Alder called Anne Wexler, and they began to reactivate the telephone network of October. At the same time, Alder began drafting a letter to Harris protesting the merger of the two commissions, to come in under the signature of those former members of the Rules Committee who had signed the Rules minority report. Alder roughed out the letter, Wexler and Joe Crangle edited it, and Alder sent it to Harold Hughes for final approval, before Wexler, Bill Sueppel, and the others would begin using it to bombard the new national chairman.

While this protest was developing, Harris began the serious labor on his new commissions. Between the meeting of the National Committee on January 14 and the unveiling of the two new bodies on February 8, the chairman and his staff concerned themselves with little else. Indeed, the major nonroutine event which intruded on membership negotiations during this three-week period was a first attempt by Harris at fundraising, and even that was largely undertaken to guarantee financing for the new commission.

Harris's style of negotiation, however, was sharply different from that of Larry O'Brien. Where O'Brien had made a show of touching base with a wide range of organizations and individuals and where he had been only a trifle more circumspect in brokering appointments with party and interest group leaders of all sorts, Harris operated far more privately and indirectly. This approach was, at least in part, a product of the existence of a prior round of appointment talks, and especially of the existence of a prior set of appointment *lists,* the ones which O'Brien had bequeathed to Harris.

Harris had many reasons for wanting to escape these tentative commission rosters. At bottom, his desire to see these commissions produce stiffer recommendations for reform necessitated the burial of O'Brien's suggestions. O'Brien had weighted his commissions toward the reformers, so that his lists were far more sympathetic than a typical subcommittee of the National Committee would ever have been. Yet this tilt was not enough to satisfy Harris.

On the other hand, Harris was forced to walk a fine line between the old Humphrey constituency which had placed him in office and the new reform constituency which he hoped to attract. He would never succeed at this if he could not create his commissions and permit them to get down to work without a major explosion by one side or the other. The high-profile names on the O'Brien roster were an automatic threat to this scenario, since they did not lend themselves to being eased past anyone and were, in fact, automatic irritants to opposing segments of the attentive public. On all these grounds, Harris almost had to conduct his discussions as quietly and privately as possible.

One other, crucial difference in appointment negotiations was confirmed soon after the accession of Harris: Most of the interested individuals had come to suspect that the key commission was destined to be Party Structure, and not Rules. The Humphrey-O'Brien call for appointment of "the rules study commission" had skewed the first round of inquiries toward Rules and away from Party Structure. After the election, the attentive public had begun to perceive, in the words of Samuel H. Beer, Harvard professor and eventual commissioner, that Party Structure was "where the action would be," and the balance had begun to shift. By appointment time, the weight of requests had reversed, and Rules had come to be seen as the secondary commission.

The logic behind this increasingly convergent view was straightforward. Control over the process of delegate selection would probably mean more than control over the rules by which these (previously selected) delegates deliberated. That is, the institutions and rules of delegate selection would inevitably shape the distribution of candidate and issue preferences among the resulting delegates, as well as their general social identities. These features, in turn, would be more important to the eventual decisions of the delegates than would the formal procedures by which those decisions were registered.

History would vindicate this point of view. The Rules Commission would admittedly make some noteworthy changes in the organization of the national convention. But it would be *Party Structure* which would engineer the second most extensive change in the institutions of delegate selection in all of American history, *Party Structure* which would contribute to a fundamental change in the nature of presidential nominations, and *Party Structure* which would open the door to a wide-ranging and consequential shift in the character of political elites in the United States. In short, once Fred Harris began to apply himself to the construction of the Commission on Party Structure and Delegate Selection, the essence of the politics of party reform was to revolve primarily around the negotiations for its appointment, around the deliberations preparatory to its recommendations, and around the maneuvering to convert those recommendations into real party law.

The first individuals to try to constrain Harris in these appointment negotiations were those associated with Tom Alder and his amorphous reform constituency. Harris remained confident that if the politics of commission appointment necessitated an arm's-length approach to these militant reformers, their support would rebound when they saw the commissions which he was constructing. Despite this, the new chairman did have to cut their access for a short period, and that, of course, was what Alder and the others immediately noted:

> After all the flak, O'Brien then developed what might have become his valedictory. That list was intact and was generally known. It was Fred Harris's mistake, the error that he made in dealing with Kennedy, Hughes, and McGovern, that Harris developed his own list, which he pulled together in unnecessary secrecy. Harris provoked more suspicion about duplicity. He was not trusted. He did things in extreme secrecy. The way he handled it, that hurt him. Why did he take the O'Brien list and dismantle it?

Harris would have preferred to avoid the New Democratic Coalition [NDC], too, but the NDC leadership was determined to negotiate with him. A delegation headed by Co-chairmen Donald Peterson and Paul Schrade, and including Earl Craig, the executive director, and Anne Wexler of the NDC Task Force on Party Reform, did manage to visit with Harris on January 18. Although the Democratic national chairman assured them that he was seeking reliable reform majorities, the fact that he would not promise to name Harold Hughes as chairman of the Party Structure Commission aroused their anxieties. In response, they tried to put Harris's reassurances on the public record, in an obviously unfriendly press release:

> Chairman Harris, although evidently uncomfortable at being forced to define his position, promised the New Democratic Coalition delegates that no persons who were opposed to party reform would be appointed to either commission.[14]

Of the groups which had held a central place in appointment negotiations under O'Brien—the Hughes Commission network, the Kennedy entourage, and the Humphrey circle—the Kennedy group lost the least in negotiations under Harris. Even here, the new Harris operation made itself less available, but Harris was at least very concerned that the product be acceptable to Teddy Kennedy. The Massachusetts senator was already, in early 1969, the morning-line favorite for the next presidential nomination, and any national chairman might have been expected to give him deference on those grounds. But Harris also had personal fences to mend with the Kennedy partisans, as well as hopes for his own future which Kennedy could certainly aid. Harris actively desired Kennedy to be content with his new commissions, and many of his ultimate choices would be recognized as "Kennedy people" first and foremost.

The new chairman was more ambivalent about a role for his most recent patron, the outgoing vice president. Given that ambivalence, he was perhaps fortunate that Hubert Humphrey was moving back to Minnesota, to accept a joint position as professor of political science at Macalester College and the University of Minnesota. The new professor could not escape some contact with appointment negotiations, but Humphrey was not continuously concerned with their details, and Harris was certainly not seeking his participation on a continual basis. Humphrey did have a former aide, William B. Welsh, at national party headquarters, as one of Harris's two top staffers, and Welsh was hardly withholding his advice. He was, however, constrained by his own belief that adverse comment should not be allowed to torpedo these commissions, and he did suffer the additional disadvantage of lacking a firm political base:

> The NDC was after Harris on this score. You had staffers, and other people around Hughes, who were after him. But there was no input from the Humphrey side. I was there; the treasurer was a Humphrey guy; John Stewart was there.

If the Humphrey operation was no longer a force which required careful, anticipatory acknowledgement, its role as protector of the party was assigned—by default—to organized labor, and especially to Alexander E. Barkan, executive director of the Committee on Political Education [COPE] of the AFL-CIO. Harris was very apprehensive about Barkan's response to his handiwork. He did not modify his lists in any major way to appease the COPE director; he did continually try to obtain an endorsement from Barkan. Vick French and Mary Zon, a Barkan aide, communicated frequently about commission rosters. As appointment time neared, Barkan himself went to visit Harris.

At that meeting, Harris went over his prospective lists in detail, defending them name by name. Barkan argued that they were, taken as a whole, thoroughly unrepresentative of the party. Worse, he asserted, they rewarded the very people who had just finished damaging that party, a scant three months before. The chairman offered no specific changes, but sought acquiescence from Barkan. The COPE director demanded no specific changes, but left without promising support. Harris judged that Barkan's attitude had been one of reluctant acceptance. Barkan felt, after the same meeting, that it would have to be "wait and see":

> Fred Harris was the chairman then, and he gave me a list of people. It was so *overloaded* with "new politics" people that I protested. So he said to me, "If you think this is loaded, look what Larry O'Brien left." Then I took another look and he had George McGovern on it. "What the hell have you got him on for?" I said. "He's a presidential candidate." The whole goddamned thing was so stacked. It looked so hopeless.

The Composition of the Party Structure Commission

The lists which Harris showed to Barkan, and to rare few others, had been constructed to meet two separate sets of criteria. Neither was so explicit as to constitute a written formula; neither was so implicit as to disappear from the discussion of any given candidate for a commission slot. The more overt set of these appointment criteria involved notions of representativeness.

First came *geographic balance.* Both commissions should have members apportioned to the various geographic regions of the country, according to a reasonable numerical standard. Strangely enough, even this presented problems, when combined with Harris's more covert criteria. On numerical grounds, the industrial Northeast was entitled to the largest bloc of commissioners by far, and this entitlement would have been even more pronounced if Democratic votes, rather than raw population, had been the guide. Yet this was exactly the region where party leaders and public officeholders were least sympathetic to changes in party rules. The inevitable solution was to shade the standard: The western and southern states were overrepresented, at the expense of the Northeast.[15]

The second overt criterion was *group balance.* Both commissions should draw their members from all of the recognized "groups" which composed the national Democratic party. Generically, these included demographic categories, official party sectors, and organized interests. Among demographic groups on the Party Structure Commission, Harris saw to it that racial minorities exceeded their percentage in the general population. He recognized women and people under thirty but did not better their percentages within the general public. And he ignored white ethnics and the aged, the other traditional claimants on Democratic demography. Within party officialdom, Harris included state chairmen, National Committee members, and miscellaneous party functionaries, but he did not name any leaders of urban party organizations. His sample of elected officeholders likewise avoided local officials, but included senators and congressmen, governors and state row officers, and state legislators.[16]

Yet when it came to the major interest group within the orthodox Democratic coalition, organized labor, all the problems associated with a straightforward adherence to these overt criteria surfaced in their most virulent form. If classical notions of representation were observed, the prospects for stiff reform recommendations—or at least for reform recommendations pleasing to party dissidents and established reformers—would decline sharply. If the United Auto Workers, perceived as proreform, acquired a commissioner, then the Teamsters, perceived as antireform, had to have one, too—and the AFL-CIO, a reliable ally of the regular party and a powerful contributor to the preceding election campaign, had to have eleven. The solution, of course, was to shade the standard again: The Teamsters were ignored, the UAW received a seat, and so did the *entire* AFL.

Last, but truly not least, came *partisan balance*. Both commissions should draw their members from associates of the leading figures in the national Democratic party. In practical terms, this meant that Hubert Humphrey, as the most recent presidential nominee, and Teddy Kennedy, as the most probable future choice, were entitled to a number of commissioners, while a second group of leaders had the right to name one member per commission. As between Humphrey and Kennedy, Harris gave the edge to Kennedy. Among the others, Harris recognized Lyndon B. Johnson, the outgoing president; Edmund S. Muskie, the losing candidate for vice president; and Eugene J. McCarthy, the losing nomination hopeful. George S. McGovern, as a stand-in contender for the nomination in 1968, was not automatically entitled to anyone, a situation which was more than rectified when he became chairman of the full Party Structure Commission. Fred Harris, of course, in some sense chose them all. Vick French helped puzzle out the practical meaning of these criteria:

> We set out on paper the categories that we should pay some attention to. Geographical distribution. Major interest groups within the party, like labor, the blacks, city organizations. Different levels of elective officeholders. Party officials. Women. We had only three women on that. That would be outrageous today, but it was because of the [Party Structure] Commission that the notion developed that it would be outrageous. We did think about it. Young people.
>
> We began by thinking that we could appoint a much smaller body of people than we ended up with. The French-Harris rule said that twenty-seven people had to be used to be representative of America. We tried to find people who represented more than one factor. It was a very conscious and deliberate approach. What does the party consist of and who would we have to represent. Who had supported who in the last presidential nomination—McCarthy, Kennedy, Humphrey.

These three overt criteria—geography, group membership, and political attachment—were intended to support the contention that the new commissions were indeed representative. If they did their job, they would ward off the criticisms which might arise from three more covert criteria, which were also central to formation of these commissions.

The first and most fundamental was *reform orientation*. Both commissions should contain reliable majorities for extensive structural change. If Harris was to be a reform chairman, this had to be guaranteed. If it were *proclaimed* so soon after he had assumed office, however, it might undermine his position at the National Committee and perhaps destroy the legitimacy of his new organizations. Hence creation of a reform majority had to be at least an ambiguous criterion. The chairman had to feel that he could predict the reform orientation of every member, but he had to refrain from spelling out those orientations too explicitly.

Beyond that, the new commissioners were to be evaluated for an explicit *Harris connection.* If the chairman was to appoint them anyway, and if their product might advance his long-run goals, there was no reason not to have their individual appointments contribute to those goals, too. This standard actually had two separate meanings, depending on the commissioner in question. For commissioners who were expected to be reliable reform votes, it meant only that they should begin with no personal animosity to the national chairman and should offer no evident threat that credit for party reform would be deflected from him. For commissioners who were not expected to support changing the rules, this standard required a more personal loyalty. Reform orientation aside, these members should be active supporters of the chairman himself and should be potentially willing to defer to him on what he defined as critical votes, even if they intended to vote no on most other proposals.

Finally, there was the question of the *symbolic character* of these commisioners. If the commissions were to be constructed for ostensible balance, while guaranteeing party reform and a personal boost for the chairman, they should not contain any obvious "red flags." In the short run, avoiding persons who were symbolic irritants to large segments of the attentive public was the only way to finesse the mutual suspicions surrounding these appointments. In the longer run, an absence of such members promised to make the commissioners easier to lead, since established figures with organized constituencies would presumably be much less amenable to Harris's outside persuasion. Harris was not so persistent with this standard in the Rules Commission, which he had come to see as the lesser of the two bodies, but he held to it strictly for Party Structure. French felt that this criterion was essential for understanding many individual selections:

> The Middle-Atlantic states had no Democratic governors or senators, and their state chairmen would have been offensive. Conversely, Bailey objected violently to Anne Wexler. He was a bright man, and understood what was going on. We had to find people who were liberal and reform-minded, but who didn't have violent objections from other party people.
> This was why people from the northeast didn't get on. This was why Christopher had powerful party support, but Wexler had powerful party opposition. Har-

ris liked English, thought he was able, thought he would work at it. A solid liberal vote. With English as with several others—or with why McGovern was chairman instead of Hughes—these were people who were very solidly in favor of reform, but who did not revive old local feuds, raise hackles.

We got some early recommendations from the NDC. The NDC national "heavy" list came to meet with Harris. All of those people were precisely the type of people who were red flags. They were no more committed to party reform than Fred Dutton or Warren Christopher, but they would have driven labor or organized party types out right away.

The complete list of regular members for the Commission on Party Structure and Delegate Selection was available to those with some rightful claim on an advance copy by Friday, February 7, the day before the two commissions were announced through press releases from the National Committee, and from their respective chairmen. The selection of several of the individual commissioners was itself a complex and delicate process; the selection of the commission as a whole, so that it embodied three overt and three more covert criteria, was even more so.

Yet nowhere were these basic criteria better exemplified than in the selection of a chairman for the Party Structure Commission. Nowhere were negotiations more delicate. Nowhere did the principals themselves bring such intricate calculations to their decisions. And nowhere, finally, was the fundamental thrust of commission-building under Harris more abundantly clear. At a minimum, this commission chairman would become the first available symbol of the new commission's orientation. If he then devoted time and energy to his commission, he would surely set its general tone, in fact as well as in appearance. If he sought active, daily direction of its staff, he might go well beyond tone, to influence the specifics of national party reform.

All of this was normal and natural. It became a problem only because there was an obvious candidate for the job, and he wanted it. Harold E. Hughes, freshman senator from Iowa, was clearly emerging as the national spokesman for formal democratization of internal party affairs. Hughes had lent his name to the unofficial commission which had kicked off this latest reform movement, at a time when others would not take the risk. He had spearheaded—or at least figureheaded—the efforts to get these official reform commissions appointed, at a time when others could not be bothered. He remained the biggest political name which could be mobilized by reform activists when they desired a national spokesman.

Moreover, Hughes himself had always been interested in the chairmanship of the Special Committee/Party Structure Commission. From the first, he had possessed an ideological commitment to reform, and this had only been reinforced by subsequent events. By early 1969, he faced a complementary political problem as well, the need to locate some major, national issue which could generate substantial publicity and which would be his alone. "Party reform" promised to be such an issue; it was not already the province of some older, more established solon; Hughes wanted it.[17]

Yet the very reasons which made Hughes the candidate of reform forces made him an expensive liability to Chairman Harris. In fact, he managed to violate all of Harris's private criteria for commission appointment, so blatantly as to risk subverting all of Harris's plans for the Party Structure Commission. Hughes had contributed critically to some of the major fights dividing the 1968 Convention, and he had capped that off by nominating Eugene McCarthy—making him one of the reddest "red flags" in the entire party. After that, he had continued to symbolize a flat-out, no-holds-barred approach to reform, so that Harris could hardly engineer a *quiet* restructuring of the party through Hughes. Moreover, Hughes was unlikely to be responsive to the national chairman, since he not only had his own programmatic goals, but his own personal constituency. French attempted to cross him off early:

> We didn't want Hughes to become chairman because that would be giving one very intense faction too much of an advantage. Fred, beyond that, did not regard Hughes as a person with whom one could have a rational discussion. That really did enter into our calculations.

In order to escape from the omnipresence of Hughes, however, Harris needed another potential chairman, one who could also be defended as "logical." It was Bill Welsh, the former Humphrey aide who had become executive assistant to Harris at the National Committee, who found the way around Hughes: "Somewhere in that early period, I tried out the names of McGovern and O'Hara. McGovern was a way to block off Hughes; he was an antiwar guy, too."

Senator George S. McGovern of South Dakota did appear to have most of the surface credentials to placate the organized reform network. McGovern had stepped in as a rallying point for dissident delegates at the 1968 Convention. He was emerging as perhaps the most active antiwar Senator, where opposition to the war in Vietnam remained an important touchstone among many of the independent activists who would fuel the party reform movement. He was publicly in favor of extensive structural reform. Despite all this, McGovern was not nearly as automatic an irritant to party regulars as Harold Hughes. The senator from South Dakota had been a much more conciliatory dissident at the convention, and he had formed up immediately behind the vice president once Hubert Humphrey was nominated, appearing with him on the platform that very night. Both French and his boss saw the advantages in Welsh's suggestion:

> The brilliant compromise was George McGovern. It was brilliant, because who could object, from the least-common-denominator view? He raised no strong hackles with the labor people. He was good with the reformers. We also appointed O'Hara [as chairman of Rules] at the same time, who was eminently acceptable to labor; we explained that very privately and deliberately.
>
> McGovern had endorsed Humphrey and had worked for him. He was very close to Kennedy. There was no doubt on the part of reformers that he was for it, although they may have doubted how vociferously he would fight for it. He was a decent, even-tempered guy in his personality.

The "brilliant compromise" did not immediately seize his opportunity. Mc-Govern was offered the Party Structure chairmanship on Friday, January 31, and he embarked on five days of discussion about its potential. His primary consideration was what the post was likely to contribute to a possible campaign for a presidential nomination in 1972. That, in turn, broke down into two more specific questions: What was the long-run value of an intimate connection with the party reform process? What would be the short-run response to the announcement of a McGovern chairmanship by key political actors?

McGovern began with the issue itself. He judged that being the leading spokesman for "clean politics" and "small 'd' democracy" could hardly hurt a presidential contender. But he worried that being chairman of the Party Structure Commission might imply constant conflict with local party leaders, whose support would be helpful in obtaining a nomination:

> I was paying no attention to these commissions. I had no contact with them at all. I had just been through a tough Senate campaign, and my mind was on winning elections, not on reforming. I was so involved with the anti-War effort at that time anyway; I didn't think it [party reform] made much difference. Procedural questions were always secondary to merging opposition in Congress and in the country to the War.
>
> I was not interested in that position until Fred Harris came to me and asked me. I felt then that Hughes would be a more logical choice, since he was more involved, and I said so. I was emerging as the leader of the anti-War effort; Hughes was emerging as the leader of the reform movement. But Harris was unwilling to name Hughes; he said that I was a more logical choice. Myself, I thought the chairmanship was also a political liability. The thought of 1972 was in my mind, and I felt that this would be a burden in 1972.

McGovern's personal constituency was split in the matter. The "senatorial McGovernites," the Senator's personal staff and principal allies in South Dakota, opposed the move. They felt that the top priority remained the security of his Senate seat, a liberal Democratic outpost in a conservative Republican state. They argued that a presidential bid had to be classed as a long shot. They concluded that activities which could advance his presidential hopes only at the cost of senatorial security should be avoided.

On the other side were the incipient "presidential McGovernites," those who had been active in the late-starting nomination bid of 1968 or who had gotten to know McGovern through press coverage of that effort. Like Richard C. Wade, professor of history at the University of Chicago, they argued that if McGovern could gain control of the reform issue and meld it with the anti-war issue, the combination would have a powerful attraction for independent activists, and even for rank-and-file voters:

> Without that [1968] Convention, there would have been no 1972. He wouldn't have been asked to be head of the Commission. I always thought, from the beginning, that his being chairman of the Commission on Party Structure and Delegate Selection would be an asset. But we had to fight against the South Dakota view, George Cunningham, Pat Donovan, and others. They have always resisted George's national success. Every time George says something nationally, it hurts him back home.
>
> I was telling him to do it. I had gotten him a few speaking engagements in the interim, so that he came to Chicago a couple of times, but we never discussed the reform commission. I came back into the picture when McGovern called and asked whether he should become chairman. I thought that he should pre-empt the reform issue as well as the War. I also felt that if someone who had not backed Humphrey were chosen, the thing would never get off the ground.

There were, however, two other sets of political actors whose advice was critical, not so much for its content as for what it revealed about their reactions should McGovern decide to heed the presidential, and not the senatorial, McGovernites. First were the other recognized contenders for the presidential nomination of 1972, which effectively meant the "big three"—Edward M. Kennedy, Hubert H. Humphrey, and Edmund S. Muskie.

Humphrey actively blessed a McGovern chairmanship. He had preferred some other candidate to Hughes from the beginning; he was a personal friend of McGovern. Muskie remained uninvolved. He had no intention of getting publicly enmeshed in appointment negotiations, beyond naming his allotted member to each commission; his vague consent was more or less automatic. Kennedy was necessarily more equivocal. He had publicly endorsed Hughes, although by the time McGovern sought his blessing, he was able to obtain direct confirmation that Hughes was not a possibility. Under those conditions, he gave full but private approval to a McGovern chairmanship.

The second set of political actors whose reaction might be crucial was the loosely connected circle of independent activists who had begun to focus on the issue of party reform. The larger pool of these individuals was composed of those who had participated in the various dissident campaigns of 1968, but the most organized, and hence best able to respond, were those associated with the continuing Hughes Commission. If any group was to attempt to make McGovern *pay* for taking the Party Structure chairmanship—for taking it away from Harold Hughes—this was certainly the group. For his initial contact with them, McGovern asked Adam Walinsky, a former aide to Robert Kennedy and a member of the steering committee of the New Democratic Coalition, to put him in touch with Tom Alder, a classmate of Walinsky's from law school and the obvious starting point with the Hughes Commission.

Alder at first urged McGovern not to take the post, citing not any ill will but the rightful claim of Hughes. The South Dakotan then confirmed that Hughes could not be appointed. Alder was not prepared to endorse McGovern on that say-so, but he did offer some detailed advice on the political costs of the position, and on strategies for minimizing them. The two men parted with the understanding that they would talk further, and McGovern left with the feeling that the Hughesites would have to be courted assiduously but could be mollified.

With this preparation, McGovern called Fred Harris on Tuesday, February 4, for one last discussion. The upshot of this conversation was the formal appointment of George S. McGovern to the chairmanship of the Commission on Party Structure and Delegate Selection, with a series of compromises on associated conditions. McGovern suggested several nominees for the commission proper, the most controversial of whom was Anne Wexler. Harris accepted them only if they were already on his larger lists, and he rejected Wexler outright. McGovern proposed that Harold Hughes be made vice chairman of the commission. Harris agreed to raise no complaint if *McGovern* appointed Hughes at some future date. McGovern requested complete control of commission staffing. Harris assented, with the proviso that he be consulted and informed.

McGovern then sounded out Harris on the reliability of political support over the next several years, and he asked for an additional staff slot immediately, so that there could be both a staff director and a commission counsel. Harris made appropriate noises on the first score and consented to the second. Finally, McGovern reminded Harris that he could promise to remain for only two years and might then run for president—a reminder which not only kept that option open but provided a means to escape the painstaking and thankless

63

work of pressuring state parties into compliance. Harris was unbothered by that prospect and agreed there too. That same day, the national chairman revealed to the press that the senator from South Dakota would be heading his new reform body.[18]

While this entire series of negotiations was occurring, the most adamantly proreform forces—at the Hughes Commission, in the New Democratic Coalition, and in self-conscious reform factions in the states—were not inactive. Those who had first mobilized to press Larry O'Brien about the timing and content of commission appointments were, in fact, deeply discomfited by post-O'Brien negotiations. The simple replacement of one better-known national chairman with another had created uncertainty. When Fred Harris had amended the Special Committee resolution at his first meeting of the National Committee, that uncertainty became anxiety. When it became clear that Harris was actively avoiding Harold Hughes as chairman of the Party Structure Commission, that anxiety became alarm.

By the end of the third week in January, at least one new response to what appeared to be increasingly ominous developments at the National Committee began to take shape, and it involved the resurrection of the Commission on the Democratic Selection of President Nominees. At first, there was only the idea, plus some preliminary conversation. If Harris's commissions were to be patently unattractive, a reconstituted Hughes Commission might brand them as "antireform commissions" and might undertake the real work of party reform. If Harris's appointments were to be more ambiguous, a continuing Hughes Commission might function as a pressure group, to keep them on the straight and narrow. If their ultimate product was nevertheless disappointing, a private commission might develop its own report, for use in a full-scale battle within the National Committee. Tom Alder saw all three possibilities:

> The decision to hold the Hughes Commission in abeyance, and perhaps hold it. I felt that the work we had done under its name was not that good. On the other hand, I really did think that if the Democratic party was to have as its chairman that guy from Missouri [Delton L. Houtchens; see below], then alternative, shadow institutions were necessary. Or if Fred Harris were to try to reassert operational control over the Commission. Or if the DNC were to convert these Commissions into study groups only, and not delegate any power of enforcement to them.

By Monday, January 27, Alex Bickel, still formally a Hughes commissioner, was pursuing the possibility of a reinvigorated private commission at a conference on the electoral process at the Ford Foundation, where he sounded out various foundation officials about support for the proposed venture.[19] Simultaneously, the drive for a coordinated protest about Resolution No. 12, the one merging two resolutions from the 1968 Convention to create the new Commission on Party Structure and Delegate Selection, was put on hold. While most potential protesters were apprehensive about Harris's appointments, many were nevertheless seeking commissions slots and were not eager to compromise their chances with a public attack on the national chairman. As a result, Alder put the mass written protest into limbo, but not the notion of a shadow commission:

> When Hughes was being snubbed, when you could never get to the enemy, there was this tremendous frustration, with everyone saying "it can't be done." There just seemed to be a lack of everything, a lack of fairness, a lack of good sense. There were just the pettiest kind of false appraisals. We were losing time if we had to start all over again.
> Hughes raised the suggestion one night shortly before the first meeting; he mused that he might not go on the Commission. This was a time when Harris was forming the Commission in secret. Nelson was appointed but Eli was not. Eli at that point says to Hughes that he hopes that he won't go on.

George McGovern set to work assembling a staff for the Commission on Party Structure and Delegate Selection with no awareness of the specific threat of a continuing Hughes Commission, but in full knowledge that those who had formed up behind Harold Hughes were suspicious and restless, and required some calming effort. Thus, while McGovern needed to assert his own control over the new commission staff, these staff appointments had to serve a second purpose. Because they were one of the few manipulable elements remaining—commission membership was almost entirely fixed before McGovern took the chairmanship—they had to contribute to the construction of a larger, external, supporting coalition, which would give the commission increased legitimacy in the longer run and neutralize the most unhappy opposing voices at once.

In theory, it was possible, even logical, to use these staff appointments to reach across to party regulars and to reassure *them* about the drift of this new reform commission. The bulk of the regular party was evidently leery of party reform, as was organized labor, the major interest group in the orthodox Democratic coalition. Moreover, regular party figures had constituted a healthy majority of the previous national convention and were obviously the dominant force within the National Committee. Indeed, they would inevitably be waiting down the road, in the National Committee, in state committees across the country, and in local organizations at the city and county level, when the Party Structure Commission reported. Their response to its recommendations would necessarily be decisive.

In practice, McGovern never seriously considered this option. Instead, he concentrated on securing his ties to the emerging reform network. This was in part a response to the political environment of the moment. The reformers were more sharply focused on, and better organized around, the issue of commission appointments than were the other relevant party factions. But the response by McGovern was a matter of longer-run calculation as well. He believed that an eventual presidential nomination required the support of these reformers first, although he did not believe that they would be sufficient, and he did hope to blend them with party regulars once they had helped get his candidacy off the ground. Finally, his route to the chairmanship of the Party Structure Commission had just run directly over the champion of the reform forces, Harold Hughes, and this fact clinched McGovern's decision: He had to cement the organized reformers to his new operation, and his staff positions had to be turned to that purpose.

The incoming chairman at least began with full appointive powers, and with two top spots on the commission staff through which to exercise them. Accordingly, one of these could be applied to his more personal needs and one to his need for external bridge-building. The first post, that of staff director, was filled quickly. Robert W. Nelson, a political associate for more than a decade, agreed to be "his man" on the commission staff. Nelson had managed McGovern's first (unsuccessful) Senate campaign in 1960, had come to Washington when McGovern secured his Senate seat in 1962, and had been deputy assistant secretary of the interior during the Kennedy and Johnson administrations. He was attracted, intellectually, by the issue of party reform; he was eager, personally, to return to a partisan role:

> McGovern wanted someone he knew. My experience in politics had been electoral and congressional, as well as executive from the administrative side. I had worked with the state party in South Dakota, so I knew something about constructing a strong, open, political party.

With Nelson in the fold, McGovern moved to appoint a commission counsel, one who could help bind reformers in general, and Hughesites in particular, to the commission. He had, in effect, begun this task by promising that Hughes himself would become vice chairman at the first meeting of the full commission. But while Hughes was agreeable to that suggestion, he remained noncommittal, and his evident ambivalence meant that the counsel slot still had to be used to assuage hard feelings among those who would have preferred a different commission chairman.

This task, however, proved easier to describe than to execute, and the difficulties were rooted in the selection of Bob Nelson as staff director. To the extent that Nelson was perceived as the man protecting the personal interests of Chairman McGovern, he was suspected of not placing party reform above personal loyalty. To the degree that Nelson had been well received in the office of Chairman Harris, he was suspected of being part of some master plan by the national chairman. And so it went.

McGovern offered the counselorship first to Tom Alder, who flirted with the possibility, to the point of bringing Geoff Cowan, his associate director from the Hughes Commission, in from Connecticut to discuss the matter and to meet with Nelson. Alder was uncomfortable from the first, however, with the notion of dual staff leadership, and he eventually turned the offer down:

> McGovern was very out-in-front about why he wanted Nelson to be on, and in some sense I appreciated that. He wanted someone who could protect his personal political interests and needs, and he felt Nelson was the guy. But he was clearly setting up two co-equal posts on the staff, and when I looked at Nelson, I knew it was no deal. He had been "hatched" for so long, and he was making such an effort to show that he could pick up new political things, but he really didn't have the fire. If he had only had some real intensity about these issues, but he was so easy-going.

The choice then narrowed to Simon Lazarus III, who had drafted the final version of *The Democratic Choice* and who had been recommended by Cowan, and Eli J. Segal, who continued to be interested in some such position and who was working through Harold Hughes. On Monday, February 17, McGovern again summoned Alder to get a comparison of the two. Alder's recommendation of Segal, seconded by Hughes himself, convinced McGovern to offer the post again.[20] Segal, in turn, confined himself to a long discussion with Hughes, to be sure that if McGovern's backing did go exclusively to Nelson, he could rely on the same support from the Iowa senator. He then took the job:

> By that time, the New Democratic Coalition had come into existence and had given some thought to monitoring the Commission, and I thought of working with them. Hughes gave me assurances that this would not be a farce. I had a long talk with McGovern, and then agreed. I felt that Nelson was an empty vessel who could go either way. At least coming from Minnesota, he didn't have that built-in anti-openness bias. Actually, though, it was months before I thought that McGovern himself was okay.

While he was still weighing acceptance of the Party Structure chairmanship, McGovern had begun to consider a panel of consultants to supplement this regular staff. Unlike the staff director or commission counsel, none of these individuals would devote full time to commission activities, but each would be available for intensive work on particular problems or for attention to the full scope of commission concerns at critical periods.

McGovern actually collected his first consultant, historian Richard C. Wade of the University of Chicago, while he was surveying opinions about the value of the chairmanship. He had queried Wade; Wade had strongly urged acceptance; McGovern had finished by asking whether Wade would become a consultant if the senator followed his advice. Professor Wade had readily consented, and he became in effect "McGovern's man" among the consultants, as Nelson was "his man" on the regular staff.

The second consultant, Anne Wexler, joined the panel immediately after McGovern agreed to accept the chairmanship. Wexler had tried to obtain an appointment to the commission proper from National Chairman O'Brien, then from National Chairman Harris, and finally, through McGovern, from Harris again. Each overture had been turned away, but her campaign was ultimately rewarded when McGovern rescued her from exclusion by placing her on the panel of consultants. As a hard-line reformer and acknowledged Hughesite, she counterpoised Dick Wade in much the same fashion as Eli Segal counterpoised Bob Nelson.

McGovern then turned to Alexander M. Bickel, professor of law at Yale University, "blue ribbon" member of the Hughes Commission, and a man who had continued to take an interest in reform politics, as his third and final consultant. With the selection of Bickel, it was possible to upgrade the intellectual status of the commission staff while helping again to cement the Hughesites to that operation, a joint virtue easily sufficient to earn him an appointment.

Even after this careful analysis of the value of his new chairmanship, and even with his careful adjustments to realize its full potential, George McGovern could not have appreciated the full significance of these staff choices at the time he made them. For from February through August of 1969, and then from December until really the next Democratic Convention, *the Commission on Party Structure and Delegate Selection would consist of little more than its chairman, its vice chairman, and its staff.* Only from late August through late November would the rest of the commissioners have much of a role. Indeed, within months, even the external actors—insurgent and regular—who had seemed so likely to try to influence the commission as it went about its daily business would largely disappear, leaving only the interactions within the commission leadership and staff to shape the development of recommendations for party reform.

These discussions about commission staff actually occurred at the same time as some additional negotiations about the official membership and in consort with some external preparations for the launching of a shadow commission, should that appear necessary. The announcement of a willingness by McGovern to assume the Party Structure chairmanship was made on Tuesday, February 4, but discussions to flesh out the staff of the new commission chairman ran through the third week in February. The unveiling of the full commission followed on Saturday, February 8, yet even here, final maneuvering over commission membership went on for another ten days. Finally, the possibility of reviving the Hughes Commission, a possibility first raised in late January, was not eliminated until the tag end of February, over four weeks later.

The Commission on Party Structure and Delegate Selection, after all the false starts, after the application of three overt and three covert criteria, and after a few postpublication adjustments, came to consist of twenty-eight members. (See table 2.1.) When the commission roster was initially published, it contained a chairman plus *twenty-six* members, but it was fine-tuned over the next ten days to cover one promotion, one addition, and one mistake.[21]

The promotion was for Harold Hughes, appointed as an ordinary commissioner but elevated to the newly created post of vice chairman. The addition was Albert A. Pena, county commissioner for Bexar County, Texas, whose late appointment was a response to complaints that the group had no Chicano member—thanks to a misunderstanding about the ethnicity of Peter Garcia. The mistake, finally, centered on the "youth" members of the Party Structure and Rules commissions, David Mixner and Dennis T. O'Toole. O'Toole was originally slated for Party Structure, but in a secretarial foul-up, Mixner got the letter inviting him to join. Despite the original plan and a press release placing him on Rules, Mixner refused to budge, and he was then allowed to retain his preferred seat.

Perhaps surprisingly, as all these personnel decisions fell into place, the plans of some party dissidents for a continuing Hughes Commission did not immediately grind to a halt. During the third week in February, Alder actually reserved a meeting room in the Carroll Arms Hotel for March 1, the day of the opening session of the Party Structure Commission, in case Hughes should decide to convene a second generation of his own commission instead of attending George McGovern's.

Shortly after that, however, events finally caught up with the idea of a shadow commission. McGovern continued to emphasize, in public and in private, his own devotion to the cause of party reform. More concretely, he continued to woo major figures from the Hughes Commission. Within weeks of McGovern's appointment, Hughes, Fraser, Dutton, Bickel, Wexler, and Segal had been drawn to the new commission, and Alder and Cowan had received

TABLE 2.1

The Commission on Party Structure and Delegate Selection

George S. McGovern, chairman, U.S. senator from South Dakota
Harold E. Hughes, vice chairman, U.S. senator from Iowa
I. W. Abel, president, United Steelworkers of America
Birch E. Bayh, Jr., U.S. senator from Indiana
Samuel H. Beer, professor of government, Harvard University
Bert L. Bennett, partner, Quality Oil Company, Winston–Salem, North Carolina
Warren M. Christopher, attorney, O'Melveny and Myers, Los Angeles, California
Leroy Collins, defeated candidate for U.S. senator from Florida
Will D. Davis, attorney, Heath, Davis and McCalla, Austin, Texas
William Dodds, director of community action, United Auto Workers
Frederick G. Dutton, attorney, Dutton, Gwirtzman, Zumas, Wise and Frey, San Francisco, California
John F. English, national committeeman from New York
Donald M. Fraser, congressman from the Fifth District of Minnesota
Peter Garcia, deputy director of community action program, Tulare County, California
Earl G. Graves, president, Earl Graves Associates, New York, New York
Aaron E. Henry, president, N.A.A.C.P. of Mississippi
John J. Hooker, president, Minnie Pearl International, Nashville, Tennessee
Patti J. Knox, vice chairman, Democratic party of Michigan
Louis E. Martin, publisher, *Chicago Daily Defender*
Oscar H. Mauzy, state senator from Dallas, Texas
George J. Mitchell, national committeeman from Maine
David Mixner, co-director, Vietnam Moratorium Committee
Katherine G. Peden, defeated candidate for U.S. senator from Kentucky
Albert A. Pena, county commissioner from Bexar County, Texas
Calvin L. Rampton, governor of Utah
J. Austin Ranney, professor of political science, University of Wisconsin
Adlai E. Stevenson, III, state treasurer from Illinois
Carmen H. Warschaw, national committeewoman from California

---

offers and attention. Even then, McGovern did not stop: He hired Alder on a temporary basis to draft both an agenda for the opening meeting of his commission and a tentative schedule for the next six months of calendar 1969.[22]

By late February, almost the entire first generation of the Hughes Commission was either *on* the McGovern Commission or irrelevant to a second incarnation. Even if Hughes himself had changed his mind, a new commission could hope, at least immediately, to have only its chairman for physical continuity with its namesake and predecessor. Under those conditions, Alder watched the idea fall of its own weight:

> I did call the Carroll Arms to arrange for a meeting room for the time of the first meeting of the commission. Then that was abandoned completely when

Hughes decided to go on the commission. I felt that we could still caucus anyway, that we didn't need a sitting shadow body.

Hughes had been subjected to unjustifiable and public humiliation in not being made chairman. But his going on the commission would be a personal achievement, in staying on the issue and overcoming his anger. If there were to be a walkout from the new commission, a new Hughes Commission could be a rump of that commission.

That seemed a more sensible approach. Dutton and Bickel might then be involved, and Kimball and Ashmore wouldn't have to be. The Hughes Commission was too ephemeral to go on anyway; we would have had to raise the money that hadn't ever been there.

In theory, the performance of the McGovern Commission would determine the ultimate response of those who had flirted with the notion of a shadow body. In practice, the absorption of key figures from the Hughes Commission was to be so total, by late summer, that the idea never again received serious consideration. In effect, then, with the arrival of an ostensibly temporary agreement to see how the McGovern Commission performed, the old Hughes Commission was permitted to expire. As it did, the new members of the Commission on Party Structure and Delegate Selection awaited orders from their equally new leadership before getting down to the task of party reform.

Implications

The empaneling of the Party Structure Commission was a crucial event in the politics of party reform. The character of its membership set undeniable if vague limits on the scope and content of the recommendations for reform which it would produce. The character of its leadership imparted a general if still vague direction to those recommendations. The composition of its staff augured a much stronger push in that same direction.

All of these effects were prospective. Yet the empaneling of the Party Structure Commission was also a critical event precisely because it guaranteed that there would indeed *be* a politics of recommendation, an ongoing politics of party reform in which these selections for membership, leadership, and staff would eventually matter. Barring implosion, the commission would go on to frame a detailed set of reform recommendations. Struggles over the content of these recommendations would constitute the heart of reform politics until they were framed. The commission would automatically become the organizational arena for these struggles. In fact, as soon as the Party Structure Commission was created, reform politics moved naturally inside, where it essentially remained for the next fifteen months.

In theory, the Party Structure Commission might never have been appointed. A national chairman who was sufficiently committed to the regular party and its associated interests could at least have chosen among numerous ways to translate the reform resolutions passed by the 1968 Convention. As events fell out, Harold Gordon, deputy general counsel at the National Committee, actually began to create a rationale for *nullifying* these resolutions, when reformers began to press for appointment at the most inopportune time possible.

In practice, however, most national chairmen would have followed through and appointed the reform commission—or commissions—suggested by the National Convention. There were, after all, official resolutions directing that appointment. Moreover, these had proceeded from a recognized crisis within the national party, a crisis which an official reform body might address, compromise, and assuage. Beyond that, an opening round of appointment negotiations had stimulated a large collection of interested persons, with implementation of these resolutions as a major continuing concern.

Nevertheless, the actual politicking over commission appointment emphasized the variability which remained even after the decision to appoint had been made. Before the general election, Larry O'Brien, Hubert Humphrey, or one of their lieutenants may in truth have considered a reform commission dominated by hard-line regulars, led by top convention figures, and aimed at shoring up the official party for the election campaign. After the November defeat, O'Brien clearly did begin to assemble a commission weighted the other way, toward the reformers, but containing major spokesmen from all factions within the party, and aimed at re-establishing party unity for the longer term.

When O'Brien departed without making these appointments, the variability inherent in the composition of these commissions was underlined. Delton Houtchens, national committeeman from Missouri, had been the one most frequently mentioned as a successor to O'Brien during the election campaign itself. He would surely have shifted these commissions to a concern with the welfare of the regular party and to a reform orientation emphasizing simple extension of procedural guarantees.[23] But Houtchens had receded by the time a succession was at hand, and when Fred Harris managed to snare the chairmanship, both the personnel and the rationale for commission appointment changed sharply, in the other direction. Harris wanted to advance the cause of party reform, not party regularity, or even party unity. His commissions, especially the key Party Structure Commission, reflected that wish.

The composition of this commission—twenty-six commissioners, a chairman and vice chairman, a staff director and commission counsel, and three parttime consultants—was hardly the determining factor in the fate of party reform, and thus of institutional change. After the commission had reported, and after the "politics of recommendation" had come to an end, there would still be a "politics of implementation," in which the institutional fate of these recommendations would be practically resolved. Despite that, the composition of the Party Structure Commission—members, leaders, and staff—certainly provided clues to the direction in which recommendations from the commission would go, as well as to their probable breadth and depth.

The commissioners had admittedly been selected to avoid the leading theoreticians and tacticians for the major approaches to party activity, and that selection had been largely successful. There were few obvious doctrinaire reformers. There were even fewer obvious defenders of the regular party and its associated interests. But what this fact concealed was a consistent if unfocused sympathy for reform in the abstract, along with a willingness to be instructed in what the details of that abstract concept implied.

If there were few doctrinaire reformers among the commissioners as a body, there were many, a clear majority, who were prepared to endorse substantial proposals for reform. This fact would become evident in short order even to the commissioners themselves. Warren M. Christopher, deputy attorney general under John Kennedy, Los Angeles attorney, and veteran of the Robert Kennedy campaign as well, saw this orientation early:

> I myself had relatively radical expectations for what the commission would produce. I think, in answer to your question, that I was much farther over toward the side of expecting recommendations for radical change out of this Commission than toward expecting moderation. After all, the commission ran the gamut from "A" to "B," not from "A" to "Z." There were guys like Muskie's man Mitchell who represented the relatively strong conservative position, but that was "B," not "Z."

If these commissioners did not arrive with specific reform suggestions of their own, that meant only that the commission remained a malleable body, dependent, as such commissions usually are, on the activities of its leadership and staff for a detailed agenda. And there, the bias toward extensive institutional change was clear and strong. It was not just that there were no committed defenders of the regular party and its associated interest groups among these key actors. There were not even any moderate spokesmen for the orthodox Democratic coalition.

As a result, the divisions which did exist pitted those who favored thorough but meliorist reforms, to increase the influence of independent actors all along the line, against those who favored more aggressive and extensive reforms *in the same direction.* Sam Beer, Harvard professor of government and former president of Americans for Democratic Action, shared Christopher's perception of the commission as a whole—and extended it to the staff:

> Any commission that has a staff with Bob Nelson as its most conservative member is not likely to produce any conservative reforms. I mean, we knew he was from one of the most open parties in the country and surely wouldn't see anything wrong with participation in any way. And if there weren't any anti-participatory guys on the staff, where would any opposition come from?

Moreover, the more committed and active individuals among these key actors were uniformly on the more militant side of this (proreform) divide—Hughes in the leadership, Segal on the full-time staff, Wexler among the consultants. Even Nelson, the staff director, whose greater moderation on the central issue and whose broader responsibilities within the commission enterprise might have given him reason to deny this bias, did not disagree:

> When Hughes was blocked, that added to their suspicion. Eli Segal was Hughes's man. He was a non-Democrat then, just an anti-war guy. He had come down to work for Javits, but he became Hughes' man.
>
> There was some comment on the staff balance at the time. But because McGovern was commission head, it was his prerogative to hire whomever he wanted. There was also no great pressure to get a Humphrey guy.

There was, then, an official commission, sympathetic to reform. Within it, the most concerned participants were even more sympathetic, indeed committed. Yet the alternative Democratic coalition itself—that amalgam of new party dissidents, established reform factions, and emerging organized interests, which conceived of itself as in opposition to the orthodox Democratic coalition and which aspired ultimately to replace it—had achieved an ironic position in reform politics while all this was occurring. The members of this coalition had begun to think of themselves as a separable, self-conscious, connected entity. They had even produced an organizational framework or two to embody the alleged unity of this emerging force. But they had ended up with little direct representation on the key reform commission. As a result, they remained dependent on a few surrogates in the commission leadership and staff.

One clear change in this larger collectivity was the birth of a self-conscious interest group for those desiring a new, participatory brand of politics. This was the New Democratic Coalition, and it quickly fielded a national directorate, as well as chapters in numerous states and cities. Another, more consequential development was the reinvigoration of the Hughes Commission, and thus of the network which it connected. The general election campaign brought the commission back to life as a staff operation; that staff then reconnected a diverse and far-flung aggregation with reform as its central concern.

Despite these developments, all of which reflected the potential vitality of an alternative coalition of Democratic elites, that coalition fared ambiguously in the politics surrounding commission appointment. Those who were most concerned with sweeping institutional change—and most hopeful of benefiting from it—were indeed welded back together and organized in a more self-conscious fashion by the effort to get official commissions appointed. But the self-proclaimed leaders of this emerging, alternative coalition secured almost no place on these official bodies, and the coalition as a whole gained little direct representation.

The response of Fred Harris to the New Democratic Coalition accurately reflected its problems with the national party. The new organization was so equivocal in its public statements—as to whether it was the nucleus of a new party to the left of the Democrats, a reform movement within the Democratic party, or the beginnings of something beyond party, something more appropriate to an antiparty age[24]—that it would have been difficult for any chairman to slate its members on official party commissions. Harris, with his special need to move cautiously between the old Humphrey entourage and the emerging reform constituency, was doubly unlikely to cater to the NDC, and he did not.

That left the looser reform network associated with the remnants of the Hughes Commission. The Hughes entourage, because it was so skeletal, could easily negotiate with the national chairman. Ironically, it was also far better able to encompass and connect party dissidents from the nomination campaigns of the spring, original supporters of the Rules minority report, and party officeholders from reform factions around the country, many of whom were unwilling to join the more radical New Democratic Coalition or were unable, because of their party ties or personal aspirations, to embrace its evidently hostile stance.

Nevertheless, the Hughes entourage, too, was only ambiguously successful on the Party Structure Commission as appointed. Very few of those on the official roster were Hughes Commission endorsees. Almost none were self-conscious members of the network which Geoff Cowan had created and Tom Alder had religiously tended. Only on the leadership and staff of the new commission—with Anne Wexler, Eli Segal, and Harold Hughes himself—did the Hughesites achieve any real success.

What this meant, finally, was that upon the achievement of this segment of the Party Structure leadership and staff would rest not just the prospects for sweeping institutional change, but the surrogate influence of the alternative coalition which hoped to benefit from it. Because this was so, it was important to note one other small but potentially consequential shift which had occurred among these individuals, the evolving central figures in a continuing reform politics.

During the days when the Hughes Commission was being created, the major actors in what was to become a reform movement were individuals who had acquired their formative political experiences in civil rights struggles or in poverty politics over the previous decade. As a result, they had explicit—and often quite radical—*policy* goals for reform politics. The two top staffers at the Hughes Commission, Cowan and Alder, personified this pattern, although most of their volunteer aides would have embodied it as well.

When the Party Structure Commission was finally appointed, however, the key individuals with ties to this alternative coalition were of a noticeably different character. *Their* formative experiences in politics, almost without exception, were the insurgent nomination campaigns of 1968. If they saluted, vaguely, an additional range of policy goals, they were focused overwhelmingly on the issue of party reform—as an end in itself. Segal and Wexler best represented this pattern, but even Hughes was a reasonable example.

Hughes, Segal, and Wexler, then, did bring the evolving values and prejudices of a larger external coalition, along with some direct political attachments to the groups and individuals within it, into the Party Structure Commission. Whether they could convert their organizational advantages there—advantages of formal position, of concentrated attention, and of technical expertise—into recommendations for sweeping party reform, recommendations desired by and favorable to that alternative coalition on the outside, remained to be seen. Upon their success in internal commission politics would depend the answer to that question. Only their complete success in internal commission politics would—could—provide a chance at realization of all those goals.

An Institutionalized Bias for Reform

Politics: A Statement of Purpose and

an Executive Committee

IN WHICH, the commission staff searches for a means to lock their interpretation of the new organization's charge into continuing commission procedures; their solution, an official statement of purpose and an Executive
Committee peopled by reform advocates, is accepted by the full commission; and organized labor, in response, walks out. AND IN WHICH, reform politics centers on the contribution of an institutionalized bias to
commission proceedings; prospects for one particular approach to institutional change are heightened by the outcome of these maneuvers; and the
last remaining organizational spokesman for the orthodox Democratic
coalition abandons the Commission on Party Structure and Delegate
Selection.

THE FORMAL APPOINTMENT of the Party Structure Commission allowed anyone with enough interest to make a personal guess about the future
course of reform politics. Many must have done so. But two opposing groups
made estimates which would themselves acquire major, direct consequences
for the subsequent politics of party reform. First were the militant reformers,
whose perceptions, perhaps surprisingly, were initially quite negative. Second
was organized labor, with equally negative perceptions and an equally consequential response.

The reformers were obviously in the best position to act on these initial
impressions. They were collectively focused on commission appointments;
they included several individuals with key posts on the Party Structure Commission. In short order, these individuals countered with an additional reform

strategy. For the first meeting of their commission, they proposed a statement of goals and purposes, to be adopted by the assembled commissioners and to represent the aggressive interpretation of convention resolutions on reform. Along with this, they suggested the creation of an Executive Committee, to be justified on administrative grounds but to be chosen to institutionalize their own control over the drafting of reform recommendations.

When the inaugural meeting of the full commission accepted both this statement of purpose and these appointments to an Executive Committee, without significant dissent, it confirmed several central developments in commission politics—and directly produced another. Most evidently, it confirmed the drift of commission engineering, by attesting to the presence of an incipient majority for extensive party reform. Simultaneously, it hinted at the probable pattern of internal commission politics, by adopting aggressive reform proposals originated and propelled by the commission staff.

Within days, the success of these maneuvers was also registered, seismically, at the AFL-CIO. The AFL's Committee on Political Education [COPE], the major voice of organized labor in American politics, had never been happy with the idea of official reform commissions. COPE leaders were even less happy with the actual appointments to the key reform body. When that commission opened its proceedings by catering to militant reformers and by tossing in an additional, gratuitous slap at the AFL, these COPE leaders concluded that the prospects for organized labor within the commission had been fatally damaged. In response, COPE washed its hands of the commission venture, pulled its lone commissioner, and dropped out of the politics of recommendation.

With that departure, the last major link between the orthodox Democratic coalition and the Commission on Party Structure and Delegate Selection was severed. As a result, the commission was free to move into the drafting of reform recommendations without consulting—or even considering—the regular party and its associated interests. This fact alone promised to affect the brand of party reform which the commission endorsed and the extent of its application. Indeed, this fact promised to affect the subsequent balance *in presidential politics* between the orthodox coalition and its aspiring replacement—if proposed reforms could be successfully implemented.

Preparations for the Inaugural Meeting

Chairman Harris unveiled both the Party Structure and Rules commissions on Saturday, February 8, and thereby offered the first concrete, public clues to what his commissions might ultimately produce. Most of those who had been monitoring the creation of these bodies, in turn, quickly developed a set of expectations, and many began to prepare for the inaugural meeting of the Commission on Party Structure and Delegate Selection with these preliminary hypotheses in mind.

The national chairman and his staff, of course, had no need to produce fresh expectations for this commission. They knew that a general reform intention had guided its construction; they believed that this intention had been successfully embodied within it. Whether they were pleased with the result, as Vick French was, or feared that it gave too much to one side, as Bill Welsh did, most believed that they knew where such a commission would necessarily proceed.

What they saw was a body guaranteed to produce recognizable and perhaps sweeping reforms, in the participatory mode, for the rules governing party activity. If they differed at all in their predictions, the difference was less over the probable orientation of this commission than over whether the commission was sufficiently—superficially—balanced to avoid immediate outcries about "rigging." While they did hope that the commission leadership would consult with them during the drafting of specific recommendations for party reform, they saw no need for any special preparations for the opening meeting of the commission, which would presumably be devoted to introductions and housekeeping.

The press reports analyzing commission appointments generally accorded with this private perception of Harris's handiwork. The Associated Press, in its account for the wire, emphasized not just the available majorities for structural reform, but the insulation of those who would have been most displeased by this prospect:

DEMOCRATS NAME TWO REFORM GROUPS
Units for Delegate Selection Omit Powerful Mayors

WASHINGTON, Feb. 8 (AP)—Two special commissions liberally sprinkled with reform advocates but with minimal representation from old-line machine leaders were appointed today by Democratic National Chairman Fred R. Harris of Oklahoma.

Senator Harris said in announcing the twenty-seven-member commissions that he had consulted with top party leaders such as former Vice President Hubert H. Humphrey, and Senators Edward M. Kennedy, Eugene J. McCarthy, and Edmund S. Muskie.

But, in response to questions, he said he had not talked directly with such powerful party chieftains as Mayors Richard J. Daley of Chicago, James H. J. Tate of Philadelphia, and Joseph M. Barr of Pittsburgh.[1]

The private expectations of the national party staff, or the public interpretations of the national news media, did not square with the immediate evaluations of militant party reformers. If they had hoped that commission appointments would consist solely of reform advocates, they had always doubted the commitment of Fred Harris to that goal. In their newspapers, on February 9, they believed that they had the evidence to justify their suspicions.

Harris's commissions might have fared better in their eyes if these party insurgents had possessed more experience in party affairs and a wider acquaintance among party elites, so that they could have moved directly to the reform orientations of these new commission members. In the absence of this background, proreform analysts turned to a number of other simple standards, and the lessons from these were uniformly discouraging.

These analysts began by looking for ties to the McCarthy for President campaign. But with the exception of the inevitable Harold Hughes himself, there was only one obvious "McCarthy person" on the Party Structure Commission, David Mixner, co-chairman of the Vietnam Moratorium Committee—and insiders knew that he was a clerical error. Next, they looked for a clear and public record of opposition to the regular party. Harris's attempt to avoid "red flags," however, had eliminated most aspirants with such an evident orientation. Finally, militant observers turned to the positions and affiliations of the new commissioners. What they discovered was that very few were even members of dissident party factions or "new politics" organizations, while many were actually party or public officeholders.

The result was not destined to inspire confidence among those who had supported McCarthy, opposed the regular party, and helped create the leading dissident groups. Geoff Cowan summarized their view:

> We thought the McGovern Commission was a disaster. There was no McCarthy person on it. It looked awful. Hughes seriously considered quitting the Commission and reactivating his own.

Eli Segal echoed Cowan:

> We felt at the time that most of these people were part of the "good old boy" network, that guys like John Bailey and Hughes of New Jersey and Joe Barr would at some point call them up and get them to go a certain way.

Some response to this situation—some early action to *prevent* the situation from unfolding as these reformers feared—seemed essential. Fortunately for those with this perception, elements of the loosely connected reform circle were present on the commission itself, and it thus fell to Eli Segal, the commission counsel, and to Anne Wexler, commission consultant, to frame their immediate response. The first official staff task, preparation of an agenda for the inaugural meeting of the full commission on March 1, gave them their opportunity. Segal and Wexler moved to see if that meeting could be used to impel the Commission on Party Structure and Delegate Selection in their preferred direction.

The two staffers settled quickly on their approach: An official statement of purpose for the commission enterprise and some institutional engineering to lock that statement into commission procedures. If they could get the commission to begin by endorsing a broad interpretation of its own responsibilities, they reasoned, they would be off and running. If they could build that interpretation into normal operating procedures, they might be able to sustain this momentum.

The first of these tactical initiatives, an official statement of purpose, had to affirm three basic points if it was to serve these general goals. First, it had to affirm that this was a "rule-making," and not a "study," commission. Second, it had to assert that whenever the convention resolutions which had created the commission were overlapping or in conflict, they should be read additively. Third, it had to designate a set of abstract values from which the staff could then "deduce" specific proposals for reform. Commission endorsement of this tripartite statement did not guarantee the success of these recommendations, but it would augment staff legitimacy in developing them, and it might help to finesse them past subsequent commission dissent.

Fred Harris, the national chairman, George McGovern, the commission chairman, and Harold Hughes, the vice chairman, were booked as the principal speakers for the March 1 meeting, but their remarks were expected to be ceremonial and hortatory. As a result, it was the fourth speaker, Anne Wexler, who received the serious assignment, presentation of the staff version of a proper commission course.

Wexler and Segal then turned to Tom Alder for help with the details of this key speech. The three enjoyed a clear positional advantage because Segal was to help in drafting the remarks of both McGovern and Hughes. These could thus be coordinated to support the specific assertions in Wexler's commentary. Alder proposed that they use as their text the letter which he had drawn up to protest the merger of the Special Committee with the Party Structure Commission, before that protest had been shelved:

> That was the draft letter that was going to go to Harris, but got saved for Anne Wexler's opening speech. This was the document about the January DNC resolution. This was an effort to do legislative history retroactively. I don't know that I think it was accurate, but it *was* what we *should have done* at the time.

With this as framework, Wexler set out to demonstrate that the Party Structure Commission had been intended to communicate the specific requirements of reform resolutions to the individual state parties and to impress upon them their obligation to implement these communications:

> . . . it was agreed that a delegation should be allowed to prove to the Credentials Committee that Republican control of the legislature made compliance impossible. The language "all feasible efforts" was accepted by the group to meet this problem after its proponents clarified two points: 1) the exception would be applicable only where the opposition party controlled the legislature at all times during which it might be reasonably possible to pass a new law going into effect in 1972 or before; and 2) a delegation establishing impossibility on this ground would also be obliged to show that it had held hearings, introduced bills and lobbied for their enactment, and that its state rules had been amended in every necessary way.
>
> It was our intent that this language establish the minimum mandatory standards for delegate selection in 1972. . . .[2]

This was point number one in the reform interpretation of the commission mandate, that it was to be a "rule-making," not a "study," commission. A careful student of the same original texts, however, could easily have produced "evidence" to the contrary. The Rules majority report, even as amended, suggested a far more intricate process:

> . . .that said Commission be charged with the duty of studying and evaluating and codifying the rules of past Democratic National Conventions, and investigating the advisability of rules changes, and that the Commission report its findings to the Democratic National Committee in a timely manner in order that the Democratic National Committee may submit said findings to the Rules Committee of the 1972 National Convention for acceptance, rejection, modification, or amendment.[3]

The Credentials majority report was equally equivocal:

> D. Report its findings and recommendations to the Democratic National Committee and make them available to the 1972 Convention and the committees thereof.[4]

Wexler, Segal, and Alder hoped that whenever these Rules and Credentials reports were obviously not parallel, they would be read additively, rather than selectively. The central issue here was the call in the Credentials majority report for "meaningful and timely" opportunity to participate, and the demand in the Rules minority report for "full and timely" opportunity. Wexler sought to extract a command of "full, meaningful, and timely" participation from this discrepancy:

When we drafted the language of the Rules Committee minority report, we already knew that the majority report of the Credentials Committee would offer language for the 1972 Call which would be intended to make the delegate selection process more meaningful. The Credentials Committee report, which the Convention adopted, used the phrase "meaningful and timely opportunity to participate." The members of the Rules Committee wanted to draft language which would give clarification to that phrase.

The Rules Committee language, which we drafted and which was adopted by the Convention after the adoption of the Credentials Committee report, says, "It is understood that a state Democratic Party in selecting and certifying delegates to the national convention thereby undertakes to assure that such delegates have been selected through a process in which all Democratic Voters have had a *full* and *timely* opportunity to participate."[5]

Apart from the slight rewriting of legislative history—the Credentials majority report had actually been a fall-back position in case the Rules minority report failed—there was still a major stretch in this textual analysis. A hard-line opposition staffer might have argued that such legislative inconsistency usually nullifies, rather than sums, the provisions in question; a softer opponent could have noted that the Rules and Credentials reports, together, offered only two specific standards for delegate selection in the future, only the first of which was truly unambiguous:

(1) The unit rule not be used in any stage of the delegate selection process; and
(2) All feasible efforts have been made to assure that delegates are selected through party primary, convention, or committee procedures open to public participation within the calendar year of the National Convention.[6]

Indeed, the "full and timely" language in the Rules minority report was not in the instructions to future conventions at all, but in the *preamble* to those instructions.

Nevertheless, there was no countervailing staff member to support these contrary arguments, and Wexler was free to make her third major point, the one which established definite values by which devices for delegate selection should be judged. Her suggested values, taken on their own terms, were directive but not determinative. Yet they would be translated, by a sympathetic commission staff, to imply the termination of three of the five institutional devices for delegate selection in use at the time:[7]

The word "full" was chosen with great care. The drafters of the minority report were concerned not only with party systems which make it impossible for delegates to participate in the selection process, but also with systems which make it possible, but also make it difficult or confusing. For example, in states where a state committee selected in the calendar year of the convention picks national delegates, the voters who select that state committee should be fully informed that one of the committee's functions is the selection of national delegates.

Similarly, if a state party makes it possible for voters to participate in caucuses or primaries to select delegates to a state convention, party officials and state and local rules must encourage such participation. While leaving the final responsibility for participation with the voters, the national and state Democratic parties must insure that such caucuses or primaries are held, that all Democratic voters know how and when to participate in them, and that no unnecessary obstacles are placed in the way of those voters who wish to do so.[8]

Once more, an opponent inclined to read the Rules and Credentials reports in a strictly literal fashion could easily have dissented from these allegedly guiding values. Moreover, such an opponent could more easily have dismissed the institutional implications which the staff would eventually draw, by demonstrating that operational sections of key convention resolutions made no distinctions among presidential primaries, state convention systems, or state committee selections, nor any distinctions within them:

> (2) All feasible efforts have been made to assure that delegates are selected through *party primary, convention,* or *committee procedures* open to public participation within the calendar year of the National Convention.[9] (Italics added.)

Wexler's statement would ultimately gain its greatest significance not from any direct contribution to reform politicking within the Party Structure Commission but as a testimonial to the elasticity in the convention resolutions addressing party reform. As a direct contribution to a strong reform document, Wexler's remarks would be only one of many similar influences, and a lesser one at that. *But as a revelation of the extent to which the practical meaning of "reform" was up for grabs in March of 1969, Wexler's statement was second to none.* In her hands, the major reform resolutions from the 1968 Convention were about to be stretched so that only committed reformers would reliably recognize the link between original and interpreted content. Yet in the hands of a different staff, these same resolutions could as easily have been snapped back to the point where an unsympathetic party regular might have wondered how they had ever been thought to "mandate" anything.

Perhaps a comprehension of this very elasticity was what drove Eli Segal to look for some additional means to support this statement of purpose, some way to engrave it on continuing commission procedures. Although he believed that Wexler's interpretation was the morally correct one and although he very much desired its approval by the full commission, Segal remained pessimistic about its larger value. He judged, in fact, that its worth would be quite transitory unless its language was enshrined in normal operating procedures through some new structural arrangement. It was Segal, accordingly, who hit upon the idea of using a newly formed Executive Committee to do exactly that.

From the first, Chairman McGovern had considered naming an Executive Committee to serve as a sounding board for early staff proposals, on the theory that a body with twenty-eight members could not meet regularly enough to stay involved with the details of its own work.[10] Segal now urged McGovern not to make this new subcommittee a mere microcosm of the larger commission but to pack it with commissioners who would provide a reform nucleus for subsequent battles. When McGovern agreed, the Executive Committee became, in effect, the concrete means for locking the legislative intent of Wexler's opening statement into the formal organization of the Party Structure Commission. (See figure 3.1.) Segal was delighted:

> The Executive Committee was important. If you took that commission and looked at the Executive Committee, then you could really see the slant toward reform. With two or three exceptions, you had the hard core there. Seven of the ten were hard-line reformers, and two of the others never came.

Segal, Wexler, and Alder hoped that careful preparation would be enough to extract this entire package—both the statement of purpose and the new organizational arrangements—from the full commission at its initial session, since the commissioners would have no good reason for immediate, coordinated resistance. Segal put the general plan into a late memo to McGovern, as a last step before the March 1 inaugural:

> Without suggesting that the first meeting of the Special Committee be stage-managed, I have prepared this memorandum with a view toward minimizing the possibility for friction on Saturday. My premise is that under the glare of TV lights, we do not want to repeat the management and confusion of Chicago.

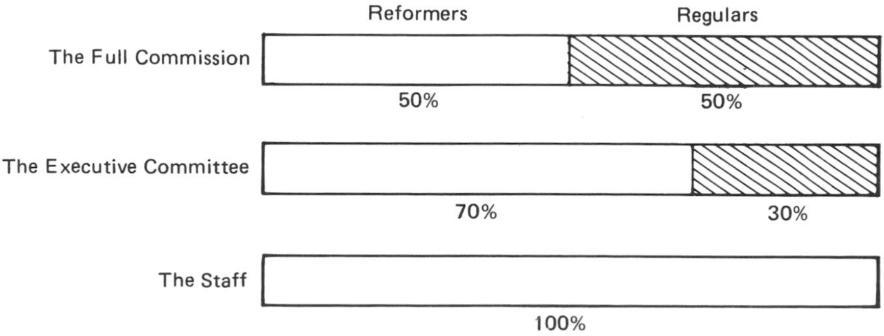

FIG. 3.1
The Institutionalized Bias of the Commission:
Eli Segal's Perspective

There should be little difficulty with your opening remarks or those of Fred Harris; nor do the reports of Senator Hughes or Anne Wexler offer the likelihood for pitched battles. On the other hand, your talk on the organizational structure, priorities, and timetable of the Special Committee must be approached with great care if we are to avoid discord. . . .

Your talk should emphasize that the organization of the Special Committee is consistent with your belief that [the] Committee has short-term and long-term needs to fulfill. The short-term needs are to assure compliance with the Call to the 1972 Convention, i.e., timeliness of delegate selection, abolition of the unit rule, integration of all Democrats into all affairs of the state party. In order to do this you are now:

(1) Urging adoption of Anne Wexler's testimony as the official Special Committee interpretation of the minority report. . . .

(3) Directing the staff to report its findings to an Executive Committee—which you are now appointing—by May 1. The Executive Committee will evaluate findings and make recommendations to the full Committee for their adoption, rejection, and/or amendment at the next meeting of the full Committee around June 1.[11]

Almost all tactical preparations for the March 1 meeting were coordinated by those who held official positions on the Party Structure Commission. The exception was a series of discussions at AFL-CIO headquarters, where a very different set of impressions about the new commission held sway. Unlike the militant reformers, the leadership of the Committee on Political Education of the AFL-CIO did see the new group much as Fred Harris did. Where they differed, of course, was over the merits of his creation. Alexander E. Barkan, executive director of COPE, and his associates were disappointed, even dismayed, and they began to search for ways to prevent the new commission from damaging the position of organized labor within the Democratic party.

In any year, the COPE leadership might have responded carefully to unspecified exhortations toward party reform, with their potential for disrupting the strong relationship between the regular party and organized labor. But in 1969, coming off the 1968 campaign, they were less inclined than ever to endorse dissident complaints. The general election campaign of 1968 had been a high-water mark for AFL involvement in presidential electioneering:

. . . The AFL/CIO set out immediately after the convention, therefore, for a classic exercise. The strategy was homely and time-honored: to register working people, then get them out to vote. But the results, effort, and technique were staggering. Volunteers card-punched names of union members across the country, by state, county, and precinct. Computers in Washington digested names, spewed them out broken down by walking lists, arranged by street numbers; volunteers, trained by the Communications Workers Union, manned telephones; others rang doorbells. Appalled at the official Party's disarray, the AFL/CIO assumed responsibility for grinding out special literature and special appeals in the thirty-one black communities across the nation.

The dimension of the AFL/CIO effort, unprecedented in American history, can be caught only by its final summary figures: the ultimate registration, by labor's efforts, of 4.6 million voters; the printing and distribution of 55 million pamphlets and leaflets out of Washington and 60 million more from local unions; telephone banks in 638 localities, using 8,055 telephones, manned by 24,511 union men and women and their families; some 72,255 house-to-house canvassers; and, on election day, 94,457 volunteers serving as car-poolers, materials distributors, baby-sitters, poll-watchers, telephoners.

Wherever an "unexpected" Humphrey surge developed, there, underbracing it, was the effort of COPE. . . .[12]

These efforts had failed to turn the tide. But they *had* resulted in a labor interpretation of presidential politics, and this did suggest an orientation toward party reform. In the COPE view, the party in 1968 had been injured by elite outsiders, who had begun without any great concern for the welfare of American working people and who had ended with an even greater unconcern for the prerequisites of electoral victory. Despite the harm done by these "party wreckers," organized labor had stepped in with all the resources it could muster and had very nearly salvaged the situation.

For national COPE leaders like Barkan this suggested a fundamental lesson for any deliberate party reform: If there were to be changes in the formal rules of the Democratic party, these changes should facilitate the rebuilding of the party as an organization, so that it could never again be damaged by those who were unconcerned with its organizational interests, so that it could never again be deprived of the resources necessary to wage a vigorous campaign, and so that it would never again suffer unnecessary electoral defeat:

> The so-called political bosses were smart enough to pick candidates who could win. These "bosses" gave us a Truman, a Stevenson, a Kennedy, a Humphrey, you name it. Invariably, the unions over time supported the Democratic Convention.

Conversely, in this view, the worst imaginable result of any reform drive would be a set of rules which actually rewarded those who had contributed to the election of a Republican and had thereby postponed the arrival of those programs—universal health care, guaranteed employment, expanded social security, and so forth—which most clearly distinguished Richard Nixon from Hubert Humphrey. Barkan believed that the reform commissions which Harris was establishing had been authorized as advisory committees only, but he saw a chance that they would be converted into rule-making bodies, captured by antiparty forces, and turned upon the party at large:

87

That became a *mandate*, instead of what everyone thought in 1968 was becoming a study to come back to in 1972. At the '68 Convention, in an effort to pacify the radicals, they adopted a resolution calling on the National Committee to *study* the rules.

After carefully studying the new Party Structure Commission, the COPE director concluded that a dissident takeover was a distinct possibility. Barkan's evaluation was derived from the same basic information as that of the leading reformers, but from radically different premises. Where reform strategists had taken the absence of public opposition to the regular party and its associated interests as evidence of devotion to established rules and procedures, Barkan looked instead for *attachments* to a strong party organization or to strong elements of organized labor, in the belief that those who lacked such attachments were, in practice, political independents. Indeed, with no party or union to constrain them, and under reliable pressure from reform activists, they were likely to side with militant reformers.

When Barkan totaled up the members who met his standards, he made the inevitable discovery. Given the appointment criteria of Chairman Harris, the Commission on Party Structure and Delegate Selection contained few commissioners with strong constituency ties. When Barkan added the fact that the commission leadership and staff was uniformly devoted to a different vision of party reform, he concluded that this commission, at best, would not offer any gains for organized labor, and might well boost "antiparty" or "new politics" interests at labor's expense: "When the membership was announced, it wasn't at all clear that we could have much effect. We complained, but we didn't cut out then. We just waited."

Barkan did complain, but he did not quite "just wait." Instead, he moved to create an additional strategic option. The only AFL member on the commission was I. W. Abel, president of the United Steelworkers. Barkan and Abel agreed that the latter would not immediately lend his presence to the new body but would send his Washington legislative representative, James C. O'Brien, in his stead. After the initial meeting, if O'Brien reported that Barkan's estimates were unduly pessimistic, Abel would rejoin the commission, and Barkan would mobilize the forces of COPE behind him.

On the other hand, if O'Brien reported that Barkan's view was essentially accurate, Abel would desert the commission for good and thereby remove even an implicit AFL imprimatur from its ultimate product. COPE would remain free to fight the recommendations of the commission from the outside; its energies could be directed—with far better hope of success—at the Democratic National Committee and at the individual state parties, rather than at a quasi-independent rules study commission.

The Inaugural Meeting and Its Products

The initial meeting of the Commission on Party Structure and Delegate Selection convened at 10:00 A.M. on Saturday, March 1, in the Caucus Room of the Old Senate Office Building. In two hours and forty minutes, the assembled commissioners heard four speeches, met the staff, established an executive committee and three subcommittees, authorized the appointment of five task forces for regional hearings, and engaged in a limited debate about their own legal status.[13]

George McGovern opened the meeting with a general welcome and some brief comments on the roots and purpose of the commission. Fred Harris followed with a pep talk, urging the commissioners to create the most open and representative party ever. Anne Wexler offered her statement on the legislative intent of the Rules minority report. Harold Hughes completed the formal speechmaking by evoking the moral importance of the commission's work.

Each of the ceremonial speakers—McGovern, Harris, and Hughes—made a set of roughly parallel points. First, that the real reason for commission existence was a decline in support for the party of the commissioners: "It is no secret that we are in trouble, especially with significant groups that have traditionally been identified with the Democratic Party." Second, that the explanation for this trouble lay with the role of regular party officialdom: "A small group of men has legal authority, if they should care to exercise it, to name the delegates without any regard to the wishes of the Democratic voter in the presidential election year." Third, that sweeping changes in party rules seemed the obvious answer: "We must—and I am convinced we will—carry through with the reforms that are essential to making the Democratic Party responsive to all of its members, from the precinct to the national convention."[14]

It was, however, the more concrete statement by Wexler which generated the only debate of the four. Her comments, in passing, assumed that the commission had the authority to dictate to the individual state parties on matters which *it* judged to fall within its jurisdiction. That assumption elicited the first of what would become a long series of pragmatic dissents from Will D. Davis, outgoing state chairman of the Democratic party of Texas. Davis contended that the commission could call for whatever it liked, but that if it did, its members should be prepared to see the state parties comply with whatever *they* liked in return:

> You can define "all feasible efforts," or whatever phrase that was, any way you like, but defining it won't make much difference when it comes up against a state

party or a state legislature. It's not just Republican states that aren't going to knuckle under to something like this. There are plenty of conservative Democrats, who control the legislatures in several southern states, for example, and they are not going to line up like sheep to pass reform legislation.[15]

But as soon as Davis opened the issue, Fred Dutton and David Mixner rushed in to argue that even the Wexler language was too weak and that the commission should simply say that state parties must comply, however they could. In the end, the commission "compromised" by staying with the initial Wexler interpretation and thereby terminated its lone inaugural debate. In effect, all sides were left free to seek the reform recommendations of their choice, and the issue of legal status was (temporarily) sidestepped.

Chairman McGovern then moved to the formal introduction of Robert W. Nelson and Eli J. Segal, the staff director and commission counsel, and he noted that they would begin immediately collecting election laws and party rules from each of the fifty states. The chairman next suggested the need for four more specialized bodies, an Executive Committee and three subcommittees, and he revealed his nominations for each.

In McGovern's proposed arrangement, an Executive Committee would provide a continuing commission presence between full commission meetings. A Model Delegate Selection Subcommittee would work on exemplary rules for delegate selection, one half of the commission mandate. A Party Structure Subcommittee would draft model rules for normal party business, the other half of that mandate. And a third subcommittee, Grass Roots Participation, would search out means to stimulate widespread citizen activity, once the first two subcommittees had guaranteed that such activity could be effective. In his final announcement, the chairman noted that he would be appointing five task forces as well, to travel the country over the next three months and take testimony on internal party politics from the general public.

The only item to which the commissioners themselves contributed was an elaboration of their own rules of procedure. On a motion by William Dodds, seconded by Fred Dutton, the commission ruled that anyone could attend its meetings as an observer, but that only official commission members could take part in its discussions. Dodds, the director of political action for the United Auto Workers, was painting James C. O'Brien, the stand-in for I. W. Abel of the United Steelworkers, into a corner:

> At the same time this was going on, the UAW was getting out of the AFL. That may have had something to do with my introducing that. It probably did, although I'm really not sure any more. I do remember being in favor of that resolution. That was one of the things you found wrong in corporations, and we knew it wasn't for us.

At the time, however, no one questioned the Dodds motion, as no one questioned the appointment of an Executive Committee, three subcommittees, or five task forces. As a result, at 12:40 P.M., having heard four speeches, having met their staff and colleagues, and having accepted an initial plan of organization, the commissioners adjourned their inaugural session.

Segal, Wexler, McGovern, and Hughes had all sensed a need for tactical planning before this inaugural meeting, in order to avoid the acrimony—or undesirable outcomes—which might follow from its opening battles. For their part, however, the commissioners had apparently seen no need to call those battles into being. Wexler's prospectus had drawn debate only on her translation of "all feasible efforts." McGovern's appointment of an Executive Committee had elicited no comment at all.

In the question of how far commission authority extended into the traditional territory of the state Democratic parties, the commissioners recognized an issue with concrete implications. They saw the implied assertion of powers, as well as the potential for conflict with other rule-making bodies, and this was sufficient to spark an argument. But the other major issues embedded in Wexler's speech—the question of the proper field for commission investigation, for example, or the question of the general values which should guide its recommendations—did not rouse anyone to more immediate debate. Possibly, a suggested range and character for commission deliberations, especially at first listening, were less obvious in their practical implications than was an assertion of formal powers. In any case, these other issues could safely, perhaps more plausibly, be deferred until there were detailed proposals to give them concrete meaning.

The creation of an Executive Committee was potentially more important than any initial statement of purpose, since that committee was intended to frame subsequent recommendations for reform and since it would thus put concrete meaning into Wexler's more abstract commentary. Nevertheless, most of the members were unacquainted with their colleagues and were unable, in principle, to judge the degree to which the Executive Committee mirrored the full membership. Only an inherently obstreperous commissioner—or one benefiting from some preparations by a countervailing organization—would have publicly questioned these appointments. No one sought a reputation for being obstreperous; no one possessed the countervailing preparations.

But if most members could not evaluate the direct impact of these maneuvers at their first meeting, David S. Broder of the *Washington Post* did not feel similarly handicapped. Broder saw both the Wexler statement and the Executive Committee appointments as important events. In a piece with a title which summarized his judgment, he awarded the substance of both to the militant reformers:

Democratic Critics Run Reform Unit
by David S. Broder,
Washington Post Staff Writer

The Democratic Party reform commission began work yesterday with a series of organizational victories by its hard-line critics of the "old politics." . . .

Putting muscle in these words the Commission members:

· Overrode the objections of Texas Democratic Chairman Will Davis and approved the toughly worded guidelines for state party reform proposed by Mrs. Anne Wexler of Connecticut, a 1968 supporter of Senator Eugene J. McCarthy's nomination bid.

· Accepted McGovern's recommendations and named an executive committee dominated by strong reform advocates and a staff whose chief counsel, Eli Segal, is a 26-year-old McCarthy campaign organizer.[16]

Individual commissioners could afford to await further developments before they decided whether these events demanded some modified tactical response. The AFL-CIO had no such luxury. The COPE leadership had watched the opening Party Structure meeting with alarm, not just at its general tone but at the acceptance of Wexler's views on the commission mandate and, especially, at the creation of an obviously stacked Executive Committee. In case they could have missed these points, the *Post*'s Broder had then driven them home again in his analysis of this initial session.

Yet what really took away their time for further reflection—what put COPE at a critical decision point—was the "gag resolution" from Bill Dodds. In effect, that resolution forced Abel to fish or cut bait: Either Abel came back in, and thus enmeshed the AFL-CIO in subsequent commission deliberations, or he took the Executive Committee maneuver as a reasonable prediction of the commission's future and dropped out for good.

During the week after the initial Party Structure session, Al Barkan, the COPE director, held his own gathering, with I. W. Abel; James C. O'Brien; Lane Kirkland, the secretary-treasurer of the AFL-CIO; and Jacob Clayman, the secretary-treasurer of COPE. Over lunch at the Hay-Adams Hotel in Washington, the five discussed the first meeting of the commission, for what it revealed about the policy preferences of the commissioners and for what these portended for organized labor.

Jimmy O'Brien began by reviewing the events of March 1. As he put them in perspective, they retained the possibility of substantial COPE influence, if the organization were to mount a full-scale, shadow staff operation and if it were to back this with pressure from the home territories of the Commissioners. O'Brien was supported in this by Jake Clayman, and the two became responsible for outlining the risks involved in withdrawal. Among these, they cited missed opportunities for affecting commission conduct, a lack of support for potential allies inside the commission, and deficient information about commission activities.

I. W. Abel, the vehicle for any strategic decision, was the neutral in the lot. He expressed a mild preference for not attending, but he was willing to do what his colleagues judged to be in the best interests of labor. He was not eager to invest time in studying the details of party rules, much less in being upbraided by reformist commissioners with no responsibility to any organized constituency, but he agreed to do so if necessary.

He would never have to. Lane Kirkland and Al Barkan, the two ranking members of the gathering, opposed a return by Abel. Speaking for himself and, on occasion, for George Meany, the president of the AFL-CIO, Kirkland recalled the general labor view that a reform commission established at the demand of party dissidents, so soon after the prodigious efforts by labor on behalf of the party, showed a disturbing sense of priorities at national party headquarters. Max Kampelman, one of the Humphrey advisers with extensive ties to organized labor, watched the arrival of the COPE decision with real sadness but saw the roots of the Meany-Kirkland view:

> Abel was being a good soldier. He was doing Meany's bidding. Labor was intransigent, stubborn, and proud. Here was labor, which had given of itself in 1968 more than it had ever given—more money, more effort, more intelligence. For that group, which did more for the party than the party did, for that group to have to go to Fred Harris and ask for something—it was not dignified, they would not do it.
>
> They saw that the only way to deal with the problem was to *cut*. They wanted to cut this McCarthy group. They said, "They'll have to come to us in 1972. Who will give them the money? Who'll give them the manpower?"

Yet it was Al Barkan who actually carried the day, by weight of argument and by force of conviction. The COPE director offered his own history of commission events and his own projection of future developments. He argued that the Rules minority report had been a vehicle for what were essentially nonparty and antiparty forces. He reported on the meetings which he and Harris had held while Harris was creating the new reform commissions. He went through the commission roster, arguing that it was indeed stacked against the policy preferences of COPE, and he summarized the analysis behind this conclusion. In passing, he noted that Walter P. Reuther, president of the United Auto Workers, had been given the option of putting his director of political action on the commission in his place, whereas I. W. Abel, president of the United Steelworkers, had not—an insult converted to injury by the antiproxy resolution with which the commission had then silenced the unofficial stand-in for Abel.

For the future, the COPE director asserted that a shadow staff could never have the impact of the real thing, because it would never have the legitimacy or constant contact with commissioners which the latter had. Moreover, he warned that the possibilities for internal pressure, even with a shadow operation, were much more limited than Jimmy O'Brien imagined. Having hit at the limited potential for labor influence inside the commission, Barkan raised the possibility that the entire venture would collapse without labor participation, and he underlined the increased potential for labor influence outside the commission if it did not:

> I had one meeting with Harris alone, and then a meeting with him and Bill Welsh. I gave them a chance. They asked me to encourage Abel to participate. I told him that he was wasting his time. Very few people thought that it would end up with the powers that it did. I think most people at that time thought the Commission would come up with a document that would be presented to the 1972 Convention.

The last straw, in Barkan's view, was the creation of the new Executive Committee. Barkan had been arguing all along that the Party Structure Commission was unrepresentative of the 1968 Convention. After its first meeting, he could also argue that its Executive Committee was unrepresentative of the full commission. (See figure 3.2.) If the staff was even unrepresentative of this Executive Committee—with every distortion in an antiparty, antilabor direction—then no response was reasonable, he concluded, except to withdraw from the entire operation and let it fall of its own weight:

> There were twenty-eight members. Then they went to a ten-member executive group. If we thought the first group was unrepresentative, this executive group was worse. These ten people held periodic meetings in 1969, with the staff doing everything. If ever there was a staff running away with things, that was it.

A recorded vote would have shown the five men to be split—two yes, two no, and one abstention. But Barkan, with the relevant formal authority and the longest list of arguments, effectively cast the crucial ballot. The decision was to boycott the Party Structure Commission. Abel would not attend any commission meetings; O'Brien would no longer go in his place.

There was no formal announcement to underline the disappearance of Abel for the outside world, but insiders registered his departure quickly. At the Party Structure Commission, Bob Nelson, the staff director, feared that Bar-

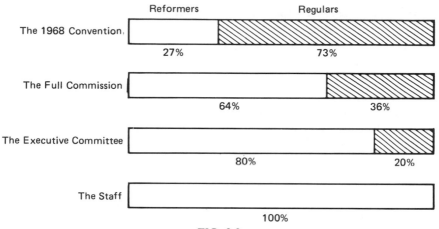

FIG. 3.2

The Institutionalized Bias of the Commission:
Al Barkan's Interpretation

kan's analysis of the long-run impact of a withdrawal by COPE might prove correct:

> The AFL-CIO was very antagonistic toward the whole operation. They had a deep disappointment with the 1968 election, the fact that McCarthy had taken a walk. They felt that this was enshrining the McCarthy wing of the party, after they [labor] had broken their necks for the Democrats in 1968. They thought we were going to impose restrictions on the real, true-blue Democrats.
>
> I felt it was important that labor get involved, and I had worked hard at that. Jimmy O'Brien actually came to the first Commission meeting. At that meeting, they passed a no-proxy resolution. Then he dropped out entirely, and that was that.

The withdrawal of I. W. Abel created an immediate tactical problem for National Chairman Harris and Commission Chairman McGovern. Each, in effect, had to choose between pursuing Abel in a manner likely to justify a return to full participation or letting him go in peace. Their decisions provided the denouement to the politics surrounding the inaugural meeting of the commission.

Harris would have preferred, in the abstract, to offer the renewed overtures which might cause Abel to return. But to do that, he would have had to risk offending the militant reformers. Because Harris had set out to create a reform-oriented body, and because he had nevertheless been assailed by the *reformers* when its membership was unveiled, the chairman accepted the departure of Abel philosophically, with no attempt to woo him back. The COPE decision represented an open break in the forces theoretically aligned behind the national chairman. But once that break occurred, Harris, too, had to choose sides, and Vick French saw that the man who was hoping to be the "chairman of reform" had no real choice:

> We didn't have any insight at the time that the Abel drop-out was coming. Nobody warned us. Neither Zon nor Barkan was happy with the composition of the Commission to start with. Harris got them to agree to accept it, but once it was appointed, Barkan reacted to the liberals' organization of the Commission. Barkan blamed Harris for not controlling it. But Harris was determined not to control it, much less intervene in its structuring. It was Harris's full intention to let it have its full head, and let it rip.
>
> We went very much out of our way to structure the thing to be satisfactory to everybody we had to deal with. Presented with this list, he [Barkan] reluctantly agreed to it. That wasn't the problem. It was the structuring of the thing immediately thereafter that made Al drop out. The structuring was what did it. We didn't foresee that, but once it was done, we decided to let them go. We didn't attempt to do much after that. . . .
>
> The creation of the Executive Committee was a quite deliberate effort to strengthen the liberal position on the Commission. It was quite deliberate. Hughes became Vice Chairman, and then they stacked the Executive Committee to build a majority. That was one of the ways in which Eli and the others were trying to increase the dominance of the liberal vote.

The COPE-Abel decision raised the same questions for George McGovern. In his ideal scenario, labor would remain on the commission, while the commission developed recommendations which lent credibility to the image of its chairman as a reformer. McGovern would then emerge as a plausible leader for the activist community; he would maintain his personal ties to organized labor; he could depart the Party Structure Commission before its recommendations caused direct annoyance to official party leaders. Once Abel had withdrawn, however, McGovern, too, had to choose between letting the Steelworkers president go and making the kind of counteroffer which could cost him dearly on the reform side.

McGovern chose to let Abel depart. In the long run, his nascent presidential campaign—the reason, after all, that he had taken the commission chairmanship—could never succeed if he did not capture the loyalty of those most interested in party reform. It was not that he was prepared to foreswear the support of organized labor and the regular party. It was only that he would never be in a position even to bid for that support if he could not corral the backing of party reformers. On the record, McGovern continued to overlook the withdrawal of Abel and to send him notes expressing interest in his attendance. But on the record or not, Abel was gone.

Implications

The first official meeting of the Commission on Party Structure and Delegate Selection, on March 1, 1969, was the formal start of the politics of recommendation. On that date, the central reform commission for the national Democratic party set to work on the central document in the politics of party reform.

From a different perspective, however, this date, too, was only one more artificial starting point in an informal process stretching back at least to late June of 1968. Some of the key events from that early period, such as the struggle over wording and interpretation of convention resolutions, were reflected again in this first commission meeting. Yet more proximate, focused, tactical preparations to influence the details of this inaugural session had also been going on for some time. When the meeting occurred and these preparations bore fruit—sweet for organized reformers, bitter for organized labor—these products merely confirmed that a serious reform politics was already under way.

The subsequent politics of party reform was to be a good deal less tidy than reform strategists hoped in March of 1969, and the Executive Committee which they secured from the initial meeting of the Party Structure Commission was to be less dominant and less predictable as well. Yet the process of creating that committee was still an instructive introduction to commission politics, for its creators, for neutral observers, and for the major interest group in the orthodox Democratic coalition. The formal products of this inaugural session—an official statement of purpose and an Executive Committee to put it in operation—confirmed the drift of commission engineering effected by Fred Harris. At the same time, these products constituted an additional, solid push in that same proreform direction. Within days, the response of the Committee on Political Education of the AFL-CIO endowed these developments with even greater significance.

The AFL-CIO was the numerically preponderant unit within organized labor. COPE was the official political spokesman for the 16 million members of the AFL-CIO. The largest independent union for which it could not speak, the Teamsters, had been written out of reform politics from the beginning. As a result, when COPE broke with the Party Structure Commission, it created a break between organized labor and the new reform enterprise. This rupture may have been invisible to all but a handful of reform actors. Yet it had substantial consequences for the character of the elite coalitions which would continue to attend to the commission during the remainder of the politics of recommendation. And it had even greater potential consequences for the character of the recommendations which the winners in that politics would secure.

The withdrawal of the major voice of organized labor in fact marked the final break between the orthodox Democratic coalition and the new Party Structure Commission. The orthodox coalition had lost most of its potential influence when Chairman Harris created this commission. Harris had not only tilted it against the regular party. He had seen that the minority of commissioners sympathetic to the party as an organization were not major figures within it, with extended ties to important others. I. W. Abel, on the other hand, clearly was a major spokesman for the major interest group in the orthodox Democratic coalition, as well as a man with evident ties to other, major, party interests. When Abel withdrew, the disconnection between the orthodox coalition and the new commission was nearly complete.

In theory, Harris himself remained as a major link between the official party and the Party Structure Commission. But Harris was determined to foster extensive reform, even at the expense of the regular party. Moreover, suspicion of Harris within reform circles was such that the reformers would work consistently to insulate him from commission deliberations. In short order, concrete actions would reveal their orientation. But it was already clear, as an attitude, by the time Tom Alder wrote to Alex Bickel about the inaugural commission meeting:

> The latest I have on the Saturday meeting makes it sound like an unveiling ceremony which everyone has to leave before the shroud can be dropped, leaving behind our trusty, woody steed, the Executive Committee. It is to be open, which seems OK to me only because Fred Harris is going to speak and should not be casually invited to do this at any other kind of session.[17]

The regular party would thus have extreme difficulty in acting to constrain the Party Structure Commission. The major interest group allied with the regular party would henceforth not act to constrain it at all. As a result, the commission would respond primarily to its own composition, to the initiatives of its leadership and staff, and to its subsequent internal interactions and struggles. This had direct implications for the character of the institutional change, the applied party reform, which the commission might ultimately recommend. That is, it promised to affect the *kind* of party reform to which the commission was drawn. It promised to affect the *scope* of its application to internal party affairs as well.

In professional writing about party structure and party activity, there are three main approaches to the topic of party reform.[18] One, in truth, counsels against the reform enterprise. This approach argues in favor of evolutionary change; it exalts decentralized adaptation to the character of society at the grass roots; it endorses deliberate alterations in the structure, rules, and procedures of a political party only when undertaken in a gradual and piecemeal fashion.

But there are two other approaches to party reform, both consistent with a more self-conscious and systematic assault on the topic. The first emphasizes the *contributions* which political parties can make to democratic governance. In consequence, this approach centers on strengthening parties as organizations, at the grass roots and at the center, while insuring that party organizations are subject to extensive procedural guarantees. "Strong and disciplined parties" are the hallmark of this perspective, and it is the clear favorite of professional reform theorists across time.

The second approach emphasizes the *obstacles* to democratic governance presented by party organizations as traditionally constituted. As an antidote, it offers easy access and free expression within mass party gatherings, which are bound by extensive regulations and which are entitled to transact major party business directly. "Open and participatory parties" are the ideal of its supporters, and they included most—perhaps all—of the self-conscious party reformers produced by the events of 1968 and 1969.

The disconnection of the orthodox Democratic coalition from the Party Structure Commission, and the gradual increase in influence of an aspiring, alternative coalition of Democratic elites within that body, had obvious implications for the fate of these three reform doctrines. Nothing about the commission suggested that it would endorse the evolutionary approach and consciously refrain from institutional engineering. If this had ever been in doubt, the inaugural commission meeting surely laid that possibility to rest. Yet the commission politics revealed at that meeting, and reinforced by the withdrawal of the AFL-CIO, implied an emerging choice between the strong and disciplined versus the open and participatory approaches to party reform as well. Indeed, this pattern of politics implied a clear, if still potential, triumph for the participatory model.

Regular party figures and leaders of their associated interest groups, with more attachment to party office and more experience in using the official party to obtain desired outcomes, were inherently more receptive to proposals for filling the gaps and correcting abuses in the rules governing strong (and even disciplined) party organizations. Insurgent party figures and leaders of their associated interests, with less attachment to party office and recent experience at being *thwarted* in their political desires by the official party, were inherently inclined to replace the ladder of party offices with mechanisms favoring more immediate and less structured participation.

In the same way, the continuing shift in commission influence from the orthodox to the alternative Democratic coalition suggested an impact on the scope of any proposed reforms. Regular party figures and leaders of their associated interests, with their greater experience in party affairs, could see more variability in any existing mechanism for party business and were less ready to prohibit and replace it. Perhaps more to the point, with more responsibility under existing arrangements and with *more to lose* under any revisions, these individuals were less sympathetic to all calls for alternative institutional change. Insurgent party figures and their interest group allies, on the other hand, were tempted to see any existing arrangement as a tool of regular party dominance. In any case, with little or no stake in the inherited mix of institutional devices, these individuals were attracted to intensive and extensive alterations, from the beginning.

The emerging balance within the Party Structure Commission thus had profound consequences for the character of the recommendations which that commission might produce.[19] It predisposed the commission toward one approach to party reform; it predisposed the commission toward extensive application of that one approach. Yet this balance itself, much less its translation into specific recommendations for party reform, was hardly a fixed equation. It remained dependent on developments in internal commission politics; it remained subject to major external events as well.

Moreover, the situation as it existed within the Party Structure Commission in early 1969, even if that situation came to govern commission recommendations, could hardly prevail thereafter within the party at large. The regular party had to re-enter reform politics when the Party Structure Commission reported and sought to have its recommendations converted into party law. At that time, organized labor might well re-enter reform politics, too, in deadly conjunction with the regular party. In short, when the politics of recommendation gave way to the politics of implementation, the regular party would inevitably be back. There was no reason to assume that labor would not be back as well.

Nevertheless, when organized labor pulled out, in March of 1969, its action did complete the detachment of the Party Structure Commission from the orthodox Democratic coalition, and this did leave the leadership and staff of the commission free to go off in the direction they preferred. It left them free to press for participatory, and not organizational, party reform. It left them free to strive for comprehensive, and not just piecemeal—much less cosmetic—institutional change. It left them at liberty to cater to the aspiring new groups in Democratic party politics, rather than to their established counterparts. It left them free to inaugurate a new era in Democratic party affairs, if they had the political skill, and if they knew how.

CHAPTER

4

The Definition of Party Reform:

The Staff in Commission Politics

IN WHICH, the commission staff undertakes diverse organizational initiatives toward a set of recommendations on party reform; practical constraints encourage this staff to concentrate on the reform of delegate selection—and hence presidential nomination; and a broad and deep, theoretically coherent set of reform proposals emerges. AND IN WHICH, reform politics centers on the private development of the substantive content of party reform; these recommendations imply sweeping institutional change, on the participatory model; and the alternative coalition of Democratic elites, preferring this package and expecting to benefit from it, first appears at its full extension.

THE ESSENTIAL CHARACTER of the reform recommendations from the Commission on Party Structure and Delegate Selection was determined during the summer of 1969 by elements of the commission staff and not during the fall of 1969 when the full commission met to address staff proposals. The small, internal, political environment within which these proposals were developed thus gained a historical interest all its own. The recommendations emanating from this environment were destined to revolutionize delegate selection and presidential nomination—and thus to gain a more obvious and extended significance.

The Party Structure Commission had no immediate occasion, as a body, to feel the loss of I. W. Abel, since the full commission did not assemble again until September 23. At its first meeting, it is true, there had been bold talk of a draft report by early June, but it was to be another six months before such a report could be put before the entire membership and another eight months before the commissioners ratified a final version.

Hindsight revealed a central—and probably inevitable—thrust to the diverse commission activities occurring during these months. The commission staff and leadership began by debating the proper substantive focus for their operation and by agreeing on the broadest possible definition. Then, as the summer wore on and as the scope of their research needs, the scarcity of commission resources, and the simple pressure of time began to converge, they narrowed this focus to one principal endeavor—systematic reform of the politically central process of delegate selection.

Along the way, the commission leadership and staff also promoted a set of commission ventures with fewer direct contributions to these eventual proposals for reform. In an initial burst of enthusiasm, for example, they suggested three subcommittees to augment the full commission. These ultimately had to be suspended, leaving them as little more than diversionary appendages. In the same way, subgroups of commissioners were dispatched to take testimony from interested persons around the country. Although these regional hearings did provide the first official rallying point for a potential reform constituency, their formal product was never integral to commission recommendations, while it did absorb (scarce) commission resources.

By the end of the summer, in any case, the commission staff was working on the substance of its major contribution to party reform, to presidential nomination, and to national politics—the systematic reconstruction of the machinery for delegate selection in the national Democratic party. As autumn approached, staff members worked intensively and singlemindedly toward this goal.

A faction within the staff actually controlled the drafting of these reforms. Its members worked only intermittently with the remainder of their staff colleagues and with the commission leadership. They worked very occasionally with individual commissioners. They never assembled the commission as a collectivity, and their written communications to the group as a whole were irrelevant to the substance of their final product. Indeed, while these staff members did keep track of individuals on the outside who might eventually be part of the constituency for this product, they paid no direct heed even to these individuals in developing their draft report.

The recommendations which emerged were remarkable for the extent to which they reflected—or rather, recapitulated—a fully developed model of participatory politics, as applied to delegate selection. Their drafters had no intention of applying a theoretical model to practical party affairs. Yet they insisted on the possibility of direct public participation as the diagnostic value in party reform, and they applied that value to every institution and every activity in the process of delegate selection. Fortunately for the drafters, their reform proposals were more than satisfactory to the emerging constituency for party reform. Even more serendipitously, these proposals offered that very constituency a practical advantage in presidential politics.

As a result, the draft proposals which went forward were remarkable for their sweep and their coherence, that is, for their approximation to a full-blown model of participatory reform. They were remarkable for their integration with both the wishes and the practical interests of their own potential constituency. They were at least noteworthy for the intimacy of the politics surrounding their development. And they were destined to be remarkable not only because they would constitute the framework for commission deliberations but because they would come to constitute the overwhelming bulk of successful proposals within that commission.

The Focus on Delegate Selection

The first attempt at defining a field of concentration for the commission—its realm for eventual recommendations on reform—came at a February meeting of the leadership, full-time staff, and consultants at the Washington home of Chairman George McGovern. All of the key individuals had been appointed, and McGovern was set to elevate Harold Hughes to the vice chairmanship, but the commission as a body had not yet assembled, so that there was still time to channel its substantive investigations.

In the face of this opportunity, an immediate split surfaced. One side argued that the commission should concentrate primarily, if not exclusively, on delegate selection. Dick Wade took the lead in their argument, asserting that reform of the process of delegate selection was at least intellectually and politically manageable, because this process was separable from total party business and could conceivably be reformed from without. Moreover, said Wade, successful, mandatory, delegate guidelines would automatically produce some leverage on state party structure, thereby broadening commission impact in a highly practical fashion. Wade was supported by Bob Nelson, the staff director, by Alex Bickel, his fellow consultant, and by Chairman McGovern.

The other side argued that the commission should construe its mission much more broadly. Eli Segal carried the load for them, asserting that failure to address any element in their charge would be a signal to the state parties that they need not be concerned with that. Moreover, he argued, such a signal might encourage them to resist the commission even on its announced priority, delegate selection, and it automatically risked letting subsequent events intervene to prevent the commission from ever attending to party structure and public participation. Segal was vigorously supported by Anne Wexler, the third consultant, and by Harold Hughes, the vice chairman-to-be.

As long as this argument remained solely a debate over the desirable impact of the commission, it would be carried by the second, more expansive side. As soon as the logistics of commission operations began to shift the argument from an abstract debate to a set of clear, practical, *forced* choices, the decision would be reversed. In February of 1969, then, it was Segal and the partisans of a wide-ranging focus who won; it was Wade and the partisans of a concentrated focus who lost:

> When I arrived at the first meeting of the consultants, when we first met at George's house, the staff had already been chosen. What we had when we first met was the staff pushing for the broadest possible interpretation of the mandate. There was a move to go toward grass-roots participation. I felt that the first job of the staff was to build the state-books, to go into each state and determine the rules of the state and the results of the party.

The decision was to plunge ahead on all three fronts—delegate selection, party structure, and mass participation—and the three subcommittees which McGovern appointed at the inaugural meeting of the full commission were a confirmation of this. The lone concession to the losing argument was organizational: Everyone agreed that Wade's proposed "state-books"—fifty individual collections of state law, state party rules, and actual state behavior—were the ideal way to proceed with commission research. Nelson and Segal followed through by converting the notion into operating procedure for the staff.

Almost immediately, the decision to remain with the broadest possible focus, as compounded by the research demands of fifty state-books, created an overload at commission headquarters. Segal had assumed that the data collected by the Hughes Commission would be sufficient to generate recommendations from the McGovern Commission as well, but it quickly became clear that this information was thin, even sketchy, for many states, and patently inaccurate for some. Moreover, Segal and Nelson were responsible for organizing numerous regional hearings and for packing their commissioners off to them. Finally, they were charged with activating three major subcommittees, with giving each a detailed research agenda, and with guiding their planned activity.

Nelson formulated the first putative response to this ultimately intractable problem. He proposed a group of student interns in Washington for the summer. Each would be given a half-dozen states on which to develop expertise; their discoveries would form the basis for the proposed state-books:

We had all these letters. How are we going to respond to this massive request for participation? Letters from people like Rick Stearns, Rich Norling, and others who later became very important. So I said, what if we could pick ten of the brightest kids, from big and small universities, balance them in other ways, bring them in on a scholarship basis? Bring them in at $1,000 per, ten of them. That's really the only way we could go through the massive amount of materials from the hearings anyway. We set all these people up over in one room at George Washington [University].

The interns however, promised to create new problems while they solved the old. Nelson and Segal would still be immersed in the regional hearings and the subcommittees, as well as the normal administrative business of any national commission. Yet they were presumably the ones who would have to coordinate the new team of summer interns, too, advising them on what to collect, how to find it, and where to put it. Beyond that, the two top staffers were the logical people to take the first cut at deciding what it all meant, in detailed recommendations for reform.

Their next response was to ask for a third full-time staff member, a director of research, to devote himself to overseeing the collection and organization of this data and to join in the development of recommendations from it. McGovern agreed to the need and pressed Chairman Harris about it. Harris agreed to the position, with the understanding that McGovern and Hughes would help with the requisite fund raising.

Kenneth A. Bode, an assistant professor of political science in the state university system in New York, thus joined Segal and Nelson on the full-time staff of the commission. Bode was a long-time acquaintance of McGovern and had moved in and out of many of the events leading up to formation of the McGovern Commission. Like Wexler, Bode had tried to enter commission politics on his own, as a commissioner. Like her, he had been turned away. Like her, finally, he was to realize his ambition by joining the commission staff.

In 1968, Bode had worked for the McCarthy nomination campaign in both Indiana and New York. After the assassination of Robert Kennedy, however, Bode had left for England, with the thought of foresaking not just American politics but perhaps American life in general. He had returned to observe the Democratic Convention, and when McGovern announced his belated candidacy, Bode enlisted in the McGovern operation. He knew the senator from college days in South Dakota, and he easily secured a role in the McGovern delegate hunt. Nevertheless, that had not been enough to gain him a commission appointment, and he had gone back to the political science faculty at SUNY-Binghamton, whence McGovern plucked him for commission research director. Bode was delighted to make the move:

> I came in on the first of June. It was clear that they would need a research director. They had dreamed up an intern program. Then I came and decided what we would do with these interns. I had ten questions for them to find out about each state. The Hughes Commission report had already firmed up the general problems.

While the commission staff was turning to the research which would, they hoped, eventuate in a set of strong recommendations for party reform, the commissioners themselves were not permitted to sit idle. Instead, each was assigned to one of five task forces and was then shipped off to regional hearings around the country.[1] Publicly, these hearings were justified as devices for gathering information and as means for publicizing commission pursuit of party reform.[2] Privately, staff members were under few illusions about these public goals. They were well aware that mere hearings would never convince skeptics of the commitment of the Party Structure Commission to thorough party reform. They knew that public hearings were poor devices, in principle, for gathering information.

If staff members were unbothered by this situation, it was because they saw three other, more explicitly political purposes for the regional hearings. First, these hearings could mobilize those around the country who were interested in the issue of party reform and allow them to meet some principals from the Party Structure Commission, as well as to meet and reinforce each other. If these individuals continued to press the commissioners for stiff reform recommendations, that would be a double virtue, but they would at least be identified and positioned for the implementation battles which would surely follow. Bob Nelson emphasized this first, more practical rationale:

> The strategy was to build on your strength. In the hearings, the effort was to get everyone who might have any interest in these to come in to have their day in court. We held sixteen or seventeen hearings in four and a half months during the pre-guideline period.
>
> The main value of the hearings was as a sounding board. You could guess what the guidelines would be before the hearings started. No concrete suggestions came in; *no one* had that. They'd tell about their experiences, and pump for more openness. Something they had suffered in the process, an example of something to avoid.

Beyond this, the hearings could expose individual *commissioners* to a strongly reform-oriented sample of elite opinion. The commissioners might be impressed by the formal content of the associated public statements. They might be impressed by the sheer number and intensity of reform advocates. Either outcome would suffice. Sam Beer was one commissioner who listened intently to the substance of these comments:

> I went to many of the regional hearings. I still use the material from these in my classes. It's marvelous, the practices, the examples, the questionable short-cuts. It gives you information on the inside of the party.

Finally, hearings could themselves be an event for the regional press to cover, thus generating additional attention for the commission. That attention would presumably draw additional groups and individuals to the cause of party reform, while simultaneously signaling all and sundry that the Party Structure Commission was pressing ahead. Moreover, if regional newsmen could be convinced to monitor commission progress, they would be available, during 1969, to pose "the hard questions" about party reform, and they would be available, after 1969, to publicize the politics of implementation. Commissioner Fred Dutton backed the hearings on these grounds:

> I was trying to use the media to make up for the lack of a constituency for this organization. I believe that the media are more important than organized labor in marshaling our society. This gave us legitimacy, so that labor could do less to us. The whole process began to take on a life of its own. This ad hoc, loose group of people developed a cutting edge.

On April 10, with this combination of public and private goals, the staff sent each task force chairman a format sheet suggesting arrangements for these hearings.[3] But while staff members expressed the hope that individual chairmen would do some advance publicity for their own sessions and would try to insure that scheduled witnesses did indeed attend, they were not about to leave those functions to the whims of these task force leaders. Instead, the staff remained actively involved with invitations to testify, and the full range of staff contacts with local reform bodies and liberal interest groups was carefully added to any autonomous inquiries which surfaced.

The hearings began in Washington, D.C., on April 25, with a special "national" session for senators, congressmen, and officials of the Democratic National Committee. Regional hearings began the next morning in Detroit, home base for Commissioner Bill Dodds and the UAW. From there, they passed through fifteen other locations, ending with a special return hearing, after conclusion of the original schedule, in New Orleans. From late April through late June, any commissioners who were willing to travel were accordingly absorbed in their personal task force duties.

The desire for interns, a research director, and regional hearings was also, of course, a desire for additional funding. Fred Harris had already agreed to underwrite both a staff director and a commission counsel, to permit access to supplies and equipment at the National Committee, and to provide housing at national party headquarters.[4] He agreed to *try* to pick up the salary of a research director as well, but 1969 was even then presenting acute financial problems for the national party, and Harris urged the commission leadership to undertake its own fundraising efforts to cover the costs of summer interns and regional hearings. After this, periodic, desperate searches for the wherewithal to pay additional bills were a fundamental fact of commission life.

Chairman McGovern and Vice Chairman Hughes undertook a series of limited, personal efforts to raise funds for commission activity during the spring and summer of 1969.[5] But the serious external subventions during this period—not great amounts but important ones, given the shortage—came from the coffers of the United Auto Workers, courtesy of Commissioner Dodds. First, Dodds secured $5,000 in direct monetary contributions, via the Committee for Good Government, a UAW-sponsored political operation. UAW checks for $3,000 in early May and $2,000 in early June went directly into the regional hearings.[6] Beyond that, the union helped keep the hearings alive with a larger collection of contributions in kind. Dodds's report of the hearing situation in Chicago was typical:

> The United Auto Workers often provided facilities for the commission along the way. In Chicago, for example, we rented the hall and got the equipment. This happened fairly often, since the commission was always strapped for funds.

Once the regional hearings had been organized and were on the road, the commission staff turned to pumping life into its three official subcommittees. The result, however, was strongly conditioned by the orientation of the respective chairmen. At one extreme, Adlai Stevenson III, chairman of the Grass Roots Participation Subcommittee, had taken hold autonomously and was seeking *extra* finances to establish a complete "mini-commission" in Chicago. At the other, Leroy Collins, chairman of the Party Structure Subcommittee, had written to his members after the first meeting of the full commission suggesting that they defer any sessions until they had "the benefit of considerable research to form the basis for discussion" and "until after the Task Force hearings are concluded."[7] In-between, Congressman Donald Fraser evinced a readiness to lead his group in whichever direction the staff might suggest.

In May, Segal pulled together a research agenda for each of these groups. His prospectuses for two of the three, the Party Structure Subcommittee and the Grass Roots Participation Subcommittee, gained historical significance largely as additional evidence of the grand ambitions of the commission staff at this early period. On the other hand, the third prospectus, for the Model Delegate Subcommittee, constituted Segal's first attempt at codifying his own thoughts on the reform of delegate selection and thus acquired additional historical consequence, although the prospectus itself would never serve as the basis for serious activity by its subcommittee.[8]

Segal quickly noted the varied orientations of his subcommittee chairmen and responded to them accordingly. He pressed Fraser and his Model Delegate Subcommittee for immediate and extensive action. He gave Stevenson and his Grass Roots Participation Subcommittee a detailed prospectus but bowed to their intention to run a semi-independent operation. He left Leroy Collins and his Party Structure Committee alone in deference to Collins's desire for a measured start.

Ken Bode formally joined the commission staff on June 1, and the summer interns began to arrive at about the same time. Bode was to become a central figure in reform politics through 1972; the interns were to be a far more varied presence. There was a core group of six or seven who remained throughout the summer of 1969 and who really developed the state-books. There were others who, while equally dedicated, arrived late enough that their major contribution was to implementation, rather than to research. There were some who used commission data to do their own work, work which promised important side benefits to the commission. And there were, of course, a number whose interest flagged and who never made much contribution at all.[9]

The interns were collectively and officially welcomed by Chairman McGovern on the afternoon of June 17. That very morning, others on the staff had turned once again to the question of a practical focus for the commission, in a meeting with eventual, powerful consequences for them all. McGovern had met with consultants Bickel, Wade, and Wexler to discuss priorities and schedules. Their meeting produced an agreement, with Wexler consenting only reluctantly, that a much heavier emphasis had to go to delegate selection. Wade summarized the outcome in a June 20 letter to McGovern:

> Alex, Anne, and I are in agreement that the scope of the project is so large and the resources available to us so modest that the establishment of priorities is obviously essential to make certain that the first commitment of the commission be met this summer. As we see it, this means that the initial emphasis should be placed on informing states which are out of compliance that they must change their procedures before the next convention. Since in many states this would require a change in legislation, that information should be presented to the state chairmen early this fall.[10]

The staffers who had to execute this agreement—Bode, Segal, and Nelson—were receptive to a shift in priorities, but Bode and Segal were not eager to curtail the work which would theoretically be the substance of the commission *after* delegate guidelines had been issued. Their interpretation of this new understanding was that a change in the schedule for reform pronouncements was desirable, but that differing ultimate priorities for party reform were not.[11]

Their resistance, however, was destined to be short-lived. At a second meeting on July 9, as the three consultants and three full-time staff members attempted to draft an actual calendar for the rest of 1969, it became clear that the investment of staff energy in topics other than delegate selection had to be sharply curtailed, if there was to be any hope for real reform. Research in three major areas was proceeding slowly. The apparent deadline for securing compliance with reform recommendations was coming up fast, especially in those states where the legislature met only biennially. In a memo summarizing the July 9 session, Segal and Bode bowed to the inevitable and made delegate selection their sole focus for the next several months:

> We had a highly satisfactory meeting with the three consultants on Wednesday, July 9. We now have the same understanding of (1) Commission priorities; (2) the nature of the "State of the States"; and (3) the nature of the compliance report.[12]

The significance of this shift was larger than any of its assenters, the willing or the reluctant, could possibly know. After this renewed agreement on commission priorities, the field for commission investigation—the realm for recommendations on party reform—would never formally expand again. Wade's original hypothesis, that the reform of delegate selection would provide some informal leverage on state party structure and on the opportunities for public participation, was to prove correct. But formally, delegate selection was to be the overriding concern of the Commission on Party Structure and Delegate Selection for all the three years to follow.

An apparent contraction in the substantive reach of the Party Structure Commission was thus a crucial expansion of the ultimate impact of the commission report. At a minimum, this refocusing accelerated development of a set of recommendations for reform. Without the effective jettisoning of party structure and grass-roots participation, these recommendations would necessarily have been delayed. Moreover, this refocusing probably increased the chances that these recommendations would ultimately be implemented, since a joint assault on delegate selection *and* state and national party structure *and* grass-roots participation would surely have generated more resistance, and much more deliberate evasion.

The refocusing of the field of investigation, then, was probably an essential step toward production of sweeping recommendations for delegate selection reform—and ultimately toward changes in the mechanics of presidential nominations more extensive than any in the preceding 140 years. The agreement to refocus was confirmed in a new official calendar, containing no items on "party structure" or "grass-roots participation" for the period from July 12 to October 17. In truth, this calendar did leave room to resume work on these other topics in late October. But by that time, the leadership and staff would be so heavily invested in the reform of presidential selection, and so close to the adoption of major recommendations for reform, that these other possibilities would be quietly, almost inadvertently, foresworn.

Once this agreement was reached, of course, several ongoing commission ventures became superfluous, became, indeed, little more than a diversion of scarce commission resources. The three official subcommittees—Model Delegate Selection, Party Structure, and Grass Roots Participation—fell into this category instantly. But even the regional hearings presented a version of the problem.

By the time this narrowing of the commission focus had been accepted by all the principal staff, the regional hearings had nearly run their course. Accordingly, there was no need to redirect or curb the hearings as such but only to think a bit differently about their product. Each regional hearing was originally slated for recording and transcription; every witness was invited to send an expanded version of his remarks to commission headquarters. All this could proceed as planned, but the previous staff efforts to compile, index, and compare hearing transcripts was abandoned for more productive endeavors.

The abandonment of this ostensibly important research tool was actually a matter of near-indifference to the commission staff. Testimony at the regional hearings had not come organized around issues and subdivided by perspectives. Some commissioners were disturbed by this fact (see below), but the staff was not, since few of the points which arose in testimony were going directly into the development of reform guidelines. This testimony would prove useful in supporting these draft guidelines—with an example of a practice which should be proscribed, with evidence that a proposed solution had worked elsewhere—but the guidelines were neither being developed from, nor tested against, these examples.[13]

Nevertheless, the hearings clearly *had* made some contributions. They did succeed in turning out large numbers of reform advocates and precious few dissenters. If these individuals could be activated again, once the commission had framed its recommendations, then the hearings would have made an essential contribution to the politics of implementation. The commissioners, for their part, were not unaware of this function of their public sessions. Warren Christopher saw that they were helping to forge the constituency for their own eventual product:

The Politics of Recommendation

The function of the hearings was largely to rally support for what the Commission was doing. The hearing format really didn't leave room for concrete suggestions to be picked up and re-used by Commission members, although this might occasionally have happened. (Pause) I can't think of any examples. It was slightly more likely to give them a sense of the interested public's wishes. But it was most useful for rallying support for actions which the Commission was to take anyway.

On the other hand, whatever their utility for rallying support, the propensity for the hearings to attract *dissident* witnesses was also not lost on the commissioners. Some saw this as a helpful counterbalance to the party regulars who would presumably dominate rules negotiations when it came time to implement commission pronouncements. But more fretted that these were precisely *not* the people who should be the principal beneficiaries of intelligent structural reforms. Carmen Warschaw, national committeewoman for California, summarized their view most caustically:

> We held testimony at four places. The only ones who were really interested were the "new politics" people, the really far-out people. No one else cared. Oh, a few nutty professors, maybe, but no one else. Extreme objectors are the main testifiers at any hearing. Moderate reformers never come. Most were saying how terrible it was, but they had all managed to be delegates. When they complained to me, I always wanted to ask, "How did you get on the delegation?"

If this sample of witnesses had been the critical aspect of the regional hearings for the commissioners, it might actually have made them less receptive to draft recommendations from the staff. The commissioners were aware that they were drawing a peculiar slice of the political world; they did recognize a sharp difference between this political sample and the ordinary citizens whom they were formally charged to empower.

That the hearings did *not* operate in this fashion, then, was traceable to a very different aspect of their impact. For the element of the hearing presentations which stayed with the commissioners once the witnesses had departed was not the social distinctness of those who appeared and testified, but the roster of specific abuses which some contributed in the course of their testimony. The hearings did expose the commissioners to real and potentially correctable shortcomings. If the members did not receive many concrete solutions, their staff would be perfectly happy to provide these later.

The commissioners did hear, for example, of a precinct meeting which had been adjourned before normal wage earners could attend; they did learn of a district meeting which had been held in the locked basement of a local party leader; they even encountered a precinct caucus which had been convened on a moving bus. If they did not simultaneously receive a corrective, they probably became more receptive to a suggested remedy from the staff, when it eventually arrived. George Mitchell, national committeeman and former state chairman from Maine, judged this to be the main impact of the regional hearings, even on himself:

> We travelled around the country to regional hearings. I got very active in studying the material. I went to Atlanta, to Chicago, to St. Louis, and to Boston, trying to familiarize myself with party rules.
> I was Chairman of the Maine Party in 1968 and the caucuses were very heated. I myself found many of the complaints in Chicago very hard to believe, because there had rarely been any abuses here. These hearings gave some substance to the charges of irregularity that were made. I can only speak for myself, but it lent substance in my mind to the need for some rules reform. When you are exposed to things like the Georgia rules, you can hardly make an argument for them.

The three subcommittees of the Commission on Party Structure and Delegate Selection were unlike the regional hearings in that they were not winding down as the decision was reached to concentrate on delegate selection. Yet once that decision *had* been reached, the subcommittees became not just a diversion but an evident detriment to the new central priority. It took a little time for this fact to sink in upon the Washington staff, but they were surely fated to put their subcommittees back to sleep once that awareness became explicit.

The first subcommittee, Model Delegate Selection, ceased functioning voluntarily when the change of focus for the full commission rendered it superfluous. The subcommittee had begun its work willingly enough, and by mid-June it possessed a fifty-five-page draft report.[14] Don Fraser, the subcommittee chairman, remained willing to contribute to the cause of party reform, but he was not interested in bootlessly duplicating the work of the full commission. The staff, in turn, preferred to pursue that work through the Executive Committee and not through this subcommittee. As a result, the scheduled subcommittee meeting of July 28 was canceled. It was never rescheduled, and the subcommittee was permitted to expire.

The second subcommittee, Party Structure, was even easier to suspend, if more difficult to dispatch. Leroy Collins, the subcommittee chairman, had resisted early staff urgings to put his subcommittee into gear, and as the summer passed, the staff simply forgot about his entire operation. This subcommittee, too, did eventually acquire a report, when Collins suggested that it was inappropriate to have an official unit with no tangible product, and Research Director Bode drafted a sizable document in response. But this report was

113

hurriedly prepared by a staff which begrudged the time; it was flown to Florida by Bode for a weekend conference with Collins; and it was filed and forgotten immediately thereafter.

The third subcommittee, Grass Roots Participation, was a very different story. Adlai Stevenson, the subcommittee chairman, had assembled his new group almost immediately after their appointment. When he discovered that his new colleagues could think of numerous projects but few ways to finance them, he had gone on to locate independent funding, in Illinois, for a full-blown "mini-commission" there. Stevenson had then drawn upon this subvention to hire a research director, a secretary, and office facilities. Moreover, he had set his membership and staff to work on an aggressive research agenda, one centering ultimately on voter registration and its obstacles.

The Washington staff moved gingerly in terminating this subcommittee, considering its independent roots. Nevertheless, by August, the fact that its major sources of data were the regional hearing transcripts and the state-books put the Chicago contingent on a collision course with the Washington operation. Washington was devoting full time to delegate selection. With fresh meetings of the full commission approaching, staff members became unwilling to have the transcripts and state-books travel to Illinois. When James Lindheim, the staff director for Stevenson in Illinois, complained about this lack of assistance, the central staff moved to terminate his operation, forcibly. On August 25, Ken Bode signaled the end of the Subcommittee on Grass Roots Participation:

> Jim, we have absolutely stopped indexing the hearings. There was general agreement that, while not counter-productive, the enterprise was of limited utility. We found that in the preparation of the state-by-state reports, we were going over all of the material anyway. That leaves us with the problem of how we can make the best use of our materials for your subcommittee. It might be that when most of our interns depart, we could spring one copy of each transcript loose for your use out there—perhaps on a rotating basis—and that they could be indexed for your purposes there. It may also be that we can locate some volunteer indexers here after the immediate press is off. That is, I would be reluctant to turn out any of the transcripts at the moment. . . .[15]

The Substance of Delegate Selection Reform

The demise of the last subcommittee removed the last organizational diversion from what had become the commission's main task—the framing of guidelines to govern delegate selection within the national Democratic party. Moreover, the commission leadership hoped to reassemble the Executive Committee on August 28, to ask its members to pass upon a complete draft of recommendations from the commission staff, and thus to begin the process of adopting a set of rules which would change the institutional character of presidential nominations in the United States. As a result, the technical details of a major report on democratic means for delegate selection became the intensive focus of staff activity.

The format for these proposals fell into line quickly, in response to an evolving political and administrative logic. The staff had originally planned to present its proposals in two stages, with an initial set of individual state reports, advising each state chairman about his state's compliance with the "full, meaningful, and timely" directive, to be followed by a more abstract report, summarizing and publicizing the general standards upon which the state reports were based.[16]

But as staff members began to zero in on delegate selection, they saw the impracticality of sending out detailed compliance reports before publication of the more abstract rules from which these were ostensibly deduced. Politically, it would be unrealistic to expect acquiescence to a specific analysis which was not clearly tied to general standards applying to everyone. Technically, the staff continued to have difficulty in confirming exact state rules and in documenting precise state practices. This technical difficulty would not prevent them from drawing up general guidelines to correct known abuses, but it did increase the risk that some of the compliance reports, if mailed early, would contain serious—even potentially discrediting—inaccuracies.

As a result, a decision to refine priorities and have the compliance letters appear after the general report arose more or less naturally. In early July, staff members had begun to concern themselves exclusively with delegate selection. By early August, they were concentrating, within delegate selection, on the production of a general set of draft guidelines, with specific applications to follow.

Within a few weeks, the staff was to see one final implication of this change in priorities and to make one final refinement in the character of its draft report. When the compliance letters had been the first scheduled item, they had been intended to convey the immediate deductions of the commission from the full, meaningful, and timely standard. The more general—and more evidently hortatory—report to follow would then have concentrated on less proximate issues like proportionality, apportionment, and the role of the regular party under reformed procedures.

When this general report was moved ahead of the compliance letters, however, it quickly expanded to assume the subject matter of *both* approaches. Thereafter, the principal public report would offer specific guidelines embodying the full, meaningful, and timely directive and addressing these other major issues as well. In passing, the distinction between the binding character of those recommendations following directly from convention resolutions and those following from autonomous commission decisions *would disappear entirely.* [17]

By early August, in any case, the permanent staff was hard at work on a draft of general standards for delegate selection. These guidelines, which were now being directed at an August meeting of the Executive Committee, had first been self-consciously collected by Ken Bode, shortly after his arrival at commission headquarters. That collection, and subsequent redrafts, had drawn on three interrelated sources.

First was the report of the Hughes Commission, *The Democratic Choice.* [18] Numerically, most of the guidelines could be traced to something in that document, and it was to remain a central reference as the Party Structure staff elaborated its own recommendations. Second was the draft report of the Model Delegate Subcommittee. [19] The subcommittee itself had never had any significant function, but its report was the first attempt by Eli Segal at codifying his thoughts on party reform, and it thus represented the initial, formal blend of those ideas with the recommendations of the Hughes Commission. Third and last were the ongoing conversations between Segal and Bode about their experiences in the nomination campaigns of 1968. If these were necessarily more amorphous as a source of guidelines than the reports of the Hughes Commission or of the Model Delegate Subcommittee, they were also more proximately influential. Often, when such discussions raised an especially useful point, Bode would excerpt and formalize it immediately afterward:

> Almost every argument made was based on 1968. This was the key. It was all based there. I would go even further. I think we developed most of the stuff. And of course, much of it went right through just as drafted.

The summer interns were also cranking out research on the politics of delegate selection. But while this would serve as the ostensible base for the Segal-Bode recommendations, and while it would be marshaled much more explicitly to support their suggestions, it never actually became a fourth source of specific guidelines. At bottom, key staff members simply felt no great need of codified "data" to produce recommendations for reform. Their experiences in hunting delegates, their subsequent activities in reform politics, and their mutual conversations were all that was necessary. Moreover, the draft guidelines were already well developed by the time data from the interns became available. Segal, accordingly, saw a supportive, rather than a creative, role for this research:

> Ken and I came up with the draft guidelines. We presented the first draft of nearly all of them. Whenever we printed a guideline, it came out of the data which the interns had collected. We had in mind the adoption of standards for all the states. Where I wanted to go was to make untimely delegate selection a thing of the past. Most of these guidelines may have been backed up with the interns' data, but they came out of the experience of Ken and me.

"Where they wanted to go" was to pursue the participatory approach to party reform and to inject opportunities for direct public participation into as many facets of delegate selection as possible. What this implied—what it *required*—became more exacting and more extensive as guideline drafting progressed. A comparison of three key documents in the drafting process—the report of the Hughes Commission, the original prospectus of the Model Delegate Subcommittee, and the later subcommittee report—showed this progression as well as any.[20]

The rise of participation as the crucial standard for party democracy, and its application to every facet of delegate selection, was demonstrated most dramatically in the fate of the basic institutional devices for creating delegates. The original prospectus for the Model Delegate Subcommittee had countenanced all five of the existing, institutional methods of delegate selection:

> *Delegate Primaries,* in which primary voters were encouraged to select individual delegates to represent them directly at the national party convention.
> *Candidate Primaries,* in which primary voters were encouraged to select among presidential candidates, thereby creating presidentially committed delegates to the national party convention.
> *Party Caucuses,* in which grass-roots party officeholders met in convention to select delegates to some higher caucus, which eventually chose delegates to the national party convention.
> *Participatory Conventions,* in which all interested persons met at the local level to select delegates to some higher caucus, which eventually chose delegates to the national party convention.
> *Committee Selections,* in which the state party's central committee, or even a subcommittee thereof, selected delegates to the national party convention.

The draft report of the Model Delegate Subcommittee, mailed to its members a scant four weeks later, had effectively sliced this permitted list to *two,* candidate primaries and participatory conventions, although the report did not outline its implications in precisely these terms, and, in fact, the ability to recognize these effects would be a crucial factor in their eventual fate.

This constriction of permissible means for delegate selection was dramatic, especially when compared with the original Convention resolutions, which appeared to endorse all five basic institutions. It was less eye-catching when compared with *The Democratic Choice,* which had also suggested a reduction to a single form of the presidential primary and a single form of the convention system. But the crucial point about both recommendations, those from the Hughes Commission and those from the Model Delegate Subcommittee, was that both would have unseated perhaps 60 percent of all the delegates to the 1968 Convention.[21]

This constriction, then, testified to the centrality of direct public participation as a touchstone for evaluating the mechanics of delegate selection. Yet the similarity between the reports of the Model Delegate Subcommittee and the Hughes Commission masked an important difference in the way their respective staffs thought about participation itself. The staff of the Hughes Commission had actually sought a ban on *everything* except explicit presidential primary elections, in the belief that no other device could produce anywhere near the same *level* of public participation and in the belief that open conventions and caucuses were little more than forums for professional caucus-packing by the elite, activist community.

The staff of the McGovern Commission, on the other hand, felt that the *quality* of participation in truly open conventions or caucuses was so superior to the simple act of voting in a presidential primary that the device should not only be retained but urged upon those states which would have to abandon other existing means of delegate selection. In this view, the ability to debate issues and not just register candidate preferences, as well as the ability to aggregate these preferences directly and personally, was a far more important characteristic than the inevitably far smaller and potentially more distorted turnout which accompanied the device.

The staff of the McGovern Commission was also developing a second major emphasis within their recommendations, and this, too, differed noticeably from the other priorities of the Hughes Commission and indeed from the limited reform initiatives previously undertaken by the regular party itself. Segal and Bode came to feel that the coupling of *formal proportional representation* with the opportunity for public participation was the essential requirement for true democratization of political arrangements. Nothing else could guarantee perfect structural equity to the participants. Nothing else could guarantee that insurgent movements would never again be restrained by the delegate selection process.

As a result, the report of the Model Delegate Subcommittee featured a special, six-page analysis of proportional representation, easily the longest item in a section called "Democratic Procedures." The need for proportionality was also introduced explicitly into the sections describing ideal forms of the presidential primary, party convention, and preference poll. In fact, Segal was prepared to call for an abstractly mathematical, even formulaic means for institutionalizing true proportionality:

> Granting the acceptance of the fair share principle, there remains the problem of its practical implementation. . . . The voting method that would come closest to the "fair share" ideal in this case would seem to be that of the single transferable vote (the *Hare system*). . . . When the Hare system is impractical, there are still valuable alternatives available that would constitute a major improvement on the winner-take-all system. One such alternative is the *cumulative vote*. . . . Assuming that neither the Hare system nor the cumulative vote is found acceptable, one can assure representation for the political minority by the *limited voting* system. . . .[22]

The elevation of proportionality to a status second only to direct participation in the reform proposals of the Party Structure Commission was also, of necessity, a diminution for the dominant issue in reform politics over the preceding decade—and the preceding quarter-century. This was the issue of racial discrimination, and it had received a higher ranking not only in the work of the Hughes Commission but in previous reform efforts inside the Democratic party.

The regular party had created the first separate reform body in its history, the Special Equal Rights Committee [SERC], to deal explicitly with the issue of participation by minorities. The SERC had responded with six antidiscrimination standards, which had been written into the Call to the 1968 Convention and which had resulted in the unseating of the entire Mississippi delegation and half of Georgia as well.

The Hughes Commission, however, many of whose staff members had cut their political teeth on southern battles over civil rights in the early 1960s, had judged that the pursuit of racial desegregation by the regular party was still clearly insufficient. They had insisted, fruitlessly, on much stiffer regulations, including numerical targets to shift the onus for discrimination onto the state party and to bring the national party within hailing distance of formal demographic quotas.

The staff of the McGovern Commission, finally, was less concerned with the entire issue, and the draft report of the Model Delegate Subcommittee mentioned discrimination almost in passing, and then in a highly pragmatic fashion:

> While it is necessary that minority groups such as racial, religious, ethnic, and economic groups, be fairly represented, practical considerations preclude that minorities always have delegates in proportion to their numbers. For example, if

119

a given state has 100 delegates and 1 % of the Democrats are Chinese and another 1 % are Greek, it is almost impossible to insure that one Chinese and one Greek will be represented, short of dictation by party functionary. Of course, delegates who live in communities having Chinese and Greek residents, should represent these groups as well as other groups in their area. In some cases, at-large delegates or directly appointed delegates (within prescribed limitations) could provide for delegates representing minority groups.[23]

This diminution in emphasis on racial discrimination and its remedies was not so much a reflection of staff indifference—the possibility of providing numerical guarantees was continually discussed at commission headquarters—as it was a reflection of the inherent institutional logic in the rest of the proposed staff package of reforms. If the overarching goal of party reform was to create open and participatory mechanisms for delegate selection, then the requirement of a large, fixed outcome was an intellectually obvious—and publicly evident—contradiction of this goal. By the same token, explicit moves toward the appointment of delegates on racial grounds were evidently more appropriate to the *other* approach to party reform, with its emphasis on having black party officials in black areas and then on bringing *these officials* to the Democratic National Convention.

Moreover, commission staffers did see that a drive toward proportionality—the essence of structural fairness, in their view—implied an emphasis on *political* rather than demographic minorities. Staff members might privately experience discomfort with these implications of their preferred path to party reform, but they did understand that this was the price of securing both participation and proportionality, and they were prepared to pay that price. There was, as Segal correctly noted, no alternative "short of dictation by party functionary."

The specific approach of the commission staff to the task of party reform, then, had been confirmed in all its essentials by late summer of 1969.[24] With hindsight, it would be clear that the *entire* politics of recommendation, during which reform proposals were developed, debated, and approved, was centralized, almost encapsulated, within the Party Structure Commission. Yet even by those standards, the internal commission politics which shaped the initial drafting of these guidelines was remarkably specialized, private, patterned—and unconnected to the political world outside.

All of the draft guidelines began within the commission staff, but this actually meant its counsel, Eli Segal, and its research director, Ken Bode, and not its staff director, Bob Nelson. Nelson was hardly inactive in commission business as a whole. He was, however, insulated from the initiation of specific guidelines, thanks partly to his greater organizational responsibilities, but largely to the maneuvers of his ostensible colleagues, the commission counsel and research director.

Segal and Bode had come out of the insurgent campaigns of 1969, and Segal had come through the Hughes Commission as well, so that both began with an emotional and ideological attachment to reform. Nelson, while an evident structural reformer, had been in federal administrative posts during the same period and brought no parallel emotional investment to his work. Segal and Bode shared a "new politics" perspective, including a preference for theoretical argument and personal confrontation, and a suspicion that most of political life was, in fact, explained by private understandings. Nelson was more attuned to empirical argument and personal accommodation and was inclined to use more direct explanations for the events of politics—explanations which were more observable and calculable, if not necessarily more meritorious. Segal (and later, Bode) had been appointed to attach the most intensely proreform factions to the commission enterprise, while Nelson had been appointed to protect the personal interests of Chairman McGovern.

As a result, Segal and Bode inherited a fairly well-developed set of reform goals, which drew upon the participatory theory of party reform and which were relatively extreme when compared with existing party practice. They topped these off with an evident antipathy to the regular Democratic party. Nelson, by contrast, began with a more detached interest in issues of party reform, and while this led him, too, toward an emphasis on participation, it did not strike him as inconsistent with a concern for party building. He arrived with a clear intention to "improve" his party. Tactically, Segal and Bode were apt to ask whether any given guideline was a sharp enough change to be worth the fight. Tactically, Nelson was more likely to ask about the balance between desirability and attainability for that same guideline, with a preference for reforms which would not jeopardize the total enterprise.

These distinctions paled by comparison with the differences between all three commission staffers and the average delegate to the 1968 Convention. But they were easily sufficient to produce a strong and continuing split within the commission staff, and this division was at the heart of the process by which reform proposals were actually developed. The split had surfaced in the very first internal debate over the appropriate focus for the Party Structure Commission, where Segal had advocated a simultaneous assault on delegate selection, party structure, and mass participation, while Nelson had preferred an immediate concentration on delegate selection. The split continued through the summer, leading Segal and then Bode, too, to try to screen Nelson off from the actual drafting of reform proposals.

Even as these recommendations were going out to the commissioners, this split remained a major fact of commission life. In an August 27 note to Chairman McGovern about the next day's meeting of the Executive Committee, Segal and Bode alluded to it directly: "Senator McGovern: Bob Nelson is unaware of this memo. His major objections to it would be . . ."[25] If he was unaware of this particular memo, however, Nelson was fully sensitive to the political and stylistic gulf which separated him from his staff colleagues:

> Bode came on in June, 1969, for the next eleven months. Bode is a conspiracy-type guy; he really believes that that's the way the world works. Segal does, too, to a slightly lesser degree. I don't. But Ken did have great rapport with these kids [the interns]. He was bringing the kids in. Some were coming in strange hours, doing projects of their own.

This split did not divide the summer interns, since they were far closer to Segal and Bode than to Nelson in background, experience, and perceptions. But it did reach into the consultants, and it did push them toward one side or the other. Again, the three consultants were probably in greater agreement among themselves than any of them would have been with the average convention delegate of 1968. But again, it was their internal division which shaped the specifics of staff recommendations on party reform.

Like Nelson, Alex Bickel and Dick Wade were largely uninvolved in the drafting of reform guidelines, because Segal and Bode viewed both as ideologically unreliable and thus as potentially constraining. In return, neither Bickel nor Wade developed an automatic stake in what was being proposed at commission headquarters, although the occasions on which they actively differed from these draft recommendations were comparatively rare. Anne Wexler, on the other hand, was enmeshed in guideline drafting from the start and was reliably allied with Segal and Bode, with whom she shared both a recent political history and an ongoing, unrestrained commitment to reform. Wexler had been central to the fight for the Rules minority report and to the appointment lobbying which followed the convention, and she kept herself in the midst of staff activities on the McGovern Commission as well:

> A couple of times I met with Bickel and Wade. I went to many meetings with the staff. I would go to Washington, or to Connecticut, or to the hearings. I made many trips to Washington. And spent much time with the staff. I would guess it was a total of maybe one week to ten days per month, plus much time on the telephone.

This division within the staff was related to, and reinforced by, continuing differences between Chairman McGovern and Vice Chairman Hughes. Once again, these differences would not threaten to pull the commission in fundamentally opposed directions. Both men were firmly committed to extensive reform on the participatory model, and both came down on the same side of most specific recommendations. Yet their histories on the reform issue, their positions within the commission, their constituencies in national politics, and even their hopes for the commission product, all diverged perceptibly and led them to approach commission business in very different ways.

As chairman, McGovern needed to stay within the ideological range of a majority of his commissioners, lest he lose control of his own commission and end up not as the great reformer but as a leader who had been unequal to the task. As chairman, McGovern also had more reason to be concerned with the *fate* of whatever the commission recommended, and this argued for a moderation in style and not just in substance. Finally, his immediate political ambition, a run for the presidency, appeared to require an appeal that could be spread well beyond party insurgents and self-conscious reformers, and this, too, suggested recognizable but not uncontrolled change, which could conceivably be implemented, without widespread hard feelings. Wade, "McGovern's man" among the consultants, noted the problems which this approach caused for the chairman with other staff and leadership figures:

> Most of the staff was Hughes-oriented, and it became more Hughes-oriented. All this time, there was a struggle over the soul of the staff. McGovern didn't get involved, but Hughes was actively raiding it. Alex and I were not involved with staff problems, while Anne knew them all. George knew this, and wanted to keep everything aboveboard. Harold Hughes was always threatening to raid the staff. I would always sit between Hughes and Bayh; *whatever* McGovern did, Hughes would be a little more liberal, *regardless*.

Hughes did indeed face a very different world. He was the man who had lent his name to the original reform report and the man who had subsequently been passed over for the Party Structure chairmanship because of his "antiparty" reputation. But if Hughes had ended up without the chairmanship, he had retained a national constituency, smaller than that of McGovern but much more tightly focused on reform. His constituents, however, expected unwavering arguments for change, and Hughes necessarily became the commissioner around whom the more extreme reform proposals were organized. His blunt personal style, finally, did nothing to mitigate any of this. These differences between McGovern and Hughes were what caused George Mitchell, eventually a highly active commissioner and one who frequently opposed both men, to categorize Hughes as the man with "real leadership" on the commission:

123

McGovern gets credit for all these rules, but the fact is that McGovern never took much part. He always had to take a leak when there was a crucial vote. *Hughes* was the outstanding guy on the Commission.

In the face of these continuing divisions at the top, proposed guidelines were launched in a predictable fashion. Bode (or sometimes Segal) drafted one up, weighed the wording carefully, and backed it with examples. Segal then began a gradual clearance process, exposing the proposal to McGovern and Nelson. McGovern, for his part, followed through by consulting Hughes, the first step in *his* larger pattern of consultation. But at the same time, *Segal* primed Hughes for that same discussion, so that the vice chairman could firm up any lack of resolve on the part of the chairman:

> I would hold meetings with McGovern in the Senate Dining Room, and with Hughes in his office. That was how it was worked out. They were both in their way excellent, McGovern for mediating things through, Hughes for anchoring them so they didn't get mediated too far.

If Hughes was at the top of the list of commissioners with whom McGovern occasionally consulted, the other members of the Executive Committee composed the rest of that informal list. While the committee as a group did not assemble between late May and late August, McGovern did discuss staff proposals with individual members, sometimes by telephone, sometimes in person. Segal and Bode, too, maintained an independent testing process, and it involved these same Executive Committee members—thereby closing the intimate circle in which reform proposals were developed:

> It was nice having an Executive Committee that was committed to reform, but it was McGovern and Hughes, and our communication with them, that mattered. There were very few Executive Committee meetings. I think essentially it was a way for McGovern and Hughes to test the water beyond their own circles.

Beyond the Executive Committee, there was, in fact, a stream of routinized communication with the other commissioners, but the staff placed little importance on it, and it had little direct impact on their emerging product. Nevertheless, as suggestions for potential guidelines were put into draft form, they were copied and mailed out to all the commissioners. Oscar Mauzy was relatively happy with the substance of what he was receiving, though less so with the procedure:

> This was primarily a staff operation. I tried to read it over, and make some suggestions by mail. At the time, there were no more than ten or twelve members and the staff who were making recommendations. In some ways, even when you

were there in person it wasn't a lot better. I would fly up on the midnight flight for an eight-o'clock meeting, and leave an hour after that. There was some grousing at the time that it was a totally Washington-oriented operation. We got called in every two months to deal with an agenda that should have taken seventy-two hours, to deal with it in twelve hours.

Carmen Warschaw, who was relatively *un*happy with the slant of the same material, expressed similar frustration with the pattern of communication:

> There was a lot of correspondence during the March–September period, especially during the latter part. Give your opinion, answer some questions. When you got through doing that and they wrote it up, the question always ended up being "How often did you beat your wife?" Our input until the end was nearly confined to that.

Implications

During the period between March and September of 1969, the Party Structure Commission found its central substantive focus, reform of the delegate selection—and presidential nomination—process. During these months, the commission brought forward its central perspective on that substantive focus, the participatory approach to internal party politics. During this period, finally, the commission drove the participatory perspective through every institution and every activity in the mechanics of delegate selection.

There was more than enough happenstance in this to satisfy the most perverse student of political history. The commission staff and leadership had explicitly discussed their focus before they began their labors and had agreed to go full-bore on delegate selection, state party structure, and grass-roots participation. Yet it was only when they threw away everything but delegate selection, under the pressure of time and of limited resources, that they found their central thrust—and achieved the possibility of a revolutionary, planned change in presidential politics.

Once the leadership and staff reached a consensus on reform of the process of delegate selection, however, the details of their assault on party reform fell rapidly into line, as, indeed, did their schedule for accomplishing those details. The staff would prepare a complete draft of a general reform document by the end of August. The Executive Committee would respond to this document and pass it along to the full commission. The commission would consider these proposals before final adoption, in as many working sessions as necessary.

125

The result would be a general guideline report, containing not just a set of "full, meaningful, and timely" strictures but as many other pronouncements on internal party democracy as the staff could secure and the commissioners could stomach.

The process of developing draft guidelines for presentation to the Executive Committee acquired some historical interest because it was the first effort at pulling systematic reform guidelines together and because it occurred in such a small, private, political environment. But that process acquired its real historical consequence because it produced a thorough, consistent, and far-reaching set of proposals for party reform; because these proposals were almost ideally suited to the ideological desires, political needs, and practical advantages of an alternative Democratic coalition; *and because they were destined to constitute the overwhelming bulk of the final recommendations of the commission.*

The process of developing draft guidelines began with the commission staff, or rather, with one side of a continuing split within that staff. These drafts moved out to, and across, a parallel division within the commission leadership. They trickled out to members of the Executive Committee, though more to utilize them for certain staff-selected purposes than to weigh their opinions for some abstract merit. Until September of 1969, these drafts did not seriously involve the rest of the commissioners.

At first, there were specific institutional devices to connect the reform drafters—principally Segal and Bode, with an assist from Wexler—to both their commissioners and their attentive public. The three subcommittees were designed, in part, to keep the commissioners involved in the drafting process. The seventeen regional hearings were designed, in part, to keep the attentive public attached to the commission. Yet as the staff found its major substantive focus, the subcommittees became more an annoyance than a contribution and were quickly put to sleep. And as the staff began to develop coherent, detailed recommendations for party reform, the transcripts of the regional hearings became merely an appendage to this evolving product, while the participants in these regional hearings became merely the *potential* constituency for this evolving party reform.

The product of this small, private, political environment was a coherent and sweeping package of recommendations for party reform, developed on the participatory model. As the staff gained control of the drafting process, its members gained the confidence—they had always had the commitment—to call openly for sweeping alterations in the institutions of delegate selection, in the rules allocating delegates among presidential contenders, in the distribution of those delegates among and within the states, and in the place of the regular party in this whole arrangement. In short, they came to call for a fundamental change in the entire process of presidential nomination.

From the beginning, crucial staff members were inclined toward the participatory approach to party reform. As they worked at converting this approach into real party rules, they extended the demand for direct public participation into every aspect of the delegate selection process. For those institutions and activities which could not be made participatory enough, they recommended prohibition, pure and simple. This staff emphasis on the virtues of participation came, inevitably, at the expense of an effort at building the party as an organization, but that expense was willingly, almost casually paid on the road to a higher goal. Indeed, some reform recommendations seemed more intent on striking out at the regular party than at increasing participation per se, as with the early proposal from Segal that "no elected officeholder can be elected a voting delegate or can be elected to a state or national party office at state or national conventions."[26]

On top of this, the staff introduced a major secondary emphasis, on formal proportional representation, and drove this, too, through every newly reformed procedure. Like the elevation of participation over organization, this stress on proportionality had its cost: It came at the expense of the ongoing, if fitful, efforts by the regular party at desegregation of party machinery. The staff was not unconcerned with this side effect, but staff members understood the implications of their desire for participation coupled with mathematical equity, and they were willing to pay its price.

What resulted, as a total package, was remarkable not just for its scope but for its theoretical coherence. The staff had always aspired to a body of reform proposals which were noteworthy for the breadth and depth of their impact on the mechanics of presidential selection. But staff members had not set out to impose an integrated version of the participatory model of partisan activity on the national Democratic party. Indeed, commission staffers doubted that professional writing on political parties had much to offer them. Yet when they roughed out a package of draft guidelines, the individual recommendations within it were additionally distinguished by the degree to which they formed a coherent theoretical whole.

The explanation, of course, was social, not intellectual. The social backgrounds of those charged with developing a reform draft were roughly similar. Or at least, none of them was a product of regular party politics or of traditional constituency identifications. Moreover, their formative political experiences were essentially identical. All had begun as party insurgents, imbued with a hostility toward politics-as-usual and crowned with a sense of citizen virtue. All had experienced a nomination campaign in which the more active—and more morally outspoken—participants were obviously on their side, facing the regular party and organized labor. All, finally, were defeated by individuals of different backgrounds, experiences, and perceptions about politics, individuals whose crucial characteristic, however, was that they occupied positions of formal power within the official party hierarchy.

When these reform drafters analyzed the institutions of delegate selection in light of their experiences, they were led naturally to an emphasis on direct participation rather than on established partisan activity. When they considered the likely beneficiaries of institutional arrangements based on participatory, rather than party-office approaches, they were reinforced in this emphasis. When they took participation as a value, a value also widely saluted in the larger circles from which they themselves were drawn, and when they applied that value consciously and persistently to every aspect of delegate selection, they inevitably recapitulated—they almost recreated—the formal model of participatory politics.[27]

Similarly, and in some sense closing the circle, the guidelines which these staff members were developing were ideally suited not just to the ideological preferences of their intended constituency, but to the practical political needs of that constituency as well. Again, the roots of this congruence—a crucial one for the ultimate impact of these reforms on national politics—were indirect and social, not direct and political. But again, these roots were easily sufficient to sustain a sweeping reform package with the desired procedural emphases and the desired potential impact.

Representatives of most of the individual elements of this eventual, alternative Democratic coalition had turned out in force at the regional hearings of the Party Structure Commission. But they were hardly even an incipient coalition at this point, and even their most evident members had presented nothing in the way of coherent demands for reform. Their explicit demands, to the extent that these could be categorized, were for "participation," that is, for opportunities to participate in a direct and unmediated fashion. These demands were not just satisfied by the reform package being developed by the commission staff. They were actually *given detailed definition* in the process of being satisfied.

A different version of the same, indirect, social coherence which had characterized the development of this reform package was necessary to explain how it could also fit, so congruently, with the practical needs—and the practical advantages—of this incipient alternative coalition. For it was the fundamental social difference between the elite actors, along with their mass constituencies, in the two opposing coalitions, along with the politically relevant aspects of that difference, which explained how one set of institutional arrangements could be so beneficial to one coalition and so disadvantageous to the other, and vice versa.

The regional hearings were a reasonable reflection of the alternative coalition of Democratic elites in the spring and summer of 1969, and the low turn-out by leaders of the orthodox Democratic coalition highlighted the contrast for all to see. Yet it would have required an impossible prescience to separate the two coalitions precisely, since neither had as yet achieved its full organizational articulation and since few of the individual witnesses were appearing as a deliberate part of any larger aggregate, although the efforts of the commission staff to secure representatives from all of the potential elements of any eventual alternative coalition did provide more coherence than chance alone would have engendered.

The commissioners, in turn, did not categorize what would become the alternative Democratic coalition in any detail. But they did recognize its presence. Sam Beer, for one, was troubled by the sample of interested persons who appeared before him:

> I went to Massachusetts, Philadelphia, Chicago, St. Louis, and Atlanta. I was impressed, at these meetings, by the fact that the Negroes and the people in the cities were not the slightest bit interested in this whole thing. This was really a suburban, white, middle-class movement.

With the benefit of hindsight, it would have been possible to elaborate this perception more fully. The orthodox Democratic coalition—the regular party and its associated interests—was almost entirely absent from the witness lists at the regional hearings. Regular party spokesmen were reliably unenthusiastic about having a semiautonomous national commission examine local party affairs. Moreover, they had little to gain, and much to lose, from an appearance before such a body. If they spoke frankly, they risked being labeled, in public, as "antireform." If they simply ignored the proceedings, they had good reason to believe that evasive actions could always be taken, if necessary, later.

In theory, their role as voices of caution—or perhaps as advocates of the other, organized and disciplined, approach to party reform—could have been assumed by organized labor, the leading member of the interest groups allied with the regular party. But labor at the top had washed its hands of the Party Structure Commission, and labor at the bottom had even less reason to get involved in a public, "antireform" effort than did the regular party. Bob Nelson noted, and worried about, this absence:

> We immediately ran into a labor position. The party that had produced Roosevelt, Truman, Kennedy, Johnson, and Humphrey didn't need reform. After that line was articulated, most labor guys wouldn't appear.

On the other side, the forces dominating the regional hearings were precisely those which would dominate the alternative Democratic coalition, when it finally emerged as a coordinated entity in the fight over implementation of proposed reforms. At the head of this list were those who had been opposing the regular party in their states and localities for years, the members of established reform factions. They provided most of the initial local contacts for the Washington staff, as well as much of the indigenous framework for the recruitment of local witnesses.

These organized reformers were joined by the leading members of *their* associated interest groups, the liberal ideological and issue organizations. Spokesmen for liberal ideological organizations like Americans for Democratic Action, and for liberal issue groups like the Vietnam Moratorium Committee, were always right behind the organized reform factions in providing witnesses for the commission. While Eli Segal and Ken Bode at the central commission accepted this distribution of witnesses as a fact of life in reform politics, it bothered Jim Lindheim, the staff director of the Grass Roots Subcommittee in Chicago:

> The people who we are recruiting have, for the most part, been active in reform groups such as the Committee on Illinois Government, Independent Democratic Coalition, etc. This is largely a function of where we have sought a list of names. However, it is also a function of the type of person who is interested in this kind of project. He is primarily a white lawyer of liberal leanings who has been connected with the Kennedy-McCarthy-McGovern wing of the party.
>
> We have no definite means of getting around this problem, beyond trying to recruit people of different backgrounds, which is proving very difficult. Hence, there is a real danger that the report will simply be active liberal Democrats talking to active liberal Democrats, while a real understanding of grass-roots participation will be lost.[28]

At the time of the regional hearings, then, the descriptive differences between the two loosely coordinated coalitions were clear. The alternative Democratic coalition consisted of a congeries of self-conscious party dissidents, established and emergent, along with the liberal ideological and issue organizations, old and new. The orthodox Democratic coalition, by contrast, consisted effectively of the regular party and organized labor.

Yet there were analytic differences between the two coalitions of a more fundamental sort, and it was these which were central to the potential impact of proposed reforms. At the elite level, among specialized leadership figures, the difference was primarily between partisan independents, in the alternative coalition, and partisan loyalists, in its orthodox counterpart. At the mass level, among the rank-and-file constituents for these leadership figures, the difference was primarily between white-collar and blue-collar individuals.

These fundamental analytic differences—partisan independence versus partisan loyalty at the elite level, white-collar versus blue-collar social backgrounds at the mass level—explained why the reform plan being developed by the commission staff was not only attractive to members of the alternative Democratic coalition but provided them with apparent practical advantages as well. These basic distinctions, of course, also explained why existing arrangements remained preferable to members of the orthodox Democratic coalition and benefited them practically, too.

The major emphasis of the reforms was on opportunities for direct participation, and the fundamental distinctions between the two opposing coalitions were immediately engaged by this emphasis. At the elite level, participatory arrangements were inherently more advantageous to partisan independents, who preferred "the person, not the party" and who wanted to participate or not as the case warranted, than to partisan loyalists, who preferred party regularity and party service as the key characteristics for influence within the party. At the mass level, participatory arrangements were inherently advantageous to white-collar Democrats, whose propensity to turn out and participate was much greater than that of blue-collar Democrats—and became even more exaggerated in low-turnout forums, like participatory conventions.[29]

The same could be said of the major secondary emphasis of the reforms, on proportional representation, especially as it interacted with their primary emphasis on participation. At the elite level, proportionality was inherently kinder to members of the alternative coalition because they were ordinarily based in areas which were less Democratic than the norm, while members of the orthodox coalition were based in areas which were heavily, often massively Democratic. This was dramatically demonstrated for organized reform factions, which were usually found in areas where *Republicans* were in the majority, and whose leaders would never have much intraparty influence if a partisan majority was free to allocate major party offices.[30] By the same token, at the mass level, proportionality was inherently kinder to the alternative coalition because it allowed white-collar participants to capitalize on their higher turnout and to restrain blue-collar Democrats from capitalizing on *their* normal demographic majorities—and using them, again, to allocate major party offices.

The commission staff had hardly sought this specific pattern of practical advantages. Much less had they used it as the central organizing principle for their proposed reforms. Yet crucial staff actors had come from the same political organizations, the same partisan factions, and the same social groups as their intended supporters in the society at large. They had shared the same, formative experiences in the campaigns of 1968. And they brought with them

131

an approach to party affairs which had seemed meritorious when they were with those groups and organizations on the outside, experiencing those formative campaigns.

As a result, these staff members did not need to seek a pattern of benefits which would advantage the alternative Democratic coalition. They needed only to identify their former political colleagues with the interests of the general public, to identify the regular party and organized labor as the leading obstacles to the realization of those interests, and to design a reform program benefiting "the public" at the expense of the orthodox Democratic coalition. The resulting fit between the assets of a potential reform constituency and the procedural preferences of the Party Structure staff became inevitably—once again—clear and strong.[31]

By early August, all this was prologue. What remained was not a question of whether the commission staff possessed the influence to draft the reform recommendations which they themselves preferred; nor whether these recommendations had a different and distinctive approach to party business, thoroughly and consistently applied; nor even whether such recommendations could attract and advantage the reform coalition which their drafters envisioned as the dominant force in party affairs after their work was done. What remained, instead, was only the question of what the Party Structure commissioners as a group would *do* with these recommendations, once they had been laid before them.

CHAPTER

5

The Internal Debate on Party Reform:

The Commissioners in Commission Politics

IN WHICH, the Executive Committee and then the full commission address proposals for party reform; the commissioners debate issues great and small within these proposed guidelines; and the product of this discussion goes forward to the final stage of decision making. AND IN WHICH, reform politics moves out to the commissioners, as a body; staff proposals for sweeping institutional change survive, essentially intact; and the commission itself becomes the organizational connector for the aspiring, alternative Democratic coalition.

BETWEEN late August and late November of 1969, the Party Structure commissioners, as a group, finally entered the politics of recommendation. In three preliminary working sessions and one final historic meeting, they adopted official recommendations for reform of the process of delegate selection, and hence presidential nomination—and hence *presidential* selection as well. A meeting of the Executive Committee on August 28, a second meeting of the Executive Committee on September 11, and a two-day session of the full commission on September 23 and 24 were the organizational prelude to the full commission sessions of November 19 and 20, where the proposed guidelines to govern delegate selection in the national Democratic party were officially adopted.

With the shift to this sequence of commission meetings, the practical contours of reform politics necessarily shifted, too. The number of relevant actors increased. Segal, Bode, and Nelson; Wexler, Wade, and Bickel; McGovern and Hughes remained as active as ever. But they were joined first by the ten-member Executive Committee and then by a sizable share of the full twenty-eight-member parent body. And they were joined in a fashion in which staff and leadership figures could no longer simply patronize these other commissioners at a comfortable, and debilitating, distance.

The process of developing officially certified recommendations became more formal as well. It centered on official sessions of the Party Structure Commission, and not on private discussions, informal gatherings, and ostensibly casual conversations on the phone. At these sessions, reform politicking centered on actual texts—real wording—and not on values, goals, and approaches. The acceptance, rejection, or adjustment of these proposed texts, finally, was accomplished by official votes, and the result automatically became the substance of commission guidelines for party reform.

All these shifts were perceptible differences from the process by which reform recommendations had been shaped during the preceding seven months. The accompanying change in the substance of these recommendations, however, was almost inconsequential. The commissioners, when assembled, were not inactive. They questioned and opined, prodded and suggested. Moreover, even when given the explicit opportunity, they declined to salute the handiwork of their staff, much less its mode of operation. The commissioners went so far as to dissent from the staff view of their own authority; they resisted the battening of proportionality upon participatory institutions for delegate selection; they differed almost commissioner by commissioner on the proper formula for apportioning delegates among and within the states.

Nevertheless, the document going forward to the final session of the full commission was not significantly different from the one which came forward to the first meeting of the Executive Committee. This distinctly anticlimactic outcome, after all the pulling and hauling of the intervening sessions, can be traced primarily to the balance of influence inside the Party Structure Commission, even after the commissioners had been invited back in. Formally, the commissioners retained the right to pass upon every guideline, every action, every phrase. Informally, the staff, as supported by their leadership, retained so great a practical advantage that their lack of an official vote became only a minor, if always annoying, inconvenience.

This anticlimactic outcome can also be traced to the absence of external attempts to upset the internal balance. When organizational difficulties, ambiguous tactical incentives, and simple inattention prevented the logical aspirants for external influence from even trying to impose their wishes, the dominance of the array of forces inside the Party Structure Commission was assured.

From late August through late November, then, the commission moved with increasing speed toward a final set of recommendations for delegate selection reform. The commissioners as a body finally came together. They worked on the staff draft of a final report on party reform. Yet they contributed little to the institutional change inherent in these recommendations, beyond a sense for the items of probable conflict at their final drafting session in November.

As a result, the commissioners confirmed the dominance of their leadership and staff—instruments, by now, of the alternative Democratic coalition— in internal commission politics. In passing, they confirmed the dominance of the Party Structure Commission—the organizational link, by now, for that alternative Democratic coalition—in external reform politics. Along the way, they contributed the penultimate chapter in the politics of recommendation.

Reform Politicking in the Executive Committee

It was the Executive Committee of the Party Structure Commission which began the process of narrowing toward an official set of recommendations for party reform. Earlier, the committee had almost acquired a life of its own, with meetings on March 19 and then again on May 26. But its members had been unable to suggest solutions to the incipient financial crisis of the commission, and their staff had been unprepared to bring these members into substantive conversation on reform. As a result, the committee had been permitted to lapse back into inactivity.

By early August, the staff was prepared to bring the committee to life again. At a scheduled meeting on August 28, staff members hoped to extract formal approval of their reading of the major issues in party reform, formal approval of twenty individual guidelines to give this reading a practical bite, and formal endorsement of a timetable for leading the full commission through these same steps.

Staff members were prepared for the possibility that individual guideline approval might require more time, perhaps at a second meeting of the Executive Committee in early September. But they felt that explicit endorsement of their general, philosophical reading of the commission mandate, and of the specific issues—and hence the need for specific guidelines—which that reading implied, could not be deferred without endangering the whole operation. If the Executive Committee was unwilling to act on this, the timetable which the staff was proposing would clearly become impossible, and the outcome of the enterprise itself would be cast into doubt.

The Executive Committee of the Commission on Party Structure and Delegate Selection convened at 10:15 A.M., on Thursday, August 28, in Room 324 of the Old (Russell) Senate Office Building. The session followed closely the scenario devised by Eli Segal and Ken Bode, and this was probably its critical aspect.[1] The commissioners continued to respond to an agenda shaped almost entirely by the most aggressive members of their staff; they continued to indulge the reform proposals on that agenda.

The August 28 session underlined two other, divergent facts about reform politics. The first was the extent to which many commissioners, including some on the Executive Committee, had come to suspect that their commission could best be described as a "run-away staff operation." Analytically, this was the question of the balance of influence in internal commission activities. At the other extreme, the meeting underscored a fear by militant reformers that the entire operation was in danger of being stifled from without, by the regular party, now that the commission was drafting real regulations for party reform. Analytically, this was the question of the direction, scope, and balance of possible external pressures.[2]

Chairman McGovern, taking a suggestion from Segal and Bode, began by emphasizing that the full commission, at its March meeting, had placed responsibility for creating a package of draft reforms squarely on the shoulders of the staff, and he followed with a letter from Alex Bickel lauding the quality of staff work to date. Instead of inducing quiescence, however, his comments threatened to start a major debate. Aaron Henry, voicing a general sense of isolation and frustration among the commissioners, immediately noted that nothing the staff *or* the Executive Committee said would be official until the full commission had reviewed it. Henry's comments, in turn, caused Bob Nelson to open *his* summary of staff activity with the assurance that "the staff is fully cognizant of its subordinate role."[3]

Nelson began to report on commission developments since March, but he was interrupted from the other side for a colloquy initiated by Harold Hughes, on the need to challenge regular party leaders to affirm publicly their support for the commission enterprise. Hughes singled out Hubert Humphrey, the titular leader, for a special challenge and went on to reveal that newsmen covering the Party Structure Commission had told him they were cynical about the scope and consequences of the ultimate commission product. He urged his fellow commissioners to take actions dramatic enough to put both newsmen and the general public on notice about their real intent.

In that atmosphere, Fred Harris arrived, and conversation switched to commission finances. Chairman McGovern outlined the nature of the problem and summarized several recent efforts to alleviate it. Harris endorsed the desirability of additional joint activities and offered the mailing lists from the National Committee as a gesture of good will. But Harris's offer, instead of eliciting gratitude, raised the specter of outside interference to Vice Chairman Hughes, who came back on the attack. A short exchange ensued, with first Hughes and then McGovern underlining their intention to keep the Party Structure Commission independent:

Hughes: But remember the Commission's legal obligation. My opinion is that this Commission is a child of the 1968 Convention, with a responsibility to report to the '72 Convention. I think it's important that we not become a stepchild of the DNC. I wholeheartedly endorse cooperation, in fundraising and other aspects, but we must remain independent of the Committee.
Harris: In spite of the fact that I appointed the Commission, I don't see how I, or the DNC, in any way could prevent the Commission from reporting whatever it decides to report. The final determination, of course, will occur when the Convention itself meets and decides.
Hughes: But the DNC has outvoted us many times.
Harris: There is no way that the DNC can prevent the people from hearing the contents of the Commission's report.
McGovern: Is it our responsibility to report to the Convention?
Harris: The ultimate repository of all power is the Convention. The DNC is an interim body. You must, as I see it, make three reports—one to the DNC, one to the Convention, and one to the states.
McGovern: As a practical political matter, we want to have a Call to the Convention in 1972 embracing the recommendations of the Commission. We want it understood that if the National Committee rejects our report, we will take our appeal to the party.[4]

The funding discussion wound down inconclusively, and Eli Segal began his presentation on the general values—full, meaningful, and timely opportunity to participate—which, he asserted, should guide commission labors. His review of potential compliance suggested that while the Hughes Commission had found sixteen state parties in violation of this standard, the McGovern Commission would probably find *forty or more*. With Harris still in attendance, Segal was questioned on the rights of National Committee members under full, meaningful, and timely strictures, an issue which would surface again and again over the next two years, but this discussion, too, reached no specific recommendation. After that, the Executive Committee broke for lunch, and Harris left on other business.

When the meeting resumed, Adlai Stevenson delivered a short report from the (dying) Subcommittee on Grass Roots Participation. Ken Bode then moved to the main business of the afternoon, his report on the individual guidelines. Bode read through the entire list of twenty and circled back to

137

discuss them one by one. The very first, A–1 (Discrimination on the Basis of Race, Color, Creed, or National Origin) provoked a mild debate. Hughes suggested adding sex and income to the language on discrimination. Don Fraser countered that this smacked of demographic quotas. Bode skirted the question by suggesting that the original language from the Hughes Commission had been "explicit, strong, and sufficient,"[5] and he hurried on with his reading.

He was stopped once again at B–6 (Apportionment). But this time, when debate broke out over the proposed "one Democrat, one vote" formula, Fraser moved more forcefully to slow discussion down. He contended that the guidelines were in danger of being steamrolled through the committee, and perhaps even through the commission. He asserted that many of the draft guidelines were not clearly within commission authority, or were at least outside the realm of subjects on which the commission was *commanded* to pronounce:

Dodds: Shouldn't the full Commission be informed of this information [on apportionment]?

McGovern: I planned to have a decision made by this committee as to whether the staff is proceeding on the right course, so that we can present the result to the full Commission. . . .

Fraser (interrupts): I think the Commission. . . .

McGovern (re-interrupts): If we are going to give general approval today that the staff has properly identified the issues, that this Commission ought to be concerned with these issues, it would seem to me that the staff's job is to summarize those issues in written form so that they can be mailed out to the Commission within eight to ten days. . . .

Wade: (interrupts): But apportionment is a very substantial change.

Fraser: I think we need a debate on this issue of apportionment.

Wexler: Can the Executive Committee approve the language on page three?

Fraser (continuing on): Isolate four or five of the most controversial issues, and send this out ahead of time, one issue at a time, requesting opinions from the Commission.

Wade: Do you mean to inform them separately on one issue, provide alternatives, and let them choose?

Fraser: The legislature has nothing to do with apportionment. I propose that we slow down. Let's split our report into two parts: One, those that relate to state legislatures; Two, . . .

Wexler (interrupts): A number of states begin their selection process in January.

Fraser: Intra-state apportionment is not as sensitive as inter-state.

Hughes: In those states where all congressional and senatorial races. . . .

Segal (interrupts): Splitting up the issues might give the impression that we are not going to be as tough in one area as another.

Dodds: But it will make our selling job so much easier if we can draw more groups into consultation.

Fraser: Ideally, we would come up with proposed findings, request comments, explore all ramifications. . . .[6]

One outcome of this midafternoon exchange, in a meeting which had begun shortly after 10:00 that morning, was a general realization that specific language for each guideline could not possibly be covered in the time allotted. Seizing upon this realization, Bill Dodds, in a parliamentary move which gave the staff almost everything it wanted, asked for a vote affirming that the listed points were indeed the major issues in party reform. When no one dissented, Chairman McGovern followed by suggesting a second session of the Executive Committee within the next few weeks, to hammer out an authorized version of all guidelines on which there was not unanimity.

The Dodds-McGovern moves, in combination, appeared to set the stage for the critical meetings on party reform. The Dodds motion affirmed the staff choice of issues as the one for debate by the full commission—as the practical agenda for party reform. The McGovern suggestion of another Executive Committee meeting guaranteed that the debate on this agenda would be channeled by the Executive Committee, a presumably more sympathetic body.

The commissioners then shifted to the arrangements for this September meeting, but Fraser broke in again to press the question of commission authority. His query, in effect, was the last obstacle to establishing the staff guidelines as the principal subject matter for the full commission. This time, however, McGovern finessed Fraser completely, arguing that there was no reason to address that issue head-on, since the commission could simply recommend whatever its members would accept:

Fraser: I still find myself hung up on the problem of which of these questions have to be resolved as a result of the mandatory requirements of the 1968 Convention. I don't sense that you have really looked at the question carefully.

McGovern: Are we ready to make recommendations, or are we still trying to decide whether we are mandated? Some things we will see . . .

Hughes (interrupts): The Executive Committee does not have to come up with a unanimous opinion.

Fraser (continued): Are we resolving the interpretation of the '68 action, or are we resolving that a [given] position would be desirable?

McGovern: I suggest that the Executive Committee be prepared to react to the recommendations of our staff. We can reject them A–1 if we choose.[7]

In the two weeks between the August 28 and September 11 meetings of the Executive Committee, the staff did not engage in a great deal of further strategic preparation. The draft guidelines which they had mailed to the Executive Committee in early August were unchanged, since discussion of their detailed language had been cut short at the previous session.[8] As a result, Segal and Bode devoted their time in the interim to the state-books. They did divide the guidelines between them, so that each one had a prime defender; they did assign an intern or two to those whose complexity or controversial nature required extra support. Otherwise, they sought no new course of action, but planned simply to address the guidelines in order and in detail, with the hope of securing an affirmative vote on each.

The Executive Committee reconvened on Thursday morning, September 11, in Room 3106 of the New (Dirksen) Senate Office Building, with all ten members in attendance. This time, however, these members quickly sidestepped the Segal-Bode plan for their gathering. In its place, they picked up where they had left off on August 28 and plunged into a discussion of the extent of commission powers, and of the manner in which those powers should be exercised.

Fraser again raised the issue, by asking that the guidelines be divided into those which the commission was commanded to consider and those which it had a right but not a duty to address. Segal and Bode tried to duck the question, by offering to discuss it in context, as it arose. Both feared that the need to demonstrate that each guideline was required by resolutions from the 1968 Convention or, worse, that each guideline *rendering* was the logical response to those commands, would leave few proposed rules intact. The commissioners, however, would have none of it. They had come to understand that every activating phrase in their guidelines—every verb—implied a level of coercion; they moved to find language reflecting their joint comprehension of their own authority.

A lengthy exchange ensued, on what various words implied about power in the Democratic party and on what they would contribute to the politics of implementation. The guidelines had been drafted to "require" some actions and "recommend" others, but after considerable discussion, a new phraseology emerged. Leroy Collins, former governor of Florida, unsuccessful candidate for U.S. senator, and chairman of the (defunct) Party Structure Subcommittee, enunciated the revision.

For cases where the commissioners possessed the direct ability to make a necessary reform, they would "call upon" the state party to take a prescribed action. For cases where the commissioners viewed a reform as necessary but lacked the direct ability to achieve it, they would "call upon" the party to make "all feasible efforts." For cases where the commissioners wanted to brand a particular arrangement as undesirable but were unwilling to demand its abolition—because they clearly lacked authority, because they felt less strongly, or because they could not approach consensus—the commission would "urge" the state party to respond.[9]

Nelson was unbothered by the Collins revision, since he felt that any language clearly and consistently used would suffice, but Segal and Bode feared that "calls upon" lacked the unambiguous thrust of "requires" and might encourage individual state parties to resist. A solid majority of the Executive Committee, however, preferred Collins' wording, and the issue was settled—at least for one meeting.

Discussion then shifted to the individual guidelines, thereafter phrased as "calls upon" or "urges." Most occasioned little conversation and no debate, once the staff had introduced them and explained their rationale, but three did generate more extensive comment. On the first, on discrimination and its remedies, the commissioners were not so much divided against each other as in search of a terminology to balance competing values. On the second, on proportional representation, they were divided into two clear camps, a situation producing the only real heat of the day. On the third, on delegate apportionment, they were split so many ways as to make a coherent recommendation impossible.[10]

The Executive Committee attacked the guidelines in numerical order, and the opener, A–1 (Discrimination on the Basis of Race, Color, Creed, or National Origin), again aroused the first substantive debate. Argument centered on two questions: What was the appropriate remedy for discrimination? Which groups were entitled to this relief?

The second question was, in fact, resolved first. Fred Dutton proposed that increased emphasis be placed upon women, youth, and minorities, rather than upon race, color, and creed, and he offered a lengthy and impassioned defense of this approach. Dutton was particularly concerned with the representation of women, but David Mixner rallied quickly to the cause of youth as well. Their point was favorably received by the rest of the committee, but rather than create an amalgamated guideline—race, color, creed, national origin, women, youth, and other minorities—the members agreed that women and youth should form the substance of a new standard. Guideline A–2 (Discrimination on the Basis of Age and Sex) was accordingly born.

Within the Executive Committee, Dodds, Dutton, Henry, and Hughes were most concerned with the issue of demographic representation and strongly favored expanding the categories to receive special mention. They were joined by Mixner, championing youth; Peden, on behalf of women; and Fraser, whose greater interest actually lay in the representation of *political* minorities. Collins, McGovern, and Stevenson were less involved, but did not attempt to block the new additions.

After expanding the roster of those who would receive explicit protection, the Executive Committee turned to the question of what this protection should entail. Three remedies surfaced: Credentials relief, that is, the reconstruction of a delegation to increase the presence of victimized groups; affirmative action, that is, procedures to boost the *participation* of previously designated groups; or quotas, that is, predetermined minimums for the presence of select groups.

While a majority of committee members had endorsed the original staff language when applied to Guideline A–1—remedy number two, affirmative action—there was no comparable majority for extending this provision to women and young people. In fact, debate was characterized by a series of attacks on anything which might be described as a "quota." Where Katherine Peden, for example, had affirmed that women were often victims of discrimination in politics and that the commission should forcefully decry this situation, she was unprepared to support actual demographic quotas for any group, even women.

Moreover, where George McGovern and Adlai Stevenson had maintained a relative silence on the addition of women and youth to the list of protected categories, they were quick to emphasize that nothing in this action should be construed as endorsing numerical requirements. Collins, Fraser, McGovern, Peden, and Stevenson all argued this explicitly, while Dodds, Dutton, Henry, Hughes, and Mixner remained comparatively quiet. No one was, at that point, really supporting a quota approach to either Guideline A–1 or Guideline A–2, but the effect of this concentrated antiquota rhetoric was to hold A–2 at the first level of coercion (credentials relief), while A–1 remained at the second level (affirmative action).

The commissioners moved rapidly through the next five guidelines: A–2 (Voter Registration), A–3 (Uniform Dates and Places), A–4 (Costs and Fees), A–5 (Existence of Party Rules), and A–6 (Access to the Ballot). Because they had created a second guideline on discrimination—the new A–2—they had to do some renumbering. At the staff's suggestion, they also combined the old A–3 and A–5 as one redrafted guideline and the old A–4 and A–6 as another. None of these actions, which were essentially editorial, created any division among the commissioners, and the staff was assigned to handle the redrafts without explicit constraints.

A second major discussion occurred when the committee reached B–1 (Unit Rule). The unit-rule language from the 1968 Convention was relatively unambiguous, banning arrangements at any level which permitted a majority of delegates to bind the rest to their will. Nevertheless, discussion of its application raised the issue, as it always did, of whether a "unit-rule principle" existed, one which applied to primary elections as well as state conventions. From there, it was but a short step to the question of proportional representation, which the staff intended to address directly through Guideline B–7.

Of the four substantive issues which would eventually create extended debate among the commissioners—demographics, apportionment, proportionality, and slating—proportionality stirred the strongest feelings within the *staff*. It received the single greatest amount of their intellectual energies; it was the focus of their most intensive lobbying efforts. Staff members did not want to fight about proportionality under the rubric of "the unit rule," since they agreed that the obvious purpose of the convention had been to forbid the binding of any delegate against his conscience. They did, however, insist that a full and meaningful opportunity to participate meant that minority views from the very lowest level should be carried to the floor of the national convention and that this implied formal proportional representation. When the fight developed around B–1 instead of B–7, then, they accepted the inevitable and focused these assertions there.

Fred Dutton took violent exception to the staff chain of argument, and it was his response when Guideline B–1 was introduced which caused debate to break out prematurely. California, his home base, was the last major state to use a winner-take-all primary, and Dutton defended the device on many levels. He contended that the crux of fair representation was social categories (demographic minorities), not candidate or issue preferences (political minorities), and that a delegation could be balanced on demographic criteria *only* if it was selected as a unit. He claimed that the winner-take-all rule, rather than proportionality, was the truly democratic procedure, because it *forced* a clear choice among candidates and put that choice in the hands of the voters. At a less grand level, he noted that winner-take-all made California the most important state in the union, and he asserted that this was always a boon to reform forces nationwide.

By sheer perseverance, Dutton managed to keep the debate alive, in an Executive Committee created to enshrine the opposite perspective. No one joined him in his defense; neither could his opponents build a majority for the staff position. The issue did achieve the distinction of being the only one driven to a formal vote by the Executive Committee. But that vote showed four in favor (Dodds, Henry, Hughes, and Mixner), one opposed (Dutton), and *five* abstaining (Collins, Fraser, McGovern, Peden, and Stevenson).

This split led to a decision-rule. Whenever the Executive Committee could not agree on a guideline, it would make no recommendation. Instead, the issue would be bumped along to the full commission for another round of the same debate. Dutton dissented from this decision-rule, too, arguing that the committee should more appropriately act as a filter. Proposals which could not obtain committee agreement, he said, should be dropped at that point. His fellow members, however, decided to forward B–7 to the full commission, and Dutton was left to polish his arguments for the commission meeting.

In the wake of the proportionality debate, the Executive Committee could get through only three more guidelines before experiencing another major disagreement. B–2 (Selection of Alternates), B–3 (Quorum Provisions), and B–4 (Clarity of Purpose) received committee approval without incident. But with the arrival of Guideline B–5 (Apportionment), unanimity disappeared again.

The formula which the Democratic party had been using to apportion delegates *among* the states was a modified bonus system, the product of twenty years of political compromise. The staff proposed to scrap it and move directly to apportionment by prior Democratic (presidential) vote. Existing formulas to apportion delegates *within* the states were even more intricate, since each state was entitled to make its own rules. The staff proposed scrapping all these, too, in favor of a uniform Democratic-vote standard.

Committee members, on the other hand, saw virtue in numerous arrangements. No one cared to defend the status quo, but there was support for a revised bonus system, for apportionment by population, and for population blended with Democratic vote. With four live options among the seven remaining members and with the afternoon nearly gone, there was no possibility of a resolution. The members, accordingly, agreed to let the issue lie over until the full commission meeting, two weeks later. As with proportionality, the staff was invited to outline the alternatives and to circulate this analysis by mail. The full commission might then have better luck with the apportionment question, but better luck or not, it would cut its teeth on the issue when it met on September 23 and 24.

Reform Politicking in the Full Commission

The next morning, September 12, the staff began to prepare for that full commission meeting. Segal and Bode again divided the guidelines between them for individual attention. This time, however, they enjoyed the added advantage of knowing which had already provoked controversy. For those guidelines which had experienced little trouble, they did a routine review of arguments. For those which had produced unmistakable warning signs, Apportionment and Representation of Minority Views, they planned for maximum supportive firepower.

Beyond this preparation of manifest arguments, the staff had a number of other potential levers through which they might hope to influence the session. Its editorial control, for example, had been carefully exercised in the past and would be tapped again for late September. Its agenda control held additional possibilities, if staff members could foresee the dynamics of the meeting. The simple knowledge of expected attendance, finally, knowledge which only the staff could have, might be used to color both their specific arguments and, especially, the order of guideline presentation.

Staff members had always been aware of their editorial power. For the Executive Committee, they had, for example, retitled their guideline on proportionality so that it became "Representation of Minority Views," to escape an expected aversion among their commissioners to "Proportional Representation." For the full commission, they produced no new euphemism, but they did discover a useful fillip. Within the Executive Committee, staff members had been forced to offer each guideline as a staff suggestion. Within the full commission, they could present these guidelines instead as recommendations of the Executive Committee.

Thus, a draft guideline going to the meeting on September 11 had been introduced with the notation that "The staff recommends that the Commission. . . ." The same guideline for the meeting on September 23 could read "The Executive Committee recommends that the Commission. . . ."[11] And here, the staff simply plunged ahead and extended this figure of speech into the seven draft guidelines in Section "C"—which had never been debated, or even examined, by the Executive Commmittee.

In planning the sessions of September 23–24, the staff also queried each commissioner about potential attendance and about the ability to remain for both days. Staff members learned, in the process, that Albert A. Pena, a reliable vote for proportional representation, did not intend to come. In response to his complaint that the timing was inconvenient and the trip costly, Bode promised to locate the necessary finances, if Pena would sacrifice the time:

> Pena was flown in for this. We knew where our votes were. And we tried to bring them in. We knew that Pena would be for us on p.r., so we brought him in. We *found* the wherewithal to get him there. Garcia couldn't be found even

then. It may well be that Louis [Martin] stayed away because of dissonance. We wanted Graves, and he would be with us on everything. We did our best, and we got him for one day. He was busy running around the country, getting *Black Enterprise,* the magazine, started.

Finally, as the crucial days approached, the commission counsel and research director turned to the agenda itself, for one more tactic to help ease their commissioners past the more explosive guidelines. In a premeeting memo to Chairman McGovern, they outlined their thoughts:

> We also agreed that it might be undesirable for us to get bogged down on the controversial issues right away. We would suggest that we specifically set aside the three issues that caused prolonged debate within the Executive Committee, begin promptly at 9:30 with the top of the agenda, and take up these three systematically at 11:00 A.M. The three issues are: (1) Unit Rule (which the Executive Committee voted on 4–1–2); (2) Apportionment; (3) Proportionality—the representation of minority views in the delegate selection process. We should probably stay with these issues until we achieve some resolution of them and, if possible, work through lunch.
>
> It is very important that we reach some resolution of the major issues tomorrow. We are very close to a minimum quorum. If some people leave on Tuesday evening, we may well be short on Wednesday. Therefore, it's important that we reach some kind of resolution—not move on and return later unless it is really imperative.
>
> There are a couple of reasons not to break for lunch: First, the matter of time and pressing issues; secondly, we are liable to be in the middle of one of the controversial items, and the press will be anxious to talk to all the Commission members individually, before we have really resolved anything. We'd urge you to plan to have lunch sent in and have the Commission work straight through.[12]

The first substantive session of the full Party Structure Commission began at 8:00 A.M. on September 23 with a breakfast in the Senate Dining Room. The group then shifted back to Room 3106 of the New (Dirksen) Senate Office Building, where the commission would sit for the next two days. Once in 3106, Chairman McGovern opened the meeting with a short speech of his own, emphasizing the magnitude of the occasion—and the desirability that his commissioners endorse proposals of a scope appropriate to it:

> We were created, not by a faction of the party, but by a strong majority mandate of the Democratic National Convention of 1968. That mandate instructed the national chairman of our party to name a commission to carry out certain specific reforms. We are instructed to assist the States in establishing a delegate selection system in which all Democratic voters have had full, meaningful, and timely opportunity to participate. In blunt language, this means that the Democratic Party in national convention assembled has asked us to spell out methods

for assuring that the people rather than the bosses select the presidential nominee of our party.[13]

The guidelines were put before the commissioners in a slightly altered sequence, in order to allow for anticipated debates on proportionality and apportionment. Otherwise, procedures for discussing each were essentially parallel. Either Segal or Bode introduced the guideline and read it through. The introducer offered a brief survey of its development and a brief explanation of its purported need. This was followed with some examples from the interns' research, and the guideline was then thrown open for general discussion.

That discussion was always conducted in the presence of, and with frequent reference to, the black, loose-leaf state-books. The extensive labor invested in these books paid heavy dividends at this September meeting, where their active utilization was a major factor in inducing the commissioners to leave most guidelines alone. Bode was delighted by their impact:

> We would hit them with all this evidence. How can you vote against requiring a political party to have rules? If you're going to have them, what should they contain? We'd hit them with a couple of extreme examples of some practice, and they'd laugh and come up with other examples like it which they knew about, but hadn't thought of. But after they had laughed, there wouldn't be anyone who wanted to deliberately *allow* that to happen. So we'd introduce the text of a guideline which would do away with it.

If the existence of the state-books, coupled with the vastly greater store of information on the part of the staff, was one reason why most guidelines met little resistance, the fact that they had already—apparently—been sorted out by the Executive Committee was surely another. The committee had, in effect, called the two highly contested items from the September 11 meeting, proportionality and apportionment, to the explicit attention of their commission colleagues. Chairman McGovern had reinforced this emphasis in his pre-meeting memorandum.[14] Most commissioners, in turn, dutifully made their major investments there, and not in the guidelines which had provoked no earlier disagreement. Warren Christopher was impressed by this damping effect of prior approval by the Executive Committee:

> The Executive Committee had things pretty well prepackaged by the September meetings. I remember being surprised by the leadership role that it took all the way along. About the only role to be played by the full Commission would be if the Executive Committee hadn't thought things through. They often got carried away by the fervor of the moment and brought back things which had logical faults in them. If there were obvious logical problems, questions might be re-opened. Sometimes the full commission would point them out to them, and then we would have debates.

On the other hand, while the commissioners ultimately deleted only one draft guideline, and while they did not veto any at the September meeting, they were to have some minor, textual input on nearly all. No commissioner reliably asked how particular guidelines would affect the Democratic party *as a party,* or how *the overall nomination process* would work under these rules. Yet the members did see particular problems with the language of individual guidelines, and they did suggest alterations to deal with these problems.

For example, the staff suggestion that at least 50 percent of a state committee be present before that committee could take any action to select delegates (Guideline B–3, Quorum Provisions) met objections from John English, national committeeman from New York, who noted that a full half of his un-wieldy State Central Committee could rarely be assembled. In response, the commissioners lowered the quorum requirement from 50 to 40 percent. In the same manner, George Mitchell, national committeeman from Maine, warned that an insistence on uniform dates and places for the activities of delegate selection (Guideline A–5, Existence of Party Rules) would work a hardship on rural states like his, where bad weather, difficult geography, and diverse local customs all ran afoul of such inflexibility. In response, the commissioners developed a specific exemption for rural areas.[15]

Apart from these minor changes—and there were certainly fewer of them than there would have been in a commission with a greater number of active party leaders—two of the four issues which had divided the Executive Committee provided the major battlegrounds for the full commission as well. At the Executive Committee session on September 11, commission authority, demographic discrimination, proportional representation, and delegate apportionment had been the major items of debate. Two weeks later, at the full commission meeting on September 23 and 24, commission authority and demographic discrimination caused hardly a stir, but some of the less controversial guidelines required more attention than they had in the Executive Committee, and the arguments over apportionment and, especially, proportionality ballooned to take up all other slack time.

Leroy Collins again raised the subject of commission authority. But this time, Segal and Bode remained silent, since they calculated that a greater percentage of commissioners were on hand who might insist on tracing their powers to precise convention instructions. As a result, after a few questions from members who were not on the Executive Committee, Collins's wording was retained intact.

The full commission also passed more easily, almost nonchalantly, over Guidelines A–1 (Discrimination on the Basis of Race, Color, Creed, or National Origin) and A–2 (Discrimination on the Basis of Age or Sex). Apparently, the compromises hammered out within the Executive Committee were sufficient to bring the full commission along, without much need for further discussion.

The longest substantive debate of the two-day session, then, came on proportionality, via Guideline B–7 (Representation of Minority Views in the Delegate Selection Process). That debate dragged on for hours, weaving in and out of arguments about political versus demographic minorities, about convention versus primary states, about appearances of equity versus incentives to participation, and about early versus late application to the mechanics of delegate selection.

This debate began with a quick voice vote on whether it was even legitimate to discuss proportionality. There were those, led once again by Fred Dutton, who argued that the 1968 Convention had never, by the wildest stretch of imagination, intended to impose formal proportional representation when it passed the Rules minority report. Notwithstanding their vehemence, these commissioners found themselves on the short end of the tally, and the inquiry moved ahead.

Shortly afterward, there was a recorded vote on whether the basic mandate evidently *required* proportionality. The result was 4 yes and 8 no, and the parameters of commission debate were set: The assembled commissioners would accept proportionality as an item for discussion; they would not be stampeded into a positive recommendation.[16]

Hours later, when the question was finally called—Should the Commission "urge" (but not "call upon") the state parties to encourage fair representation of minority views through the device of proportional representation at all levels?—the membership split in half: 8 said yes; 8 said no; 3 were out of the room. Even then, if Harold Hughes, who was chairing the meeting, had not responded when his name was called, the issue would have been settled. Hughes had followed normal parliamentary practice on the vote requiring proportionality and had abstained; he violated that practice on the vote recommending proportionality and voted aye. Without his vote, Guideline B–7 would have been dropped from the package, and proportionality would not have been on the agenda for the commission's final session.

Yet Hughes did vote, his vote did produce a tie, and the commission did in effect decide to make no immediate recommendation but to query a wider range of interested persons and then return to the issue. The staff was directed to prepare a special paper on the subject, presenting issues and enumerating options, so that this paper could both inform debate within the commission and stimulate the general public in its response. The commissioners would reassemble in perhaps six weeks, fortified by whatever came back in the mails, and presumably break their tie.

The final major debate at the September meeting came on Guideline B–5

(Apportionment). The content of B–5 had, in fact, changed substantially *since* the Executive Committee meeting on September 11, thanks to some old-fashioned horse-trading between the staffs of the Party Structure and Rules commissions. At a breakfast meeting between staff members on September 15, an agreement had been reached to partition the topic: The McGovern Commission would confine itself to the apportionment of delegates *inside* the individual states; the O'Hara Commission would tackle the more politically explosive question of apportionment *among* the states. The staff of the McGovern Commission thus gained the right to plunge ahead on delegate selection reform, secure in the knowledge that the O'Hara Commission would not subsequently undercut or contradict them. The staff of the O'Hara Commission gained the largest substantive area in dispute between the two bodies.[17]

The jettisoning of interstate apportionment, however, did not appreciably change the level of controversy on the issue within the Party Structure Commission. Support for a bonus system, in which states receive delegate bonuses for interim electoral successes, had pretty well disappeared by September 23–24, but the pure Democratic-vote system, the pure population system, and various mixed plans each retained a cadre of adherents. The upshot for apportionment was the same as for proportional representation: The commissioners agreed to postpone the issue until their next meeting, to invite the staff to outline available options in the interim, to query a much broader range of interested observers, and to face the matter upon their return five or six weeks hence.

By the time the full commission had worked its way through the rest of the "B" guidelines, it was well into its second day of deliberations. With the seven "C" guidelines still to come—still, indeed, untouched—there was again no chance that the commissioners would actually finish by the end of the day. Given those conditions, the remaining commissioners decided to mail out the full set of guidelines for public review, including the text of Guidelines C–1 to C–7 and the special staff reports on proportionality and apportionment. After sufficient time for a response, they would reassemble and go through the entire process one more time. At that point, they could accept all of the noncontroversial guidelines which they had tentatively approved in September, unless public reception justified reopening the issue. The commissioners could then concentrate on B–5, B–7, and the "C" guidelines. With that limited agenda, they could still potentially fulfill their responsibilities without delaying their recommendations.

A few administrative tasks remained before the staff and leadership could focus all their energies on this final session. The major one was a mass mailing of the draft guidelines for public review. In the first week in October, the commission staff copied the guidelines, Chairman McGovern dictated a covering letter, and the staff put the entire package into the mails, with the promise of two follow-up papers on proportionality and apportionment. McGovern assigned these supplemental papers to Alex Bickel for proportionality and Dick Wade for apportionment, and consultants Bickel and Wade completed the package of reform proposals for external review.[18]

Perhaps because these two supplemental papers did not go out until October 20, recipients were slow in replying to the entire collection. Their tardiness was one reason that the November meeting was pushed back from the twelfth to the nineteenth. Eventually, 110 people, roughly 3 percent of those solicited, did answer, and their judgments became the public response to the guidelines. To convey these answers to the commissioners and to suggest changes which might follow from them, the staff sent out a series of four memos during the second week in November.

Nelson presented a quick overview of public responses. Segal and Bode addressed the activating language in the guidelines and suggested, once again, a return to "requires" instead of the more recent "calls upon." Nelson offered a review of the debate on proportionality and apportionment, complete with highlighted issues and options. Segal and Bode closed with an eight-page note on technical wording, a note which actually redrafted twelve of the nineteen guidelines, either to correct professed confusions which had surfaced in the public review or to eliminate alleged ambiguities which they themselves had discovered.[19]

When the last of these memos had gone out, on November 13, the staff was free to turn to the orchestration of the crucial sessions of the Commission on Party Structure and Delegate Selection, by then scheduled for November 19 and 20. Nelson, Segal, and Bode had mailed their commissioners forty-five pages of single-spaced material in the period since September 24; they had reserved the remaining week to anticipate questions which this material might raise. In truth, however, these staff members had been over the relevant arguments so often that they could do little more than weigh the agenda for the coming meeting, worry over the roster of attendees, and wait for the two-day period which would determine the short-run fate of all their efforts.

Implications

As the leadership, staff, and commissioners waited for the November sessions of the full commission, the process of developing recommendations for party reform—and thus the politics of recommendation itself—entered its critical phase. Fifteen months before, this process had begun with an informal meeting of a faltering nomination campaign in a private home in Connecticut. Now, it was to reach a climax in a formal meeting of an official reform commission at national party headquarters.

This chain of events—from the creation of the Hughes Commission, through the appointment of the McGovern Commission, to the construction of a reform agenda and the development of draft guidelines by key commission personnel—was moving relentlessly toward one final, showdown session. That session was intended to produce the official report of the Commission on Party Structure and Delegate Selection. It was destined to contribute the practical definition of party reform for the next three years—and the central issues in party reform for the next fifteen.

Three preliminary meetings set the stage for this crucial session. The opening meeting of the Executive Committee on August 28 was actually devoted to housekeeping and to recurrent organizational problems. But in its closing moments, with the adoption of the staff's proposed guidelines as the commission's working agenda, the Executive Committee took a formal action of major consequence. Ironically, this first committee gathering also attested to the restiveness of many commissioners, to their fear that they had lost control of their own operation. More ironically still, it testified to the contradictory fear that the regular party, which appeared to have so much to lose from the developing reform effort, might finally move to restrain the commission.

At a second meeting of the Executive Committee on September 11, those commissioners who were most anxious about their own role in the reform process insisted on having their concern addressed. The vehicle for this was a debate on the activating language of the guidelines; the result was a new phraseology reflecting the commission's—and not the staff's—perception of its responsibilities and powers. Beyond that, the members created a new guideline saluting the aspirations of women and youth within the party and surfaced strong disagreements over proportionality and apportionment, thus calling those issues to the attention of the full commission.

Two weeks later, on September 23 and 24, the full commission confronted the same agenda. Again, the commissioners went round and round on proportional representation. In the end, however, only a lenient decision-rule and a charitable vote-count permitted the issue to survive for the decisive meeting in November. Again, the issue of apportionment generated extensive argument. But here, even the shape of the likely options remained unclear. Beyond that, the commissioners contributed numerous minor changes to the less controversial guidelines, adjusting them sometimes to achieve greater precision, sometimes to meet practical implications uncovered in the course of discussion.

Yet a summary of the issues and conflicts at these preliminary meetings obscured more than it clarified—and *that* was ultimately the most significant fact about these sessions. For reform politics, a concentration on evident issues and conflicts obscured the actual balance of influence with the Party Structure Commission. For institutional change, a concentration on the evident substance of debate obscured the fate of the overall package of institutional reforms. For the circulation of elites, finally, attention to the appearance and content of disputes within the commission obscured the relationship of that commission—and its dominant figures—to contending coalitions on the outside.

During the six months leading up to the August 28 meeting of the Executive Committee, the balance of influence within the Party Structure Commission was clear. The commissioners, if they were active at all, were out on the hustings, listening to testimony which would serve only to buttress staff proposals. The staff was in Washington, developing the commission report. Even under those conditions, the extent of this disjunction was striking. The commissioners had little or nothing to say about the formal structure of their own enterprise. They had nothing at all to say about the initial broadening and subsequent narrowing of its substantive focus.

The shift to a sequence of official commission meetings necessarily altered this pattern of influence. Or rather, it altered the way in which that influence had to be exercised. For the crucial fact about the addition of the commissioners as a body to the politics of recommendation was the extent to which prior patterns continued.

Formally, the commissioners had the upper hand. They could introduce entirely new emphases; they could delete established staff suggestions; they—and only they—could certify any compromise product. Part of the explanation for the restrained fashion in which they seized upon these formal advantages, then, lay with motivation. The bulk of the commissioners had been appointed to be receptive to reform; most lived up to their notices.

Yet there was room for a great variety, in proposals and even in fundamental approaches, under the broad banner of reform. Moreover, a significant number of commissioners were restless, even suspicious, by the time these proposals appeared before them. If these formal advantages and mixed motivations did not contribute to a major reworking of staff proposals, then, it was largely because the *practical balance* in the means of exercising influence had not shifted nearly as much as the formal situation might suggest.

Many initial staff advantages carried right over into the official meetings in the fall of 1969. Staff members remained more expert and better prepared. The commissioners could have compensated only with countervailing staff assistance, but the staff was not divided, and its aid went only to reliable allies. Staff members knew precisely what they wanted. The commissioners had far less opportunity to develop an understanding of their own wants; when they did know that they disliked the staff solution, they rarely possessed an alternative.

In fact, the commissioners, as a full and functioning collectivity, met *only twice*—March 1 and September 23–24—before the November session at which they had to adopt final recommendations for reform. As a result, a majority of the commissioners were addressing the guidelines in person *for the first time* when they assembled on September 23. The staff, of course, had been living with these guidelines for all the months before.

Even when the commissioners were assembled, this situation changed in degree but not in kind. The staff retained control over the editorial content of its working document; it retained control over its formal agenda; it retained some mild control over the composition of its active membership. Indeed, after the commissioners adjourned to await their final drafting session, the staff continued to tap these advantages, through four memos aimed at creating the context for this session.[20] The commissioners were not unaware of this effect, but awareness was not an antidote. Fred Dutton complained openly:

> I often felt that even when we did get a consensus, the staff would distort it in the rewriting, and they would come back after having run with the ball again. You have to get back to the problem where they weren't working enough with us, so we were doing things without them, because they wouldn't accommodate to us. They thought that we should just take papers from them, because that was the way the Hughes Commission worked.

Because staff members knew what they wanted and how they hoped to extract it, they could coordinate not only their own activities, but the activities of a small set of militant reform commissioners. The bulk of the commissioners, by contrast, because they were unacquainted at the time of their appointment and because they had met very little in the interim, never developed the working relationships, much less the division of labor, which might have allowed them to neutralize these assets.

As a result, the commissioners never threatened to rework the guidelines in wholesale fashion. The continuing fear of the staff, that these commissioners would turn out to be part of a functioning "old boy network," proved groundless. The staff, of course, was able to use its position at the center of commission communications to influence the ultimate product. No countervailing communication among disenchanted commissioners ever developed.

This continuing balance of practical influence within the Party Structure

Commission was itself a major explanation of a second, major, analytic surprise in this series of fall commission meetings. For in the realm of institutional change, the critical fact about these preliminary sessions was the tiny amount of substantive amendment which they—and hence the assembled commissioners—produced. Despite a parade of issues and conflicts, the recommendations going forward to the final drafting session were remarkably similar to those which had come forward to the first fall meeting of the Executive Committee.

The obvious tussling of various commissioners with the details of individual guidelines, and their fierce debate over several, could easily mask this fact. The commissioners did come out to their meetings. Once there, they did press staff members about the implications of proposed reforms. They were, in no sense, mere rubber stamps. Nevertheless, a precise inventory of commissioner accomplishments told a very different tale.

The commissioners added only one new guideline, and it was apparently honorific. They deleted none at all. They introduced new activating language into all the guidelines, their most distressing intervention from the point of view of their staff. But this was the sort of change which looked much larger from within than from without; it had no direct effect on what the commission would (or would not) endorse. At the same time, the commissioners never managed, at any of their meetings, even to *address* the last full third of their intended recommendations, the "C" guidelines. Numerous lesser adjustments to the "A" and "B" guidelines certified that these commissioners were neither napping nor quiescent, but those adjustments did not promise any serious institutional impact.

If the *disputes* at the fall commission meetings emphasized a few items as major issues for the final drafting session, it was still the *absence of disputes* on the vast bulk of staff recommendations which was by far the most significant substantive aspect of those meetings. In particular, *the drive toward participatory—nonparty—institutions of delegate selection,* the dominant theme, the principal connection, and the prime institutional consequence in all these staff proposals, *was never explicitly challenged at all* and did not even indirectly provoke debate.

Again, it was not that the commissioners uniformly approved of the institutional impact of the proposed guidelines, an impact that would banish two of the five fundamental devices for delegate selection and radically curtail a third. Instead, the commissioners as a collectivity simply failed to see this impact or, in a few cases, to appreciate its significance. But this very misperception—this nonperception, really—had additional bearing on the final meeting of the commission. Having been through the guidelines without ever having discussed this effect, and having surfaced several major items which they had not only discussed but heatedly debated, the commissioners were that much more unlikely to address what was the central institutional impact of their entire guideline package.

The result was a lack of consequential alterations—and precious few open questions—in the reform draft going forward to the final meeting of the full commission. That result, in turn, was partially explained by an imbalance in practical influence between the commission staff and leadership, on the one hand, and their commissioners, on the other. Yet both of these results were also dependent on a third, partially independent, nearly invisible fact about reform politics in the fall of 1969.

In a fashion so simple as to be easily overlooked—a fashion predictably obscured by a focus on the issues and conflicts of the day—the internal balance of commission influence might not have determined the drift of commission actions, so totally and directly, had there been major efforts at shaping these actions by groups and individuals on the outside. That is, the ability of the internal workings of the Party Structure Commission to determine the content of its recommendations rested, in part, on the absence of serious external efforts at upsetting this internal balance.

The absence of attention by the general public was not difficult to understand. Individuals with no organizational stake or specialized interest could hardly have known of these deliberations. There was no press coverage of the Executive Committee meetings of August 28 and September 11. The scattering of accounts which followed the full commission sessions of September 23–24 appeared *after* those sessions were completed.[21]

On the other hand, there was no shortage of politically specialized, apparently organized, potentially interested candidates for the role of external influencer. The regular party, in particular, appeared to have an obvious stake in the outcome. Moreover, if party officialdom was to have any role in the politics of recommendation, it had to come in the fall of 1969. From the other side, militant reformers had an evident stake in these meetings, and thus a reason to act, too. Reformers could always seek more expansive reforms than the commission staff had proposed; they could certainly mobilize to oppose the dreaded countermobilization by the regular party. In short, the most active members of both the orthodox Democratic coalition and its aspiring replacement had apparent cause to approach the Party Structure Commission in the fall of 1969 and to attempt to sway its internal balance.

Simple inattention erased much of this possibility. Commission activities had been geographically dispersed and temporally intermittent from their inception. The process of framing official recommendations for party reform had bubbled along below the surface during months of apparent inactivity. And then, suddenly, that process had surfaced for a quick public resolution. State and local party leaders, in particular, were likely to miss this development.

On the other hand, a significant minority of these state and local leaders must still have known that the commission was moving toward dramatic recommendations on party reform. Some of these leaders had been sensitized to commission events by their own attempts to gain commission appointment; others had been alerted by the regional hearings, which had featured several public confrontations between the commission leadership and the regular party.[22]

Yet party leaders who saw that a turning point was at hand still faced major—and eventually decisive—organizational obstacles. The various state and local Democratic parties suffered an initial handicap, of course, in their lack of representation on the commission proper. Fred Harris had made it a point to ignore direct lieutenants of major party organizations, but even those commissioners who were actively sympathetic to official party perspectives were not generally tied to functioning regular parties.

The obvious way for these diverse and decentralized parties to address the Party Structure Commission, in light of their lack of direct membership, was through their national chairman. But the office of chairman was still occupied by Harris, and he was still a strong supporter of reform. A sensible party leader who opposed the guidelines would not have bothered to contact the chairman; the chairman would not—did not—convey any message of restraint to the commission.

That left only the difficult task of developing some other, coordinate, opposition vehicle, and of developing it on very short notice. No one made the attempt. The job required substantial time and energy. It was guaranteed to brand its movers as (public) enemies of reform. Yet there was no guarantee that the product of the commission would be of any consequence. If its proposals really did threaten to achieve a concrete impact, the state and local parties retained the option of dealing with that later, in the National Committee or on their home turf.

In the face of those incentives, regular party leaders across the country uniformly opted out. When they did, the orthodox Democratic coalition—the regular party and its associated interests—essentially abandoned any coordinated role in the politics of recommendation and left the product of that politics to be determined in one final, two-day session of the Party Structure Commission.

In theory, militant reformers might also have mobilized to influence the deliberations of the Party Structure Commission. Their failure to do so reflected, in part, the positive prospects of the reform package with which they had become identified. It reflected, even more, the success of the commission staff in becoming the major organizational link among proreform forces around the country. It reflected, finally, the desperate organizational disarray of these forces in the absence of coordination by the Party Structure Commission.

One of the major implicit developments in reform politics during the fall of 1969, unmarked by any specific event, was the emergence of the Party Structure Commission—really of its headquarters staff, using the commission framework—as the central link for reform forces nationwide. As with the movement of the commission staff to the center of internal reform politics, this was based upon formal position. It was the Party Structure Commission, after all, which would eventually produce the certified recommendations for reform. Moreover, as a quasi-independent arm of the National Committee, and despite its financial difficulties, the commission was better institutionalized, and hence more likely to continue, than were most unofficial competitors.

As with the movement of the commission staff to the center of internal reform politics, however, its emergence at the center of external reform politics was the result of more than formal assets. Staff members had shown the "proper" orientation; they had shown themselves aggressive in its pursuit; they had reached out, individually and through the regional hearings, to interested groups and individuals around the country. Potential, alternative, coordinating mechanisms had logically deferred to them on all these grounds. Some, like the old Hughes Commission, the original coordinating device for reform politics, had actually ceased to exist.

A combination of deliberate calculations plus the press of events, in turn, prevented the commission staff from trying to remobilize its external reform network for the fall commission meetings. Staff members were unsure that such pressure would not backfire; they did believe that rallying their potential supporters inside the commission was a far more productive activity. When the fall meetings began to unfold in rapid succession, then, staff members concentrated on strategies and arguments for the commission forum, and forswore a costly and potentially ineffective attempt to rally outside support.

The organizational disarray of these putative external allies was both a reason why such an effort would have been extremely costly and an explanation for why it did not occur on its own. The New Democratic Coalition, the umbrella group for advocates of a "new politics," remained the obvious, nominal vehicle for this effort. Yet the very ability of the commission staff to usurp the coordinating role of the NDC during the summer of 1969 reflected its declining organizational capacities. By fall, this decline had become catastrophic. As a framework, the New Democratic Coalition would survive through the 1972 campaigns. As a political instrument of consequence, it was finished by late 1969.[23]

In theory, independent reformers might still have thrown up an ad hoc organization to press their views. In practice, this effort would have suffered all the difficulties faced by the regular party—and more besides. A large portion of what had appeared to be the constituency for such an organization in the fall of 1968 had come directly out of the insurgent nomination campaigns of that year. By the fall of 1969, that portion had largely disappeared. This did not mean that that constituency would not coalesce again when the campaigns of 1972 began to stir. It did mean that its members were not easily located as the Party Structure Commission approached its final drafting session.

In the absence of attempts at affecting internal commission deliberations by the plausible candidates for external influence, it was impossible to say that such efforts would have altered commission proposals. The peculiar, partially self-contained character of the commission as a political system might have been sufficient to produce the same outcomes in spite of such efforts. The commissioners were not well connected to major external interests. Their staff would have retained many of its practical assets even in the face of external assault.

Yet a serious attack on commission decision-making in the fall of 1969 by major external actors would at least have injected more uncertainty into possible commission outcomes. Moreover, there were obvious candidates for the role of outside influencer, and they were reputed to have the political strength to upset this internal balance—and perhaps to produce a different set of recommendations for reform.

No one, however, found enough incentive to undertake a major effort at influencing the deliberations of the Party Structure Commission in the short period before its intendedly final session. The national chairman continued his policy of detachment. State and local party leaders, those who even bothered to follow the matter, concluded that an approach to the commission was not worth the effort. The New Democratic Coalition, lacking stimulus from the commission staff and facing extreme organizational disarray, failed to move. Nothing else sprang up in its place.

As a result, by early November, the likelihood that the content of commission guidelines would be resolved by forces from anywhere other than inside the commission had declined almost to zero. The orthodox Democratic coalition had passed. The alternative Democratic coalition possessed crucial surrogates on the commission leadership and staff; otherwise, it had passed, too. One final application of the internal balance of influence within the Party Structure Commission, as measured by one final, historic session, was nearly all that remained of the politics of recommendation.

CHAPTER

6

The Content of the Mandate:

A Final Meeting and a Reform Text

IN WHICH, the commissioners assemble to frame final recommendations for party reform; extended debates over demographics, proportionality, apportionment, and slating dominate their discussions; and the major developments in commission politics to date combine with the internal dynamics of this particular meeting to create an official outcome. AND IN WHICH, the first stage of reform politics, the politics of recommendation, reaches its climax; proposals for sweeping institutional change, built on the participatory model but with certain noteworthy emendations, become the concrete definition of party reform; and the prospects for an impact on the character of elites in national politics are tied specifically to the fate—and effectiveness—of this reform package.

THE Commission on Party Structure and Delegate Selection reassembled on November 19, 1969, for a two-day assault on the remaining issues in its drive toward a comprehensive statement on party rules reform. That session, which began shortly after 9:00 on Thursday morning, stretched through the late afternoon of the following day. It reached the final collective decisions on commission guidelines for delegate selection. In the process, it capped the most thorough effort at recommendations for party reform in the history of the world's oldest continuing political party.

By intention, this meeting was to frame a final reform text for the national Democratic party, in as many hours of concentrated effort as a two-day meeting could, or needed, to provide. By definition, the product of this effort would be a set of formally certified recommendations for institutional change, the official translation of the original "mandate" for national party reform and thus the climax of the politics of recommendation. By extension, that product would become the document which the National Committee and the fifty state parties would have to address during the politics of implementation to follow.

The *final* character of this meeting gave it more than a heightened significance as the site at which all these things would necessarily occur. It gave it a peculiarly consequential place in the *sequence* of reform politics as well. That is, because the meeting was intended to frame the final recommendations in that politics, the possibility was ever present that the peculiar internal dynamics of this meeting—the interactions which materialized there, the arguments which arose there, the forces which collided in the process—would powerfully affect the document which was destined to lie at the center of reform politics afterward.

In practice, the continuing influence of the actors, proposals, and events of the preceding nine months—or the preceding seventeen, if the chronicle ran back to formation of the Hughes Commission—remained central to commission deliberations on November 19 and 20. Yet there was also a major, meeting-specific development which flared suddenly and then ramified through many other conflicts at this final two-day session.

The staff, and presumably those commissioners who had attended the preliminary meetings, expected two major battles in November. The first was on proportional representation; the second was on intrastate apportionment. Both battles did indeed arise. They were, however, joined by two other, unforeseen counterparts. The first of these, at the very beginning of the two-day stretch, was on demographic representation; the second, at the very end, was on slate making. Moreover, the opening battle over demographic representation was so extended and so intense, and achieved such a muddled but portentous resolution, that its fallout appeared continually in the discussion of the other guidelines. This included the key standards on proportionality and slating; it included several lesser strictures, too.

Again, this dramatic surface politics obscured but did not override the principal fact about the outcome of the meeting. The recommendations of the commission staff, for extensive reform on the participatory model, survived largely intact—and characterized the institutional impact of this reform package in the fundamental, analytic sense. Yet the debate over demographics, especially as ramified through numerous other guidelines, was easily sufficient not just to stand as the obvious main conflict of the two-day session but to give that session its distinctive character and contribution.

The result was the organizational climax of the politics of recommendation. The full commission meeting of November 19 and 20 produced the final collective decisions, though not necessarily the final wording and not always the final interpretation, of the central document in the politics of party reform. That document, after the peculiar interactions and intermittent high conflict of the November meeting, still called for sweeping institutional change in the national Democratic party. That institutional change, if it could be implemented, retained the potential for producing a significant shift in the character of political elites in presidential politics. That shift, finally, promised to reach into every institution of American national government and to alter the fabric of American national politics.

The Framing of Party Reform, Day One

The Party Structure Commission returned to the site of its first meeting, the Senate Caucus Room, for its final session of 1969. The meeting followed what had become a standard order of business. George McGovern offered a few opening comments about the commission's roots, its two-day task, and its possible future. Bob Nelson reviewed developments in the nation at large, and especially in the counterpart reform commissions in the fifty states. Ken Bode provided a similar review of commission events since the last meeting, consisting, this time, of a short rundown on responses from the public review of draft guidelines. Eli Segal led the commission into the text of the guidelines themselves.

The commissioners then moved through these guidelines in alphabetical and numerical order, with only two deviations. In midafternoon of the first day, they took up the issue of proportional representation; in late morning of the second, they tackled the question of intrastate apportionment. These deviations were intended to provide the commissioners with extra time for the most potentially controversial issues. Yet their very first stop, at Guideline A–1, was to embroil the commission in what would be measurably the longest, probably the most heated, and surely the most unexpected debate of the entire meeting.

Before any of that occurred, however, A–1 was to play another familiar role—as the catalyst for one more discussion of commission powers and of the semantics which should be used to convey them. Leroy Collins had theoretically settled this matter, with "calls upon" and "urges." But Collins was no longer present to defend his handiwork; Eli Segal knew that Collins would not be present; and Segal had laid the groundwork for a return to the original "requires" and "recommends": "Leroy Collins got everything screwed up with urges and calls upon. I slipped that through with only recommends and re-quires for the final Commission meeting."

After the September meeting, Collins had gone back to Florida and had tendered his resignation from the Party Structure Commission, citing business opportunities which demanded his complete attention. With Collins out of the way, Segal and Bode had gone back to their concern with activating language and had designed a set of maneuvers to cancel Collins's earlier contribution. First, they had written the memo on guideline verbs, which had been sent to all commissioners in advance of the November meeting.[1] Then, they had alerted their personal allies on the commission to the "fact" that this issue would surely rise again, and they had urged these commissioners to speak up immediately when it did. Last, with their troops in line, they had notified Chairman McGovern that "several members" would predictably insist on discussing the question one more time:

> The definition of these terms is the most important single decision the Commission faces. Almost all of the respondents recognize this, the staff agrees, as does the writing press. We have ideas on each of these terms which we should discuss with you. For the time being, you should be made aware that several members of the Commission are unhappy with the sloppy way in which the Commission addressed these questions at the last meeting; these members, among other things, plan to reintroduce the word "requires" into the discussion.[2]

The course of the politics of implementation would affirm that the definition of these terms was *not* one of the more consequential decisions which the commission ultimately faced. Yet the issue did indirectly reflect several central features of the politics of recommendation, both retrospective and prospective. The issue had originated in a fear by many commissioners that their operation had somehow gotten beyond their control and was about to plunge them, personally, into extended conflict with the regular party. While they would fail to perceive any number of institutional implications in the text of their proposed guidelines, implications which were far more likely to create this conflict than was the difference between "requires" and "calls upon," they did insist on manipulating guideline verbs to avoid this conflict if possible. Their success in this insistence, then, only underscored the reality of influence within the commission, since the staff was about to overturn one of the few conscious initiatives from the commissioners and substitute the original preference of militant staff members.

On the morning of November 19, in his carefully considered introductory remarks about Guideline A–1, Eli Segal complained that the guideline was inherently ambiguous because the phrase "calls upon" could not, in principle, be given any real precision. His comments produced a short exchange with Will Davis and Aaron Henry, not so much over specific wording as over the right of the commission to discuss "mandating" anything. By November 19, however, some of the commissioners were sitting through this debate for the third time, and there was comparatively little left to say. As a result, the topic of commission authority was not so much resolved as allowed to drop. Chairman McGovern suggested that the commission adopt the linguistic conventions in Segal's memo of November 12. No one objected. And the commissioners as a body moved into the substance of their antidiscrimination guidelines, A–1 and A–2.

The commissioners moved, as well, into the largest surprise in their final drafting session. The commission staff arrived at their meeting prepared to do battle in several areas—the activating language for the guidelines as a group, the issue of proportional representation, the question of intrastate apportionment. Yet even they arrived in the belief that the content of Guideline A–1 (Discrimination on the Basis of Race, Color, Creed, or National Origin) had been effectively resolved.

To this point, the staff had been able to shape at least the context for every major commission debate; this time, staff members were prepared to pitch their battle around formal proportional representation. They were to discover, instead, that *demographic* representation was the central issue of the November sessions not just because of the substance, length, and emotionalism of its debate but because of the way in which its resolution would color subsequent commission decisions, including the one on proportionality.

The key sections of Guideline A–1, as they entered the meeting, were familiar to most commissioners:

> To supplement the requirements of the 1964 and 1968 Conventions, the Commission:
>
> 1. Recommends that State Parties add the six basic elements of the Special Equal Rights Committee to their Party rules and take appropriate steps to secure their implementation;
>
> 2. Recommends that State Parties overcome the effects of past discrimination by affirmative steps to encourage minority group participation (e.g., specifically inviting black Democrats to attend Party meetings).[3]

Three separate alterations—from the staff, from Austin Ranney, and from Birch Bayh—were to rework this text substantially. The first occasioned little comment. Eli Segal reported that many mailback respondents had asked that subsections one and two be required, not merely recommended. The commissioners had no objection.

The second amendment, proposed by Austin Ranney, professor of political science at the University of Wisconsin and former editor of the *American Political Science Review,* represented a more sizable change. Ranney opined that a simple switch from "recommends" to "requires" was insufficient and that his colleagues ought to demand not mere steps, but results. McGovern tried to slip past the notion, by suggesting that the matter had been addressed at the September meeting, but Ranney, who had been absent, refused to be bypassed:

> *Ranney:* Our fellow black Democrats feel that something more is needed than a no-discrimination rule. I want to suggest that the Commission add a clause to A–1 in which we at the very least urge that the state party organizations make every effort to see that there be included as members of the delegation adequate, fair, whatever the word may be, representation of minority groups in the population.
> *McGovern:* I should advise you, Professor Ranney, that we discussed this matter at some length at the September meeting. The Commission, as I recall, unanimously decided after some discussion that it was not feasible to go on record for a quota system.
> *Ranney:* I don't think we could "require," because that would mean quotas, but we would like to "urge" that members of minority groups be adequately, fairly, whatever adjective you want to use, represented in the personnel of the delegation.[4]

The staff, remaining more concerned with proportional representation, did not immediately seize upon the Ranney proposal. Instead, it came back with language which followed McGovern's lead: "We urge that State Parties make every effort to secure adequate representation of minority groups."[5] The commissioners, however, buffeted this provision from both sides. Dutton and Henry, who admired the quotalike aspects of Ranney's suggestion, fell to arguing about the proper numerical base for assessing compliance; Davis and Mitchell, who were repelled by the quota possibility, focused on securing a specific, restrained translation of "adequate." After a bit, McGovern made another, unsuccessful effort to subsume the entire argument:

> *McGovern:* I must say I find it hard to understand where this proposal has much concrete meaning unless we're talking about a quota system. Now perhaps, it's the kind of thing that has to be left that way, but really, in concrete form, it's one of two things: Either we're talking about a quota system with some kind of formula, or we're simply stating a moral principle.
> *Ranney:* I think you are essentially right, except that you shouldn't assume that

a statement of moral principle doesn't mean anything. I would like to move that we urge state parties to make every effort to assure adequate representation of members of minority groups in the delegate selection process.

Shortly after that, Birch E. Bayh, Jr., Senator from Indiana, brought the third and crucial amendment into the discussion, by attempting to strengthen Ranney's proposal:

> *Bayh:* Certainly we could take the professor's motion as verbalized by the staff, and add two or three words to sort of give guidelines saying that to meet this requirement, that there should be some *reasonable relationship* between the representation of delegates and representation of the minority group to the population of the state in question. This doesn't "require," it doesn't make it absolute, and I don't think it should. But it sort of gives a guideline so that those who are in the process of setting up slates can realize, well, that we do have to shoot for this target. And I think if we don't do that, we're really being very moral, but we're not really putting the emphasis behind how we make that morality reality.

Sam Beer immediately tried to finesse Bayh through new language ostensibly incorporating both Ranney's and Bayh's suggestions:

> *Beer:* We're talking about overcoming the effects of past discrimination, and that's what we're really getting at. We're not talking for quotas here. So I would suggest that we add so that it reads: The Commission requires that state parties overcome the effects of past discrimination by affirmative steps to encourage minority group participation, including representation on delegations to the National Convention.

Bayh, however, was not pacified, and reamended Beer's motion with the phrase "in reasonable relationship to their appearance in the state's population as a whole."[6] Thereafter, the Bayh amendment would be the crux of Guideline A–1.

That Bayh should be the proponent of this "reasonable relationship" language, rather than the black members, the leadership, or the aggressive reformers, came as a surprise to many commissioners. The Indiana senator, after a vigorous effort to get on the commission, had been nearly inactive in its subsequent affairs and would be present for only a short time after the debate on A–1 and A–2. Fred Dutton, however, who was to play a more influential role in adapting the Bayh amendment to Guideline A–2 than its author would play in working it into A–1, admitted no surprise:

> There were a number of people on that Commission who were trying to get some political mileage out of being on it. McGovern and Hughes obviously, since

both were heavily identified with the reform issue, but also Bayh, who I wouldn't have even thought would want to be on it, although he very much did, and Stevenson, who kept trying to do reform things which he could point to with pride, without getting tarred by other reform things that would not go down well at home.

Bayh's exact phraseology—"reasonable relationship to their appearance in the state's population as a whole"—had actually been formulated by Dick Wade, commission consultant:

> I gave Bayh the "reasonable relationship" language. I was worried about the blacks. There had been an earlier argument pushing percentage in the national Democratic vote instead; I was for that. The argument in the Executive Committee had broken this out on the basis of opposing quotas. "Reasonable" was my word to get around quotas. Yet you knew when you sat there that sooner or later someone would have to say what was "reasonable."

After Bayh had tacked this language onto Beer's version of the guideline, debate came to focus on two basic questions: Would this inevitably imply demographic quotas? How would that mesh with the main commission thrust toward participation and openness? The first concern—the possible presence of an incipient quota system—surfaced repeatedly:

> *Davis:* I like the word "reasonable" much better than "adequate," if you want my viewpoint, because it implies reasonable efforts, and "adequate" is a mathematical sort of thing . . . .
> *Beer* (interrupts): If you talk about "reasonable relationship" to numbers in the population, I don't see how it can mean anything but a quota. If you want to vote on that, than I'll vote on it, but if you don't want that, then we can still say something meaningful by adopting my suggestion.

The second concern—the potential conflict between a fixed target and an open process—bothered even some of the reformers. Proponents asserted that the party would remain practically closed if this language was not adopted; opponents argued that it would be artificially closed if it was, because every state party would be commanded to rig the result:

> *Henry:* I would like to say that we aren't talking about quotas. I suggest that those who are not willing to drive for the inclusion of various groups within the party apparatus are the ones who are trying to defeat such a move by the innocuous [sic] term, quota, that we have already agreed would not be.
> *Davis:* But you can't deny that with Bayh's language, you've got to look at the percentages, and say, "Okay, we've got to have so many of this group, and so many of that group."
> *Bayh:* I'm willing to concede that in the structuring of a delegation to meet this

requirement, that whoever's doing it, our leaders who are doing it in each state, are going to crank that information into their own thought process.

Davis: Let's say that a white would want to seek an office, to seek to be a delegate. Who's going to tell him, "No, you can't seek that office, because if you are elected, that would throw our quota system out of alignment." So you delete his chance to participate. You say, "Okay, you can't run. We're going to have to get a black to run against that black, a Mexican to run against a Mexican, so regardless of who wins, we still maintain our little quota system."

In a last attempt to head all this off, Beer drove his motion to a vote. McGovern noted that this would be only the first of a series of ballots and that it could be further amended. He then called the roll. On Beer's language—"requires that state parties overcome the effects of past discrimination by affirmative steps to encourage minority group participation, including representation on the national convention delegation"—the commission voted 17 yes and 2 no. Only Davis and Hughes dissented, the former because he found the resolution too strong, the latter because he found it too weak. Bayh then reoffered *his* amendment, and the ensuing vote was the closest of any at the final sessions. When the last name was called, however, the amendment had squeaked by, 10 yes and 9 no.

Guideline A–2, which the staff read to the group as soon as the tally on A–1 was completed, had a very different history from Guideline A–1. Nevertheless, the outcome of the vote on A–1 raised immediate questions for A–2 as well. Until September 11, there had been no guideline for Discrimination on the Basis of Age and Sex, but only an occasional suggestion that youth or gender (or income, age, and so forth) be added to A–1. At the meeting of the Executive Committee on September 11, Fred Dutton had convinced his colleagues to make women and youth the explicit subject of a regulation, and Guideline A–2 had been born. At the meeting of the full commission on September 23, the members had been unbothered either by the creation of this new stricture or by the fact that it was significantly weaker than its counterpart, Guideline A–1.

On the morning of November 19, then, A–1 had begun by asking specifically for "affirmative steps," while A–2 still commanded its readers merely to end "all vestiges of discrimination."[7] This difference in coercive status, however, was considerably widened through the Bayh amendment, and extension of the new "reasonable relationship" wording thus became the central question for the disposition of Guideline A–2. One potential answer was not long in arriving:

Dutton: I would say that, in connection with this proposal, we ought to consider whether or not we shouldn't also represent and write some sort of adequate or fair representation for young people and for women as for ethnic groups. I just don't see how we can separate out one from two.

Shortly after this, Chairman McGovern tried, once more, to rein the notion in, by commenting on the extent of the change which this would represent. In return, Dutton merely affirmed his willingness to expand the proposal even further, to any groups which the commissioners might designate. His response, in effect, guaranteed that the matter would be driven to a vote, and not just to some intermediate understanding.

Opponents of a "reasonable relationship" provision for Guideline A–2 found themselves in a nearly untenable position. Having lost the parallel vote on A–1, they had to draw the distinction between blacks, as a social group, and women and youth—without losing partisans of the latter. Ranney, already regretting his contribution to Guideline A–1, reversed his field for Guideline A–2, accepted the evidently delicate assignment of differentiating blacks from women and youth, and tried to put the cat back in the bag:

> *Ranney:* I think you must draw a distinction between the problem as it relates to racial minorities and to women and youth. The whole historical pattern of discrimination is simply, basically, very different.

In their efforts to stave off extension of the "reasonable relationship" clause, opponents hit hard, first, at the inconsistency of such a proposal with the over-all thrust of commission proposals, and second, at the impact which such a provision might have on implementation of the total reform package. Beer limned the argument about inconsistency:

> *Beer:* The job of this Commission is to eliminate discrimination, not tell the voters who they have to select as their representatives.

Mitchell raised the prospects for implementation, predicting futility for everything the commission might propose if it insisted on attaching this particular provision to Guideline A–2:

> *Mitchell:* If the Commission adopts quotas for racial groups, women, and young people, I think we are going to undermine the rest of the report, because it's just going to look ridiculous. And I think that's very serious. . . .

After these arguments had been produced, elaborated, and pushed back and forth, McGovern moved to bring the discussion to some resolution. In doing so, he tried to substitute a scaled-down version of the original Dutton motion:

McGovern: Let's have a compromise here, just looking at this thing pragmatically, and keeping in mind that in our last Convention only 13 percent of the delegates were women and a much smaller percentage under thirty. If we could adopt or consider the language that's been put before us and proposed, but in this case as distinct from Guideline One, adopt the word "urges" rather than "requires." I say this simply because I can see that there is going to be an enormous problem in many states with long traditions . . .

Mitchell (interrupts): All right, George, I'll go along with it, although I think it's bad politics.

McGovern: Well, I'm concerned about bad politics, but I just wonder, as a pragmatic matter, if we're not being more reasonable about it to use the word "urge" rather than "require." There's no point of us adopting something that's going to lay on the shelf.

McGovern heard a little more discussion and began to call the question. He was never to complete his sentence. Katherine Peden, former secretary of commerce for Kentucky and defeated candidate for U.S. Senate, cut him off in a highly peremptory fashion and reprimanded him sharply for changing the thrust of Dutton's idea:

McGovern: Well, subject to that modification, then, those in favor of Mr. Dutton's motion that we use the same language that we did with reference to the ethnic groups, those in favor will say . . . .

Peden (interrupts). I realize that you've called for the question, but as a matter of principle, before we take the vote moving from "require" to "urge," we all need to look at the make-up of this Commission. Only 11 percent are women, only one person is under thirty years of age, less than 10 percent are black, *on this Commission.* This morning The *Washington Post* quoted Elly Peterson, the Assistant Chairman of the Republican National Committee, pointing out the position that women were in political office now. That in 1959, there were 18,000 women serving in county elected positions, but by actual count in 1969 she found the number to be 3,862. That with these facts in mind—and I realize that it's a matter where we are going to be striving for things, and as Senator Bayh said, it's more a thing where we're going to require as much as we can, and we'll urge—but I think for us to back down, for this Commission to back down on the position of women in the Democratic Party would be just as substantial a mistake as we would make if we had backed down on race, creed, or national origin.

McGovern: Katherine, I want to make my position clear. I didn't think that I was proposing a back-down. I thought I was suggesting something that might get a majority here. I have no problem voting for the strongest possible language, and if the Commission prefers to have the motion worded in some other way, I'm just raising a possibility here, not offering a motion.

The chairman declined to finish his introduction to the vote—which had gone well beyond being a "possibility"—and an involved colloquy developed among Bayh, Beer, Davis, Dutton, Henry, Knox, and Ranney, with each getting in a few additional licks before another motion could be called. Eventually, the original Dutton proposal became the question of record:

> *Segal:* . . . Furthermore, the Commission requires that State Parties overcome the effects of past discrimination by affirmative steps to encourage representation and participation of young people and women in the National Convention delegation, representation which will bear some reasonable relationship to the group's presence in the population of the state. Young people are defined as all people under the age of thirty.

The motion passed comfortably, 13 yes and 7 no. Five switchers explained its ease of passage. Peden and Warschaw, the two women who had voted against the Bayh amendment on Guideline A–1, voted for it on A–2. Hughes, who had voted no to protest the lack of even stronger wording when A–1 was before the group, rejoined the strong-language advocates for Guideline A–2. McGovern, who did not vote on A–1 and who had been developing more conciliatory phrasing on A–2 until he was chastised for timidity, then moved to demonstrate his personal resolve by going with the more extreme, substitute motion—and recording his vote. The lone switch in the other direction was by Ranney, who already saw his contribution to the Bayh amendment as unfortunate and who deemed that amendment even more inappropriate when transferred to Guideline A–2. Had previous lines held, this shift by Ranney would have been decisive. They did not, and the commission moved farther down the road to which Guideline A–1 pointed—whatever its ultimate terminus.

After the vote, the commissioners repaired to the Senate Dining Room for lunch, where the prime topic of conversation was the general outcome on A–1 and A–2 and the specific question of whether it implied demographic quotas. Those who were convinced that it did, Beer among them, pressed that case upon McGovern, urging him to move for reconsideration: "I got after McGovern over lunch. I said, You know that we have quotas. You've got to do something about them. But he didn't." Perhaps mindful of his public scolding before the vote on A–2, McGovern was unwilling to ask for reconsideration. What he was willing to do was to suggest a clarifying footnote, to the effect that "it is the understanding of the Commission that this is not to be accomplished by the mandatory imposition of quotas."[8] The footnote was intended for both A–1 and A–2; the chairman introduced it as soon as the commission reassembled.

McGovern's action provoked a short but lively debate. Hughes responded that the "reasonable representation" language was indeed a quota and should stay that way, without the footnote. Rampton countered that it was *not* a quota and should stay *that* way, with a footnoted guarantee. Ranney suggested that it *was* a quota, and averred that there was little point in adding a footnote to deny the obvious. Dutton, finally, asserted that it was *not* a quota, so that it mattered little whether it was further footnoted or not. Rampton then moved adoption of McGovern's codicil, and it passed on a voice vote.

The remainder of the "A" guidelines were a welcome respite from this level of conflict and confusion.[9] Both the staff and the commissioners were in favor of liberalized procedures for voter enrollment, the subject of Guideline A–3 (Voter Registration). Neither staff nor commissioners were much engaged by the subject, however, and they ratified it quickly. In preparation for the November meeting, Segal and Bode had redrafted Guideline A–4 (Costs and Fees/Petition Requirements) to provide a definition of "excessive" costs and "burdensome" requirements. The commissioners struck one sentence in this redraft and adopted five revised paragraphs unanimously. With Guideline A–5 (Existence of Party Rules), the staff had also done a new text, enumerating the items to be covered by published rules and restricting the rural exemption which the commissioners had added at their last meeting. Both changes were adopted without debate.

While there would, in fact, be two major battlefields at the end of the "B" guidelines, the bulk of these standards were noncontroversial, too. As a result, the immediate significance of the guidelines from A–3 to A–5 and B–1 to B–5 for the politics of party reform lay in their implicit comment on the drafting process. In only two of these guidelines did the commissioners make a substantive—a noneditorial—adjustment. Overall, then, it was the staff which created these regulations. It was the staff which had the satisfaction of seeing them adopted roughly as created. It was even the staff which contributed the larger share of the adjustments between creation and adoption, through its intervening drafts.

The substance of the noncontroversial "B" guidelines was quickly addressed. B–1 (Proxy Voting) banned all proxies in delegate selection. B–2 (Clarity of Purpose) insisted on a separable process for delegate selection, where this had previously been mixed with other party business. B–3 (Quorum Provisions) set the minimum attendance for action by state central committees. And B–4 (Selection of Alternates; Filling of Vacancies) confirmed that the other guidelines applied to these designations, too, and not just to the initial choice of the front-line delegation.

Guideline B–5 (Unit Rule) had previously served as the jumping-off point for a major debate about proportional representation. But having agreed in September to treat this guideline as a ban on binding delegates against their conscience, rather than as a backdoor requirement of proportionality, the commissioners were not tempted to wander off into extraneous debate. B–5 was, however, the occasion for the first of two meandering, inconclusive discussions of "favorite son" candidacies, those arrangements by which purely local champions entered the delegate selection contest to unite and preserve a state delegation for subsequent bargaining.

Vice Chairman Hughes spoke strongly in favor of prohibiting these candidacies and closed by suggesting that Guideline B–5 had already done so. No one disputed Hughes, there were general murmurs of assent, and the members moved on to their next item. The same discussion would resurface when C–1 (Adequate Public Notice) came under review on Friday the twentieth, but Chairman McGovern would cut this short by noting that the group had previously handled the issue, presumably through B–5. Ultimately, in the absence of any formal language, the staff would simply provide a footnote in the published report, asserting that "it is the understanding of the Commission that the prohibition on instructed delegates applies to favorite-son candidates as well."[10]

When the commissioners arrived at Guideline B–6 (Adequate Representation of Minority Views), they faced the possibility of another extended debate. In September, they had devoted hours to this one guideline, without reaching consensus. For November 19, they had earmarked the heart of the afternoon for the same debate, so that they could argue into the dinner hour if need be.

All such precautions proved unnecessary. Perhaps because the commissioners had already held one lengthy and emotional argument on the 19th, perhaps because they had already sat through such a debate on proportionality in late September, or perhaps because nearly everyone's position had hardened, there was little sentiment for a prolonged brawl. Fred Dutton remained ready to take on all comers over the folly of banning winner-take-all primaries; few were any longer interested in meeting his challenge, at least point by point. Moreover, Alex Bickel, commission consultant, had begun shaping an alternative in his written analysis to which a clear majority of commissioners could subscribe.[11] There was, arguably, little room left for maneuver.

The major protagonists were unchanged. The commission staff cared intensely about proportionality, which was second only to participation in its canon, and Bode, Segal, and Wexler provided the principal energy for the reform side. Hughes, Knox, and Mixner backed them consistently; Beer offered more restrained support. Bode came prepared to fight:

> Proportionality came out of the Connecticut challenge of 1968, when John
> Bailey would not give the McCarthy people their fair share. It was something

the staff wanted very, very much. We lobbied our asses off. The *debate* was never districting versus winner-take-all. It was always real p.r.

From the other side, Dutton was still the leading antagonist, with active assistance from Christopher and Warschaw, fellow Californians, and more general reinforcement from Davis and Rampton. Dutton was fully the equal, at least in adamancy, of the commission staff:

> The original staff recommendation was against the winner-take-all primary. My own experience was with the California primary, and there was some truth to the California chauvinism charge. But I still believe that you have to make the stakes high enough to bring people into the fight. Then, too, I'm not interested in moving from one form of backroom process, with the labor and party guys, to a new backroom process, with the super-activists, the intellectuals, and the professors.
>
> This was just one example. I'm terribly concerned about the whole reform thrust. We may have gotten to the point where we are separating the society from the political process. We may be boring or alienating people instead. How do you involve people? How do you keep the society integrated?

The issues, too, remained much the same. Supporters of proportional representation still argued for its abstract fairness, and for the practical virtue of convincing everyone that he had gotten a fair shake. Winner-take-all partisans still countered with the notion that their arrangement heightened public interest, attracted the serious candidates, and kept the nomination in the hands of the voter. The crucial new element, of course, was the prior commission response to Guidelines A–1 and A–2.

To the extent that the new "reasonable relationship" language required demographically balanced slates of delegates, it provided an additional, powerful argument against formal proportionality. Or at least, the more fully the grass-roots participants could register their *political* wishes, and the more directly they could select their *individual* representatives, the less likely these delegates were to conform to a demographic mix endorsed by national reformers. Winner-take-all regulations, at the other extreme, possessed the undeniable "advantage" of requiring delegates slates. The associated slate-makers could then guarantee any given demographic outcome. Beer, who cared a great deal more about political than demographic representation, was dismayed that the commission had been pressed away from his preferences by its morning decisions:

> I felt that there should be some very strong language on p.r. By that time, we were all worn out. That ended up being gone over very fast. The big fight had been on quotas. Personally, I wanted something done so that these people would feel that they had had their say. But once Dutton had those quotas, he

more and more saw the advantage for his California thing. At lunch, after the quota debate, I said to him, "Well, Fred, you've gotten your way on quotas. I hope now you'll go with us on p.r." But he didn't.

The essence of Guideline B–6 as drafted was a requirement of formal proportional representation from the first stage of delegate selection to the floor of the national convention. When the Executive Committee and then the full commission had been unable to reach agreement on this or any other text, however, the task of spelling out the alternatives had been assigned to Alex Bickel. Bickel responded with five separate "propositions," at five different points on the continuum between uncritical endorsement of winner-take-all and complete acceptance of proportional representation. These propositions effectively replaced the staff draft as the starting point for commission discussion on November 19.

While Bickel's text was to provide the basis for the November debate, the author himself would not figure in it. Bickel could not get to Washington before the morning of the twentieth, and Chairman McGovern, after gaveling the Thursday session to order, had proposed that the agenda be altered. The presentations by Bickel on proportionality and Dick Wade on apportionment could be reversed, he suggested, so that the commission would benefit from the wisdom of both men. Dutton, who expected to miss the *second* day, had taken vigorous exception, arguing that many commissioners had geared their attendance to the announced schedule. The chairman had withdrawn his suggestion, and Dutton had won the first skirmish of the battle of Guideline B–6.

Later Thursday afternoon, the commission began by examining Proposition I in the Bickel text—that the principle of statewide majority rule be endorsed, for use with the proper safeguards, at the discretion of the individual states. While there was never any chance that this would become commission policy, its appearance did produce the usual argument over whether the commission had any business addressing the issue. Dutton again asserted that it did not, since the question of winner-take-all rules had been before the National Convention numerous times and had always met the same supportive response. McGovern conceded that there were grounds for finding a lack of jurisdiction, but he ruled that the commissioners should vote. On what was thus the first ballot of the proportionality debate—Should the commission consider the *issue* of proportional representation?—the ayes triumphed solidly, 12 to 5. Davis, Dutton, English, Rampton, and Warschaw dissented. Everyone else voted to go on.

Alex Bickel had told the chairman that his own preference was Proposition

III—that the commission "recommend" that state parties adopt proportionality immediately, that it "recommend" that the 1972 Convention "require" proportionality thereafter, but that it not "require" such a basic change, which had undergone such limited scrutiny, on its own. McGovern noted Bickel's view, George Mitchell spoke on its behalf, and it became the main reference point for subsequent arguments.

Those arguments, however, were hardly constrained by the appearance of Proposition III, and debate continued for some time. Dutton, Mitchell, Mixner, and Ranney exchanged opinions about the effect of the two allocation systems, proportionality and winner-take-all, on voter interest and participation. Beer, Davis, Mixner, and Rampton traded judgments on the right of highly popular individuals to be selected as delegates, regardless of the division of the presidential preference vote. Christopher, Dutton, and Ranney argued over the practical distinctions between primary and convention systems, as they affected delegate allocation.

After all that, Mitchell began the process of refining some operational language, by turning Proposition III into a formal motion. Mitchell's proposal did appear to occupy the middle ground within the Party Structure Commission, and after some additional discussion, McGovern asked that someone call the question, noting that this proposal could serve as the baseline for further amendments. Dutton, however, temporarily blocked confirmation of its majority status by offering an alternative of his own, affirming majority rule in primary states.

The tally on Dutton's alternative, disregarding absentees, was the exact converse of the vote on whether the commission should consider proportional representation at all. As such, it met with a decisive defeat, 5 yes and 11 no. The vote also indicated that lines on the issue were sharply drawn, and were probably immune to additional argument. A majority of the eleven negatives would in all likelihood get to draft the substance of B–6, unless some unforeseen subissue split them.

With the defeat of the Dutton amendment, Mitchell restated his motion, but with a twist: He proposed that *direct election of delegates by district*, along with formal proportional representation, be recognized as sufficient means of insuring some presence of minority political views. Districted election was logically a form of proportionality, but it was also, structurally, a real step back from an explicit mathematical formula. Mitchell had thus shifted the focus of commission debate from Bickel's text to his own. He had found an even more moderate way to move toward proportionality. In doing so, he had found a way to consolidate his position in the center of the votes which would determine the outcome.

rambled off in various directions. While the commissioners would thereafter pursue no coherent sequence, their conversation did return continually to three general questions:

1. What was the *fairest formula* for delegate apportionment?
2. What was the *proper scope* for this fairest formula?
3. What was the *practical effect* of a formula with this content and scope?

Because these three questions—the proper content, scope, and impact of any formula—overlapped but did not duplicate, they led the commissioners continually from point to point, without conducing toward substantive agreement. The first tentative move toward a resolution came from George Mitchell, but Mitchell left his motion open to debate and the floor was eventually gained by John English, who called the question on his own proposal:

> *English:* I move that the Commission require state parties to apportion their delegations to the national convention on the basis of representation which reflects the Democratic vote in the last presidential election.

The tally on this suggested text was 8 yes and 6 no. A majority had gone with English; the commission had apparently resolved the issue. But before Chairman McGovern could move on, Katherine Peden asked to be recognized and to have her opposition to the successful resolution, along with her reasons for dissent, written into the record. She was less forceful than she had been in silencing McGovern on Guideline A–2 the previous morning; she was about to gain a second substantial revision nevertheless:

> *Peden:* Just for the record, because Mr. English was recognized before I was, I wanted to amend the Mitchell motion to include the vote for senatorial and congressional candidates in the last election. You've just handicapped 60,000 people that voted for a Democratic nominee for the United States Senate in Kentucky, who didn't vote for the Democratic presidential nominee. I ran 60,000 ahead of Humphrey/Muskie, and I think they were loyal Democrats, and I think that frankly, in my state, there's going to be resentment that—I stood straight for the Democratic party, after all—and I think that as a matter of record Kentuckians will resent the fact that this standing by the Democratic candidate for United States Senate is not going to have some influence in the way their vote is apportioned. Just for the record.

Peden's comments were not intended to do more than dissociate her from the outcome. But Harold Hughes, who had also run ahead of the national ticket, took the opportunity to agree with her. Bill Dodds, who had arrived just before the vote and who had been deliberately queried by Chairman

McGovern to see if he understood the issue, then asked for additional discussion.

The commission returned to the major issues on which it had already touched—the proper base (or bases) for apportionment, the proper scope of the resulting formula, and the practical impact of this formula and its alternatives. After these themes had re-emerged, Dick Wade threw out an idea destined to move the commission away from its first solution:

> *Wade:* You know, we could do what the DNC has done in the past on interstate apportionment. We could use a combination of population and presidential vote. That would lead from your strength by rewarding voting Democrats, but also would allow you to reach for new constituencies, in the suburbs for example.

In response, Dodds moved formally to reconsider. Although his motion seemed to have passed on a voice vote, the nays were assertive in their displeasure, and a roll call was taken. The result was a 10 to 5 majority for setting aside English's version of Guideline B–7, with Christopher, Dodds, and Hughes switching sides.

The vote on reconsideration did not produce an immediate counterproposal, and discussion continued. After a short while, Wade offered a new compromise, a blend of presidential vote, gubernatorial vote, and population. Before anyone could convert Wade's suggestion into a motion, Mixner attempted to cut off debate with a different combination, and Peden moved to void Mixner by substituting her own amalgam. Peden's text, and then Mixner's, each failed on a voice vote, after which Warren Christopher found the key:

> *Christopher:* The Commission requires an apportionment formula to be based on a mandatory combination of straight population and Democratic vote in the last presidential election, with the provision that there can be no apportionment based on pure geography.

This language sailed through, minus only those commissioners who had voted against the motion to reconsider. The group had thus affirmed a second version of B–7, by a ballot of 9 to 5.

Even then, debate was not finished. Mitchell immediately questioned the scope of the new formula, whether it covered only the final stage of delegate selection or reached all the way to the precinct. Ranney proposed that this arrangement be confined to the "top level" of the selection process. Ranney's motion passed by a vote of 9 to 4. Even *that* did not terminate debate. Segal came back on the attack and asked whether, in convention states, this applied to the national delegation, to the state convention which picked the national delegation, to any district conventions which also selected national delegates, or to any lower conventions which selected delegates to an authoritative state convention. The commission launched back into debate, with most commissioners restating previous positions.[13] Finally, Christopher again offered the clarifying proposition:

> *Christopher:* In convention or committee systems, this Commission requires the body actually selecting the delegates to be based upon an apportionment formula based on population or some measure of Democratic strength.

This recommendation received unanimous approval, the commission had apparently dispatched the issue of apportionment, and the commissioners turned to the question of lunch.

From time to time, the commissioners had considered a second type of apportionment, involving the share of a state delegation which should be selected at each level of the process. There was not a great deal of debate on the issue, since most commissioners seemed tacitly to accept Mitchell's suggestion of a maximum of 25 percent at large and a minimum of 75 percent from districts. Nevertheless, the debate on other aspects of apportionment had so overshadowed this question that the commission never adopted a provision addressing it.

The staff was not inclined to let the matter pass, because staff members viewed it as one more way to regain territory lost in the fight over proportionality. Such a rule would at least prevent *convention states* from selecting all their delegates at large, and hence winner-take-all. Accordingly, apportionment by level became one more item on which the staff, before publication of the final report, simply added language converting an earlier suggestion into an eventual party rule.[14]

A second, more substantial, and undeniably independent revision of Guideline B–7 was also contributed by the staff. In answer to a question from Ranney, Christopher had confirmed that "the motion before us relates solely to the convention or committee that chooses the national delegates."[15] In transferring this provision into the final document, however, the staff rendered it as "the Commission requires State Parties to adopt an apportionment formula *for each body actually selecting delegates to State, district, and county conventions* which is based upon population and/or some measure of Democratic strength."[16] (Italics added.) In the process, they created an additional apportionment formula and applied it to *all* levels below the top.

When the members returned from lunch, they still faced the entire list of seven "C" guidelines. While the *staff* regarded all seven as noncontroversial, there was no guarantee that the commissioners would share this view. At a minimum, they had virtually no acquaintance with this part of their report, so that section "C" would surely require as much attention as its earlier, non-conflictual counterparts. Beyond that, the "C" guidelines, by virtue of their unexamined status, had the potential for hiding another explosive standard. By Friday afternoon, on the other hand, there was a major, new factor working against any such explosion—time itself. The commissioners were in the final part of what had been an unstinting two-day session. They had already covered twelve guidelines and had endured intense debate on four. They were just returning from one such argument, on apportionment.

In the interplay between these opposing influences, all but the last of the "C" guidelines were to move expeditiously through the commission. This would not mean, in contrast to the lesser "A" and "B" guidelines, that they drew no serious attention. Some would even create a clear division. But none would slow the commission appreciably. Yet despite a general exhaustion, the very last, Guideline C–6 (Slate Making), was to generate an extended argument, one ranking just below demographics, proportionality, and apportionment in length, convolution, and intensity.

While none of the guidelines preceding C–6 produced substantial controversy, all reflected a major theme in reform politics, the appropriate role of the regular party. Several emphasized a second theme as well, participation and participatory arrangements for delegate selection. As a result, their treatment by the commissioners, and hence the treatment of both of these themes, still commented implicitly but powerfully upon the nature of reform politics.

The bulk of the text for Guideline C–1 (Adequate Public Notice) concerned detailed strictures on convention states. But the political heart of the guideline lay in a stiffly worded provision on what adequate public notice should mean in presidential primaries or in state committee selections. The staff wanted every contender for a delegate slot in a primary, and every candidate for state committee if that committee would select any delegates, to put either a presidential preference or the word "uncommitted" beside that person's name on the ballot.

Both institutional impacts of this provision, on presidential primaries and on state committee selections, disturbed some commissioners. But they were unable to generate much discussion, perhaps because their colleagues were still unwinding from the morning session or perhaps, as Bob Nelson, the staff director, thought, because opponents were badly outnumbered:

> Presidential preference was not much of a matter of debate. The thing that would be wrong with it would be to force your party leaders out of the process;

you were taking flexibility out of the system. That argument was rejected; the purist theory won out. You could line up the people with experience in campaigns against the rest on this—Davis, Mitchell, English.

Lining up the people with experience in state party affairs did, in fact, produce a very short line. A few of their commission colleagues argued that state party leaders would always be selected anyway, but most failed to see any reason to anguish over the presence or absence of state and local party officialdom.

This same general orientation—indifference or even hostility to the role of party officials—characterized both the draft of C–2 (Automatic Delegates) and the response of the commissioners to it. Guideline C–1 had been calculated to make life more difficult for those regular party leaders who had always been forced to compete for seats at the national convention; C–2 was intended to guarantee that all such leaders would indeed have to compete. In essence, it removed various party and public officeholders from previously automatic positions at local and state conventions, by barring ex officio delegates. A unanimous voice vote affirmed that essence.

The staff had actually proposed extending this prohibition all the way to the National Committee, via a special guideline barring committee members from the seats which the 1964 Convention had awarded to them. Here, however, the commissioners decided to duck, and this proposal became the one draft guideline which was deleted entirely. Mitchell argued that the guideline was impolitic, because it affronted the one body whose support would be crucial to implementation. Davis argued that it was superfluous, since other guidelines effectively handled its substance. Only Mixner, the antiwar activist, put serious energy into the opposing arguments, and Nelson watched the guideline fall gradually of its own weight:

> There was one guideline that got dropped along the way. It related to the National Committee. Too few people felt that it was in the mandate. Its impact was covered by other guidelines, and it would have been an insult to the DNC. Even then, I was surprised that it failed: There was much more enmity toward the DNC than toward the Republicans among the reformers.

The lone guideline concerned with orthodox partisanship, and perhaps the lone guideline following the organized and disciplined theory of party reform, was C–3 (Open and Closed Processes). The purpose of the guideline was to protect reformed nomination arrangements from manipulation by non-Democrats, while insuring that anyone who wanted to *join* the party could still do so. The draft which Bode and Segal had used to prime the commissioners for the November meeting offered the tough approach to this goal:

> The Commission calls upon State Parties to provide for a party enrollment provision that (1) assures identification of the party membership of each voter, (2) facilitates the enrollment as Democrats of unaffiliated voters and members of other parties, and (3) allows that a voter may participate in the delegate selection process of only one party.[17]

Immediately below this, however, the two staffers had flagged the option of moderating their draft, and when the guideline reached the commission floor, Austin Ranney leapfrogged over this staff suggestion and led the fight for an even weaker variant. Ranney offered a motion to take the original text of C–3 *before* its pre-November toughening, to strike the demand for a procedure which "assures identification of the party membership of each voter," and to make even the remaining language "urged" rather than "required." Only Warschaw spoke insistently against Ranney's proposal, upbraiding her colleagues, fruitlessly, for deviating from one of the few draft guidelines which should have been attractive to reformers who favored organized and disciplined political parties. Immediately thereafter, Ranney's motion passed.

Guideline C–4 (Timeliness) achieved the distinction of having the shortest adoption time. C–4 had been drafted in late summer; it had survived until late November with no revision. When Chairman McGovern read the text aloud on Friday, November 20, there was no discussion. In fact, the only substantive change in its provisions came *after* the November meeting, when the staff added a phrase forbidding untimely bodies—which presumably meant any state or local Democratic party—from so much as endorsing a slate of delegates, even if that slate had been created in an approved manner.[18]

The staff had drafted Guideline C–5 (Committee Selection Processes) with an active antipathy toward this method of delegate selection but under an annoying constraint when translating that antipathy into party law. The Rules minority report appeared, very plainly and explicitly, to place committee selections on an equal footing with conventions and primaries in terms of their democratic acceptability.[19] As the November meeting approached, Segal and Bode nevertheless developed a two-step strategy aimed at elimination. Step one, in the memo on "clarifying language," suggested a limit of 10 percent on committee selections. Step two would be a coordinated argument by the staff, at the November meeting, that this 10 percent be squeezed to zero.

When the guideline was introduced in this form, Davis immediately objected, noting that it violated the obvious intent of the 1968 Convention. But perhaps because they had spent the previous two days consulting their own judgment about reasonable and unreasonable ways to reform the mechanics of delegate selection, his fellow commissioners were uninterested in that argument. In its stead, they produced two new lines of attack. The first contended that certain key public and party leaders should be on *any* state delegation. The second asserted that if the commission was to insist on demographic balance in the final delegations, it should at least provide a means for creating that balance when the voters themselves did not. Wade watched the prior action of the commission on Guidelines A–1 and A–2 come back to haunt yet another party rule:

> The C–5 debate went from 25 percent to 0 percent. In these cases, "discussion" was the thing, not "debates." There was a good deal of talk. Arguments for some percentage, put your Governors or Senators on; this was the argument of a number of Commissioners. The other argument was that you "replace the divots." You put on blacks or women or Puerto Ricans or youth.

The commissioners did indeed stay with a limit of 10 percent. Accordingly, with the passage of C–5, those commissioners who remained were at last able to hope for a rapid conclusion to their deliberations and for the opportunity to join those of their colleagues who had already slipped away. That these hopes were not to be realized was instantly clear from the reception of the final draft guideline, C–6 (Slate Making):

The staff had drafted C–6 for one basic purpose—to extend public participation in the nominating process not just to its final stage, but to the point where individuals acquired the right to stand for election as a delegate under the name of a particular candidate, that is, to the slate-making stage. As a result, Guideline C–6 automatically divided the commissioners into three discernible blocs:

- A "private slate" faction, whose adherents argued that *anyone* should be able to put together a delegate slate and submit it to primary voters or convention participants.
- A "modified public slate" faction, whose partisans demanded that procedural guarantees extend to the slate-making stage, but who insisted that a presidential candidate retain the right to *refuse* any delegate campaigning in his name.
- A "pure public slate" faction, whose believers argued that *no one*—not even a bona fide presidential contender—should be able to overrule a democratized slate-making caucus.

The guideline, as it had been drafted in August and as it had stood, unexamined, until November 20, incorporated the "modified public slate" approach. If holding the middle ground had been the determining factor—especially when buttressed by the press of time and the rush to adjourn—the fate of C–6 would have been settled. What unsettled it was a chain of commission decisions stretching all the way back to Guidelines A–1 and A–2.

In this chain, the commissioners had first amended the draft guidelines on demographic representation to beef up requirements about the race, sex, and age of state delegations. Having done that, they had been less receptive than ever to the staff call for formal proportional representation. But having resisted *that*, they had cornered those who still cared about proportionality, and even some who merely saluted public participation: If the commission did not introduce participatory elements into the slate-making process, there would be neither proportionality nor consequential public participation in the selection of individual delegates in those primary states which remained winner-take-all.

The "private slate" people—Beer, Mitchell, and Warschaw—did make an initial attempt to control debate. Beer was considerably annoyed with the draft guideline as placed before them, and labored diligently to move it back toward a "private slate" interpretation:

> I was very much against Slate Making. I had long battles with Nelson over the phone about procedures in this state [Massachusetts]. That's where I think the differing experience of people came in. You *cannot* democratize slate making. Every political initiative must begin with one man or a small group. They would say, "You don't know what Daley does." I would say, "You can't have some bums off the street come in and wear Muskie's label." I think the fact that they were from convention states, not primary states, was crucial.

These arguments were destined to make little headway. The commissioners as a group had been endorsing uniform efforts to democratize the formal procedures of delegate selection during the preceding day and a half. They were unlikely to desert this orientation to the point of allowing *anyone* to draw up a delegate slate, *in private,* if it might then be elected *winner-take-all.* Moreover, the committed proponents of proportional representation were doubly reluctant to allow any compromise on slate making, because this guideline represented the last chance to see any of their wishes written into party law in the winner-take-all states. In case they could have missed this implication, Segal hammered it home for them early in the debate:

> *Segal:* The ambiguity here is caused by a situation, a situation I guess we all know well is California, where any three people can designate themselves a nominating committee and put together a delegation of 174 people for a presidential candidate.

The battle quickly devolved into a "modified public slate" versus "pure public slate" contest. As a result, the crucial issue became the role of presidential candidates or their agents in the slating process. "Modified public slate" partisans believed that the candidate was entitled to an ultimate veto; "pure public slate" advocates claimed that a process free from *anyone's* control was the ideal.

Despite having drafted the existing text, with its "modified public slate" approach, Segal and Bode were actually in the "pure public slate" camp and were, in fact, the moving forces in commission argument. They were joined by Vice Chairman Hughes and Chairman McGovern, but their most powerful allies were really their superior preparation, their sense of personal injury from the outcome on proportional representation, their willingness to stay on the issue, and the clock. From the other side, they were most actively opposed by Christopher, filling in for the absent Dutton, by Wade, and by Beer who, once the "private slate" position disappeared, fought to hold the line at a "modified public slate."

Christopher, Wade, Beer, and an occasional kindred spirit produced three main counterarguments. The first asserted that uninterested or even hostile participants might capture a candidate's slate, if he were not given a full veto. The second alleged that without candidate control, delegate slates might proliferate to the point where the result was artificially affected. The third said that some degree of control, by *someone*—and the candidate was almost the only one left, once the other guidelines had eliminated the official party—was necessary if the delegates were to live up to the requirements for demographic balance in Guidelines A–1 and A–2.

After these arguments had been presented, rebutted, and repeated, a series of motions began. Christopher asked that the section on challenges to slated delegates apply only to convention or committee systems, and not to presidential primaries; his motion went down to substantial defeat on a voice vote. Davis then went after the section on candidate right of approval and made the reverse argument, namely, that it apply only to primary and not to convention or committee states, where delegates could be directly selected.

The vote on this motion was interrupted, after the ayes but before the nays, by a point of order to the effect that there was no longer a quorum. After a short digression on that issue, Christopher introduced a new motion, subsuming Davis's. He proposed to erase all three original subsections of the guideline, gutting its text, stripping it of its substance, and leaving it as an exhortation toward more public involvement:

> *Christopher:* I move that we adopt the first paragraph of Slate-Making, dropping everything that starts with "furthermore," but of course the staff will know that as part of the legislative history, there have been certain abuses that fall under [deleted] paragraphs one, two, and three.

The immediate effect of Christopher's motion was to confuse discussion further. Warschaw suggested that the commission defer action on C–6, so that it could mail the options to its entire membership. Ranney backed her up. Christopher returned to an argument in support of his proposal. McGovern countered with the case of South Dakota, where he asserted that the alleged abuses did indeed occur. This exchange, in turn, provoked, not a call for the vote, but a second protest about the absence of a quorum, and discussion moved off in that direction.

After a second agreement to keep talking, Segal rushed in with language ostensibly equivalent to Christopher's, but lacking its radical surgery. If Segal's motion were not successful, the commission appeared headed for a very weak form of the "modified public slate" approach:

> *Segal:* It seems to me that there are two different problems we're trying to get to in this paragraph. One of them is the burdens placed on challengers. The second is the opportunity for people to participate in the slate-making process. Quite apart from these questions—it's a separate thing, I think—is the presidential veto or lack thereof. Why don't we say the challenges are one problem, and the second problem is open processes, and instead of the proviso in there, why don't we say that the process should be done "in consultation with the presidential candidate or his representatives"?

Christopher, apparently seeing no great contradiction between this language and his own, offered to withdraw his motion in favor of Segal's, but Hughes again interrupted with the question of a quorum and drew the commission off onto that. In answer to his own query, however, Hughes suggested that while the commission no longer had 50 percent in attendance, it did have 40 percent; since Guideline B–3 required only that for state party business, the commissioners might consider themselves legitimate and continue. After a murmur of assent, Christopher converted *Segal's* language into a formal motion:

> *Christopher:* I move the approval of the Slate-Making guideline, with the first and third paragraphs unchanged. . . . Paragraph two would read: Those persons making up each slate have adopted procedures which will facilitate widespread participation in the slate-making process, with the proviso that any slate presented in the name of a presidential candidate in a primary state be assembled with due consultation with the candidate or his representatives.

The commissioners, on a voice vote, adopted Christopher's suggestion with no audible nays, thereby shifting the content of Guideline C–6 substantially. Christopher's *semi*final motion, the one which Segal had managed to waylay with his substitute, had been a very weak version of the "modified public slate." Final authority would have been left in the hands of the candidate, the state convention leadership, or state party officialdom, depending on state

189

law. Segal's reinterpretation, on the other hand, which became Christopher's final motion, moved far over toward a "pure public slate," with only the sop of "due consultation" for presidential candidates and with nothing at all for state party leaders.

Nevertheless, the guideline did pass in the form which Segal, and not Christopher, had proposed. With that passage, the remaining participants congratulated each other for surviving their ordeal. Chairman McGovern went to face the press. And the commissioners scattered for home. They were not to reassemble as a commission for almost twenty months. They were never to affect the definition of party reform again.

Implications

With the arrival of the final drafting session of the Commission on Party Structure and Delegate Selection, there was no longer any need to search out the true *arena* for reform politics. For two days, on November 19 and 20, that arena was a formal meeting of the Party Structure Commission. With the arrival of this final drafting session, there was no need to search for the effective *agenda* in reform politics either. On the morning of November 19, that agenda was the collection of draft guidelines set before the Party Structure commissioners; by the evening of November 20, it was the composite record of their formal decisions.

That record, needless to say, encompassed recommendations for major change in the matrix of institutions for delegate selection in the national Democratic party. These recommendations promised major changes in the practical fabric of presidential politics. Those changes, finally, implied shifts in the composition of national political elites and impacts on all those political institutions affected by the presidency.

Much of this was the culmination of trends, relationships, and forces established well in advance of the crucial commission meeting. The most fundamental shift in the entire reform package, a radical restructuring of the basic institutional mechanisms for delegate selection, had been in the staff draft before the commissioners were ever brought into the drafting process. That shift had remained in this staff draft, jealously guarded but, in truth, largely unchallenged, during the preliminary meetings leading up to a final session. It had survived that session without major amendment, or even major attention.

Yet what was true of the basic institutional forms for delegate selection was

190

true, in a less dramatic way, for the total package put before the commissioners. If their final session did contribute numerous minor amendments and several major changes, that session never altered even the general contours of the original reform package. The vast bulk of what came out of the November meeting was the vast bulk of what went in.

That said, it was also true that there were meeting-specific developments, major as well as minor, nearly everywhere one looked. If the commission had not been determined to make this its final drafting session, if it had been prepared to reassemble and reconsider its actions of November 19–20, there would have been fewer of these effects, and they would have been less substantial. But the leadership was determined to complete the politics of recommendation, and under those conditions, the membership was to produce some noteworthy amendments of the day, idiosyncratic decisions destined to be permanently enshrined in their official report.

One of these amendments was so substantial, in fact, as to contribute a cast to nearly everything which followed on November 19 and 20. In their adjustments to the opening guidelines, A–1 and A–2, the commissioners created not just a new proposal for two related strictures, but a new emphasis for their entire reform package. The impact of these adjustments—the introduction of "reasonable relationship" language to both standards—was unclear when the commission adjourned; indeed, it would necessarily depend on the subsequent politics of implementation. But the fallout from these adjustments appeared and reappeared immediately.

The first major impact of these opening amendments was on the staff drive for proportional representation. Having emphasized *demographic* representation, the commissioners were even less receptive to formal proportionality. Again, the practical impact of their reticence should not be overstated; their actions on proportionality were like those on demography, in that the meaning of these actions would necessarily be determined in the subsequent politics of implementation. But the commissioners had refused to follow the staff lead on proportional representation, their major revolt of the day, and this refusal had been linked to prior amendments on demographic representation.

More fallout was to come, as staff members tried to adjust to this apparent defeat. In fact, the major unexpected battle of the second day, over Guideline C–6 (Slate Making), sprang largely from a staff effort to recoup some of what had been lost on proportionality—and this time the effort was successful. Staff members were to continue this effort even after the commission adjourned. Because the staff had lost on proportional representation, its members would amend the commission rule on intrastate apportionment, in their published report, to insist that three quarters of the delegates be selected *below* the state

191

level in convention states, thereby injecting an element of proportionality into convention-state proceedings.

The staff had never *opposed* the commission response to A–1 or A–2, so that this was hardly a victory of commissioners *over* staff. While staff members were far more concerned with participation and proportionality, they had done some preliminary statistical work on the presence of blacks, women, and youth at prior conventions, and they were not unreceptive to a guideline addressing their lot. The participatory rhetoric of the day usually included these three groups as a unit; so did arguments about a deliberate realignment of the Democratic coalition, as Segal noted:

> The mandate was for opening up the process, for participation. The mandate was *not* for getting more blacks and women and youth. But in America of 1969, I would make these speeches, too. It was a way of showing that there was discrimination, and a need for reform. We were interested in opening that door. I don't believe Bode or I would ever have proposed what finally came out of the quota discussion. But we ran into a whipsaw. We had Mixner, Dutton, Aaron Henry, all of whom felt that this was absolutely vital. That was my constituency. I had to go with them. I had no choice.

The ramifications of commission amendments to Guidelines A–1 and A–2 emphasized a second fact about this single, two-day session. Because the session was so determinedly final, the order of appearance for individual items could condition their fate. Had the commissioners begun with their unexamined standards, the "C" guidelines, for example, and had they then worked back from these, their eventual decision on C–6 (Slate Making)—perhaps the most heavily influenced by their prior action on A–1 and A–2—would have been very unlikely. Indeed, if A–1 and A–2 had come on the second day instead of the first, neither Bayh, who introduced the crucial amendment, nor Dutton, who actually drove it through, would even have been in attendance.

What was true with the sequence of guidelines as a whole was also true, less dramatically, with the parliamentary initiatives and tactical maneuvers on individual guidelines. The attempt by Mitchell to channel debate on intrastate apportionment with an early motion, the ability of English to circumvent Mitchell by calling his own motion and recasting the debate, and the success of Peden at interrupting and securing reconsideration made Guideline B–7 the strongest case of this. But lesser syntactic and procedural engagements were not uncommon in the other guidelines, and they, too, were frequently influential.

Even these influences, however, with the exception of those following from commission amendments to A–1 and A–2, worked more often in favor of *staff* preferences than against them. It was the staff, after all, which was prepared with additional, restrictive amendments for many of the guidelines—and with new activating language for *every* guideline in the list. It was staff members who were prepared to *pull back* on others, in response to expected opposition from their commissioners, but who, seeing no such opposition, quietly stifled those preparations. It was the devoted persistence of the staff on C–6 (Slate Making) which converted an apparently successful attempt by the commissioners to weaken the guideline into an evident strengthening of this final rule.

Once again, all these twists and turns in the final meeting must be kept in perspective. For the crucial fact about this final session remained the limited nature of the adjustments it contributed to the extended, systematic, and tough document which the staff had placed before it. Neither peculiarities of agenda or argument, whether capitalized on by commissioners or staff, could hide this crucial consideration. The staff plan for sweeping party reform had passed with numerous smaller amendments and with several new, open questions, but with precious little impact on its central thrust.[20]

A focus on the internal dynamics of this final drafting session cannot place this meeting in the full sweep of reform politics to date. A detailed chronicle of the meeting—surface appearances to the contrary—cannot reveal even the scope of the institutional change which it proposed, unless the observer or reader is exceedingly skilled at institutional analysis and reconstruction. The story of this meeting cannot offer more than hints about the ultimate impact of this institutional change. These, because they complete the practical account of the politics of recommendation, are inevitably topics for an additional analytic chapter. (See chapter 7.)

Yet by the time this meeting had adjourned, several other facts about its contribution to reform politics, institutional change, and elite circulation were established. The meeting had been the organizational climax to the politics of recommendation. It had contributed the institutional centerpiece to the politics of implementation. And it had seen the last of the Party Structure Commission, as a full-blown collectivity though not as an organizational framework, in the total politics of party reform. Whether as an embodiment of or an obstacle to the alternative Democratic coalition, whether as a contributor to or a brake upon a new national politics, the commission, as a collective rule-making operation, was gone.

CHAPTER

7

The Meaning of the Mandate:

Formal Rules and Practical Effects

IN WHICH, institutional analysis of the reform text adopted by the Party Structure Commission reveals a plethora of practical demands; re-examination of these demands for the extent to which the commissioners intended them uncovers a major perceptual factor shaping their adoption; and a review of the politics of recommendation puts these practical demands and this perceptual contribution in political perspective. AND IN WHICH, reform politics at the final commission meeting is used to summarize the politics of recommendation; institutional change on an unprecedented scale emerges as the theoretical implication of the resulting reform package; and elite replacement becomes the most grand of the potential impacts from implementation of these reforms.

WHEN the Commission on Party Structure and Delegate Selection adjourned in the late afternoon of Friday, November 20, it left in its wake an undifferentiated trail of major and minor actions, touching nearly every aspect of delegate selection in the national Democratic party and culminating in the largest planned change in presidential selection in American history. Press accounts tended to obscure this fact, by concentrating on items of conflict rather than consensus, by seeking out opposing views of commission accomplishments, and by abjuring systematic analysis of the total package.[1] But when the individual texts embodying these various actions were examined for their institutional implications, when formal rules were translated into practical effects, the final product of the commission stood out, quite simply, as unprecedented and monumental.

Perception of this potential impact did require a systematic effort at institutional translation, an effort at converting a formal text into its practical impacts. The need for this translation, in turn, was surely a major reason that few participants or professional observers appreciated the cumulative potential of the commission product. Yet there was more to the absence of controversy surrounding adoption of this total package than the presence of stiff analytic demands. For even the attentive commissioner sitting through the final two-day session—and perhaps even the attentive reader working through a detailed account of that session—was likely to miss the practical consequences of these formal actions.*

Most fundamentally, of course, the commission had insisted on the detailed codification of state party rules, and this in itself—the promulgation of national party standards to govern state and local party business—was a change of historic proportion. Beneath this umbrella, the commission had gone on to specify particular rules to govern most realms of party activity in delegate selection, and many of these specifications could be expected to have a significant, independent effect on the politics of presidential nomination.

In its most important substantive decision, the commission had sharply constricted the permissible mechanisms for selecting delegates, entirely repudiating over half of all state plans and demanding major amendments in all but a handful. The commission had then constrained the procedures by which state parties might allocate delegates from these institutions to the contenders for a presidential nomination, although the scope of this constriction remained a matter of debate. Less debatable was the commission move to redistribute the delegates which these states would be allocating, through a formula guaranteed to cause consternation for most state parties.

The commissioners had demanded newly democratized arrangements for creation of these individual delegates as well. That is, they had required participatory arrangements even for the process by which an individual gained the right to run for delegate. On top of all this, the commissioners had imposed explicit demographic targets for the outcome, although the constriction in these targets, too, would depend on subsequent politics. They had gone on to prohibit ex officio delegates of all (other) sorts, and while this prohibition constituted a significant change in and of itself, it was really only the most obvious case of a far more extensive effort to redefine the role of the regular party—of party officialdom—in presidential politics.

The most dramatic fact about these institutional implications, then, was their scope. They were, without exaggeration, the most extensive planned

---

*Readers for whom this claim seems intuitively overstated may want to pause at this point and try to reconstruct the composite process of delegate selection envisioned by the commissioners at the end of their final drafting session. The remainder of this chapter will, in part, do precisely this.

change in the process of delegate selection—and hence presidential nomination—in all of American history. But the most curious fact about these institutional implications was their differential visibility even to the Party Structure commissioners. It was not that the commissioners shied from debate when they saw practical implications in the guidelines put before them. They addressed such guidelines with gusto. Yet the commission as a body varied enormously in its ability to locate—or miss—these inherent effects.

Nevertheless, there was a pattern to commissioner perceptions. Among the guidelines, the crucial influence on collective response was not potential impact on the institutions of delegate selection, grand though that impact might be. Instead, it was the evident tendency of a guideline to demand a change in the outcome of the selection process. With this as a standard, the oldest and most common form of the convention system for selecting delegates was abolished without any debate whatsoever, while the formula for intrastate apportionment, with a deliberate but marginal effect on concrete outcomes, drew immediate and sustained attention.

By the same token, the strongest factor in attracting an individual commissioner, and then in getting that commissioner to seek the attention of the larger group, was the interaction of a guideline text with the personal experience of one or another participant. Thus, one phrase within a single guideline abolished the oldest form of the presidential primary, with only the most desultory debate, while the proposed guideline on proportional representation, through its impact on the commissioners from California, forced the entire commission to stay on the topic hour after hour and meeting after meeting.

This implicit pattern of perception was, in fact, the crucial link between ongoing influences in commission politics and the peculiar dynamics of the final commission meeting. Or, said differently, the tendency of the commissioners to perceive—or not to perceive—individual items as consequential was a central element in explaining why established influences in internal commission politics worked as they did in the final drafting session. As such, this tendency completed the set of factors which molded the commission's official product.

The major explanation for what the commissioners actually did in their final meeting was contained in the contours of reform politics before that historic session—in its major actors, their organizational context, their resources, and their goals. (See chapters 1–4.) But the perceptions which the commissioners developed when they as a group came to grips with their reform text, during a series of meetings in the fall of 1969, became their continuing, collective approach to these reform recommendations. (See chapter 5.) The application of this approach to the particular interactions of their final meeting then contributed directly to their ultimate decisions on party reform. (See chapter 6.)

When the commission adjourned on November 20, this product was essentially completed. The resulting document touched almost every facet of delegate selection. It promised a new matrix of institutions for the nomination of presidents. It implied a new practical politics to go with this institutional matrix. It contained the potential for an extensive restructuring of political elites within the national Democratic party, and thus within national politics at large.

A Practical Translation of Reform Proposals

The fate of all these pronouncements remained an open question as the commissioners turned for home on that Friday afternoon. But the institutional impact of these pronouncements was, in large part, deducible from the text of the guidelines themselves, if anyone had cared to make the effort. Or at least, it was possible to take the existing array of institutions for delegate selection and to contrast that array with the formal arrangements demanded by the Party Structure Commission. This would highlight the alterations explictly mandated by commission guidelines; it would isolate those other changes where the subsequent politics of implementation would inevitably determine guideline effect.

The commission had insisted on *detailed codification of state party rules*, and it had specified a minimum of seven items to be included. In the direct sense, this meant that the discretion of those who had previously interpreted local party regulations, usually on the basis of experience and custom, would necessarily be curtailed, while the influence of those who specialized in mastering and then manipulating formal rules would simultaneously be enhanced.

But in a less direct and more portentous sense, this insistence on detailed party rules meant that the national party (or an appendage of it) was assuming the right to demand compliance with *national* party regulations from the individual—and previously independent—*state* political parties. This was itself a sharp break with American political tradition, and everything else which the commission recommended was in some sense subsidiary to such a fundamental change.[2]

By far the largest and most consequential, specific change demanded by the commission was the *redefinition of permissible mechanisms for delegate selection.* This redefinition, in turn, inevitably implied a *reconstitution of the total matrix of institutions for presidential nomination* in the national Democratic party.[3] When the commission began its work, there were five basic institutional forms for creating state delegations:

- *The Party Caucus.* In party caucus systems, the bottom level of party officers, usually precinct committeemen and committeewomen, met to select delegates to some higher party gathering in a tiered system of party meetings which eventually chose the delegation to the national party convention. States using this system varied according to the level at which the process began and the number of levels which intervened between the bottom and the top, but tiered meetings of party officials or their designees were its hallmark.
- *The Participatory Convention.* The participatory convention system was formally similar to that of the party caucus, except that participation on the bottom level was open to *any* party member, and usually to anyone who claimed to be a member. States using this system also varied according to the unit which formed the bottom level and the number of levels intervening between bottom and top, but the wide-open character of participation at the first stage always distinguished it from the party caucus.
- *The Delegate Primary.* In delegate primaries, all candidates for delegate to the National Convention appeared on the ballot under their own names only. They could, of course, campaign for election by publicizing their loyalty to a presidential hopeful, but they could also campaign by emphasizing community ties, celebrity, or whatever they preferred. Direct election of individual representatives was its hallmark.
- *The Candidate Primary.* In candidate primaries, the name of the presidential candidate, rather than that of the potential delegate, was featured. In a few states, the delegate merely put a presidential preference after his own name; in others, individual delegates were grouped under the name of the potential president; in many, only the name of the presidential candidate appeared, and the delegates who won with that candidate were actually chosen through some other procedure. Emphasis on a presidential contender, with more or less indirect selection of the delegates, distinguished this system.
- *State Committee Selection.* In a committee selection system, the central committee of the state party—or occasionally just the state chairman or incumbent governor, as a committee of one—selected the National Convention delegates. A few states used the device to select their total delegations; many more used it to select some share. The dominant role of the top party committee in a state marked the system off from all others.

The Party Structure Commission never addressed these five basic institutional mechanisms by name, not even individually, much less as a group. Yet the eighteen guidelines adopted by the commission had unequivocal implications for the fate of all five. The party caucus, for example, was not just the oldest convention system for creating state delegations to the national party convention; it was by far the most widely used system across American history. The commission banned it completely. Because the commission actually abolished the party caucus through the interaction of a set of guidelines, it never trumpeted this abolition, and it never announced an intended replacement.[4] Yet the assumption among those commission personnel who focused on the issue was that participatory conventions would replace party caucuses in the convention states and would thus become the dominant device for delegate selection nationwide.

The delegate primary was likewise the oldest form of presidential primary election; it had, in fact, been a major reform in the last great round of reform activity, at the turn of the century. Again, the commission banned it outright. Its prohibition was more explicit than that of the party caucus and was localized in a single guideline. Even then, the commission did not attempt to endorse a replacement, but simply left the candidate primary as the logical, available alternative. Presumably, the candidate primary would become the other leading device for delegate selection in the postreform world, along with the participatory convention.[5]

The commission was most explicit in addressing a basic mechanism of delegate selection when it turned to appointment by state central committees. Most commissioners freely admitted that they were stretching their authority by pronouncing on this device. That said, they went on to limit its application to a maximum of 10 percent of a state delegation and to regulate both the means of election to committees used for this purpose and the character of the decisions which they might reach about this (paltry) 10 percent.[6]

This massive retailoring of the institutions of delegate selection was only the beginning of commission impact on the probable fate of their delegates, and thus on the process of presidential selection. Indeed, within these very devices, the commission had given major impetus to the *constriction of the procedures for allocating delegates to the various contenders for a presidential nomination.* When the commissioners began their work, there were three main allocation rules:

- *Winner-Take-All.* In a winner-take-all primary, the plurality leader among presidential candidates received the entire state delegation. In what could be called a winner-take-all convention, although it went by other names as well, a convention majority, however constructed, was entitled to select all the delegates.
- *Districted.* In a districted primary or convention, delegates ran from geographic units, and the plurality leaders within those units were elected. Delegates were sometimes grouped by slates within these districts, in which case the system was effectively winner-take-all by district. Otherwise, it was more usefully thought of as direct election.
- *Proportional.* In a proportional primary or convention, delegates were divided among presidential aspirants according to some explicit mathematical formula. The unit to which proportionality was applied and the threshold above which a candidate could receive delegates provided elements of variation from state to state. But the requirement that participants vote for candidates rather than

delegates and an explicit mathematical standard for converting those votes into delegate allocations were hallmarks of the rule.

The 1968 Convention had done away with some winner-take-all provisions in convention states, by outlawing the unit rule. Whether the Party Structure Commission had done much more would depend crucially on the politics of implementation. The commission had condemned the remaining applications of winner-take-all; it had urged the states to move immediately to some form of proportionality; it had urged the 1972 Convention to require proportional representation in the future.[7]

Whether these signals were followed for 1972 would obviously depend both on the extent to which the guidelines in general were implemented in the states and on the extent to which partisans of proportionality were able to emphasize these urgings in the course of implementation. Whether these signals were followed by the 1972 Convention—and beyond—would depend on the real, practical contribution of these reform rules to the composition of that convention and, again, on the extent to which the partisans of proportionality could focus the energies of the convention on this issue.

In a more evident and more automatic fashion, the commission had demanded an *internal redistribution of state delegates,* the ones who would be selected through these reformed institutional devices, who would be awarded through these reformed allocation rules, and who would collectively determine presidential nominations. Here, however, the commission had redistributed these delegates so explicitly and to such a degree that only a few state parties could escape the need for a totally new delegate dispersion.

The commission had demanded that every state delegation to the national party convention be apportioned internally through a formula based 50 percent on raw population and 50 percent on prior Democratic (presidential) vote. For states with a tiered system of delegate selection, it had included a looser set of stipulations for the apportionment of delegates at lower levels.[8] This was a major departure for the average state party in two ways. First, it countervailed both the most common basis for internal apportionment, which was population alone, and the next most common basis, which was some measure of *state* Democratic vote. Second, and more painfully, it implied that states could no longer reserve a minimum of state convention delegates to their smallest geographic units, a practice which most state parties had followed since the birth of national party conventions.

Most of these reforms were aimed at guaranteeing public participation in the choice among presidential contenders and among candidates for delegate to the national party convention. Yet the commission had also addressed itself to the prior stage of this presidential nominating process, the stage at which individuals acquired the right to stand as delegates for particular presidential aspirants. In fact, the commission had demanded *explicit extension of parti cipatory reform to this initial process of slating delegates for subsequent selection.* [9]

Some of the commission demands in this realm were clear. It had eliminated the regular party as a slating committee, by refusing to let any sitting body undertake the task and then by refusing to allow the party even to make an endorsement of a slate created elsewhere. It had eliminated the electorate as a repository for the slate-making function, by demanding a participatory process which unfolded prior to the balloting on delegates. But at that point, the commission had left a fundamental ambiguity. For it had leaned toward lodging the task of slate making in some new body created expressly for the purpose, some prior, open caucus of candidate supporters. Yet it had noted a need for "due consultation" with the candidate, too. The comparative authority of caucus and candidate was thus left undefined, to be resolved, inevitably, in the politics of implementation.

In what many would later argue to be a thoroughly inconsistent move, the commission had also endorsed the *imposition of explicit demographic targets* for the presidential politics occurring within this reformed process of delegate selection. Specifically, it had named race, color, creed, national origin, sex, and age as characteristics of the American public which were worthy of careful recognition in the construction of a state delegation. In doing so, of course, it had ignored income, social class, occupation, and educational attainment, the distinctions most commonly thought to separate Democrats from Republicans in the society at large. More to the point, whatever the key guidelines *said,* it was race, sex, and youth which were really deemed worthy of recognition—not color, creed, national original, or age—and everyone, opponents as well as proponents, understood this.[10]

But while the commission had selected blacks, women, and young people as the beneficiaries of a requirement of "reasonable relationship" to their presence in the state population as a whole, the exact meaning of this phrase was subject to general disagreement, even among the commissioners. If pressed, most would have agreed that its implications would have to be hammered out along the way, in the politics of implementation. Beyond that, they might or might not have confessed to having contributed a major fixed outcome to a process which was otherwise intended to be open and participatory.

Although the commission had obviously (if imprecisely) expanded the guaranteed role at the national convention of delegates drawn from certain demographic groups, it had eliminated numerous other automatic spots. Indeed, in a less internally controversial but more clear-cut decision, the commission had prohibited ex officio delegates of all (other) sorts, thus forcibly and explicitly compressing the guaranteed role at the national convention of the regular Democratic party. Whether this would remove the national committee itself was not immediately obvious, but the intended elimination of counterpart figures in the states and localities was there for all to see.[11]

In a larger sense, however, the ban on ex officio positions was only part of a general effort at the *separation of party officialdom from the delegate selection process,* and the preference for demographic groups over the regular party was more usefully seen in this light. In the vocabulary common to most other advanced democracies, many of the guidelines were, in fact, aimed at isolating *the party itself* from what was, at least rhetorically, "the party's nomination." Some of the minor guidelines had acquired this as their surface rationale in explicit commission debate; many others had acquired it as their projected impact at the time when the guidelines were being drafted.[12]

An obvious example was the prohibition on proxy voting—banned not because independent activists might collect too many proxies and overwhelm the regular party, but because party regulars might collect too many proxies and overwhelm the independent activists. Yet what was true of these minor strictures was even more true of the commission's most substantial decisions, like the ban on party caucuses, the ban on delegate primaries, and the constriction of state committee selections.

The Perception of Practical Effects

The proposed guidelines of the Party Structure Commission could thus be translated—on paper—to reveal profound impacts on the process of presidential selection. Yet the substance of these practical effects was only an indifferent guide to the character of the debate which had preceded adoption of the guidelines producing them. Group discussion, in short, both the amount of attention and the intensity of debate, had been tied only partly to institutional impact.

The expected debates on proportionality and apportionment had indeed surfaced, but so had surprise contests over demographics and slate-making, issues which entered the November meeting with no great institutional significance. Beyond that, the most consequential actions of the meeting, the commission's radical surgery on the fundamental institutions of delegate selection, had actually arrived and departed without any real heat, without even sustained group attention.

This was not the last occasion when warfare over reform guidelines would be characterized by a degree of practical disconnection. When the Democratic National Committee and the fifty-five state, district, and territorial parties had to determine which elements in these recommendations could safely be implemented and which should logically be resisted, the same sorts of calculations would be required. At that point, too, the items which did—and did not—become centers of debate would present only the same mild relationship to their institutional impact.

In all such cases, of course, the art of making institutional translations from textual provisions—of eliciting practical effects from formal rules—was at issue. In all such cases, accordingly, the means by which decision-makers evaluated the triviality or importance of substantive proposals was important. In this case, in November of 1969, an analysis of the institutional effect of commission guidelines was obviously an erratic predictor of commission propensity to see a reform of consequence, and to stop and argue about it.

This difference between the apparent meaning of the guidelines as they were being discussed in commission and their institutional implications when they were subjected to subsequent analysis resulted, in part, from the manner in which the commissioners had addressed their proposed reforms—one by one, with lesser and greater strictures mixed together, in the midst of irrelevant as well as insightful argument. Yet much of the difference between apparent meaning at the instant of adoption and institutional impact upon subsequent reflection resulted from the peculiar character of debate itself.

The pattern was simply described: Where the commissioners saw a provision which would reliably alter the *outcome* of the delegate selection process, whether by a great deal or only by a little, they were moved to argue, and occasionally to amend or reject. Where they did not see such an impact, where they believed that a formally large change would produce a practically small one, or where they were able to *put off* the question of concrete outcomes until some (unspecified) later date, they accepted staff recommendations.

The debate over commission policy on intrastate apportionment exhibited one extreme in this pattern. A revised formula for internal apportionment had absorbed the entire morning of November 20, putting it on a par with new requirements for demographic representation and ahead of altered institutions of delegate selection, altered rules of delegate allocation, and altered procedures for the construction of delegate slates. This was out of all proportion to the significance of the change.[13] Yet an intrastate apportionment formula was still the ideal stimulus for extended debate, because it was so concrete, because everyone could see that real changes would follow, and because the impact of each alternative was precisely calculable. All three facets appeared in an exchange among Dick Wade, Will Davis, and Aaron Henry:

> *Wade:* I would think the best you could do would be to use congressional districts and weight them, so much for enrollment, so much for presidential and guberna-torial elections.
> *Davis:* Yes, you can work this out mathematically, but now try to think about it as to what effect it has in what we're trying to achieve in politics. That's the whole point, what we are trying to achieve politically, not in the mathematical, political science judgment as to how to weight all these things. What you're doing is strengthening yourself where you're strong and weakening yourself where you're weak. That's what you're doing in the panhandle of Texas, for example.
> *Henry:* If you don't vote Democratic, you don't get no votes. Then you gonna vote Democratic.
> *Davis:* But also, I've got a guy out there who's working his rear end off for the Democratic party, fightin' a battle that's tough. It's a hard, tough battle to win elections in the panhandle. And he's working his guts out. And I tell him, "Now you keep on working, but you can't go to the national convention because you didn't get enough votes." He won't work next time![14]

At the other extreme on this criterion of obvious impact was the ban on party caucuses, the archetypal device for delegate selection by organized and disciplined political parties. This was a historic alteration, one with the very greatest potential impact, but one which passed the commission with hardly an aside. The explanation lay in the peculiar, piecemeal fashion in which the device was proscribed. It took a combination of *three* guidelines to dispatch it—A–5 (Existence of Party Rules), B–2 (Clarity of Purpose), and C–4 (Time-liness). These three had to be reassembled in reverse order—C–4, B–2, A–5—to produce their joint effect. The first of these, C–4, had never previ-ously been discussed by the commissioners and came up only after the others had been endorsed separately. Anne Wexler watched the device disappear, with delight but without comment:

> We knew all the time what this meant. We knew that we were going to change the face of American politics. We knew that it would mess up *every* convention state. We knew that the entire process would be affected, even internal commit-tee politics. The reason I knew what would happen was from knowing Connecti-cut.

A general awareness that a guideline portended real change in the concrete outcomes of delegate selection, then, was the most reliable stimulus to com-mission inquiry. As a result, the *surface impact* of a guideline was critical. If the text itself claimed to be making such a change, the commissioners were usually roused to action. If the institutional meaning of that text was obscure or ambiguous, the members could glide rapidly by. Ken Bode saw an almost eerie quality in this frequent nonresponse: "My hair would tingle when something went through. I'd say, 'Do they know what is going on? Do they know what they are doing?' "

There was a second way in which the arrival of a proposed guideline might create this same general awareness of an inevitable impact on outcomes. If an individual commissioner had some *personal experience* which fell within the scope of the guideline, if this experience suggested that the new rule might work quite differently from the description which the staff was providing, and if the commissioner was able to communicate this experience forcefully, the commission as a body might well be moved to investigate, to amend, or even to table.

The starkest example was the guideline on proportional representation, euphemistically presented as "Adequate Representation of Minority Views." All such rhetorical camouflage quickly became irrelevant when Fred Dutton read the suggested text. Dutton saw the implication for the winner-take-all primary; he knew that his home state (California) would be the most strongly affected; he cared intensely about that possibility; he went to war on the proposal with all his energies:

> I spent a lot of my time resisting the staff. Staff was very much for proportional representation. I thought they were acting on intellectual-theoretical grounds. They couldn't show you how this had worked anywhere. They tried to keep you from asking how it would work, and just kept hitting you over the head with the argument that it was "fair."

This "California connection," however, was only the most dramatic instance of the way in which personal linkage could make guideline impact appear serious. The quorum provision in Guideline B–3, for example, was amended because John English of New York offered a detailed argument about the way the staff draft would actually work in his home state. The requirement of uniform dates and places in Guideline A–5 was altered when George Mitchell drew on his experience in Maine to demonstrate some additional, unintended consequences for local convention activities.

By the same token, when the obviously relevant commissioners were absent, or when they failed to perceive the implications of a proposed reform, it passed without difficulty. Guideline C–1 (Adequate Public Notice) was such a case. C–1 dispatched the delegate primary, but while most commissioners did see the formal effect of requiring delegates to run with a presidential preference attached to their names, they suspected that this would make little practical difference. Several of those with actual, *contradictory,* home-state experience—I. W. Abel, Louis Martin, and Adlai Stevenson—were not in attendance. The few others who believed that the general perception of the impact of C–1 was wrong were then numerically overwhelmed. Eli Segal, like Bode, watched these incidents with surprise:

> If you say it's a runaway staff operation—I don't know if you think it was a runaway staff or not. But there were only maybe half a dozen people—Davis, who was the smartest, and then Mitchell of course, Dodds *probably,* Dutton, McGovern of course, *maybe* Hughes—they were the only ones who knew what they were actually doing, who understood what the votes meant in political terms. The others never knew. Warren Christopher would introduce things if we asked him, but he never paid attention. Bayh was out of it most of the time; Stevenson, too. I must admit I was amazed at the way they let us run things. There wasn't even any lobbying in advance, any calling back and forth between members. There was only us.

This characteristic of commission debate—its reliance on a general perception of some automatic effect on outcomes—helped to explain not just the ultimate fate of many guidelines, but the course of discussion along the way. Guidelines A–1 and A–2, on demographic representation, were the classic case. Both, as they had advanced through the series of fall meetings, had contained nothing to alarm commission members. They seemed decent and desirable, but largely hortatory. The instant Birch Bayh injected his "reasonable relationship" language, however, they gained a pointed and dramatic character—or at least, everyone's attention was called to the fact that they *might* possess that character.

A lengthy and heated discussion followed. In fact, the commissioners were unable to leave these guidelines alone until they had returned to add a footnote which *denied* that a shift in outcomes was required, which asserted that the apparent concrete impact of these guidelines was not really there. Carmen Warschaw and Oscar Mauzy, both of whom voted for the "reasonable relationship" language *and* the footnote to it, showed the diagnostic difference. Warschaw denied the existence of quotas:

> To us, it meant no quotas. To me, this was the closest you could come without saying quotas, and still have some action toward improving the situation. It was difficult to arrive at this as a formulation.

Mauzy, on the other hand, viewed a quota interpretation as an eventual inevitability:

> That was window dressing, the sixteen-to-nothing statement [the footnote]. The debate was full of the word "quota." There was a lot of harangue over semantics and language, but at bottom, everybody knew what was there.

A more detached appraisal of A–1 and A–2, even at the time, would have said that the fight over their practical meaning had been postponed, not resolved. Several other guidelines received this treatment in an even purer form. That is, the commissioners recognized an inherent effect from the text alone; they argued about it as a group; but they redrafted the guideline so that its eventual meaning remained open-ended.

The proposed guideline on participation by the National Committee was one of these. The guideline entered the November meeting with a clear if not necessarily major impact on the process of delegate selection: It ejected sitting committee members from their ex officio seats. The commissioners were immediately unsettled, and they deleted the proposal, but the majority for deletion was actually composed of those who felt that the National Committee should not be offended *and* those who felt that Guideline C–2 (Automatic Delegates) had already wiped it out. A subsequent interpretation would obviously have to award the decision to one half of this majority or the other.

Commission language on slate making was left in a similarly ambiguous condition. Slates were to be developed in "due consultation" with the candidate for whom they nominally stood, but this might mean that such consultation included a veto and the right of substitution, or it might imply only that the candidate, too, had the right to contest in an open process for the formation of "his" delegate slate. Despite the distance between these positions, the commissioners were again disinclined to stay around and narrow the gap, once they had found language which could garner a majority. Dick Wade watched them let such issues slide away into the future:

> It was crazy in that Commission that you left the candidate bereft of any control over the delegation. Candidates could "accept" the nominees, but that was all. At the Commission, the consequences didn't seem so bad. McGovern, Bayh, and Hughes all thought that they would be candidates, but none of them ever raised that point. They were all looking for some grass-roots movement.

The one category of recommendations for which these considerations were least relevant were the provisions which staff inserted into the commission report after the commissioners had departed. Scattered throughout the various guidelines, these provisions included a requirement that three quarters of a state delegation to be selected below the statewide level, an extension of the apportionment formula to the bottom level of the process, a prohibition on favorite-son candidacies, and a ban on state or local party endorsement of a slate of delegates. Some of these had been arguably intended by the commissioners. Others had never been foreseen. None had been formally adopted.[15]

Implications

With the adjournment of the Party Structure Commission in the late afternoon of November 20, 1969, the first phase of reform politics, the politics of recommendation, was drawing rapidly to a close. The larger, longer, and more consequential politics of recommendation was still, of course, to follow. But major attempts to influence the formal texts of the recommendations at the center of this subsequent politics were not. With the exception of a few tactical questions about the presentation of the reform report itself, the recognizable decisions, the political turning points, in the chronicle of official recommendations for reform were all in the past.

With the adjournment of the Party Structure Commission on that Friday afternoon, the potential scope of this party reform, of the institutional change associated with its recommendations, was almost completely resolved. Eighteen principal guidelines, with sweeping institutional implications, had been adopted by the official reform commission. A set of technical and editorial tasks remained before this complete commission report could be put before party leaders and the interested public. Major political tasks did not.

With the adjournment of the Party Structure Commission, finally, the outer boundaries of practical impact from its reform recommendations came, for the first time, into general public view. The guidelines as a detailed and publicly available text were presumably a matter of weeks from publication and dissemination to interested elite actors, within the orthodox and alternative Democratic coalitions. The institutional implications of these guidelines were presumably a matter of months from exposure to those state party officials who would be asked to realize them. The practical results of these institutional implications were waiting immediately beyond.

The most limited of these practical outcomes was a massively reshaped composite process of presidential selection. This would follow automatically if the attempt at implementation were successful. If nothing more followed, the formal change from this successful implementation would still be the greatest shift in the mechanics of presidential nomination since the creation of national party conventions themselves, in the 1830s. And it would still be the largest systematically planned change in these procedures in American history.

Yet if this direct, organizational reform were realized, it could hardly avoid facilitating—triggering, really—an indirect but even more serious, practical change in the politics surrounding these mechanics. This was, in fact, a less definitional but almost equally automatic response to sweeping changes in the institutional arrangements of presidential politics.

The logical fallout from realization of this reformed process was, in fact, a substantially changed pattern of political activity by candidates, specialized participants, and the party rank and file. Stated differently, these new arrangements promised practical change in nearly every operational aspect of presidential selection, including the type of candidates likely to compose the field, the nature of the resources needed to participate successfully, the character of the issues raised along the way, and the identity of the beneficiaries in society at large.

The grandest potential outcome, finally, was a transformation of the character of elite actors in presidential politics, and thus of national political elites in general. This was *guaranteed* if these reforms were implemented and if they worked as their drafters intended. It was *likely* if these reforms were extensively implemented, period—whether they worked as their drafters intended or in some new, different, unforeseen, but still evidently substantial manner.

The official recommendations of the Party Structure Commission, then, were impressive by nearly any standard. At a minimum—and the fact of these impacts as a "minimum" deserves emphasis—they proposed central, national rules of great breadth and depth for the practically independent, almost formally independent, state and local political parties. These rules, in turn, promised to restructure the fundamental, continuing institutions of delegate selection, not only in the individual states but as a composite national matrix. In the process, they threatened to alter a broad range of associated arrangements and procedures, from the distribution of the delegates themselves, to their initial slating for the right to be selected, through the awarding of these delegates to presidential contenders, to the demographic composition of the resulting delegations.

These automatic impacts, contained—and sometimes hidden—within eighteen reform guidelines, had been shaped most proximately by the particular dynamics of the final commission meeting on November 19 and 20. That is, they had been most directly affected by the arguments presented as each draft guideline appeared, by the receptivity of other commissioners to these arguments, by the parliamentary and other tactical maneuvers which surfaced as discussion proceeded, by the *order* in which reform proposals were addressed, and by the ramifications of each resolution on subsequent decisions.

Had the commissioners as a collectivity been a less atomistic body, and had their leadership and staff not been determined to make this their final drafting session, these idiosyncratic effects would have been less decisive. But the commissioners had met only once as a working collectivity before these final sessions; their staff and leadership were determined that these sessions indeed be final; and a clear, meeting-specific impact on the total product of the commission did result.

Nevertheless, the primary impact on the contents of this total product—indeed, the primary impact on the course of this final meeting—was still the balance of influence within the commission as it had evolved during the nine months before the November sessions. Much of this influence, especially the balance between independent and intermittent commissioners versus a cohesive and continuing staff, had, in fact, been established before the commissioners had even been brought back into the politics of party reform.

The November meeting confirmed the importance of Fred Harris's initial criteria for commission appointment, by demonstrating a solid, working majority for extensive party reform. The meeting confirmed as well the substantive and style differences within the commission leadership, between Chairman McGovern and Vice Chairman Hughes, differences which had earlier been important to the development of reform recommendations.[16] Most fundamentally, of course, the meeting confirmed the persistence of inherent staff advantages. The staff, for example, retained its formal, positional assets. It was full-time, expert, and at the center of reform communications. Moreover, staff members knew what they wanted and how they hoped to attain it. They were far more dedicated than any individual commissioner, and dedicated to one overall, desired outcome.

The commissioners were never simply acquiescent. They did contend directly and actively with the draft text put before them, as well as with the staff members aligned behind it. Their contentions did result in the recasting of that document, to accommodate a new and potentially major action on demographic representation. Despite this, the overwhelming share of the document going out to publication was effectively identical to the draft document preceding it.

Again, the carry-over from earlier, major influences on internal commission politics was primarily responsible for this limited intervention by the commissioners. But a peculiar way of responding to reform proposals by the commissioners themselves, a pattern of response surfacing in the fall meetings and appearing again in November, was also integral to this limited intervention. Or at least, this pattern translated those earlier influences and thus became an additional, indirect influence on the proposed reform document.

The pattern involved an active response to guidelines which promised a reliable impact on the *outcome* of the selection process. It involved an indifferent and erratic response to guidelines which promised to affect the *institutional* structure of delegate selection instead. The pattern appeared most commonly when stimulated by the face impact of a guideline. Guidelines which asserted in their very text that they were affecting outcomes drew reliable debate; others were likely to escape without debate, or discussion, or even attention. The pattern surfaced secondarily as a result of commissioner experiences. When an individual commissioner had prior political experience which gave that guideline an apparent impact on outcome, the other commissioners were frequently drawn to debate; when no one had that experience, or when no one could communicate it forcefully, the commissioners frequently passed on by.

The key aspect of this pattern—a tendency to credit impact upon outcomes but not upon institutional arrangements—appeared and was confirmed in the series of fall meetings leading up to the final drafting session in November. There, it became the collective filter through which the commissioners as a body addressed their staff draft for the last time. Yet the pattern itself was largely a product of prior influences in commission politics, so that it served not so much to redirect those influences as to provide an additional, indirect expression of same.

For example, while the commissioners were more likely to exert themselves and question staff suggestions when an individual commissioner had immediately relevant experience, it was also the case that comparatively few commissioners possessed that experience—and that the commission had been expressly designed to create this condition. Numerous individuals on the Party Structure Commission had some public or party office behind their name; few had contemporary statewide responsibility for organizing campaigns and electing candidates.

Moreover, while Fred Harris had hardly concentrated on this contribution to commission perceptions when he created the Party Structure Commission, he *had* deliberately reduced the number of commissioners with contemporary organizational responsibilities in a state or local political party. This characteristic not only made the commissioners as a group more receptive to reform in the abstract; it made them less likely to examine specific reform suggestions in light of some potentially countervailing experience.

When the commissioners did not see an obvious, surface impact in the text of a guideline, they could still be roused to discussion and debate by a pointed example putting concrete impact into the formal text. Yet it was still *staff members,* rather than the commissioners, who were in the best position to provide these examples. Staff members tried to prepare supporting evidence for every guideline. They tried to prepare extra support for those with the potential for controversy, should the commissioners make a divergent connection to experience. They tried to anticipate what key commissioners would say in response to certain guidelines, so as to counter them with arguments and examples. Ken Bode recalled these efforts:

> Eli and I would prepare to meet what Will Davis and George Mitchell would say. What will they say on this? What will they say on that? Everything was marked "K" and "E" to set it up for the arguments.

On the commissioners' side of the aisle, Sam Beer found this preparation, and the subsequent activity associated with it, to be powerfully annoying:

> To my knowledge, *no* Commission members had any input into the staff. And among the consultants, the only person who regularly showed was Anne Wexler. It was almost as if she were being made an added member. She held forth all the g.d. time. She *was* like a member.

What was true for staff provision of supporting examples was, of course, equally true for the withholding of this crucial stimulation. As the abolition of the party caucus strongly suggested, when the impact of a guideline was indirect, the role of the staff in underlining its institutional implications became critical. Had there been an abstract student of the process of delegate selection, which is to say a staff member, who wanted to step forward and pull together the guidelines which would jointly abolish the party caucus, he could surely have induced a far more extensive debate. Indeed, a personal warning that a venerable device for delegate selection was about to go out of existence might have sufficed, by itself, to produce a different result. But as the case of the party caucus also suggested, there was no such person—and existing staff members were not inclined to fill in for him. Bob Nelson noted the staff role here:

> Davis and Mitchell both argued that, on many of the guidelines, the national convention had no idea that we would go into this. We would always fall back on the "all feasible efforts" language. Nothing would keep them from making the effort, but then keeping their old rules. But as you went on, what "all feasible efforts" meant concretely became tougher and tougher. Maybe some of the Commissioners couldn't see that.

It would not do to overstate staff comprehension of their own recommendations. The practical effects of successful implementation of a package of reforms this broad and deep would surely—and surely did—contain surprises for everyone associated with their creation. Beyond that, staff members, too, never explicitly outlined the combination of institutional impacts which would result from acceptance of their guidelines—and might not have been able to do so. But they did strive for the introduction of opportunities for participation at every step of the nomination process. They did seek to remove the regular party along the way. And they did cross-check the individual recommendations which resulted, to see that they were internally consistent. In this sense, then, they were at least more aware of combined institutional implications than were their official commissioners.

What resulted, in any case, was the most extensive set of recommendations for reform of the process of presidential nomination in the history of the Democratic party—and of American parties in general. What did not result, by the same token, was any guarantee that these proposals would actually become party practice, or even party law. At a minimum, they were an unsolicited demand on the time, energy, and resources of party leaders across the nation. For most, they were more than that: They were nothing less than an attack upon traditional ways of handling delegate selection, and thus upon practical influence over presidential nominations and upon the internal organization of state and local party affairs.

Whether these recommendations achieved the institutional impacts inherent in their reform demands depended on the course of the politics of implementation, and on the ultimate scope of its success. Whether these recommendations achieved the larger practical impacts on presidential politics associated with their institutional arrangements depended, in turn, on the scope of implementation and on the character of the politics associated with it. Whether these recommendations achieved their ultimate possibility, the replacement of one established coalition of elites with another aspiring alternative in the national Democratic party, and whether this elite replacement was merely an introduction to a more general circulation of elites in national politics, depended critically both on the character of implementation politics and on its results.

CHAPTER

8

The Promulgation of Party Reform:

Compliance Letters and a Published Report

IN WHICH, the commission staff and leadership adopt a strategy for presentation of their handiwork to its relevant publics; these individuals address themselves specifically to compliance letters for the fifty state chairmen and to a general report for a wider audience; and detailed maneuvering for the development of these central documents occurs in an atmosphere of anxiety about the response. AND IN WHICH, reform politics shifts from a politics of recommendation to a politics of implementation; the detailed requirements of institutional change are revealed to state party officials while a grand picture of these required changes is painted for the attentive public; and the influence of crucial surrogates for the alternative Democratic coalition reaches a peak, just before the return of the regular party as the major arena for conflict over party reform.

THE PERIOD between late November of 1969 and late April of 1970 saw the final product of the Party Structure Commission converted into various official communications and presented to the various audiences which would be critical to its impact. As such, this period became the inevitable transition between the politics of recommendation and the politics of implementation. On the day after the final drafting session of the commission, on November 21, 1969, the remaining commission leadership and staff were still clearly focused on what would be the denouement of the politics of recommendation. On the day after publication of the commission report, on April 29, 1970, that leadership and staff were equally, evidently involved in the opening phase of the politics of implementation. In between, this five-month transition was a mix of characteristics from both brands of politics.

Only two additional tasks remained in the aftermath of the November meeting before commission proposals could be pressed upon the outside world. A general report had to be developed, to inform the interested public of commission recommendations. Individual compliance letters had to be developed, to inform state party chairmen of the specific implications of these general recommendations. Both tasks were apparently straightforward and mechanical.

Despite expectations of dispatch, these two undertakings were to stretch out for a full five months. In part, this was due to a simple overestimate of the ease with which the technical end of these jobs could be accomplished. In part, the delay was due to related strategic considerations, involving the composition, tone, and audience for both the compliance letters and the published report. In part, this delay, this extension in the period of transition, resulted from a shift at national party headquarters, a shift which raised both immediate and long-run questions for the fate of the commission product.

The process of moving toward a published report and fifty-five individual compliance letters began, and then ended, with the technical labors inherent in drafting a comprehensive report and in organizing background information on the fifty-five state, district, and territorial parties. In spite of substantial prior research, the latter task, the application of individualized detail to fifty-five separate cases, came to require more time than eager staff members had hoped.

The technical aspects of these tasks, however, were immediately enmeshed in larger strategic questions. The first of these was the timing of an approach to the National Committee, the crucial body in rule making for the national party. The resolution of that question, a conscious hesitation while individual successes were sought in the states, fed back into decisions about format and content for both the compliance letters and the published report. Each of these tactical elaborations then implied substantive adjustments and added technical activity.

By the time these questions were resolved and the commission staff was again pressing forward, their plans received an additional shock. Fred Harris resigned abruptly as national chairman; the commission was presented with yet another strategic decision. Should it push for publication on its own and risk offending Harris's successor? Or should it await that unknown successor and risk not only wasting time but encountering an indifferent sponsor? The commission response—deliberate, independent publication—closed the transition from the politics of recommendation to the politics of implementation, in a posture not of conciliation but of continued opposition and implicit defiance.

While all this was occurring, the cast of characters for the politics of party reform changed in a correlate, and highly consequential, fashion. The shift began at the Party Structure Commission, where it appeared as a constriction in the number of relevant actors. But it continued, courtesy of the compliance letters and the published report, with state and national party officialdom and with the interested public at large. And that, of course, was a corresponding expansion of far greater scope.

After this, state party leaders, National Committee members, organized reformers, and especially the national chairman would share crucial reform activities with the remnants of the commission enterprise. In the process, the focus of reform politics—negotiations over implementation of reform guidelines—changed profoundly. The institutional implications of reform politics—the practical meaning of these struggles over guideline implementation—changed as well. So, finally, did the nature of the elites contending for reform—and this shift promised to affect not just the fate but the meaning of proposed institutional change.

The Development of Compliance Notices

The question of the moment, as the Party Structure Commission recessed from its final drafting session, was not how long it would take to convert commission decisions into detailed compliance letters and a published report. The answer to that question would admittedly spawn a five-month interim in reform politics, with interesting—even consequential—developments all its own. Yet for those who possessed immediate acquaintance with commission recommendations, the central question was hardly narrow and administrative. Instead, it concerned the practical fate of the eighteen guidelines which had been framed at their final meeting.

A healthy majority of the commissioners themselves were favorably inclined toward their final recommendations. Not all were as enthusiastic as Anne Wexler, who told an Associated Press reporter that "I never dreamed we'd be able to accomplish this much,"[1] but most were prepared to endorse their handiwork, taken as a whole. Where this consensus broke down was not on the virtue of the guidelines as a package, but on the question of that package's probable fate. At one extreme, George McGovern projected an unflinching faith that the complete report would become party law:

> I was entirely confident that we could pull it off. I thought that resistance
> would be stronger on the part of the National Committee and on the part of

the state parties. I was pleasantly surprised to see them [the guidelines] approved first by the Chairman, then by the Executive Board, then by the full Committee. There was good acceptance that they had to be implemented.

Warren Christopher, a similarly strong partisan of the guidelines, was a trifle less certain:

> I remember feeling that the final report of the Commission was good. It achieved a certain sense of minimal goals that I had had going into the Commission. I did not perform very well myself on it, but I thought the result was good. I wasn't sure whether it would be implemented or not. I would say that I had hopes rather than expectations. I thought some part of it would go into effect, but I didn't know how much.

Still less optimistic was Don Fraser, the eventual successor to McGovern as commission chairman:

> I expected some difficulty. There was the question of what the role of the National Committee would be. The Commission's position would be that what it did would not require further action by the National Committee. That argument was advanced by the staff. But if the National Committee decided to contest parts of it, there would have been a brouhaha. That was one concern. The other, related issue was whether the states were likely to follow through.

Finally, on the far pessimistic end, Sam Beer felt that there was no guarantee of any concrete result:

> You know what happened. Nobody thought these would amount to a damn. Everybody thought it would be a great big joke. Organized labor thought by boycotting it, they could make it nugatory. In the days of Rayburn and others, this would have been true. Even some of us at times thought we were going through symbolic exercises. And then, by God, it was law. But even most of us didn't expect it to have the impact that it did.

It was this same aspect of the guidelines—not their abstract virtues, nor their concrete implications, but their probable fate—which engaged the press. As the remaining commissioners departed in the late afternoon of November 20, Chairman McGovern talked with newsmen in an impromptu press conference. A few reporters did pick at the practical effect of particular guidelines; most focused on the issue of their legal status. McGovern bravely offered the staff position, that the commission was a creature of the national convention and that the guidelines had become party law a half hour before. But he was willing, when pushed, to admit that these new rules would come a lot closer to being party law, in fact as well as in theory, if the National Committee gave them a boost:

Reporter (unidentified): Senator. Senator, just what is the legal situation of these guidelines which have been passed here today?

McGovern: We have always taken the position that they are party law, that they become effective once this Commission has approved them.

Reporter (same voice): But Senator, isn't it really true that they won't have much muscle behind them unless the National Committee approves them, too, and that if it doesn't, they will be pretty much a dead letter?

McGovern: Well, there's no denying that the Commission will be in a much stronger position after the National Committee has endorsed its report.[2]

An approach to the Democratic National Committee was indeed the nub of commission strategy on guideline implementation. It was the National Committee, after all, which issued the "Call to Convention" for 1972. That Call, in turn, presented the mandatory rules for delegate selection and convention activity. If these rules ignored the commission guidelines, and surely if they differed from them, the guidelines would instantly become optional. State parties which wanted to conform to commission recommendations could still do so; state parties which preferred to conform to the Call would predictably do that; and some might even pick and choose, taking this provision from the commission report, that one from the official Call. Dick Wade, at least, had few doubts on this score:[3]

> The question was, did the Commission report back to the Convention, where it would not need the endorsement of the Democratic National Committee, or did it report to the body which had, after all, appointed it. My assumption was that no matter what the legalities were, if you couldn't get it through the National Committee, you couldn't get it. You had to get strong support to get it by. . . . The only way to make it workable was to have the Call to the Convention include the guidelines, and who makes up the Call? Can you imagine if the Mc-Govern Commission made up one Call and the National Committee made up another? The issue was hanging around, but it was not being pressed. In my mind, I never had any illusion that fifteen members of the party could change the rules of fifty states.

So, the National Committee had to be approached. The issue then became one of tactics and timing, and here, there were two obvious options. The commission could take the guidelines to the National Committee immediately, building on a first rush of enthusiasm for their newly completed product, and press for official acceptance. If this effort were successful, the commission would possess a powerful weapon for bringing the individual state parties into compliance—far more powerful than independent assertions of legal authority. The risk, however, was equally evident. If the effort failed, the entire move for party reform might be over.

The second option also featured a partial resolution at the National Committee, but more indirectly and farther down the road. Under this plan, the guidelines would be pressed first upon the individual states. During the period of decentralized activity which would ideally follow, some state parties would begin moving into conformity on their own. Then, at some later point, perhaps when the National Committee came to adopt a Call, the guidelines could be pressed upon the committee, too. By that time, they would already be law in at least a minority of states; these state parties would provide a bloc of votes for adoption by the National Committee; National Committee endorsement—with its threat of sanctions in the Credentials Committee—could serve as the means for encouraging conformity in the remainder of the states.

The choice between these two options was partially shaped by circumstance. The National Committee was not slated to meet until well past the first of the year; even then, it was unlikely to act on commission recommendation until the commission report had been exposed, in detail, to the state party chairmen. But beyond this initial nudge toward the delayed approach, there was, it developed, a kind of consensus within the commission entourage as well.

The more moderate and pragmatic members—McGovern, Nelson, Wade, and Bickel—believed that it was tactically wiser to hold off. With Nelson, they believed that they were more likely to lose an immediate confrontation and less likely to lose one farther down the road, especially if they could accumulate some successes:

> Our feelings were, and I remember this very strongly, at some point in time we've got to get a Committee vote, but let's *wait* until we have the votes. Obviously, the National Committee members were informed at all times. There were only a few who were antagonistic all the way along. J. Marshall Brown had a small group like that.

On the other side, the more militant and dogmatic strategists—Hughes, Segal, Bode, and Wexler—preferred this option, too. With Bode, they saw it as a way to continue to maintain, first, that the guidelines were *already* party law, second, that the commission (and *only* the commission) should now focus on "aiding" the states into compliance, and, third, that the National Committee need not even be approached, ever:

> Our theory was always that the guidelines *were* law, without being adopted by the National Committee, without being included in the Call. Later, there was a legal opinion to that effect, the Califano memo. O'Brien wanted the National Committee to vote, to have it legitimizing. Our feeling always was that

the vote was unnecessary and irrelevant. If they wanted to read and study the guidelines, that was fine; everyone had the right to do that. But that was all they were entitled to do, and they didn't have to do that.

The staff thus set to work on its two initial tasks—publication of a general report and development of fifty-five individual compliance letters—with this peculiarly consensual strategy in mind. The National Committee would be ducked; the state parties would be explicitly addressed; sympathetic forces in the nation at large would be put on notice that crucial reform issues were hanging in the balance.

Once an initial strategy had been chosen, the tactical details for both the report and the compliance letters began to fall into place. The target for each document, for example, followed logically from the decision to bypass the National Committee. The report could now speak directly to the attentive public for reform politics, which meant, primarily, those who were most in favor of structural reform. Indeed, this was a necessity if the report was to help mobilize them for battles over implementation. By the same token, the compliance letters could speak even more directly to the state party leadership, taking these leaders through the precise requirements of the new party rules, but in the privacy of their own offices.

Once these targets were established, the tone of both documents was also well on the way to being set. If the report was to speak to the reform constituency, and certainly if it was to *mobilize* that constituency, it would have to be hard-hitting and hortatory. If the compliance letters were to move even closer to private correspondence, they could be detailed, factual, and conciliatory. Indeed, that was the only plausible approach if they were to avoid alarming some state party leaders, while eliciting the maximum in spontaneous compliance from others.

The principal actors who would uncover these implications and make these tactical adjustments were a sharply reduced sample of those who had participated in the commission meetings of November 19 and 20. Then, the task of framing a set of reform recommendations had guaranteed a central role for the full commission. Afterward, the mechanics of converting these recommendations into a formal product, published and disseminated, provided no similar role. As a result, the commission again came to consist of its leadership and staff. These six individuals—McGovern, Hughes, Nelson, Segal, Bode, and Carol Casey, summer intern and eventual staff assistant—got to manage presentation of the commission product to the outside world.

That presentation, on the other hand, vastly expanded the realm of outside actors who would—or at least could—play a role in reform politics. The largest group of these individuals was ultimately reached by the published report of the commission. But the most critical and immediate segment of this expanded roster was the state party chairmen, the recipients of fifty individual compliance letters. From November of 1969 through April of 1970, then, a published report and particularized compliance notices were both the major focus of this reduced commission entourage and the means whereby the list of relevant actors for reform politics was unavoidably increased.

Between the two documents, it was the letters which absorbed by far the largest share of staff time. Their demands for information were large—comprehensive facts about actual practices in delegate selection. So was their number—fifty-five, for the fifty states, the District of Columbia, and the four territories. The character of their audience, finally, was crucial—the Democratic state chairmen themselves. Staff members like Bode approached these individual interpretations with some anxiety:

> We took a very cautious view of implementation. We did compliance letters. They were carefully fashioned to offend nobody. We used those letters to establish that these rules were binding on the states themselves. This was another step toward establishing the authority of the Commission. We tried to analyze those rules to them very neutrally. We would not release those letters to anybody until everybody got them. We did everything we could to make those things clear. We were really paranoid that we would make some major mistakes.

In theory, the necessary information for these letters was in the state-books, and there had even been a preliminary effort at retrieving it in the late summer and early fall. In practice, this had proved to be a false start, because preparations for the critical, formal commission sessions of September and November had soon absorbed the attention of everyone.

By the time the November meetings were past, the plan to recast the state-books for the compliance letters had stalled again, this time over the poor quality of existing commission data and over the impact of the academic calendar on the labor available to bring these data up to standard. By late September, both undergraduate and graduate interns were being drawn inexorably back to their colleges and universities. By late November, it was no longer possible to assign "summer interns" to compliance research. The loss of this volunteer labor was doubly felt, since the staff, with actual implementation and not abstract argument in mind, came to view their data on delegate selection with markedly decreased confidence.

This information had served, and served well, to impress the commissioners with the need for particular reforms. But when the time came to plug it directly into compliance letters, staff members lacked sufficient faith in its accuracy, especially when it had to explain a state system of delegate selection *to the state party chairman.* Renewed digging for state party data thus became the order of the day.[4] Despite this, the impending arrival of compliance letters was revealed to the state party leadership on December 9 by Chairman McGovern, in a note addressed to each state chairman, with a copy to the national committeeman and committeewoman:

> In order to aid you in meeting the standards established by the Commission, we will be sending you soon a preliminary staff analysis which details your State's delegate selection process as it relates to the guidelines. If there is any way in which the staff can be of assistance to you before that time, either in the form of information or technical assistance, please let us know. In any case, we will arrange for people who are thoroughly familiar with the guidelines to contact you soon.[5]

Within a week, the staff had developed a prototype for these letters, including a covering note, four individually applied descriptive sections, and a warning on how to avoid credentials challenges at the 1972 Convention.[6] At that point, however, the process slowed. The distance between possessing an approved prototype and possessing the data to fill in the blanks—fifty-five times—was ultimately measured in another ten weeks of staff effort. The "soon" which Chairman McGovern had promised state party leaders began to stretch out accordingly.

It was not until February 27, 1970, then, two days short of a year from the first meeting of the commission, that fifty-five compliance letters went out to state, territorial, and district chairmen. The six-page letter to Pennsylvania was representative, and its covering note was a reasonable summary of its contents:

Dear Mr. Minehart:

> In December 1969, we sent you a copy of the Official Guidelines for Delegate Selection of the Commission on Party Structure and Delegate Selection. In keeping with the Commission's obligation to "aid the states" in meeting the requirements of the Call to the 1972 Convention, the Commission staff has analyzed the delegate Selection process in your state as it relates to the Guidelines.
>
> The enclosed analysis is based on the best information available to the Commission at this time. For each state, we have compiled and evaluated the election laws, Democratic Party rules and practices, testimony taken at our public hearings, statements submitted to our offices, and newspaper accounts of the delegate selection process. If your understanding of the process in your state differs from the analysis, we hope you will contact us at your earliest convenience.
>
> This analysis is limited to: (1) those laws, rules, and practices in your state that are inconsistent with the mandatory requirements of the Commission Guidelines; and (2) those Guidelines that the Commission urges State Parties to adopt.

In most cases, conformity with the Guidelines—a copy of which is attached for your ready reference—can be achieved in several ways. We are prepared to offer whatever technical assistance you may need to evaluate and respond to the analysis. You will note that we specifically deal with the following Guidelines for the state of Pennsylvania: A–2, A–5, B–1, B–4, B–5, B–7, C–1, C–4, C–5, C–6.

Since the beginning of Commission deliberations, we have been encouraged by the commitment to reform demonstrated by Party leaders. We believe that the adoption of the Commission's Guidelines, along with the local reform efforts, will ensure a strong and winning Democratic Party.

Sincerely yours,
George McGovern
Chairman[7]

Pennsylvania, in being judged out of compliance with ten of the eighteen guidelines, was relatively typical. Four states were in violation of twelve, the high score. Nine states were in conflict with only six, the low, although these summary figures reflected neither the severity of individual violations nor the prognosis for rapid correction. Six guidelines had at least forty of the fifty states out of compliance. Only one featured fewer than ten states delinquent.[8]

As a result, no state chairman received a letter from which he could draw immediate satisfaction. Some fared better than others; all were faced with an unsolicited demand upon their time and their political credits. Yet if this mailing constituted a guaranteed irritant for them, it was also an opportunity to vent any resulting displeasure. Indeed, the release of the compliance letters seemed, to many insiders, to be the obvious point at which the counterattack against party reform would begin.

It was not the first plausible occasion. For most state parties, that had come with the mass mailings in October, preparatory to the final commission meetings. At that time, state party leaders had been given their first real evidence of how extensive commission recommendations might be. Despite this, there had been precious little response from the states, and most of that had come from staunch reformers, protesting the *moderation* of proposed reforms.[9] After that, the November meetings had provided a second focused opportunity for dissent, when their final decisions were announced. This, too, passed without major comment. Carol Casey was surprised at this passivity:

> It seemed that the general public reaction was favorable, at least as far as we could judge. On the other hand, there wasn't really much coverage of that meeting. Many reporters came, but few wrote stories. Naturally, there wasn't much public reaction either.

But the third and most serious opportunity for spontaneous, public opposition—or even for coordinated resistance—came with the dispatching of the compliance letters. With their arrival, the state chairmen, the chairmen of state reform commissions, and the members of the National Committee could at last see, unavoidably and in detail, how much would be required if they were to bring their states into line. Some would see a demand for root-and-branch change, in state party rules and even in state law. None would enjoy the knowledge that they were already near compliance and were thus free to sit back and watch their neighbors struggle. Segal and his fellow commission staffers expected some stiff protest from those whose ways of doing business were most strongly under challenge:

> All through 1969 and 1970, we made lots of efforts to attract attention. Whatever the reason, nobody paid us any attention. Then we thought when we sent out the compliance letters—we thought that they were tough yet diplomatic—we thought that the shit would hit the fan. Instead, nothing happened. No states' rights arguments, very few comments about errors, just nothing.

A minority of states, though not an inconsequential minority, actually accepted the guidelines as intrinsically virtuous. If the labor associated with implementing them prevented party leaders from trumpeting their admiration, these leaders did knuckle down and begin the process of institutional translation. And the rest of their counterparts, the solid majority, simply held their peace.

It was not clear—and, many felt, not reasonable to assume—that the guidelines would ever have much effect. The Party Structure Commission might choose to call them "rules." State party leaders might as easily see only the recommendations of a quasi-independent study group, recommendations which lacked even a token endorsement from the National Committee. Under those conditions, it was comparatively foolish to take a public stand against these proposed reforms. Such a stand would automatically brand its contributor as "antireform"; if there was no good reason to suppose that the guidelines would be implemented anyway, there was little reason to pay that price. Instead, party leaders who preferred the unreformed political world and who had contempt for those who were pushing its revision simply accepted their correspondence and awaited developments.

The concrete embodiment of these more general responses varied considerably from state to state. In some, nothing happened at all; Hawaii was to remain in this category for a long time. In some, the state chairman saluted the work of the national commission while opining that it had little relevance to his own bailiwick; Texas was one of these. In others, the state chairman actually appointed an indigenous reform commission, which addressed its responsibility at a snail's pace; Pennsylvania was an example. In still others, a reform commission was appointed, met, and produced a plan for reform, a plan which had little congruence with national commission guidelines; this was essentially the California situation. In some, finally, the state chairman began immediately to translate commission strictures into state party rules; Alabama, Maine, and Minnesota fell into this group.

Overall, then, the minority who were unbothered by the guidelines began to put them into effect, or at least to make some preliminary moves toward compliance. The majority who were either uninterested or actively unhappy did not engage in any coordinated display of disaffection, or even in individual public complaint. Instead, they bided their time—and trusted their opposite numbers across the country to do likewise.

The Publication of a Reform Report

The drafting of the other major reform announcement, the published report of the Party Structure Commission, had also begun immediately after the meetings of November 19 and 20. Staff members came to see the report as a means of communicating with the interested public, and especially with the proreform public, whose assistance would be essential if its contents were to become the institutions of delegate selection in the national Democratic party. Because the report was explicitly hortatory, and because it did not feature the detailed statistical demands of the compliance letters, staff members turned to it with a good deal of enthusiasm.

A nearly complete draft of this final report went to Chairman McGovern on January 26, along with a two-page memo from Bode and Segal offering possible additions and raising questions about the tactics of presentation.[10] Much of the factual content of this draft, and some of its organization and argument as well, was based on the doctoral dissertation in political science of Richard G. Stearns.[11] During the summer of 1969, Stearns had benefited from the interns' research in launching his own. By January of 1970, the tables had turned, and Bode and Segal were drawing on his draft chapters to inform their work.

McGovern basically approved what he saw, and by January 30, a copy was ready to go out for review by the other commissioners. A covering memo from the commission staff emphasized, however, that there was nothing left to say:

> Enclosed is a draft report on delegate selection in 1968. We have prepared it for two reasons: (1) our mandate requires us to "report to the Democratic Na-

tional Committee concerning (our) efforts and findings," and (2) we have had numerous requests for a narrative of our history and our rationale for the guidelines.

We view this draft as an analytical account of our origins and our work to date. It offers nothing in the way of recommendations or requirements beyond those the Commission adopted in November.[12]

Staff members had worried continually that finances might crimp their publication plans, and the January 30 mailing put the commissioners on notice about that, too. But their real fear, as they circulated this draft, was quite different. During the final commission meetings in November, there had been periodic rumblings about the need for this or that "minority report." The arrival of a purportedly final document would inevitably crystallize any such sentiment which remained.

The possibility that dissident commissioners would seize this chance to pull their views together was looked on by the staff with real trepidation; the possibility that they would ask to have those views included in the report itself produced genuine horror. Public displays of dissension would be an obvious signal that the report contained items about which party leaders should be concerned. Moreover, such displays would testify to an absence of unanimity, even within the commission, on the substance of its recommendations. Finally, official dissent would provide uneasy party leaders with the initial arguments—with weapons—to use against the entire document.

To the extent that simple manipulations of the text were likely to reduce this risk, the staff was willing to make them. Thus, while Chairman McGovern was going with generally tougher language for the report as a whole, he did overrule Bode on the handling of proportionality, after Segal argued that a stiff position was the surest route to minority reports:

> We also differ on the need for the last paragraph on p. 29, Ken (and Alex) believing that proportional representation occupies a very special status in the Commission's work, Eli believing that it does not belong in this section (and is inappropriate for other sections). Ken thinks we may want a special section on this whole matter; Eli fears a proliferation of Minority Reports if this is done.[13]

Beyond such minor adjustments, however, the staff and leadership could do little to avert the most immediate danger to the goal of implementation, except to sit, and wait, and see what came back in.

Two commissioners, Fred Dutton and David Mixner, had voiced explicit intentions to use the minority report device; two others, Will Davis and George Mitchell, were widely believed to be considering the possibility. But by the time the commissioners recessed, few believed that Dutton or Mixner would follow through. Dick Wade watched a climate of good feeling begin to meliorate the irritation of proreform commissioners:

> At lunch, I thought there was a very good chance that there would be Minority Reports. Somehow, though, when we got to the end after two days, there was a great deal of camaraderie. I wasn't even worried about Minority Reports on both left and right. There was just the Minority Report from the right by itself that was the risk. The only real risk was that Mitchell and Davis would write one. They were the only ones who were able to, and who would have any clout.

For the most part, Dutton had *won* the battles which led to his complaints. Twice at the November sessions, he had openly asserted a willingness to draft a minority report, once on demographic representation and once on proportional representation, and he was known to be unhappy with slate making as well. Yet the full commission had acceded to his preferences on demographics; he had at least stopped it from banning the winner-take-all rule, even if its language on proportionality remained offensive; his agents had secured the same mixed outcome on delegate slating.

The situation of Mixner was less clear-cut, since he had necessarily lost on proportionality when Dutton prevented the adoption of stronger language. In November, Mixner had warned that this failure required a written dissent condemning commission timidity. Yet most other proreform commissioners felt that a minority report was not the logical way to recoup lost territory, and Mixner's closest confidants within the commission, Segal and Bode, pressed this view upon him in the days following the meeting. By then, they had adopted implementation as their primary goal; shortly afterward, Mixner dropped the idea of protesting any part of the final document.

This perception that the commission report was essentially attractive did not so obviously constrain either Davis or Mitchell. Mitchell, with an intuitive talent for translating printed words into real political behavior and with the ability to produce unforeseen critical arguments based on these translations, had become a principal opposition spokesman on the commission proper. On the other hand, the fact that he had been uncomfortable with this role did have implications for the fate of his criticism, both at the time and subsequently.

At the time, the ambivalence of Mitchell about his role as a major critic had meant that Davis, in addition to firing the opening shot at most guidelines, had been forced to stand nearly alone in pressing the staff for the implications of those proposed rules which did not arouse major controversy within the commission. Despite the apparent futility of his position—and unlike Leroy Collins, who had begun with somewhat the same orientation but who had become discouraged and had withdrawn—Davis continued to attend commission meetings and to punch away at what he saw. Davis and Mitchell were thus the members whose reactions most frightened the commission staff; Wade saw reason for those anxieties:

> The two ablest people on the Commission were Mitchell and Will Davis. That was my fear, that they might issue a Minority Report. At which time, that would be the end of the report. In any debate, they could run rings around the reformers. Both of them told me at one time or another that they might issue a Minority Report. Davis demurred on apportionment, Mitchell on proportionality, as I remember. When we left, I had a clear feeling that we would get a Minority Statement; not a Minority Report, but a Minority Statement. This would have left the Commission report bereft of its unanimity. If this happened, it would be opened to the Democratic National Committee, where the whole thing would go on all over again, and it would be lost. Especially with people of the quality of Davis and Mitchell.

Wade was not far wrong in his assessment of the initial frame of mind of either man. Immediately after the November meetings, Mitchell returned to Maine in the belief that the commission had far overstepped its authority in even urging proportional representation and had, in fact, *instituted* stringent demographic quotas. On the other hand, in an opinion unknown to commission staffers, he saw most of the other guidelines as noncontroversial, and perhaps overdue:

> I think, on balance, they were good. Most of them represented fundamental fairness. Many of them were things we had done for years here in Maine. Things like written rules were inevitable. . . . I did have serious reservations on A–1 and A–2, and I took the position that proportionality was too fundamental a change for them to make on their own.

The passage of a little time further dampened the interest of Mitchell in a formal protest. At first, when his discomfort was at its most intense, there was no occasion to develop a written dissent. Later, when the draft report arrived, his emotional involvement had lessened:

> A Minority Report was widely discussed. I think it was ultimately outweighed by the feeling that there was more good than bad in here. If we divided it up, no rules would be passed. This, at least, was what deterred me. Dutton was always threatening to write a Minority Report if we didn't do such and such. The attitude that *I* would not write a Minority Report just gradually grew.

This perceived balance of good over bad was reinforced by the larger political forces surrounding Mitchell. By March of 1970, his patron, Senator Edmund S. Muskie of Maine, had become a clear possibility for the Democratic presidential nomination in 1972. Mitchell had been the personal choice of Muskie for the Party Structure Commission; his stance on its product would inevitably appear as an indicator of the candidate's own feeling. Even if Muskie shared his lieutenant's dislike of some elements in the commission report, any plausible nomination strategy counseled him to avoid the politics of implementation, rather than to become a public enemy of reform. Bill Dodds thought that *this* was the key to Mitchell's change of heart:

> Mitchell's ties to Muskie explain his change. Muskie recognized the time of day. He knew he had to have the liberal element of the party, or at least not have its opposition. Plus, I got to know Mitchell very well after that, and he was not the conservative I had thought he was.

Will Davis was the other potential, serious dissident. While he had never brandished the minority report club in commission debate, his dislike for the total package was no less evident for this rhetorical restraint. He was, indeed, thought to be so disturbed by the issue of apportionment (Guideline B–7) as to be ready to follow this course. On the other hand, the crucial preconditions for a *coordinated* written dissent had been lacking from the first. Staff perceptions to the contrary, there was no common bond between Davis and Mitchell, in political experience or in prior social contact. The two had come out of recognizably different wings of the national party. While they had become leading critics of staff proposals, that development had not been premeditated, much less orchestrated.

Moreover, when the question of a minority report finally arose, the crucial similarity between Davis and Mitchell lay not in their discomfort with the commission product, real though that discomfort was. Instead, it lay in the way their personal political environments had changed. The shift had actually begun first for Davis, before a Muskie candidacy had started to color Mitchell's world. In 1969, Preston Smith had replaced John Connally as governor of Texas, and Elmer Baum had replaced Will Davis as chairman of the state Democratic executive committee. Thereafter, *ex*-Chairman Davis retained only a diminished personal stake in influencing even local, much less national responses to commission guidelines. Thereafter as well, he lacked the institutional base from which to mount such a response.

Davis's dislike of what he had seen pass before him was still sufficient to involve him in subsequent reform politics in Texas and to draw him intermittently into negotiations between state party officials and the national commission staff. But he would never again appear in the guise of a Party Structure commissioner. If he remained unenthusiastic about the guidelines, and if he invested some energy in seeing that they did not disrupt his home state, he left it to other state officials to do the same, without the guidance of a minority report.

The probability that minority reports would influence the course of implementation politics was thus falling sharply by the time the draft report went out to the commissioners, although the staff members could not know that this was the case. By the time they had gained their first firm indications, at the end of the second week in February, a substantial danger of a different sort was already visible. On February 6, Fred Harris resigned abruptly as chairman of the Democratic National Committee, thereby placing all committee operations—including the Party Structure Commission—in limbo.[14]

Neither the past activities of the Party Structure Commission nor the future conflicts which might follow from publication of its guidelines were critical to the resignation of Harris. Rather, the declining leadership potential of the chairmanship itself was the crucial factor. The burden of this declining potential was exaggerated by financial problems at the National Committee, but the Party Structure Commission was, at worst, only one more contributor to these. Vick French, Executive Assistant to Harris, recalled the decision to depart:

> On Harris' February resignation, there were several elements. Harris was an activist kind of pol, and this was something he had to do to turn from an obscure Senator into a viable presidential nominee. What he didn't understand was that it could not be done from the position of the Chairman of the Democratic Party. He was more controversial in his way than Paul Butler. As Chairman, you don't want an ideologue, you want a manager. . . .
>
> A terribly unproductive fund-raiser in Miami Beach in January of '70 was the final blow. The original idea had been for a twenty-city, private-screen hook-up, but that never got off the ground. Bob Strauss took a planeload of Texans to that in Miami, or there wouldn't have been any return at all. That was a major blow to Fred. If, after five or six months of planning, they couldn't do better than that, it was over.

In any case, the instant Harris announced his resignation, the commission leadership and staff were faced with a tactical decision. They could alter their publication schedule, await the appointment of a new national chairman, and trust that his good will—and talent for raising money—would bail them out with reasonable speed. Or they could determine to maintain their original schedule, bypass the National Committee, and try to amass the necessary funds on their own.

The choice had larger strategic implications. The first option—reschedule and wait—had the advantage of not even appearing to encroach on the prerogatives of the new chairman, an offense which might cost the commission crucial support later; it had few other attractions. This option entailed a minimum delay of more than a month, until the National Committee reassembled. It risked a significantly longer period of marking time, while the incoming chairman organized his office, undertook some initial fundraising, and cleared those expenses, like staff salaries, which had unavoidable priority. It raised the specter of the ultimate cost, if the new chairman was not partial to commission guidelines and if he decided to squeeze them to death financially.

The second possibility—an immediate attempt to go it alone—thus became the guiding consideration. All the principal commission personnel preferred this option, preferred, that is, to raise the money for publication independently if they could. If these efforts nettled the incoming chairman, so be it: They would simultaneously present him with a major accomplished fact, in the form of a widely circulated report from his Party Structure Commission. And that, at least, should be sufficient to keep any resulting displeasure private.

Having reached this decision to finance, publish, and disseminate their own report, commission staffers began in a familiar fashion, with the list of individuals and organizations which had already made some financial contribution to the commission's work. After some unsuccessful feelers, they came to a familiar resolution as well. The United Auto Workers, through the active intervention of Bill Dodds, promised the funds necessary to convert the draft report into a final, circulatable document.

That promise effectively guaranteed that the commission would have a finished product, that this finished product would constitute an early tactical problem for the incoming (and still unnamed) national chairman, and that this tactical problem would prevent the national party from simply letting conflict over party reform peter out, as an unforeseen side benefit of Harris's resignation. The report would exist, publicly; the new chairman would have to address it, publicly; his response would be the next focus for the politics of party reform.

As a result, ten weeks after Chairman Harris resigned, a sixty-three-page, orange-covered, six inch by nine inch booklet entitled *Mandate for Reform*[15] was finished and ready for distribution. It contained four items of front matter, four chapters in the text proper, and three subsequent appendices. The booklet opened with a list of Party Structure commissioners, including Peter Garcia, who may never have known of his membership, and Leroy Collins, who had terminated his. It followed with a complete roster of staff members, grouped as titled staff, research staff, summer interns, volunteers, and consultants.

231

Bracketed between these lists and a "Dear Fellow Democrat" letter from Chairman McGovern was the one piece of front matter which contained any potential clues to the report's reception by party officials. This was a two-page collection of remarks by national party leaders, a category which eventually included Fred Harris, Hubert Humphrey, Edward Kennedy, Eugene McCarthy, Edmund Muskie, and Lawrence O'Brien. All these men were complimentary, yet they differed perceptibly in their intimations about the coercive status of the report. Teddy Kennedy hewed closest to the staff interpretation:

> The members and staff of the Commission deserve the Party's thanks for reporting early enough *so that all state and local party organizations will have ample opportunity to achieve full compliance in time for the next convention.* [16] (Italics added.)

Hubert Humphrey, on the other hand, treated the issue as much more of an open question:

> I commend the McGovern Commission for giving the Democratic Party the most comprehensive and detailed *analysis and recommendations* in its history on delegate selection. [17] (Italics added.)

A five-page introductory chapter, "Mandate for Reform," kicked off the text. This introduction painted an unflattering picture of existing procedures for delegate selection, branding them as unduly discretionary, untimely, closed, and discriminatory. It posed the resulting choice as one of scrapping this system in its entirety or of reforming each constituent element. It went on to associate the commission with the second, more moderate approach. In closing, it characterized this as an attack on all rules and practices which inhibited access to the institutions of delegate selection, which diluted the influence of those who did attain access, or which contained elements of both failings.

The three-page second chapter, "History of the Commission," was exactly that, an outline of key events from the creation of the Hughes Commission in June of 1968, through the mailing of the compliance letters in February of 1970. Then came a review of preconvention politicking in the most recent presidential contest, "Delegate Selection in 1968," with sixteen pages on available systems for selecting delegates and on the practical problems inherent in them. These problems—divided into "procedural irregularities," "discrimination," and "structural inadequacies"—were then further classified into categories leading logically to the eighteen guidelines. "Discrimination," for example, was additionally parsed into "blacks" (Guideline A–1), "women" (A–2), and "young people" (A–2 again); "structural inadequacies" were carved into "untimely delegate selection" (C–4), "costs, fees, and assessments" (A–4), and so on.

The heart of the booklet, a chapter called, appropriately, "The Guidelines" followed. There, a short summary of all eighteen was followed by a two-page statement about their legal status and then, from page 39 through page 48, by the text of the regulations themselves. (See appendix A.) For everyone but Party Structure commissioners, state and national party officials, and a few newsmen, these ten pages were the first real opportunity to gauge what the new rules might imply for presidential politics, if they were implemented.

The last chapter, a three-page "Conclusion," sketched the "antipolitics" which might result if these rules were not implemented. In this vision, the publication of commission guidelines represented a crossroads. If the party did not move toward systematic implementation, peaceful change might henceforth be impossible. The chapter did, however, close on a hopeful note, by listing the state parties which were allegedly moving ahead and by predicting that more would surely follow.

To the extent that there was a larger argument to the report, it was found in several recurring themes, themes which the staff had been emphasizing since the very start of commission activity. Number one involved the range of investigation which the 1968 Convention had assigned to the Party Structure Commission. The staff had always endeavored to construe this range broadly, to include anything bearing on full or meaningful or timely participation. Accordingly, it sought to underline, one more time, the *additive nature* of key convention resolutions. The opening chapter of the final report plunged so boldly into this task, in fact, that it cited a nonexistent passage from these convention reports and then footnoted the combination of other quotations which had gone into this citation:

> The delegates to the Convention, concerned by the chaos and divisiveness, shared a belief that the image of an organization impervious to the will of its rank and file threatened the future of the Party. Therefore, they took up the challenge of reform with a mandate requiring State Parties to give "all Democratic voters . . . a full, meaningful* and timely opportunity to participate" in the selection of delegates, and, thereby, in the decisions of the Convention itself.[18] [Quotation marks, ellipsis, and asterisk all in original].

A second major theme was the legal status of commission recommendations. Appearing later in the report, this argument suggested that the guidelines were, of course, mandatory and that they should rightfully be viewed as the *sole* available means for realizing the goal of full, meaningful, and timely opportunity to participate:

> Because the Commission was created by virtue of actions taken at the 1968 Convention, we believe our legal responsibility extends to that body and that body alone. We view ourselves as the agent of that Convention on all matters related to delegate selection. Unless the 1972 Convention chooses to review any steps the Commission has taken, we regard our Guidelines for delegate selection as binding on the states.[19]

To provide a practical impetus toward this interpretation, the report returned continually to a third and final theme: That the disastrous 1968 Convention was only a harbinger, an example of the logical outcome of unreformed presidential politics. If the national party did not do its business under guidelines like the commission's own, it might expect to see that outcome repeated again and again. This moral might have emerged naturally from the way the old institutions of delegate selection were described in the commission report, but Chapter Two introduced it explicitly, and Chapter Five, the conclusion, hammered it again:

> If we are not an open party, if we do not represent the demands of change, then the danger is not that people will go to the Republican Party; it is that there will no longer be a way for people committed to orderly change to fulfill their needs and desires within our traditional political system. It is that they will turn to third and fourth party politics or the anti-politics of the street.[20]

These same themes received one more airing at Chairman McGovern's press conference to release the report. On Tuesday, April 28, at 11:00 A.M., *Mandate for Reform* was officially unveiled in Room EF–100 of the U.S. Capitol, although selected party officials, newsmen, and interested outsiders had received copies four days before. At the Capitol ceremony, McGovern read directly from the report, and especially from its concluding section on the consequences of nonimplementation. The *New York Times* opened its story with his reading:

> Washington, April 28—A Democratic party reform commission warned today in its final report that the only alternative to broader citizen participation in politics was the antipolitics of the street.[21]

In his prepared statement, and again in response to a reporter's question, the Party Structure chairman subscribed, once more, to the staff position on legal status—that commission proposals had already become party law and that arguments over their appropriate meaning were finished. R. W. Apple of the *New York Times*, however, apparently suspected that matters might not turn out to be quite that simple. As he put McGovern's remarks in perspective, they became instead the opening shot in what might well be a protracted battle for implementation:

> Speaking at a Capitol Hill news conference, Senator McGovern predicted that the commission's guidelines for the selection of delegates to the party's convention in 1972 would be followed by state Democratic organizations.
> "I suspect there'll be some struggles," he added. "Certain party leaders in some states have been critical, but they are a tiny minority. I expect that we will get a broad compliance."
> But other sources in the Democratic party indicated that the guidelines would not go into effect without a fight, possibly a long and bitter one.[22]

Implications

With the press conference announcing publication of the official report of the Commission on Party Structure and Delegate Selection, the politics of recommendation was indisputably over, and the politics of implementation had begun. The process of converting formal recommendations into practical institutions of delegate selection would still involve negotiations about the precise institutional requirements of individual guidelines; in that sense, the debate over the meaning of commission recommendations would never end. But with publication of an official report and with its delivery to a variously waiting world, the process of developing the formal proposals which would be at the center of these negotiations was unequivocally completed.

A public announcement of the official commission report did not so evidently reveal the scope and content of the institutional changes implicit in these reform guidelines. The report was available to those with the energy to seek a copy; an appreciation of its potential impact still required substantial skills at institutional translation. Copies of the compliance letters for the fifty-five state, district, and territorial parties would have helped in this translation, but even they required considerable analytic sophistication before yielding their secrets to the curious reader. In any case, no one except the commission leadership and staff possessed copies of all fifty-five compliance letters, so that the precise scope and detail of the demanded institutional change remained elusive.

Despite that, the members of the alternative Democratic coalition were presumably alerted to imminent battles over implementation by the press conference announcing the commission report. If these incipient reformers did not perceive the precise institutional content of projected battles, the commission report was certainly not reticent in asserting that the scope of reform was large and that the struggles surrounding its realization might be fierce. From the other side, the highest-ranking figures within the orthodox Democratic coalition—the top officeholders in the regular party—had already been notified, explicitly and personally, about the approaching politics of implementation through the individual compliance letters. Presumably, they, too, were alerted to the battles which might result, and even to the roles which they themselves might be called upon to play. Presumably, publication of the official report reinforced this warning.

The drafting of the two key documents conveying the product of the Party Structure Commission to these critical, interested publics—the official report of the commission and the fifty-five compliance letters applying that report to each of the individual Democratic parties—began immediately after the November meeting of the commission. And for the next five months, the progress of the report and the compliance letters was intertwined, technically and politically.

One central, strategic question inaugurated this process: How to approach the National Committee. When the remaining commission figures chose to approach it indirectly and after an attempt to accumulate some successes in the states, most of the other, tactical decisions about the report and the compliance letters fell into place. The report could be addressed to the general public, and especially to the attentive—proreform—public for party reform; the letters could be addressed to a small, semiprivate, absolutely crucial audience, the top party leaders in the states and on the National Committee. The report, then, could be general and hortatory; the letters could be pointed and specific, but conciliatory.

A series of technical tasks occupied most of the following five months. A prototype for the letters, being considerably shorter than a published report, was obviously ready first. The report, on the other hand, while longer, was still a single document, not a start on fifty-five separate projects. Its contents were considerably more appealing to the commission staff than were the lesser details of, say, delegate selection in Wyoming; these contents made considerably fewer demands for minute but accurate facts and figures. As a result, a theoretically final report was ready by late January, a full month before the last compliance letters were assembled. At that point, however, a particularly acute attack of the commission's chronic fiscal problems—this one caused by a dramatic shakeup at the National Committee—stalled the report. The compliance letters could be officially posted in late February; the report was not officially published until late April.

Even at the time, when the compliance letters had been dispatched and as the complete report was being published, these events contained some evident portents for the course of reform politics, for the fate of institutional change, and for the likely character of elite replacement. Indeed, the letters, which had been in the hands of major party figures for two full months by the time the report was publicly unveiled, gave rise to another of those events which had become almost typical of the politics of party reform—an expected event *which never occurred.*

Insiders had uniformly expected these letters to unleash the flood of resistance by regular party leaders which reformers had dreaded since the reform movement was institutionalized in the Party Structure Commission. Instead, the more sympathetic party officials, of whom there were a significant minority, made at least some responsive noises. And the rest of the party simply held its peace.

One result of this pattern of reaction was an absence of dramatic conflict, which might have alerted all observers—the press, the reform public, and especially other party officials—to the possibility that significant changes were at issue. A second result was an implied license for the Commission staff to continue pumping out recommendations to the states, albeit without any corresponding assurance that this communication/pressure was having much effect. A third and final outcome was a generalized inability—among reporters, state party leaders, organized reformers, and even commission personnel—to judge the progress of the recommendations of the Party Structure Commission.

This mixed and undecipherable response by party leaders created an ambiguous political climate which would last well into the following year. This ambiguity would ultimately alarm party reformers far more than it would disturb their regular party counterparts. Yet this quiet, private, and individualized response by party officialdom could at least as reasonably have been cause for alarm by party regulars, too. For the absence of coordinated opposition to the guidelines at the time the compliance letters were released, and the absence even of spontaneous but unconnected statements of public opposition by party leaders around the country, served as the first concrete indication that the politics of implementation might indeed be successful, that reform of the process of delegate selection might actually, possibly succeed.[23]

On the other hand, the reaction by commission personnel to the resignation of Fred Harris—the last tactical decision in the politics of recommendation or the first strategic decision in the politics of implementation—was probably a portent in the other direction. Or at least, the plan to bypass the successor to Harris and to confront this new national chairman with another accomplished fact in reform politics—the decision to go it alone on publication of the commission report—guaranteed that the commission's own transition from recommendation to implementation would be much sharper than it might otherwise have been.

In the period from commission appointment through the framing of official guidelines, leading reform actors within the commission had driven for as extensive a reform agenda as they could muster and had pursued its adoption as aggressively as they knew how. Then, once the guidelines had been adopted and the job became one of translating them into compliance letters and a published report, these same actors had moderated their approach and had carefully adjusted the format and content of both the letters and the report, to secure maximum acquiescence with minimum complaint.

But when faced with the choice of pressing ahead and publishing on their own or of delaying and seeking publication in the fashion most likely to secure the approval of the National Committee, these remaining commission actors opted, once again, to ignore the regular party, to assert their independence, and to risk a confrontation. By doing so, they guaranteed that nothing would prevent the commission from having a final, generally available report. At the same time, they made the overriding goal of subsequent reform politics—bringing the report of the Party Structure Commission back in from the outside and making it the dominant operational doctrine of the national Democratic party—appear even more distant.

PART II

---

*The Politics
of Implementation*

CHAPTER

9

The Mandate at the National Level:

The National Chairman and the

Commission Report

IN WHICH, after a series of portentous maneuvers, a new national chairman is selected; one of the first tasks facing that chairman is the development of an orientation—public and private—toward the report of the Party Structure Commission; and the activation of this newly developed strategy sets off an additional round of political maneuvering. AND IN WHICH, reform politics comes to center on selection of the most influential actor in the politics of implementation; institutional change receives a crucial, if hesitant, boost from this new national chairman; and the regular party and its associated interests are again pressed away from their expected role in the politics of party reform.

A SHORT but convoluted struggle over the naming of a successor to Fred Harris, and the elaboration of a strategy for party reform by the winner of that struggle, were the first major events in the politics of implementation. The politics of recommendation had begun to achieve an institutional focus with the selection of one national chairman. The politics of implementation began to achieve its institutional focus with the selection of another. Unlike his predecessor, however, this second chairman entered a political world in which a major reform report already existed, in published and disseminated form. Accordingly, the development of a chairmanly orientation toward that report, and the discovery of tactical measures to embody that orientation, became one of his first priorities.

By resigning abruptly in early February, Harris—the architect of the Party Structure Commission—guaranteed that the politics surrounding implementation of the commission report would begin in the regime of a new national chairman. Harris had been a crucial early influence on the politics leading up to adoption of an official reform document. His successor would be a crucial influence—early, middle, and late—on the politics of securing compliance with it.

Despite the protestations of committed party reformers, this was largely inevitable. If the National Committee was ever to be rallied behind the work of the commission—and cooler heads already saw this as essential to its success—then the national chairman had to play a central role in assembling committee support. If the report of the commission had to be amended along the way, the national chairman would again be the central figure in hammering out these compromises. If the report of the commission was to be actively buried, or merely encouraged to die a quiet death at home, the national chairman would once again be essential to permitting—or facilitating—this outcome.

Once a new national chairman had been selected, in turn, one of his first policy decisions involved a strategy for dealing with the issue of party reform. This had been true in the time of Harris, when there was not yet a reform commission, much less a reform report. It was to be true in the time of his successor, and the orientation of this second chairman would be no less integral to the success or failure of the reform movement. Despite the disparagement of committed party regulars, this was nearly inevitable, too. There had been an officially recognized reform process. It had produced a published report, *Mandate for Reform.* Both process and report had created an audience of partisans, concerned with the fate of reform and focused on the response of the new national chairman.

So, there would be another national chairman. He would become a major actor in the politics of party reform. He would need some personal strategy for addressing the reform issue almost as soon as he entered office. That strategy itself would become an influential fact of reform politics. Its construction, in passing, would provide a particularly clean and dramatic instance of the making of political strategy within the context of a national party, and even of the role, nature, and limits of strategic brokerage in democratic politics more generally.

The search for a replacement for Harris began with a rapid and easy consensus, on Larry O'Brien, the man who had served as chairman during the desperate days of the 1968 campaign. But when this consensus came unglued, the contest split wide open, and the various factions within the national party began to look for individual champions. The emergence of these divisions, however, led other party leaders, regular and reform alike, to press for a second approach to O'Brien. When the principal, this time, agreed to return, the National Committee acquired a new national chairman—and a crucial actor in reform politics for the duration.

It also acquired him in a manner which left O'Brien singularly free of factional attachments, free, that is, to develop a reform orientation all his own. In short order, O'Brien discovered the fundamentals of a strategy, one which would guide him for the next two and a half years. Stripped to its essentials, this approach involved a cautious but unequivocal advocacy of reform, coupled with a deliberate and persistent attempt to bring reform negotiations inside the office of the national chairman.

Two major initiatives activated this strategy. The first was a memo to all state chairmen and members of the National Committee, drafted by the general counsel but authorized by the chairman himself, averring that commission guidelines should be treated as party law. The second was a special subcommittee of the National Committee, charged with helping the state parties into compliance with those guidelines. Strangely, this combination aroused more fear than hope among committed reformers, and negotiations between the national chairman and the Party Structure Commission over the true meaning of these initiatives became the last step in establishing a national environment for reform politics.

When these negotiations had been played out, it was manifestly clear that the politics of implementation, the period of conflict over the realization of commission reforms, had arrived. When these negotiations had been played out, it was clear that the prospects for sweeping institutional change were greater than they had been while the appointment of a new national chairman hung in the balance, though by how much no one could tell. When these negotiations were finished, finally, it was established—though it was hardly clear, even to interested actors—that the orthodox Democratic coalition had been pressed away from coordinated influence over the fate of party reform, while the alternative Democratic coalition had been given new, major, and unexpected assets.

The Selection of a National Chairman

While the leadership and staff of the Party Structure Commission were still hunting for the funds to make *Mandate for Reform* a published reality, others, with no specific interest in that document, were trying to influence another decision which would shape the fate of that report far more strongly. By maneuvering to fill the vacant national chairmanship, these others were manipulating what would ultimately be the largest single influence on guideline implementation.

The task of organizing the search for a successor to Fred Harris devolved, as it traditionally did, on the titular leader of the party. Hubert Humphrey readily took up the challenge. Although the Humphrey operation, as such, was a bit rusty—the hunt for a new national chairman was their first coordinated maneuver since the term of the vice president had ended—their job appeared remarkably simple. Humphrey zeroed in quickly on an "obvious choice," his own former chairman, Larry O'Brien; the Humphrey entourage was left with the leg work for O'Brien's impending return.

There was little doubt, either in the Humphrey camp or among newsmen who followed these events, that O'Brien could be confirmed. Humphrey's connections within the National Committee seemed sufficient to install nearly anyone, as long as he respected the dignity of individual committee members. O'Brien's connections within the committee seemed sufficient to secure his own installation, at least in the absence of opposition from Humphrey. When Humphrey announced that he had constructed a full leadership slate, with the former chairman at its head, any remaining doubts were banished.[1]

In the face of this, O'Brien confounded most political observers, on Thursday, February 26, by turning down the chairmanship. In a statement released through his public relations office in New York, he offered only a vague explanation:

> I have concluded that there are some within the party structure and some among those with whom the party traditionally has had close relationships who do not share the view that I should return as chairman.[2]

O'Brien's refusal changed the nature of the hunt. No longer did potential influencers feel a need to defer to the titular leader. No longer did potential *candidates* feel a need to defer to his choice. Some of these newly energized actors were explicitly concerned with the fate of reform. All represented predictable orientations, implicit but strong, toward that issue and that fate.

The mantle of the Humphrey operation came to rest on Matthew E. Welsh, former governor of Indiana. Welsh had been out of the office for the preceding four years, but he was a solid political organizer and he did possess statewide experience. Moreover, he had been an early partisan of every Democratic nominee of the 1960s and had even headed the stand-in Humphrey slate in the Indiana primary of 1968. William J. Connell, one of the several Humphrey advisers who opposed O'Brien because they believed that he had never been loyal to their principal, pressed the move for Welsh:

After we regrouped in mid-1969, we began to think about the presidential election of 1972. Humphrey and I did try to find a successor for Harris after Harris resigned. We tried to move in former Governor Matt Welsh. Welsh had agreed to do it, but then O'Brien began lobbying around him and took the job. My analysis was that O'Brien went this way because he didn't want to be associated with Humphrey in any way. This was his first public move to the left. It was a track leading straight to the 1972 Convention.

Committed reformers, this time, deliberately rejected the lead of the Humphrey operation and settled around an explicit candidate of their own. He was Joseph F. Crangle, county chairman for Erie County, New York. While Crangle was the head of a bona fide party organization, he had also been the one to introduce the Rules minority report—the start of all this—at the 1968 Convention. He had kept in touch with reform actors in the interim, and they rallied to him as a potentially sympathetic national chairman with regular-party credentials.

Several other contenders, with highly varied prospects and strategies, rounded out the field. The most serious of these was Gordon St. Angelo, sitting state chairman in Indiana, who aspired to become the candidate of committed party regulars. St. Angelo undertook an active campaign, with a "national headquarters" in Washington and a whirlwind tour of the states. At some remove was Joseph A. Doorley, Jr., mayor of Providence, Rhode Island, who announced that he was available but would not campaign. Beyond Doorley, there were only rumors and speculations.

While this was occurring, Fred Harris came back into action, too, by calling a meeting of the Executive Committee of the Democratic National Committee in Washington for Sunday, March 1. Harris had resigned on February 6, effective four weeks later; he had stayed out of subsequent negotiations except to schedule the National Committee meeting which would theoretically confirm a successor. His summons to the Executive Committee, however, created a new and unpredictable arena for the contest, one not directly under the control of the Humphrey search team.

The Executive Committee met on Sunday afternoon, March 1, at 4:00 in the Mayflower Hotel. Humphrey was present to advance the name of Matt Welsh, but the combined efforts of Welsh's competitors were already enough to deny him a quick consensus. Welsh did possess a working majority. St. Angelo (and Doorley) were unable to show any support. But Crangle held the remainder of the committee, and his partisans were not prepared to retire from the field. The members decided to reassemble after dinner and to hear the major candidates in person.

Welsh, Crangle, and St. Angelo did appear, but when their presentations were over, no votes had changed. By the end of the evening, in fact, all that had been clarified were the strategies of the two sides. Those backing Crangle were determined not to accede to Welsh and to drive the issue to a vote in the full National Committee. They were prepared to gamble that the vision of a heated floor fight, emphasizing old divisions and impairing the prospects for any eventual winner, would deter Welsh's backers from ever bringing their candidate out of the Executive Committee.

They were, at least, on the right track. Humphrey, as the leading Welsh partisan, was clearly able to crush his opponents in the full committee; he was just as clearly reluctant to do so. While both sides could see that an exercise of muscle would underline the impression of a deep and continuing split, Humphrey was perhaps uniquely situated to understand, viscerally, what that might imply for the fate of the party—and for his own. Indeed, the spector of a rerun of the politics of 1968 was being raised explicitly in newspaper accounts of the dispute:

> The split of the executive committee appeared to be developing along roughly the same lines as the 1968 division between the supporters of Mr. Humphrey and those of Senator Robert F. Kennedy of New York. One source characterized the fight as "an argument between young and old, establishment and innovaters, standfast and antiwar" elements.
>
> A supporter of Mr. Crangle commented, "It's beginning to look like the convention in Chicago all over again."[3]

The Executive Committee reassembled on Monday morning, March 2, to discover that a good night's sleep had changed no minds. But what at first promised to be only a replay of arguments from the previous day began to suggest a compromise, if Larry O'Brien could be convinced to reconsider. Crangle supporters still preferred using Crangle to batter Welsh, but they favored winning with O'Brien to losing with Crangle. Welsh backers had hardened their preference for Welsh over Crangle, but some of them favored a peaceful coronation of O'Brien to a bloody installation of Welsh.

Col. Jacob M. Arvey of Chicago, in particular, saw the triumph of the regulars as potentially costly, since it would emphasize divisions and damage hopes for reducing the party's overwhelming debt. It was Arvey, the arch-regular, who took the lead in bringing O'Brien back into the negotiations, with the private encouragement of committed reformers like Jean M. Westwood of Utah:

> Joe Crangle and Gordy St. Angelo were putting on tremendous campaigns. Humphrey was backing Welsh. The idea came up: What would happen if we could get Larry O'Brien back as the candidate of *the party?* Millie Jeffrey and I discussed the idea, and liked it. Jake Arvey liked it, too. We all got it through the Executive Committee, then the Executive Committee members lobbied their regional caucuses.

Once the Executive Committee had agreed on the need to draft O'Brien, Arvey phoned him and noted that the committee had created the consensus "that he indicated he needed." O'Brien promised to respond within twenty-four hours, after he had checked to see that the purported consensus extended outside the Executive Committee. Arvey then called Humphrey and put *him* on record as being "delighted" with the result. The Executive Committee recessed to await the answer of their nominee.[4]

The next morning, in a telephone call to Arvey at the Watergate complex, O'Brien accepted nomination to the position of national chairman.[5] While the formal result was thus exactly what it would have been had O'Brien accepted five days earlier, the political result was substantially different. By delaying for this second round, O'Brien had avoided identification with any one faction of the party; by delaying, he had avoided identification with Hubert Humphrey as well. In the process, the new national chairman had teased out a superficial unity—artificial and transitory though it might be—from the national leadership of the party. If that unity could be maintained, an attack on the party's organizational and financial problems, the key to its fate in 1970 and 1972, might plausibly follow.

The field of opponents for O'Brien shrank rapidly. On Monday, after the Executive Committee again tendered the chairmanship to O'Brien, Welsh withdrew from contention. On Tuesday, after O'Brien accepted, Crangle dropped out, too. Only St. Angelo, citing the need to maintain an open selection system and a desire to prevent the National Committee from becoming another "House of Lords," promised to remain in the race, although Doorley did concede that he would be available if O'Brien and St. Angelo should cancel each other.[6]

With the return of O'Brien imminent, however, the titular leader himself—as a way of maintaining his own standing with both the National Committee and the incoming chairman—went to work on O'Brien's behalf. Those few committee members who were still willing to stand up for a challenger, then, received only an energetic lobbying effort from Hubert Humphrey for their pains. St. Angelo ultimately allowed his name to be put in nomination, but he withdrew it at once, citing his satisfaction at having "contributed a small measure to reopening the process." Other party figures who had been unhappy with the selection of O'Brien then closed ranks, some by making major nominating or seconding speeches:

> Mr. O'Brien was nominated by John Powers of Massachusetts, who had told intimates as recently as last week that he opposed Mr. O'Brien. He was seconded by, among others, Gov. Robert E. McNair of South Carolina, who had been a leader of a stop-O'Brien movement last week.

> Mr. Powers, a stout, florid, orator of the old Boston School, cried out at one
> point that "the overbearing decision is what is best for the Democratic Party,
> the people of this great country, and the whole free world."[7]

With that, Lawrence F. O'Brien succeeded Fred R. Harris, and the Democratic party had a new national chairman.

The condition of the national Democratic party which Harris bequeathed to O'Brien, along with the normal mechanics of assuming the national chairmanship, generated most of the new chairman's initial decisions. Like any incoming leader, O'Brien had to begin by selecting and organizing a top staff for the National Committee. Unlike some luckier incoming chairmen, he had to develop a long-range strategy for retiring a growing party debt, as well as some immediate arrangement for meeting current payrolls. But unlike any earlier incoming chairman, he also had to adopt a stance toward a comprehensive proposal for party reform.

O'Brien had not been monitoring the progress of recommendations for reform while he was a private citizen; he had not engaged in any explicit discussion of their fate when he agreed to return:

> I had had no contemplation of going back. I was paying no attention to
> the guideline business. I had been firmly persuaded that I had cut the cord and
> gone on. When discussions did begin, I was most concerned with being sure that
> there was a broad-based desire for my leadership. The guidelines were still not
> important to me then, except as they affected that. I came in without any
> promises.

If O'Brien had not been pondering a response to proposals for sweeping party reform, the environment to which he returned would nevertheless effectively demand one within weeks. The Party Structure Commission was about to publish its final report. The contents of that report had already been communicated to state and national party leaders and to reform activists around the country. These contents were about to be communicated to the news media and to the interested public as well. Inevitably, then, a new national chairman would need a public posture toward this report. Inevitably as well, he would need some strategic orientation toward its substantive provisions.

The narrow realities of power within the national party, as they applied to this response, were clear. In an immediate showdown over party reform, the national chairman could easily lead the National Committee *against* this commission report; he could not so obviously place his committee behind it. The National Committee, the site for such a showdown, was the formal embodiment of party regularity; the orthodox Democratic coalition, that is, the regular party and its associated interests, was clearly larger and massively better established than was the reform network.

Yet an immediate showdown was an unlikely response to the larger political environment of the new national chairman. His absolute priority was some means of reversing the growth of the enormous—the crushing—national party debt. After that, the need to provide widespread assistance, financial or at least technical, to Democratic candidates across the country in the midterm elections of 1970 was coming up fast. Beyond that, finally, the campaigns for the presidential nomination of 1972 were beginning to stir, and the clear responsibility of a national chairman was to provide a functioning party for the eventual nominee.

All of these concerns, at bottom, revolved around "party unity"—the reality of unity if possible, the appearance of unity at the very least. *Any* opening battle would shatter even the appearance of party unity; that, in turn, would sharply reduce the new chairman's chance of accomplishing all—or any—of his other goals. In his autobiography, *No Final Victories,* O'Brien placed more emphasis on this elusive unity than on the enormous party debt as a factor influencing his calculations about a second term as national chairman:

> In early March of 1970, soon after my return to Washington, I had a breakfast reunion with some friends in the press corps. Their blunt attitude was: "O'Brien, you're crazy! What are you doing here?"
>
> They knew, as I did, that the party was a shambles. Not only did our debt total some $9.3 million; despite Fred Harris' efforts, it had increased rather than decreased in 1969.
>
> Even more serious than our financial plight was the deep division within our party, the worst I had ever seen. The problem encompassed far more than our loss of the 1968 election. We had lost in 1952 and 1956 and remained reasonably united. But in 1970 the bitter divisions of 1968 still existed—hawk versus dove, liberal versus conservative, reformer versus regular—and no reconciliation in sight.
>
> The National Committee was, I thought, the proper forum, indeed, the only forum, through which the party might be united.[8]

The dominant, practical incentives in the political environment of the new national chairman, then, suggested avoiding any immediate conflict over party reform, especially one which embroiled the entire party. Yet if there was not to be an immediate, central decision on the fate of reform, the chairman, more than ever, needed a public posture of his own toward the concept.

Organized reformers—the network connected by the Party Structure Commission, the continuing reform factions in the states, and individual party dissidents across the country—would predictably demand a response at the point when the commission's report was published. If the chairman did not publicly endorse reform, they would just as predictably create the overt and ostentatious divisiveness which he dreaded. Indeed, aspiring spokesmen continually surfaced to remind the new chairman of their potential presence and of their willingness to incite a renewed internal war if proposed reforms were not accepted.[9]

From the other side, the regular party was far more easily able to choke off the reform movement at once and to deflate it in the longer run as well. Yet party regulars would have some difficulty in mounting a national attack without the active assistance of their national chairman. More to the point, they would be extremely unlikely to undertake this initiative, with its obvious prospects for further division and organizational decay, *unless* the new chairman were to press them for specific and concrete steps implementing the more offensive of the individual guidelines.

As a result, his personal political environment encouraged the new national chairman not just to avoid immediate conflict but to adopt a public posture of vague but general benevolence toward reform in the abstract and toward the guidelines in particular. Early public statements of support might placate—though hardly disarm—organized reformers. An absence of specific pressures toward concrete implementation with those party leaders who were actively opposed should prevent explosions from the regular party. Despite the differences between Harris and O'Brien, the staff of the outgoing chairman, in the person of Vick French, perceived the situation of the incoming chairman in precisely the same way:

> O'Brien also saw that after the reformers had gotten as far as they did, to undo it would have instantly created open warfare. There was no other way to go, at that point. His internal party position was impossible otherwise. He was too smart and polished a pol not to know that.

While this disingenuous resolution might not last forever, French believed that the new chairman might hope to escape temporarily from alienating all but the most militant party reformers and the most intransigent party regulars:

> I think O'Brien thought that he could do what Harris wasn't able to do, which is to keep the support and regard of the moderates, and some conservatives, and still keep the respect of the reformers, or most of them. And to a large extent, he did just that. He also felt that it was the inevitable course of history, so why not make it a virtue?

Yet there were additional incentives, over and beyond these, which constituted a rationale for an even more active support, public and private, for the reform package. These factors were less determinative in character; that is, they were more open to interpretation by the particular incumbent of the national chairmanship. But they did suggest an approach to the guidelines which was much more than detached benevolence and delay. In short order, this approach, too, became that of Chairman O'Brien.

Foremost among the factors leading to a more active and aggressive endorsement of party reform was the widespread view that some new party rules might be beneficial. Among reformers, it was axiomatic that 1968 had shown the need for comprehensive rules reform. But among many regulars, too, the events of 1968 had generated a tolerance for some comprehensive code to govern delegate selection. The numerous credentials challenges which McCarthy supporters had launched at the 1968 Convention had unquestionably contributed to its disastrous character. The 1972 Convention would surely feature more of the same, unless there were some precise, advance standards to obviate most such challenges and to resolve the rest. Bill Dodds, the UAW representative on the Party Structure Commission, heard this argument repeatedly:

> You'll have Chicago all over again. Many party leaders had the feeling that they couldn't cope with that, but that they could survive this. O'Brien felt, I think, that you could have this boat rock a little, and still get it to shore.

In theory, the rules which the party ultimately adopted did not have to be the guidelines propounded by the Party Structure Commission. Any detailed, publicized set of regulations would do. But in practice, if commission guidelines were not to become party rules, then the reform process had to begin again. The new chairman was not, in private, terribly happy with any number of proposed reforms, but he never believed that a new rules study was a serious option:

> There was a bothersome aspect in the cuteness of writing in A–1 and A–2, for example. But if you're committed to the concept, you go along. I went along. If I had been on the Commission, the guidelines would have been different.

The combination of all these factors, as filtered by O'Brien—the existence of a major reform report, the desirability of maintaining short-run party unity, the potential usefulness of an official code for delegate selection—created a strategy: Make an early, public move of support, and do all you can privately, as well, to produce widespread adoption without controversy. At the same time, avoid becoming identified with specific reform proposals, so that the option of pulling back or seeking amendments remains available—should those who oppose implementation turn out to be an even greater threat to party unity over the longer run than those who favor it. John G. Stewart, the new director of communications at the National Committee, saw this plan assuming concrete form:

> What O'Brien felt when he came in was that the only way to handle the damned fool things was to go ahead with them. The best thing was not to open them up again, but to do the best job you could at carrying them out. He was more concerned about what the left was going to do than what the regulars were going to do. The only way to handle it was just to push on. His *instincts* were that this was how you should go about it; it was just a gut feeling. He doesn't pressure easily, so I doubt that anyone directly forced him into it. These rules weren't perfect, but you had to go ahead and try them, and try to make an asset out of them.
>
> I think it was just a judgment on what had happened at the Convention, plus the basic documentation that the McGovern Commission had collected. It also leaves completely open what a state must do, if you don't adopt these rules ahead of time. That would become a terrible bottomless pit of acrimony and chaos, if you didn't do this. If he had just left it to the 1972 Convention, you would never work your way out of that swamp. It was not a choice that was clear on either side, but there *was* the Commission, and they *had* reached these rules, and they *were* there. He concluded that what you had to do fairly soon was just get on with them. It would have been more disruptive to wrangle over them than to just go ahead.

A Chairmanly Strategy for Reform

While the new chairman was still considering his most productive strategy toward the issue of party reform, and well before he had taken any concrete actions in the reform realm, he had to think about arrangements for managing the National Committee. Some of these arrangements were narrowly technical, involving staff appointments with skilled, substantive responsibilities. But some were more directly political, including appointments to the other positions of official leadership within the committee proper.

Given the character of the National Committee, as the capstone organization of the regular party, these appointments would normally be slanted toward evident party regulars. If O'Brien was to adopt a proreform orientation toward the product of the Party Structure Commission, his need to cement relationships with committee regulars—who were, after all, the dominant faction on the issue of party reform, too—would obviously increase. Beyond that, it had been elements within the regular party, more than apprehensive reformers, who had grumbled about the choice of O'Brien when it was first announced, and who had openly resisted that choice when it was proffered for the second time.

These individuals differed crucially from their opposite numbers in the reform coalition, however, in terms of the response which might keep them united behind the leadership of O'Brien. This difference, in turn, produced an additional, tactical elaboration in the chairman's evolving strategy for party reform. Where the reformers wanted public endorsements, and then actual procedural change, the regulars were much more amenable to private conversations, backed by personnel decisions which appeared to lock the substance of those conversations into the structure of the National Committee.

To exploit this crucial difference, O'Brien developed a tactic which he would use continually during the ensuing two-year period: He met discontent among the reformers by moving toward their substantive demands; he met discontent among the regulars by naming individual representatives to various official slots at the National Committee. In other words, he gave rules to reformers, appointments to regulars—procedures to one group, personnel to the other.

Within a month of his return to Washington, O'Brien had rearranged the executive cadre at the National Committee in accord with this approach. By April 4, when he announced the appointment of Robert E. McNair, governor of South Carolina, as his second vice chairman for the national party, this element of his leadership strategy was fully realized. Besides the chairman himself, the top officers at the National Committee would include Geraldine M. Joseph, first vice chairman; McNair, the other vice chairman; and Robert S. Strauss, national treasurer.

The disgruntled groups within the regular party were understood to include southern party officials, organized labor generally, the Democratic governors, and continuing Humphrey partisans.[10] O'Brien's executive slate incorporated something—someone—for each. Geri Joseph was a longtime Humphrey associate, putting the Humphrey people back at the center through her surrogate participation. If her personal ties to organized labor were not as strong as they might have been, Humphrey's own ties remained exceptional. Bob McNair was a governor, a southern party leader, and one of those known to have been unhappy with the idea of O'Brien. Bob Strauss was a second southerner, a committed regular, and a Humphrey supporter, to boot.

As this general strategy for managing the National Committee—and this specific strategy for facing the issue of party reform—began to take shape, it came to require one other, major element in order to have some serious chance at success. The national chairman could cater publicly to party reformers; he could press privately for compliance with recommended reforms; he could try to use appointments at the National Committee to bring the regular party along. But if he was to remain in control of this increasingly complex and interrelated strategy—and if he was to remain able, in particular, to modify specific reform proposals, either to protect the regular party from the impact of reform or to protect his hard-won party unity from eruptions by party regulars—he needed to assert his personal primacy in negotiations over compliance.

As the final element in his emerging strategy for party reform, the national chairman needed to shift the center of reform politics into his own office and to develop the means for channeling that politics once it was centered there. Only then could the chairman put the influence of his position behind the implementation of party reform. Only then could he assess the response from the state parties and press ahead or pull back accordingly. Only then could he be sure that the politics of implementation would contribute to his other goals—debt reduction, candidate recruitment, and pursuit of the presidency—rather than damaging those goals on the way to its realization.

By early May, Chairman O'Brien was ready to take specific steps to put himself on record in support of party reform, to urge the state parties in that same direction, and to assert his own primacy in the negotiations to follow. The financial crisis at the National Committee had been stabilized, though hardly ameliorated. The official report of the Party Structure Commission, *Mandate for Reform,* had been published, adding extra pressure for a response from the national chairman and emphasizing the fact that the commission, not the chairman, remained at the center of reform politics.

The logical opportunity for O'Brien to begin converting his general strategy into specific actions was the scheduled meeting of the Executive Committee of the Democratic National Committee on May 22. This meeting had been called because the previous session of the full committee had been devoted to the installation of O'Brien and because the chairman expected to have numerous items from the new O'Brien regime ready for ratification by that time. It could also serve, however, as a crucial site—and hence as a benchmark—in the ongoing politics of party reform.

Four days before the Executive Committee session, on May 18, 1970, Lawrence F. O'Brien opened what was to become a personal, twenty-six-month campaign for reform of the process of delegate selection. Few, including the chairman himself, could have known that this was the first concrete move in a continuing campaign for implementation and compliance. Despite that, this initial move was carefully crafted, sharp and distinctive, and historically noteworthy.

O'Brien's opening shot was a four-page, single-spaced, advisory memorandum on the legal status of commission guidelines. The memo was drafted by Joseph A. Califano, general counsel to the National Committee. O'Brien added a covering letter of his own and mailed copies to all state chairmen and members of the National Committee, thereby signaling his intention to be intimately involved in the politics of party reform. The Califano memo jumped directly to the question of the coercive status of proposed reforms:

> You asked for an opinion on the status of the Guidelines adopted on November 19–20, 1969, by the Commission on Party Structure and Delegate Selection (the McGovern Commission) contained in its report to the Democratic National Committee, entitled "Mandate for Reform."
> Briefly stated, my view is that the Guidelines should be respected by the State Parties as their guide in assuring that the delegate selection processes within each state provide all Democrats with a full, meaningful, and timely opportunity to participate, in line with the requirements applicable to the 1972 Convention established by the 1964 and 1968 Conventions of the National Democratic Party.[11]

Califano skipped over arguments about the *scope* of commission proposals. Throughout 1969, the commission staff had worked to expand the range of topics which they judged to fall within their purview. The national counsel had no interest in a debate over whether the 1968 Convention had foreseen that they would roam so freely. Instead, he merely listed the convention resolutions preceding commission action.

If Califano was willing to advise the states to accept the recommendations of the commission, and if he was willing to second those recommendations across their full range of application, he was unlikely to hesitate in mentioning the sanctions which might follow if a state should fail to heed his warning. He did not. Califano raised the ultimate threat—a credentials challenge, a negative report, and then expulsion—as the penalty which might accrue if a state party did not take his advisory opinion to heart:

> The ultimate remedy for the failure of a State Party to comply with the requirements set forth above is to deny seating to a delegation from such a state. All questions of credentials are ultimately decided by the Convention, applying in the instance of the 1972 Convention the delegate-selection requirements which were laid out by the previous Conventions.[12]

Califano had left no question about the direction in which a wise state chairman should move. His notice could thus serve, variously, as the green light for those states which were already inclined to accept reform, as ammunition for reform factions in those states which were ambivalent, or as a set of personal suggestions for those states which were not inclined to go along on their own, but which might be willing to defer to the national chairman. O'Brien commissioned the memo in full realization of these possibilities:

> The Califano memo was an interpretation. We worked very hard on this. It was a means on my part to express my *personal* point of view, and, I think you could say, in a way everyone could see.

Despite this unambiguous statement of preference, O'Brien's strategy also called for preservation of a way out, or at least of a way to retrench, in case the opposition to implementation should prove the more serious threat to his other goals. Not surprisingly, the Califano memo contained an escape clause. For those state parties which were adamantly opposed to reform, those which were not interested in whether Larry O'Brien was endorsing the guidelines or not, Califano offered a reminder that "the ultimate decision on compliance with the requirements established by the 1964 and 1968 Conventions will reside with the 1972 Convention"[13]—phraseology which could be defended as simple, accurate, legal exegesis, but which could also be read as permission to wait.

Finally, O'Brien's evolving strategy called for the centralization of reform politics in his own office; the Califano memo made several contributions there as well. In a sense, the simple act of circulating this memo was a step toward establishing the authority of the national chairman. But the obvious organizational impediment to an increase in that authority was still the Party Structure Commission, and Califano attempted to put its role in perspective. Indeed, the provision noting that ultimate responsibility in these matters rested with the 1972 Convention was actually embedded in a larger section addressing the formal position of the commission and its recommendations:

> In the McGovern Commission's report, there is a discussion entitled "Legal Status of the Guidelines" (Report, pp. 36–37). While it is possible that some will interpret this discussion as asserting a legal, binding effect for the Guidelines, the fact is that the discussion proceeds on the correct theory that the ultimate decision on compliance with the requirements established by the 1964 and 1968 Conventions will reside with the 1972 Convention.[14]

With this closing notation, then, Joe Califano slapped down the countervailing assertion of legal authority which the remaining commission personnel were trying to advance. By doing so, he underlined the primacy of the political process surrounding implementation—and the intended primacy of the new national chairman at its center.

The Califano memo was actually the first half of a one-two punch which

O'Brien planned to deliver in late May; the second half followed quickly upon it. Four days later, at the May 22 session of the Executive Committee, the national chairman suggested creation of two Ad Hoc committees, one to work with the Party Structure Commission, one to work with the Rules Commission, and both to work with the state parties in implementing the two commission reports. His suggestion was introduced amidst a lengthy series of procedural matters, but the idea itself was not casually put forth. Rather, the potential joint effect of the Califano memo and the Ad Hoc committees had been carefully considered.

For the state parties, the Califano memo was intended as additional pressure toward action on party reform. The relevant Ad Hoc Committee might then come along and provide an official, yet obviously sympathetic, means to ease the states into compliance. For the National Committee, the memo was intended, generally, to reduce the potential for that body to become a focus of opposition, and specifically, to predispose the members of the Executive Committee toward authorizing the Ad Hoc committees. These committees could then assure the full National Committee of its own window on the implementation process, while they simultaneously aided and encouraged compliance. O'Brien viewed this special window as absolutely essential, to enhance the legitimacy of the reform process within the National Committee and to increase the chances of slipping the entire reform package past it without a major battle:

> I think there was a basic view, which I certainly understood, that the McGovern Commission, by itself, could not be responsive to party needs, because it was not representative of the party. The COPE guys certainly took this view, although they were not active.

The Ad Hoc Committee arrangement had one other potential advantage: It increased the chairman's own control over the politics of implementation. The final section of the Califano memo had been one step in this direction, with its reminder that the National Convention, not the Party Structure Commission, would ultimately decide the requirements of compliance. The Ad Hoc committees were a second step, because they moved more of the negotiations over compliance back inside the National Committee and thus, on a day-to-day basis, inside the office of the chairman. O'Brien was well aware that this prospect would look less attractive to the commission leadership—and to its allies—than to the National Committee:

> The Commission was a slight hang-up, because they were of the view that once their work was completed, that the guidelines were in effect, and that there

was no role for the Democratic National Chairman or the Democratic National Committee. I made it clear that this was not my view. I wanted the National Committee to perform.

The McGovern Commission leadership and a bare majority took this view. My view caused them to feel that I might be playing a game. I told them that this would come up at full and open meetings of the Democratic National Committee. Bode took the position that I was putting roadblocks in the way.

The national chairman opened his resolution establishing these committees by commending the Party Structure Commission for its labors to date. Next, he sounded a theme which would become a mainstay in his public arguments about Democratic party reform—that his party was making a precedent-breaking attempt, on its own, to improve the character of American democracy, and that no other party had the initiative or the courage to do likewise. After that, O'Brien suggested (as Califano had) that the guidelines were only the logical extension of requirements adopted at the 1964 and 1968 conventions, and that they deserved deference on these grounds as well. In conclusion, he ordered himself to appoint two new ad hoc bodies.

The resolution passed on a quick vote, but then Mildred Jeffrey of Michigan called a halt and started to probe its implications:

> *Jeffrey:* I'm not sure of the meaning in the last paragraph beginning on the second page: "The Chairman of the Democratic National Committee is directed to implement the reports of the Commission." Is this the implementation at the Democratic National Party level, insofar as setting forth the Call, Rules, etc., or what does "implement" mean?[15]

Jeffrey was searching for the practical connection between the Party Structure Commission and what would become Ad Hoc Committee No. 1. Her evident fear was that this second body might "aid" the first right out of existence. Califano succeeded in meeting what became a series of questions from Jeffrey by minimizing the role of the new Ad Hoc committees and by asserting that they would work in tandem with the official commission staff. The Executive Committee then moved on to other matters.

Jeffrey's suspicions were not out of character, since she herself was a committed reformer. More surprising was the absence of parallel suspicions from the other side. Any number of Millie Jeffrey's fellow members on the Executive Committee—Jacob M. Arvey of Illinois, for example, as well as Joseph M. Barr of Pennsylvania, J. Marshall Brown of Louisiana, or Beatrice H. Rosenthal of Connecticut—might have been expected to prefer seeing the commission struggle along on its own, while keeping the National Committee unentangled in the reform process.

The immediate criticism from Jeffrey probably helped tamp down their discomfort, but so, surely, did the actual appointments to these two new bodies. Chairman O'Brien had brought his proposed membership lists with him to the meeting, and he put them on the table with the enabling resolution.[16] Only Carrin M. Patman, the new and politically unknown committeewoman from Texas, held even the possibility of becoming a militant reformer; each of the others had some symbolic attribute which made them unattractive to reform partisans.

The crucial Ad Hoc Committee, in other words, was not constructed to strike terror in the hearts of regular party leaders. In effect, O'Brien had held both sides together, once again, by giving institutional arrangements to the reformers, individual appointments under them to regulars. At the same time, he had managed a net contribution, moderate and controlled though it might be, to the overall progress of party reform. For their part, the appointees to these new bodies were not unaware of the strategy behind their selection, nor of the contribution to reform which it implicitly constituted. George Mitchell, the link between the Ad Hoc Committee and the Party Structure Commission, saw both aspects of the device:

> There was, of course, continuing opposition from the regulars to the idea of these rules. This would be useful for a guy like Larry, to have a committee like this to look at these rules and give them a stamp of approval. I don't think that the committee ever actually did anything. People from other states would inquire about different aspects of this. I would do my best to explain and defend the guidelines. This is sometimes difficult if you don't agree with it all.

Passage by the Executive Committee of a resolution authorizing two new Ad Hoc committees completed the formal and organizational inauguration of the O'Brien approach to party reform. But that passage was not quite the end of the informal maneuvering behind initiation of this strategy. The appearance of two new "reform" bodies, made up of members of the National Committee and under the obvious suasion of Chairman O'Brien, alarmed the remaining members of the Party Structure entourage. They retaliated quickly, and O'Brien's first concrete approach to the issue of party reform could not be said to be fully in place until he, in turn, had dealt with their response.

The opening period of the new O'Brien regime was a time of great anxiety for the staff and leadership of the Party Structure Commission. As a potential chairman, O'Brien did not occasion the outright horror associated with several of the others who had loomed briefly as replacements for Harris. But if the appointment of O'Brien was not perceived as the most deadly threat to the commission's handiwork, neither did it appear to promise significant benefits. Ken Bode spoke for most of his colleagues in analyzing the selection:

The Politics of Implementation

O'Brien was Humphrey's manager, remember. There was dissatisfaction among the regulars that Harris had let this thing go too long, had let it get out of hand. Harris quit amid reports that he had let it get away. Someone had to come in to rein it back in.

Moreover, the first practical contacts between the new chairman and the commission entourage came in the form of inquiries about the size of the commission budget and staff—and about the opportunities for making reductions in same. Carol Casey found a source of anxiety in this, too, despite the kind words of the chairman in public:

> At that point, we thought that O'Brien really had little choice. To the extent that there was any publicity, it was good publicity. If he tried to turn it around, he would have alienated the liberal wing, which was more vociferous then. We were, however, very paranoid about cuts in money. We never knew how much of this was attributable to politics and trying to dump the reforms, and how much to normal financial problems.

O'Brien had moved initially to calm these apprehensions. For his official installation on Thursday, March 5, he had invited both George McGovern, the Party Structure chairman, and Jim O'Hara, the Rules chairman, to make short presentations. Not long afterward, he met privately with the Party Structure leadership, Chairman McGovern and Vice Chairman Hughes, and emphasized his good will.

These gestures did not significantly comfort the rest of the commission staff. Bode, Segal, and Casey quickly came to see that the national chairman was not going to denounce their reforms and abandon them, but they continued to fear that he might accomplish the same end by dismantling the commission and assuming its responsibilities. Even Bob Nelson shared this uncertainty:

> I felt, in the O'Brien change, for a six-week period, that there was a chance that funding would be cut off. I felt that that might be the end of the thing. I didn't know what commitments had been made. O'Brien began to assemble a budget. For a period of a number of months after that, we were getting negative reactions from the Chairman's Office from time to time. We would get those vibes from Ira Kapenstein [deputy director of the National Committee].

When his initial approaches to McGovern and Hughes proved insufficient to quiet these concerns, some of which were spilling out in quasi-public ways, O'Brien assembled the entire commission entourage. In McGovern's Senate office, the national chairman spoke to the commission leadership, staff, consultants, and remaining volunteers about his developing support for reform. Dick Wade was one of those on the receiving end:

260

I always expected that O'Brien would accept it. *I* thought he was a pragmatic guy, but the staff was very upset. He was a Kennedy man, and the notion was that I could best talk to him. I did, and he said he thought they [the guidelines] were good, that they were overdue. But the staff didn't believe it. So then he came over to McGovern's office, and he gave a very flat commitment. There were ten or fifteen people there. Then, his phrase was, "This is my survival kit." He said this when we were all together in one room. I remember his words very clearly.

The Califano memo appeared to give practical substance to these reassurances, and despite continuing reservations by commission personnel, their response to the memo was almost uniformly positive. Chairman McGovern was pleasantly surprised, not only by the contents of the memo but by the fact that it had arrived without commission prompting: "O'Brien deserves full credit for instigating the Califano memo. O'Brien went on this by himself. I remember Eli Segal keeping me posted on that."

Any incipient good will was dissipated four days later, when the Executive Committee of the National Committee adopted O'Brien's proposal for two new Ad Hoc committees to help with implementation. The absence of prior discussion would itself have led commission personnel to view these new organizations with suspicion. The evident overlap in functions between the commission and Ad Hoc Committee No. 1 raised the possibility that this committee was, in fact, the opening move in a campaign to defang and then dissolve the commission.

The National Committee had authorized creation of the two Ad Hoc bodies on Friday afternoon, May 22. On Saturday morning, Segal, Bode, and McGovern met in McGovern's Senate office to respond. Bode attended in the belief that Ad Hoc Committee No. 1 represented a serious danger:

> When the compliance committee was appointed, there was no notice. It was Friday, and there was no notice. Eli and I went up with McGovern to the Hill and wrote a letter asking that this committee not have any authority to "interpret" the guidelines. We sensed this as the first wedge. It was *how* O'Brien did it; the list came out of his pocket. Absolutely nobody knew about the 1970 compliance committee.

The three commission figures settled on an aggressively worded letter from McGovern to O'Brien, underlining their insistence that any new committee have no authority even to analyze the guidelines, much less to modify them. This went by special messenger to the office of the national chairman, while copies were circulated, privately, to some of the newsmen who had been following reform politics.

O'Brien had no trouble recognizing a threat to the truce which he had been forging between regulars and reformers, and he offered an answer by letter that same day. In this, the national chairman stressed the fact that the Ad Hoc committees would be a step *toward* implementation, and he included copies of the resolution establishing them and of their membership lists. As additional evidence for this interpretation, O'Brien adduced the Califano memo, a copy of which was also included. He pointed directly to the parts of that memo which advised the state parties to treat the guidelines as party law and which averred that these new rules were only simple elucidation of the actions of previous conventions. In closing, he noted that even though the Ad Hoc committees were designed to help with implementation, they would still have only a circumscribed role, one which would supplement, and never supplant, that of the Party Structure Commission:

> Finally, I want to emphasize that the ad hoc committees' responsibility reinforces the commitment to reform by the Democratic Party. The ad hoc committees have no power to alter, dilute, or in any way veto the guidelines, but rather they are a means by which the National Committee can now fulfill its obligations, in cooperation with the Commission, in carrying out the mandates of the 1968 Democratic Convention.[17]

O'Brien did not stop there in his efforts to calm whatever fears had been aroused by these new committees. The following Monday, he drafted a note to all Party Structure commissioners and enclosed a copy both of the Califano memo and of his Saturday letter to McGovern.[18] Then, in a final exchange on the matter, McGovern, Hughes, and O'Brien stanched the flow of quasi-public letters and gathered in the same room, to be sure that the situation had been clarified to the satisfaction of everyone. This meeting produced no move to disband the Ad Hoc committees, nor any additional public definition of rights and responsibilities. It did, however, generate verbal guarantees that the Party Structure Commission would be funded as long as, or longer than, Ad Hoc Committee No. 1 and that the Ad Hoc Committee would rely upon the commission for its expertise, especially when a state party was seeking advice on its options.

As a result, McGovern emerged with a guarantee that the reform commission which he had headed since its inception would continue to exist and would thus, at least potentially, remain a major influence upon the politics of party reform. O'Brien departed with the mechanisms for an expanded role in reform politics, something which he had desired since returning to the national chairmanship. In passing, most of the major institutional actors for the politics of implementation were established, or confirmed, as well.

Implications

The parallels between the inauguration of the politics of recommendation and the inauguration of the politics of implementation were striking. The initial turning point in the politics of recommendation had been the selection of one national chairman, Fred R. Harris. The initial turning point in the politics of implementation was the selection of his successor, Lawrence F. O'Brien. The alternatives to Harris at the time he was selected had represented clear and divergent approaches to the main reform task of that time, appointment of the Party Structure Commission. The alternatives to O'Brien represented clear and divergent approaches to *his* initial reform task, addressing the report of that commission.[19]

Nevertheless, these parallels should not be overdrawn. The fundamental task of each new chairman in reform politics was recognizably different. Harris was appointing a reform commission only, albeit one which aspired to be historic. O'Brien was being asked to implement the product of this commission, its recommendations for sweeping institutional change. Moreover, the political environment which each chairman entered—the institutional context in which he found himself, coupled with the principal developments in internal party politics which preceded his arrival—shaped his response in major ways, almost in spite of himself. Both men represented crucial implicit directions for subsequent reform politics. Both were still constrained in major, specifiable ways, and the case of O'Brien was particularly revealing.

In a sense, there were five serious options for chairman at the time of the appointment of O'Brien, and each presented strong if implicit portents for the course of reform politics. The first was Larry O'Brien as supported by Hubert Humphrey. The second and third were Matt Welsh and Joe Crangle, after O'Brien withdrew and the party split. The fourth was O'Brien as a subsequent, independent compromise. The fifth was Gordon St. Angelo, as a last-ditch alternative to O'Brien.

The process of arriving at the fourth of these options—O'Brien on his own—had unavoidable implications for the course of reform politics and, especially, for the role of national elites in that politics. By returning to the national chairmanship in the way he did, O'Brien shook loose from a specific attachment to Humphrey, and from a general attachment to the regular party. This made him more receptive to the drive for party reform from the beginning. It made him less potentially responsive to the regular party at any—at every—subsequent point.[20]

Harris, by aligning himself so consciously with the emerging reform wing of the party but by failing at the same time to win the trust of that wing, had failed completely at resolving the problems contributed by the 1968 Convention. Factionalism along the lines present at the convention had invaded the National Committee itself. More crucially, the huge party debt left by the 1968 campaign had actually increased, thereby limiting—almost eliminating—the help which the National Committee could provide to Democratic candidates across the country.

Unity thus became the immediate public theme for O'Brien; the appearance of unity became his immediate operating goal as well. That appearance seemed central to an assault on the disabling party debt. The stabilization of party finances, in turn, seemed the only hope for supporting party candidates around the country in the general elections of 1970. Beyond that, the reality of unity stood as the major potentially available contribution to the election of a Democratic president in 1972, whoever he might be.

Every candidate for Democratic national chairman—Welsh and Crangle and St. Angelo as well as O'Brien—would have faced this need for an appearance of unity. Every candidate would have faced an immediate need for a public posture toward party reform as well, thanks to the decision of the Party Structure Commission to go it alone and publish a major reform report. An evident public endorsement of that report by the new national chairman was probably the sole way to prevent the automatic fracturing of this incipient party unity. Every potential national chairman without a death wish—without, that is, a desire for instant civil war—would have made this endorsement. O'Brien, having maneuvered so carefully to arrive as an independent compromise for the entire party, was not about to violate these constraints.

At that point, however, the implications of choosing one individual over another did diverge sharply. Every candidate would have given the commission report an obvious public blessing. Not every candidate would have followed through with public actions to give that blessing a practical content, or with private urgings toward implementation and compliance. O'Brien followed through by having the general counsel of the National Committee issue a memo advising state party leaders that the report of the commission should be treated as the rules of the party and by appointing an Ad Hoc Committee of the National Committee to help ease the states into compliance with those rules. Welsh, the previous leading contender and the man charged with protecting the interests of Humphrey—and indirectly of the regular party—would hardly have taken the same course. It would have been too great a risk for his major patron; it would have represented too much of an assault on the dominant faction which had placed him in office.

It was O'Brien, however, who acquired the need for some precise course of action in the realm of party reform. As a result, it was O'Brien's strategy which became the major new influence on reform politics. O'Brien quickly gave the guidelines his general public blessing. But he went on to give them a major specific push, through the Califano memo and through strong private endorsements to those party leaders whom he judged susceptible.

At the same time, O'Brien understood that while organized reformers might be the short-run threat to party unity—the regulars were unlikely to disrupt what was, after all, *their* party, at least without more concrete provocation—regular party officialdom was perfectly capable of being a greater threat in the long run. Or at least, it was the regular party leadership which would ultimately decide the fate of reform in both the National Committee and the fifty states. Indeed, the delay in an immediate confrontation over party reform presumably *increased* the likelihood that the regular party would force an eventual confrontation—and thereby strain (or smash) the unity teased out to that point.

As a result, O'Brien elaborated his strategy. He attempted to centralize negotiations over the implementation of reform in his own office, so that if it became necessary to amend the central reform document, in order to attain substantial compliance while retaining party unity, he would be able to do so. At the same time, he attempted to remain personally detached from the specific guidelines in the commission package, so that he would have the necessary freedom to maneuver—and to amend. Finally, in order to bring the regular party along with all this, he used his appointive powers to cement a broad range of party regulars to the new O'Brien regime, including representatives of those who had been most unhappy with the prospect of his own return.

The Califano memo could be broken down, almost paragraph by paragraph, as an embodiment of this strategy. Ad Hoc Committee No. 1, while not subject to such textual analysis, fit the pattern, too. Both conduced the regular party toward implementation and compliance. Both moved subsequent negotiations toward the office of the national chairman. Each contained escape hatches for the regular party, should that prove necessary.

The construction of this strategy, with all its adjustments and convolutions, became a particularly detailed and compact example of the common wisdom about the way in which democratic politicians normally construct political strategies. O'Brien did not lack for values and goals of his own. Much less did he lack a peculiar personal filter for analysis. But he did begin with the world as he found it, and he did build his strategy—jerry-build his strategy, really—primarily in the role of a broker.

In this, O'Brien tried to encompass each—all—of the relevant constraints within his emerging plan for party reform and to rally a sufficient coalition behind this plan to give it some chance of success. The approach of the new

National Chairman, then, besides being a major influence on the subsequent course of reform politics, was a classic case of the construction of a political strategy by a small *d* democratic politician, especially a regular party politician in the American context.

None of this put O'Brien in particularly good standing with the individuals who would benefit most from his approach to reform. Indeed, the mere arrival of O'Brien as a determinedly major actor in reform politics, even if most of his initial actions were manifestly proreform, disturbed key figures at the Party Structure Commission. These individuals had rallied behind a different candidate for chairman. They were decidedly not reassured by the party history of O'Brien. They focused on the small but real elements of ambiguity in his reform strategy and saw them as a possible opening wedge in a potential effort to rein in the guidelines.

Accordingly, they protested appointment of Ad Hoc Committee No. 1, in order to secure its removal if possible, in order to limit its impact if not. But what they gained from this protest was an assurance that the commission itself would continue for the duration of reform politics. This had not previously been guaranteed, since the commission had absorbed a large amount of scarce financial resources, while the arrival of a chairman with an interest in party reform made it arguably redundant. Yet within days of the appointment of Ad Hoc Committee No. 1, the continuation of the Party Structure Commission, too, was assured.

The implications for institutional change were simple and straightforward. The new national chairman would inevitably be a major actor in the politics of implementation—in the implementation of sweeping recommendations for party reform. When that new chairman turned out to be not just sympathetic to reform in the abstract but publicly supportive of the commission guidelines *and privately supportive as well,* the prospects for major institutional change brightened at once.

Moreover, while this new chairman would still try to maintain his freedom of maneuver, even his vague public blessings served as an additional pressure—upon himself—in the same, proreform direction. What could be said of vague public blessings was, of course, even more true of strong, specific, public and private actions aimed at bringing the state parties into line with this public posture. Every one of these actions became an event which would have to be implicitly disavowed if the chairman was to change course in a major way. Those actions which produced a response from other party actors became *specific compromises* which would have to be violated explicitly in order to change course.

Finally, as individual state parties followed the public lead of the chairman—as they responded to his public and private prodding toward reform—the pressures on the chairman to maintain, or even expand, his proreform activities would increase accordingly. Every new success at implementation reduced the corpus of those with incentive to resist. Every new success added to the collection of those who were potentially willing to stand up for reform.

Larry O'Brien may have been especially sensitive to the divisions within the national Democratic party, and thus to the apparent, associated need for unity which underlay his entire strategy. His most recent experience in party politics, after all, had been with the divisive 1968 Convention and the disastrous presidential campaign which followed. Two years later, an incumbent without that experience could have noted that there were no ongoing nomination campaigns to provide a framework for insurgents and that the aspiring "new politics" organizations which had sprung up in the aftermath of the 1968 campaign had already deteriorated, severely.

Be that as it may, it was O'Brien who had to find a response. It was the appearance of party unity which guided that response. It was an aggressive, proreform strategy which became the embodiment of that search for party unity. This strategy, finally, had clear and positive, though not irrevocable, implications for the fate of proposed institutional change.

Ironically, when the remaining members of the commission entourage objected to the initial moves by O'Brien in the reform area, as insufficiently proreform, their very objections became yet another cause of improved prospects for these proposed institutional changes. This would not have been so if these objections had provoked a counterattack from the national chairman. But his desire to begin immediately to build at least the facade of party unity caused him instead to try to placate them by promising that the commission, too, would remain in place through the politics of implementation, and would thus remain a powerful force for the realization of institutional change.

The continuation of the Party Structure Commission was likely to have this effect because of the relationship between the commission—and O'Brien's overall reform strategy for that matter—and the major elite coalitions contending for dominance within the Democratic party. When the politics of recommendation gave way to the politics of implementation, the orthodox Democratic coalition might have expected to regain the influential role in reform politics. But to do so, it needed to act, or at least it could act most easily, through the Democratic national chairman. When he instead endorsed reform, and especially when he turned to activities giving his endorsement practical impact, party regulars were forced back to individual, decentralized, case-by-case resistance.

The Politics of Implementation

The accession of O'Brien himself, then, as augmented by his public and private urgings toward implementation and by the Califano memo in particular, served to push the orthodox Democratic coalition away from control of reform politics. When O'Brien closed the initiation of his reform strategy by promising to retain the Party Structure Commission, he made a direct gift to the alternative Democratic coalition. The commission had become the major link among self-conscious reformers around the country. If the national chairman was holding the regular party at arm's length from national reform politics, he was simultaneously returning the commission to its previous place, right there at the center.

As a result, the commission, too, would be around to press the state parties toward implementation and compliance. It would be around to continue to press the *national chairman* toward additional initiatives on party reform, thereby making it increasingly unlikely that he would turn back. It would be around, finally, as the continuing link among external reformers, to encourage them to continue to press for implementation and compliance in the states and for additional reform initiatives from the national chairman.

CHAPTER

1 0

The Mandate at the State Level:

The State Parties and the Commission Report

IN WHICH, the national actors assemble for the politics of implementation; the state parties respond, according to local needs, practices, and pressures; but the state response assumes a clear and patterned character, one
that will reappear continually. AND IN WHICH, negotiations among national actors and autonomous state counterparts become the essence of reform politics, a subset of state parties proves less resistant to institutional
change than national reformers had feared; and as a result, the national
party becomes more likely to resemble these volunteer-based parties, rather
than their office-based counterparts.

BY THE TIME Larry O'Brien had been installed as national chairman, the
politics of party reform had already begun to move out toward the individual
states and away from a focus at one central, national site. Indeed, the maneuvers surrounding the return of O'Brien and his development of a first approach
to the reform issue were the last, major, nationally focused events in reform
politics until early 1971. In the interim, the politics of implementation was
composed of autonomous developments in the fifty-five state, district, and territorial parties. It was composed of jockeying among institutional actors at the
national level for the right to negotiate with key figures in these subnational
parties. It was composed, especially, of the resulting negotiations between
state and national reform actors.

Between August of 1968 and May of 1970, the constituent units of the
Democratic party had played little part in the politics of party reform. Until
November of 1969, the mechanics of rules revision had effectively required
that reform politics be concentrated at the national level, in Washington, at
the Party Structure Commission. The commission did reach out to the state

parties through its regional hearings, albeit in a perfunctory fashion. The states were urged to create their own, parallel, "little McGovern commissions," as an initial commitment to the cause of party reform.

Yet the practical constraints on state reform politicking were nearly immutable. Until the Party Structure Commission issued its national guidelines, anyone with an interest in party reform was well advised to follow this national commission and to slight its state counterparts. Indeed, until the Party Structure Commission reported, almost nothing which the states might do could be guaranteed to matter. If their reform commissions, by some happy accident, settled on recommendations identical to those of the national body, well and good. If they did not, the recommendations of the national commission would still become the official definition of party reform.

Between November of 1969 and May of 1970, all this changed. The transition from a politics of recommendation to a politics of implementation was defined by a shift in the central goal of reform politics, from the development of a set of reform proposals to the translation of those proposals into real institutions of delegate selection. Yet this shift was accompanied by a change in the character—and number—of the relevant actors in reform politics, and that was its crucial, practical difference.

By late May of 1970, this transition was completed. Some of the change was still explicitly focused at the national level. The number of institutional actors in reform politics increased as the national chairman moved more deliberately into reform negotiations and as his Ad Hoc committees were added to the mix. The membership of most of these institutional actors, old and new, altered as well with a new incumbent in the national chairmanship and with a shuffling of personnel at the Party Structure Commission.

Most of this change, however, came from the introduction of the individual states into reform politics. Fifty state parties, along with counterparts in the District of Columbia and the four trust territories, became the crucial arena(s) for reform politicking. For implementation to succeed completely, all fifty-five units had to be brought into compliance with all eighteen commission guidelines. For implementation to succeed at all, a very substantial share of these units had to be brought into substantial compliance, so that it was clear that the recommendations of the commission were the effective rules of the national party.

Yet the introduction of fifty-five state, district, and territorial parties multiplied the number of decision-points in the politics of party reform by more than fifty-five. All these units possessed a state chairman and a state central committee, whose acceptance was usually essential. Most possessed an indigenous reform commission as well. Many had a sitting Democratic governor, the highest elected officeholder of the state party and the person most frequently recognized as party leader by outsiders. Some featured organized reform factions, factions which had been fighting their party regulars for years. All contained a range of major, local, organized interests, which might enter reform politics or not as their perceived stakes dictated.

As a result, a good deal of the subsequent politics of party reform, then, was played out in California, Minnesota, Pennsylvania, or Texas, and not in Washington, D.C. Indeed, a good deal of this subsequent politics, at least by bulk, consisted of independent activities within these individual states, activities which were the product of interactions among a range of state and local actors, including party leaders, indigenous reform commissions, incumbent governors, established reform factions, and diverse, other, organized interests.

Beyond this, the essence of the politics of implementation after May of 1970 was really an extensive and decentralized set of negotiations *between* this range of relevant actors in the states and localities and a counterpart group of national actors. Independent state initiatives drawing a national response, or state responses to national prodding, along with struggles at both the state and national levels to influence the outcome of any such exchange, were the dominant activities in reform politics from May of 1970 until July of 1972, until, that is, the next national convention.

This did not mean that there was no pattern to the specific communications about compliance emanating from the national level. Nor did it mean that there was no larger national strategy behind these individual communications. More surprisingly, the arrival of this extensive and decentralized politics of implementation did not mean that there was no pattern in the state responses to national exhortation. Nor did it imply that any initial pattern was merely transitory, the result of a coordinated national strategy and idiosyncratic state reactions.

The national strategy, in fact, emerged largely by default. Both the national chairman and the commission staff began with those states which were most receptive to reform, rather than those which were least. Beyond that, the staff at the Party Structure Commission, because it produced the vast bulk of reform communications, augmented this pressure by making a conscious effort to harvest the most receptive states early.

The emergence of a patterning in the response of the individual state parties, however—a patterning which was tied to fundamental characteristics of these state parties as organizations—was more surprising. The peculiarities of individual state politics did condition the way in which each state addressed each successive stage of the reform process, and no state could be understood individually without attention to these local factors. Yet for the state parties as a group, the reaction to national urgings proved highly patterned and predictable. That is, basic characteristics of state party structure conditioned the response not just to the call for creation of a state reform commission, but to every activity thereafter.

The crucial distinction was between volunteer state parties, those which relied upon independent activism in pursuit of party affairs, and organized state parties, those which could turn to a perpetually staffed set of party offices for the same party business. Volunteer parties, through the nature of their incentives, the character of their participants, the form of their electoral campaigns, and the overall party structure which these, together, created, were far more responsive to national urgings toward party reform. Organized parties, for these same reasons, were far less responsive at every analogous stage.

This difference in behavior between volunteer and organized state parties, then, became more than a means of comprehending the progress of the states as a whole. Indeed, it became more than a central *explanation* for that progress. For this difference became an immediate asset to those who were pushing for sweeping party reform. Indeed, it became an immediate contribution, strong though hardly decisive, to widespread institutional change. Beyond that, this difference in the response of volunteer and organized state political parties became a crucial clue to the prospects for elite replacement in the national Democratic party—and thus to the character of the elite political actors who might dominate party politics in a reformed party in the post-reform era.

The Presentation of National Demands

With the arrival of an agreement to maintain the Party Structure Commission, the institutional actors at the national level for the opening of the politics of implementation had been confirmed and put into place. Much of the subsequent reform politics would consist of activities within the various states and not in Washington. But a substantial share would involve negotiations *between* individual states and these national actors, and there would be a significant, explicitly national politics of implementation, too. In any case, the national aspects of this new brand of reform politics had clearly been inaugurated by the end of May, 1970.

The collection of organizations which would speak for the national party during the politics of implementation—or more accurately, the collection which would *attempt* to speak for the national party, sometimes in coordination, sometimes in competition—was changed substantially from the politics of recommendation. Some of this change was in the creation of new, relevant organizations, as with Ad Hoc Committee No. 1. Some was in the reintroduction of existing, relevant organizations, as with the Democratic National Committee. Most was in the restructuring of the continuing, obviously relevant organizations, as with the office of the national chairman and the Party Structure Commission.

Ad Hoc Committee No. 1, the newest institutional actor in this aggregation, never acquired the influence which its supporters, much less its detractors, had envisioned in May of 1970. As a body, the committee was overwhelmed by the national chairman, from one side, and the Party Structure Commission, from the other. It did comparatively little over the next two years. Indeed, its most obvious contribution to reform politics would come when it served as a vehicle for the reform resolutions of Chairman O'Brien in early 1971.

As individuals, the members of the Ad Hoc Committee were somewhat more active, answering queries from individual state leaders. Yet even here, their activity may have contributed as much confusion as clarity. For when the members of the Ad Hoc Committee *were* making an independent contribution to reform politics, it was because they were differing—and hence competing—with the other organizations and individuals trying to speak for the national party and claiming to be the authoritative interpreters of reformed party rules.

The National Committee itself had obviously re-entered the politics of party reform, indirectly but powerfully, when it served as the arena for the selection of a new national chairman. Like Ad Hoc Committee No. 1, the National Committee was destined for only a very infrequent, collective opportunity to operate in reform politics. Unlike Ad Hoc Committee No. 1, however, its two major opportunities were crucial to the fate of reform. In February of 1971, the National Committee would assemble to adopt a Preliminary Call to the 1972 Convention, thereby confronting the guidelines as a package and passing on them in their entirety. In October of 1971, the committee would take a second—and last—look at the guideline package, in an up-or-down vote, and would appoint the convention officials who would interpret these guidelines once real delegate selection was under way.

As a decentralized group of individuals, however, the members of the National Committee played a more varied, if informal, role in reform politics. Individually, they served as emissaries from their state parties to the national chairman, informing him of developments at home and pressing him in their preferred direction. Individually, they were also tapped *by* the national chairman, to communicate with their state parties and to seek support for his own reform preferences. In either guise, some members played these roles frequently and with gusto; others never experienced them at all.

The major, continuing, "new" actor in reform politics—new not in an institutional sense but in the degree to which the incumbent exerted himself and all his institutional resources to acquire an influence over the fate of party reform—was the office of the national chairman. Larry O'Brien had signaled his intention to be actively involved from the beginning. He was to remain actively involved throughout his tenure as national chairman, and that, in turn, was to stretch through the 1972 Convention.

The Party Structure Commission, too, continued throughout this period and served, along with the national chairman, as the other major source of interpretations—and pressure—for party reform. The commissioners as a group had recessed indefinitely on November 20, 1969. They were not to meet again until July of 1970, twenty months later. They were never to meet again in sufficient numbers to satisfy their own quorum requirements.[1] A few commissioners, though far fewer than the staff had hoped, played a role similar to that of select members of the National Committee, as communicators between state and national reform actors and as interpreters of national reform regulations. Many, on the other hand, had made their last commission appearance at the November sessions.[2]

For the next twenty months, then, the commission would consist, as it had for all but three months in the fall of 1969, of its leadership and staff. But this time, even that skeleton crew was further reduced by aspects, formal and informal, of the shift from a politics of recommendation to a politics of implementation. Formally, the staff component continued to shrink as financing became more difficult and as the technical responsibilities of staff members changed. Informally, the leadership component began effectively to shrink as well, as both the chairman and vice chairman withdrew to pursue other political interests.

Part of this change traced to financial problems at the National Committee. Chairman O'Brien was not enthusiastic about maintaining a heavily staffed commission in a period of budgetary crisis. Yet his desire to cut staff support did not engender major resistance at the commission, because of a change in its role in reform politics and in the willingness of individual staff members to undertake its inevitably altered functions.

All the key participants at the commission understood that the next phase of reform activity required the writing of solicitous letters to distant party officials and the drafting of detailed interpretations to help bring these officials into conformity with commission guidelines. All admitted that this task was essential, that it could, in fact, contribute to the realization of party reform. Yet neither Ken Bode nor Eli Segal was attracted by this prospect, while Bob

Nelson was uniformly acknowledged as more adept at the intricate discussions with state party leaders which the task demanded. Bode recognized the obvious solution:

> In April of 1970, Eli and I left together. Neither of us had any vision of being *clerks* for the next three years. McGovern invited both of us to the Hill. I went on his staff; Eli went on the Nutrition Committee.

By the time *Mandate for Reform* was published, these personnel adjustments had been made. Bode and Segal were still available in late May, when O'Brien created his Ad Hoc committees and when McGovern reacted with quasi-public dismay. From their posts on Capitol Hill, both helped prepare the salvos which McGovern fired at O'Brien, and both advised him on the best way to accept reassurances from the national chairman.[3] This was, however, the last major contribution from either for some time.

Segal drifted away first, going from the commission, to a post as general counsel to the Senate Select Committee on Nutrition and Human Needs, to a short stint in private legal practice, to the Hughes for President campaign, with only one brief venture back into reform politics:

> From May of 1970 to February of 1971, the McGovern Commission was essentially Bob Nelson and Carol Casey. I got discouraged at the Nutrition Committee. I did take a trip to Wyoming, North Dakota, and Idaho, to encourage them to come into compliance. Otherwise, I was out of action. I was, after that, not directly involved with party reform until the Hughes-Harris fight of 1971. I went to work for Hughes in October of '70 through July of '71, until the campaign ended.

Bode foresook commission activities a trifle less quickly. Initially, he joined McGovern's senatorial staff, and the shift by McGovern to a serious quest for the presidency provided Bode with an automatic role in reform politics, as McGovern's monitor, liaison, and occasional surrogate. But as the senator shifted even further into his presidential campaign, his disengagement left little for the former research director to do, and no real base from which to do it. As a result, Bode, too, disappeared from reform politics until the early months of 1971, when he would return in a new, independent, organizational guise.

The Pattern of State Response

By the time these various national actors were free to devote themselves more intensively to the progress of party reform, their state counterparts had already received a series of communications about the need to implement reformed party rules. Most of these came, as they would continue to come, from the Party Structure Commission. More were also coming, with the ascension of Larry O'Brien, from the office of the national chairman as well.

In late November, the commission had adopted its final recommendations for party reform with as much public fanfare as it could muster, and it had mailed copies of the substance to state party leaders almost instantly. In late February, the commission had followed up with individualized compliance letters to every state chairman and National Committee member, applying its recommendations specifically to their state parties. In late April, the commission had published *Mandate for Reform*, reminding these state party figures of the existence of the guidelines while simultaneously informing all interested state residents about the content of these proposals.

When O'Brien ascended the national chairmanship, he began almost immediately to add to this flow. By early March, he had endorsed an investigation by each state party of the commission report, but his endorsement, while public, was vague and nondirective. By late May, however, he had authorized the Califano memo, advising all state party leaders that commission proposals should be treated as party law. Within days, he had set up his own compliance committees, to draw the National Committee into reform politics and to emphasize his commitment to the cause.

No major state official could have missed the injunction to begin work on party reform, repeated, as it was, in different forms, in different forums, by different individuals, but always with the same general thrust. The response to this series of exhortations, however—both the nature of the response and its timing—varied enormously from state to state. Some were quick to note that they had been moving faster than the national party. Others were prepared to note that they did not intend to move at all. Most were neither powerfully energized by the issue of party reform nor automatically opposed to a locally controlled investigation.

Four states—California, Minnesota, Pennsylvania, and Texas—illustrate the variety of these responses as well as any. Two, California and Pennsylvania, were presidential primary states; two, Minnesota and Texas, selected their delegates through party conventions. One pair, California and Minnesota, were widely considered to be crucibles for "the new politics"; the other pair, Pennsylvania and Texas, were symbolic bastions of old-line regularity.

All four of these states were major elements within the national party. All four had played major roles in the presidential politics of 1968. The four, together, were strung out along the continuum of responses to the call for state action on party reform. As a result, they provide a sense for the detailed fabric, first, of the response to the call for appointment of state reform commissions and, second, of the response of these commissions to national recommendations for party reform.

The Minnesota Democratic party had come the farthest on the route to concrete reform by the time implementation of the guidelines had become the priority for national reform actors. In fact, the Minnesota party had come so far that a few of its indigenous reforms would have to be *retrenched* in order to bring the state into compliance with the guidelines. Minnesota was one of the first to appoint a local reform commission. Its commission was one of the very first to produce comprehensive recommendations for state party reform.

The Minnesota Democratic-Farmer-Labor Party, known locally as the DFL, had been about as badly divided by the presidential politics of 1968 as any state party could be. Its long-time senior senator, Hubert Humphrey, was the national nominee; its current senior senator, Eugene McCarthy, was his principal opponent.[4] After the National Convention, in order to preserve some semblance of unity for state campaigns, Warren S. Spannaus, DFL chairman, had turned at once to the device of a reform commission, in the hope that newly alienated factions within the state party would work to extract the reform rules they preferred, rather than to defeat each other's candidates for elective office in November.

Spannaus's committee then pressed ahead and developed a comprehensive revision of the party charter. Indeed, its revised party code was *adopted* before the Party Structure Commission had issued so much as a single reform guideline.[5] DFL officials thus found themselves in a position to take a mildly patronizing attitude toward their national counterparts, an attitude which surfaced early, when Spannaus mailed McGovern the deliberations of the Minnesota party as potential precepts for the national commission:

> This letter and the enclosed materials are in response to your letter of March 6th requesting information on party rules and delegate selection revision. . . .
>
> In September 1968, I appointed a new Commission which is charged with a complete revision of our State Constitution, including delegate selection procedures. This Commission will develop recommendations which will be acted upon by a reconvened State Convention (about August 1969).
>
> Enclosed are minutes of the Commission meetings which have been held. These minutes are not for general publication, nor has any specific language been drafted yet. Rather, they represent the formative meetings of the Commission. They are therefore available for your personal use only.[6]

The Pennsylvania party had authorized an indigenous reform commission well before Minnesota, although the Pennsylvania leadership did not actually appoint its version until after the Minnesota commission had settled down to work. The quick action of the Pennsylvania hierarchy, however, was highly misleading. Where the Minnesota commission, once appointed, addressed its charge with dispatch, the Pennsylvania body, despite a similar mandate, served as an active obstacle to party reform. Indeed, motion toward the implementation of revised party rules could not begin in Pennsylvania until this commission had been discharged and replaced.

Pennsylvania was unlike Minnesota in that divisions between party regulars and self-conscious reformers were an established fact of political life. Existing divisions, however, had been exacerbated by presidential politics in 1968, and the blame for that could be placed squarely on state rules for delegate selection. Under those rules, Pennsylvania Democrats gave Eugene McCarthy an overwhelming majority of their preference votes; they gave Hubert Humphrey a solid majority of their national delegates. McCarthy activists threatened a credentials challenge; Thomas Z. Minehart, the state chairman, countered with the proposal of a state reform commission, to placate party dissidents and to defuse the situation.[7]

To that point, the Pennsylvania and Minnesota cases possessed a surface similarity. From the moment of the creation of their reform commissions, however, they diverged sharply. The Rules Revision Committee of the Pennsylvania Democratic party was unveiled in February of 1969. It met only twice; it held a lone public hearing; it never reported at all. Its appointment had satisfied the letter, though hardly the spirit, of a bargain struck the previous year, and the commission which resulted was sent off into the wilderness. Chairman Minehart, its creator, had no desire to hear from it again. Horace J. Culbertson, its chairman, shared Minehart's feelings:

> Most of us were old-liners. We did not represent that group—the dirty-mouthed, long-haired people—but we didn't care either. The Rules Revision Committee met maybe twice in 1969. Usually, State Committee meetings were at one in the afternoon. Our meeting would be at ten in the morning, so that we could make a report to them. . . . I'll tell you what I wanted. I wanted to kill off every god-damned move that was coming out of this turmoil.

The California Democratic party delayed far longer than the Pennsylvania party in creating a local reform commission. Yet its state body turned around and produced a far earlier report on local party reform. The party in California had long been self-consciously reformist, but it emerged from the 1968 campaign with no great internal demand for reform. As a result, a California commission was summoned into being principally through pressure from above. Once that commission was imminent, however, state leaders gave it a broader mandate than the one upon which the national commission had settled, and the California body went on to produce, quickly, its own independent—even conflicting—report on party reform.

Existing arrangements for delegate selection in California had produced little debate among the 1968 participants—the drama of the California primary had been located in other realms [8]—so that the various contending factions were content to let state procedures stand. Accordingly, Roger Boas, the state chairman, delayed in forming a state commission, through 1968, through 1969, and into 1970. At that point, the leadership and staff of the Party Structure Commission turned their attention to Boas in a concentrated fashion, in a series of communications emphasizing that a majority of states had already established state counterparts and that California would be outrun on the reform issue if it did not follow suit. With this stimulus, and with the opportunity to use a new commission to address numerous internal party needs and several personal goals, Boas created the California Commission on Democratic Party Reform.[9]

While California was comparatively late in having a reform body of its own, Chairman Boas sought to make up for any apparent tardiness with a more aggressive mandate. Unlike its national counterpart, which had made delegate selection its principal target, the California commission allocated only one of its five subcommittees to delegate selection and focused on four other aspects of party structure and public participation. Indeed, in the press release announcing formation of a California commission, Boas took pains to emphasize the comparative ambitions of his group and the national body:

> Boas said he had submitted a much broader mandate on party structure to the California commission than that asked by the National Democratic Party's McGovern Commission on Party Structure and Delegate Selection. The McGovern Commission's guidelines dealt with changes in delegate selection. "Also in need of reform are other areas such as internal state party structure and practices which will be studied by the California Commission," Boas said.[10]

The Texas Democratic party illustrated a further pattern of response—or really of nonresponse—to national importuning for state party reform. Like the California leadership, the Texas hierarchy felt no immediate need, coming off the presidential politics of 1968, to create a state reform commission. But unlike the California party, the Texas party was so strongly opposed to national party reform that it was unwilling even to have a local reform body on the loose. Moreover, the Texas party remained in this posture until a new national chairman with personal credits in Texas convinced it to take its first, hesitant steps toward party reform. Even then, the resulting commission was so carefully constructed—and so carefully restrained—that it never threatened any serious change and, indeed, simply faded away with the passage of time.

The Texas delegation had been made to serve as a national example of the evils of party regularity at the 1968 Convention, and party regulars returned to Texas with no inclination, or need, to apologize to their critics. Moreover, the Texas State Democratic Executive Committee (the SDEC) was advised on its response by Will Davis, SDEC member, Party Structure commissioner, and vocal critic of national reforms. Not surprisingly, the SDEC concluded that it was uninterested in reform in the national manner. After that, the party turned a deaf ear to the national commission.[11]

Throughout 1969 and into 1970, the Texas party managed to maintain this stance. In fact, its chairman, Elmer C. Baum, never really changed his mind. He did, however, relent long enough to appoint a state committee to investigate the guidelines, out of respect for a new national chairman. Larry O'Brien had a considerable personal following within the regular party around the country; that following was one of his major assets; Baum was in this legion:

> There was a tranquil period between 1968 and 1971. Reform of the party wasn't too much discussed. We heard about reform, of course. We got a lot of material. But the SDEC never did get too excited, because we had a unified party, and the SDEC was functioning well.
> The Committee to Study the Guidelines came about through Larry O'Brien. O'Brien is a fine man. I'm a great admirer of his. He asked me to form a study committee, and I did, although we already had an open party. Our party was ahead of the national people. We were doing our work, successfully.

These four states did not include any from the handful which would be certified in full compliance by the end of the summer of 1970. They did not include any from the contrary handful which would refuse even to appoint a state reform committee, through 1970 and into 1971. Otherwise, they encompassed the full range of initial responses to the national call for state party reform.

The details of commission appointment in these states, when coupled with the course their reform commissions would eventually adopt, contained an obvious lesson about the progress of party reform. For any given state, the time at which a particular step in the reform process was accomplished was not an invariable guide to the time at which the next logical step would be completed. For example, the Pennsylvania party was an early appointer of its state reform commission, while the California party was just as evidently late. Yet the Pennsylvania commission was ultimately discharged for nonfeasance, while the California commission, when finally appointed, moved to its task with dispatch. Individual state politics thus shaped state activity on party re-form in major ways, even when the Party Structure Commission and the na-tional chairman were both pushing all state parties in the same clear direction.

Nevertheless, neither the peculiarities of state party politics nor the disjunc-tions in state progress from one stage of reform to another can obscure the fact that these states still followed a quite reliable course through the total reform process when observed across the nation as a whole. That is, despite the variety of local factors which did condition the appointment and subse-quent energy of state reform commissions, they came into existence, and swung into action, in a very regular fashion for the country at large. Four state cases cannot, of course, demonstrate this regularity. But a more superficial ex-amination of the full range of state parties can easily do so. Indeed, one crucial distinction among these parties immediately reveals a precise patterning in their response to national reform directives, *and this patterning continued through every step of the reform process.*

This distinction is between volunteer and organized state political parties. *Volunteer parties,* those which rely on independent activists to mount election campaigns, were much more likely to move early. *Organized parties,* those which can turn to the incumbents of a hierarchy of party offices when election time approaches, were much more likely to shy away from the entire reform process. The two types of state party are most easily defined by the divergent character of their normal political actors. But they are also distinguished by the political incentives which call forth this normal pattern of participation, and they are most commonly recognized by differences in the resulting cam-paigns for elective public office.[12]

Volunteer parties are perhaps best classified through the activist character of their campaign workers. In general, those who do the work of the party are motivated by comparatively intangible, even transient considerations, like issues, personalities, or a sense of civic duty. As a result, individual candidates build their own campaign operations, out of personal supporters. Often, no two candidates have the same campaign coalition; often, any single campaign worker cannot be expected to be active in two successive elections. In 1970, within the national Democratic party, these volunteer state parties were con-centrated in upper New England, the Southeast, the upper Midwest, the Rocky Mountains, and the Far West. (See figure 10.1.)[13]

Organized parties, conversely, feature a continuing collection of party of-ficeholders, who are reliably present in several campaigns at the same time, and in successive campaigns over a period of years. Ordinarily, a significant number of tangible, divisible rewards are necessary to guarantee this large ag-gregate of reliable party workers, and to guarantee that they will subordinate

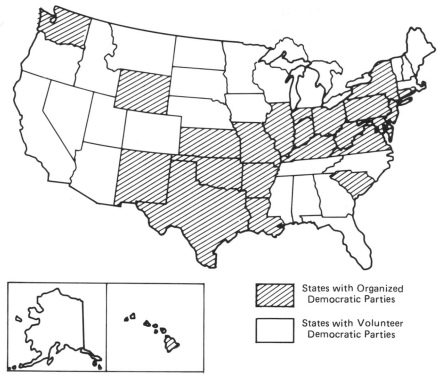

FIG. 10.1

The Distribution of Organized and Volunteer
Democratic State Parties in 1970

their personal preferences to a common, loosely connected ticket. In some places, however, ethnic, religious, or geographic ties, reified by the experience of working together, can substitute for jobs, contracts, and favors. In 1970, within the national Democratic party, these organized state parties were concentrated in the middle-Atlantic, near midwestern, border, and south-central states, although a few were scattered elsewhere. (See figure 10.1.)

These differences, in the nature of party actors, in the incentives for party activity, and in the pattern of party campaigns, produce different structural characteristics for the political party as a whole. In volunteer parties, partly as cause and partly as effect of the ease of intermittent participation, party offices are hard to fill and are not reliably valued for their own sake. At the extreme, "the party," as an institution, may be difficult to locate. In organized parties, on the other hand, the party is far more likely to possess a progression of occupied offices and a range of formal authority to go with them. At the extreme, a functioning statewide hierarchy may exist.

Despite a century-long decline in the number of fully articulated and disciplined organized parties, the differences in 1970, at the margins, could still be striking. Organized parties like those in Connecticut, Pennsylvania, Missouri, or Texas had all the classic characteristics: tangible rewards which could be used in a discretionary fashion, a substantial corps of party officeholders (and their dependents) who were reliably at the service of the party, and the consequent ability to intervene in nomination politics and to mount coordinated election campaigns. At the other end, volunteer parties like those in California, Minnesota, Vermont, or North Carolina presented all the standard opposites: Personalities as the sole means of mobilizing campaigns, independent activists as the major source of political manpower, and a skeletal hierarchy of party offices which could not begin to intervene in nomination contests or coordinate a slate of election campaigns.[14]

In between, these differences were more blurred, and many state parties did share some characteristics of both types. Thus, an organized party like that in New York could include a very substantial number of independent activists, while an organized party like that in New Mexico could be relatively poor in concrete, distributable rewards and could be forced to rely more heavily on social ties and regional alliances. Conversely, a volunteer party like that in Massachusetts could show sizable pockets of regular organization, while a volunteer party like that in Iowa could feature an impressive continuity in participation by its large cadre of formally independent actors.

What separated such parties, when they were not in the clear-cut mold of a Pennsylvania or a California, a Minnesota or a Texas, was the way state-wide electoral coalitions were constructed. In organized parties, such coalitions were still assembled from smaller chunks of preexisting *organization,* that is, from clusters of incumbent party officials and their political associates. In volunteer parties, on the other hand, electoral coalitions were necessarily created from formally independent *volunteers,* that is, from intermittently active individuals who would affiliate on the basis of personal preferences.[15]

These distinctions were important—even critical—to the politics of implementation because they created an institutionalized predisposition for a particular response to national calls for state reform. The resulting difference in state party response was so pronounced and so persistent—rooted, as it was, in a basic structural characteristic of these parties—that it surfaced at every step of the compliance process. It was present in the very first, involving appointment of a state reform commission; it was present in the very last, involving final approval of a certified reform package.

Volunteer parties were institutionally sympathetic to the reform of state party rules. Such parties possessed few potentially active participants whose abstract concerns—or personal fortunes—would be automatically disturbed by shifts toward participatory rules. Moreover, volunteer parties usually needed the (voluntary) support of precisely those individuals who were most attracted by the reform issue. Indeed, these parties were frequently *led* by individuals who had been drawn into politics by considerations of citizen duty or by an explicit interest in reform. These individuals were thus predisposed toward institutional tinkering in the name of party democracy.

Organized parties were a different story. By definition, they had more at stake in any alterations affecting the powers of party office. Moreover, they had more *people* in those offices to try to prevent any losses of this sort. The party, as a whole, had organizational resources associated with its existing procedures; party leaders could be expected to oppose some reforms on these grounds alone. Beyond that, reliable participants often had pecuniary interests in party arrangements, so that their real well-being might be affected by a misjudged party reform. As a result, the members of organized parties had both institutional and personal reasons for looking askance at externally ordered change, regardless of its particular substance.

In practice, the purity of this organizational logic was muddied by the peculiarities of individual state politics, by the fact that most state parties themselves were not pure types, and, especially, by the practical demands of compliance politics. Even the purest of volunteer parties did not necessarily welcome nationally imposed directives, since those directives often appeared to ignore crucial facts of local political life and since their implementation always demanded the investment of time and the expenditure of political credit. Even the purest of organized parties could see no harm in *some* commission guidelines and could often see practical advantage in local reform initiatives.

Nevertheless, these muddying factors were not enough to cancel the underlying logic of party structure and organization. Volunteer parties remained much more likely to get going early, to establish state-level reform commissions, and to move from there to actual reform. Organized parties remained much more likely to resist such commissions for as long as they could, to encourage inaction once these commissions had been created, and to isolate them from party decision-making if they began to function actively. (See figure 10.2.a.)[16]

By May of 1970, when national reform actors turned serious attention to state party reform, they discovered that those state parties which had actually begun to *change* their local rules were overwhelmingly in the volunteer-party category. They discovered that those with active reform commissions were primarily volunteer. They discovered that those with state reform commissions

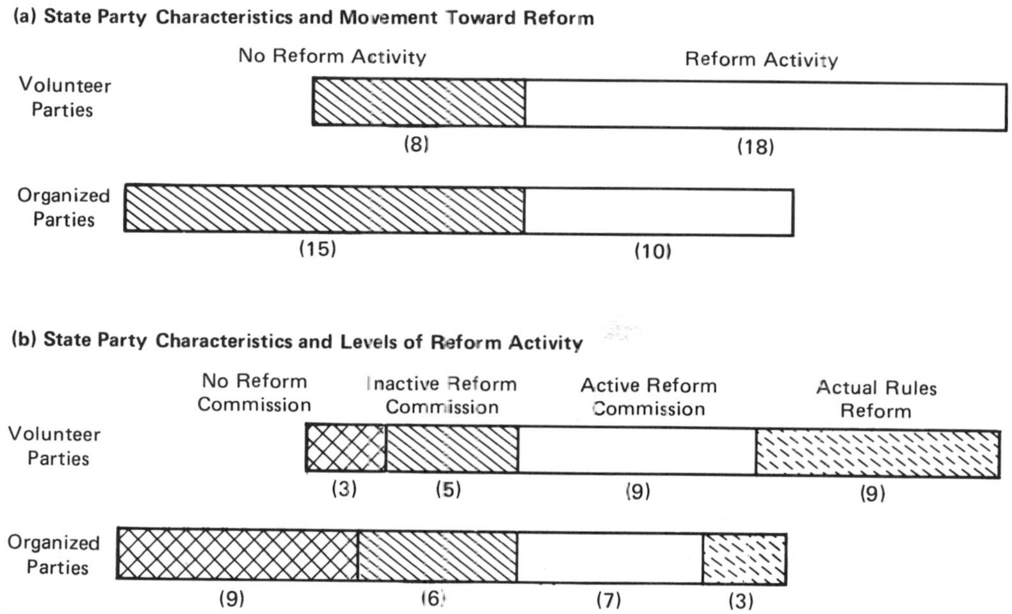

(a) State Party Characteristics and Movement Toward Reform

No Reform Activity   Reform Activity

Volunteer
Parties
(8)   (18)

Organized
Parties
(15)   (10)

(b) State Party Characteristics and Levels of Reform Activity

No Reform   Inactive Reform   Active Reform   Actual Rules
Commission   Commission   Commission   Reform

Volunteer
Parties
(3)   (5)   (9)   (9)

Organized
Parties
(9)   (6)   (7)   (3)

FIG. 10.2

The State Parties and Compliance: March–April 1970

which had been allowed to languish were primarily in the organized-party category. And they discovered, of course, that those state parties which had refused even to appoint a local reform commission, despite letters from the national commission and calls from the national chairman, were overwhelmingly organized. (See figure 10.2.b.)

This underlying distinction between the two types of state political parties, and its impact on their reaction to rational calls for state party reform, were not lost on those who had some reason to observe the wider scope of state responses. These observers may have grasped this distinction much more impressionistically; they still saw it as central to events around them. Bob Nelson, who was in communication with nearly every state party, who had occasion to visit a substantial number, and who would be the moving force within the commission during all of 1970, had his version of the difference, and of what it meant for the success or failure of reform politics:

> Kansas and Missouri were very tough states; Hearnes was not very reform-minded, and he had the regular organization behind him. West Virginia. Jay Rockefeller could help in West Virginia; otherwise, it was tough. We were in the hands of regular party people. Texas, Louisiana, Rhode Island, New York. The older the state, the more difficult it was. The system had been entrenched for so long, and a network of people had grown up around it who believed in it, or who benefitted from it. Pennsylvania. Maine would have been tough except for Mitchell and Muskie. Certainly New Jersey.
>
> Most of the western states were quick and easy. Either their leadership was very progressive, or else they didn't have much of a party to get in the way. . . . The easy states, Alabama, North Carolina, Minnesota, South Dakota because of McGovern, Nebraska, Tennessee, which adopted very wide-open rules, but they went through easy and early. Virginia, because the regular party guys, the Byrd people, didn't seem to care. Virginia could have been trouble, but for some reason it wasn't. Wisconsin, Colorado, Oregon. But Washington was tough; they have machinery there.

From the other side, Joseph M. Barr, national committeeman from Pennsylvania, product of a strong organized party, and confirmed critic of commission guidelines, used a different vocabulary to make the same point:

> The small states weren't paying attention to the needs and problems of the big states. The big states, especially here in the northeast, have the kind of parties that mean something, that can get out the vote, win elections. The only one that isn't like that is Michigan, where the party doesn't seem to mean much, and where they always send crazy people to the National Committee. But all those other states, they couldn't see what this would mean to us. They can't do anything on their own, they don't deliver, but they were going to tell us how to do business. It was the tail wagging the dog.

The Nature of Opening Negotiations

The central role in negotiations with these individual state parties over the implementation of national party reform fell, largely by default, to the major actors at the Party Structure Commission. Chairman O'Brien did put continued general pressure on the states, but he entered specific negotiations only when explicitly solicited by the state party leadership or the commission staff. In fact, the central role in these negotiations really fell to Bob Nelson, the staff director, and to Carol Casey, the staff assistant, since the commission leaders, Chairman McGovern and Vice Chairman Hughes, were busy inaugurating their respective campaigns for a presidential nomination.

For a time, from February through May of 1970, the job of communicating with the state parties, volunteer and organized alike, was entirely the province of Nelson and Casey. After May, the national chairman was more active. After December, the commission would have a new chairman, Don Fraser, and he would be more active, too. Yet even then—and indeed, for the rest of the politics of implementation—the *bulk* of the communications from the national to the state level was still from the staff director and staff assistant and not from the commission chairman or even the national chairman.

For this entire period, Nelson and Casey would necessarily undertake one or more of four general tasks. First, they had to coax the laggard state parties into creating a local reform body. Second, they had to energize those state reform commissions which existed only on paper. Third, they had to channel those state commissions which were actually in session toward the proper conclusions. Fourth, they had to convince those state parties which faced acceptable recommendations to move ahead and adopt them.

The initial step in the Nelson-Casey approach to these tasks was simplicity itself: Find a person in each state, a contact, who had some obvious relevance to party rules and then maintain direct communication. Even at this trivial level, however, the tactic was more easily described than accomplished. In some states, party officials themselves seemed almost eager to receive the latest suggestions from commission headquarters. In others, Nelson had to search methodically to find someone, anyone, who would take delivery of his memos. For every Minnesota, which was trying to eclipse the national operation, there was a Pennsylvania, which was obviously inclined to forget the whole thing—and which provided only a lone student intern as a correspondent for commission staffers.

Once a reliable contact had been located, Nelson concentrated on funneling detailed information and suggestions to that person and on checking with him often enough to create the impression that someone from the national operation was watching. At the same time, Nelson sought every opportunity to strengthen those within the state who were cooperating with his efforts, by introducing them to each other, by boosting them for relevant party positions, and by securing press coverage for anything they might undertake. Both activities required a sizable flow of personal exchanges with Washington.

The sum of this communication, when pursued over fifty-five subnational units, was more than enough to absorb the staff director and staff assistant. The volume of the correspondence they generated was noteworthy even from the perspective of a single state, as Carmen Warschaw, national committeewoman from California and Party Structure commissioner, attested:

> Early on, there was no other persuasion except those letters. Occasionally, Larry O'Brien himself would send something, but mostly it came from Nelson. Nelson writing on this, Nelson writing on that. I mean, he buried them under the biggest pile of paper you ever saw.

This specific method of operating was fitted into a more general strategy, too. From the beginning, the staff had planned to concentrate on those state parties which were expected to be most receptive, to use successes there to press the issue with those which appeared to be next in susceptibility, and so on. In this way, those states which had some inherent sympathy for reform could be harvested early. Those states which were neither enthusiastic nor actively hostile might be convinced that reform could be accomplished without undue strain, and even with some side benefits. And the more recalcitrant state parties might then find themselves in a deteriorating position, with a growing number of states in compliance and with a growing prospect of a—successful—credentials challenge. Ken Bode, who would later specialize in these recalcitrants, supported the general strategy: "We did want to find states, like Iowa, where we knew there would be a response. Get them into compliance, and use them as a wedge."

This approach was made even more attractive by the way in which a number of state parties geared up quickly and showed an evident interest in being first. Alabama, Iowa, Maine, Minnesota, and North Carolina all had Democratic parties which evinced immediate enthusiasm for reform, but the real duel came down to Maine versus Alabama. Nelson, of course, was delighted with the contest:

> Bob Vance, Chairman of the Alabama party, said he wanted to be the first one to comply with these guidelines. The first two or three states were Alabama, Maine, North Carolina, etc. Vance had been an enemy of Wallace. Maine had George Mitchell as Chairman. They were both proving a point, we thought.

It was Alabama, home base for the major splinter candidate in 1968 and target of a major credentials challenge at the 1968 Convention, which ultimately won the duel. Robert S. Vance, Alabama state chairman, had decided immediately after the convention that he would try to bring his state party into compliance with whatever the Party Structure Commission recommended and, moreover, that he would try to be among the leaders in doing so:

> My own reaction was that this was a crock of shit, but it was something I could live with. The problem that arose out of the McGovern Guidelines was that footnote, and it wasn't apparent what that meant at the time. I was elected as an anti-Wallace Democratic leader, and I was offended when I got to the '68 Convention and was challenged. It didn't seem right that I would get into a knock-down, drag-out fight with George Wallace down here, and then get to the National Convention and get attacked in Credentials, so then I decided that I would never get out-lefted again in Credentials. Since then, I've always swung from the left on this. I never wanted to get challenged again.
>
> Steve Mitchell and a former South Carolina congressman, in 1968, said, "How many votes can we get from Alabama?" I said, "One-half of a vote." And they said, "That's not enough." Well there wasn't even a primary yet, and they hadn't filed *any* delegates, but they said they'd challenge me anyway, unless I found them some votes. I won that challenge, but I had to go through a lot of pain, and it made me very cynical.
>
> So I was a little disillusioned after my first "reform" experience. I decided that the thing to do after this was to play to win. These idealists are total phonies, so we'd just acclimate to the situation. I told them in the rule-making process, "You adopt any set of rules, and we'll be in total compliance." We made a conscious effort to be first in 1972. We knew we were going to be under the gun, and we tried to be spectacularly first.

Vance had, in fact, moved very early to put himself in a position to comply with new regulations from the national party, if they did not seem too internally painful. In gradual stages, he first waged a campaign for control of the Alabama State Committee, then for re-election as state chairman, then for reform of state committee rules. In the process, he strengthened his own faction and weakened the others:

> Wallace does care about the party, but I keep winning. In '66, I won 44–29; in '70, Wallace didn't make much effort, and I won two-and-a-half to one. Because I got overwhelming control of the State Central Committee, we undertook to adopt a model set of party rules. July of 1970 is when we made those reforms.
>
> We started in January of 1970 with just enough reforms to control the election of the State Committee. It was a comprehensive package, but there was little debate. We took the selection of the National Committee people off the ballot,

because they kept electing people like "Bull" Connor. So then in adopting the party reforms, we didn't have to pay much attention to them.

In the perspective of history, Vance was extremely acquiescent—and extremely prompt. *Mandate for Reform* had not been officially published until late April; Alabama had fully embraced it by late July. Viewed from commission headquarters, however, the entire process was excruciatingly slow. The commission had announced its recommendations in November of 1969; it had sent out compliance letters in February of 1970; there was not one state in full compliance by early July. Vance's efforts were thus an early ray of sunshine.

The combination of these factors, a willingness to act on the part of Vance and a perception by the national staff that a success was desperately needed, produced the certification of Alabama. While the Alabama party met nearly all of the new reform standards, its proposed rules were still out of conformity with Guideline C–1 (Adequate Public Notice), and C–1 was a guideline with major institutional impact. Alabama proposed to elect its delegates to the national convention by placing delegate contenders on the ballot, by district, under their own names only. This formal plan violated the requirement in C–1 of an indication of presidential preference; the resulting institution for delegate selection was little more than a sanitized version of the old delegate primary, which C–1 ostensibly proscribed.

Despite that, the staff was eager to have *someone* in compliance, the Alabama rules did meet seventeen of the eighteen guidelines, and Nelson certified them officially on those grounds. Casey saw the larger strategy behind this evident concession—and this initial "victory":

> There was only one instance in which we flip-flopped, on Alabama. They didn't have presidential preference on the ballot, but they were certified anyhow early. We did this to get someone in compliance, and to help Vance with his political problems there. Plus, Alabama would be such a marvelous example: If *they* can do it, *you* can do it.

The Alabama party, in altering its rules for delegate selection, kicked off a small flurry of other successes. Maine and North Carolina followed almost immediately, without the need for special dispensations. Minnesota and Iowa appeared headed for the same result, even if their proposed reforms required greater adjustment. By the end of the summer, then, the commission staff could point to one bloc of states which were in conformity for all practical purposes and to another bloc—Colorado, Maryland, Michigan, Mississippi, New Mexico, Oregon, and South Dakota—which showed real promise.

Again, those states which had already initiated some concrete reform were characterized, on about a two-to-one basis, by volunteer rather than organized state parties. Conversely, those in which reform was obviously, publicly dormant were characterized by organized rather than volunteer parties, by the same two-to-one margin. Those which fell in the middle, finally, with evidence of reform activity but without enough practical success to guarantee momentum, were split about evenly between the two party types. (See Figure 10.3.)[17]

Implications

By the fall of 1970, the character of reform politics had evidently changed. Until November of 1969, and really through May of 1970, the politics of party reform had possessed a pointed, national focus. After May of 1970, it came to consist instead of a diffuse web of decentralized negotiations—among relevant national figures, among relevant state and local figures, and between relevant actors at the state and national levels. These negotiations still involved a continual jockeying among national reform actors, in an attempt to speak—authoritatively—for the national party. Intermittently, they also involved specifically national decisions reached in obviously national arenas, and these always had a greater impact on the resulting institutions for delegate selection than did the decisions reached in any given state.

Yet the far greater share of total reform conflict had already begun to occur inside the fifty-five state, district, and territorial parties, a situation which would not change until the individual states had selected their delegates to the 1972 Convention and, indeed, until those delegates had assembled in one central site. Until then, the status of party reform would be measured by the number of subnational units at each stage of the compliance process. Until then, the impact of party reform would be judged by the sum of institutional changes occurring in the individual states.

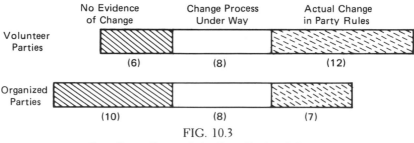

FIG. 10.3

Compliance Status of the State Parties: July 1970

These two realms of reform activity, the national and the local, were of course connected by an ongoing set of negotiations *between* their principals. In fact, the negotiations between this range of national actors and this counterpart—and vastly expanded—set of relevant individuals at the state and local level became the practical heart of reform politics after May of 1970.

Surprisingly, the state response to national pressure had already begun to assume a clear and distinctive pattern by the fall of 1970. More surprisingly, this pattern was to continue throughout the remainder of the reform process. Volunteer state parties, those with intangible incentives for participation, independent activists as major participants, temporary and discontinuous electoral coalitions, and a fluid and volunteer-based party structure, were more likely to move early on the issue of party reform. Organized state parties, those with tangible incentives for participation, party officeholders and their associates as major participants, coordinated and continuing electoral coalitions, and an organized and even hierarchical party structure, were more likely to resist national urging toward state party reform at every stage of the compliance process.

The initial appearance of this pattern was surprising because it emerged from tremendously varied political histories and indigenous pressures. Its persistence was even more impressive because it followed neither from the distribution of national efforts at securing state compliance—except tautologically—nor from the peculiar details of compliance politics within the individual states. Nelson and Casey, the leading national protagonists for reform during this period, did weight their efforts toward those states which they hoped would be most responsive. Yet their selection criterion, the location of those political parties with the most reform-oriented leadership, reflected, at bottom, primarily the difference between volunteer versus organized state parties.

The appearance of this consistent patterning had a major, summary implication for institutional change: The tendency of state party structure to determine state response meant that there would be some immediate, *positive* reactions to national reform initiatives. By the same token, it meant that the hypothesized—and widely feared—inclination of sitting party officials to resist reform had been evidently exaggerated. Later, the tendency of organized parties to oppose reforms might slow, or even stop, the resulting momentum. Now, the tendency of volunteer parties to comply was the more important event, for it suggested that there would indeed be a proreform momentum, which would eventually have to be addressed.

This initial patterning, then, was a contribution to widespread institutional change. The tendency of organized parties to *resist* reform could still eventually serve as a brake on the reform process. But when that process began with such extensive demands for institutional change—when it featured *no* states in full compliance and few with the prospect of quick and painless conformity—this "institutional sympathy" by the volunteer-party states was surely the matter of consequence.

Because this was so, the arrival and persistence of a patterning in state party responses to national reform demands contained two larger implications. These involved the probable character of the national party under reformed party rules and, especially, the character of national elites within a newly reformed political party.

The character of a reformed—and unreformed—national party had always been central to the concerns of reform drafters. They had believed that existing procedures for selecting delegates and nominating presidents were powerfully beneficial to the orthodox Democratic coalition, to the regular party and its associated interests. Institutional analysis suggested that this view was essentially accurate; the fact that these rules had evolved incrementally *within* the regular party supported that institutional analysis.

The newly developed reform rules, on the other hand, had been drawn up to be just as powerfully beneficial to an alternative Democratic coalition, to party reformers and *their* associated interests. Those most responsible for the reform draft had often acted in a conspiratorial manner, but this aspect of their proposed reforms, including even the nature of their intended beneficiaries, was never really hidden from view. Moreover, the institutional analysis behind their estimate of the practical impact of party reform was supported by the fact that the political experiences of those in the alternative coalition were so precisely similar, were based on such similar social backgrounds and organizational assets, and led to such clearly similar institutional preferences.

As a result, when volunteer parties across the country proved more responsive, right from the start, to national demands for state reform, more was at issue than improved prospects for widespread implementation of sweeping institutional change—critical as those improved prospects might be. For the type of internal party politics already occurring within volunteer-party states was much more evidently consistent with the institutions, rules, and procedures required by commission guidelines than was the internal party politics of organized-party states—and party leaders in both groups were well aware of that fact.

In essence, then, *the differential attraction of this reform package for the two types of state political party*—its active attraction for volunteer state parties and their consequent contribution to widespread adoption—*implied a move by the national party toward the volunteer, rather than the organized, mode of party politics.* That, in turn, seemed likely to influence not just the fate of contending party elites, but the utility of various political resources, the relevance of available public issues, and the nature of aspiring presidential candidates.

Again, the impact of these reforms on contending coalitions of party elites was the best clue to this potential effect. For the differing types of state party structure already coincided with differing social mixes among the active participants in state party politics. This difference was still only a tendency; there were still many evident sympathizers to the organized-party model even among officials in volunteer-party states. Yet the difference was already perceptible not just to the analyst, but to active participants as well.

Those in party office in volunteer-party states were clearly closer, in their personal background, in their political history, and in their philosophical approach to politics, to those who were pushing reform at the national level. Those in party office in organized-party states were more likely to face as *enemies* in internal party politics precisely those sorts of persons who were supporting reform at the national level. Moreover, the fact that these social differences among elite actors were already associated with the distinction between volunteer and organized state parties was not lost on the actual participants in reform politics. In fact, a general perception of these social differences exaggerated the difference in response by the two party types.

When these reforms proved, in practice, to be much more acceptable to one type of state political party than to the other, and when these parties offered a rough congruence, in their actual composition, to the split between supporters and opponents of participatory reforms, the stage was set for a major elite replacement. As that became a possibility, as it became possible that the initial circulation of elites under reformed party rules would substitute an aspiring, alternative coalition of Democratic elites for an entrenched, orthodox coalition, the stage was set as well for a larger and continuing replacement of elites in American national politics more generally.

CHAPTER

1 1

Reform as an Ideology:

The Elections of 1970 and the

Functions of the Mandate

IN WHICH, the elections of 1970 serve to reorganize the array of institutional actors with an interest in party reform; the roster of key reform actors undergoes an especially consequential shift in the states; and the practical requirements of abstract reform guidelines are elaborated and focused. AND IN WHICH, reform politics is increasingly shaped by certain symbolic attributes of reform; the prospects for institutional change are enhanced by the arrival of a new group of Democratic governors, with reform as at least their implicit ideology; and these new reformers are melded with the old to begin an explicit alliance of alternative Democratic elites.

THROUGHOUT the summer and into the fall of 1970, there was visible motion on national calls for state party reform. Volunteer parties, in particular, showed a general acceptance of the argument that some deliberate change was inescapable. By the same token, there were few unambiguous portents of the fate of these developments, when summed for the national party as a whole. Organized parties, in particular, rather clearly did *not* accept the notion that sweeping party reform was either logical or desirable. By fall, there had been several obvious breakthroughs, with a handful of states officially certified as being in full compliance. By fall, these were still offset by an equal number which were ostentatiously resisting so much as the *appointment* of an indigenous reform commission.

This ambiguity in the progress of party reform, when coupled with the impact of the normal calendar of electoral politics, reshaped the roster of key reform actors at both the state and national levels as 1970 drew to a close. The heart of the politics of implementation remained the negotiations among reform figures at each level, and between these state and national figures as well. Yet the identity of key actors at both levels changed in crucial respects, and this shift had powerful, long-run implications for the fate of party reform.

At the national level, change resulted from the varying interpretations which major national figures placed on the progress of party reform and from the way in which the arrival of the November elections affected the activity of some national actors and the analyses of others. Some of this change consisted of little more than a temporary shift in focus by continuing national participants. Part of it was more substantial, consisting of an actual change in the incumbents of national institutions. Some, finally, contributed an expansion in the circle of relevant institutions itself.

At the state level, the most important change in the identity and character of key reform actors resulted directly from the 1970 elections and far overshadowed the counterpart shifts at the national level. A remarkable number of state electorates replaced one gubernatorial incumbent with another, thereby altering—always perceptibly, often sharply—the indigenous influences on party reform. An unusually large share of these changes involved the replacement of a Republican governor with the Democratic alternative. By itself, this altered the environment for state reform politics in important ways. Beyond that, a number of these incoming governors—concentrated in states which had been anchoring the opposition to reform—were self-conscious "reform Democrats." Needless to say, this was an even greater shift in the state reform environment.

The presence of this large, new group of major state actors, with their inherently greater sympathy for reform as an issue, emphasized the centrality of the process by which that abstract concept was converted into specific institutional requirements. At the heart of this conversion process, in turn—partly by intention, largely by accident—was the Party Structure Commission. While the remaining commission staffers waited for the products of the 1970 election to arrive in statehouses across the country, they moved to capitalize on their own organizational position, by drafting a highly detailed set of institutional deductions from established commission guidelines. In doing so, they further constrained the continuing negotiations between national reform actors and indigenous counterparts in the states and localities.

The immediate result was a new chapter in reform politics. But the practical outcome was another boost for the prospects of widespread implementation and compliance, and hence of widespread institutional change. This outcome was associated with a crucial addition to the alternative coalition of Democratic elites, an addition which began the broadening of that coalition as an explicit political entity. The upshot, finally, of the improved prospects for institutional change and of the increasing concreteness of the alternative coalition, was an increased likelihood of a major elite replacement, of a major circulation of elites, within the national Democratic party.

The Midterm Elections and National Pressure

By early fall, most party officials and many independent activists, whether they were concerned with the progress of party reform or not, had begun to turn their attention to the general election of 1970, to concrete electoral politics. The common argument, among Democrats and Republicans alike, was that this election would provide a referendum on the new Nixon administration.[1] A reasonable showing by Republican candidates would be an affirmation of the president's policies; clear gains for their Democratic opponents would suggest that the outcome of the election of 1968 had been an accident, an artifact of Democratic misadventures.

In such an environment, the Democratic national chairman was naturally eager to throw all his resources into the fray. For Larry O'Brien, this could not include major financial resources, but it could at least include the efforts of everyone at the National Committee. In O'Brien's view, this did not exclude the staff of the Party Structure Commission, Bob Nelson and Carol Casey. Nelson, in particular, with his history at the interior department, possessed an expertise which might be useful in areas where the Democratic party was traditionally weakest, in the midwestern farm states, the Rocky Mountains, and the Far West.

This desire to apply both Nelson and Casey to electoral politics might have produced another clash between the national chairman and "his" commission. Instead, it produced an understanding. These commission staffers would devote nearly full time to campaign affairs until after the November election. At that point, the national chairman would make party reform his number one priority. Casey saw a cost to this arrangement but believed that it was far outweighed by potential benefits:

> Minnesota, Iowa, Alabama, Maine, and North Carolina were easy and early. In the other states, they were trying to get definite timetables. The 1970 elections were taking most people's attention at this point. Even Bob himself was writing position-papers for the state elections, with his Interior Department background, at that point.

This agreement at national party headquarters was hardly the cause of a concurrent slowdown in state reform activity. That had arrived along with the fall campaign. Most state party officials were directly concerned with the November elections. Many had the central office in state party politics, the governorship, at stake. Party reform, by comparison, had no immediate pay-off—and could always be pursued later.

The general perception of those few observers who were following the politics of implementation—that reform activity had risen slowly during the summer and then declined again—was thus clearly accurate. In principle, there was nothing alarming about this, given its connection with the normal cycle of electoral politics. In practice, however, the pattern, as acknowledged by the understanding between the commission staff and the national chairman, proved to be the last straw for Ken Bode, former director of research for the Party Structure Commission. As such, it led directly to an expansion in the circle of institutional actors for national party reform.

Since May of 1970, Bode had been drifting away from active participation in state reform negotiations, worrying all the while about the progress of reform nationwide and languishing unhappily in his enforced isolation. By the end of the summer, he was considering an attempt to get back into the action, despite the lack of an official position. He had begun to look for financial support for his new vehicle, an independent, proreform pressure group, which he himself would direct and then target at the hard cases in party reform.

While the mix of reform activities in the states during the summer of 1970 had been grist for varying interpretations of the status of party reform, Bode had been inclined, all along, to believe that this mix was primarily evidence of troubled prospects. Three fully certified state parties in the year since the commission had reported were, in his view, all that could be logged on the positive side of the ledger. On the negative side, there were clear and evident reasons why any number of other state parties, including most of the truly significant ones, should resist implementation. When the coming of the 1970 elections led to a general, recognizable, and admitted slowdown in state reform activity, Bode felt that there was no longer any reason to hesitate in establishing his own reform operation:

> They always ran a dog-and-pony show: Food's good, everything's happy here, and all's well with party reform. I said this wouldn't happen unless there were another side. Even though each state was urged to have a reform commission, it often didn't amount to much. Let's have an independent organization, pull together some expertise, and find somebody to help if there wasn't anybody doing anything.

Bode's notion for addressing this collective "dog-and-pony show" was an independent pressure group, the Center for Political Reform, which would operate in a distinctly adversary fashion—toward the state parties, toward the National Committee, and, on occasion, toward the Party Structure Commission itself. Such an organization would search out and identify reform factions and independent reformers in the various states. It would then serve as a source both of expertise and of strategic coordination among them:

> I first had the idea for an independent force who would mobilize things for party reform in the states with Phil Stern. I raised $50,000 in autumn of "up-front money." Financers were Bronfman, Stern, Peretz, Sheinbaum; Steward Mott was at first not interested at all. We held a meeting at Bronfman's, where Howard Samuels made the pitch.
>
> Well before January 1, I had the money. Then I set up the Center. Technically, it was set up January 1, but from September on, I was beginning to get things under way. A woman named Carol Randles was my Administrative Assistant. She drafted and typed the first Pennsylvania primary proposal, for example. I took a task force of law students from Harvard; Joe Gebhardt headed that up, from Commission days.

His intimate knowledge of the McGovern Commission and his acquaintance with key figures from its predecessor, the Hughes Commission, provided Bode with access to most of the resources needed to launch his center. The idea was indeed hatched in conversation with Philip M. Stern, who had been active in bringing the Hughes Commission to birth and then in shepherding its product through the 1968 Convention. The staff was drawn primarily from those legal interns and their friends who had worked for the McGovern Commission during the summer of 1969. The money came mostly from those who had been solicited in the external fundraising efforts of the McGovern Commission or from those who had underwritten the Hughes Commission.

The November elections marked one other change in the political calendar of the national party. For the coming of the November elections meant the passing of the midterm period—and the arrival of presidential politics as the obvious focus for all those with a concern for national political affairs. The coming of presidential politics, in turn, affected the immediate leadership and subsequent activity of one of the major, continuing, institutional actors in national reform politics, the Party Structure Commission.

The transition to this next phase of electoral politics was of immediate consequence to the commission because its chairman, George McGovern, was an active candidate for the Democratic nomination and henceforth needed to be free to pursue it. A change in the formal leadership of the commission was thus inevitable. Yet the arrival of a more intensive presidential politics not only removed the incumbent chairman; it colored the selection of a successor as well—the man who would see the commission through to whatever its ultimate impact might be. Indeed, the external course of presidential politics, after this, was never entirely separate from the politics of party reform, and it would impinge quite directly on reform politics at occasional, crucial intervals.

Implicit presidential politicking had never really been absent from reform politics. The presidential ambitions of McGovern, for example, had been an open secret since his eleventh-hour candidacy for the nomination in 1968. Yet the pace of presidential politicking and the explicitness with which it was conducted had increased gradually from early 1969 through mid-1970, and then sharply from the fall of 1970 onward. In fact, the pace of this new presidential politics affected everyone who had reason to consider the connection between commission activities and a possible presidential run, including Harold Hughes, the vice chairman, and Birch Bayh, the other potential nominee among the commissioners.

The short-lived Subcommittee on Youth Participation, a one-shot venture in the summer of 1970, was a good example. All of the potential presidents on the commission—Hughes and Bayh as well as McGovern—had found the time to sit on the subcommittee. But it was McGovern, as chairman, who got to put a personal stamp on the subcommittee report. His preface was ready well in advance of the report itself; it came down heavily on the alleged link between disillusion with party processes and disillusion with the war in Vietnam—the twin themes of the nascent McGovern campaign:

> America's young people are terribly frustrated, and in many instances their frustrations are manifested in unfortunate ways. Our party must seek to understand these frustrations, not exploit them. The War in Indochina is a major cause of the growing discontent among American young people from all walks of life. . . . They have had no voice whatever in the process by which that war is prolonged, yet they are impelled daily to "work within the system," and seek change through established channels. We cannot keep urging them to stay within the system when they are excluded from the system. If taxation without representation was tyranny, then conscription without representation is slavery. . . .[2]

By fall of 1970, McGovern was criss-crossing the country on behalf of Democratic candidates for state office, and this activity was absorbing all the time he could spare from his senatorial responsibilities. In truth, however, this tendency for the chairman to withdraw from commission affairs had been evident since the spring. McGovern had remained available for spot duty on national issues. He had otherwise been so preoccupied with the groundwork for a presidential nomination that he had found little time for negotiations with state party chairmen over particular changes in individual state rules.

By late November, in any event, McGovern knew approximately when his formal announcement of a presidential candidacy would come. He began to plan his official departure from the Party Structure Commission:

> I tried to make sure that nothing in the presidential effort would interfere with the reform effort. Up until April, there was no presidential consideration that in any way hampered the reform commission. After that, I felt that the reform commission could then go it alone. I had given some private notice to a few key people that I would not let the presidential effort conflict with the reform effort. I wanted to make sure it wasn't jeopardized in any way by my own candidacy.
>
> I recommended Fraser as the guy to take over for me. I felt that he was knowledgeable, felt that he had a real commitment, which was deeper than mine. That was my only recommendation, I think; my best recollection is that I told O'Brien that Don Fraser knew more about reform and how to carry it out than anyone else. I may have mentioned a few others, but the implication was that he was my first choice. Again, he was not a McGovern supporter. I knew by then that he would be a better Chairman than Hughes, although I had not thought that in 1969 when he was first appointed.

The need to replace McGovern generated two political questions. First and most obvious was the issue of who the new chairman should be. Second was the issue of who should select him. The effective answers to these two questions were in turn constrained by the general context of reform politics. The progress of reform to date appeared to dictate that any new chairman be committed to reform, lest the whole operation explode under him; that he be based in Washington, so that he could be available for ongoing negotiations with the states; that he be thoroughly familiar with commission history, so that he would maintain the web of understandings which surrounded commission politics.

If Harold Hughes, the vice chairman, had not been headed toward a presidential bid of his own, he might well have replaced McGovern in a manner which would have prevented either of these questions—the identity of a new chairman or the identity of his selector—from surfacing. Indeed, if Hughes had not acquired a presidential appetite at about the same time as McGovern, he might well have begun to function as the effective leader of the commission during the summer of 1970, discussing strategy with Nelson and Casey, calling state party leaders to press them along the road to reform, and so forth. But Hughes had been drawn down the same path as McGovern, and he could not become the heir apparent when his former chairman departed.[3]

The three major contextual criteria for a new commission chairman—a commitment to reform, a base in Washington, and a history with the commission—thus cut the pool of potential replacements to three: Bill Dodds, director of political action for the United Auto Workers; Don Fraser, congressman from Minnesota; Adlai Stevenson, newly elected senator from Illinois. The nearly automatic generation of this short list then forced commission actors back on the question of who had the right to pick within it.

The commission staff, like its chairman, felt that Dodds was too clearly a spokesman for one special interest and that Stevenson could not be relied upon to pursue the issue with sufficient vigor—and sufficient indifference to the regular party. That left Fraser, their first choice all along. Rather than explicitly argue their right to appoint him, however, Nelson, Casey, and McGovern took their informal consensus to the members of their Executive Committee by telephone. The members were uniformly supportive, and Fraser's name was formally transmitted at the top of a short list. In this way, commission nominators hoped to constrain the national chairman, without making a show of this constriction.

If O'Brien had been sufficiently antagonistic, that might not have been enough. His predecessor had named the original chairman; he presumably retained that authority with a successor. O'Brien, however, had not failed to notice McGovern's withdrawal during the summer of 1970. Nelson, it is true, bore the brunt of McGovern's lessened involvement, since Nelson had been forced to speak for the commission by himself, without official backing. Yet O'Brien, who had promised to make reform a personal priority after the November elections, was equally aware that there had been no one playing the commission chairman's role during much of 1970. He, too, was prepared for a change. "McGovern by mid-1970 was no longer paying much attention. I was handling my end, Bob Nelson was handling the commission's end, but no one was handling the chairman's end." From the other side, Don Fraser was ready and willing to take the job. In 1969, he had been interested enough to take over the Subcommittee on Party Structure. In 1970, he had volunteered to reactivate that subcommittee. He remained interested in some larger commission role:

> I had been chairman of the Subcommittee on Delegate Selection, which didn't have much point to it. Then I wrote and asked to become chairman of the Party Structure Subcommittee. Instead, they picked me as Chairman.

On January 7, 1971, Larry O'Brien, the national chairman, announced the elevation of Don Fraser, congressman from the fifth district of Minnesota, to the chairmanship of the Commission on Party Structure and Delegate Selection. In the official press release announcing this transition, O'Brien saluted Fraser, Fraser saluted McGovern, and both men emphasized the magnitude of the task ahead. Of Fraser and his mission, O'Brien noted:

> Don Fraser assumes the chairmanship of this commission at a crucial time. It has completed its deliberations and developed the guidelines needed to make the party processes truly democratic. And now the job is to assist the state parties in meeting the guidelines so that throughout the nation, party processes and procedures will be open to full participation by all Democrats. . . .
>
> Because of the work of Senator McGovern and his colleagues on the Commission, the 1972 Democratic Convention and all subsequent conventions promise to be models of a truly democratic process at work. We shall be demonstrating to the American voters in unmistakable terms the vitality of the Democratic Party and its readiness to resume national leadership in the White House. . . .[4]

The Midterm Elections and State Response

The changing political calendar produced these alterations indirectly at the national level. In effect, major national actors, established and aspiring, took the arrival of the November elections as the occasion to assess both the progress of party reform and their own place in reform politics. After that, each settled on a particular strategic response to these assessments.

At the state level, the impact of the November elections was far more direct. In essence, the general election of 1970 created a major actor—often *the* major actor—for reform politics in a remarkable number of states. This actor, of course, was the governor. Of the thirty-five states holding gubernatorial elections in November of 1970, twenty-one changed the identity of their incumbent. Of these, fourteen actually replaced a Republican with the Democratic alternative. At a stroke, then, statewide electorates across the nation shifted the collective incumbency—and the partisan balance—of the formal post with perhaps the greatest prospective influence on the progress of party reform at the local level. (See figure 11.1.)[5]

The potential relevance of these new Democratic governors to reform politics was substantial. Most governors were widely believed by their general publics—and by national reformers, too—to have major responsibilities for the conduct of party affairs within their states. More to the point, most governors, willingly or not, were deeply enmeshed in state party politics. Many had been forced to address their party in order to arrive at the governorship. Most, re-

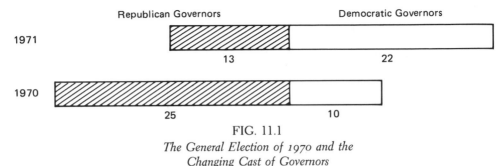

FIG. 11.1

*The General Election of 1970 and the
Changing Cast of Governors*

gardless of their route into office, would find a need to use the state party in the course of attempting to govern.

This swelling of the ranks of Democratic governors, however, was more than a neutral shift, or even a neutral expansion, in the cast of available reform actors. For new Democratic governors almost automatically made their states more sympathetic to national party reform than these states had previously been. This was true even where new incumbents were merely replacing another Democrat; it was much more impressive in the larger group of states where they replaced a Republican.

In part, this drift was the result of formal positional logic. The introduction of a Democratic governor in a previously Republican state effectively increased the number of major pressure points for state party reform. Where once there was mainly the state party chairman, now there was a Democratic governor, too. The number of significant targets for national party actors had accordingly grown; the number of state figures who might reasonably attempt to manipulate the state party from above had precisely doubled.

Yet far more was at issue even than this simple, mathematical contribution to reform. For the tendency of this bumper crop of new Democratic governors to move their states toward compliance was also a result of the practical logic of continuing state politics. At bottom, governors were likely to be responsive to a different, and more proreform, set of indigenous pressures than were sitting party chairmen. Beyond that, governors often had specifically national concerns, productive of a more sympathetic response to national party reform, which state chairmen were quite unlikely to share.

These institutionalized considerations were, in fact, the more important factors driving incoming governors toward a more sympathetic stance on state party reform. State party chairmen, in institutional practice, needed to be concerned primarily with the maintenance of the political party as an organization, with the political needs of state and local party officials, and with the fate of party candidates at the polls. If they worried about social groups, they worried about those which constituted the orthodox Democratic coalition. If they worried about issues, they worried about those which helped to hold that coalition together.[6]

An incoming governor, on the other hand, was predictably responsive to a broader range of factors. The concerns of his state party chairman might be his as well—although in a surprising number of cases they were not. But an incoming governor had his own public image to consider; he had cause to weigh the wishes of social groups not reliably allied with the Democratic party; he had a *personal* coalition to maintain; he had reason to attend to the link between state and national party affairs.

Even a governor with no personal interest in party reform was likely to think about how he was publicly perceived on the issue. While the press coverage given to reform was thin and sporadic, it was uniformly positive. More concretely, a governor was likely to desire political understandings with constituents who *were* sympathetic to reform, even if they were not particularly influential in his state party. These groups and individuals had representatives in the state legislature; they were often directly relevant to the success or failure of his policy initiatives; they might even have significant (minority) representation within the state party itself. Beyond this, governors had some explicitly national concerns within the Democratic party; these, too, led in the direction of greater support for party reform. By 1971, for example, many incoming governors could think about leading their state delegations to the 1972 Convention. In this, of course, they desired to reap the benefits in publicity, public policy, or personal advancement, and not to spend their time in battling public charges of bad behavior.

As a result, most incoming governors encountered a set of incentives leading toward greater sympathy for national party reform than their state party chairmen were ordinarily manifesting. At the same time, the arrival of these new Democratic governors created incentives for these state party chairmen to accommodate, within limits, to gubernatorial preferences. In short order, then, these chairmen, too, could be expected to show more attention to party reform than they had previously shown in the absence of a new chief executive from their own party.

There were good and traditional reasons for this. The governor usually became the symbol of the state party, whether his state party chairmen liked it or not. More to the point, the governor was usually the largest single source of those rewards, tangible and intangible, pecuniary and honorific, which were most useful to the maintenance of state party operations. Beyond even that, the influence of the state party over day-to-day politics in its home state was inevitably tied to its working relations with the incumbent governor.

All these incentives, for incoming governors and state party chairmen, would have existed, in principle, in any given year. But in 1970, thirty-five of the fifty gubernatorial seats were up for election. And in 1970, the winners of those elections, at least within the Democratic party, faced a major national proposal for state party reform as soon as they assumed gubernatorial office. When the Democratic party then picked up fourteen gubernatorial chairs, lost only two, and replaced three sitting governors with new Democratic incumbents, the conditions had been met for these state incentives to affect the course of reform politics, if they were capable of doing so at all.

Within the year—in fact, within months—those states which received a new Democratic governor in the election of 1970 were indeed to prove much more receptive to national reform recommendations than were those states which retained an incumbent or actually dismissed a Democrat and replaced him with a Republican. The full effect could be seen only in the concrete details of reform politics in the individual states. Yet the presence of a substantial impact could be seen in even the crudest measures of aggregate change, like the record of movement into full compliance between December of 1970 and December of 1971.

Of the thirty-five states holding elections in 1970, a clear majority of those which obtained a new Democratic governor were in full compliance by the end of 1971, less than a year after their newly elected chief executives had been formally installed. Conversely, a clear majority of those states which did not obtain a new Democratic incumbent were just as clearly *not* in compliance. (See figure 11.2.a.)[7] Again, such a crude measure, with such an arbitrary cut-off, inevitably understates the contribution of new Democratic governors to reform politics in their home states. The extent and variety of ramifications from such an apparently routine, idiosyncratic, and decentralized change can be suggested only through careful examination of an individual state, such as Pennsylvania. (See chapter 12.) Yet again, the impact of this ordinary and institutionalized shift is sufficient to register even with such a crude and arbitrary indicator.

Abstractly, the effect of a shift in the incumbent of the governorship ought to have been more pronounced in those states with organized, rather than volunteer, political parties. By the approach of the 1970 elections, volunteer parties had already proved more receptive to national demands for state party reform, so that there was less room for an electoral impact. At the same time, organized parties were more concerned with the concrete resources which newly elected governors possessed—jobs, contracts, and favors—and incoming governors in organized-party states were likely to have more such rewards to

FIG. 11.2

Compliance Prospects Among States with
New Democratic Governors

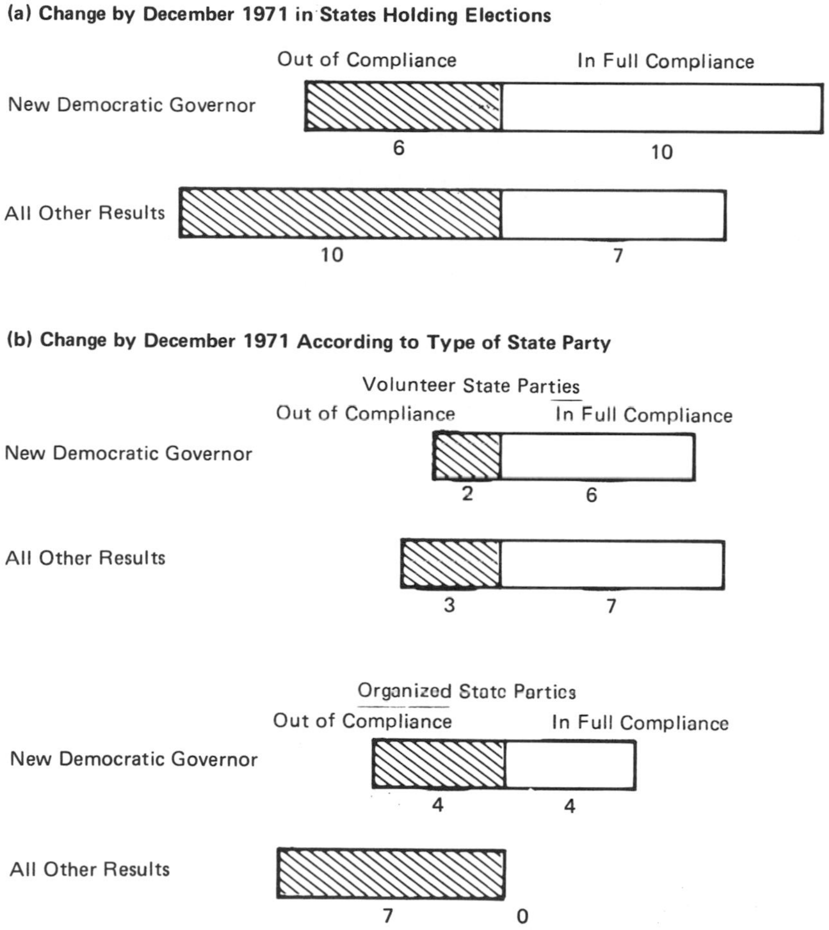

(a) Change by December 1971 in States Holding Elections

Out of Compliance   In Full Compliance

New Democratic Governor

6   10

All Other Results

10   7

(b) Change by December 1971 According to Type of State Party

Volunteer State Parties

Out of Compliance   In Full Compliance

New Democratic Governor

2   6

All Other Results

3   7

Organized State Parties

Out of Compliance   In Full Compliance

New Democratic Governor

4   4

All Other Results

7   0

NOTE: The numbers exclude the three states which were in full, certified compliance
by the time of the general election of 1970.

distribute. As a result, organized parties ought to have been more responsive to the wishes (or at least the assets) of a new Democratic governor, even if they had not had more room for such a response.

This, too, turned out to be very much the case. Both a detailed investigation of a single state (see chapter 12) and a summary examination of aggregate measures (see figure 11.2.b) suggest the projected difference between volunteer and organized state parties. Those volunteer-party states which acquired a new Democratic governor as a result of the election of 1970 were slightly, but only very slightly, more likely to move into full compliance during calendar 1971 than were those volunteer-party states which retained a sitting Democrat, remained with a Republican, or actually replaced a Democratic incumbent with the Republican alternative. In contrast, those organized state parties which received a new Democratic governor in the 1970 elections were *far* more likely to move into full compliance by the end of 1971 than were those organized parties which received some other outcome. In fact, *none* of the organized-party states which held elections in 1970 but which did not opt for a new Democratic alternative moved into full compliance during 1970.

These incentives, both from the simple, mathematical addition of a new governor to the state political equation and, especially, from the impact of continuing reform politics on any new governor, would have fallen on the winners of the November election without regard to their personal backgrounds, political histories, or ideological dispositions. When the election of 1970 created an unusually large group of potential respondents, then, a neutral event (the 1970 election) became a very biased contribution to the cause of party reform.

Yet real and powerful though they were, these incentives did not exhaust the contributions of the 1970 election to that cause. For scattered among the seventeen new Democratic faces in statehouses across the country was a second, smaller group of new chief executives who shared a characteristic which would have propelled them in the direction of party reform even in the absence of formal or contextual incentives. These were the self-conscious "reform Democrats"; their deliberate and professed attachment to party reform constituted an additional, separable pressure for compliance with national reform directives.

Among the most militant of these self-proclaimed reformers, there had been a stereotypical path to the governorship. The candidate had begun as a political outsider, with few, if any, ties to the regular party. When that party closed ranks around an officially endorsed candidate, this aspiring contender had been forced to challenge the party's choice. Perhaps he had been at-

tracted to politics by the desire to be an instrument of reform; perhaps he acquired the reform ideology in the process of bumping up against the regular party and established state politics. In either case, when he went on to defeat the party's preference for the gubernatorial nomination, and when he was then successful in the general election, he entered office as a confirmed reformer, *with a publicized devotion to the cause and with allies who shared that same general goal.*

In fact, the stereotype was a reasonable approximation to the political experience of an important subset of incoming governors. Perhaps the clearest example was Milton J. Shapp of Pennsylvania. Shapp was a wealthy businessman-reformer, who had a history of tilting with the organized party. But if Shapp was the archetype, John J. Gilligan, the incoming governor of Ohio, was not far behind. Similar individuals with similar scenarios surfaced even in volunteer-party states, when existing party officialdom or a sitting Democratic governor had opposed reform, and when a challenger identified with the concept had managed to prevail. Perhaps the clearest case was James E. Carter, Jr., of Georgia.[8] But if Carter was the archetype, another relatively sharp example was Reuben O'D. Askew, incoming governor of Florida.

Beyond these obvious (and self-announced) cases, there was a larger group of incoming governors who, while they had not hitched their star so explicitly to reform as an ideology, were clearly perceived—and interested in portraying themselves—as "progressives." They included Dale Bumpers in Arkansas, Cecil B. Andrus in Idaho, Marvin Mandel in Maryland, Wendell R. Anderson in Minnesota, Richard F. Kneip in South Dakota, and Patrick S. Lucey in Wisconsin. Most had been less directly the product of an explicit, crystallized, regular-reformer confrontation than had Shapp, Gilligan, Askew, and Carter. Most were less narrowly allied with reform factions or independent activists who possessed direct ties to national reformers. Yet all were interested in portraying themselves as dynamic, forward-looking figures who were concerned with changing the character—and by extension, the structure—of government and politics in their home states.[9]

These two groups together, the self-conscious "reform Democrats" and the less deliberately militant "progressives," were the final, additional, differentiable product of the midterm elections of 1970. A bumper crop of new Democratic governors was itself an inherent contribution to the cause of party reform, thanks to the positional and political logic which they encountered upon assuming office. These other individuals within their ranks, the reformers and the progressives, then brought deliberate attachment to reform per se to the highest public office in the state—and in the state party.

Content for the Ideology of Reform

The arrival of this large cadre of new Democratic governors, the presence within its number of a significant group with a public (if vague and undefined) commitment to reform, and the presence in *their* midst of a smaller sample of explicit reformers emphasized the importance of the process by which an abstract concept, reform, acquired concrete institutional meaning. All of these incoming governors were likely to make their state parties more receptive to reform, regardless of its specifics. The self-conscious reform Democrats were likely to *begin* by searching for specific proposals to give substance to their ideology.

By early 1971, both the relevance of political parties to the drive for abstract reform and the specific definition of reformed party rules had, in fact, been established. The political party had become an obvious—almost a definitional—focus for attempts at reform. The prior activities of the Party Structure Commission had largely settled the detailed definition of reform in the realm of the political party. As a result, the contents of *Mandate for Reform* had become the definition of party reform for the national Democratic party. In theory, there were other approaches to this goal; the model of disciplined and hierarchical political parties offered one of these. In theory, there were other practical deductions even from a participatory model; the commission's own guidelines contained several strictures which seemed actively inconsistent with the participatory approach.

In practice, none of this mattered. The commission had been certified by the national party; anyone who preferred his own plan for party reform had to confront an immediate lack of legitimacy. The commission was a *national* body; anyone who preferred a reform plan of his own had to speak for one state only, and to go against most others. The commission had already reported, in a set of aggressive recommendations; anyone who preferred a different report had to produce it first and then acknowledge that pursuing it might undermine the cumulative prospects for reform nationwide. The product of the commission had long since acquired the support of most self-conscious reform partisans; anyone who intended to be for reform but against the guidelines could expect only the active animosity of these other reformers—could expect, in fact, to be labeled as an enemy of reform.

Under those conditions, it may have been impossible for an incoming governor to impose an extensive, new, and different definition of party reform in place of the commission report. In any case, no one tried. The guidelines from the Commission became the working definition of party reform for all incoming Democratic governors; each chose his response within their parameters.

Some, those who were sufficiently militant about reform in general, embraced these recommendations in toto. Most accepted them as a package, but strove to modify those individual recommendations which were most incongruent with local conditions. Some, being sufficiently repelled by the overall content or potential cost of commission proposals, simply pulled back from reform politics.

Yet the effectiveness of this translation—between the abstract concept of party reform and the practical detail of commission guidelines—extended well beyond the circle of incoming chief executives. The attraction of the concept itself had been sufficient to mobilize a network of independent activists and established reformers on several critical occasions. In a different fashion, it would eventually prove sufficient to capture the working press. Thanks to both of these developments, finally, the attractiveness of the concept—and its halo effect for specific institutional suggestions—would become a problem even for regular party leaders.

Before there was a Party Structure Commission, there had been a loose network of individuals vitally concerned with party reform. At the 1968 Convention, they had worked to extract reform resolutions. In the aftermath of the general election, they had lobbied to secure appointment of the authorized—reform—commissions. A year later, they had, with rare exceptions, accepted the detailed contents of the report of the Party Structure Commission as the practical definition of reform. Their continued acceptance was a major reason why no major redefinition was likely.

The attentive press followed much the same trajectory. During the politics of recommendation, comparatively few reporters had actually bothered to cover the progress of party reform. Nevertheless, there had been little reason for those who did cover the development of commission recommendations to treat them as only one among several options, since there had been no other live alternatives. Once these recommendations were adopted, reporters, too, were prepared to treat them as the operational content of party reform. They would continue to do so throughout the politics of implementation.

The press was destined to make further practical contributions to the course of reform politics. Much of the published press which continued to follow the progress of party reform was itself committed to reform in the abstract, and thus to the success of this particular reform package. To the extent that their reportage influenced the course of reform politics, it was surely in a proreform direction. Moreover, even those reporters and publications which attempted a more analytic approach still permitted this institutional definition of reform to stand for reform in general, and thus to accrue any abstract virtues associated with that general concept.

Those virtues certainly existed. At a minimum, they included a figurative connection between reform and improvement. Political life can always, by definition, benefit from more of the latter. Beyond this, reform was normally associated with notions of democratic responsiveness and accurate public representation. Again, at least in the United States, these are unassailable values.[10]

From the other side, these positive abstract associations were a continuing *problem* for regular party officials, as it came time to address the concrete recommendations of the Party Structure Commission. By late 1970, interested party regulars could hardly fail to see that the specific content of commission guidelines had become the effective translation of party reform—and had borrowed many of the virtuous associations of reform in the abstract. Yet these defenders of the regular party experienced a continued difficulty in meeting the public arguments of reform partisans, phrased, as they were, in more abstract terms.

This inherent difficulty was exaggerated by the differing political skills of reformers and regulars. Reformers were more adept at abstract argument and at the symbolic presentation of ideas. Regulars were more adept at organizational maintenance and at the assembly of political coalitions.[11] The difficulty was exaggerated by the existing imbalance in the development of the rhetoric supporting reform and resistance. Reformers had an explicit, elaborated rationale for their proposed changes. Regulars lacked a carefully constructed, fully articulated rationale—touching on other, equally appealing values—to justify opposition.[12]

These difficulties were not a constraint at all times and in all places, nor were they the determining factors in any given case. But they did remain a consistent problem for party regulars, and a consistent asset for party reformers. Geraldine M. Joseph, vice chairman of the National Committee, chairman of Ad Hoc Committee No. 1, and a deeply ambivalent observer of reform politics, noted the difficulty of organized party leaders in countering the arguments of reform proponents, especially in the absence of contrasting proposals and a contrary rationale:

You have to remember that mind-set for reform. Things *must* be done. Yes, it *is* right to have more women and blacks involved in the party. No, we *can't* have 1968 again. People didn't have any sense for how these rules would work in practice. It looked all right, so you did it. Those who feel most strongly about the thing are those who will get out for it. Those who were against it weren't really, *really* against it. Many who did oppose it and didn't know how to express themselves said, "We can't possibly do this. We'll just have a primary. What can be more democratic than that?"

The abstract attraction of reform as a program, and the concrete success of the Party Structure Commission in providing a practical content, were not lost on the remaining staff members at commission headquarters. They had hardly created this translation process, except indirectly and in pursuit of other goals. They were not even explicitly aware of the translation process as such. Yet they were about to capitalize on it—and thereby channel the proreform pressures which the election of 1970 had created.

Between November of 1970 and February of 1971, while they were waiting for key personnel changes at the state and national level, Bob Nelson and Carol Casey, with a late assist from Don Fraser, moved to elaborate the specific requirements of commission guidelines. In doing so, they put the abstract attractions of party reform at the concrete service of these more detailed elaborations; in doing so, they further constrained all those who were even potentially coming into compliance with official commission recommendations.

The device for doing this was a set of "Model Party Rules."[13] Formally, these were intended to address the situation in which a state party was willing (or claimed to be willing) to come into compliance, but lacked the expertise necessary for a comprehensive revision of state party law. Practically, these Model Party Rules had any number of additional, potential, political functions. At a minimum, they were calculated to set the effective boundaries within which state parties could develop their own procedural preferences. Simultaneously, they would narrow these boundaries. In passing, they would further transfer the evaluation of indigenous state reform proposals—state counterproposals, really, in the aftermath of the Model Party Rules—to the operating part of the Party Structure Commission.

These new Model Party Rules took the guidelines one by one, offered a short justification, summarized the requirements of each in tabular form, and then provided a specific formulation or two to give them institutional meaning. Careful detail and precise phraseology characterized all these elucidations. A further constriction of their institutional implications, akin to, if not as great as, the constrictions which staff members had added to some guidelines after the final commission meeting, characterized a number.[14]

In the face of all this, acquiescent state parties might simply select a developed alternative and adopt it as state party policy. More innovative—or more resistant—state party leaders could still develop their own alternatives, but these would hereafter be debated back and forth between the Model Party Rules and the indigenous state suggestion, and not just between that suggestion and the guidelines themselves. As a result, the institutional reach of national guidelines was expanded; the institutional freedom of the state parties was constricted; and the abstract virtues of reform as a concept were put in the service of an increasingly concrete and detailed set of proposals for institutional change.

Implications

The hiatus in reform politics in the fall and winter of 1970–71 was, ironically, a crucial period in the development of that politics. Most reform actors in the states were diverted from any possible attention to party reform by the approaching elections of November 1970. Most reform actors in Washington were similarly diverted. Yet this interregnum in the states rearranged the political landscape across the country. And this interregnum in Washington not only rearranged the political landscape there, but contributed a crucial twist to the negotiations between state and national reform actors.

At the national level, the coming of the general election of 1970 drew even those actors who were most explicitly and deliberately centered on party reform off into electoral politics. The national chairman, of course, had the nationwide fate of the party as one of his personal responsibilities during this period, and he was eager to contribute as much as he could. But the remaining staff at the Party Structure Commission were also drawn, more intermittently, to electoral politics. Nevertheless, even this apparent shift *away* from reform politics resulted in several major contributions to party reform.

In order to leave the reform realm and concentrate on electoral politics, for example, and in order to bring the commission staff along, Chairman O'Brien promised to make implementation and compliance his top priority after the first of the year. His commitment was a major, if indirect, contribution. Simultaneously, the Party Structure staff, even with these new electoral duties, found itself with time on its hands. There was no point in urging state party leaders to attend to implementation and compliance when they had the decisive elections in state politics to concern them. There was no point in urging Chairman O'Brien to concentrate on reform politics, when he faced an implicit referendum on the Nixon administration.

While it waited for this period to pass, the commission staff turned back to the official text for party reform. There, it turned to an elaboration of the guidelines, a translation of these eighteen general strictures into very detailed, alternative formulations for state institutions of delegate selection, and for state party processes more generally. These new formulations were automatically a constriction on any states which eventually came into compliance, since they became the sanctioned meaning of "party reform." They gained an additional influence, far beyond anything which their drafters could reasonably intend, through the outcome of the 1970 elections.

Those elections contributed a total of seventeen new Democratic governors to state parties across the nation. All of these new governors were likely, for simple mathematical and more explicitly political reasons, to be more sympathetic to party reform in the abstract—and thus to these specific elaborations of the guidelines. A subset of these new governors, the self-conscious reform Democrats, were deliberately committed to implementation and compliance—and hence, without knowing it, to these new elaborations as well.

The simple introduction of a new Democratic governor, especially when he replaced a Republican, was a contribution to party reform. Or at least, these governors automatically constituted an additional pressure point for national party reformers. More crucially, the political environment which these new governors entered made them additionally responsive to party reform, far more responsive than their lone, sitting, state chairmen had been. These new governors needed to be concerned with reform as a public issue and as an element of their own public image; they had to be concerned with *press treatment* of the issue—a uniformly positive treatment—and of their own role in it. Moreover, incoming governors had reason to consider the political activities of those who were supporting reform, both in the legislature and in the state party, even when these individuals were hardly a dominant force in either. These new governors, finally, faced an almost instant need to consider their role in the national party, through their state delegation to the 1972 Convention.

There was, then, a quiet, essentially bureaucratic process by which commission guidelines were converted into detailed formulations for implementation in the states. There was a recurring political event, the midterm election, which produced a comparatively unusual outcome, a strong shift in partisan balance among governorships. As a result, the interaction of this quiet, bureaucratic process with this routine, recurring event became a classic case of *the practical power of an abstract concept*, of a vague and general public ideology which was to alter the course of reform politics, the extent of institutional change, and the nature of elite circulation.

This was clearest in the case of the self-conscious reform Democrats scattered among the new chief executives. These men were personally committed to reform; they had been portrayed by the press, before and after the election, as partisans of reform; they had built their campaigns, and their continuing supporters, from those who were also attracted to the issue. When they arrived in office, they discovered, if they had not already known, that the operational meaning of reform in state party politics had already been defined—by the Model Party Rules of the Party Structure Commission.

It was clear, in turn, who had rendered this definition. Bob Nelson and Carol Casey, with the subsequent blessing of Don Fraser, had elaborated, refined, *and constricted* the institutional requirements of the guidelines during their period of forced inactivity, from November through February. When they began, they could hardly have known the outcome of the November elections, much less the significance it would give to their revision. Even afterward, they did not proceed in the thought that they were the instruments by which an abstract ideology was being given precise, concrete, operational requirements. But they were in place; they were committed; they did fill that role.

When a new group of Democratic governors entered office, then, and when the formal and political logic of the environment which they entered encouraged them to move toward compliance, the significance of these detailed elaborations, these Model Party Rules, was magnified—as was their significance as the embodiment of reform in the abstract. The implications of all this for institutional change were obvious. The implications for elite circulation were no less profound for being less immediately apparent.

In the case of institutional change, almost every noticeable event which occurred in this period had the potential for *increasing* the degree of implementation and compliance within the state and national parties. This was true of the major contribution from Chairman O'Brien, a commitment to upgrade his personal priority for reform. It was manifestly true of the major contribution by the commission staff, the Model Party Rules. It was true for the least publicly evident of these developments, the creation of the Center for Political Reform.

What was true and impressive at the national level was far more so among the states. The large number of new Democratic governors was admittedly an unplanned—even uncoordinated—contribution to reform. Yet within months, its impact was profound. By even the crudest measures, those states which received a new governor showed a progress on implementation which did not characterize those which remained with a Republican governor, which retained a sitting Democrat, or which went from Democratic to Republican.

Less obvious, perhaps, were the implications of these events for the circulation of elites within the national party. With improved prospects for institutional change, of course, came increased prospects for extensive elite replacement, and hence for the ascension of the alternative Democratic coalition. Moreover, that alternative coalition itself had begun, in the period from November of 1970 to February of 1971, both to expand and to achieve a more explicit and self-conscious identity, as a continuing coalition. Yet this period also saw the appearance of a distinction between the aggregate of those who were supporting reform and the coalition of those who aspired to benefit from it, and that distinction became its final, noteworthy nuance.

All those supporting reform had prospered tremendously during this period. At the national level, the principal addition to the institutional actors which were supporting reform was the new Center for Political Reform, founded and led by Ken Bode. It would come into its own during 1971. Yet the major institutional actor committed to implementation and compliance remained the Party Structure Commission, and the significance of its institutional continuity—the significance of the earlier agreement by Chairman O'Brien to keep the commission as a functioning entity—was never more evident than when it issued the Model Party Rules and saw them constrain the seventeen new governors created in the general election. Even in an emaciated state, with two staff members and an occasional volunteer, the commission managed to issue the Model Party Rules. By early 1971, it possessed a new chairman, Don Fraser, and the promise of renewed energy and an even more active part in reform politics.

At the state level, the principal additions to the reform coalition were more numerous, more obvious, and even more important. Some of the new Democratic governors created by the election of 1970 put themselves at the service of continuing reformers with deliberate forethought; others responded more to the logic of their political environment. Either way, most swelled the ranks of the reform coalition. Some of these governors, however, also illustrated the way in which the aggregation which supported reform could differ, in small but important respects, from the coalition which was forming up to benefit from these new rules. Stated differently, those who were supporting reform were not always deliberate and continuing members of the alternative Democratic coalition. As a result, the success of reform would not uniformly benefit those who had supported its realization, while it might well help others who had little to do with that success.

This fact became clear in late 1970 and early 1971 when the alternative Democratic coalition began to acquire a series of additions, additions which not only swelled its ranks but gave it a self-conscious identity—in opposition to the orthodox Democratic coalition and in aspiration of replacing it. Originally, what hindsight would reveal as the beginnings of this alternative coalition had been merely a sample of actors from the dissident nomination campaigns of 1968. These had coalesced more broadly around the effort to get national reform commissions appointed. They had then been expanded and held together, though only tangentially and intermittently, by the Party Structure Commission itself.

Once the politics of implementation began, however, this alternative coalition achieved a more precise, self-consciously coalitional character. This began when individual reform partisans and remaining party dissidents were joined by organized reform factions in the states, as efforts at compliance became the heart of reform politics. In late 1970 and early 1971, it continued apace.

At the national level, the creation of the Center for Political Reform was the harbinger of the arrival of the liberal ideological and reform interest groups in the alternative Democratic coalition—and of their abandonment of the orthodox coalition. Most of this would occur during 1971, when continuing ideological organizations like Americans for Democratic Action and new reform groups like Common Cause would explicitly join the alternative coalition. The Center for Political Reform, however, was the first of these recruits, and it would play a major role in recruiting the others.

At the state level, the self-conscious reform Democrats among the new governors were a more obvious, and far more immediate, counterpart. These individuals aspired to lead the alternative Democratic coalition in their home states; they automatically became important members—champions, really—for that coalition nationwide. They would remain with it through 1972; some would remain with it long after that.

Yet there were contrary examples as well, of individuals who swelled the ranks of those seeking procedural reform without ever joining the alternative Democratic coalition and without any serious hope—if they only knew—of benefiting from the implementation of reform. They made serious contributions to institutional change and elite circulation; they were not destined to benefit from either.

At the national level, the dramatic case—the symbol, really—was Chairman O'Brien. In late 1970, O'Brien was still temporizing on party reform. By early 1971, he was fully committed to its realization. Yet at the 1972 Convention, the first reformed gathering of the full national party, he would go within days from being the man who was promised the chairmanship again, as a bridge between the old politics and the new, to the man who was discarded by the alternative Democratic coalition, as unfit to lead the party.[15]

Again, however, the more numerous examples were on the state level. Among these, the most obvious were those new Democratic governors who were not deliberately attached to reform as an ideology, who were pushed by political and institutional incentives toward support of party reform. Realization of these reforms did not have anything to contribute to them personally; the *supporters* of these reforms did not intend to rally behind these governors in the aftermath of implementation—and they did not.

With equal irony, the leaders of the regular party in volunteer-party states fell into this category, too. Volunteer political parties were more receptive to reform at every step of the reform process. The leaders of these parties were often personally responsive; they were reliably responsive to the incentives in their environment which encouraged support of reform. Yet most of these individuals did *not* join the alternative coalition, in opposition to the orthodox version. Reformed party rules did not, in consequence, promise them much additional attainment. As a result, many of these individuals—the members of the National Committee from these states were only the most glaring examples—would be retired from office by the delegate politics of 1972.

Time alone would tell whether the period surrounding the general election of 1970 had made enough contribution to the progress of party reform to make this apparent hiatus in reform politics a critical turning point for the overall fate of reform. The period had contributed new reform actors at the national level and an elaborate new translation of the requirements of reform, to boot. It had contributed new reform actors at the state level, actors who threatened to dwarf these national figures not just by their number but by their centrality to implementation. Yet the impact of these actions would have to be registered individually, state by state, before it could be said to be decisive. And this individual impact would have to be registered collectively, at the national level, before it could be judged to have contributed a turning point.

CHAPTER

1 2

The Politics of Implementation Writ Small:

Pennsylvania Accepts Reform

IN WHICH, a classically developed, organized political party addresses the issue of reform, defeating both an indigenous reform faction and national reform actors; a new governor, a "reform Democrat," activates the moribund reform process; and heavy investment of resources by the governor, coupled with an intricate set of compromises with the regular party, produces compliance with national party rules. AND IN WHICH, the elements of national reform politics are present, in concentrated form, in a single state; institutional change results from traditional bargaining at the state level; and the local version of the nationwide coalition of alternative Democratic elites scores a victory which will aid their cause at the national level, too.

THE ELEMENTS of reform politics established by the midterm elections of 1970 played out their impact in state after state as 1971 progressed. Some states featured one or another of these elements as the dominant influence. All states mixed them in locally varying proportions. Yet if some sample of these elements was at work in most states, they received perhaps their most striking expression in Pennsylvania. There, one of the strongest, old-fashioned, organized parties confronted all the reshuffled and augmented, proreform influences which followed the election of 1970.

In that confrontation, the impact of shifting forces at the national level, of shifting actors and alignments at the state level, of the symbolic pull of reform in the abstract, and of concrete demands from specific recommendations for party reform could all be seen, in action, in a particular locale. As a result, Pennsylvania can serve as a specific—if overdrawn—embodiment of the general forces playing upon the Democratic party nationwide.

Reform politics in Pennsylvania, as elsewhere, consisted in part of negotiations between national and state reform actors, and every one of the new or newly invigorated principals in national reform politics had a counterpart who served as his entree to party politics in Pennsylvania. Yet the heart of reform politics in the Keystone State consisted of the interplay among indigenous political actors. And here, the confrontation was a classic.

Ranged on one side was the regular Democratic party and its traditional associated interests. At first the official party leadership, and later an informal group from the dominant faction, carried the ball for this alignment, with the effective endorsement of a strong labor movement and the implicit support of black party officialdom. Ranged on the other side was an indigenous reform faction and its emerging associated interests. This alignment was joined, energized, and then led by one of the most explicit reform Democrats among all the new gubernatorial incumbents, but it enjoyed the support of most independent activists and liberal ideological organizations as well.

The eventual triumph of the reform side, partial and convoluted though that triumph would be, provided forceful testimony to the importance of one crucial change in these alignments—the addition of a self-conscious reform governor, courtesy of the general election of 1970. Yet along the way, the abstract character of "reform" as an ideology, the concrete way in which it acquired a practical definition, and the role of national actors in enforcing that translation were highlighted, too.

Despite the introduction of a new governor to the reform coalition in Pennsylvania, the outcome remained in doubt up to the instant at which reformers recorded their victory. The previous history of local reform politics explained this air of uncertainty. The first indigenous reform commission simply sputtered out; a second exploded; a rump faction then failed dramatically, at a public meeting of the state committee, to secure its reform plan.

Nevertheless, the governor managed to keep the issue alive until his own staff, in consort with that of the state party chairman, could develop a new reform package, for presentation to another meeting of the full state committee. Even then, only a recess in the middle of that meeting, for a long-distance phone call from the governor to the "boss" of the Philadelphia City Committee, produced the additional understandings—in procedural guarantees and in general principles for the distribution of patronage—which permitted these reforms to go through.

The result was substantial institutional change in Pennsylvania. The result, simultaneously, was improved prospects for institutional change in the national party as a whole, especially since Pennsylvania was one of the largest and most reliably Democratic states. But the triumph of reform in Pennsylvania also testified to the ascendancy—temporary though it might be—of a new coalition of elites. This outcome, too, made a similar victory more likely at the national level. If that occurred, finally, then developments like those in Pennsylvania held the prospect of *institutionalizing* this aspiring alternative coalition, through a reformed politics of presidential selection.

A Reform Commission for the Regular Party

The division between regulars and reformers which had flared into prominence in many states during the presidential politics of 1968 was a matter of long standing in Pennsylvania. It had characterized state party affairs for years; it would form the basis for a first round of reform politics in 1969 and for a second round in 1971. Moreover, this political division was rooted in social distinctions precisely parallel to those at the national level.

The reform faction in the Pennsylvania party was based in the white-collar, suburban counties around Philadelphia, although it drew substantial support from counterpart areas in Allegheny County (metropolitan Pittsburgh) and in those counties with a substantial university population, especially around Penn State University in central Pennsylvania. All these areas tended to be Republican in state and national politics; their Democrats tended to be reformist in internal party affairs.

The regular party, by contrast, had long been described in terms of an "iron triangle"—Philadelphia, Pittsburgh, and the coal regions of northeastern Pennsylvania. The Philadelphia City Committee provided the longest side to this triangle, but the organized parties in Pittsburgh and along the coal seam (the Scranton–Wilkes-Barre metropolitan area) were not far behind. These areas were overwhelmingly Democratic in partisan preference; they had to deliver a preponderant margin if statewide candidates were to be successful. Over time, party officialdom in most rural areas had allied with this regular coalition, although its base, like that of the reformers, tended to be Republican in state and national affairs.

The resulting division was accompanied by a split among associated interest groups. On the reform side, perhaps the most consequential established organization was Americans for Democratic Action, especially the Southeast Pennsylvania Chapter. Among newer ideological groups, the most active was the Pennsylvania branch of the New Democratic Coalition, although by 1971 it, too, was suffering the disarray of its national parent.

On the regular side, the Committee on Political Education of the state AFL-CIO and the various international unions headquartered in Pennsylvania, especially the United Steelworkers, were an important force in state politics. Indeed, Pennsylvania labor often extended this role to the national scene,

as it had in supporting Hubert Humphrey in 1968—and as it would in supporting him in 1972. State civil rights organizations were in a more ambiguous
position, but black voters in Pennsylvania were a mainstay of the regular party,
and black party politicians were uniformly regulars.

These divisions had been given sharp focus by the gubernatorial campaign
of 1966. The regular party had closed ranks behind Robert P. Casey of Scranton, the state auditor general. But Milton J. Shapp of suburban Philadelphia,
a millionaire industrialist, had come on to serve as a rallying point for reformers, and after spending an estimated million and a half dollars of his own
money, Shapp had managed to overcome the organizational advantages of the
regular party and secure the nomination. He had sought no subsequent accommodation with party regulars; these regulars had sat out the general election;
the Republican had won decisively in November.[1]

Instead of reconciling these differences in the aftermath of this gubernatorial debacle, both sides found a vehicle to resurrect them in the presidential
politics of 1968. The reformers went with Eugene McCarthy; the regulars
supported Hubert Humphrey. When McCarthy won the statewide preference
vote, effectively unopposed, while individuals loyal to Humphrey won most
delegate elections, and when the regular party went on to name only one Mc-
Carthyite, Milton Shapp, among the at-large delegates from Pennsylvania, a
nadir of bad feeling was achieved.[2]

The desire to avoid a credentials challenge to this controversial delegation,
along with the desire of the state party to reorganize for the elections of 1970,
produced a compromise, the first tentative step toward reform in Pennsylvania. The State Central Committee would upgrade the position of state chairman and permit its incumbent, Thomas Z. Minehart, to step aside as auditor
general, so that Robert Casey, the former gubernatorial aspirant, could be appointed to that slot. Chairman Minehart, in return, would appoint a state reform committee, charged with investigating both state party rules and delegate selection procedures, as long as Pennsylvania reformers did not contest
his organizational maneuvers.

When this arrangement was accepted, Pennsylvania became one of the first
states to possess an indigenous committee studying local party reform. Anna-
Maria Malloy, state committee member from suburban Philadelphia and informal chairman of a subsequent reform commission, was one of those who
went along, grudgingly, with the procedural compromise:

> At that time, Minehart was running for Treasurer or Auditor General alterna-
> tively with Grace Sloan. The party could not accommodate him, but they talked
> him into staying on as State Chairman, with pay that equaled the money that
> he would have gotten as Treasurer. Reformers got the Rules Revision Committee

in return for their votes. Then Minehart double-crossed us on this because he appointed antireformers. This enraged the suburban Committee members.

This first reform commission was to abort spontaneously within a very short period. At the initial state committee meeting of the new year, Chairman Minehart did indeed appoint a Rules Revision Committee. But from the first, its chairman, Horace J. Culbertson of rural Lewisburg in central Pennsylvania, defined his responsibility as the containment of a potentially explosive situation. He assembled his subcommittee sparingly, under conditions which would prevent it from causing any serious upset. Two short work sessions and one public hearing were, in fact, the sum of its activity, in 1969 and forever. When the coming of summer provided an excuse for temporary suspension, that excuse was quickly taken. The first Pennsylvania reform commission never met again.[3]

In all this, the Pennsylvania party was not very different from other organized parties. It had, of course, appointed a local reform committee when many of these other parties were deliberately taking no action. But it had restored its reputation by putting this body back to sleep at the earliest opportunity. Where Pennsylvania differed from even the stronger organized parties was in its willingness to oppose reform publicly. Most unenthusiastic state parties contented themselves with spiking reform proposals in their own bailiwick, on the assumption that others would do the same. Spokesmen for the Pennsylvania party, however, put their reservations on the record at every official opportunity.

Indeed, these spokesmen went on to offer an active defense of organization, discipline, and hierarchy in state party politics. The mailing of the draft guidelines for public review, in October of 1969, provoked one of the sharpest defenses of the Pennsylvania way, from Ernest P. Kline, minority leader of the state senate:

> Our nation has operated as a Democratic Republic, not a pure democracy, and our political parties have been fashioned in the same way. The extremely sensitive area is that point where we get the elected party officials to properly reflect a broad cross-section of political views. I look forward to the back-up paper on this subject.
>
> It is my feeling that a declaration of Presidential preference, if a delegate chooses to make one, should be optional and non-binding. The convention system in the past has worked amazingly well, and credit for this to a great extent is due to the fact that most delegates go to the convention prepared to select a candidate on the basis of many practical factors, but not for hard-line ideological reasons. Our parties have survived because of their flexibility, and delegates should be reasonably committed to any candidate.

Proposal C–2, which covers the question of ex officio delegates, is of great concern to me because of my general view of what a political party is and who it represents.

If we were to prohibit ex officio delegates, we would be ignoring the place party officeholders have achieved, either through loyal and knowledgeable representation or through their election to some high party post. It seems to me to be unfair to penalize persons who have devoted themselves to party affairs and/or have already proved their credentials as representatives of the party and the people, by winning and holding some prestigious and important office. Party loyalty and participation should mean something.

The Party is a party, and therefore should reflect the interest of all those concerned with party affairs. The party as a unit must concern itself with satisfying the public need for progress. The party process is indirect, not direct, and our objective should be to strengthen and democratize the two-party system, not to weaken or destroy it.[4]

In the face of a somnolence on the part of the official reform commission and of this active criticism from top party officials, Bob Nelson sought to intervene from above and generate some state reform activity. When the compliance letters had been mailed, in February of 1970, Nelson began the search for a contact within the Pennsylvania party, a person who would receive his memos and coordinate some local response.

The hunt was diagnostic. After four months of searching, the best he could do was Stephen P. Mahinka, a junior staffer in the office of the House majority leader, with no direct connection to the State Central Committee. Mahinka took commission desires seriously and pumped out numerous reform communications of his own, but there was to be no practical upshot.[5] Horace Culbertson, chairman of the Rules Revision Committee, summarized the situation:

I had no contact with the national commission. They *were* in touch with Tom Minehart, because he said to me that he met with them in Philadelphia. He said it was the damnedest bunch of crackpots he ever saw. They were meeting with him once or twice, but never with us, and we didn't look for it.

Those letters came to Tom Minehart, and he said, "Forget about them." I think Tom just gave them lip service. He didn't believe they could do anything, and he didn't want me to do anything.

Another Commission for Party Reformers

The Pennsylvania party might have remained in this situation indefinitely, were it not for the arrival—and outcome—of the 1970 election. Milton Shapp, the reformer, again defeated Robert Casey, the regular, for the gubernatorial nomination in the spring of 1970. Yet this time, Shapp was less inclined to send the regular organization into the wilderness. And this time, the state committee was less precipitous in washing its hand of an unwanted nominee. Shapp needed a united, active party in what was generally viewed as a close contest. The state committee, after a four-year hiatus, needed renewed access to the concrete rewards of office.[6]

Discussions on a compromise party leadership were the logical result. National party reforms were never central to these discussions; neither were they ignored. The Shapp forces did want an understanding which would facilitate implementation. The regular party did want the ability to constrain any ensuing change.

The resolution was an interlocking set of agreements, similar to the one which had produced the first reform committee. The state chairmanship would remain in the hands of the regular party; the vice chairman, the secretary, and the treasurer would be ceded to the gubernatorial candidate. The state committee would work diligently for the election of Milton Shapp; the new governor, if such he became, would see that the committee shared the fruits of victory. The new state chairman, John N. Scales of Greensburg in western Pennsylvania, agreed to create a second reform commission and was authorized to make its individual appointments, but he promised to weight them in the direction of reform.

Shapp did indeed win the governorship in November, and the self-described "reform Democrat" thus became eligible to assist the cause of party reform. Norval D. Reece, special assistant to the governor, saw not the slightest hesitation: "The issue was never much of a problem with Milton Shapp. He put his own prestige on the line. He said he did not want to head a delegation to the 1972 convention that would be challenged." Scales, the state party chairman whose appointment completed an intricate array of bargains, saw the same orientation when the candidate became the governor:

> The whole idea of Shapp coming in with a reform image—he wanted to establish a name on issues like this. He felt that there should be much more involvement of the public in selection committees of all kinds.

Milton Shapp assumed the governorship on January 19, 1971. Three days later, the new chairman of the Party Structure Commission, Don Fraser, mailed the new chairman of the Pennsylvania party, John Scales, his first official communication about party reform. This was the standard, year-opening review of progress in the individual states; it centered on legal changes which would have to be made in 1971, the last full legislative session before the start of delegate selection.[7]

In Pennsylvania, the major compliance issues were, of course, unchanged. The initial compliance letter of February 27, 1970, had categorized Pennsylvania as deficient on ten of the eighteen guidelines. Several of these were deficiencies of some scope, including violations on Guideline B–7 (Apportionment) and on Guideline C–5 (Committee Selection Processes).[8] But the major institutional change required of the Pennsylvania party, and the major sticking point for reform politics, was implied by Guideline C–1 (Adequate Public Notice).

C–1, in effect, required Pennsylvania to terminate its delegate primary, in use since 1908, and to move to a candidate primary instead. Pennsylvania had been one of the first states to select its delegates in a primary election, and its delegate primary was a major reform of its time. Through the years, a presidential preference poll, entered at the option of the candidates, had been appended above the election for individual delegates, who were still voted under their own names only. The official compliance letter had proposed, at a minimum, adding the presidential preference of every aspiring delegate to the ballot. State reformers proposed grouping those delegates into slates, according to this presidential preference. National reformers preferred removing delegate names entirely, leaving only the names of the presidential candidates.

The arrival of Milton Shapp had no immediate impact on the status of these proposals. Instead, a second Pennsylvania commission took the first—eventually pointless—steps toward reform. The Fraser letter to Scales must actually have crossed in the mails with a note from Shapp to O'Brien, revealing the creation of a Pennsylvania Rules Reform Commission.[9]

The new commission possessed twenty-four carefully selected members. They included commissioners who were not members of the State Central Committee; they featured a slight tilt toward organized reformers. Nevertheless, the chairmanship went to Genevieve Blatt, former statewide candidate and long-time party regular. Horace Culbertson, Blatt's predecessor as chairman of a Pennsylvania reform commission, saw her group as precariously balanced:

> The first chairman was Genevieve Blatt. She became a judge. I think Gen would have followed the same path I was following. The members of the State Committee did not turn over, and that meant, had Genevieve Blatt continued, that the organization might have stayed anti-Shapp. But she stayed in there to hold the line on that for only a short time. By then, Shapp had had time to use his resources to bring over some of these people.

Blatt did indeed remain for only a short period, before resigning to become judge of the Commonwealth Court. During her tenure, the commission was organized into two subcommittees and met twice for internal work sessions. Otherwise, it accomplished little more than the collection of some necessary background information—and the division of its membership into clear and self-conscious reform versus regular factions.

Once Blatt announced her resignation, however, the commission moved off in a quite different direction—and ultimately off into oblivion. AnnaMaria Malloy, the designated vice chairman, immediately assumed the chairmanship, an action which drove the two internal factions to a full-blown split: "I was in good touch with the national commission. I was never appointed chairman of the state commission; I just grabbed it. Or, you could say that I just offered myself as Chairman." From the other side, Eugene E. J. Maier, commission representative for the Philadelphia City Committee and unofficial spokesman for party regulars, refused to acquiesce in this maneuver:

> AnnaMaria Malloy did in fact just announce her Chairmanship. One of the problems was that Scales' assistant [Gerald A. New; see below] was trying to be all things to all men. Malloy just sort of got in there as chairperson, and there was never a formal appointment.

After that, relations within the commission, never cordial, deteriorated rapidly. By early April, Maier and other commission regulars were no longer attending meetings. Malloy, in the face of this unofficial boycott, reorganized the group. Boycotting commission members branded subsequent sessions as nothing more than "rumps." Commission reformers resolved to push on to a formal result. The Pennsylvania Rules Reform Commission held one more public hearing, on April 12 in suburban Philadelphia. The remaining commissioners then set about writing a draft report, to go before a June meeting of the state committee.

This draft was substantially aided by Ken Bode and his new Center for Political Reform. Bode had been contacted around the first of the year by Jeanne M. Simon and Stephen D. Sheller, both of the southeastern Pennsylvania chapter of Americans for Democratic Action and both about to become members of the Rules Reform Commission. They had asked him for information and suggestions; Bode served as adviser to the reform caucus from that time forward. In large part, he drafted the document which would emerge from the truncated reform commission:

> In Pennsylvania, Jeanne Simon called the Center, or maybe it was Steve Sheller. I went to a Philadelphia meeting, held in Sheller's law firm, late at night.

> I went back and wrote a report. *We* wrote the report, but it went out under the imprimatur of the Pennsylvania reform commission subcommittee. We had such good access that we could do this.[10]

During April and May, while the functioning part of this commission was going about its business, those who had withdrawn from its proceedings were largely inactive. Their real leadership remained with Peter J. Camiel, chairman of the Philadelphia City Committee. It was Camiel who had recognized the need for his personal rules experts and Camiel who had asked Gene Maier to gear up for the job:

> I did not ask for a seat on the second reform commission. But I was a vocal expert on the rules, and someone had to negotiate. I had demonstrated an interest in writing rules, and I was competent to do it. There weren't a lot of other people who could say that on the State Committee.

In part because the extent of this breakdown was itself an item of disagreement, outsiders, even in the office of the governor, did not fully appreciate its significance. Moreover, the reform faction on the commission continued to press ahead. On June 12, it formally adopted recommendations for reform of the Pennsylvania Democratic party, not just of its regulations for delegate selection but of its internal rules of procedure as well.

Despite the bravado, this was to be the commission's last act. Another month would pass before the demise of this second commission was generally recognized, but its collapse would then be evidently, dramatically, confirmed. Nevertheless, in an attempt to rally the party behind its proposed rules, Gerald A. New, chief assistant to John Scales, notified the members of the state committee, the members of the reform commission, and National Chairman O'Brien of a meeting of the full state committee at which party reform would be addressed.[11]

Gene Maier was enraged by his notification, by the draft report he received, and by the scheduled meeting to consider it. He fired back immediately with a document of his own, which, he asserted, might just as well be taken as the commission's report. He covered it with a broadside to all members of the state committee, urging them to disavow the Malloy proposal:

> The AnnaMaria Malloy draft never went through the Rules Commission at all. I had to come up with my own draft as a response. The Commission never really had a report. The AnnaMaria Malloy draft triggered a letter from me censuring her. That was a letter to all State Committee members. "She is not the Chairman. This is not a document from the Rules Commission."

Jerry New continued with his preparations for the meeting on June 26, crossing his fingers all the while. When the day came, however, the proposed reforms failed simply for lack of a quorum. Some of the missing committee members surely faced legitimate scheduling conflicts, since the session was a special one, announced on short notice. But many just as surely stayed away from sheer dislike of the substance. Their inclination to boycott, rather than fight, stemmed from a desire not to stand publicly against Governor Shapp, with whom they might still hope to develop a working relationship. Their response was as effective as any veto.[12]

For a short period after the June meeting, the Rules Reform Commission continued to serve as the framework within which private negotiations about party reform took place and as the legitimizer from which key members drew their warrant to participate. Gene Maier, for one side, and Steve Sheller, for the other, met several times to try to develop a plan which would satisfy both factions. The sticking point continued to be the required change in the basic institution for delegate selection. The regulars were not inclined to surrender the delegate primary; the reformers saw no way to maintain it and still meet the letter, much less the spirit, of national guidelines. With no real room for compromise, and with no external incentive for creating room, Maier and Sheller could make little headway. Their conversations gradually petered out:

> Steve Sheller and I began to hammer out the rules privately. I would have my draft, and Sheller would try to change the language. After three or four such meetings, we finally had no more meetings.
>
> We may actually have agreed on Senatorial Districts [as the units for electing delegates]. But the central issue was presidential preference, which is to say, different wording on the notice requirement.

A "Deal" on Party Reform

By the summer of 1971, the status of party reform in Pennsylvania was confused even for indigenous actors—and was incomprehensible to outsiders. Bob Nelson, watching from the Party Structure Commission, could make little sense of developments in the Keystone State but felt pessimistic about them:

> We did not have a warm relationship with the State Chairman in Pennsylvania at any time. He ignored our letters and did not return our phone calls. We then dealt with House Majority Leader Leroy Irvis, and he and his staff came down several times. But even in 1971, there was not much contact. Fraser had begun

going to state legislatures, and we offered them this. They said, "No, we're doing okay. Don't worry about us." We could not really force ourselves on the state. We didn't know whether their assurances were real; we usually assumed when we got the brush-off that the state did not intend to comply.

Confusion, at the very least, was justified. On the state level alone, there were four major operating entities in Pennsylvania reform politics. There was the office of the governor, backed by the prestige, commitment, and perquisites of Milton Shapp. There was the office of the state chairman, where John Scales had formal authority but was informally pressed between his governor on the one side and his state committee on the other. There was the organized party, centered on the state committee but ceding effective authority to Pete Camiel of the Philadelphia City Committee. And there was the established reform faction, based largely in the activist community outside the regular party, coordinated, to some extent, by groups like Americans for Democratic Action and the New Democratic Coalition, and featuring almost as many aspiring leaders as ostensible members.

Moreover, the issues raised in Pennsylvania by national reform directives played across these indigenous actors in unpredictable ways. The biggest substantive issue of all, the mandated switch from a delegate to a candidate primary, did feature the governor and the reform faction against the organized party, with the state chairman tiptoeing in between. But there were other, lesser questions, like the standard for intrastate apportionment and the district appropriate to delegate selection, which produced noticeably different alignments.

Matters were made worse by the fact that there were three separate sources of advice and pressure on the national level, each of which had one primary contact within the state and each of which offered its own interpretations and suggestions without much concern for the advice of others. The office of the national chairman worked principally with the governor and his staff. The Party Structure Commission worked principally with the state chairman and his staff. The Center for Political Reform provided ideas and initiatives to the indigenous reform faction. Only hard-line regulars used no national counterpart—there being none to complement the regular party—and relied on a technical spokesman from the local level, Gene Maier of Philadelphia.[13]

This entire mix of national actors, state actors, and national reform directives was compounded, finally, by a set of state reform issues. As an indigenous reform process had emerged, fractionated and nebulous though it was, local actors had appended their favorite causes, in the hope of using national pressure for state party goals. Because the regular party intended to maintain a role in delegate selection, for example, and because the governor wanted to restructure its highest official organ, the State Central Committee, he had insisted that its reapportionment be grafted onto the reform of delegate selection. By the same token, because the regular party wanted to remain central to delegate selection at other levels as well, and because state reformers hoped to break up the regular party organization, they had insisted that all party officials with a role in selecting delegates be directly elected.

At any rate, when the state committee turned down the product of the second Pennsylvania reform commission in June of 1971—or rather, when it failed even to muster a quorum—the reform process might have been pronounced moribund by all. Or at least, it might easily have been ignored until the winter of 1971–72, when it would be possible to count the number of other state parties in compliance with national recommendations and to judge whether Pennsylvania was practically forced to act.

That this did not occur was a reflection of the commitment of the governor to reform in the abstract and thus to compliance with these particular reform guidelines. In July and August of 1971, Governor Shapp began to press Chairman Scales again, and Scales's assistant, Jerry New, began to shuttle back and forth among the governor's office, the reform faction, and the state party organization, seeking a way out of the existing impasse. The state legislative calendar added urgency, since if the state committee could not ratify a reform plan by fall, the legislature could not act on it until delegate selection was already under way. New saw his informal consultations as the last hope for reform in Pennsylvania:

> The logistics of holding those meetings wore people out. The working element of the party just couldn't sustain those people who had nothing else to do, like the reformers.
> I always tried to play the "third man" role, which works better when you're not in a meeting. . . . I became the broker. A set of rules would come from southeastern Pennsylvania, what they would like to see. The National Committee would send us rules. You could say that a set of rules, then, came out of a *process*, but it was not coming out of *commission* meetings.

Gradually, as this three-cornered discussion moved into September, the less proximate issues—and some of the participants—were stripped away. First, Scales jettisoned the locally generated reforms for the election of party officials. Their backers, the state reform faction, had been initially handicapped by their inability to settle on one clear, unofficial spokesman. They were ultimately overridden because of their weakness within the state committee, which would have to adopt any successful compromise. In the course of telling state reformers that their proposals had gone by the boards, New told them that their role in reform negotiations had been abrogated:

> The southeastern Pennsylvania people tended to like me or hate me, depending on what was going on. Malloy, Sheller, Patane, and Pevar, they had a real problem of acceptability with the regular Democrats because they had never won anything, except their own posts, which down there don't mean anything. Gene Maier spoke, but Pete Camiel did the negotiating. Pete said that the Democratic party had to *win;* he wanted a technique that he could win with.

Next, the governor agreed to defer efforts at reapportioning the State Central Committee. Shapp had come to believe that adoption of new rules for delegate selection would in fact make it *easier,* over time, to obtain his wishes. If he withdrew his demand for reapportionment temporarily, he might create a procedural trap: The reform of delegate selection would be nearly accomplished; the members of the state committee would want to retain a role in this reformed process; their own apportionment would be the only item standing in their way.

What remained was a partial agreement on national reform demands including a specific agreement to move to the candidate primary. Most state actors were apparently united on—or resigned to—this package. National actors were sufficiently isolated to prevent their overturning this resolution. The key question remained the commitment of the state committee and, behind it, of the organized party in general. Aspiring reform plans had been killed before by last-minute opposition from the regular party. Reform drafters hoped that they had removed the incentives for similar action again.

This hope was based specifically on the substance of the proposed reform package. But it was buttressed generally by growing practical links between the governor and the organized party. Since his inauguration, the governor had been seeking a modus vivendi with sitting party officials. The key element had been gubernatorial patronage, and while its application had been a source of continuing tension, the passage of time had still built some ties based on that application. Within this framework, then, Chairman Scales and his staff prepared to present a reform document to the fall meeting of the State Central Committee. They believed that a committee majority was available for this document, but because they only *thought* so, Scales invited Shapp to attend, in case a few words from the governor were needed to solidify a shaky consensus.

The state committee assembled in the Penn Harris Hotel in Harrisburg on September 25, 1971. After a substantial amount of procedural business, the proposed new rules were introduced, described, and offered for adoption. At that point, Gene Maier rose and moved to strike the provision requiring candidates for delegate to indicate a presidential preference. The impact of Maier's motion, of course, was to retain the delegate primary—and to refuse the major national demand upon the Pennsylvania reform process.[14]

A standing vote followed, and the call of the affirmatives suggested that Maier's motion would pass decisively, so decisively that it could not be overturned by rhetorical flourishes from the governor. New had hoped that the crucial votes of the Philadelphia City Committee had been corralled behind these rules, but city committee members were voting yes on the amendment before the house and taking many other members of the state committee with them. Maier offered their continuing opposition to an institutional change which would diminish the role of the regular party as the justification for his move:

> Basically, the position that our side took was that anyone who wanted to run for an office should be able to do so, and should *have* to do so on his own merits. You run as a fraud now, because you aren't being forced to honor your commitments. There is no way to enforce his decision, because you can't disfranchise him if he doesn't live up to them. You're taking a lottery four months in advance.

At that point, Governor Shapp requested a temporary recess, before the final tally could be completed. Chairman Scales obtained the recess, and Shapp, Scales, Maier, and New retreated to a private room on the second floor. Shapp asked Maier to call Pete Camiel in Philadelphia, to see if some understanding could be reached then and there:

> There was a meeting on the presidential preference provision. I could have kept that out. The Governor attended the meeting and waited through all the other State Committee business. Shapp was incredulous when I turned out to have the votes against it; New had said that they had the votes.
> Scales quickly recessed the meeting and went upstairs. Scales brought in Shapp to talk to me. I said Camiel opposed this, even though New had told Shapp that he had the votes. Shapp got Camiel on the phone, and he talked to me, and I then agreed to defer to Shapp.

Part of this conversation, perhaps the larger part in elapsed time, concerned the reform package before the house. Camiel expressed anxiety that the rules being voted might include provisions extending beyond delegate selection; Shapp repeated his belief that they did not and promised to support removing any such provisions which did turn up, at least for that session. Camiel requested specific assurances that some local party rules which had been included in earlier drafts, like the direct election of county chairmen, would never reappear; Shapp again assented. On those grounds, Camiel agreed that the remaining standards for delegate selection could be termed acceptable.

Part of this conversation, however, and perhaps the crucial part for its substantive outcome, concerned not provisions for delegate selection but operating norms for the channeling and dispersal of patronage. Camiel was interested in a central place in an evolving dispersal arrangement. Once he had demonstrated his political relevance—once he had shown that he could hold up reforms which the governor had sought for a year but about which he (Camiel) cared much less—the chairman of the Philadelphia City Committee relented and agreed to support those reforms. New believed that the issue of future working relationships was really the dominant, if less explicit, consideration in the understanding which Shapp and Camiel reached on the long-distance line:

> I could judge the details of that conversation, from being there and from being told things afterwards, but I don't think it would be right to talk about them. You should remember, however, that the patronage battles were going on at this time. Not just the usual battles over patronage but also the fight by Shapp to get control of the State Committee through patronage.

After this telephone exchange, the four princpals—Shapp, Scales, New, and Maier—returned to the meeting below and called it back to order. Maier withdrew his proposed amendment. Scales requested a motion on the original reform package. And this time, with the active support of the Philadelphia City Committee, extensively revised rules for delegate selection easily passed within the Pennsylvania Democratic party.

Implications

Even after passage of a comprehensive reform plan, there were still a series of minor substantive adjustments, and thus of minor political conflicts, before Pennsylvania could be certified as complying with all eighteen guidelines. Despite these, the big event in Pennsylvania reform politics had been the state committee meeting; the big substantive change had been the shift to a candidate primary; the remaining issues and conflicts were resolved, almost ineluctably, in line with these earlier developments.

The story of reform politics in Pennsylvania offered all the elements characterizing state reform politics nationwide, on a scale a trifle larger than life and with a touch of last-minute drama not consistently attained elsewhere. In the first phase of reform politics, a classic incarnation of the orthodox Democratic coalition—a strong organized party, along with a major labor movement—squared off against a classic version of the emerging, alternative coalition—an established reform faction, along with a range of militant, liberal groups. The confrontation was no contest. Party regulars did, admittedly, appoint an indigenous reform commission, in the aftermath of the 1968 primary. But they first stacked its membership and then encouraged these members to follow their instincts. The reform commission expired from inactivity; party reform appeared to die with it.

The reform process, however, was resuscitated at a stroke by the election—in fact, the mere nomination—of a "reform Democrat" for governor. When Milton Shapp actually secured the governorship, a second reform commission followed quickly. This second commission was tilted toward the reformers; after an internal split, reform members pressed ahead to an aggressive report. Yet during the time that reform politics was the province of this commission, party reform was destined to languish. Indeed, regular party members killed the report of this commission in the most ignominious way possible: They failed to show up for the state committee meeting which addressed it. Party reform appeared to die again.

Only when the governor himself stepped in and pressed for immediate, decentralized, private negotiations did a reform process worthy of the name finally emerge. Even then, the governor could secure the resulting reform package only by delaying his own local preferences, by discarding the local preferences of the established reform faction, and by securing a last-minute deal with the "boss" of the Philadelphia party.

The role of a new, reform governor was highlighted by contrast with the neighboring state of New York. New York faced roughly the same procedural violations as Pennsylvania, including the central demand for an end to the delegate primary. But while New York was also an organized-party state, its regular party was in fact weaker than that of Pennsylvania, while its established reform faction was far stronger. With that as framework, New York, too, went on to nominate a self-consciously reform-oriented candidate for governor, the former justice of the Supreme Court, Arthur J. Goldberg. Where New York differed from Pennsylvania, of course, was that this Democratic candidate lost. Nelson A. Rockefeller, the incumbent Republican, was re-elected, and that was ultimately the determining event in reform politics. Pennsylvania, with its new Democratic governor, moved haltingly toward compliance. New York, with no change in its effective party leadership, never came into compliance at all.

The introduction of a new Democratic governor, especially one with a self-conscious attachment to reform, was thus the critical event in reform politics in Pennsylvania, as it would be in many of the seventeen states which acquired new governors in the general election of 1970. Yet even then, and even in a "tough case" like Pennsylvania, the influence of national party reformers—and of the elaborated reform interpretations which they had developed—was ever present and consequential.

In fact, the insistence of the Party Structure Commission on abolishing the delegate primary provided the substantive context for reform politics in Pennsylvania from February of 1970, when the compliance letters were mailed, through September of 1971, when the state committee capitulated. Earlier, in the case of Alabama, national reformers had been the ones to capitulate, when they waived the demand for a shift to the candidate primary. Six months later, in the case of Pennsylvania, they refused to waive the same rule, and protracted negotiations—followed by an eventual, hard-won victory—resulted.

Local rules experts were unaware of the differing treatment accorded Alabama and Pennsylvania. But they were very conscious of the apparent maneuvering room in the national guidelines as adopted. They were, accordingly, also conscious of the deliberate constrictions introduced into these guidelines by the Party Structure staff, through the Model Party Rules. If there had been an alternative source of expertise at the national level—within the National Committee, among the state chairmen as a collectivity, or even at the AFL-CIO—rules experts in Pennsylvania would certainly have used it to try to loosen these constrictions. But there was no such operation, and Gene Maier was left railing bootlessly at national constraints:

> I went to Washington several times. AnnaMaria Malloy, Pevar, New, and I went to see Fraser and Nelson. I said that the rules implied that you didn't have to do it [indicate presidential preference] on the ballot. I said that we would publicize it in the newspapers instead. They said we couldn't do that, although they had no rational reason for it.

The resolution in Pennsylvania, a trade for gubernatorial patronage in return for institutional structure, was an archetypal "deal" in the old-fashioned sense, and this was its final, distinguishing feature. Deals were hardly new to Pennsylvania politics; they were hardly new to democratic politics in general. The regulars perceived them as normal; the reformers derided them but, in the name of reform, endorsed them on the crassest level.

It was possible to stigmatize both sides.[15] Yet this was probably unfair and inappropriate. For what was really at issue were the normal—essential— activities of party politics in a democracy. Perhaps the usual brokerage approach of continuing party officials should have been restrained in the case of *the rules of the game,* but those raised in the brokerage ethic were not guaranteed to perceive that. Perhaps those who touted a "new politics" should have accepted a defeat in the name of principle, but if the principle in question was inconsistent with democratic politics, there was no reason to demand that reformers reject political reality as they found it.

At any rate, the acquiescence of Pennsylvania, in and of itself, was a major contribution to institutional change. A substantial element of that change—the fundamental shift from a delegate to a candidate primary—came directly out of the state committee meeting of September 25, 1971. Pennsylvania would have the third largest delegation at the 1972 Convention. The selection of that delegation was effectively reformed.

Yet the acquiescence of Pennsylvania was a contribution in several other ways as well. The fall of Pennsylvania automatically raised the total of states which were going to be in substantial compliance, thereby raising the potential penalty for those inclined to resist. Moreover, as a large and reliably Democratic state, the value of Pennsylvania was increased for reformers, because Pennsylvania itself was an obvious candidate for resistance and an obvious leader for other, potential holdouts. When it fell, the cause of party reform gained by far more than an addend of one.

Pennsylvania was perhaps even more significant for what it implied about prospects for elite replacement in the national Democratic party. As always, these prospects were tied to institutional change; in a direct sense, Pennsylvania had obviously contributed to that. But beyond this, reform politics in Pennsylvania had formed up exactly as it had at the national level when these reforms were being drafted, with similar social coalitions backing similar policy preferences.

In Pennsylvania, reform politics had pitted a well-articulated, local version of the orthodox Democratic coalition against a well-articulated, local version of the emerging, aspiring alternative. Moreover, each side had not only manifested its expected abstract posture toward party reform, but had gone on to recognize its specific, practical stake in the existing arrangements or their proposed substitute. When the reformers, after two false starts and a last, desperate deal, then won the contest, the stage was set—the institutions were in place—for the circulation of elites in presidential politics in the state of Pennsylvania and presumably in presidential politics at the national level as well.

The triumph of party reform was hardly guaranteed to be permanent, either in Pennsylvania or in the national party. In Pennsylvania, that triumph had been evidently dependent on a peculiar conjunction of circumstances. Even then, it had required the stripping away of all other, state-based reform proposals. Beyond that, it had left the regular party in position to attempt a recovery of its institutional influence in the future. Despite all this, it had come within a whisker of failing.

Yet these qualifications on the triumph of reform could be easily overstated. For the institutional rules which were the immediate embodiment of this triumph were not easily displaced. And the elite replacement associated with them, even if it required several elections for its realization, was likely to receive those elections. Over time, these new rules would at least have their full opportunity to produce new political actors who had benefited from their implementation—and who would be prepared, in turn, to fight for their retention. Beyond that, there would be other, intrinsic, automatic mechanisms for their defense as well.

Foremost among these was the normal inertia of politics. Existing arrangements enjoy an inherent advantage. Their continuation requires no mobilization, no coordination, no negotiation; their alteration does. Moreover, intervening events frequently, inadvertently, change the agenda of politics. Institutional reform can thus decline, and not just rise, as a matter with a claim on the attention of political actors. When it does, the institutional forms which are already in place ordinarily remain there.

More concretely, the politics contributing to the adoption of new institutional arrangements had created some additional buttresses of its own. The most obvious of these were the allied reformers, who had been mobilized between 1968 and 1972 and who would presumably remain available to sustain their product between 1972 and 1976, when these reformed rules became the ones with the organizational advantage of inertia. Indeed, if these rules worked as their drafters intended, the ranks of the reform coalition should be increased, win or lose, in the aftermath of the 1972 campaign. By the same token, the advantage in being publicly allied with reform in the abstract would presumably continue, too. This was hardly sufficient to protect the resulting institutional matrix if most active participants judged that it had worked badly. But it would make it very difficult to mount a coordinated, public campaign to "turn back the clock" and return to prereform, party-based arrangements.

Under those conditions, the political world itself could shift as a result of events in states like Pennsylvania during 1970 and 1971. The temporary triumph of a local reform coalition, as coordinated and supported by a national counterpart, could produce institutional change at the local level. These local institutions, when summed for the nation as a whole, could create a sharply different matrix for delegate selection and presidential nomination.

If that matrix succeeded in removing the regular party from the politics of presidential selection—and it had been designed specifically with this in mind—then the contours of the political world would shift sharply. If these new institutional arrangements also advantaged a noticeably different group of political actors—again, they had been designed to correspond with the political experiences and attributes of some members of an aspiring, alternative coalition—then a replacement in national Democratic elites would be one of the clearest signs of an altered political world. Finally, if reformed rules responded to a changed set of political attributes, and if different social groups possessed these attributes and thus succeeded under reformed rules, then the elite structure of the national Democratic party, or even of the national Republican party, should be markedly different—and in all probability there would be no turning back.

The Battle for Official Status:

The Preliminary Call and the Fate

of the Guidelines

IN WHICH, relevant actors prepare for the appearance of the guidelines before the National Committee; the national chairman, the key actor in this presentation, develops an elaborate strategy to guarantee passage, and most other, potential influencers either pass up the meeting or find their influence severely limited. AND IN WHICH, reform politics reaches a climax within the national party; proposals for sweeping institutional change, with the potential to rebound and alter the National Committee itself, finally go before the committee; and the orthodox Democratic coalition fails to discover any vehicle to coordinate its opposition to reform.

WHILE the state developments triggered by the 1970 election were only beginning to unfold, the politics of party reform moved back to Washington for one short, sharp, explicitly national interlude. In early 1971, the National Committee assembled to address a Preliminary Call to the 1972 Convention. That Call inevitably contained an official, national policy on delegate selection. The process of framing that policy provided an unavoidable encounter between the regular party and the issue of party reform. To date, the National Committee, the highest continuing organ in the regular party structure, had been carefully and deliberately screened out of reform politics. On February 19, 1971, it would enter that politics in the most portentous way possible—it would confront the recommendations of its national reform commissions. What survived would become the certified definition of party reform, for regulars and reformers, for the national party and its constituent units.

Two successive national chairmen, for quite different reasons, had kept the National Committee at arm's length from the reform process. During the politics of recommendation, Fred Harris had tried to insulate the committee, so that the Party Structure Commission could produce an aggressive set of proposals for reform. During the politics of implementation, Larry O'Brien had tried to keep the committee at a similar distance, so that he could become the central figure in negotiations over compliance with those proposals.

With the arrival of the first meeting of the National Committee for 1971, this policy had to change. The winter meeting of the National Committee in the year preceding a national convention is traditionally the one at which a Preliminary Call to that convention is adopted. The Preliminary Call traditionally contains the rules which will govern the convention itself. Before 1971, this situation was rarely worth remarking, since these rules rarely changed in ways worth the attention of committee members. In 1971, however, the Preliminary Call was qualitatively different from its predecessors: It contained a proposal for comprehensive, historically unprecedented, planned reform of party procedures for delegate selection and presidential nomination.

As a result, the meeting of the National Committee on the Preliminary Call became the occasion for the national embodiment of the regular party to enter the politics of party reform. Nevertheless, the maneuvering to influence this crucial meeting featured a curious disproportion to its place in the total chronicle of reform politics. Not only was the jockeying in preparation for adoption of a Preliminary Call confined almost entirely within the National Committee; effective maneuvering there was confined almost entirely within the office of the national chairman.

There was no shortage of other actors with an apparent stake in the response of the National Committee. State and national reformers, state party leaders, incoming governors old and new, and the leaders of organized labor—to list only the most obvious—had extended grounds for concern with the committee response to the Preliminary Call. Yet most of these groups passed up the attempt at influencing this crucial meeting, and the rest discovered that the committee context reduced their efforts to insignificance. By design and by default, then, the principal actor in reform politics before the February meeting of the National Committee was its formal leader, the national chairman. His wishes became the draft for committee consideration. His maneuvers became the buffer between that draft and the normal, institutionalized disposition of the committee to oppose systematic reform.

Chairman O'Brien started with an ambitious goal. He aspired to take the handiwork of the Party Structure Commission through the National Commit-

tee, essentially intact. To that end, he began by manipulating the text of reform recommendations, the substantive content of the committee meeting.
The chairman followed by lobbying his committee members, offering a mix
of arguments and incentives to the major blocs which he perceived among
them. He closed by adjusting the formal agenda for the committee session
itself.

When this was done, the crucial meeting of the National Committee in
the entire politics of party reform had arrived. If the committee reacted negatively, a reform drive which had begun at the 1968 Convention might not
endure until 1972. If the committee tinkered extensively, the fate of implementation would be more dependent than ever on subsequent negotiations
with—and within—the individual state parties. If the committee was basically
agreeable, or merely acquiescent, these reform proposals would acquire the
largest grant of formal authority they could practically attain.

Should the National Committee follow this latter course—willingly or un-
willingly, knowingly or not—it would contribute to a major institutional
change within the Democratic party. In doing so, however, it would also contribute—by how much, no one could know—to a second, major institutional
reconstruction, in the organization and composition of the National Committee itself. In the process, it would summon to power an alternative coalition
of Democratic elites—and institutionalize that coalition so that it could not
easily be dislodged and replaced.

The National Committee as an Arena for Reform

The National Committee which had to reach these decisions was widely
perceived as hostile to party reform. Most analysts, and certainly most reformers, used a grand, gross, institutional extrapolation to come to this conclusion.
They saw the committee as the capstone of the regular party. They reasoned
that this ultimate bastion of party regularity ought naturally to oppose reforms
aimed at reducing the value of party office.[1]

On this grand level, these analysts were not inaccurate. Yet the premises
upon which they based their deductions were so flawed, and the lack of discrimination in their picture of the committee was so extreme, that they seriously misconstrued committee operations. The committee encompassed considerable diversity in the character of its members, a diversity not irrelevant
to the course of reform politics. If other, equally ill-perceived factors still made
the committee an inhospitable environment for reform, its peculiar internal

character also permitted a broader range of potential responses than outside observers might credit.

The standard external analysis of the National Committee, and of its probable response to specific proposals for party reform, ignored the variation internal to the committee. Half of the state parties which composed the national party, after all, were volunteer rather than organized; volunteer parties had consistently been more responsive to exhortations toward party reform. The presence of delegates from both party types was, in fact, the essence of complaints from committee members like Joseph M. Barr of Pennsylvania, an unrepentant spokesman for party regularity:

> You had the tail wagging the dog in the National Committee. Pennsylvania and the others could not resist. A state like South Dakota had the same number of representatives as Ohio or Pennsylvania or California. You've got two people from every state. Smaller states don't look at the voting power of the big states. They're not practical on these matters. They just expect us to do their business.

Moreover, many committee members, especially in organized-party states, were less immediately attached to state party politics than an uninformed observer might suspect. It was quite common for a seat on the committee to be a reward for *past* party service; individuals holding their seats on this basis did not experience the direct problems which implementation and compliance were presenting to their state chairmen. These were the members whom Don Fraser had in mind when he characterized the committee:

> The other thing is that many of the National Committee members are not involved in the day-to-day operation of the parties. One of the major complaints is that they are not tied into ongoing politics. It was a way to kick people upstairs, to reward good *old* Joe Blow. That was another reason not to think about what it would mean.

On the other hand, despite the numerical importance of members from volunteer parties, and despite the practical detachment of some members from organized parties, too, the committee was not even close to a practical balance between sympathizers and opponents of reform. Two *other* factors—the method of selecting members for the committee and the career patterns in politics of those who eventually arrived—were far more central to its composite orientation toward reform.

Perhaps the primary factor shaping the orientation of National Committee members was the institutional method of their selection. At bottom, most members were still chosen through a regular party structure, that is, through a ladder of party offices, and members chosen in this way were likely to share an aversion to party reform. Even committee members from volunteer-party states normally came up through a regular party, skeletal though it might be. Many of these individuals still identified strongly with that party structure and remained concerned about its organizational health—and organizational perquisites.[2]

Beyond this, the detachment of some members from their local political parties made these members on average more, not less, committed to party regularity—and thus more hostile to party reform. Senior members who had arrived on the National Committee in return for prior party service were often the product of a political party closer in operation to the organized-party model than the one which currently operated in their home territory. Their reference points had been developed in an environment where party regularity was far more demanding. Joe Barr of Pennsylvania was an excellent example:

> I paid some attention to the McGovern-Fraser Commission at the time, when they were drawing those up. When the commission published those rules, I refused to read them because they were so silly. I thought a lot of it was deliberately provoking, in fact. . . .
>
> You had to be practical, cold-blooded, but have forward-looking programs. That's what I wanted. I favored progressive programs but very practical party business. That's what I did here in Pittsburgh. That's what the national party used to do, too, with Kennedy, Johnson.

The National Committee which emerged from closer examination, then, was much like the one more distant observers perceived. It was characterized by a strong and general, if vague and unfocused, hostility toward reform, along with a much more explicit concern for the well-being of the regular party. Indeed, if there *had* been any creeping reform sympathy among this overwhelmingly regular group, it was surely counteracted by one other characteristic of reform politics. This was the fundamental *social* difference between most committee members and the partisans of party reform. The members almost uniformly perceived this distinction, in social background, in prior political experience, and in contemporary views about political life. They felt the very real hostility associated with the division; they did not desire to advantage those on the other side. Barr vented these feelings strongly:

> All these do-gooders, *they* were the ones who were raising hell. They agreed to let us *sit* with the delegation if we weren't elected. Can you imagine that? *They,* people who had never given a damn for the party, were telling *us* that *we* could sit with *our* party!

345

Where the moderating factors in this analysis—the differing character of the state parties and the detachment of some state representatives—came back into the picture, then, was not in shaping basic orientations toward reform. Instead, it was in contributing some additional possibilities to the outcome within an inherently suspicious National Committee. The existing variability in party background among committee members did suggest that member-by-member attempts to rally support for particular options on the Preliminary Call might not be entirely fruitless. Moreover, the comparative detachment of many committee members from party politics in their home states went on to suggest that these individuals might be responsive not just to the views of local party leaders, but to other pressures which could be introduced on the way to the National Committee meeting and, in fact, to the internal dynamics of the meeting itself.

As a result, the National Committee which emerged from a close examination in 1971 was not unlike the National Committee which had long been recognized by professional students of party politics:

> The literature which purports to be about the national committees is mainly about the chairmen and national staffs of the committees. It could hardly be otherwise, for the national committees themselves are large groups of people variously selected, representing different amounts and kinds of local political interests, who come together now and then to vote on matters of undifferentiated triviality or importance, about which they are largely uninformed and in which they are often uninterested.
>
> This may appear to be a harsh or smart-aleck description of the national committees of the major American political parties. It is neither. There are many good reasons that the committees, as groups of committeemen and committeewomen, cannot be more significant bodies at this stage in the evolution of the American party system. The committee chairmen and national bureaucracy may be, and often are, people who have considerable personal and institutional influence. But the committees, as committees, are important mainly for what they will acquiesce in, rather than what they will propose or decide.[3]

One facet of state party politics, however, did promise a more direct, if still imprecise, impact on the fate of reform within the National Committee. This was the compliance status of the individual states in early 1971. Compliance status alone was unlikely to determine either the response of individual members to the guidelines as a package or the response of the committee as a whole to any individual guideline. But it did constrain the committee in one important respect.

A small group of states—Alabama, Iowa, Maine, Mississippi, and North

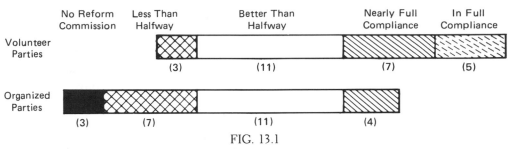

FIG. 13.1

Compliance Status of the State Parties: January 7, 1971

Carolina—had been certified in full compliance by January of 1971. Another small group—Hawaii, Kansas, and Rhode Island—had refused even to appoint a state reform commission. Of the forty-three states strung out in between, eleven were rated by the commission staff as in nearly full compliance; twenty-two were said to be better than halfway there; ten were considered to meet less than 50 percent of commission guidelines. (See figure 13.1.)[4] Geri Joseph, vice chairman of the National Committee, noted the situation at the time:

> All the states were attempting to come into compliance with *some* of the guidelines. You have to remember what the reforms said that they were trying to do. They had all the good words. They had all the things we say we believe in, and a lot of people in the party really do believe in.

The overall compliance mosaic could predict little about the response of the National Committee to specific suggestions for reform. A majority of states, after all, could be in compliance with one guideline and out of compliance with the next. Beyond that, the transfer between the compliance status of a state and the vote of its committee members was inevitably inexact. Yet this compliance mosaic did compress the *range* within which the committee was likely to act.

If a healthy majority of states could already satisfy over half the guidelines, there was little likelihood that the National Committee would rise up and strike them down in their entirety. Such an action would bootlessly invite open warfare within the national party; it would deliberately court a bad press from those predisposed toward reform in the abstract. On the other hand, if an overwhelming majority of states were not yet in compliance, and if solid majorities were out of compliance with a number of individual guidelines, there remained a great potential for amendment. The search for these amendments, then, was likely to be the heart of committee politics on the Preliminary Call.

347

A Strategy for the National Chairman

Formal responsibility for arranging the committee meeting on the Preliminary Call rested, of course, with the national chairman. Beyond that, practical accountability for the outcome of this meeting would be lodged primarily at the chairman's door, regardless of the formal situation. Together, these factors, as magnified by the substantive importance of this particular Preliminary Call, would probably have thrown any national chairman into action. Yet Chairman O'Brien had long since invested his political fortunes in the outcome of this session, so that he possessed personal as well as institutional stakes. As the time of decision approached, the orientation of O'Brien became crucial.

He never evidently wavered. From the first, O'Brien planned to take the guidelines through the National Committee; in doing so, he hoped to make those guidelines the official rules of the national party. This course of action was in part a response to incentives present in O'Brien's political environment since the day of his return. The need for some detailed rules to govern delegate selection, for example, appeared even more pressing with a Preliminary Call to the 1972 Convention at hand. Time had run out for any new reform process, to develop a different set of rules for examination by the National Committee. Dick Wade, commission consultant, saw O'Brien press ahead on his previously chosen course:

> Larry had made a simple calculation: There's less trouble in going with them than in trying to turn them down. What Larry thought about the idea *in toto* I don't know, but by the time he got to that stage, he showed not the slightest reservation.

The continued, aggressive support of the chairman for commission guidelines was in part a response to newer, parallel incentives as well, some of which he had indirectly generated. At a minimum, the report of the Party Structure Commission was no longer merely a document on the political landscape; it was in effect in a number of states and on the way in a number of others. This motion could not steamroll the National Committee, but it was an added pressure. More critically, the chairman had been actively facilitating this improved compliance situation by his emphasis on the virtues of reform. Privately, this had created a set of implicit commitments to those who had followed his exhortations. Publicly, it had created perhaps a more serious pressure through the continued emphasis on reform as a public relations device. Jean Westwood, national committeewoman from Utah, saw the new pressure which these stands, public and private, had generated for their proponent:

Larry kept stressing the "good faith" efforts. They [the state chairmen] thought that if you changed the bylaws, you would have made the effort, and that was all that mattered—you'd never use them anyway. There had also been enough favorable press over the opening of the party, so that many members felt that if you rescinded this, it would look very bad. That was looking at the practical end.

A number of observers closer to the national chairman believed that something more was at work, however, more than old incentives, reinforced by new pressures. They believed, in essence, that O'Brien had become committed to party reform. These observers perceived him as arriving either at a belief that reform was inherently right, given past injustices and existing procedures within the party, or that reform was the wave of the future, and that he could either ride that wave or be swamped by it. Geri Joseph, much less convinced of the desirability of this outcome, noted the transformation in her national chairman: "We all had a general interest, but were also leery, of course. Larry, however, was totally committed to reform. Somewhere along the way he had gotten religion, and he never really gave it up."

Victor S. Navasky, a political journalist who had profiled O'Brien while the latter was helping to coordinate the Humphrey nomination campaign, had seen the seeds of this conversion even then.[5] Later, when O'Brien appeared to be facilitating the reform drive, Navasky took the actions of the chairman as presumptive evidence that these seeds had begun to germinate:

I don't remember whether I described O'Brien as a bridge between the old politics and the new politics or not in that article. I do know that I toyed around with the idea. I know that O'Brien did, too. And he did have this alter ego, this apparatchik [Ira Kapenstein], who believed it very much, and said it to me from time to time. I didn't think Kapenstein was as much of O'Brien's total story as many other people did, but they did. Anyhow, the idea was certainly around, and O'Brien certainly knew about it.

That got much stronger four years later, when there were all those rumors about a Vice Presidency, all those attempts to dangle it in front of him, all those closets reputed to be full of O'Brien bumper stickers, and so on. My piece that year was about Mankiewicz, not O'Brien, but I have no doubt that he had the bug by then. So maybe he was driven by that notion. Too bad if he was, since the bridge collapsed.

In any case, by the time an agenda for the February meeting of the National Committee had begun to take shape, the national chairman had put any private doubts about the guidelines behind him and had decided to marshal his resources to place them in the Preliminary Call. John G. Stewart, director of communications at the National Committee, watched him continue —indeed escalate—his previous support for reform:

It just reflected his sense that you have to go ahead. However difficult it may be, it can't be worse than redoing the work of the Commission, or of leaving them up in the air for later fights. You're dealing in a situation where the McGovern candidacy was hard to imagine. The Nixon candidacy looked vulnerable. The Muskie operation was leading Nixon in the polls, and getting organized.

The national chairman began his preparations for this crucial committee meeting with its substantive content. The core of the Preliminary Call actually involved not just the rules governing delegate selection, proposed by the Party Structure (McGovern) Commission, but the rules governing preparatory functions of the national convention itself, proposed by the Rules (O'Hara) Commission. Within the initial draft, O'Brien located four items which he believed would arouse general concern among National Committee members—and which aroused a parallel anxiety for the national chairman. Two of these, apportionment and credentialing, were, in fact, the province of the O'Hara Commission. The other two, ex officio and demographic representation, came from the McGovern Commission report.[6]

The proposed formula for interstate apportionment of delegates struck the chairman as most likely to inflame his members. The recommendation of the Rules Commission, based 50 percent on population and 50 percent on prior Democratic vote, was a major change from the existing bonus system; its costs and benefits were easily calculated; these would evidently injure the states which were most *over*represented in the National Committee. There seemed to be no chance of avoiding a battle over this proposed reform, and little chance of avoiding a defeat.

Under those conditions, O'Brien decided to add a formula of his own to the list of options. His new middle position, one far better suited to the committee context, was a formula based 50 percent on Democratic vote but 50 percent on size in the Electoral College, instead of raw population. This would recognize the winner-take-all character of the Electoral College; it would be far more charitable to the smaller states, and thus far more acceptable in a National Committee apportioned on strict state equality.

The other major provision from the Rules Commission, a set of regulations governing challenges to state credentials, was likely to provoke argument for a different reason. The arrangements coming forward to the National Committee had actually been a last-minute victory for conservative forces within the commission. Commission reformers were already planning an effort to overturn these provisions and substitute the version which they had replaced. In response, O'Brien decided to go with the original proposal for credentials reform. He could thus identify with the reform side of the commission debate. In the process, he could balance a move toward moderation on apportionment with a move toward stringency on credentialing.

In the report of the Party Structure Commission, O'Brien also found two items of concern. The first, and the one most likely to provoke discussion and then combat, was the commission stand on ex official delegates. Guideline C–1 (Automatic Delegates), appeared to eject outgoing members of the National Committee from promised seats in their state delegations. Committee members seemed unlikely, if they noticed anything, to miss this fact. Having noticed it, they seemed unlikely to accept it with grace.

O'Brien was not unsympathetic to his members on this provision. The sitting members of the National committee, after all, were the ones who sustained the party in the period between conventions, and who created the convention itself. Nevertheless, an ex officio entitlement ran patently counter to the thrust of most guidelines in the commission report. To ease the pain of dispossession, O'Brien proposed giving every current member of the Committee, who was not re-elected or selected as a normal member of his state delegation, all rights and privileges of delegate status, *except* the right to vote.

The national chairman also expected a good deal of questioning—steady, hostile, and perhaps intense—on the commission proposal for demographic representation. There was no conceivable majority for demographic quotas within the National Committee, so that the tendency to fight about demographic representation hinged crucially on whether the members believed that Guidelines A–1 and A–2 implied demographic requirements. O'Brien determined to assure his members that they did not, by pointing to those aspects of the commission report which supported this interpretation and by providing whatever additional guarantees were necessary.

With those four provisions—a new formula for interstate apportionment, the original proposal for credentials proceedings, augmented privileges at the national convention for outgoing committee members, and systematic reassurances about the status of demographic quotas—O'Brien completed his initial substantive review. The attempt to sell these revisions to the members, as desirable changes and as the *only* desirable changes, might turn up additional needs for amendment. Barring that, these four policy proposals, with only two real policy amendments, would be the personal position of the national chairman.

As a package, these adjustments had one other noteworthy characteristic: They altered both major proposals from the Rules Commission; they touched nothing, except rhetorically, in the entire report of the Party Structure Commission. Stated differently, if the national chairman had gauged his committee correctly, and if he could sell these proposed changes as the necessary amendments to his two commission reports, *the recommendations of the Party Structure Commission would go through the National Committee and become national policy essentially intact.*

These substantive adjustments were a plausible anticipatory response to the National Committee context. Having developed them, the national chairman turned to rallying the committee behind his draft Preliminary Call. In the weeks leading up to the February 19 meeting, O'Brien worked his committee intensively. On the long-distance telephone, the chairman, or occasionally his assistant, Bill Welsh, sought out individual members and urged them toward the chairman's preferences. O'Brien, in effect, divided his committee into four rough blocs, with four differentiable orientations toward party reform. To these blocs, he presented four separate, comprehensive arguments, mixing and matching assertions about the ethical virtues of proposed reforms, the practical impact of formal rules, the strategic constraints on the national party, and the personal wishes of the chairman himself.

At one end of this spectrum were the self-conscious reformers, those members who had deliberately taken the reform side of most issues across time and who would reliably take the reform position on the items in the Preliminary Call. In a limited sense, these members were an asset to the chairman, since they did not have to be convinced of the need to endorse the guidelines. On the other hand, they presented tactical problems as well, since they would reliably *oppose* the principal substantive amendment from O'Brien, the altered formula for interstate apportionment, and since they might, in consequence, open a conflict which committee regulars would then use to introduce their own, far more extensive amendments. Bob Nelson appreciated their presence, but conceded their propensity for self-defeating conflict:

> People like Dutton from the Commission were pushing the fracture line. On the National Committee, Jeffrey and Reinhardt and the North Dakota National Committeewoman, ten or twelve of them, were militant on this score.[7]

The straightforward predictability of these individuals influenced, and limited, O'Brien's approach. They did not need to be urged to support reform in general; they could not be brought around to his particular tactical amendments. Accordingly, the chairman largely took their support—and their opposition—for granted. He did touch base with most of them during the weeks preceding the National Committee meeting; he did run through the arguments about his own contributions to reform. Yet he accepted their opposition to his major amendment and did not try to do much more with them.

Shading off from the reform bloc was a group of members who received a great deal more attention from the chairman, and for whom he had much higher hopes. These were the comparatively detached party regulars, those who had paid little attention to the politics of party reform or to the substance of reform recommendations and who were experiencing little pressure to go with—or to oppose—reform in general. Some of these members were truly distant from state party politics, because their seats had been consolation prizes to losing party factions or because they had attained such seniority that most party issues passed them by. Others were from states where the reform issue had not generated significant internal politicking. Some were merely unconcerned with reform politics, or more concerned that conflict over state party rules not contaminate their major political interests, whatever those might be.

With these members, O'Brien emphasized the public side of his arguments about party reform. He began with the virtues of reform as an activity. Reform showed the concern of the Democratic party for responsiveness to the general public; it demonstrated a readiness to assume national leadership; it contrasted sharply with the approach of the Republicans. O'Brien then added an emphasis on his restraining amendments, underlining their special attraction for party regulars. These amendments had neutralized the excessive aspects of proposals by party reformers; they gave the regular party a means to go with reform and yet oppose the individuals behind it; they offered stability in the process of change.

After all this, the chairman appealed for personal support from these members, if they could possibly provide it. George Mitchell, national committeeman from Maine, judged that this general approach was very persuasive to committee members who had no direct involvement with the politics of implementation: "There was a feeling that this was a good thing, that 'reform' was a good thing. There was a widely held feeling that there had been some wrongs done."[8]

Many committee members who could be classified as party regulars, however, were more attentive to the content of proposed reforms—and held more serious reservations. Such members were not attracted by the content of the guidelines, because their implementation would clearly disadvantage the regular party back home, because their impact was unpredictable, because compliance itself, whatever its impact, was politically costly, or just because these new rules were being pushed by outsiders, renegades, and troublemakers. The standard arguments about the abstract virtues and tactical advantages of reform could make little headway with them.[9]

Accordingly, O'Brien used a different approach. The chairman began by arguing the practical costs of *opposing* reform. He stressed the danger of fracture within the national party; he raised the possibility that this would produce a rerun of 1968. From the other side, O'Brien argued that these reforms would have little practical effect. Politics at home would work as it always had; reform would correct undeniable abuses, while serving a largely cosmetic function.

To cap the argument, O'Brien emphasized the changes which he himself was introducing. The chairman suggested that they would function as a clear assertion of authority by the regular party; he labored long and hard to impose the notion that *these particular amendments* were the changes which suspicious members themselves desired. Joe Doorley, national committeeman from Rhode Island and no fan of the chairman on a regular basis, found this package of assertions convincing:

> Our feeling was that they were rewarding constituencies that went against Humphrey. But Larry was saying, "Don't worry, Joe. This won't matter. You'll get elected, the same as ever." And I felt the same way. It was only later that I realized that we'd been duped. When we got to that Convention, we knew.
>
> There wasn't that feeling at the time of leaving the pros out. These reforms at that time looked like you had to do them, I mean if you were a liberal party. Where we started to learn what these rules meant was in the Credentials Committee. I don't think at that point that many of us felt that anything was going on. There were no percentages, no quotas, for example.

At the far end of this spectrum, finally, were the rock-ribbed party regulars, generally from states with organized political parties, who recognized an assault on regular-party prerogatives and did not intend to countenance it, and who recognized—and resented—the social distinctions between themselves and reform enthusiasts. Some of these members, like J. Marshall Brown of Louisiana, had been opponents of the reform movement from the first and could not conceivably be moved by argument or suasion in the weeks before the February meeting. Like the militant reformers at the other end, they would offer their views firmly and without equivocation. O'Brien left them strictly alone.

Even within this hard core, however, the chairman possessed one last, major resource. With some of these members at least, the chairman could fall back on extensive social ties, built up during a common political history—from electoral politicking with John Kennedy and then Hubert Humphrey, from programmatic endeavors during the Kennedy administration (when O'Brien had been chief tactician of patronage), and from shared experiences in national party politics during two separate tenures as national chairman. In fact, O'Brien shared these ties with a remarkable proportion of his National Committee. With the most intransigent party regulars, they had to carry the entire load:

Hard work and long-time friendships, and personal credit. I was just saying, "Trust me. Trust the chairman." I was just saying, "You can go along with me. Nothing bad will happen."

Chairman O'Brien, then, offered four different sets of reasons for supporting the Preliminary Call. With confirmed reformers, he merely emphasized that he, too, was backing implementation, and that they might damage their cause if they strayed too far from his positions. With those who were comparatively indifferent, he underlined the larger strategic and ethical reasons for endorsing this package. Reform would surely be "good politics"; it possessed a fundamental virtue, to boot. With orthodox party regulars, he focused on a more limited logic, internal to the party. An attempt to reverse directions would be disastrously divisive; the real change resulting from compliance would be inconsequential. Finally, with those who expressed no interest in any of this, he fell back on personal loyalties, hitched to personal desires. O'Brien called upon the basic social attachments which some of these members had for him as a party leader, and he urged them to add these to the general equation before they cast a dissenting vote.

The major substantive contribution by the national chairman to the committee meeting of February 19 was his pair of amendments to the reform package. The vast bulk of his time and energy before the February sessions went into personal negotiations—into lobbying. Yet O'Brien did not neglect the edge which might be gained from careful orchestration of the meeting itself.

The first aspect of this, the process of arranging for explicit statements explaining and supporting the Preliminary Call, was easily handled. The two commission chairmen, Don Fraser of Party Structure and Jim O'Hara of Rules, were the obvious expert witnesses; the national counsel, Joe Califano, was the resident rules interpreter. Fraser and O'Hara could speak on behalf of their respective reports in whatever terms they chose. As nonmembers of the National Committee, however, they were not invited to take part in its subsequent deliberations.[10]

The expert witness who *was* expected to engage in give-and-take with committee members, and who was thus charged with a detailed explanation and defense of reform proposals, was Califano. The national counsel began with the belief that many in his audience would not have read the report on which they were being forced to pass, but would be instinctively hostile to *any* formal rules drafted outside the confines of the National Committee. To counter these initial prejudices without fueling an eventual reaction, Califano planned to lead the members through the entire document, section by section and guideline by guideline:

I was not involved in counting heads. My job was to operate on the assumption that they would not have read them, that they would have to be explained clearly and precisely to them. We did not want to be in a position that the DNC members could say that they didn't know what was in the rules when they passed them. By God, we'll take them through it.

The second source of potential leverage in these meeting arrangements was the agenda, the order of presentation for various reform proposals. If there were to be sharp disagreements about the details of the Preliminary Call, and if the location and result of these disagreements were not preordained, then the ability to manage the order and timing of this conflict might be a valuable asset. In any case, there was no reason for the chairman not to prepare for this eventuality, and he gave it serious consideration.

Here, O'Brien returned to his original surmise that the most evident source of conflict at the meeting was not the guidelines from the Party Structure Commission but the apportionment formula from Rules. O'Brien had already *guaranteed* this conflict, by offering his own, proposed substitute. When he considered the meeting's agenda, he took the final step by scheduling interstate apportionment *first*. If conflict broke out in this area, and if that conflict was protracted, his manuever would automatically compress the time in which the National Committee could tinker with the recommendations of the Party Structure Commission. If the chairman himself was then successful on apportionment, he might parlay that success into an implicit bargain which assured passage of commission guidelines.

When these preparations were completed, the chairman needed only a vehicle for bringing his full reform package before the National Committee, one which would reduce any appearance of heavy-handedness on his part. He found that vehicle in Ad Hoc Committee No. 1. The committee was renamed the Ad Hoc Committee on the Preliminary Call; O'Brien assigned it to report out his tactical adjustments—the new apportionment formula, the semifinal credentials language, and the nonvoting, ex officio provision for outgoing members of the National Committee. Since there was no time to bring the Ad Hoc Committee to Washington in advance of the full committee meeting, O'Brien merely turned these items over to its chairman, Geri Joseph. George Mitchell, the member of the Ad Hoc Committee with the most substantive expertise, was surprised but not distressed by the unveiling of "their" report:

That may have been the same compliance committee I was on. It would have been easy for O'Brien to float this in, and then have it floated back. I don't remember. If we recommended it, I'm sure I never did anything on it in advance.

The Irrelevance of Other Actors

The extent of the attempt by Chairman O'Brien to influence this National Committee meeting and the degree to which this effort was harnessed to the cause of party reform were impressive to those who observed them first-hand—and would have been more impressive to those who knew the chairman only by reputation or position. Even more surprising, however, was the shortage of other, independent efforts to influence the meeting—and the unimportance of the few which did materialize.

The list of actors with a hypothetically sizable stake in the meeting's outcome was long indeed. Yet for many, institutional constraints, internal to their own organizations and reinforced by their political history, prevented so much as an approach to the National Committee. For the rest, a deliberate attempt at influence was reduced to insignificance by the peculiar character of the committee itself.

Party reformers, national and local, had a self-evident stake in the response of the National Committee. The most revolutionary planned reform in the history of American party politics was about to receive its major, formal, national test. It would come up in the company of amendments by Chairman O'Brien which seemed, on balance, to reduce its scope. Moreover, reformers possessed an effective consensus on both aspects of this package. All favored inclusion of the guidelines, as written, in the Preliminary Call. Most favored the original, stronger formula for interstate apportionment; the others preferred an even stiffer alternative.

Yet despite the presence of an obvious concern and a substantive consensus among reform-minded individuals, most organized frameworks for rallying external reform support were either defunct or neutralized by the time the National Committee met. The original, ad hoc network of reform enthusiasts, coordinated by Tom Alder through the remnants of the Hughes Commission, had passed away when the Party Structure Commission was empaneled. Some elements of that network, it is true, had been institutionalized in the New Democratic Coalition. But by 1971, the NDC, too, had largely disintegrated.

The real coordinating mechanism for reform forces since the empaneling of the Party Structure Commission was, of course, the commission itself. But for the National Committee meeting of February 19, the commission was on the sidelines. The national chairman was doing the work of the commission; indeed, he was supporting its report, unchanged, in its entirety. The chairman, however, preferred to do its work his way; since he *was* doing it, and since the commission remained partially dependent on him for organizational support, its members were not inclined to break with him in order to provide additional support for a course which he was already pursuing.

The one organization to which none of this applied was the new Center for Political Reform, launched by Ken Bode in late 1970. As a result, the battle for National Committee acceptance became the first major national engagement for the Center. Even then, the early stage of its own development, coupled with its inherent difficulties in approaching the National Committee, sharply limited its impact. Bode did not learn of the proposed amendments to the Preliminary Call until the chairman had inaugurated an intensive lobbying campaign behind them. In that situation, with the late hour, few resources, and limited access, Bode concentrated on the alternative formulas for interstate apportionment.

Bode began by contacting former staff members of the Party Structure Commission, full-timers and volunteers, and urging them to contact National Committee members whom they might know. He himself then telephoned those members who were part of the self-conscious reform faction on the committee, to bolster their opposition to the major amendment from O'Brien and to provide additional arguments for their position. After that, he attempted to reach out to other members who were not a part of the reform faction but whose states would be injured by the substitute apportionment formula, through a modified form letter translating that injury state by state:[11]

> We had the apportionment thing that we were concerned about. Why would O'Brien go with this formula? The small states would have gone along if he hadn't raised this. The small states never would have caught on. That formula! In all the O'Hara hearings around the country, not once was *that* formula suggested. Did the Joseph Committee ever even meet? This was *O'Brien's* device.
>
> What we did to prepare for it was on the apportionment question. I knew that the guidelines would be in, because O'Brien had already agreed to that. He had an opinion from Califano; he had McGovern's harsh statement. O'Brien was already with us on the guidelines, so let him fight that.

These efforts had only marginal impact on the National Committee. Most of the lobbying from Bode was concentrated on members who were already committed to reform. Committee members outside this minority faction eventually reached their decisions on grounds quite unrelated to a written communication from Bode's Center. Most members never received such a communication, since their states would clearly *benefit* from the O'Brien revision.

What gave these efforts their distinction, then, was not their impact on the proceedings of the National Committee, but the fact that they were the only external lobbying attempt of any scope beyond that of the national chairman. The absence of other attempts, especially from the antireform side, was additionally striking because the chairman was, of course, going with recommendations for reform. This meant that he was not available to press the stereotyped position of the regular party. It meant that someone else had to coordinate that position, if it was to be pressed at all.

The state party chairmen were the obvious, formal candidates for this role. They were the ones charged with implementing national recommendations for reform—and with paying the political price. By February of 1971, they were well aware of the specific substantive demands of implementation—and of the institutional changes which would be required in their home states to move into full compliance.

That they produced no systematic lobbying effort traced directly to the absence of machinery for coordinating such an effort, and indirectly to long-standing traditions of state independence. By tradition, state chairmen dealt with the gaining and holding of public office within their own state boundaries; they expected their counterparts in other states to do the same. If the National Committee was functioning effectively, it could provide some intermittent and rudimentary negotiations *among* the states. Otherwise, and on most occasions, the norm was one of noninterference and reciprocal deference.[12]

Individual state chairmen, of course, had been complaining to their national chairman since the day he resumed the chairmanship. At first, O'Brien simply reassured these more overtly resistant state counterparts and counseled patience. Then, as he gained assuredness in reform politics, he began arguing, even in private, that some of these reforms were inescapable, and he began urging even recalcitrant chairmen to comply with whatever they could. By early 1971, he was attempting to take the recommendations of the Party Structure Commission through the National Committee. Bob Nelson watched with approval:

> The big-state guys were giving Larry an earful by this time. But he was telling them that "It's a new day. You had better get with it. We have an opportunity here to strengthen and build our party. We've got to get with it."

The national chairman, then, was unavailable to coordinate contrary pressures on behalf of his state chairmen. Because he was unavailable, he removed the rest of the national party bureaucracy from their potential service. Because he was unavailable, the state chairmen had to produce any coordinating machinery *de novo*, and on short notice. They did not. Some of these chairmen, those whose committee members were not tied into state party politics, may not even have realized that a Preliminary Call with extensive recommendations for reform was about to come before the National Committee. Most did not become explicitly aware until O'Brien began to alert committee members to the coming session—and to press them for support of his personal position.

If any of them looked for some means of coordinating a response at that point, they found none. The Democratic governors at least possessed the semi-annual Governors' Conference at which they might occasionally develop collective policy statements. The Democratic state chairmen lacked even so evanescent an institution. What they had instead was a long-standing custom of minding their own business. The frustrations in this were sufficient, in the spring of 1971, to lead to the creation of an Association of Democratic State Chairmen.[13] But in January and February, there was no such operation. Bill Welsh, who was helping O'Brien in his lobbying effort, saw the organizational discomfiture of the state party chairmen:

> But for practical purposes, there was no institution of state party chairmen; there was no *body* for them. That was important. There was no input from labor on the outside. Labor was still completely dissociated. The DNC was on its own.

The election of 1970 had contributed a second source of potential influence at the state level, in the form of numerous Democratic governors. By early 1971, there were thirty of these; by late 1971, most would be major actors in reform politics. Yet as the crucial committee meeting approached, there was never any serious possibility that they would take coordinated action. These individuals were probably too divided on the issue of reform to make any collective stand possible. In any case, many of their number were too new to their positions to mount even individual, much less coordinate, attempts at influencing the National Committee.

If there was to be any systematic attempt to predispose the committee toward a more cautious view of the Preliminary Call, then, it had to come from outside the regular party structure. By definition, such an attempt had to come from some organized, external component of the orthodox Democratic coalition, from the major organized interests associated with the regular party. In practical terms, this effort had to come from organized labor.

The major voice of organized labor in American politics, the Committee on Political Education of the AFL-CIO, suffered few of the evident drawbacks restraining committed party reformers or state party officials. COPE already possessed a fully articulated organizational framework. It had a national office with the possibility of focused action; it had local counterparts in most states in the union. Moreover, the national leadership possessed a clear and contrary view of the roots, development, and prospects of party reform. Al Barkan, executive director of the national COPE, spoke forcefully of these perceptions:

> We were of course getting reports, privately, about developments inside that commission, even if we were no longer associated publicly with it. And I must say that those reports were not very encouraging. These zealots were running off on their own crusade, and they weren't much concerned about what would happen to the American working man in the process.

Yet when the time came for concerted action, COPE, too, was absent until the very end, when it was left with a limited, indirect, and ultimately unproductive approach to the National Committee. In part, this failure to act in a more broad-gauge fashion was rooted in the political history of COPE within the Democratic party. In turn, the failure was reinforced by a set of internal, organizational constraints, which prevented attention to the Preliminary Call until only a limited and indirect option remained.

The history of COPE on the reform issue had led the national office away from concern with the February meeting of the National Committee. In March of 1969, after the inaugural meeting of the Party Structure Commission, COPE had pulled its lone commissioner, I. W. Abel, and had deserted the commission for the duration of the politics of recommendation. While Barkan did receive occasional reports on commission developments in the interim, he and his staff were uninvolved with the progress of party reform from that point.

This detachment was reinforced by the more general history of COPE within the Democratic party. COPE had been central to recent presidential campaigns, providing manpower, advertising, and even some financial contributions. But labor issues had rarely arisen in the National Committee, and other matters had traditionally been handled through direct negotiations at the top, between the national chairman and the executive director of COPE, or even between a Democratic president and the president of the AFL-CIO. As a result, when O'Brien went the other way on party reform, Barkan was immediately cut off:

> There were one hundred ten members of the Democratic National Committee. We didn't have a single one. This gets back to our policy. We were never involved, never. It was kind of a peripheral thing. There wasn't any fight on the McGovern-Fraser thing, for example. The Pat Harris thing was really an isolated event; O'Brien asked me to help, and we did. We never attended the DNC meetings, even as observers.

Added organizational constraints, internal to COPE itself, prevented the annulment of these traditions in February of 1971. The annual meeting of the Executive Board of the Committee on Political Education was scheduled for mid-February, in Florida. In a trivial sense, this meant that the national COPE leadership would be out of Washington when the National Committee met. In a more consequential sense, it meant that the COPE leadership did not begin to focus on the National Committee meeting until Chairman O'Brien began to line up support for his version of the Preliminary Call.

Given the traditional dissociation of COPE from the National Committee, given the institutionalized focus of its leadership on its own internal calendar, and given the late hour at which these leaders woke up to the impending vote on reform, their options were severely limited. With time running out, Barkan reached for an indirect strategy. He called the contenders for a Democratic nomination in 1972, those who were sympathetic to organized labor and likely to be supported by it, and he urged *them* to call National Committee members and request a postponement of the committee vote:

> We didn't have anyone on the DNC. Not one guy was an AFL member. And besides, we didn't usually go to them anyway. But we went to the candidates. We called Humphrey, we called Muskie, Jackson. We said, "Just get your people to wait a little, will you?" Christ, Humphrey couldn't even deliver Minnesota. Many of these people said yes, yes, but when they got into that Committee, they voted the wrong way.[14]

The strategy, in fact, was a complete failure. Of the three contenders contacted by COPE, only Humphrey could be expected to have extensive ties within the National Committee. But more to the point, none of these contenders was likely to risk an assault on the National Committee on the issue of party reform, especially on short notice. All knew that they would attract the immediate and continuing enmity of reform partisans if they answered the call of labor. Each possessed an exemplary record on labor issues and knew that this would hardly be the last—or even the major—policy request from organized labor. All simply passed.

As a result, the last prospect of organized opposition from the orthodox Democratic coalition failed to materialize. The National Committee itself still provided a spontaneous rallying point for the regular party. The National Committee meeting still promised opportunities for unforeseen interactions which could affect the course of party reform. But organized opposition to the Call as the national chairman envisioned it—and especially opposition to its proposed reforms—would *have* to appear spontaneously at that meeting, if it was to appear at all.

Implications

The meeting of the National Committee on February 19, 1971, was to be a crucial event in the politics of party reform. That meeting would address a Preliminary Call to the 1972 Convention. The Call would contain the rules to govern delegate selection and convention activity. The process of addressing these rules would bring the National Committee—the formal embodiment of the national party—into reform politics in an intimate and consequential fashion. The outcome—whether endorsement, adjustment, or decimation—would be the official definition of party reform from that time forward.

Three grand factors would inevitably affect the fate of this Preliminary Call. The first was the continuing character of the National Committee as a political institution, both the nature of its membership and of its ongoing operations. The second was the advance preparations of those who desired to mitigate the normal response of this institution, both the strategic thinking of these lobbyists and their lobbying itself. The third was the particular dynamics of the committee meeting. The fundamental character of the National Committee could not be altered in advance of this meeting, but those who aspired to influence its outcome could adjust their strategies in light of this character, and they could try to anticipate the dynamics of the crucial meeting.

As a political institution, the National Committee was organizationally unsympathetic to reform, though in a more complicated manner than most observers realized. Formally, the committee was the capstone organization of the regular party. It might contain as many delegates from volunteer state parties as from their organized counterparts, but any softening contributed by this volunteer presence was more than compensated by the fact that most members were products of a regular party structure.

Moreover, delegates produced through a regular party structure did care, in practice, about the organizational health of the regular party. Their attitude might be mitigated by the distance of many of these delegates from continuing party politics in their home states, but any softening contributed by this detachment was, again, more than balanced by the fact that senior committee members had actually grown up in parties which were stronger—closer to the organized model—than the current ones in their home areas.

As a result, the National Committee was an inherently hostile arena for reform politics. If this orientation had ever been in question, it was reactivated, once again, by the social differences between committee members and national reformers, and by the fact that most members did perceive these distinctions. On the other hand, if the committee was a bastion of regular-party sentiment, its internal diversity—the extent to which it was far more complex than simple elucidations suggested—did mean that there was room for maneuver—room, that is, for lobbying campaigns with the prospect of some impact.

In the weeks leading up to the committee meeting, Chairman O'Brien undertook a classic example of such a campaign. He weighed the substance of the Preliminary Call and proposed several substantive amendments, including a major one on interstate apportionment. He went on to rally the National Committee behind his revised preferences, varying his arguments according to the member in question and the bloc structure of the Committee as a whole. He closed by attending to the order of business, the agenda, for reform proposals.

The scope and intensity of this effort was impressive. So, however, was the absence of countervailing efforts. Reformers managed a minor lobbying attempt by the new Center for Political Reform. Otherwise, they were collectively inactive. Regulars—those with the apparent, central stake in the outcome—managed even less. The state chairmen, the party figures with the most to lose in the politics of implementation, failed to mount any collective attack. Organized labor, through the Committee on Political Education, mounted only a late, indirect, desperate, and bootless campaign.

By the time these maneuvers had occurred—or more commonly, failed to occur—the crucial meeting was at hand. And there, the fundamental character of the National Committee and the dynamics of the meeting itself might still counteract the dominant strategic preparations of its chairman. Yet whatever the actions of the committee, the process of preparing for its meeting had revealed several key facts about the prospects for institutional change and for the circulation of elites in the national Democratic party.

The most obvious, and most immediately consequential, of these facts was the status of this meeting as a crucial encounter in the pursuit of institutional change. If the National Committee acquiesced in the preferences of its chairman, even though these preferences included a revised formula for interstate apportionment, it would give the largest grant of formal authority which it could practically muster to sweeping proposals for party reform. *Every* state party would be under orders to implement these reforms. Some concrete number would *automatically* follow through and implement this explicit directive.

By early 1971, there was a possibility that even this would be only the beginning. By the time the National Committee addressed the Preliminary Call, with its extensive proposals for the reform of delegate selection, extensive proposals for reforming the *National Committee* were also in the air. The sitting committee would never, under the most extreme lobbying campaign from its chairman or anyone else, endorse these proposals. But if the committee accepted the Preliminary Call, and if delegate selection under reformed rules produced what the drafters of those rules intended, then the *National Convention* of 1972 would have the authority to restructure the National Committee—and might well do so.[15]

This chain could be drawn out indefinitely, with a reformed National Committee guaranteeing the continuation of a reformed process for delegate selection, with the guaranteed continuation of that reformed process insuring the rise of the alternative Democratic coalition, and so forth. Yet the preparations leading up to the pivotal committee meeting revealed far less about the direct character of any subsequent—substitute—coalition of Democratic elites, and the reasons for this were a final, ironic comment on reform politics, institutional change, and elite circulation in the national party in early 1971.

The intrinsic charity of existing institutions of delegate selection to the orthodox Democratic coalition and the contrasting charity of reformed institutions of delegate selection to the alternative Democratic coalition were, of course, unchanged by any politicking in advance of the committee meeting. The beneficiaries of these institutional arrangements would be determined by the way they worked in presidential politics, not by whether the National Committee could be reconciled to them.

If the preparations leading up to the crucial meeting of the National Committee revealed little about the *current* health of the two contending elite coalitions, then, this was because so few elements of these coalitions were involved in lobbying the committee. What these preparations confirmed instead was that reform politics had finally moved inside the regular party. Once, reform politicking had occurred largely outside its confines. Now, it was centered inside and would not predictably progress unless the regular party gave its endorsement. Once, the underlying question for reform politics had been how a set of reforms developed so conspicuously outside the regular-party framework could ever be brought back in. Now, those reforms were within hours of being there.

If there had been a central political puzzle during the period when these reforms were being developed, it was how the alternative Democratic coalition—more aspiring than actual, more talked of than seen—could have such an influence in advance of its apparent numbers. If there was a related political puzzle as the National Committee prepared to address reform, it was how that alternative Democratic coalition could be on the verge of securing an endorsement of widespread institutional change when it was apparently so weak within the national party. At the very least, it was patently clear that the alternative coalition, as an organized political entity, could compel almost nothing from the National Committee proper.

The practical power of the alternative coalition was, of course, more ambiguous than that. Organized reformers had generated the procedural substance of the reform debate; they had helped to propel that substance to the point where it required serious attention by the regular party. At about the time when the National Committee was meeting to address the Preliminary Call, these reformers were receiving a crucial increment to their coalition through a new crop of Democratic governors with an institutionalized sympathy to reform—a testimony to the practical power of an abstract notion which was nevertheless hitched to a concrete political alignment. Within months, a functioning alternative coalition would be hammered together as an active political entity as well and would be highly relevant to the interpretation of many reforms, once it was clear that these would be implemented.

Yet as the day of decision for the National Committee approached, it was easily, equally clear that the conflict over party reform was being fought out not so much between the orthodox and alternative Democratic coalitions as within the orthodox coalition itself. It was the regular party which had to reach the key decisions at the national level, just as it was the regular party which had to reach those decisions concurrently in Pennsylvania and as it would be the regular party, without much effective pressure from party reformers, which would have to reach them in many other states.

The final irony in this situation—the return of the regular party to center stage in reform politics along with a sharp reduction in the direct influence of party reformers—was that it did not automatically determine the fate of reform. For while the highest official of the regular party was indeed taking the major role in shaping the response of the National Committee, *he was working actively on behalf of party reform.* For reasons tracing to his return as national chairman; in reaction to pressures which had been added since that return; with an eye toward maintaining a surface calm in party affairs; in the belief that history might treat any other approach unkindly; perhaps even in the belief that these reforms would matter far less than proponents thought—Chairman O'Brien was devoting all his energies to making problematic the otherwise instinctive response of the National Committee.

In any case, all that could be said with surety by the second week in February was that these potential developments were about to be immersed in the internal dynamics, the very concrete and practical politics, of the next meeting of the National Committee. The committee might never explicitly address any of them in coming to grips with the Preliminary Call. But its decisions would necessarily affect—positively, negatively, or ambiguously—the realization of these historic possibilities. And the outcome within the committee—the draft Call or whatever was left of it—would automatically become the official position of the national party on proposals for extensive party reform.

CHAPTER

14

Climax on the National Level:

The National Committee and the Triumph

of the Guidelines

IN WHICH, the Executive Committee and then the full National Committee address the Preliminary Call; the committee amends the Call on
ex officio representation and fights extensively over interstate apportionment; and the guidelines are essentially endorsed as presented. AND IN
WHICH, the maneuvers of the national chairman remain central to reform politics; National Committee members fail to perceive much institutional change in the recommendations they adopt; and the alternative
Democratic coalition, while unable to influence the proceedings directly,
realizes its wishes through the regular party leadership.

IN A THREE-DAY PERIOD in February, 1971, the guidelines of the Party
Structure Commission met their principal test before the National Committee. The Executive Committee assembled first, and its response became the
new working draft of the Preliminary Call. The full committee assembled two
days later, and its decisions became the specific content of that Preliminary
Call, the official definition of party reform, and the concrete program of the
Democratic party for institutional change at the state and national levels.

Reform politics did not remain focused exclusively at the national level for
much more than this three-day period. The National Committee as a collectivity was not focused on party reform for more than a single day within it. Yet
when the committee finished its day-long labors, it had adopted rules which
would influence the selection of a sequence of presidential nominees and
which would influence the basic elite structure of presidential politics—and
even of national politics more generally—for some undefined period to come.

In a small break with tradition, the Executive Committee was given the opportunity for serious and detailed consideration of the draft Preliminary Call. Chairman O'Brien brought the final report of the Party Structure Commission, the partial report of the Rules Commission, and the ostensible report of the Ad Hoc Committee before the Executive Committee on Wednesday, February 17. The committee heard Counsel Califano discuss these materials through the morning. In the afternoon, its members endorsed everything except the revised formula for interstate apportionment, which they debated at length. When the members closed by accepting that, too, the proposal from the Ad Hoc Committee became the text of the Preliminary Call, and O'Brien departed with everything he had desired from the Executive Committee.

The full National Committee addressed this package that Friday morning, and its encounter produced significantly more drama. Califano again engaged in a detailed and spirited defense of the document presented. But this time, the members cut open another of the areas in which O'Brien had sought to avoid conflict. In a short, almost surgical attack on the draft Call, they rejected his nonvoting provision for outgoing committee members and awarded themselves full convention privileges, including the right to vote. After that, the full committee addressed the formula for interstate apportionment, in an even lengthier and more intense debate than the one in the Executive Committee, before settling on the proposed compromise from O'Brien as the position of the national party.

Yet when the National Committee adjourned, in the late afternoon of Friday, February 19, the single, dominant, substantive fact about its session was that it had accepted—and officially endorsed—the guidelines of the Party Structure Commission *essentially intact.* The result was an evident contribution to sweeping institutional change within the national Democratic party. The result was a concomitant contribution to a thorough circulation of party elites.

This outcome had been shaped most directly by the strategic maneuvers of the national chairman. Those maneuvers, in turn, had been powerfully conditioned by the basic character of the National Committee as a political institution. Yet both of these factors had influenced the dynamics of the crucial committee meeting *through* an implicit pattern of perceptions among committee members, through a patterned tendency to identify, or miss, the institutional significance of the rules which passed before them.

The pattern is easily described. A mandated change in the outcome of delegate selection, or an evident connection with the personal experience of a substantial number of committee members, was enough to draw these members into sustained debate. A formal rule whose practical effect was on institutional structure, or a rule whose effect was indirect and therefore not very evident at all, was likely to escape committee attention, no matter what its institutional significance.

Nevertheless, all these influences were matters of the moment. National Committee members may not have seen the institutional impact of everything they endorsed. They may not have believed in the practical consequence of some of the institutional impacts they saw. But after their endorsement, the fate of all these institutional changes, and the fate of the elite circulation associated with them, was largely out of their hands.

The National Committee and the Preliminary Call

An invitation for the Executive Committee to pass on so potentially important a document as the Preliminary Call was itself a minor break with precedent. The convening of the Executive Committee a full two days before the National Committee meeting gave emphasis to that break. Chairman O'Brien, however, had clear strategic reasons for summoning this committee and for giving it the privilege and the time to address the Preliminary Call. He was guided by those reasons.

Most fundamentally, the chairman hoped to extract a full and detailed endorsement of the draft Call, *as amended.* This would constitute an additional asset in tackling the full committee, since the draft Call would arrive with the explicit endorsement of a range of recognized party figures. This endorsement might even relieve full committee members of the need to pry further into the Call. At the same time, the chairman would hear a round of arguments about the document he was presenting, from committed regulars and committed reformers. Since he continued to have serious doubts about his ability to bring both—or either—side along, he counted this an additional advantage.

The Executive Committee assembled on Wednesday morning, February 17, and the session began routinely. Chairman O'Brien named Governor Robert W. Scott of North Carolina to replace Governor Robert E. McNair of South Carolina as one of two vice chairmen at the National Committee. O'Brien followed with a summary of a meeting he had called the previous week for all announced—and unannounced but widely touted—contenders for the Democratic presidential nomination. The chairman had urged upon them his "speak no evil" philosophy, under which they would mount vigorous attacks upon the Nixon administration but not upon each other, and he expressed some hope that the idea had taken hold.[1]

Then, in the first procedural hint of the day's potential, the chairman changed schedule slightly and offered a short speech on the historic significance of the actions which the Executive Committee was about to take. That done, he reverted to the norm and recognized Robert S. Strauss, the national treasurer, and Mary Lou Burg, director of women's activities, for their regular reports. At the conclusion of their comments, O'Brien turned to Geri Joseph to introduce the major business of the day. Joseph read carefully through the "report" of the Ad Hoc Committee—the text of O'Brien's proposed substitute for the Preliminary Call.

The motion that Joseph's report be adopted provoked an opening dispute. Stephen Reinhardt of California and Mildred Jeffrey of Michigan—moved in particular by the substitute apportionment formula—objected strenuously, asserting that the Ad Hoc Committee had been assigned to "implement" the reports of the Party Structure and Rules commissions, not to comment upon, much less amend them. In return, Jacob Arvey of Illinois and Joseph Barr of Pennsylvania insisted that the content of that original charge, as well as the content of anything the Ad Hoc Committee subsequently produced, were beside the point, since the Executive Committee could integrate either, or neither, into its own recommendations.

O'Brien interrupted this discussion and moved the Executive Committee back into the details of the Preliminary Call, where he asked Counsel Califano to go through the draft text, item by item. Califano opened with the section on apportionment, then followed with the proposed rules for delegate selection. He preceded a reading of the rules with a review of the resolutions passed at the 1968 Convention and an outline of the standards which these resolutions appeared to demand. In launching into the guidelines themselves, Califano divided them between "required" and "recommended" standards, and he offered a full reading along with his own running commentary.

The national counsel lingered for some time, right at the start, over Guidelines A–1 and A–2, to show that commission pronouncements on demographic representation were not mandatory quotas:

Califano: Implementation of the antidiscrimination standard which, again, we read as required by the 1968 Convention, to encourage minority representation, and to encourage 18-year-old participation. Minority representation is essentially directed at women and young people, who the McGovern Commission felt had been underrepresented in the past.

The word "encourage" is specifically used, and the report provides that this is not intended as establishing a quota system, that you must have exact number of women if you have exact number of women in the population, or exact number of people between 18 and 30, which is the definition of young people in the McGovern Commission Report, or exact number of blacks if you have that number in the population.[2]

No one, however, stopped the counsel on any facet of A–1 or A–2. In fact, Califano continued until he reached C–2 (Automatic Delegates) before the Executive Committee came to life. Barr of Pennsylvania interrupted by asking for clarification. Califano responded by revealing that National Committee members could be given voting status only if they had been selected within calendar 1972, but that the committee might otherwise do for them whatever it wished.

Both Barr and Arvey rushed to label this as wrong-headed, asserting that the sitting, not the incoming, committee members deserved voting representation. In return, Reinhardt and Jeffrey asserted, even more vehemently than before, that the Barr-Arvey proposal lay outside the authority of the Executive Committee, or indeed of the National Committee itself, since it would countervail the timeliness injunction of the 1968 Convention.

Give-and-take on this issue continued for some time without a resolution, and O'Brien then returned the floor to his counsel, who continued through the remaining required guidelines and all of the recommended ones. None of these produced dissent, and Califano next covered both the original and the amended language from the Rules Commission on credentials procedures. Individual members of the Executive Committee jumped into his presentation at various points along the way but without major substantive difference or evident emotional involvement. As the noon hour came and went, and as this discussion began to peter out, the Executive Committee recessed for lunch.

After lunch, Barr reopened the meeting by moving adoption of the Preliminary Call, as amended by the Ad Hoc Committee. Before that vote could be called, O'Brien asked the Executive Committee to be a trifle less precipitous and to ballot on the draft Call, if not item by item, at least section by section. In response, however, Reinhardt suggested that since the previous discussion had shown most items to be nondivisive, the Executive Committee should adopt the Call as presented, save for the apportionment provision, which had provoked his original dissent and which could now be debated at length. The other members concurred and focused on apportionment.

Easily the longest discussion of the day ensued. After a considerable period, and after the examination of a multitude of possible formulas, a series of motions began. Jeffrey kicked them off by offering the original language of the

Rules Commission, 50 percent Democratic vote and 50 percent pure population. Reinhardt and Jean Westwood of Utah spoke for the Jeffrey proposal, and that was its entire supporting cast: It failed, 3 yes and 7 no. Reinhardt offered a more extreme substitute, apportionment by pure Democratic vote, and it lost even Westwood, failing by a tally of 2 to 8.

The Ad Hoc Committee amendment then came to a vote. Some initial confusion, a request for clarification, and a consequent revote all intervened before a final ballot. But when that ballot was completed, with 7 yes and 4 no, the amended formula had passed, and the Executive Committee had sent a Preliminary Call to its parent body.[3] Shortly after this, with its substantive business completed, the committee adjourned.

If anyone had been keeping a more personal tally, the meeting would surely have been scored as a full triumph for Chairman O'Brien. He had foreseen every item of potential conflict; he had secured his preferences on every one as well. At no time had the meeting appeared likely to slip from his grasp. Demographic representation had generated less concern among Executive Committee members than the chairman had originally anticipated, and Califano had been able to dispatch the issue with simple, textual exegesis. Credentials regulations and ex officio representation had produced more discussion but no additional amendments, so that the chairman had again imposed his own preference while avoiding all others. Interstate apportionment had generated by far the largest debate, but O'Brien had actively defeated the position of the Rules Commission and of the Preliminary Call as drafted and had substituted his preferred alternative.

Yet as with so many other incidents in reform politics, a focus on the items of discussion and debate obscured the most significant development at this meeting. For in passing, without a specific vote and without even comment, the Executive Committee had accepted the entire text of the recommendations of the Commission on Party Structure and Delegate Selection. The institutional changes which this implied were the most revolutionary since the creation of the national party convention, 140 years before. The specific wording which accomplished this change was nevertheless as unremarkable and unobtrusive as the manner in which it had been adopted:

> The Call adopts those required guidelines as the standard for judging a state's compliance for full, meaningful, and timely participation. It urges states to undertake action on those guidelines as the Commission urged.[4]

The transcript of the Executive Committee meeting gave further testimony to the peculiar lack of attention which these standards for delegate selection had received. Apart from thirty-five pages of introductory formalities, there were forty pages of debate on apportionment, twenty on ex officio status for members of the National Committee, twenty on credentials procedures, ten for Califano's explanation of the draft Call, and only ten for everything else, including informal byplay, honorific motions, a lunch break—and adoption of eighteen guidelines for party reform.

Curiously, press reports exaggerated this disjunction. The debate on apportionment, because it was the most extended controversy, because its impact was concrete and literal, or because it lent itself to simple, schematic portrayal, dominated the accounts of reporters. The success of a revolutionary change in the mechanics of presidential selection received short shrift. William Chapman at the *Washington Post,* for example, allotted twelve paragraphs to the apportionment dispute and exactly one sentence, his last, to endorsement of the commission guidelines:

> The Executive Committee also approved all 18 major recommendations for delegate selection reform approved by another special committee headed by Sen. George S. McGovern (S.D.).[5]

Indeed, in looking for practical consequences from the Executive Committee meeting, what most reporters credited was not the raw amount of proposed reform which had passed the Executive Committee. Nor was it the strategic success of the national chairman in foreseeing the items which would draw comment and in imposing his view of their proper resolution. Instead, it was the character of the one division which did emerge—a classic reformer-regular split. The portent which this seemed to offer for the meeting of the full National Committee, a portent of high conflict and additional defeats for reform, became the centerpiece of analyses which went beyond the narrow reporting of events. R. W. Apple, Jr., in the *New York Times,* suggested that the fate of party reform had become increasingly problematic:

> The split was almost the same as the one that occurred last March when Senator Hubert H. Humphrey tried unsuccessfully to put across former Gov. Matthew E. Welsh of Indiana as national chairman. Mr. O'Brien was later named in a compromise.
>
> It was, in effect, a new politics vs. old politics split, not a big state vs. small state split. Mr. Arvey, Mr. Barr and Mr. Strauss all voted to cut their states' votes.[6]

If these predictions were to come to pass, they would do so at the meeting of the full National Committee, a day and a half later. The committee remained a haven of regular-party sentiment. The dynamics of its meeting would provide the opportunity for party regulars to make themselves heard. Still, the Executive Committee had provided Chairman O'Brien—literally—with everything he wanted. There was no reason for O'Brien to modify his strategy in the interim, and he contented himself with making a few additional calls during Thursday the 18th.

As a result, at 9:30 A.M. on Friday, February 19, Lawrence F. O'Brien convened the Democratic National Committee for the purpose of considering a Preliminary Call to the Democratic National Convention. In order to set a tone for the day's proceedings, and without waiting for the usual, opening formalities, the chairman launched into an expanded version of the speech which he had given to the Executive Committee:

> *O'Brien:* The meeting will please come to order. Welcome this morning, friends.
> We are gathered today to chart a new course for the oldest political party the world has known.[7]

In rapid-fire order, the chairman introduced a number of themes which might predispose his listeners toward party reform, from the public attractiveness of reform as an enterprise, through the tactical utility of reform as a means to avoid a recurrence of the divisive events of 1968. After a relentlessly negative review of the Nixon presidency, O'Brien offered more focused comments for the regulars, and then the reformers, in his audience. From the regulars, he asked for sacrifice, including, by implication, their personal perquisites in delegate selection. From the reformers, he asked for restraint, insisting that since his return to the national chairmanship, the reform drive had been at the forefront of party activity. The chairman closed with an effort at uniting them all behind the Preliminary Call:

> *O'Brien:* How we perform today, and on into 1972, will demonstrate to the American voter in unmistakable terms that the Democratic Party is prepared to assume national leadership in the White House. The stakes are vital to our party, to our country, and to those who will follow us in trying to preserve and strengthen American democracy. Let us begin. Thank you.
> The Chair will now entertain a motion for adoption of the agenda.[8]

O'Brien then reverted to the normal order of business. The Credentials Committee of the National Committee reported on the admission of several new members, and these were duly seated. The roll was called. Mary Lou Burg, who had been acting as national vice chairman, was officially installed. Bob Strauss, the national treasurer, reviewed committee finances. Burg returned to cover political developments among Democratic women, the chief concern of her former post as director of women's activities.

After this presentation, Joe Barr rose to introduce the Preliminary Call, as forwarded by the Executive Committee. The former mayor of Pittsburgh outlined its general content, with particular attention to the apportionment formula. When Barr had finished, Steve Reinhardt requested permission to distribute a written complaint about that formula and about the legality of the Ad Hoc Committee proceedings which had contributed to it. Permission was quickly granted.

O'Brien brought on Joe Califano for a scheduled one-hour briefing, after which there was to be a question-and-answer session of whatever duration the members desired. This time, Califano began with the part of the Call derived from the work of the Party Structure Commission. Again, he moved from the reform resolutions of the 1968 Convention, to the abstract standards which had been extracted from them, to the specific rules by which the commission had given these standards life. Once more, he distinguished between required and recommended guidelines before turning to their individual content, which he surveyed in a discursive and informal fashion, with numerous asides.

Despite this informality, the Califano brief for the guidelines of the Party Structure Commission was a stern one. It even incorporated, without question, the "full, meaningful, and timely" directive which the commission staff had carpentered together out of very disparate pieces:

> *Califano:* These requirements are not within the power of this body, or any body except the 1972 Convention itself to change. These are, one, resolutions barring discrimination in the selection of delegates to the National Convention. Secondly, providing full, meaningful, and timely opportunity to participate. And thirdly, specific requirements relating to two matters: One, the unit rule is barred at every stage of the delegate selection process, and secondly, the selection of all delegates to the 1972 Convention must be made within the calendar year of 1972.[9]

Because the Executive Committee had accepted O'Brien's full package of amendments to the Call, Califano needed to devote some additional remarks to the convention status of National Committee members. In doing so, he attempted to insure the Executive Committee amendment—nonvoting, observer status for outgoing committee members—against assault either from those who would remove it or from those who would take it further.

Counsel moved next into the territory of the Rules Commission, beginning, this time, with its elaborate new process for evaluating credentials. Because this procedure was so very comprehensive, Califano settled for alerting committee members to a lengthy appendix containing its full text. His discussion of credentialing did, however, provide the opportunity to underline an aspect of delegate politics under reformed rules which might make the entire agenda more palatable to committee members, the fact that the *national convention* retained authority to evaluate credentials and thus to determine what these reforms required:

> *Califano:* I am sure you all recognize that it is the Convention that decides whether a delegation is to be seated or not, or a particular delegate is to be seated or not. It is the Credentials Committee that makes recommendations to the convention. . . .
>
> The Hearing Officer would not recommend whether the challenged delegation, or the challenging delegation, were the delegation he thought would be selected. He would simply try to find the facts.[10]

Finally, Califano addressed the apportionment section of the Call, where he discussed both the original formula from the Rules Commission and the new arrangement from the Ad Hoc Committee, which the Executive Committee had preferred. He touched on the lesser provisions which any such system had to include, an allocation for the territories, the ratio of alternates to delegates, and so forth, but a comparison of the underlying formulas was the heart of his presentation. With the end of his comments on apportionment, Califano reached the end of his prepared remarks on the Call. He threw the meeting open for questions.

Discussion circled through a variety of topics, at varying levels of abstraction. Easily the largest share of questions centered on the apportionment formulas. Three other items attracted some comment: The convention role of National Committee members, the mechanics of credentials review, and the legally and/or morally binding quality of the O'Hara and McGovern Commission reports. *Not a single question* addressed the content of the guidelines from the Party Structure Commission per se.

About a half hour into this interrogation, the issue of the legal character of commission recommendations—a staple of debate in reform politics since the day the commission had been appointed—made its appearance. Marjorie C. Thurman, national committeewoman from Georgia, broached the subject and offered Califano her view, that the guidelines carried no special authority or intrinsic obligation. Counsel, however, refused to be lured into the theoretical argument and answered with the obvious, practical truth:

> *Thurman:* I am Marjorie Thurman from the state of Georgia. I would like to inquire if you are taking the legal position that this party is bound by the guidelines of the McGovern Commission although they have never been submitted to this Committee, or to the Convention itself.
>
> *Califano:* I always think of that as sort of a theological point. This body is consid-

ering a Call to the Convention, a Call to the Convention which specifically, by the rules of the Democratic National Committee, [which] were passed at the 1968 Convention, and which is the function of this body to perform. What this body is considering is whether in that Call it will place language that one "adopts," and that is the word used, the required guidelines of the McGovern Commission, and two, "urges" the states to adopt, to put into effect the recommended guidelines of the McGovern Commission, and it is clearly the function of this body to decide whether or not it wants to put that into the Call to Convention, because it writes the Call.[11]

Califano's response was apparently satisfactory, and questioning moved off in other directions. After perhaps thirty more minutes, the committee found itself well into the noon hour and recessed for lunch.

Before the recess, John E. Powers, national committeeman from Massachusetts, had been seeking the floor. When the committee reassembled, Chairman O'Brien recognized Powers, and the latter wasted no time unveiling the initial amendment of the day:

> *Powers:* Thank you very much, Mr. Chairman, and my fellow National Committeemen and Committeewomen. . . . I would move, and so move, Mr. Chairman, to amend Section 8 on Page 3, to strike out the words in the second line, second line from the bottom, "Except the right to vote."[12]

This was, of course, the provision on ex officio representation for National Committee members. O'Brien had foreseen it as a possible point of friction with the entire National Committee. An anticipatory amendment had been created to avoid that possibility. The Executive Committee had gone along with this circumvention. John Powers did not. Instead, the Massachusetts Democrat backed his motion with a classic argument for party regularity:

> *Powers:* Now, Mr. Chairman, in the short time since you have been on this job, I think if we allow ourselves to be put in the position of eroding the National Committee, by taking away rights that we now have—say to us that we should go shoulder to shoulder with Bob Strauss in our respective states, to wipe out a $9,300,000 deficit, that we should be the individuals upon whom revolves the matter of party politics naturally, that we should come here as we do at your call, Mr. Chairman, that I should come as I have on occasion as a member of the O'Hara Commission, paying my own expenses—and that is a contribution we expect all to make, time, effort, money, and many other things, and inconvenience, to carry out the traditions as a National Committeeman—and I think until such time as the Convention takes this right away from us, that we should not sit and preside over our own liquidation and our own demise, and this is exactly what we are going to do if we adopt in total this Call. . . .
> Why should you be invited to my home, and then I refuse to let you sit down

at the table? In substance, this is what it is, and you are destroying the very thing that has kept [us] alive, during very lean years, Mr. Chairman, when you are not going to get any recognition because of the turn of political events, not because we have been remiss.[13]

Two days before, Joe Barr and Jake Arvey had put Powers's position before the Executive Committee, but O'Brien had slipped past them by having Califano continue to read and explain the draft Call. Steve Reinhardt had then prevented the discussion from resurfacing, by proposing to accept all of the Ad Hoc Committee recommendations except the one on apportionment and to debate that recommendation at length.

Powers, however, could not be finessed in this manner, since he had introduced the subject in the form of a motion. That motion had to come to a ballot; the response of the National Committee had to be the first test of O'Brien's anxieties—and of press speculation—about an impending revolt of the regulars. The question was, in fact, called as soon as the committeeman from Massachusetts finished speaking. His proposal passed overwhelmingly on a voice vote.

With this initial amendment out of the way, Liv B. Bjorlie, national committeewoman from North Dakota, followed with a second, on apportionment, and thereby inaugurated the longest battle of the day. Bjorlie offered the original formula from the Rules Commission, and her offering brought the National Committee to life. It was followed by five alternatives from the floor. For more than two hours, discussion shifted back and forth among these alternatives, in an unpatterned but intense manner.

As the competition to speak at last slackened, the vote on each was called. Each, in turn, fell by solid majorities. The favorite of the reformers, apportionment by pure Democratic vote, did not possess enough support to merit a division. Not surprisingly, the most popular of the losing measures, given the existing apportionment of the National Committee, was apportionment by size in the Electoral College, but even it failed to threaten passage, with 38 yes and 60 no. When the last of these proposed amendments arrived, the original mixed formula from the Rules Committee, it, too, failed overwhelmingly, 27 yes and 68 no.

At that point, in a clear anticlimax, Bob Strauss moved the Executive Committee version, and the members confirmed the obvious by adopting it on a voice vote. The result was so absolute that the usual, pro forma request for a roll call was not forthcoming, although John English, national committeeman from New York and Party Structure commissioner, did signal the absence of complete resignation when he announced, immediately after the meeting, that he would seek a reversal in the courts.[14]

Although no precise clocking was maintained, the period from the introduction of the initial amendment by Bjorlie to the passage of its ultimate successor from Strauss covered 70 of the 85 pages of transcript which the National Committee generated that afternoon. By that same measure, the members had already been sitting for about 160 of their eventual 175 pages. They were coming off a lengthy and emotional debate, one whose substantive character had demanded a high degree of concentration. Many were facing comparatively inflexible deadlines, in the form of scheduled flights to distant parts of the country; others had less ironclad, but still prescheduled, social appointments for the early evening.

In this atmosphere, the guidelines of the Party Structure Commission finally arrived for their moment of truth. With an apportionment formula in hand, Chairman O'Brien was at last ready to lead his committee into the text of these reform recommendations and to see what awaited him there. O'Brien paused once more for additional questions, but only a few surfaced. They centered this time on Guidelines A–1 and A–2, on the issue of whether these might under any circumstances become de facto quotas, but Counsel Califano successfully dismissed that possibility. After that, O'Brien asked for a motion, and Barr immediately moved that the draft Preliminary Call be accepted, *in toto*, as a package—guidelines, credentials regulations, and all.

As he had in the Executive Committee, O'Brien protested this undifferentiated and overly expeditious approach and suggested that the recommendations of the Party Structure Commission, at least, be separated out and voted up or down individually. This time, however, it was Barr (rather than Reinhardt) who argued that such procedural nicety was not required, and he settled the issue by calling his own motion. It passed on a heavy voice vote. Guidelines had been placed in the Call, as the ostensible rules for delegate selection to the 1972 Convention. Geri Joseph noted the speed and lack of fuss with which this apparently historic change was accomplished:

At the first quarter meeting of 1971, February, the McGovern stuff came up. This [apportionment] comes up mid-afternoon, and occupies a tremendous amount of time, and that was it. You would have thought that they would have taken up that booklet [*Mandate for Reform*] page by page. That never happened. You would have at least thought that they would have taken up those recommendations one by one. Unh-unh. That never happened that way.

The success of Barr's motion transferred everything endorsed by the Executive Committee into the Preliminary Call, along, of course, with the National Committee pronouncement on ex officio representation, added by John Powers. No sooner had Barr's motion gone through, however, than Powers's amendment came under fire, as George Mitchell of Maine came back immediately with a request for reconsideration.

Mitchell juxtaposed the rule barring ex officio delegates, Guideline C–2, with this amendment guaranteeing seats to his fellow committee members. He went on to emphasize the inequity in elevating these members above other deserving party workers. Powers, of course, was not inclined to let this stand and volleyed back as well, arguing that Mitchell's reasoning was in fact the *rationale* for his own amendment. Steve Reinhardt tried to finesse the entire debate by questioning the national counsel on whether the Powers amendment was not in principle "untimely" and thus prohibited by the 1968 Convention. Counsel, however, remained unwilling to use a legalism to choke off a political argument:

> *Califano:* The words of the 1968 Convention in this regard are as follows: "Be it resolved that the Call to the 1972 Democratic Convention . . ." and it goes on.
>
> Now it would seem to me that if the motion of the Committeeman from Massachusetts passes, if the reconsideration fails, then the provision stays in, and it is something that the 1972 Convention will have to confirm, as they will confirm the whole procedure.[15]

After a few more comments, O'Brien himself called the question. He found the ayes and nays insufficiently clear, however, and asked for a division. The result on that was unambiguous—31 yes and 57 no. The reconsideration motion failed. The Powers amendment stayed in the Preliminary Call. Substantive business for the day was completed. All that remained was for Strauss to offer a series of ceremonial resolutions, honoring various individuals who had aided Democratic causes in the period since the last committee meeting. When he finished, a motion for adjournment came quickly, and at 4:20 P.M., on a voice vote without dissent, the meeting was adjourned.

Practical Influences on the Committee Response

The adoption by the National Committee of eighteen guidelines for the reform of delegate selection—and presidential selection, too—was a potentially historic act. If even a handful of additional states moved into compliance as a result of this adoption, the response of the National Committee would rate a footnote in the history of party reform. If a substantial share of the remaining states eventually followed this directive, the response of the National Committee would constitute a landmark in the progress of the most sweeping planned reform in American party history.

That landmark owed a great deal to the internal dynamics of the committee meeting itself, that is, to the order in which items appeared, to the response to each as it ramified upon the others, to the pace of activity and the progress of the clock. In this light, even the thorough exposition of the Preliminary Call by the national counsel on the morning of February 19, while it clearly made most members better informed than they had been in advance of the meeting, was also a compression of the time available to debate—and alter—the Call. In the time which did remain, the members had found a major issue, interstate apportionment, which they debated—and attempted to amend—at length. With almost no time remaining after that lengthy, convoluted, and intense debate, they had gone on to endorse the rest of the draft Call, in bulk, without further ado.

Yet simple recognition of the role of internal dynamics was immediately a tribute to the role of the national chairman in foreseeing—indeed, in facilitating—these dynamics. Larry O'Brien had guessed at the items which would produce the most intense committee concern; he had organized them in the agenda so that the first of these, interstate apportionment, might actually take care of the rest. When the day came, he was proved correct in his substantive estimate, and he got away with his strategic maneuver. Even Eli Segal, former counsel to the Party Structure Commission and a confirmed critic of the national chairman, was moved to salute this tactical skill: "O'Brien did schedule this by design. He said, 'Let's have this fight on apportionment.' It was very well done. You had to admire his craftsmanship."

In truth, there had been one pivotal moment when it looked as if all this preparation might go awry. That had come when John Powers introduced his amendment on ex officio representation, restoring the members of the National Committee to their automatic seats at the National Convention. O'Brien himself confessed a certain nervousness while the Powers amendment was before the house: "I must say that I had my fingers crossed on that first vote. We were asking them to throw on the table the only thing that a National Committee member got."

But when the amendment succeeded, despite the careful, anticipatory maneuvering of the chairman, the meeting still settled back on its intended course. Those who had been preparing to fight over interstate apportionment immediately gained the floor and took the members off onto that issue, in a debate which would preclude all others. The return to apportionment was effectively a return to the scenario mapped out by O'Brien in the days leading up to this session. When that return occurred, he breathed a sigh of relief:

> There was plenty of concern, of wonderment. The intricacies of the whole thing may have missed many of them. You don't take these things to the floor if you don't have your ducks in a row. In a meeting format, it's not unusual to take things to the floor, and have them exhausted, and while they catch their breath—and it's late, they have to catch planes, they have other engagements—you try to have a motion made from the floor, and you always know where that motion 'is coming from.

At the same time, of course, the success of these maneuvers owed something to the fundamental character of the National Committee as a political institution. Indeed, the nature of the outcome—formal endorsement of sweeping party reform on the participatory model by the highest organ of the regular party—served to emphasize the variability inherent in the committee structure and the possibility of alternative results inherent in that variability.

At a minimum, committee members had obviously been free to follow their national chairman and not just their state party leaders. In fact, the nature of committee organization—its intermittent character, the place of the chairman in its interim activities—made it difficult for these state party figures to mount any coordinated challenge when their national chairman went the other way. Even the more involved committee members, like Mitchell of Maine, understood that the formal post of national chairman in such an arrangement offered inevitable, substantial, institutional leverage:

> Any chairman with any degree of skill, the larger the committee and the less often it meets, the easier it is to control. The National Committee was one hundred and some, and met twice a year. This played much more of a role than the [Ad Hoc] Committee of Geri Joseph and me.

In the face of extreme intermittence—the National Committee had not assembled since the meeting which appointed O'Brien in February of 1970; it would not meet again until October of 1971—the national chairman was the major link among Committee members. He was also the controlling force in the national party bureaucracy. This was one more reason why the national staff was not available to coordinate the complaints of state party leaders; it was one more reason why the national staff could close out entirely the complaints of organized labor. In the absence of these countervailing efforts, of course, the influence of the chairman was additionally, vastly enhanced. Joseph summed it up with asperity:

> It's not in the nature of things that when you have people coming in from fifty states, that they will be able to keep track of what is going on. Also, the DNC has never been noted for communication. You're out in the states; you don't know what the [national] party is doing.

This fundamental character of the National Committee, along with the specific content of commission guidelines, had provided the framework for the encounter which resulted in the endorsement of party reform. Within that framework, the modal perceptions—and misperceptions—of committee members (see below) and the peculiar dynamics of the committee meeting itself contributed centrally to the outcome. Yet the interaction of all these factors in producing a historic outcome only underlined the fact that they had been connected, at bottom, by the strategy, the particular machinations, of the national chairman.

It was Chairman O'Brien who teased out the likely items of conflict from the formal text for party reform. It was O'Brien who revised that text to fit the basic character of the National Committee as he understood it. He then worked long and hard to sell these revisions to committee members, reinforcing or combating their instinctive perceptions as he uncovered them. He foresaw—and managed—the dynamics of the crucial meeting. The principal himself was more modest in describing his role, but he did not deny its centrality:

> Many of the southern Democrats were very concerned. Those that had labor affiliations were very concerned. You would not have had the National Committee meeting that took place if there hadn't been a very hard sell. To achieve that at that meeting, when you have conservative party members go along on a vote like that, well you have something.

Bob Nelson, who saw these committee actions as a great victory for party reform, was far less bashful on the chairman's behalf:

> O'Brien's leadership was so strong with the Democratic National Committee in February of 1971 that he could get them to go along. He was well convinced by that time; he exerted his leadership. We had some fairly sharp discussions with the members. He made one hell of a speech to them; he made it a personal matter.
>
> The National Committee didn't ever really have much power. The post was ceremonial; many of them had bought their positions with service. At that point, National Committee members had such an incredible respect for O'Brien—they gave him a mystique—that they would go along with him on nearly anything. O'Brien was using his personal credits.

The central role of O'Brien in this crucial chapter of reform politics emphasized, one more time, the peculiar personal distinctions which he brought to the chairmanship. It emphasized, as well, the way these differed both from his immediate predecessor, Fred Harris, the man who desired to restyle himself as the archetypal party reformer, and from his predecessor in the first O'Brien regime at the National Committee, John Bailey, the archetypal party regular.

Harris would have been in favor of the same ultimate outcome. Indeed, he would have been unlikely to add O'Brien's conservatizing amendment on interstate apportionment. Yet Harris never possessed a similar influence with the National Committee, and if he had failed to cater to them on as obvious a matter as interstate apportionment, he might well have endured a revolt of considerably greater scope. Bailey, by contrast, would have opposed more of the total reform package, right from the start. Even he might not have tried to sabotage the package in toto, but he would surely have put more resources from the National Committee at the service of committee regulars. The result, just as surely, would have been far less party reform.

Committee Perceptions of the Impact of Reform

Yet even then, even after acknowledging the pervasive influence of Chairman O'Brien, the crucial, final contribution to the response of the National Committee remained unacknowledged. For the character of the strategic initiatives which the national chairman had developed, the character of the institution to which they had been applied, and the dynamics of the meeting which had seen these initiatives achieve almost complete success were not enough to explain the outcome, to explain how the guidelines of the Party Structure Commission could go through the National Committee essentially intact and *with hardly a whimper.*

Committee members were—and remained—predominantly hostile to broad-gauge, externally imposed, party reform. Moreover, the reforms which they had been asked—and consented—to approve promised centrally planned institutional changes which were not only extensive but thoroughly inconsistent with current practice. Polled privately, in the comfort and seclusion of their own homes, most members would have preferred, at the very least, to postpone a decision. Most did care about the regular party structure; most saw the social and stylistic gulf between party regulars and those who were pushing reform.

384

Beyond that, the reforms at issue really did promise sweeping change in the entire matrix of institutions for delegate selection and presidential nomination. The basic institutions for choosing delegates, the institutional bedrock of the entire system, were being altered in the most extensive fashion since the creation of the national party convention. The rules governing allocation of delegates through these mechanisms were being amended. The distribution of the delegates to be won or lost was being shifted in a far-reaching manner. The character of the delegates themselves was potentially at issue. The fundamental structure of American political parties—the relationship between theoretically autonomous state party units and the national party committee—was undergoing a historic change. The place of the state and local parties in this delegate selection process was being retailored—indeed, erased.

Committee members would never have endorsed these proposals, then, without a fourth and final factor, beyond the strategy of the chairman, the structure of the National Committee, and the dynamics of this particular meeting. They would not have endorsed these proposals without a general—and influential—pattern of perception about the impact of these reform guidelines. In other words, the tendency of committee members to spot, or overlook, practical effects in formally codified rules was the final contribution to the rapid and quiet acquiescence of these members in reforms which purported to alter the entire structure of national party politics.

By 1971, an observer focused centrally on the fate of these reforms should not have found the influence of this perceptual factor surprising. The Party Structure commissioners, after all, in addressing their proposed guidelines, had been heavily swayed by their propensity to perceive, or miss, practical impacts in a formal text. National Committee members, in converting the recommendations of these commissioners into party law, were similarly affected.

Indeed, the elements constituting this general pattern of perception were essentially the same. When committee members—like commissioners—saw a recommendation which appeared to mandate specific changes in the *outcome* of the process of delegate selection, they were moved to stop, to question, and to debate. When committee members—like commissioners—had personal experiences which made the practical impact of a formal rule appear substantial, even when it was less consequential statistically, they were moved to stop and debate as well. When they failed to see a mandated change in outcome or a practical impact based on experience, they moved rapidly by.

Chairman O'Brien was not unaware of this pattern. Or at least, his instinctive responses were such that he read the guidelines much as his committee members did. This did not prevent him from seeing the myriad additional demands which these guidelines would place—were placing—on his state party chairmen. It did permit him to zero in, unerringly as it turned out, on the precise items which would cause conflict in the National Committee.

In the original draft of the Preliminary Call, O'Brien found two items which fell afoul of this particular approach to interpreting proposals for reform. The first was the formula for interstate apportionment, which announced in its text that it was altering *by precise numerical figures* the earliest concrete outcome in the process of delegate selection. The second was the provision removing ex officio seats for National Committee members, *the ultimate personal attack* on their direct political experience.

Yet the degree to which an impact on outcomes or on personal experience colored the perception of the meaning of reform really came through with the secondary items about which the chairman also worried—and in the major items about which he worried not at all. Thus, the chairman also prepared detailed arguments to deal with commission recommendations on demographic representation, because he saw that these, too, might—or might not—be seen as demanding precise numerical changes in the outcome of the process. By the same token, he paid special attention, to the point of proposing another amendment, to the credentials process, because his experience—and that of many committee members—was that the real requirements of most party rules were ultimately nailed down in the Credentials Committee.

By contrast, the items to which the chairman devoted no preparation were breathtaking in their scope. The mandated shift in the fundamental institutions of delegate selection made this point most clearly. But all those items whose evident impact was on the institutional structure for delegate selection and not on delegate outcomes per se, as well as all those items whose impact even on this institutional structure was difficult to detect, would have made the point as well. Despite their consequence for the operation of a reformed political process, they were not expected to receive much inquiry from members of the National Committee. They received no advance preparation from the national chairman.

The outstanding example of an item whose impact was on institutional structure but not on outcomes per se was the prohibition of the delegate primary and the implicit demand for a move to the candidate primary in its place. A careful reader might discern that the requirement of a statement of presidential preference by every contender for delegate status effectively doomed the direct election of *delegates* and shifted the emphasis to *candidates* instead. But even that careful reader might be unsure that this would produce a substantial impact on numerical results. Larry O'Brien—the biggest careful reader of them all—paid no attention to this possibility.[16]

By the same token, the abolition of the party caucus and the implicit demand for its replacement with a participatory convention was the perfect example of an impact on institutional structure which was itself almost impossible to discern without staff assistance. Despite its status as the device by which the largest share of delegates to national party conventions in all of American history had been selected, the party caucus was abolished by rules which were not assembled in any one guideline, which were not presented in the order in which they had to be assembled, and which did not at any point claim to be making their actual, aggregate, institutional impact. The average committee member would be extremely unlikely to perceive this impact as a concrete outcome. O'Brien never gave it a second thought.

When the crucial day came, of course, the aggregate National Committee followed these same standards to a remarkable degree. In the only explicit questioning of the guidelines, the committee stopped to examine its pronouncements on demographic representation, to see whether these demanded changes in the practical outcome of a reformed process. The committee debated interstate apportionment at length, eventually accepting a substitute provision from its chairman, one which was still a quite radical change from the existing formula. Finally, feeling no need for debate and brooking no request for delay or reconsideration, the committee took decisive action on ex officio representation, the issue of its own convention seats.

The National Committee, then, did locate items which appeared, to a clear majority of the members, to have real implications for the politics of presidential selection. Having located them, it did bring these provisions into conformity with the collective preference of the members. Yet the overlap between these disputed provisions and those which promised the most institutional impact was slight indeed. John Stewart, director of communications for Chairman O'Brien, watched the members at work:

> What most of them perceived was the immediate threat to their position. No longer was an incumbent National Committee member going to be a delegate. If they got that changed, they as individuals were not taken out of the process. Their feeling was that if they preserved that, they preserved their own participation. In fact, most of them wouldn't think of themselves as members of an "organization." They didn't look down the road. There were very few people at the time who could see what would be going on in 1972. The rest of it might have been vaguely unsettling, but it didn't present the immediate, definable threat that losing their seats did. Many of these people resented less the content of these things than the people who were pushing them, Eli Segal and all those alphabet groups.

The influence of this perceptual factor should not be overstated. All the other major influences on the product of the committee meeting—the strategy of the national chairman, the structure of the National Committee, the dynamics of the meeting itself—were reasons *not* to search for institutional implications in proposals for party reform. Moreover, any remaining inclination to search for these impacts ran up against an additional set of problems.

The lack of staff support for anyone who did aspire to ferret out institutional effects was a serious handicap. The translation of formal rules into practical effects is never a simple task; the assistance of staff experts would have been invaluable. Because the national chairman had firm control of the national party bureaucracy and was leading it in quite another direction, however, countervailing experts would probably have had to come from organized labor. Labor ultimately failed to seize its opportunity, but Don Fraser, at least, believed that an attempt by COPE to underline the implications of key guidelines might have paid substantial dividends:

> COPE didn't track very tightly on this. It wasn't so much that they didn't like the product, as that they didn't like the whole operation. COPE was not actively concerned about the guidelines.
>
> A better tactic for COPE would have required intimate knowledge, and then finding problems. But they didn't have anybody in their organization who was tracking on it. They *should* have said, "What about this?" or "Doesn't this seem to imply this?", but they didn't.

Instead of this prior, independent, institutional analysis, what the members had was a set of reassurances which appeared to mitigate the impact of formal rules and which were emphasized by proponents of these rules, including the national chairman. Some of these reassurances appeared to provide the state parties with their escape route from party reform, even after the national party endorsed it. Others appeared to provide the national party with its escape route, even if many of its state units complied.

In the first category, of provisions limiting the apparent pressure on state parties, was the "all feasible efforts" clause in the commission guidelines.[17] This might permit the national party to endorse reform, the state chairman to endorse it, too, the state party to comply only partially—and all sides to announce that they had done their best. Carmen Warschaw, Party Structure commissioner and national committeewoman from California, found that scenario plausible:

> All you had to do was make the effort, remember. But if the Governor vetoed it, or something like that, you had made your effort. You had a prima facie effort. This 'reasonable effort' language was supposed to be a way out for the states.

In the second category of obvious exits, of provisions permitting the national party to draw back at some subsequent point, was the credentialing procedure of the National Convention. Battles in the Credentials Committee had always determined what the rules actually required; battles in the Credentials Committee would still, inevitably, do so. Geri Joseph heard a good deal of this reasoning within the National Committee: "There was a feeling that a lot of this would come out in the wash at the Credentials Committee. It seemed that it would have to."

Finally, there were a number of ultimate institutional implications which were not even implicit in the guidelines at the time the National Committee met. Several of the most consequential guidelines, in fact, were to generate substantial, subsequent battles over their interpretation. The outcome on these—the result on demographic representation would be the most striking, followed by the result on proportional representation—was invisible, in principle, as the National Committee met. Don Fraser watched some members take implicit comfort from their absence:

> You should understand that the guidelines as initially perceived by an average party member were not seen as a major problem. The controversy came later. A lot of the requirements were hard to argue against. Some of the implications were not very evident.

All these factors reduced the practical significance of typical committee perceptions. They decreased the number of committee members who would search for practical impacts from formal rules; they raised the threshold of impact which those rules had to obtain before they gained the attention of those committee members who did search. Yet the inability of many committee members to see a concrete impact in a procedural change, much less their inability to notice the extent of the procedural change itself, remained the crucial, final influence on the events of February 19. Later, Joe Califano put his impression of this perceptual failure on the public record:

> But even those Democratic party leaders involved in the presidential quest believed that the newly established McGovern-Fraser Commission procedures would be of little significance. They assumed that the rules of the presidential nomination game would be basically the same. The presidential nomination, they believed, would go to the man who won the most primaries, or at least the key ones, and who obtained commitments from state and local party leaders with national impact, as far in advance as the shrewd political instincts of those leaders would permit. Their failure to appreciate the depth of the procedural revolution reflected in the new rules left them standing, mouths open, shocked into political impotency during the preconvention and convention rites both in Washington and in Miami Beach in 1972.[18]

Given the importance of these (mis)perceptions to the fate of reform within the National Committee and given the centrality of Chairman O'Brien in shaping those perceptions, the extent to which O'Brien himself appreciated the institutional impact of reform became a matter of some debate among major actors in reform politics. At one extreme, Vick French, the former executive assistant to Chairman Harris, believed that O'Brien saw many of these implications from the first:

> Reform staffers were very apprehensive about O'Brien. We had no reason to think that they shouldn't be apprehensive. He understood far better than Fred what was required by the rules.

At the other extreme, Carol Casey believed that O'Brien was yet another long-time participant in national party politics who underestimated the significance of these changes in formal party rules:

> I don't think O'Brien realized how much this would change the structure. I don't think any of us did. The ex officio ruling and the limit on state committee selection were the only ones that people really understood. These were the ones that professional politicians were concerned about. It looked like instead of lobbying the state committees, they would have to change their focus to lobbying the state convention. There was still a lot of concern for having a nice, orderly, unified National Convention. These rules would help to do that, but if there was foot-dragging on party reform, there would be disaffection on the left, and that would bring 1968 back, only worse. O'Brien saw the attraction of reform without any real costs, I think.

It was true, at a minimum, that the chairman had never at any point undertaken (or commissioned) a study of the matrix of institutions for delegate selection which would prevail if these reforms were uniformly successful. On the other hand, and far more consequentially, the chairman was already privy to the specific demands which these reforms were making on the individual states. Moreover, he had certainly acquiesced in the dissemination of the Model Party Rules, which gave these reforms an added institutional reach. If he never assembled these understandings in one central framework, then, he was certainly closer to comprehending their cumulative institutional demands, intuitively but concretely, than anyone except perhaps Bob Nelson.

There was, however, one final, concrete indicator available to the National Committee (and the national chairman) in interpreting the practical impact of reformed rules. The members might not be able to conjure up the composite institutional framework—the political process—created by these eighteen guidelines. They might have even more trouble specifying the elite structure associated with implementation. Yet they still possessed this other, giant, concrete indicator of the practical effect of new, formal rules. Indeed, no less a figure than Chairman O'Brien himself was centrally concerned, through related party responsibilities, with this practical measure.

This indicator, of course, was the identity of the probable *nominee* under a reformed process of presidential selection, and some members surely factored this into their judgments about how reform would work. By early 1971, the potential field for a nomination contest was already emerging. By that time, in fact, a consensus on the probable winner, the next Democratic contender for president, perhaps the next president of the United States, was emerging as well.

That man was Edmund S. Muskie, senator from Maine. Muskie had begun to attract national attention as the vice-presidential nominee in 1968. Indeed, he was one of the few prominent Democrats to enhance his personal standing in that divisive and discouraging campaign. The incident at Chappaquiddick bridge had then scratched Edward Kennedy, senator from Massachusetts, from the list of presidential hopefuls, making Muskie the logical heir, more or less by default. Muskie had moved from default status to an active attraction in his own right through a speech on election eve in November of 1970, one which followed and contrasted sharply with that of the incumbent president, Richard Nixon.[19] If Muskie had a major rival remaining, it was Hubert Humphrey, who had just returned to the United States Senate. Humphrey, however, was tamping down speculation about a second run of his own and was putatively supporting Muskie.

Perhaps alone among the obvious contenders, Muskie promised the ability to unite party factions and heal party wounds. George McGovern represented party insurgents and the reform wing. If proposed reforms had seemed likely to bring McGovern to power, party regulars would have had to resist those reforms, tooth and nail, at home and in the National Committee. Humphrey removed this particular incentive for resistance, but only because he represented party regulars and their associated interests, thereby rubbing salt in the wounds of the reform coalition and inciting *them* to further resistance.

Muskie had neither liability. He was busy attacking the Nixon administration, while neither demanding nor resisting the imposition of reform. In fact, he seemed likely to be nominated under any rules. Moreover, Muskie himself was widely thought to favor liberal policies but conservative politics, in the manner of Harry Truman, John Kennedy, or Lyndon Johnson. As Muskie began to come into his own, then, it became possible for party regulars to believe that the advantages of reform could be obtained without its costs, that the public relations assets of party reform could be combined with the normal product of unreformed politics. Joseph watched this belief—this aspiration, perhaps this delusion—mollify some potential opponents of reform:

Political people do not tend to be abstract theoreticians, or even very philosophical. When they get into a situation, they think in terms of a candidate. If
they can see who it's for or against, they can be for or against it. But the rules
didn't fit into any of that, so they weren't able to come to grips with this. At
the time the rules were being formulated, in '69 or '70, they didn't know who
the rules were for. Later, in 1971, it didn't seem likely that anyone other than
Humphrey, Muskie, or Kennedy would come out of them anyway.

The use of an emerging nominee—of Ed Muskie—as an indicator of the
likely impact of party reform accorded neatly with a general belief about the
impact of formal change, a belief which committee members shared with numerous outside observers, including most political journalists. This was the
belief that basic social forces and the grand issues of an era, coupled with and
operating through candidate personalities, campaign strategies, and issues of
the day, inevitably determine the outcomes of politics—and thus reliably overwhelm the effects of institutional arrangements.

In early 1971, this view was reinforced by fifty years of stability in the presidential nominating process. Anxious party reformers, of course, saw this as
a half century of inertia, dragging on any procedural innovation. When proposed reforms reached the point of a formal vote in the National Committee,
however, these reformers could instead have viewed this as fifty years in which
there had been *no experimental evidence* of the effect of altering the process,
a half century in which the central role of the rules had been permitted—by
a lack of change, not by a decline in influence—to recede almost to the point
of invisibility.

Under these conditions, with a lifetime of behavior in an unchanged institutional framework as the standard, it became possible to believe that this behavior, by itself, was the dominant factor in presidential politics. It became possible to believe, in short, that patterns which had reliably surfaced, year in and
year out, for at least half a century, would be the dominant patterns under
new arrangements as well as old. Richard M. Scammon, analyst of elections
and student of political participation, saw this as a crucial element in the failure of many party officials to worry themselves into a more active opposition:

> Many of the people in the south were convinced that the rules didn't make
> much difference. They didn't measure the depth of anti-war sentiment, for exam-
> ple. These people didn't understand that the participation of their own people
> was so low that—they didn't realize that—they could be knocked off by a busload
> of kids. They just didn't recognize what could happen. . . .
> Many of the politicians, themselves unknowing, not believing that they could
> be taken, were saying, "Gee, we've got to listen to those kids." I think to a large
> extent many of these people simply got overwhelmed. Many of the Democratic

pols never believed it would go this far. But most of them, they were inhibited by the past—they simply made a gross tactical error. "This is a new element of the party. We don't want to antagonize them. But of course they can't win anyway."

Eli Segal, one of the most committed partisans of those reforms, concurred in essence with the argument of Scammon:

> I often think that the reason we did so well was that no one understood the revolution. We were always waiting for some people to wake up and say, "Hey, they're stealing our party from us," and it never happened. We were always in a state of suspended animation, suspended anxiety.

Implications

The national press had found little worthy of coverage in the first two years of reform struggles within the Democratic party, and the National Committee's manner of adopting a Preliminary Call—an apparent benchmark in those struggles—was not calculated to alert reporters to any portentous new developments. Nevertheless, this time, a few reporters did not let the potentially historic character of committee action go unremarked. R. W. Apple, Jr., for example, observed not only the potential importance of the Preliminary Call, but even the peculiar fashion in which it had been adopted:

> Washington, February 19. After a daylong dispute on a relatively minor issue, marked by parliamentary bickering and impassioned speeches, the Democratic National Committee approved without debate today a far-reaching set of reforms in the selection of delegates to the party's national convention.
> The Committee approved without major changes the guidelines of the reform commission headed until recently by Senator George S. McGovern of South Dakota. . . . In general, they will make it harder for party leaders to dictate the choice of a presidential nominee—a change sought by the party's more liberal elements, particularly since the clashes at the convention in Chicago in 1968.
> The party conservatives said nothing as the McGovern proposals were approved. . . .
> All the decisions made by the committee were incorporated into the "call" to the convention, which sets the rules for the convention itself. These can be modified by the convention after it meets, but the incorporation of the McGovern and O'Hara recommendations into the call almost intact was a triumph for the reformers.[20]

Almost exactly two years had passed from the appointment of a Commission on Party Structure and Delegate Selection to the endorsement of its—sweeping, historic—recommendations by the Democratic National Committee. Once, the entire reform movement had been little more than a convention tactic of party insurgents. Now, the central manifesto of that movement was the official policy of the national Democratic party.

The enactment of that policy was not, of course, the ultimate triumph of party reform. The scope of the compliance negotiations which remained prevented such an easy extrapolation. The state parties had a long tradition of going their own way; they had little precedent for following national party directives. The language of the Preliminary Call was loose enough to permit good-faith arguments about the failure to comply; it was ambiguous enough to allow interpretive arguments about the practical requirements of individual rules.

Nevertheless, the enactment of this policy did usher in a new phase of reform politics. At a minimum, it was no longer possible to hope that the National Committee would serve as the bulwark against extensive, externally imposed, party reforms—although the committee would cause even optimistic partisans of reform to hesitate, once again, when it re-entered reform politicking in the fall of 1971. Beyond that, it was now the opponents of reform who were necessarily on the defensive. The official status of reform rules was established. The formal onus in rules negotiations, and the need for superior political muscle, would clearly fall upon those who did not wish to comply.

Two major questions remained for this next phase of reform politics. First, would the state parties go along? Would they implement these newly endorsed reform rules? If they did, would they honor these rules in execution, when 1972 arrived? Second, would the alternative Democratic coalition come together in some organized and coordinated fashion? Would it put itself in a position to capitalize on these newly reformed rules explicitly and directly? Or would the aggregation of those who ought logically to benefit from these rules have to be forged, if at all, in the presidential campaigns of 1972?

These were, of course, questions about institutional change and the circulation of elites, about the extent of institutional change and elite replacement which would follow from the action of the National Committee. There were clues but not answers in the proceedings of the committee itself. Obviously, the regular party had just endorsed the comprehensive reform program desired by party insurgents. This national endorsement clearly made the regular parties in the states more likely to go along with that program as well. The combined effect of these developments was surely a victory *for* any emerging, alternative coalition of Democratic elites.

On the other hand and ironically, this endorsement had been almost entirely an internal matter among party regulars. That is, the aspiring beneficiaries of these reforms had been almost irrelevant to their extraction. In fact, on the one issue where party reformers had tried to shift the inclinations of the full committee, on interstate apportionment, they had been crushed on their own proposal and then humiliated, on a simple voice vote, by Chairman O'Brien. The surprise for party reformers, then, at receiving nearly everything they had asked for, including a revolutionary change in the process of presidential selection, occasioned some whimsy among national party staffers like John Stewart:

> The dynamics of the day. They had to spend the whole day arguing over the O'Hara Commission and the apportionment formula. O'Brien and his staff had opposed the liberal position on the apportionment formula, and had prevailed there. Califano gets up and goes over it all, guideline by guideline. I think if that had come up first, you might have had a much more spirited debate. But the reason they came up second was that O'Brien didn't *want* a spirited debate, he wanted them to go through without. In that sense, it was a very skillful operation. It was just reflective of that judgment of a year earlier that it was better to accept them with all their warts. But I do think the key thing in terms of not having a major floor fight over them was that they came up second, after lunch, and by the time Califano was through explaining them, it was late, and people had to catch planes. The Ken Bodes and Eli Segals were walking around wondering what had happened.[21]

That the realization of these reforms depended on the political credits of a national chairman who was personally rooted in the political tradition being supplanted was, of course, a political irony of major proportions. Yet it did not, at this point, have many additional implications for the fate—and impact—of reform. The National Committee had just made a powerful, though by no means definitive, contribution to institutional change. The role of the national chairman in that contribution suggested that he was unlikely to reverse himself and try to restrain this change at any point down the road.

Yet if this institutional reform were substantially implemented, the political roots of the contemporary chairman would acquire a primarily historical interest. For if these rules were capable of the impact upon presidential selection which their supporters desired, that impact would predictably include an extensive replacement of party elites. And at that point, the contributions of a sitting party chairman, in getting the existing National Committee to endorse reform, would pale beside the raw fact that the committee had been convinced to go along and had helped bring a new Democratic order into being—one which might well swallow up Chairman O'Brien and many of his regular-party colleagues.

CHAPTER

15

The Debate over Implementation:

State Compliance Politics and National

Press Analysis

IN WHICH, the state parties address the guidelines in the aftermath of the Preliminary Call; debate breaks out in the national press about the real progress of party reform; and additional groups, new and old, are moved by this debate to gear up to and participate in the politics of implementation. AND IN WHICH, reform politics returns to decentralized negotiations with the state political parties, played out, this time, in the national press as well; institutional change proceeds apace in the states, while national anxiety about its realization does not abate; and major, new elements of the alternative Democratic coalition are mobilized and melded.

WITHIN HOURS of the National Committee meeting on the Preliminary Call, reform politics reverted to decentralized negotiations with the individual state parties, where it remained, on balance, for the next eight months. The immediate reality of that politics, as it had been for the eight months before the National Committee meeting, was a composite of dispersed and piecemeal but cumulatively impressive developments in the effort at implementation. This time, however, the national press essayed an interpretation of the progress of party reform, and its composite account, coming to a very different conclusion, gained a reality all its own—one which influenced national actors as much or more than particular negotiations with individual states.

The first stop for the Preliminary Call, after passage by the National Committee, was the desks of state chairmen across the country. The Call had become official policy for the national party; the office of the national chairman was quick to let its state counterparts know. In case these party leaders could have forgotten, the principals at the Party Structure Commission, seeing in the Preliminary Call an expanded grant of commission authority, contacted them as well, underlining not just the official status but the coercive requirements of commission guidelines.

The response was immediate. Everywhere, indigenous reform commissions and other extraneous actors were pushed out of the way, and state party officialdom itself tackled the question of implementation. Differences between volunteer and organized state parties persisted, even in this period of intensified negotiations, with volunteer parties more likely to bargain directly with national reform actors and organized parties more likely to hammer out their arrangements internally. Yet the crucial development was the move toward compliance, within volunteer and organized parties alike.

It was also during this period that the national press began to focus on reform politics. Previously, the nonpartisan press, and even the journals of political opinion, had paid scant attention to the progress of party reform. Ironically, when press analysts turned to that progress, at a time when the state parties as a group were moving closer and closer to compliance, the press as a whole pronounced the outcome very much in doubt, with a possibility that reform had peaked and was now decelerating.

There was, of course, a concentrated jockeying among reform principals to influence this emerging press portrait. There was an institutional dynamic within the news media which was even more central to the character of this evolving press view, a dynamic involving both the distribution of those news sources which paid attention to reform politics and the professional norms which operated within those that did. But beyond these, the mere fact of an active press debate, much less its essentially pessimistic character, was enough to produce additional developments in reform politics.

Established institutional actors in reform politics, and most especially the Party Structure Commission, were remobilized in partial reaction to the national press debate. Don Fraser had intended to bring the full commission back as a source of pressure for implementation and compliance. He found himself forced to contend, simultaneously, with a national press portrait as the "reality" which his remobilized commissioners wanted to address.

Beyond that, existing institutional actors with a less automatic interest in party reform also took this press portrait, again in part, as reason to move explicitly into reform politics. Among issue organizations with a focus on reform, Common Cause was especially important here. Among ideological organizations with a liberal leaning, Americans for Democratic Action was most noteworthy. These organizations, and others like them, spun off subunits with the progress of party reform as their official focus.

The fundamental consequence of all this, and the one most likely to be obscured by the character of the press debate and by the mobilization of new reform allies, was the accelerating drift of the state parties into compliance with national reform directives. But a simultaneous consequence was the discovery by the news media, at long last, of reform politics, a discovery producing a set of pressures on national party officials which disposed them additionally toward support for reform while placing the attentive press itself on the side of the reformers. While all this was occurring, finally, the alternative Democratic coalition began to form up as a practically organized political entity, linked through interlocking participants—almost an "interlocking directorate"—and prepared to act in concert not just in reform politics, but in the presidential politics to follow.

Reform Politics after the Preliminary Call

The Preliminary Call was copied and sent to the state party chairmen by the office of the national chairman as a matter of administrative course but as a means of pressure as well. Yet it was at the Party Structure Commission that the Call was most enthusiastically received. The commission entourage was looking for new activities—and new influence—in state reform politics. Its members seized happily upon the Preliminary Call as a potential source of both.

In the weeks following the National Committee meeting, the commission was only beginning to resume its active life. Bob Nelson and Carol Casey had been diverted somewhat by the election campaign of 1970. They had then used the period between early November and mid-February to develop the Model Party Rules. But they had been forced to restrain their efforts at imposing these upon the states, since the state party leadership had been involved first with the election campaign and then, like Nelson and Casey, with a wait for the assumption of office by those who had been victorious in the November elections.

The commission had received one crucial, additional "gift" during this period, in the form of a new commission chairman. Don Fraser did not plunge immediately into commission activities in the early months of 1971, reserving his major attention for congressional politics. But by the early spring, Fraser would be ready for concentrated commission activity, and his accession would appear to Nelson almost as another turning point in the history of party reform:

> The staff had to do the implementation end. Don Fraser was a real activist; this was his "thing." He took a tremendous personal interest in this. Don, much more than George McGovern, was the key man. It was actually Don and myself that got that through. I was interested; I found in Fraser a guy who was tremendously interested.

In this environment, the arrival of the Preliminary Call was an event of major consequence. That arrival became the warrant for renewed negotiations with state party leaders. Simultaneously, it augmented the authority of commission personnel in these negotiations—as the principal interpreters of the requirements of party reform. Its mere existence took the edge off countervailing arguments that they were using their positions to advance their own peculiar vision of appropriate party behavior or that they were really providing aid and comfort to their own allies in state party politics. Instead, after February 19, 1971, they were acting on behalf of the Democratic National Committee. Nelson moved quickly to communicate that fact to anyone with a potential interest:

> When the National Committee then acted, the Preliminary Call went out by the thousands. We made sets available to every leader, every organization, rules for every state. We gave everyone notebooks which could be changed as the states changed their laws.

This redoubling of efforts at the Party Structure Commission, in conjunction with formal approval from the national party, also coincided, of course, with the arrival of a bumper crop of Democratic governors in the party politics of their individual states. These governors were assuming office precisely as the National Committee was endorsing an official text for party reform. A crucial subset of them was arriving with an explicit, publicized attachment to reform in the abstract—translated immediately into an attachment to the contents of the Preliminary Call.

Most of these individuals were destined to be major actors in state party politics, even if most had been too new to their offices to influence the February meeting of the National Committee. By the spring of 1971, they *were* becoming central to party politics in their home states, and they were thus ideally placed to take a fresh look at the substance of party reform—and to convert the Preliminary Call into acceptable institutions for delegate selection. The interaction of the previous drift toward state compliance and the adoption of the Preliminary Call with the introduction of these new Democratic governors thus became a substantial force for state party compliance. Within months, a sharp-eyed observer could see the result, the acceleration of the initial drift toward implementation, and this became the critical fact about the shape of reform politics during this period.

The first indication of this shift was a change in the character of key actors in the states themselves. Previously, most states had adopted a formally similar pattern of addressing party reform. An indigenous reform commission was appointed; it assembled, held hearings, and issued a report; that report was presented to the central committee of the regular state party; that committee met to endorse, amend, or reject the report of its reform commission. When pressures for compliance became serious, however, one of the first responses of state party officialdom was to short-cut, perhaps even to dismiss, the local reform commission and to move to take personal charge of negotiations with relevant local interests and national reform actors. State reform commissions were collective bodies which could not, in principle, bargain effectively with local interests and national actors. Moreover, many were not well linked to the regular party, the crucial linkage for adoption of a local reform package.

When reform negotiations became a serious matter, then, many such commissions were thrust, sometimes rudely, out of the way. The movement of the governor and the state chairman to center stage in reform politics was not a guarantee of acquiescence and implementation, for these individuals still had other state interests to protect and the state committee to mollify. But that movement was normally a crucial step forward, and in most states it did indicate an intention to find some local incarnation of national rules which could win national approval and not destroy established local arrangements.[1]

At that point, the pattern of negotiations among the states did differ, once again, according to the presence of a volunteer or an organized state political party. In volunteer-party states, negotiations tended to occur directly between the state party leadership (that is, the state chairman and the governor, if any) and national reform actors (that is, the commission entourage and, often, the office of the national chairman). In organized-party states, on the other hand, these negotiations remained internal to the state political party, with much more emphasis on hammering out an internally acceptable arrangement and much less direct discussion with national reformers.

Actually, the very first states to comply had reached that status through direct negotiations between the state party leadership and the national commission. That was the only way they could be certified so quickly. Eventually, the very last states to comply, those which were still resisting in 1972, would follow the same route. That proved the only way to bring them along. But for all those in between, even after an indigenous reform commission had been shucked aside and state party leaders had themselves seized the central role, reform negotiations differed between volunteer and organized parties.

400

Party leaders in volunteer-party states had always been more receptive to national suggestions for local reform. Whether they operated through an indigenous reform commission or whether they bargained directly, these leaders gave more credence to the interpretations of national reform actors and made more effort to be sure that local reform initiatives were satisfactory to them. Party leaders in organized-party states, on the other hand, had always been primarily concerned with local party affairs. Even when the pressure for compliance began to suggest serious local consideration and even after they had pushed a local reform commission aside to make this consideration possible, they looked to national reformers only when it was time to argue that their local suggestions should be accepted as fulfilling national goals.

Observers on the inside saw these patterns develop rapidly in the aftermath of the National Committee meeting. Joe Barr, national committeeman from Pennsylvania, saw the difference in response between volunteer and organized political parties. But he also saw the overall drift toward compliance in both cases, and it distressed him greatly:

> The small states went along quickly. But only Michigan of the big states went along early. Most of the smaller states went along quickly because they didn't care. It didn't mean much one way or the other. Many of the smaller states look on the National Committee as a body with more authority, too. In Pennsylvania, we don't have to care what the National Committee is doing. And we don't. In Colorado, maybe they do.[2]

From the other side, Carol Casey saw the same trends in reform politics, even more richly in individual cases and even more fully for the nation as a whole. She was, however, as delighted by what she observed in the aftermath of the National Committee meeting as Barr was distressed:

> In the little states, the state chairmen weren't that upset about it. The 1968 Convention had said that they had to do this. If you're still angry, call Larry O'Brien, and he'd tell them that they had to live with it. We did, with the help of O'Brien, have them convinced that they had to do it. . . . We would say with a very straight face, "You have to do it or you'll be thrown out of the National Convention." We would give them specific language. We had model rules; they could look these up. Then when they sent their plans for us to look at, we would always give them direct language for them to adopt.

By May, Chairman Fraser was ready to announce this nationwide progress on party reform, to capitalize on it as an additional source of pressure for the recalcitrants, and even to berate these recalcitrants publicly. In a press conference which confirmed his own place on the national reform stage, Fraser high-

401

lighted the generally favorable movement which he and his colleagues observed, and went on to "name names" among those states standing against the alleged tide:

> Washington, May 29 (AP)—Seating fights can be expected at the 1972 Democratic National Convention if state parties do not change their delegate selection process, the head of a reform commission says. Representative Donald M. Fraser of Minnesota, Chairman of the panel that drafted 18 delegate selection guidelines, said yesterday that at least a dozen states were moving slowly on reform. About three-fourths of the states are making substantial progress, he added.
>
> Kentucky and Virginia are moving slowly on a small number of guidelines, he said, and six others—Florida, Georgia, Kansas, Louisiana, Massachusetts, and Pennsylvania—are taking vigorous action. But Mr. Fraser said he was disappointed with the pace of reform in Connecticut, Delaware, Michigan, and Washington. "If they don't act," he said, "there are going to be some problems."[3]

The National Press and the Progress of Reform

When Chairman Fraser gave his press conference on the progress of party reform, the first of a series of journalistic articles on that same topic was already under research. This article, which appeared shortly afterward in *National Journal,* was to offer radically different conclusions about the status of compliance. These conclusions would lead other news sources to take their own look, in a string of reports stretching through the summer and into the fall. These reports, cumulatively, were to achieve a separate and significant influence on the course of reform politics.

Previously, the general news media, and even the journals of political opinion, had paid scant attention to the progress of party reform. Indeed, between April of 1970, when *Mandate for Reform* was officially released, and June of 1971, when *National Journal* broke this pattern of inattention in a major way, the argument over state compliance had been almost entirely the province of national reform principals, in lonely debate.

During this period of decentralized gestation in the states, the national news weeklies had touched on reform politics, if at all, only in the process of covering the National Committee. Most major newspapers had done no better, and the two national reporters who had sensed that something of consequence was afoot, R. W. Apple, Jr., of the *New York Times* and David S. Broder of the *Washington Post,* had still confined themselves to developments on the national level. Even among journals of political opinion, only the *New Re-*

public had offered *any* deliberate analyses of developments in the individual states, and most of its state references were still in pieces on national reform politics.[4]

This situation changed sharply in June of 1970, when *National Journal* broke open what would become a continuing press debate. In its issue of June 19, Andrew J. Glass and Jonathan Cottin collected numerous contrasting interpretations of the progress of party reform and served them up en masse, along with a relatively balanced assortment of brickbats and plaudits for nearly all the relevant personnel. When it came to a title for their piece, however, they settled on "Democratic Reform Drive Falters as Spotlight Shifts to Presidential Race," and their initial paragraphs possessed such an unequivocally pessimistic tone that the rest of their commentary never succeeded in restoring an overall sense of ambiguity:

> An ambitious effort by the Democrats to reform their party structure—an effort rooted in the chaotic and divisive 1968 convention in Chicago—is faltering.
> In state after state, the reform drive has bogged down as party leaders concern themselves more with the race for the Democratic Presidential nomination than with improving the machinery under which the party's candidate is finally chosen.[5]

Glass and Cottin did lighten this assessment with some immediate rebuttals, the first from Chairman O'Brien:

> Nevertheless, he has vowed to carry the reforms through, largely by his own selling efforts.
> "I think it will have a dramatic effect on the tone of the convention," O'Brien said in an interview. "It's the greatest goddamn change since (the advent of) the two-party system."[6]

The perceptual damage, however, had been done. Glass and Cottin went on to solicit the views of potential candidates for the Democratic nomination, all of whom were comparatively optimistic. But a survey of commission personnel was concentrated among militant reformers, returning the article to a bleaker view. The nadir was reached when the authors came to Ken Bode:

> "I want the nutcutting to start now," Bode said. He said every state Democratic Party failing to implement the guidelines will be challenged. "We will bring a suit in any state before giving it up. I don't trust O'Brien."
> Bode's aim is "to start a liberal, independent constituency," Bode said. "The lack of aggressive enforcement by the DNC leaves open the possibility for development of such a constituency."[7]

Bode took the opportunity, three weeks later, to expand on his analysis, in an essay in the *New Republic* entitled "Turning Sour: Democratic Party Reform." There, he went after the alleged lassitude of the commission leadership and staff, the apparent indifference of national party officials, and the purported recalcitrance of state political parties:

> Eighteen months ago, the McGovern (now Fraser) Commission of the national Democratic Party adopted 18 "guidelines" as binding on all state Democratic parties in their selection of delegates to the 1972 convention. These guidelines are the fulfillment of the 1968 national convention's promise of party reform. . . .
>
> The reform is on the verge of turning sour. By this time next year, all of the 23 to 25 state primaries will be over, the convention will be scant weeks away. Yet, according to official Democratic National Committee statistics, here is how matters stand:
>
> • *Only 8 states (Alabama, Iowa, Maine, Mississippi, Missouri, New Hampshire, North Carolina, Oklahoma) are in full compliance with the commission's guidelines. These states will have about 10 percent of the 1972 delegates.*
>
> • Not one of the 11 largest states (New York, California, Pennsylvania, Illinois, Ohio, Michigan, Texas, New Jersey, Massachusetts, Florida, Indiana) has satisfied all of the guidelines. Together, these states will account for a minimum of 1968 delegates, or 56 percent of the total.[8]

After covering the situation in the very largest states in more detail, Bode lit into Chairman O'Brien, implying not only that the chairman was uninterested in reform but that he was, in reality, starving out the cause:

> While stressing his commitment to the reforms and their implementation, National Chairman Lawrence O'Brien has done little to speed compliance beyond periodic reminders to state chairmen. Meanwhile, the McGovern-Fraser Commission staff has been reduced to one man, who admits that he has little time to do more than keep track of compliance and advise state parties whether their proposals satisfy commission standards.[9]

These two pieces, the Glass-Cottin article in *National Journal* and the Bode analysis in the *New Republic,* were destined to bring the debate on state compliance to the surface and to sustain that debate for months to come. Together, they suggested the existence of a "story" and thus the need for other news sources to take a look at compliance progress. Together, they set off a chain reaction of comments and retorts, reassurances and demurrers. Beyond this, they fueled a surprising range of concrete organizational responses, by official party bodies and by an assortment of interest groups, all of which struggled to cope either with the deteriorating reality pictured in these reports or with the practical side effects of an unduly negative portrait.

The Glass-Cottin and Bode investigations were actually destined to reappear, in part or in nearly whole cloth, in many of the subsequent analyses which they spawned. A week later, for example, R. W. Apple took a look at the progress of reform in the pages of the *New York Times*. Direct citations to both preceding summaries figured prominently in his account:

> The *National Journal,* an independent, nonpartisan Government journal, reported after an extensive study in June that "in state after state, the reform drive has bogged down."
>
> Kenneth A. Bode, who served the reform commission as director of research before becoming director of the Center for Political Reform, said in the July 10 issue of *The New Republic* that "the reform is on the verge of turning sour." With the convention only a year away, he wrote, not one of the 11 largest states, with at least 56 percent of the total delegate strength at the convention, has satisfied all the guidelines.[10]

After another ten days, Apple returned to the subject in a more speculative piece. His central theme this time was not the progress of reform per se, but whether its success might bring problems as severe as those it sought to eliminate.[11] But having raised that issue, Apple circled back to the status of implementation, and to the ongoing debate about its pace and diffusion:

> Then there is the vexing question of whether most states will be in even technical compliance. Mr. Fraser predicted the other day that 40 states would come around by the end of the year, although only nine states have completed action so far.
>
> Outside analysts—including Ken Bode, the commission's former research director—have argued that the reform effort is faltering and will fail unless the states feel more pressure from the national level.[12]

By July 27, when the second *Times* report appeared, the debate had begun to acquire a life of its own, one related only in part to advances or reversions in the real world of party reform. The self-feeding character of this argument was illustrated most clearly in the fall, when the October issue of the *Progressive* brought back Andrew J. Glass for a reprise with "Are the Democrats Serious About Reform?" In his answer, Glass relied primarily upon material from his earlier (co-authored) article:

> For inquiring visitors, officials of the Democratic National Committee produce a fancy dog-and-pony show on the great strides that have supposedly been made on the path to reform. But, in truth, these officials do not know whether most of the fifty-five state and territorial parties will comply with proposed changes in party rules. So far, most of them have not.[13]

405

Glass plugged in quotations from the earlier *National Journal* piece, from McGovern, Muskie, Bayh, O'Brien, Humphrey, Hughes, Reinhardt, and more, but in a much less balanced and far more explicitly pessimistic fashion. The words remained the same; their impact became cheerless. O'Brien again came in for special censure, as he usually did in analyses which viewed progress on reform as halting and uncertain:

> O'Brien is not at all upset that Fraser and his commission colleagues appear both unwilling and unable to carry the major burden of the enforcement battle—a battle that the national chairman equates with the amount of energy that should be expended in a Presidential campaign. "Don't worry about it," O'Brien told me, rapping his chest with his fist. "I will get it done."
> Maybe he will. But O'Brien has already dulled his credibility in some pro-reform circles by engaging in an unseemly feud with Kenneth A. Bode, thirty-two, the commission's former research director.
> Since January, Bode has been running a small Nader-like organization called the Center for Political Reform advising Fraser and Harold Hughes of Iowa, another commission member, while pressing on a state-by-state basis for implementation of the "guidelines."[14]

The tenor of this debate, as well as its lingering character, almost demanded published responses from those who were officially charged with overseeing implementation—and who were unofficially accused of laxness or duplicity. These responses were not long in coming. The Cottin-Glass piece, the first to hit the stands, was met with published silence. The Bode analysis, however, moved Don Fraser to take pen in hand and to write back directly. Within the week, Fraser had mailed off a letter to the editor, and it ran ultimately in the August 21 issue of the *New Republic.* In that letter, Fraser refrained from impugning Bode directly, but he did present a very different statistical overview, and he did suggest that the former research director might be not just overly negative, but insufficiently informed:

> His article helps to dramatize the importance of an all-out effort to achieve compliance with the reform Guidelines during the coming months. But his conclusion that progress toward reform is lagging badly is more pessimistic than is justified by the facts.
> ·Each of the 50 states has set up a Democratic Party Reform Commission.
> ·Each state has taken some action toward compliance with the 18 guidelines adopted by our Commission and incorporated into the Call to the 1972 Democratic Convention.
> ·10 States are in full compliance with the Guidelines.
> ·Another 28 states have informed us that they expect to complete action within the next 6 months. We hope to get similar word from the remaining 12 states shortly.

> Mr. Bode's figure of 24 states that have still not met the "timeliness" requirement, under which the selection must not begin before the calendar year of the Convention, is not current. This figure is now down to 15, of which 8 have indicated that they are awaiting final action on party rules that will eliminate the problems. This does not mean that the remaining 7 will not comply. . . .[15]

This riposte from Fraser, in turn, called forth a restatement of the opposing view. When the August 21 edition became available, Marvin L. Madeson, national chairman of the New Democratic Coalition, read the letter from the commission chairman, took exception, and kept the issue churning in the pages of the *New Republic* by mailing back a letter of his own. Citing the case he knew best, his home state of Missouri, the NDC chairman argued that it was Fraser who was insufficiently perceptive—and overly sanguine, to boot:

> I wish to reluctantly demur from the optimistic tenor of Representative Fraser's communication in the August 21 *New Republic* in regard to Democratic Party reform.
>
> From my own experience as a member of the Missouri Reform Commission, and from information that I have received from New Democratic Coalition chapters around the country, the commitment of the Democratic Party state organizations to party reform is generally nonexistent. While a number of states, including Missouri, have formally met national guideline requirements, the intent to use the new rules to maintain "the old gang" is quite apparent.[16]

Madeson had been applauded in his forensic endeavor by none other than Ken Bode, who had, of course, kicked off the entire sequence some four months previously:

> Dear Marv:
> Thanks very much for sending a copy of the letter that you wrote to the *New Republic*. I hope they print it because explicit rejoinders from people like yourself will be necessary to give the lie to the hyped up publicity that the Party and the DNC have been putting out about reform being an accomplished fact for 1972.[17]

In the same manner, Fraser and Nelson were eager to reinforce others who might take the initiative in combating these negative assessments, so that these critiques would not go unanswered, and so that they themselves, with their evident stake in the matter, would not have to do all the answering. When the second Glass piece had been slated for publication, Austin Ranney wrote to Nelson, volunteering to counter the contentions from Glass in a succeeding issue of the *Progressive:*

> Dear Bob:
> Enclosed is a xerox of the galley proofs of the Glass article for the October

issue of *The Progressive.* As I told you on the phone, Morrie Rubin, the editor, invites me to write a 500–600 response to be printed in the November issue in the letters-to-the-editor column, and to make that issue he specifies a deadline of September 29 for receiving my copy. Accordingly, I would be grateful if Don and you would look over these proofs and call me here (608-262-2596) with whatever points and facts and figures you feel should be emphasized.[18]

Nelson, of course, called back, endorsed just such a response, and offered a few suggestions of his own. Ranney followed through, and his demurrer appeared in the November edition:

> Equally unwarranted but more offensive is Glass' suggestion that Commission Chairman Don Fraser is going easy on reform enforcement because "he is running for the chairmanship of the credentials committee." Fraser knows very well what Glass should learn: that the chairmanship of that committee has long been a nasty chore taken on by a loyal party leader who usually leaves the post with some political wounds. . . .
>
> The story of whether these formidable obstacles can be overcome will not be finished until next spring. But even if the Commission achieves something short of perfect success, its efforts will still constitute what two leading political scientists have already called the greatest effort ever made by a major American party to set national standards for its state parties. Moreover, it is an effort which will not end after 1972, and for liberals of all parties or none, perhaps that is the most important story of all.[19]

National reporters might have lifted this interpretive burden had they been drawn toward an inevitable consensus. But a sensible generalization, from a central site, on a previously understudied event, was inherently difficult to develop. Guideline compliance, after all, took place in more than 50 decentralized theaters. It was composed of numerous small but cumulative actions. Its interpretation required extrapolation from these acts to the ultimate behavior of party figures who were themselves largely unknown to national reporters. Moreover, the relevant experts were sharply divided, and their division added more heat than light to the inherent analytic problem.

There were, of course, objective summary measures of reform progress, but those which could be introduced by one side could be undermined by the other. The commission staff could point to a number of states which were in full compliance, to a number of guidelines which had achieved universal acceptance, and to a remarkable total of guideline adoptions—682 out of 918—almost all of which represented gains from the prereform era.[20] Commission critics could dismiss the number of complying states as minuscule, the universally accepted guidelines as trivial, and the raw total of adoptions as masking the large percentage of the largest states which were actively resisting the crucial reforms. The result occasionally exploded not in revelations, but in acrimony:

> Robert W. Nelson, the commission's staff director, reacted angrily in an interview to Mr. Bode's charges. He and Mr. Fraser, he said, have worked furiously to bring about compliance, and with considerable success. Mr. Bode's kind of argument, Mr. Nelson added, could lead to a "psychology of defeatism" that would prompt recalcitrant state parties to drag their feet even more.
>
> William B. Welsh, an assistant to the Democratic national chairman, Lawrence F. O'Brien, suggested at the same time that Mr. Bode's real interest may lie in promoting a leftwing fourth party, based on the argument that the Democrats were unable to reform themselves. Mr. Bode has consistently denied that.[21]

Yet the debate over the progress of compliance was fueled even more by events on the other side of the aisle, among individual reporters, within individual news operations, and among the institutional news media as a whole. Not all reporters, even among the theoretically nonpartisan press, bothered to strive for neutrality in reporting this debate, and there were no *antireform* partisans among those who deviated from professional neutrality. But individual reporters did not set out to create the topic as one worthy of continued coverage, nor did they determine the clear and striking pattern which that coverage eventually assumed. These developments, instead, were a response to the character of individual news organizations and of the interested media collectively.

Once *National Journal* broke the topic of the progress of reform in a major and controversial piece, involving all the major reform actors, the dynamic for a continuing debate was established. Or at least, the subject was suggested as one of potential importance. When other members of the elite press, like the *New York Times*, weighed in, and when all the journals of liberal opinion, for whom the topic was a "natural," followed suit, the progress of reform was established as an item of newsworthy value. When opponents and proponents began to volley back and forth in the pages of the press, the continued vitality of the topic was guaranteed.

The character of the nonpartisan press, the first half of those news media which did attend to the story, then shaped the course of this continuing debate. Within publications like *National Journal* and newspapers like the *New York Times*, the professional norm in reporting any item of controversy was to solicit views from participants and experts on *both sides* of the issue. A rough balance, between those who asserted that reform was progressing apace and those who asserted that it was not, became the logical outcome.[22]

Many individual reporters in the nonpartisan press did credit the staff and leadership of the Party Structure Commission with better and more current information. Yet all retained a powerful skepticism about the upshot of these "facts," an occupational skepticism activated by the unprecedented character of what they were hearing. Moreover, most of these reporters, even in the nonpartisan press, *wanted* reform to succeed and thus implicitly aligned their views with those of self-conscious party reformers.

Occasionally, the private agenda of those doing the reporting went much further. Andrew Glass, for example, who co-authored the original "nonpartisan" piece in *National Journal,* resurfaced four months later in the pages of the *Progressive,* a partisan journal of liberal opinion. There, with the same information, Glass shifted from a search for balance to an explicit attack on the national chairman and the Party Structure Commission and an explicit endorsement of Ken Bode and the Center for Political Reform.

But the character of press attention, once that attention had been gained, was hardly nonpartisan overall, and it was this *distribution* of press coverage which further shaped the course of the published debate. Indeed, easily half of the total coverage of the progress of party reform was generated by journals of political opinion, with evident programmatic biases, and all of these were on one side of the issue—aligned with one set of the discussants.

Journals of conservative political opinion, which might in theory have looked upon reform itself with a jaundiced eye but which would certainly have discounted the views of militant reformers, never attended to the story at all. Possibly this was because "reform" as an abstraction did not stimulate their editors; possibly it was because conservative journals tended naturally to focus on *Republican* politics.

Journals of liberal opinion, on the other hand, were uniformly supportive of participatory rather than disciplined party reform. They were uniformly aligned, as well, with party dissidents and liberal interest groups, rather than with the regular party and organized labor. Clearly, these journals were populated by reporters and editors who shared the views of militant reformers; probably, this could be traced all the way back to their—white-collar, reform-oriented—readership.[23] In any case, from the beginning, these journals were predisposed to the point of view of the doubters. They never gave it up.

Press Accounts and the Mobilization of Reformers

This national press debate inevitably called the attention of a greatly expanded audience to the fate of party reform. Having done so, however, it also magnified the ambiguity inherent in tracking the progress of reform in the states. Indeed, as events began to favor one side of the debate, press opinion began to lean toward the other. There were more data behind one interpretation; there were more commentators behind the other.

Despite this—or perhaps because of it—the debate went on to influence the activities of a surprising range of organizations. And here, the impact was not ambiguous at all. Groups concerned with the issue of reform and groups focused on liberal causes, groups which had always been implicit members of the national reform coalition, became explicit members in the course of this debate. The Party Structure Commission itself, dormant as a collectivity since November of 1969, came back to life and undertook new organizational responses of its own.

Curiously, none of these groups had noticeable difficulty in sorting out what they read in the national press. A truly detached organizational observer might have experienced analytic difficulty in coming to secure conclusions. The organizations with the greatest propensity toward participation in reform politics had essentially social means for reaching their operative interpretations, and these were sufficient to overcome any analytic doubts.

Initially, each of these newly activated organizations contained influential members with clear, pre-existing sympathies and suspicions. When they then encountered interpretations of the progress of state reform which were congruent with these values and beliefs and when the propounders of these interpretations were individuals who were socially familiar and who shared the same prejudices, the problem of sorting out the reform debate was effectively solved. Prior sympathies and preferred sources of information were united by parallel social contacts to produce a clear, unambiguous view of the "true" status of party reform for each of these potentially active organizations.

In none of these cases—the reform issue organizations, the liberal ideological organizations, or the national reform commission itself—was the national debate about state compliance the initial goad to more active participation in reform politics. Some initiatives in that direction would have occurred within each, even in the absence of a national press debate. Yet in every case, a central awareness of this debate and a dominant belief about the truth within it were reinforcing factors for actions previously considered. And in every case, this debate further shaped the public statements and strategic activities produced by these organizations.

The first group to act was Common Cause, the new reform organization founded by John W. Gardner. Gardner had turned his attention to the possibility of forming a "citizens' lobby" in March of 1970; he had launched it with a mass mailing and a series of newspaper ads in August of that same year.

By February of 1971, when the Democratic National Committee was address-ing reform for the first time, Common Cause had 100,000 dues-paying mem-bers and was searching for its full, appropriate, substantive agenda.[24]

A focus on voter registration and citizen participation, a cluster of issues tailor-made for a nonpartisan, progressive, reform body, came naturally. But because a sizable percentage of Common Cause members were also reform Democrats and, perhaps more importantly, because a sizable percentage of national officers and volunteers were concerned with participatory rules for internal party affairs, the leadership decided to append the cause of party re-form to the cause of franchise extension, and to create a special unit to pursue both. On February 8, before the National Committee had even put the guide-lines in the Preliminary Call, President Gardner announced formation of a Voting Rights Project:

> Washington, Feb. 8—John W. Gardner, chairman of the new public interest lobby called Common Cause, announced today that his organization had opened a campaign to eliminate restrictions on voter registration and on voting itself. It will be the first Common Cause lobbying effort at the state level. Earlier at-tempts to revitalize the public process have been directed at Federal issues such as the seniority system in Congress and national campaign spending practices.
>
> The new project will be headed by Mrs. Anne Wexler, who helped push through voter reform in her home state of Connecticut and was manager of the Rev. Joseph D. Duffey's unsuccessful campaign for the Senate last fall. Mr. Gard-ner said that Common Cause would also lobby for reforms in the selection of party delegates to the national nominating conventions, in an attempt to give rank-and-file party members greater say in the choices.[25]

The project swung into action almost immediately. Despite its initial focus on the lowering of the voting age, the appointment of Anne Wexler, former consultant to the Party Structure Commission, was a patent clue that the state chapters of Common Cause would be encouraged to help with local party re-form. Wexler and her new subcommittee had to tread carefully, since as a nonpartisan body, one which really did have registered Republicans and inde-pendents on its governing boards, Common Cause was limited in what it could comfortably—consensually—undertake in the internal affairs of a particular party.

On the other hand, Wexler herself remained free to advise interested indi-viduals within the organization about the requirements of Democratic party reform, by drawing on knowledge gained from the McGovern Commission and from the Hughes Commission before it. She remained free as well to put interested individuals in touch with other reform activists, by drawing on a network of social and political acquaintances dating at least to the McCarthy campaign of 1968. In return, the state chapters of Common Cause were free to give more or less priority to internal party reform, depending on their own partisan mix.

As a result, when the debate on the progress of reform in the states broke into the open, in June of 1971, it provided additional incentive for Wexler to urge her state counterparts toward helping with the reform effort and for amenable state chapters to shift toward pressing their local (Democratic) parties for reform. Wexler's new operation would never serve as the official leader—the recognized organizational umbrella—for reform forces in the states. It would provide one more unofficial framework to assist state reform actors, and it was often turned to precisely that task.[26]

The internal constraints which led Common Cause to intervene indirectly in the party rules arena did not impinge on the next organization to establish a specific subunit on party reform. Americans for Democratic Action, under the chairmanship of Allard K. Lowenstein, the former coordinator of the "Dump Johnson" movement, set up its own Convention Task Force as a device for prodding the state parties toward reform.[27]

Lowenstein was elected chairman of the liberal interest group on May 1, 1971. Within two weeks, he had committed it to assist the Democratic reform effort. In this, he was encouraged by the ubiquitous Ken Bode, although there was little need for urging, since Lowenstein retained a strong personal interest in the subject. In any case, his new Convention Task Force was announced on June 19, the same day that *National Journal* released its analysis of compliance politics in the states.

Washington, June 19—Americans for Democratic Action announced today the formation of a study group to oversee democratic processes in the 1972 nominating conventions. Allard K. Lowenstein, national chairman of Americans for Democratic Action, said after a national board meeting that the group would be headed by the Rev. Joseph D. Duffey, former chairman of A.D.A., with legal counsel consisting of Ken Bode, director of the Center for Political Reform, and Joseph L. Rauh, another A.D.A. chairman.

The study group, Mr. Lowenstein said, will now concentrate on the following aspects of preparations for the conventions:

—It will watch the delegate selection process in an effort to ensure that all party members, including racial minorities, get opportunities to participate;

—It will provide legal assistance in the preparation of lawsuits against states and state parties whose laws and rules erect barriers to citizen participation in the Presidential nominating process. It will also help prepare credentials challenges for the national convention in cases of racial discrimination or closed, undemocratic delegate selection.

—It will seek support for reforms to be adopted by the national conventions.[28]

The Politics of Implementation

From its inception, the Convention Task Force was explicitly focused on party reform and, within that, on internal reform of the Democratic party. In theory, ADA, too, was bipartisan; in practice, the interested members were Democrats. Moreover, it was the *Democratic* party which possessed sweeping new rules to implement, elaborate, enforce, or challenge; there was no counterpart handle on the Republican side.

From its inception, the Convention Task Force was also closely attuned to the debate over the status of state compliance—and clearly aligned with one side of that debate. In fact, the first item of business at the first meeting of the task force was a report from Bode on compliance politics in the states. That meeting, on July 7, also confirmed the role of the new group as a coordinating mechanism for nonparty, proreform groups of all types. Indeed, the roster of attenders was a cornucopia of independent reformers:

· The national ADA itself contributed Leon Shull, its executive director; Joseph D. Duffey, its immediate past chairman; and Joseph L. Rauh, Jr., a former national chairman who would later be special counsel to Ken Bode at the Center for Political Reform.
· That Center contributed Bode, its director, as cochairman of the ADA task force, along with his counsel, Joseph Gebhardt, a former intern with the Party Structure Commission.
· Common Cause was represented by Kennedy J. Guido, legal director for the national operation; by Rich Norling, another member of the national staff who had also been a commission intern; and by the Rev. Duffey, again, as cochairman of the ADA task force but as an influential member of Common Cause, too.
· The old Commission on the Democratic Selection of Presidential Nominees, the Hughes Commission, was even represented, contributing both its executive director, Thomas P. Alder, by then editor of the *Selective Service Law Reporter,* and its associate director, Geoffrey Cowan, a fellow at the Center for Law and Social Policy in Washington.
· Also in attendance were a number of individuals without current ties to reform organizations, but with an equally long connection to reform politics, including John R. Schmidt and Wayne W. Whalen, who had generated legal back-up for McCarthyite credentials challenges in 1968 and who had subsequently provided legal support to Eli Segal at the Party Structure Commission.[29]

On June 14, Don Fraser had moved to add yet another group to this aggregate of concerned organizations, when he announced the resuscitation of the Commission on Party Structure and Delegate Selection. On the 14th, Fraser revealed that the Executive Committee of the Party Structure Commission would meet on June 29 and that this meeting would prepare the way for a reassembly of the full commission sometime in July. The Executive Committee would thus end a twelve-month span of inactivity; the full commission would terminate a twenty-month hiatus.[30]

In this effort at resuscitation, Fraser was motivated primarily by a desire to follow up on his May press conference, the one in which he had promised additional difficulties for state parties which continued to drag their feet. He and Bob Nelson had conceived several new procedural weapons which they could use to augment those difficulties; the commission seemed entitled to create these weapons. By the time the Executive Committee assembled, however, the Cottin-Glass piece from *National Journal* would be available. By the time the full commission assembled, the Bode analysis in the *New Republic* would be available as well. As a result, these articles were to shape both commission meetings in ways unforeseen, and surely unintended, by Fraser and Nelson.

The Executive Committee session on Tuesday, June 29, was a comparatively short, luncheon affair. The substitution of Patti Knox for Katherine Peden and of John English for Leroy Collins meant that the original attempt to engineer a strong reform bias into the Executive Committee was now overwhelmingly, crushingly successful. The appearance of an open debate over the progress of party reform in the pages of *National Journal*, quoting several of those in attendance—on opposite sides—guaranteed a lively meeting.[31]

Nelson and Fraser began by covering the situation in the ten largest states and then painting the total compliance picture, with further asides about specific states to illustrate particular points. The members of the Executive Committee responded in a highly animated fashion, questioning and prodding as to whether so-and-so could be believed, whether such-and-such was likely to happen, and whether there were additional actions which the commission could take to facilitate all this.

Such queries led naturally to consideration of an agenda for the full commission meeting, tentatively scheduled for July 16. Proposed agenda items centered on a commission role in the implementation process and ranged from establishment of a separate compliance review body all their own, through preparation of *amicus curiae* briefs in court cases and of advisory judgments in credentials challenges, to the more neutral provision of rules interpretations and of alternative means of correction. No specific language was drafted, but an agreement to raise these same issues at the full commission meeting did emerge. With that, the Executive Committee adjourned.

In the weeks before the reassembly of the full commission, Chairman Fraser, in part alarmed by the response of the Executive Committee, circulated a modified form letter to every state chairman, requesting a detailed and definite calendar for implementation. He underlined the right of the commission to ask for such a plan; he brandished the threat of commission intervention in the credentialing process at the 1972 Convention if that plan turned out to be fanciful:

> As you know, the 18 Guidelines of this Commission have been adopted by the Democratic National Committee and are incorporated in the Preliminary Call to the Convention. The Guidelines and the extent to which each state has complied with them will be central in the evaluation of the credentials of that state's delegation.
>
> This Commission under its mandate from the 1968 Convention has final responsibility of reporting to the 1972 Convention. Our intention is to provide that body with as clear and concise an accounting as possible of how fully each State and Territorial Democratic Party has complied with the Guidelines. . . .
>
> So that we may begin now to prepare our final report, we urgently request that you provide us by August 1, with the date by which you anticipate completion of work and action on the Guidelines by your State or Territorial Democratic Party. We also need this information to respond more accurately to press inquiries and in making public statements from time to time.
>
> May we also ask that you provide us with draft copies of your proposed new party rules or rules changes, whichever the case may be, as early as possible before adoption, so that we may provide appropriate assistance in this endeavor.[32]

Early response to this request allowed Nelson and Fraser to develop a new compliance summary for the commission meeting on July 16, one emphasizing the strides which *had* been made and thus giving the lie to less favorable published accounts. This became doubly important when the Bode article in the *New Republic* appeared in print, one week before the commission was slated to reconvene, since commission members could be expected to arrive with the Bode analysis as their major recent review. In the introduction to his new report, Fraser offered a notably different interpretation, in tone as well as content. His document went on to assign every state to one of seven distinct levels of implementation and to provide additional, single-paragraph descriptions of progress in each.[33]

What these descriptions and statistics showed, overall, was an evenly balanced world, but one moving ever more clearly in the direction of compliance. About a quarter of the state parties were either in full conformity or were awaiting only pro forma certification. About half were willing to provide an explicit timetable for arriving at that point, although the accuracy or sincerity of any given schedule could, of course, be challenged. Another quarter were unwilling to commit to as much as a written schedule. As always, the bulk of those in the first group were volunteer parties; the bulk of those in the third group were organized parties; those in the middle were split about equally between the two party types. (See figure 15.1.)

These preparations for additional pressure on compliance actually raised the greatest anxieties, not among those party leaders who refused to provide a timetable, but among those in the office of the national chairman. Larry O'Brien feared that a reconvened commission might follow its more militant members and establish a compliance body of its own. At that point, his own centrality in the negotiations over state compliance, along with his efforts to maintain the appearance of party unity while reaping the abstract advantages of reform, would be endangered; at that point, the long-awaited clash between the commission and the chairman might actually come to pass. Bill Welsh watched O'Brien work to contain this possibility, first with a direct approach to Fraser and Nelson:

> A lot of effort went into dealing with these points of resistance on a one-to-one basis. The DNC staff was a buffer between the Commission and the state chairmen, but we were basically going for the reforms, too. The DNC was trying to keep the Commission from setting up its own compliance review group, by saying that this was a Credentials matter. We didn't need that kind of help from them.

O'Brien followed this with a letter to every commissioner, underlining his own commitment to reform and its progress to date, and congratulating *them* on that progress.[34]

The commission itself assembled at about 9:30 A.M. on Friday, July 16, in Room 2712 of the Rayburn House Office Building. The group which gathered there, thirteen commissioners in all, was a substantially scaled-down version of the body which had last met twenty months before, in the two-day session of November 19–20, 1969. Chairman Fraser opened by addressing Commissioners Beer, Dodds, English, Graves, Hughes, Knox, Mauzy, Mixner, Pena, Ranney, and Warschaw; staffers Nelson and Casey; and ex-staffers Bode and Segal:[35]

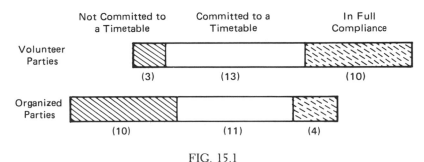

FIG. 15.1

The State Parties and Compliance: July 16, 1971

417

It was just a matter of laying down a standard and a guideline for the staff. Along toward the middle of 1971, we were concerned with the states that were not complying. The problem was how to bring them around. We were taking a tougher stance, and looking for ways to bring them around. Participation was low and not at all broad in these latter meetings. People who were sympathetic to the reforms came out.

Fraser moved quickly into a review of the material he had presented to the Executive Committee, the summary of staff activities, and the report on the compliance of individual states. From the beginning, a consensus on strengthening the commission leadership in negotiations with state party officials was evident. As a result, the meeting focused rapidly on the question of appropriate areas for additional policy statements and on appropriate wording for these resolutions.

These discussions featured a surprising twist, one attesting to the influence of the ongoing press debate. For while the possibility of new commission meetings had been one of Fraser's earliest ideas, and while it had been intended to support a more aggressive posture in reform politicking, the environment for these meetings had shifted so substantially by the time Fraser actually assembled his commission that he found himself playing a very different role.

Part of this shift resulted simply from the character of turnout among commissioners. But part reflected the arrival of a public debate over compliance progress and the way that this, too, had altered perceptions of appropriate commission action. In any case, despite his initial intention to rally his members behind aggressive resolutions, Chairman Fraser found himself with the task of holding these resolutions within sensible limits. Otherwise, they were likely to arrogate powers which were the province of the Credentials Committee or to appear as an assault on the state parties or even on the national chairman.

The very first motion to come before the meeting raised all these dangers. Ken Bode offered language which put the commission in the business of evaluating compliance in a fully independent, evidently adversary fashion, and the tug of war over commission policy had begun. The resolution from Bode suggested going so far as to initiate a credentials challenge on occasion; it endorsed assisting in *all* challenges which the commission deemed legitimate.[36] Fraser was forced to note, in return, that this was a patent usurpation of functions belonging to others; he argued that the commission could more effectively advance its goals by acting as a neutral element of the party apparatus. Fraser's view prevailed, over strong objections from Bode and David Mixner, and it became the heart of this initial policy statement:

> With regard to the procedures that are proposed to be used or have been used in selecting a delegation, the Commission will continue the practice of advising any bona fide Democratic group whether such procedures are in compliance with the Guidelines.[37]

Undaunted, Bode came back immediately with a position on commission involvement in state compliance suits, in which he advocated participation as a friend of the court whenever the commission agreed with the suit in question and possessed the necessary resources to support it. Again, the commissioners appeared willing to accept his draft as offered. Again, Chairman Fraser had to pull it back, less completely this time, with an amendment asserting that the resolution did not interfere with the legitimate jurisdiction of the Credentials Committee and that it would never produce legal action without a vote of the full commission.[38]

The assembled commissioners quickly assented, with very little comment, to a third official position. In adopting this resolution, however, the commission did finally put itself on a collision course with the National Committee:

> We commend the Democratic National Committee for incorporating the 18 Guidelines adopted by this Commission in the Preliminary Call to the 1972 Democratic National Convention in its action of February 19, 1971. However, we respectfully draw the attention of the Democratic National Committee to the Guidelines and express our concern that the action of the Committee in granting automatic delegate status to its present members in 1972, is in violation of the Guidelines. We urge that the members of the Democratic National Committee reconsider this action at their next meeting.[39]

Originally, two years before, the commission staff had brought its commissioners a separate guideline banning ex officio seats for members of the National Committee. At their final drafting session in November of 1969, the members had deleted this guideline, as a needless affront to the one body whose support was essential to any progress on reform. When the National Committee then placed an ex officio provision for its own members in the Preliminary Call, in February of 1971, it was thus unclear whether this had violated the commission guidelines or not.

In July of 1971, the Party Structure Commission clarified the question. In doing so, it confirmed that the decision of the National Committee, the superior body in both organizational position and formal power, *was* a violation. In passing, it moved the guidelines beyond what they had evidently required in November of 1969—a form of subsequent translation to which the commission would return at several critical points before the 1972 Convention.

In the course of these discussions, Eli Segal also introduced a resolution, aimed at tightening the provisions of still another guideline. The former commission counsel recommended an extended specification of Guidelines A–1 and A–2, permitting no more than a 40 percent divergence from the state percentage of women, youth, and minorities in the ultimate state delegation.[40] Here, however, the commission refused to go along with a narrowing of reform requirements. Indeed, the commissioners not only resisted a numerical standard from Segal but declined to pass any policy statement. Fraser, in July of 1971, was relieved that his members had not attempted to rewrite the interpretation which Chairman O'Brien and Counsel Califano had used so explicitly in maneuvering these guidelines through the National Committee:

> In mid-1971, there was some suggestion that they should deal in numbers. That was dropped in favor of something more general. There was a feeling that A–1 and A–2 would be regarded as pure rhetoric; the problem was how to give it some force. Mainly the division was over numerical goals versus a broader statement. I favored the broader statement; Bode [Segal] was pushing for numbers.

On the other hand, among the items which *were* adopted at the July meeting, the lengthiest, and perhaps the most consequential, was not a resolution at all, but a four-page definition—of "all feasible efforts." This definition, however, shared a crucial characteristic with the resolution on ex officio representation: It sharply narrowed the field of permissible variation in reform compliance.

The most militant commissioners wanted their colleagues to go even further. The commission should, they argued, merely outline the requirements inherent in its reforms and then tell the state parties to establish parallel procedures of their own if they could not extract a change in state law. This approach had been offered by Bode to the initial meeting of the ADA Convention Task Force; the task force had authorized him to convert it into a resolution; Bode has passed this along to Harold Hughes; Hughes had given it to Fraser.[41]

Fraser did lay it on the table as the draft version for commission consideration, but a majority of those in attendance were unwilling to go this far. They were, however, prepared to specify the details of an acceptable attempt at overcoming legislative obstacles, and they did consent to *urge* the state parties to fall back on the device of parallel procedures. Their compromise language—applicable to all the guidelines—began to squeeze the leeway out of what many had believed was an escape clause in party reform:

> There are several things that a challenged delegation could point to in order to demonstrate that all feasible efforts had been made to comply where state statutes control.

Legislation—The party shall:
a. Introduce appropriate legislation.
b. Secure the endorsement of the party leadership. . . .
c. Actively campaign for the passage of the legislation. . . .

In addition, further illustrations of other measures available to state parties in demonstrating that they have made all feasible efforts, are as follows:

Institute Litigation—In the absence of remedial legislation, the state party could institute legal proceedings to eliminate obstructing elements of state law, especially where there may be Constitutional questions involved. . . .

Party Rules—Even if obstructive statutes are not repealed or struck down, the state party should work toward compliance within the statutes.

For example, where the delegate selection power is vested by law in an untimely or malapportioned convention or committee, the State Committee could hold parallel meetings at each level at which delegate candidates are to be selected. The State Committee and party leadership could then officially sponsor the delegates chosen at these parallel meetings before the untimely or malapportioned convention or committee which is legally empowered to make the selection. Such support could be accompanied by a full explanation of the Commission requirements.[42]

With this long statement and three other resolutions to their credit, after numerous side discussions and after a full briefing on the compliance status of the states, the commissioners judged that they had put in a full day's work and adjourned at 4:30 P.M.

Nevertheless, while the meeting itself broke up late Friday afternoon, the immediate procedural results of the session would continue to appear for another few weeks. Four days later, for example, Chairman Fraser added a short covering letter to the three resolutions which the commission had adopted at its meeting of July 16 and sent these along to Chairman O'Brien. He took special care to emphasize the qualms which the commission had expressed about the provision in the Preliminary Call on ex officio representation, the Powers amendment from the National Committee:

On behalf of the Commission, I wish to particularly call your attention to the resolution concerning the National Committee's actions of last February 19, in seating itself as automatic delegates to the National Convention in 1972.[43]

Two weeks after that, Fraser took the four-page commission interpretation of "all feasible efforts," placed an additional covering memo on top of it, and mailed the package to all party chairmen in states where legislative change was necessary to attain compliance. In his own note, Fraser came down hard on the sections of the statement which endorsed parallel, extra-legislative arrangements when the institutions of state government would not oblige. In doing so, of course, he further narrowed the range within which a state party could claim to have done its best, but simply to have failed:

> The attached statement was adopted at that time for the purpose of providing guidance to State Parties where this situation pertains and also to clarify the matter for party leaders at this crucial point in our reform endeavors.
>
> Some states are actively exploring the possibility of acting through new party rules to establish procedures which comply with the Guidelines, even though State law prescribes otherwise. In states in which the law requires procedures that substantially handicap access to the process by voters in 1972, we urge that this possibility be seriously considered. We will be happy to further advise you on this matter and answer any questions which you may have.[44]

Implications

For eight months, from February to October of 1971, reform politics reverted to decentralized negotiations within the individual state parties, and between the state parties and national reform actors. Superficially, these were not very different from counterpart negotiations preceding adoption of the Preliminary Call. But this time, they were resumed upon affirmation that the guidelines of the Party Structure Commission were the official rules of the national Democratic party. And this time, they were resumed in the face of intensified pressures by national reform actors.

In short order, reform politics within the states was different, too. Compliance was hardly instant. Yet signs of serious intent—the circumventing of indigenous reform commissions, the assumption of direct state and national negotiations by the state party leadership—were present almost at once. The drift of reform politics in the states had always been toward implementation and compliance. The National Committee meeting on the Preliminary Call pushed that drift from above; the arrival of a large batch of new Democratic governors with an institutionalized sympathy for party reform pulled it from below. The existing trend was confirmed and accelerated.

The implications for institutional change and for the circulation of elites were evident. By the summer of 1971, it was clear that a large number of state parties would be in full compliance with extensive national reforms. As a result, the total institutional matrix for delegate selection—and presidential selection—would be radically altered. Beyond that, it was almost as clear, it was at least highly likely, that additional state parties would come into compliance in partial response to pressures generated by the acquiescence of this first, large bloc of states.

Much institutional change, then, was guaranteed; more was sure to follow. From the first, it had been argued—indeed, it had been intended—that this particular brand of institutional change would be the harbinger of a major elite replacement within the national Democratic party. Now, with extensive formal change guaranteed, the opportunity for this elite replacement was guaranteed as well. New institutional arrangements were on the way. New elite coalitions—the crowning elements of an ostensible new politics—could not be far behind.

It was during this period that the national press finally arrived in the politics of party reform through an effort to assess the progress of state compliance. Before the spring of 1971, a grand disjunction had characterized press treatment of reform politics. If there was a revolutionary restructuring of delegate rules, party politics, and presidential selection under way, it had been occurring without the attention of the national news media. During the spring of 1971, disjunction was replaced by irony. For the distribution of news organizations which attended to this issue, the character of the individual news operations within that distribution, and the particular views of individual reporters within those operations combined to create a fundamentally pessimistic composite portrait of the progress of party reform—at exactly the point when widespread resistance to reform had been broken, and when the state parties were falling rapidly into line.

Some of this growing press interest was attracted by prior coverage of the National Committee meeting. Reform was now official policy in the national party; newsmen became curious about its reality in the states. Some were attracted by anguished cries from national reformers who feared that the pace of reform was *de*celerating. They regarded the press as a natural ally in any attempt to prevent that development. But the largest share of this growing press interest was contributed by a chain reaction in the news business, as an initial, major article succeeded in identifying the topic of reform as "newsworthy." That topic was then addressed by numerous other news operations, and the balance of interested media, by itself, largely explained the character of the press portrait which emerged.

The journals of liberal political opinion were uniformly active in addressing the issue, and they were uniformly identified with the viewpoint of militant reformers. The nonpartisan media were also activated, but they were guided by the norm of "balance," of allowing each side equal weight in the debate about the progress of reform. When formally balanced accounts were added to the analyses of consciously biased journals, the result was a composite press judgment that compliance progress was indeed decelerating.

The practical consequences for institutional change were themselves open to debate. Nelson and Fraser clearly believed that motion toward compliance was crucially dependent on a perception by individual state leaders that more and more states were coming into compliance, and that their own states would ultimately be injured if they did not follow suit. To the extent that national press analyses suggested that other states might not be complying, they presumably encouraged these hesitant states to wait, too.

On the other hand, militant reformers, besides suspecting that the reform drive was stalled, obviously believed that press accounts focusing on that "fact" were useful in holding national party officials behind the reform effort. Chairman O'Brien was the diagnostic case. In the face of pessimistic published assessments, with their associated attacks on his own morals and motivations and having come this far in the effort to secure thorough party reform while maintaining surface party unity, O'Brien was not likely to change course in reform politics or even to ease up on recalcitrant state parties.

The impact of the composite press portrait on prospects for the circulation of elites was much clearer. In the spring of 1971, the national press had put itself in the service of the reform coalition. Press accounts of the progress of reform accorded, overwhelmingly, with the views of party reformers and not party regulars, even as the reality of reform ran increasingly in the other direction. For 1971, then, the national press had effectively joined the reform coalition.

There were indications that it had joined that coalition for the longer run as well. On the individual level, national reporters were closer in background *and perception* to party reformers than to party regulars. This was axiomatic within the journals of liberal opinion. But even within the nonpartisan press, where the norm of "balance" was saluted, reporters who deviated from that norm always did so with a bow to the reformers, not to the regulars.

On the organizational level—surely a more crucial level for the long-run allegiance of the national press—the same tendency was evident. At bottom, there were national media allied explicitly with organized reformers and the ideological interest groups; these were the liberal journals of political opinion. There were *no* national media for party regulars and organized labor, unless one counted house organs like the *AFL-CIO News.*

Moreover, even within the nonpartisan press, the debate about the progress of reform was consistently framed to favor organized reformers and liberal interest groups. The debate was always between those who asserted that reform was progressing and those who asserted that it was stalled. It was never between those who asserted that reform was desirable, progressing or stalled, and those who asserted that it was a curse. Yet the latter was, of course, precisely the viewpoint of the regular party and organized labor. Thus, they lacked partisan media specifically sympathetic to their point of view. And that point of view lacked access to the nonpartisan press, where even norms of formal balance did not serve to bring it to the attention of the general public.

The emergence of the national press as a major participant in reform politics was one consequence of the press debate about the progress of party reform in spring and summer of 1971. After this period, the news media would never again so thoroughly ignore the events of reform politics; after this period, key actors in reform politics would make continuing and consistent efforts to play out their own activities so as to influence the perceptions of the press.

Yet the emergence of this press portrait had another, far more pointed and concrete effect on the character of reform politics, through its impact on the character of the alternative Democratic coalition. For the picture of reform progress which the press as a collectivity offered *became* the reality of reform politics for a set of national actors, and their response went far to shape—indeed, explicitly to *create*—an alternative Democratic coalition which was a functioning political entity and not just an analytic aggregate.

The palpable impact of this press portrait could be seen even within the Party Structure Commission, whose principals presumably had the best available information on the true status of party reform. Yet the perceived political world changed so much between the time Chairman Fraser began to consider reconvening his commission and the time it actually reassembled—a change composed entirely of the emergence of this press portrait—that Fraser had to work to *rein in* the reassembled commissioners rather than to convince them to provide him with additional tools for the aggressive pursuit of implementation.

More consequential for the long-run character of elite coalitions was the response of those ideological and issue organizations which became explicit allies of organized reformers in the course of this press debate. Originally, in 1968, newly mobilized party dissidents began to speak self-consciously of an "alternative Democratic coalition." They were joined by established factions of organized reformers in the states, and by 1969 these were the numerical bulk of that putative coalition. The general election of 1970 then contributed numerous implicit allies in party leadership posts, along with a subset of self-conscious "reform Democrats" who were explicit members as well.

In late 1970, the Center for Political Reform began the process of providing associated, organized interests for this evolving reform coalition. While the center would never be a numerically significant member, it would serve as a crucial device for attaching other organizational members. In mid-1971, the crucial step in the creation of a continuing, fully articulated, alternative coalition was reached with the connection of established liberal organizations, like

425

Americans for Democratic Action, and of coming reform organizations, like Common Cause.

These organizations were reinforced, at every turn, by the emerging, pessimistic, media picture of the status of reform politics. Both ADA and Common Cause would probably have taken an interest in the issue without a national press debate, thanks to the established interest of their leaders, Allard Lowenstein and John Gardner, and of major members like Ken Bode and Anne Wexler. Yet this press debate certainly reinforced the decision to create specific subunits with party reform as a major focus, while it made that decision more palatable to the membership as a whole. Moreover, the press debate immediately became a central input to decisions about the direction and activities of these new subunits.

There was never an explicit decision to create and organize these units so as to realize an "alternative Democratic coalition." But they *were* seen as ways not just to move their parent organizations behind the general reform effort, but to mobilize those organizations behind a "new politics" which would in theory emerge from the success of that effort. Moreover, they were linked explicitly from their creation, so that there was indeed an effective *coalition* among them. A small group of principal actors—Bode, Wexler, Segal—provided informal overlap. Explicit, interlocking appointment of officeholders from the relevant organizations—ADA, the Center for Political Reform, Common Cause, the McGovern Commission, even the Hughes Commission—gave that overlap a formal embodiment as well.

The significance of the creation of this alternative coalition could easily be misperceived. Despite its intent to be a major force in supporting implementation and compliance in the states, it would have little direct influence there. By the time groups like ADA and Common Cause were drawn explicitly into that effort, reform politics had become a matter of internal negotiations within the regular party. Moreover, by the time these organizations were drawn in, the states with any remaining intention to resist were precisely those with organized parties, where the reform coalition possessed the least influence.

If the creation of this alternative coalition retained major significance, then, it was not because it would be important in driving recalcitrant states into certified compliance. Instead, it was because there was still—unforeseen by any of the participants—a major round of reform politicking to come, a round concerned with the appropriate *interpretation* of various guidelines, a round which gained consequence now that most states would indeed be in formal compliance. This struggle for appropriate (re)interpretations would take place on the national level. Organized interest groups from the alternative Democratic coalition would play an important part.

Beyond this, and with much more evident potential impact, the creation of a real alternative coalition meant that as sweeping institutional change was locked into place, there was an organized coalition of Democratic elites, roughly similar to the one which had been envisioned from the beginning, in place and ready to reap the advantages which new institutions were designed to provide. Upon the success of this coalition would rest the final impact of reformed rules. A crucial precondition for that success was creation of an explicit, organized, and coordinated framework among potential members. That precondition was now met. That framework, linked by formal officeholders and buttressed by the national press, was in existence. Its members were determined to claim their institutionalized reward.

CHAPTER

16

The National Party Revisited:

The Final Call and the Triumph of

the Guidelines—Again

IN WHICH, the National Committee addresses the Final Call to the 1972 Convention; a potentially tranquil meeting explodes over the identity of a temporary chairman for that convention's Credentials Committee; and the remainder of the Final Call, the complete reforms of the Party Structure and Rules Commissions, is accepted without dispute. AND IN WHICH, reform politics centers, once again, on appointments rather than institutional rules; sweeping institutional change, in both delegate selection and convention procedure, passes unscathed in the accompanying conflict; and the orthodox Democratic coalition and its aspiring replacement are mobilized for a contest in which regulars dominate all encounters, but reformers receive the consequential prize.

THE spring, summer, and early fall of 1971 was indeed the period when the fate of reform in the individual states was effectively resolved. Before this time, the pattern of reform activity did not conform unequivocally to any given interpretation. Afterward, the politics of implementation was largely a matter of "mopping up." Two national events bracketed the period, giving it not just formal definition but practical, political shape. The first was the National Committee meeting of February 1971, the meeting which adopted the Preliminary Call. The second was the National Committee meeting of October 1971, the meeting which framed a Final Call to the 1972 Convention.

If the committee had failed to incorporate the guidelines of the Party Structure Commission into the Preliminary Call in February, or if the state political parties had failed to heed the injunctions of the Preliminary Call during succeeding months, the political world would have looked sharply different as the October meeting on a Final Call approached. Had the committee failed to incorporate the guidelines, its failure would have been an inescapable signal to those state parties which even potentially wanted to resist. Had the state parties as a group continued to avoid reform on their own, the stage would have been set for an expanded counterattack at the October meeting of the National Committee.

But the Preliminary Call had put the national party on record as formally in favor of these particular reform rules; indeed, it had made them the law of the land for Democrats. Moreover, the succeeding months had seen more and more state parties fall into line, producing reformed rules of their own which were approved by the Party Structure Commission, along with precise timetables for the implementation of these reformed rules.

As a result, the committee meeting on the Final Call, despite an impressive—even historic—agenda, promised little explicit conflict. The Call would inevitably contain the guidelines of the Party Structure Commission, along with the full set of reforms from the Rules Commission, restructuring the national convention itself. Yet the previous action of the National Committee, coupled with the progress of reform in the states since its last meeting, appeared to dampen the possibility of any further, significant conflict.

This situation changed dramatically a week before the meeting, when organized reformers rallied the alternative Democratic coalition behind their own candidate for temporary chairman of the 1972 Credentials Committee, the body which would interpret compliance with reformed party rules. Harold Hughes became that candidate. Chairman O'Brien countered with Patricia Harris, a candidate of his own. Both sides mobilized to shape the response of the National Committee, in what was surely the most complete and intense effort at committee influence in the entire postwar period.

Nevertheless, despite extended lobbying efforts on both sides, efforts which marked the return of organized labor to active participation in the politics of party reform; despite the entry of many of the aspirants for a Democratic presidential nomination, an entry stimulated by the mobilization of both the orthodox and the alternative Democratic coalitions; and despite detailed press attention, in continuing reports which emphasized the apparent closeness of the contest, the result was anticlimactic. The Executive Committee of the National Committee met and endorsed Harris over Hughes, unequivocally. The full National Committee reached the same decision by a margin only a trifle less overwhelming.

This anticlimax, in turn, only masked another—and a final, grand irony as well. For largely unattended in the battle over a Credentials chairman was the acceptance of the complete and unanimous reports of the Party Structure and Rules Commissions. A choice among nominees for temporary chairman of the Credentials Committee became a major conflict. An attempt to remove the sole amendment to reform recommendations, the ex officio provision from John Powers, became a major, secondary contest. The broadest and deepest matters of consequence at the entire meeting—reforms of historic scope and historic potential in the selection of delegates to the national party convention and in the governance of that convention itself—passed without dispute, debate, or even discussion.

The irony in all this was related to the disjunction between a comparatively minor—and as it developed, truly inconsequential—decision on personnel and a set of structural reforms of immense portent. For while the orthodox Democratic coalition was confirming its domination of internal party politics, and while it was confirming its massive political superiority to the alternative Democratic coalition, it was also endorsing the procedural desires of this aspiring alternative, by enacting reforms essential to a change in the balance of influence between the two coalitions.

In the contest between Harris and Hughes, the regular party was caught off guard; it was still able to rally and crush the opposition, overwhelmingly and decisively. Yet once more, the party won a battle and lost a war. It fought impressively on a matter of little consequence; it triumphed decisively there. At the same time, the party went along with far more consequential changes, institutional changes which its members also opposed but which they did not fight, changes designed to rebound and supplant those very members themselves. For the first time in reform politics, both the orthodox and alternative Democratic coalitions were displayed in full mobilization and in full battle array. The orthodox coalition won decisively. The alternative coalition won completely.

The Final Call and a Credentials Chairman

The pace of reform had quickened perceptibly during the summer of 1971. More and more state parties sent fully realized sets of reform rules to the Party Structure Commission. More and more of these rules were accompanied by a specific date for formal adoption. There were, of course, still some noteworthy foot-draggers. There were still compliance packages which "might" be adopted "soon." Yet thoroughly revised rules were arriving almost daily. They were satisfying the increasingly stiff demands of commission principals. They were, by their certified conformity, increasing the pressure on the hold-out states.

By the time the National Committee prepared to assemble and address the Final Call to the 1972 Convention, twelve states were in absolute, certified compliance. Another *twenty-one* had received national endorsement of their proposed rules. Even among the eighteen which lacked national approval, six had made substantial alterations but were being stymied on a key guideline by a Republican legislature, while another six were led by allies of the national reform coalition and could not possibly be written off at this point. (See figure 16.1.)[1]

The usual difference between states with volunteer versus organized political parties was still evident in October of 1971. But now, the critical fact was that majorities of both categories were in possession of officially certified reform rules. If 73 percent of volunteer state parties, and only 55 percent of organized state parties, were over this procedural hump, the difference could not obscure the fact that thirty-three states had developed local reform packages in compliance with the most sweeping national reforms in American party history—and that these thirty-three were surely the minimum, not the maximum, in the chain of compliance.

Determined doubters could still find grounds for anxiety. Only twelve states, after all, had gone through every stage of the reform process. Yet the extent to which nearly everyone in the attentive public had accepted the inevitability of widespread compliance was revealed, strikingly, by the way in which the central question in the debate over reform progress had shifted. For a long time, from late 1969 through the summer of 1971, the major issue in this debate had been the status of formal implementation, that is, "Will the state parties comply?" By the fall of 1971, however, the issue had shifted to the real behavior of state officials under reformed party rules, that is, "Will the state parties actually *follow* their newly adopted regulations?"[2]

A second, indirect, but telling indicator of an emerging consensus on the formal triumph of party reform lay in the preparations of relevant participants

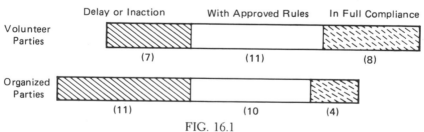

FIG. 16.1

The Status of State Party Compliance: October 13, 1971

for the October meeting of the National Committee. In the month leading up to the scheduled committee sessions of October 12 to 14, there was no evidence of orchestrated attempts by *anyone* to influence the substance of those sessions.

This was not for lack of an impressive agenda. The meeting had to reconsider the reform guidelines of the Party Structure Commission and install them officially (or not) in the Final Call. Moreover, the committee, for the first time, had to address the product of its second reform commission. These newly framed recommendations from the Commission on Rules promised to restructure the national convention; they had never previously been examined by the National Committee; yet they had to be included in the Final Call.[3] Beyond that, the committee had to endorse a convention manager and a temporary chairman for the Credentials Committee, the major convention posts subject to early decision.

Nevertheless, Chairman O'Brien planned no major lobbying efforts in advance of the meeting. He did plan to be available for any questions which his members might have about the new recommendations of the Rules Commission. He did want to receive early warning of lobbying efforts by anyone outside the office of the chairman. But communications for these purposes were largely delegated to his executive assistants, and even their canvass was leisurely and sporadic.

The apparent consensus on the inevitability of reform was so extensive, in fact, that the major element of conflict which the chairman foresaw at the meeting of the National Committee was one he intended to introduce himself. Before the technical work of producing a Final Call began, Joe Califano, the national counsel, brought the attention of the chairman back to the ex officio amendment which John Powers had introduced in February of 1971. Califano urged O'Brien, insistently, to excise that amendment:

> I got concerned about the viability of that rule. I told Larry that if that rule stayed the way it was, that all those people would be challenged, and that this might affect whole delegations. My view as a lawyer was quite simply that the DNC could not change this rule because it was set by the Convention. I was very conscious of the fact that there would be a tremendous amount of controversy and challenges, no matter what the rules were. Knowing that, I didn't want anything that was a clear-cut challenge to go in.

O'Brien needed little persuading, and he formulated an amendment to put his counsel at ease. But this time, he decided not to amass support beforehand and to try instead to carry the day with a carefully prepared argument, one which could be unveiled on the spot. As a result, O'Brien had no plans for a preparatory lobbying campaign. When his executive assistants turned up no evidence of a similar campaign by others, O'Brien was confirmed in his approach.

What looked, then, to be a meeting which would merely confirm the consensus among elite actors about the prospects for sweeping party reform was quickly transformed on October 5, eight days before its convocation, when Harold Hughes called Larry O'Brien and revealed that he was seeking the position of temporary chairman of the Credentials Committee. By then, Hughes was already soliciting support from individual members of the National Committee. For a variety of reasons, O'Brien was actively desirous that Hughes *not* assume the position. The catalyst for organized conflict, so noticeably missing before, was suddenly present.

The intellectual interests and political fortunes of Harold Hughes had been tied to the issue of party reform since its first institutionalized appearance. He had lent his name to the original Commission on the Democratic Selection of Presidential Nominees, the Hughes Commission. He had sought the chairmanship of its official successor, the Commission on Party Structure and Delegate Selection, and had received the vice chairmanship from the successful contender. On that commission, he had been an unwavering reform vote, a bloc leader for other reform commissioners, and, on occasion, a thorn in the side of Chairman McGovern. When the Party Structure Commission adjourned, in November of 1969, Hughes had taken the reform issue on the road, in a quest for a possible presidential nomination. By fall of 1970, he was one of the widely recognized, long-shot contenders for the Democratic nomination.

Nine months of active soundings, however, had failed to detect—or produce—the groundswell for which the candidate had hoped, and by the summer of 1971 he had given up the direct quest. Despite that, his statement of withdrawal showed that he was not foreswearing activities which might be conducive to a Hughes presidency at some time in the future:

> Washington, July 15—Senator Harold E. Hughes of Iowa withdrew from the race for the Democratic Presidential nomination today after having implied to his staff that he would not be displeased if they went to work for Senator George McGovern of South Dakota.
> Mr. Hughes said at a Capitol Hill news conference that his decision was "clear-cut and irrevocable," although he added that if he were offered the Vice Presidential nomination next year he would "be forced to give it serious consideration."[4]

In the aftermath of this suspension, staff members from the presidential effort continued to discuss with Hughes the possibility of some formal post at the National Convention, from which he could contribute additionally to the reform cause and in which he would remain available—and visible—should lightning strike. These staffers were especially interested in the Credentials chairmanship, and on September 14, Eli Segal, chief political strategist for the defunct campaign, endeavored to heighten this interest in the principal himself:

> The Democratic National Committee meets on October 13 and 14 to decide, among other less important things, who will be Temporary Chairman of the Credentials Committee. The Temporary Chairman, a new position created by the O'Hara Commission, has extraordinary convention powers. . . .
> You and I have discussed the possibility of your taking the Chairmanship of the Committee from three perspectives:
> (1) would it be in the interests of the party for you to be a chairman?
> (2) would it be in your interests?
> (3) could you get it?
> On Wednesday when we meet, I would like to discuss this with you again. If you want to go ahead, there is a lot of work to be done.[5]

Hughes did indeed rise to the bait; by the beginning of October, he, Segal, and a few others were at work on a campaign for the temporary Credentials chairmanship. An external effort to round up support for a candidate for this post did appear, in late 1971, to make more sense than usual, since the formal procedures from the Rules Commission prescribed a vote by the National Committee on the incumbent of this office, rather than simple appointment by the national chairman. Hughes did, however, want to reveal his intentions to Chairman O'Brien. If the chairman was receptive, the matter would be resolved. If he was neutral, Hughes would have paid the proper courtesy, and his campaign alone should otherwise be sufficient. But if O'Brien was discouraging, the Iowa Senator intended to persevere.

O'Brien was not at all receptive. The call from Hughes caught the chairman in the midst of seeking his own nominees for the various convention posts, a task in which he had been engaged, on and off, for some days. By then, he had found his convention manager, in Richard J. Murphy, a principal assistant from O'Brien's tenure as postmaster general. He did not, however, have his desired candidate for the Credentials chairmanship, and the slot was causing problems. O'Brien noted the interest of Hughes and thanked him for the call, but he regarded the nomination of a Credentials chairman as his personal prerogative, and he did not interrupt the hunt:

> Well, first of all, under the O'Hara guidelines, the Chairman of the party would recommend the Temporary Chairman of the standing committees. I had given an awful lot of thought to this. I had a lot of conversation with party people.

You would be amazed at the number of people who turned me down. You try to present a balanced picture at the convention. I couldn't find anybody to bless these rules. I myself was Permanent Chairman because I couldn't find anybody else.

During this period, I got a call from Hughes. I told Hughes that he could have some thoughts on this, but it was my responsibility. Lo and behold, at that very moment Hughes was wiring all of the members of the National Committee.

The question of personal prerogative was hardly O'Brien's major reason for wanting to avoid Hughes. That resided in O'Brien's continuing attempt to institute party reform while maintaining party unity. Hughes, of course, was a symbol of one sharply defined faction, the militant reformers. Indeed, he had been turned down for the Party Structure chairmanship two years before because he was even then too militant for all but factional loyalists. O'Brien felt that by easing commission recommendations through the National Committee and by slowly but steadily pressing the state parties into compliance, he had already pushed the regulars—who were, after all, the committee majority—as far as they could reasonably be expected to go. John Stewart, his director of communications, agreed:

O'Brien did feel that a sense of fairness in the guidelines would be violated if Hughes were Chairman. He needed someone who wouldn't come in with a set of notions about where the right solutions could be found. It would have been the last straw as far as labor and the others were concerned. Having pushed through the report in its entirety, and then having to live with Hughes, too, would have been more than anybody should be expected to live with.

The staff of the national chairman saw other liabilities, beyond Hughes's preconceived and predictable notions about the application of reform. The most critical of these was his personal style, especially his reputation for being quixotic and for having a fiery temper. That style, coupled with those views, seemed likely to reduce the chances of tiptoeing through the convention without major disruption. Accordingly, they kept looking. Their ultimate selection, Patricia Roberts Harris, emerged originally in a conversation between Stewart and Bill Welsh:

John Stewart and I came up with Pat Harris. She had been in the '68 Humphrey campaign and was attractive. Hughes was emerging again. We felt that Hughes was a nut; you can't have a guy like that, that unstable, dealing with this problem. Hughes was a candidate for President. And his people were the ones who were floating the reform argument.

We also saw that the toughest elements at the convention were going to be on quota matters. If you had Pat Harris, you would have credibility for your whole effort. She was tough; she was black.

Pat Harris had first achieved some prominence in Democratic party affairs when she gave one of the seconding speeches for Lyndon Johnson at the 1964 Convention. Subsequently, Johnson had appointed her both ambassador to Luxembourg and an alternate delegate to the United Nations. She had been an active Humphrey supporter in 1968, then dean of the law school at Howard University, then a partner in the prestigious Washington law firm of Fried, Frank, Harris, Shriver and Kampelman.[6]

When Welsh and Stewart proposed her as a potentially able chairman and a tactically sound choice, O'Brien first saluted her in the abstract. But after a few additional names had turned him down, the chairman found himself in desperate need of a candidate with whom to counter Hughes. He returned to Harris as his best hope and pressed the case with her personally:

> I remembered her very favorably. She had good recommendations from Kennedy and Johnson. She had an impressive background. I'll admit she was low down on the yellow-pad list. She and I and Bob Strauss had lunch. I had this hard-sell lunch with Pat. She resisted and called back the next day. I said, "I name the positions," and I would make it totally hers. Pat called back and said she would go, but she would not seek it. If the National Committee supported it, she would serve.

The selection of Harris by O'Brien, in response to the self-selection of Hughes, was enough to guarantee another extended lobbying war in advance of the National Committee meeting. The two contenders served naturally as rallying points for the major factions on the issue of party reform. Moreover, the two fit neatly, though not perfectly, with the revised debate over the fate of specific party reforms. If the central question in reform politics was not the extent of formal adoption but the degree to which formally adopted rules would be followed in practice, then the choice of a Credentials chairman might—just might—be crucial.

At a minimum, the selection of a Credentials chairman might reveal something about the way these new rules would be interpreted and applied within the Credentials Committee. Beyond that, the selection of a Credentials chairman might send a signal about the need to observe the new rules on the way to that convention. Hughes had been a militant reformer from the outset. He would brook no exceptions in the Credentials Committee. He would send an unavoidably chilling signal to party officials in advance of the convention. Harris was hardly the product, or advocate, of party regularity. Nor was she perceptibly soft on issues of legal procedure. But she was the choice of the highest official in the regular party structure. And she was selected, obviously and deliberately, as a way to derail Hughes. The major news media, in watching the confrontation evolve, gave it the same strategic—and symbolic—overtones:

> Vowing to reform itself, the party appointed a 28-member commission to come up with ways of giving "all Democratic voters a full, meaningful, and timely opportunity to participate" in choosing convention delegates. The commission issued an array of "guidelines," which were adopted by the Democratic National Committee. Any state party organization ignoring the reforms, the National Committee warned, did so at peril of losing their seats at the 1972 Convention.
> But would they? That would depend partly on the temporary chairman of the convention Credentials Committee, who, for the first time, would select examiners to go into the states to probe reform challenges. The examiners' recommendations on whom to seat would then be accepted or rejected by the full committee. But by picking the judges, the temporary credentials chairman will be able to influence the outcome of disputes.[7]

The Lobbying War in the National Committee

For close to a week, the battle between Hughes and Harris—really the battle between Hughes and his partisans versus O'Brien and his allies—raged on telephones across the nation. Hughes strategists had the advantage of a head start, behind a candidate who was active in his own behalf. When they found themselves under fire, they quickly came to regard this as a crucial combat, one which might determine, once and for all, whether the Democratic party was committed to reform. Segal, who coordinated the Hughes effort, put his perceptions into print:

> The selection of temporary chairman is one of the first indicators of the extent to which the major Democratic Party reforms, instituted after the debacle of Chicago, will be put into practice. The temporary chairman of the Credentials Committee often becomes the permanent chairman, and the identity of this chief certifier or bouncer will say a lot about how the new rules will be enforced.[8]

Harris partisans were forced to begin in the hole, and without the active participation of their candidate. On the other hand, they possessed the most influential campaign manager of all in Larry O'Brien, and he, too, regarded the contest as crucial. No one on this side took pen in hand to record their perspective, but Geri Joseph noted the speed with which many regulars, having been frustrated for so long in their attempt to confront reform and the reformers, transferred their energies into the battle over credentials staffing: "By late 1971, those who had any doubts said, 'Okay, so be it. We'll fight it out in the Credentials Committee.' "

O'Brien began his delayed campaign by moving to expand the array of pressures on his side, by mobilizing organized labor. The Committee on Political Education of the AFL-CIO had branches in most of the states; state COPE officials often possessed continuing social ties with party officials there as well. The coordination of the regular party and organized labor in the fight over a Credentials chairman thus became a classic effort by the orthodox coalition.

This effort began at the top, with Larry O'Brien, the Democratic national chairman, calling Al Barkan, the executive director of COPE. It resulted in the activation of a network of allies in the states, within both the regular party and the union movement. It continued with both state and national pressure, from central and local, party and union officials. Top labor officials had felt all along that O'Brien was catering disastrously, needlessly, to party insurgents. Despite this view, the COPE leadership had missed its opportunity when the guidelines had come before the National Committee in February. If COPE was to play any role in reform politics, then, it had to come at the National Committee meeting in October 1971. Barkan was immediately responsive:

> On the Pat Harris–Hughes fight, I was visited by O'Brien and Bill Welsh. They had this Patricia Harris, who I never met, and they said, "She's a natural. They're going to have a hell of a time opposing her." I put my blessing on the thing. I didn't want anyone who was definitely playing for the new-politics peoples.
>
> So I made calls, and we beat Hughes. Then Pat Harris never called to thank me, to ask what I thought she should do.

While O'Brien remained the dominant lobbying agent on behalf of Harris, Barkan did undertake a substantial effort of his own. O'Brien and Barkan, however, made similar efforts from very different motivations. O'Brien saw Hughes as a threat to the entire reform scenario which he had been orchestrating since the spring of 1970. Barkan viewed that scenario itself as pernicious. He was drawn into the Harris-Hughes fight not because he had changed his mind, but because he saw Hughes as beyond the pale—as the apotheosis of all the horrors which reformers had been trying to foist upon organized labor since the spring of 1968.

Barkan saw the reformers, at base, as individuals who had never had the party's—not to mention labor's—best interests at heart. More crucially, he saw the reforms as little more than a deliberate device, a self-conscious route to power, for independent activists and their associated interests and, thus, for white-collar Democrats generally. In his lobbying efforts, he emphasized the need for the friends of labor to line up behind Harris, as a hedge against all such developments. Joseph A. Doorley, Jr., national committeeman from

Rhode Island, was one of those with whom the COPE chieftain pressed his case:

> Barkan was more concerned over appointments to Credentials, to Rules, and so forth, than he was with the rules by themselves. Labor guys were trying to get me to go with Pat Harris. They wanted Pat Harris. Barkan thought he had a regular, a woman, and a black. Not having known Pat Harris or Hughes, and having Claiborne Pell [senator from Rhode Island] talk to me about Harris, that was enough.
>
> It was the Humphrey-labor group. They said, "This is what we want, Joe, and we'll vouch for her." There's the guy who should have been attuned. In October, they [labor] were very active. Local guys would ask me to call people. They even had me down to meet with Meany. It was the labor-Humphrey support that went for Pat Harris.

From the other side, the major gambit, once combat had been joined, was even simpler: Get Harris herself to withdraw or, failing that, get her to shift to the temporary chairmanship of the *Platform* Committee, thereby accommodating both Harris and Hughes. The gambit was a brainchild of Jean Westwood, national committeewoman from Utah:

> McGovern asked me to help him and asked me to nominate Hughes. Mary Lou Burg then called me and said that the women were going for Pat Harris. I said, "Let's see if we can get one or the other to get on one of the other committees." I tried to get Pat Harris for Platform Committee.

When this approach drew no response, Hughes partisans took a second tack.[9] Symbolically, the contest between Hughes and Harris might be a perfect confrontation between reformers and regulars, and between the alternative and the Orthodox Democratic coalitions. Yet it also featured a white, older, male against a black, younger, female—precisely the *wrong* alignment from the point of view of reformers. To counteract that symbolism and to break up the unity of the orthodox Democratic coalition, Hughes supporters mobilized all available black spokesmen on behalf of their candidate.

The central figure in this effort was Shirley A. Chisholm, maverick black congresswoman from Brooklyn. Segal had suggested recruiting Chisholm; she had committed to Hughes when the candidate called her personally. When O'Brien unveiled Harris as a second candidate for the temporary chairmanship, however, Chisholm had had second thoughts, and Thaddeus Garrett, a staff assistant, was quoted as saying that the congresswoman would "stay committed unless Mrs. Harris campaigns actively for the job."[10]

When that campaign did not materialize, Chisholm's position hardened, and she joined the other black leaders who were backing Hughes and urging Harris to withdraw. They attempted to press their case directly over the weekend of October 9–10, but Garrett reported that "she wouldn't even take calls from our people."[11] After that, Hughes partisans merely concentrated on accumulating endorsements from black leaders of all sorts, from Coretta Scott King through the members of the Democratic Central Committee for the District of Columbia.

An internal party conflict of this scope, in the fall of a prepresidential year, inevitably drew the attention of one other group of Democratic elites. The party's aspiring presidential nominees, announced and unannounced, active and inactive, could hardly remain aloof from the contest over a temporary Credentials chairman. Some of these potential contestants had specific influence to contribute to a Credentials struggle within the National Committee, a fact which encouraged the principals to seek them out. All had a theoretical stake in the outcome, since the person who adjudicated the new party rules might directly influence the fortunes of these contenders.

But beyond these secondary factors, and much more to the point, many aspirants had a direct stake in pleasing, or mollifying, the other party actors who were already deployed for battle. A major, national, party fight in the fall of 1971 inevitably attracted many of the groups and individuals from whose ranks a nomination campaign would eventually have to be fashioned. The independent activists and organized reformers were heavily committed, either as active participants or as very attentive spectators; so was the official party, at the national level and in many states; so, obviously, was organized labor. Since most of the aspiring nominees were courting these very groups and individuals, they were not in a position to treat this as just another extraneous conflict.

The dozen eventual contenders for a Democratic nomination varied widely in their direct influence within the National Committee. (See table 16.1.) Of the five candidates with no direct influence, one, John Lindsay, was not yet a Democrat and passed up the session automatically. Two others, George Wallace and Sam Yorty, had no hope of being supported by *either* major coalition and took no public notice of the conflict. Fred Harris, however, was pulled by a desire for the support of those rallying behind Hughes, and Gene McCarthy was pushed by the wishes of his former campaign loyalists, some of whom were working in the Hughes campaign. Both publicly endorsed the senator from Iowa for temporary chairman of the Credentials Committee.[12]

Of the five candidates with potential home-state influence, one, Birch Bayh, was about to drop from the race and was not about to take on the animosities of this conflict as his final campaign activity. Another, Henry Jackson, while

TABLE 16.1

Presidential Contenders and the
Harris-Hughes Conflict

Campaign Status of Commonly Acknowledged Contenders		
Already Withdrawn	Announced and Active	Yet to Announce
Bayh	Harris	Chisholm
Hughes	McGovern	Humphrey
		Jackson
		Kennedy
		Lindsay
		McCarthy
		Muskie
		Wallace
		Yorty

Reputed Influence Within the National Committee		
None	Home State	Extended Influence
Harris	Bayh	Humphrey
Lindsay	Chisholm	Kennedy
McCarthy	Hughes	Muskie
Wallace	Jackson	
Yorty	McGovern	

Strategic Responses		
Remain Detached	Endorse Hughes	Endorse Harris
Bayh	Chisholm	—
Humphrey	Harris	
Jackson	(Hughes)	
Lindsay	Kennedy	
Wallace	McCarthy	
Yorty	McGovern	
	Muskie	

his hopes lay solidly with the regular party and organized labor, concluded that there was little to be gained from any public stand at this stage in his long-shot campaign.

Harold Hughes, of course, was one of the two principals in the conflict. But while Hughes did possess some influence with his home-state members, that influence was, in fact, redundant: The Iowa members would have gone for the reform candidate, whoever that might be. Where Hughes *was* able to add something extra—once again—was through his personal friendship with Warren E. Hearnes, governor of Missouri. As he had with the Missouri delegation to the 1968 Convention, Hearnes again swung his representatives into the Hughes column, thereby delivering two votes which would otherwise have gone to Harris.

Shirley Chisholm was the lone presidential contender with a vote—her own—to contribute directly. Her aspirations for the Hughes-Harris fight, however, were much broader than being lobbied for her ballot. Like Fred Harris and George McGovern, she hoped to inherit a slice of the activist community. To that end, after a slight hesitation when Pat Harris entered the race, she worked actively on behalf of Harold Hughes. Chisholm would ultimately be the one to put Hughes's name in nomination.

George McGovern shared Chisholm's goals but in a much more strategically focused fashion. McGovern had been the earliest announced candidate for the Democratic nomination; he was the earliest public endorser of Hughes for Credentials chairman. While he was still far back among potential presidential nominees—polls showed him with minimal name recognition in the general public[13]—McGovern was making major inroads among independent activists, and this progress could only be accelerated by an evident public contribution to the Hughes campaign. McGovern quickly blessed that effort, as a logical extension of his own presidential drive, but he remained far less concerned in private with the comparative merits of the two contestants:

> I testified for Hughes at the Hughes–Pat Harris credentials fight, but I never really wanted Hughes to be Chairman, for fear he would blow things up. I was more unopposed to Harris as Chairman, feeling that she was impressive and fair. I testified for Hughes, because my people were for Hughes, and they wanted him to win. Also, some of the reform commission people were for Hughes for the post, like Anne Wexler.

The one potential contender for a Democratic nomination who was widely discussed in the fall of 1971 but who would never enter the race at all was Edward Kennedy. Kennedy was believed to have some extended influence within the National Committee; he was inherently more responsive to the alliance around Hughes; but he was sufficiently distant from a presidential bid to see little personal stake in the outcome. He contented himself with endorsing Hughes and with trying—with only partial success—to line up the votes of the Massachusetts members.[14]

Hubert Humphrey was *known* to have some extended influence, and while he was also formally a noncandidate, he was edging closer to a return run. Humphrey, however, saw the conflict as one from which he could extract only losses. His principal support lay with the regular party and organized labor. But he, more than anyone else, needed to avoid enlisting in a tableau featuring Humphrey *versus* the insurgents, activists, and organized reformers. As a result, he asserted personal friendship with both contestants, and he confined himself to responding privately to members who might seek him out.

The one candidate left out of this tally, and the one most obviously caught in the middle, was Edmund Muskie. Muskie's dilemma, of course, was the product of his blessings, of his status as the evident front-runner. But this did not prevent him from being pursued aggressively by both sides or from facing the most tortured strategic options of any presidential hopeful. On the one hand, Muskie partisans wanted to cement his relations with organized labor, while improving his standing with the national chairman. A vote for Patricia Harris would make a clear contribution. On the other hand, Muskie's people wanted at least a chunk of the activist community, so that their candidate could claim to represent all party factions, so that this stratum would not be united in someone else's column, and so that it would not be united *against* Muskie, as it had been united against Humphrey four years before.

Under those conditions, the simplest option would have been to remain detached from the entire conflict. Yet this, too, was more difficult for Muskie than for a candidate with a lower profile. From the moment the Hughes campaign began, at the start of the first week in October, Hughes strategists tried to entice Muskie into their corner. They tried pulling him, by publicizing the notion that this was the "acid test" of his reform sentiments.[15] They tried pushing him, by getting Warren Hearnes and his senators, Stuart Symington and Thomas Eagleton, to endorse Hughes for temporary chairman *and* Muskie for president in the same public statement.[16]

By the end of the week, these tactics appeared to be working. R. W. Apple, Jr., discovered major Muskie operatives working actively for Hughes, and the *New York Times* broke the story with "Muskie May Back Reform Bloc in Key Preconvention Dispute":

> Two of Senator Muskie's principal political operatives, John F. English of New York and George J. Mitchell of Maine, both members of the National Committee, will almost certainly vote for Senator Harold E. Hughes of Iowa, the reform candidate, at the committee's meeting next Wednesday.
> "I never really had much alternative," Mr. English said. "We need a man who knows the intent, not just the words, of the new rules, and Hughes is that man. I think George Mitchell feels the same."[17]

Apple's report was premature. By Friday, Chairman O'Brien was only unveiling his own candidate for the position. A phone call from Hughes had been the original stimulus which shook the chairman out of his more stately search; the threat of defection by Muskie was the follow-up which truly galvanized him:

> I didn't go into the head-hunting business on this until Ed Muskie advised me one night that he was backing Hughes. The DNC should be involved in this; it's theirs by right. I called in the staff, told them that there was a split in the DNC among Hughes and Harris, and then we went to work. Every member of that National Committee was checked and rechecked by my staff.

The chairman immediately contacted Muskie and asked him to reconsider. Barkan then went after the senator as well, and by the time the report from Apple was on the stands, Muskie had pulled back. He moved closer to a public endorsement over the weekend of October 9–10, but O'Brien reached him again on Monday and threatened to resign the national chairmanship, leaving it up for grabs at this crucial point, if Muskie acted. Once again, the candidate hesitated. George Mitchell, who favored a Hughes endorsement, saw a no-win situation developing:

> John English and I wanted Hughes's support [for Muskie]. I had become a great admirer of Hughes. Larry was very active, and wanted Pat Harris, and *didn't* want Hughes. Larry threatened to quit if Muskie supported Hughes. It was mixed up with presidential politics. I was *for* Harold Hughes; I wasn't *against* Pat Harris. Larry lobbied tremendously on that, and made it a personal contest.
> At that time, Muskie was trying for liberal support. They kept saying that he doesn't take stands, and so on. At the time, too, we didn't know we were going to get beat. Early on, we thought that Hughes might win. But the last few days, the vote was clear.

As the handful of available days passed and as the crucial ballot drew closer, there was little to distinguish the mechanics of the two campaigns, the Harris and the Hughes efforts. Both operated largely via the telephone. Hughesites issued more press releases and public statements; Harrisites relied more on informal social contacts. Most members of the National Committee had already been contacted by Hughes partisans by the time O'Brien, much less Barkan, swung into action. Many had been willing to indicate support when there was no one else in the field. The subsequent approach by O'Brien, then, intensified their sense of pressure, since O'Brien was asking many to *switch* endorsements. Ordinarily, committee members emphasized their status as fully independent decision-makers. This time, they alluded continually and publicly to their feeling of being squeezed.[18]

On the Hughes side, much of the calling was handled by Segal and Wexler, with liberal assistance from the candidate and from reform activists like Westwood. Once O'Brien entered the fray, these individuals were forced to *re-*call many of their prior contacts, to make sure that those previously uncommitted were not going for Harris. In the process, the Hughes forces probably accomplished the more impressive telephone feats, like tracking F. Grant Sawyer, national committeeman from Nevada, all the way to a stopover in London.[19]

While they were doing this, Hughes's leading supporters were regularly announcing their ostensible head counts, which unfailingly implied that they were within striking distance despite the O'Brien-Barkan barrage. As late as Tuesday, October 12, they were claiming that they had forty-three of the maximum fifty-five votes needed for victory. In response, the staff of the national chairman was regularly disputing their figures, with ill-concealed contempt. Indeed, as early as Monday, October 11, they were asserting that Harris would win by at least two to one and that Hughes might not get over thirty votes.[20]

The telephone network on this other side was worked directly by the national chairman and his staff and by the COPE director and his assistants. The chairman reached almost all his members by phone; he spoke with many of them more than once. Many committee members received a call from the national office of COPE as well, and many received one from a state labor operative, too. In this, neither O'Brien nor Barkan confined themselves to members of the National Committee. Both urged any responsive labor, party, or public official to call his state committeeman and committeewoman and register his views.

In these conversations, O'Brien emphasized not just the lack of detachment represented by Hughes, with his allegedly roughshod approach to party reform, but the qualifications of his own preference, Patricia Harris. Moreover, the chairman tried to spin out the reform scenario with Hughes as credentials interpreter:

> Mr. O'Brien's opposition to Senator Hughes, sources close to him said, stems in part from a belief that Kenneth Bode and Eli Segal, strong-minded reform advocates who served as staff members of the commission that drew up the new party rules, were behind the Hughes candidacy.
> "Larry is telling us," one committeeman said, "that if we want to get pushed to the wall with left-wingers like Eli Segal and Ken Bode, then we should go ahead and vote for Hughes."
> Mr. Hughes issued a statement today pledging that Mr. Bode, now the director of the Center for Political Reform, would not serve as the committee's counsel if he was elected as committee chairman. He did not mention Mr. Segal, who has been working actively in the new Hughes campaign.[21]

Barkan was to keep these contacts up through Tuesday, October 12, the day of the Executive Committee meeting. O'Brien would continue right down to the wire, down to the early hours of the morning on Wednesday, October 13, when he could still reach committee members from the west coast who had not yet flown east, and then again through the following morning, as he talked to wavering members who were already in Washington for the afternoon meeting.

The National Committee and the Final Call

The Executive Committee met at national party headquarters on Tuesday afternoon, October 12. The lateness of the hour—the session did not convene until 2:15 P.M.—belied the imposing character of its agenda, for the committee was being asked to write the guidelines of the Party Structure Commission into the Final Call; to address, endorse, and then transcribe the proposed reforms of the Rules Commission as well; and to recommend the appointment of a Convention manager and a temporary Credentials chairman. If Chairman O'Brien had expected more argument about proposals for reform or if he had not been sure of the vote on Harris-Hughes, the session might have convened earlier. But he possessed little anxiety on either score, and he found better things to do than to dawdle with his Executive Committee.

Even with the limited time available, the bulk of the committee session went to pro forma matters. A set of procedural resolutions, a grocery list of commendations, and a number of automatic convention arrangements all had to be cleared before anything with the potential for serious disagreement surfaced. Accordingly, the meeting was about two-thirds completed when O'Brien placed the Final Call on the table. Marshall Brown of Louisiana moved it immediately; Joe Barr of Pennsylvania seconded it.

No sooner had they acted, however, than the one topic raised by the Final Call but not on O'Brien's public agenda made its appearance. This was the Powers amendment on ex officio status for members of the National Committee. Doris Banks of Colorado introduced it by asking whether these ex officio seats would be added to the number of delegates allotted to each state or whether they would have to come out of previous state totals. Brown of Louisiana, Barr of Pennsylvania, and Arvey of Illinois, apparently fearing that the initial establishment of the right of a state to forego these privileges was only a prelude to an attempt at legislating that forbearance, acted to cut off this possibility, with a colloquy on the full meaning of the Powers amendment. Banks, however, was not to be put off and persevered with exactly that suggestion:

> *Banks:* The other half of my question relates to the automatic vote for present members who do not otherwise have votes. And I am wondering if it might not

be appropriate for this Executive Committee to act on that particular provision in the recommendation.

Joseph: We did vote on that, Mr. Chairman, but there has been a good deal of concern, I think, expressed by Governors, if I am told correctly, as well as by State Chairmen, the fact that here we are, you know, sweeping out the old—the only old we allow are those two old National Committee people who got an automatic vote.[22]

O'Brien was not eager to have the Executive Committee take action. He and Califano had already agreed to spring the matter on the floor of the National Committee; to that end, they wanted no early warnings. Moreover, since O'Brien was in the process of arguing that his fellow members should retain their prerogatives in the Harris-Hughes selection, branding the Hughes campaign as illegitimate because it was "externally initiated," he did not want to have to argue that these same members should simultaneously divest themselves of a related prerogative, one which they might see as more consequential. As a result, the chairman tried persistently to put the issue to sleep, so that it could be raised afresh at the Thursday session of the full committee, on the day *after* the Harris-Hughes vote. Banks bearded him on the topic once again, Westwood of Utah returned to it, and even Joseph reraised the question, before O'Brien moved to cut off the argument once and for all by pressing for a vote on the entire document:

O'Brien: Do I hear a motion on the Final Call? May I have a motion made and seconded?
Jeffrey: Is this the same as it was the last time?
O'Brien: Date and time and place.
Joseph: Could we know what is new in this?
Jeffrey: Yes, that is my question, Geri.
Welsh: This is essentially announcing the place and date of the Call, taking the traditional loyalty provisions that have been handed down since 1956. I am taking the O'Hara Commission's recommendations on convention procedures, the rules procedures for the convention conduct of business meetings, adopting them as the temporary rules of the convention. And that wraps up all the things that we need to have in the Call.[23]

Mildred Jeffrey of Michigan moved the whole package, but the mention of the loyalty oath by Welsh had accidentally injected a new issue, and several members wandered off in pursuit of that. Brown of Louisiana, in particular, sensed a means to embarrass those militant reformers who were talking openly of a bolt to some fourth party if reform rules were not scrupulously followed. He attempted to put this threatened *dis*loyalty on the formal record, and Welsh began to waver under his questioning, but O'Brien skirted the entire issue by driving the motion for adoption to a vote:

Brown: Are you taking out the loyalty oath?
Welsh: No, the loyalty oath is essentially what it has been. Well, yes, that is correct.
Brown: We are taking it out for everyone but. . . .
Welsh (interrupts Brown): The main loyalty oath is for the National Committee members. . . .
O'Brien (interrupts Welsh): A motion is before the house. Made and seconded. All those in favor, aye. Opposed, nay. The ayes have it.[24]

With that, the Executive Committee ceded its last chance to tinker with the specific content of reform rules for delegate selection. In the process, the committee endorsed—without change—all of the recommendations from the Rules Commission on the conduct of convention business. Committee members had attended to only one provision in the combined recommendations of both commissions, the recommendation on ex officio status for National Committee members, and they had taken no action on that. Otherwise, they had dispensed with amendment, discussion, *or even a rereading* of either reform report.

After a few procedural questions about implementation of the Final Call, the Executive Committee moved to its recommendation for temporary chairman of the 1972 Credentials Committee—and moved rapidly through this, too. If the contest between Harris and Hughes was likely to absorb a great deal of attention at the meeting of the full committee, it never seemed likely to do so in the Executive Committee. The members had predictable positions; those positions had hardened since the lobbying campaign began; there was little point in expounding them at length, before they really counted.

As a result, the entire discussion on the relative merits of the candidates took up slightly more time than the discussion of a stance on the ex officio provision. Hughes and Harris partisans did rehearse some arguments in a formalistic fashion. Even then, they managed to remember that the crucial battle was yet to come, and none of these arguments was joined in any serious way. The ballot arrived quickly and wound up as expected, in a 9 to 3 commendation of Harris over Hughes.[25] Having reached their expected conclusion, the members hurried through a few more pieces of routine business and adjourned to await the decisive contest on the morrow.

While Chairman O'Brien, the principal lobbyist for Harris, had been engaged with his Executive Committee, the major actors around Hughes had not been idle. In fact, they had been mildly buoyed on Tuesday morning, after several days of declining fortunes, when Ed Muskie finally dropped the other shoe and endorsed Hughes for temporary Credentials chairman. In deference to O'Brien and the COPE leadership, Muskie refrained from making a public announcement, but his leading political operatives began telephoning members of the National Committee with the private news early that morning.[26]

Both sides, the Hughes and the Harris contingents, worked the telephones well into Tuesday night and then picked up the campaign in person the next morning. Both Hughes and O'Brien had reserved suites at the Mayflower Hotel where the full committee would meet later that day, and both ran a steady stream of visitors through these rooms in the hours before the luncheon which would inaugurate the formal events of the day. Newspaper reports continued to suggest that the vote would be close, with Muskie perhaps providing the margin for victory, while National Committee sources were ever more insistent that the contest was over.[27]

The noon meal which opened the National Committee meeting of Wednesday, October 13, in the Colonial Room at the Mayflower Hotel, was accompanied by five short speeches from five presidential aspirants: Fred Harris, Hubert Humphrey, Henry Jackson, George McGovern, and Edmund Muskie. Each saluted the Democratic party, excoriated the Republicans, and directed the attention of their audience to the presidential race. All expressed the hope that their listeners would remain united after the crucial ballot of the day. Where they differed, of course, was in their specific comments about that ballot. Jackson essentially skirted the matter. Humphrey produced the most effusive and balanced analysis, insisting that "whatever decision you make, I'm going to like." Harris and McGovern spoke primarily about the virtues of Hughes, delivering their expected, personal endorsements. Muskie, while he did not name his preference, said simply, "You know my position."[28]

The luncheon and associated festivities lasted until 3:00 P.M., when the full committee was called to order. Arvey of Illinois opened this scheduled two-day gathering with the report of the Executive Committee. He covered its views on the creation of standing committees for the 1972 Convention, on the apportionment of expenses for its Arrangements Committee, and on the staffing decisions which would give these bodies life. Arvey presented a slate of fifteen members for Arrangements, forwarded unanimously; a nominee for convention manager, Richard J. Murphy, forwarded unanimously as well; and a candidate for temporary Credentials chairman, Patricia Roberts Harris, forwarded by a vote of 9 to 3.

Arvey was followed by Bob Strauss, the national treasurer, with a survey of party finances and of progress on convention preparations. Strauss introduced the proposed convention manager, Dick Murphy, who presented his own summary of preparations to date, thereby suggesting that the National Committee was about to confirm what had long since been his practical, functional status. Murphy was succeeded at the rostrum by James G. O'Hara, chairman of the Rules Commission, with the one element of his proposed reforms which could not be delayed until the following day.

This was the first true reapportionment of the standing committees of the national party convention—Credentials, Rules, and Platform—since the convention itself was created. Ever since that far-off Jacksonian era, every state had possessed numerical parity on each committee—originally one member, subsequently two.[29] The Rules Commission recommended an expansion of the three committees, a reduction to one guaranteed seat per state, and distribution of the remaining seats by prior Democratic vote. Nevertheless, perhaps because the members had come to view reapportionment as inevitable or perhaps because they were looking ahead to the fight over the temporary chairmanship of the (reapportioned) Credentials Committee, the motion passed unanimously.

Having established the structure of their convention committees, the members plunged directly into the key staffing decision. Surprisingly, despite the intense lobbying efforts on both sides during the preceding week, despite appearances by the presidential candidates in one final lobbying push, and despite impassioned speeches from the chosen nominators and seconders, the debate was comparatively short, occupying only twelve pages in the total committee transcript. This relative verbal containment probably resulted from the fact that so much had already been said, from the fact that the nominating speeches again covered most available arguments, and from a generalized belief that nothing was likely to change at this late date by the production, application, and repetition of arguments.

The ballot confirmed what most National Committee members had known from the start of their meeting: Pat Harris was to be the temporary chairman of the 1972 Credentials Committee. In fact, by the time Maine, the home state of Ed Muskie, got to cast its ballot—two votes for Harold Hughes—Harris had accumulated more support than Hughes would ever receive. At the end, the tally stood at Harris 73 and Hughes 29. Harris had achieved an absolute majority of the total committee; Hughes, strategic leaks and press projections to the contrary, had failed to break 30.[30]

The vote contained few internal surprises either. The usual distinction between committee members from volunteer versus organized political parties remained, although majorities of both categories actually went with Harris, thereby confirming, once again, the essential regularity of many committee members from volunteer-party states. The one newly significant element in the ballot was its relationship to the compliance status of the individual states.

Committee members from states which were in final, certified compliance with the guidelines of the Party Structure Commission actually gave a majority of their votes to *Harold Hughes,* despite the overwhelming vote in the other direction for the committee as a whole. (See figure 16.2.) Moreover, as the distance of a state party from certified compliance increased, moving from simple absence of fully implemented rules to an active resistance to their adoption, the percentage of committee members preferring Harris to Hughes increased as well. Indeed, in the final category of states, those which possessed organized parties well out of compliance and which thus had the most to lose from an inflexible interpretation of reform requirements, a full *90 percent* of committee members expressed a preference for Harris.

The lack of any surprise in the identity of the winner, coupled with the decisiveness of the vote itself, took most of the steam out of the afternoon session. A unanimous vote accepted the proposed organization of the Arrangements Committee, the body which would oversee the normally mundane convention functions of housing, security, and communications. A second voice vote accepted the nominees for membership on this committee. A third approved Richard Murphy as convention manager. By 4:40, with the only major item of business out of the way and with no further disputes attaching to these lesser decisions, the committee felt comfortable in recessing until the next morning.

The National Committee reconvened at 10:30 A.M. the following day, to tackle the contents of its Final Call. Many in the Hughes camp were still smarting from their defeat of the previous afternoon, unequivocal though it had been. Accordingly, if there had been any obvious threat to the recommendations of either the Party Structure or Rules Commissions, these Hughes partisans would presumably have been more than ready to throw themselves into the fray. No one, however, knew of any such threat, and there had been no additional maneuvering in the eighteen hours since the committee recessed.

The members were greeted on Thursday morning by their newly appointed, temporary Credentials chairman. Pat Harris read a statement thanking them for their support and pledging to administer the new rules as impartially, even sternly, as she could. Chairman O'Brien then recognized Chairman Fraser of the Party Structure Commission, for a report on implementation and compliance. Fraser began by emphasizing the real progress which had been achieved, and its congruence with his earlier predictions:

Fraser: Thank you very much, Larry. Fellow Democrats, three months ago, at a meeting of our Commission, I predicted that by the end of 1971, there would be 40 states in full compliance with the Guidelines which our Commission adopted and which are now incorporated into the Call. I can report to you today that that figure is in sight.[31]

451

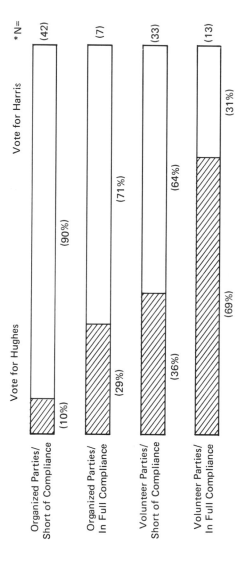

Vote for Hughes   Vote for Harris   *N=

Organized Parties/   (42)
Short of Compliance   (10%)   (90%)

Organized Parties/   (7)
In Full Compliance   (29%)   (71%)

Volunteer Parties/   (33)
Short of Compliance   (36%)   (64%)

Volunteer Parties/   (13)
In Full Compliance   (69%)   (31%)

*NOTE: N is the total number of members of the the National Committee present and voting in each category
of party type and compliance status.

FIG. 16.2

*State Party Characteristics, Compliance Progress,
and the Vote on Harris-Hughes*

Fraser went on to confirm that neither he nor his commission was about to relax, despite these optimistic projections. To underscore his point, he reviewed the full commission meeting of July 16, the one which had drafted a set of resolutions on guideline enforcement. Moreover, he described these resolutions in a fashion which emphasized not their essential moderation within the commission, but their aggressive potential within the national party as a whole. Fraser closed his substantive comments with "the interaction, if you will, of Guidelines A–1 and A–2 with the spirit of the guidelines."[32]

The original tension between "reasonable relationship" standards and a participatory institutional structure had become a topic of speculation for some reporters and a source of stress for state party leaders who were bringing their parties into compliance. Fraser summarized their concern as: "How can you say that we are to come in with this result, when the whole thrust of the guidelines is that there are no more smoke-filled rooms, no more predesigned results, we want an open and democratic system?"[33] Rather than attempt to reconcile these perspectives, however, he called the attention of his audience to a longer memo on the subject which his commission would discuss the following day.[34]

Immediately after Fraser's speech, Chairman O'Brien set the committee on the major business of the day, the adoption of a Final Call. He took a quick motion and second on a resolution authorizing the Call. He then recognized Geri Joseph for a carefully prepared parliamentary maneuver:

Joseph: Mr. Chairman, I would like to propose an amendment to the Final Call. I would like to present the amendment first, and then an explanation as to why.

The amendment would come, I believe, in Section 1, called "Delegate Votes," Nummer 8, following the remarks, "With full rights and privileges of a Delegate on matters coming before the Convention." I would like to add the amendment, "Except for the right to vote."[35]

This was, of course, precisely the language which O'Brien himself had recommended in February, when he took this amendment through his Executive Committee as a potential—and ultimately unsuccessful—attempt to head off further opposition in the full committee. Then, John Powers of Massachusetts, with overwhelming support from the members, had gone on to strike the phrase "except for the right to vote." On Thursday morning, October 14, eight months later, Joseph was moving to put those same six words back in.

Powers would again argue heatedly against this provision, but it was Thomas C. Carroll, outgoing chairman of the Kentucky party, who got in the first blow:

Carroll: What I do want to say, Mr. Chairman, is that it disturbs me, because I know so many of you all, and I have known so many of you all for so many years, to see you emasculate this Committee—and that is what you are about to do if you vote for this.

You are all elected by the Democrats in your state. You serve for four years. If you are as those in Kentucky, and I am sure most of you are, you pay your own expenses; you devote to the Party service for four years; you are the continuity of the Party; you are the thing that keeps the Party alive in good times and bad; you are the thing that has kept it alive these past three years.

To me, it is incredible that the mere argument of "democracy"—if that is the word for it—would be an excuse for you to take away from yourselves that which you give so much to the Party. You know, you can take this thing of democracy to the point where it becomes anarchy. We need this Committee. We need the wisdom of the members of this Committee. We need the voice, *with a vote,* of the members of this Committee at the National Convention. We are talking about a small number of votes.[36]

After Carroll, the discussion bounced back and forth in an emotional manner. Richard B. Stoner of Indiana spoke in favor of the amendment, as did William J. Dougherty of South Dakota. Leif Erickson of Montana spoke against it, as did Jake Arvey of Illinois. Arvey was not just opposed, but angry. He viewed the amendment as a betrayal of committee trust, since many states had already acted on the basis of the Preliminary Call. Chairman O'Brien was evidently nettled by Arvey's argument, for he interjected the notion that such states had acted on "our mistake," but Arvey retorted that they had acted in good faith nevertheless.[37]

A chain of spokesmen favoring the Joseph proposal followed, interrupted and supported by Counsel Califano. Finally, after this parade of positive witnesses, Powers obtained the floor. While the balance of *speakers* had clearly been on the side of the amendment, the balance within the National Committee remained ambiguous and, indeed, appeared little changed by the argument these speakers were presenting. As a result, while the debate ground down and while Powers spoke, Califano and a few key members circulated on the floor, arguing, cajoling, and seeking personal support for the change. Powers was incensed by what he saw:

What more could you tell them than that they were voting themselves into extinction? They didn't realize the impact of their votes when they changed their position. They realized it later.

Powers was followed by Gorman H. King of North Dakota, who offered one last endorsement of the amendment, and the question was called. Ruth

J. Owens and Robert S. Vance of Alabama were the first members polled. Both voted no, and that was the high-water mark of the opposition. Both ballots from Alaska and Arizona, the next two states, went for Joseph, and her amendment was never in jeopardy again. The final tally, 65 to 35, sustained O'Brien and defeated Powers in unambiguous fashion.[38]

As in February, members from volunteer-party states were more sympathetic to the elimination of ex officio seats for the National Committee. Yet this time, the intervention of Chairman O'Brien and Counsel Califano had been sufficient to turn the tide, and the crucial fact was that majorities from both categories of state political party—volunteer and organized—had gone for elimination.[39] When the tally on the Joseph amendment was announced, Bob Vance, who had been on the negative side there, moved for adoption of the Final Call. His motion carried unanimously, and the meeting was, for all intents and purposes, over.

O'Brien did hold his members on the scene for one more short speech, on the developments of the day, before permitting them to adjourn:

> *O'Brien:* As of the moment, we now approach adjournment of this truly historic meeting of this Democratic National Committee. I think it is appropriate, and I would hope that our friends in the press who are here would give us their attention, too, because this is not a press release, and I would like to have you hear my words. I think it is appropriate to review the extraordinary record of party reform that has been compiled in the past year. Never has a political party so totally changed its way of doing business in such a short period of time.
>
> Upon the mandate of the 1968 National Convention, the Commission on Rules and the Commission on Party Structure and Delegate Selection were organized and staffed. These two Commissions went about their work with extraordinary commitment and diligence. They wrote a new charter of democracy for the Democratic party.
>
> At the last meeting of this Committee, the eighteen guidelines for delegate selection were unanimously adopted and included as an integral part of the Call to the 1972 Democratic Convention. This action removed whatever ambiguity might have surrounded the status of the guidelines. . . .
>
> This meeting has now completed the basic reforms recommended by the Commission on Rules relating to the organization and the conduct of the 1972 Democratic National Convention. Once again, there has been overwhelming support for these recommendations, a testament to both the wisdom of the Commission on Rules and the good sense of the members of the National Committee. . . .
>
> By the time of the National Convention, there also will be recommendations for the restructuring of the Democratic National Committee itself that can be considered and voted upon by the Convention's delegates.[40]

Implications

The usual disjunction in reform politics between investment and outcome—between actions and effects—had characterized the October meeting
of the National Committee. Reform politics had returned to the national
level, through consideration of a Final Call to the 1972 Convention. That
Call had contained institutional changes of the greatest possible moment. Yet
preparations for the committee meeting had indicated no great concern, by
anyone, with the fate of these items.

This situation had changed dramatically with the announcement of an independent candidacy by Harold Hughes for the temporary chairmanship of the
Credentials Committee. Hughes had begun by notifying Chairman
O'Brien—and by mobilizing national party dissidents and organized reform
factions in the states. O'Brien had countered by mobilizing the regular party
and organized labor behind a candidate of his own. In short order, the orthodox and alternative Democratic coalitions were locked in a conflict as intense
and extensive as any in the lifetime of current committee members.

The outcome came as a surprise to many, probably because Hughes partisans had assiduously courted the national press, and because national reporters
had unduly respected the tactical forecasts of the reform side. But when the
dust had settled, the candidate of the orthodox coalition was overwhelmingly
successful. The extended lobbying war leading up to a vote in the National
Committee had served only to firm up existing dispositions. Party regulars
composed between two-thirds and three-quarters of this crucial arena for reform politics. Party regulars delivered 70 percent of the National Committee
to Patricia Harris, their candidate.[41] The truth of the matter, as at any point
in the preceding twenty years, was that within the national party the orthodox
coalition was overwhelmingly dominant. The alternative coalition, with a head
start and at full mobilization, could not cause it serious inconvenience. Reform
politics had moved solidly inside the regular party. The regular party could
dispose as it wished on reform politics.

The irony in all this, of course—almost "the usual irony"—lay in its implications for institutional change. The orthodox coalition had triumphed on the
major item of conflict, an appointment as temporary Credentials chairman.
The alternative coalition had been awarded the victory, in spite of itself, on
the major items of substance, the reform reports of the Party Structure and
Rules commissions. Indeed, it had received an extra bonus in the retraction
of ex officio status for National Committee members. John Stewart watched
a major, preliminary battle cover passage—unscathed and undiscussed—of the
most sweeping planned reforms in American party history: "The big issue was

Pat Harris, and the more conservative guys won on that. You always had another fight going on that got everybody's attention and energy."

The details of the conflict only reinforced this irony. An all-out lobbying war had come down to a division vote, in favor of the regulars, on a temporary committee assignment. Preparatory indifference had culminated in a unanimous voice vote, of benefit only to the reformers, on sweeping institutional change. Once again, party regulars had secured the personnel decisions in reform politics. Once again, party reformers had secured the rules, the institutional structure around which that politics would revolve. Joe Califano watched with a mix of fascination, satisfaction, and horror:

> I think that if DNC members had been candid about what they thought, even in October, that the vast bulk of them did not understand the ramifications of those rules. At the October meeting, while the press regarded the Harris-Hughes fight as the big issue, we did not. Pat Harris so clearly had the votes that there was no question. She was not part of a strategy, at least this time. I was not trying to trade provisions; there was no strategy on this.

The final compounding of this irony, of course, came from the fact that no one on either side who was acquainted with Harris believed that she was likely to turn out to be "soft on reform." Even George Mitchell, who was arguing forcefully in public for Harold Hughes, agreed in private that Hughes's defeat was hardly the major event of the two-day meeting: "You take Pat Harris. She is a person of integrity. She won't do anything blatantly wrong. Once the procedures are adopted, that's it."[42]

Outside observers might be excused for missing the reality of the situation, since the national press again emphasized the items of open conflict and de-emphasized the associated institutional change, thereby ignoring the closing oration from Chairman O'Brien almost entirely. The *New York Times*, for example, headlined its first article with "Mrs. Harris Wins Democratic Post" and its second with "Mrs. Harris Vows to Fight Mistrust." But it was *Newsweek* which best represented the press response when it noted that "almost lost in the battle over the credentials chairmanship was the fact that the traditionalist National Committee had unanimously approved the major recommendations of the two party commissions"—in the second-to-last paragraph of a seven-paragraph piece focused on the Harris-Hughes dispute.[43]

The press remained true to form in a second sense as well. For the summary message of these reports followed inevitably from their pattern of attention: If the Harris-Hughes conflict had been the major development at the committee meeting, then that meeting had testified to the resurgence and renewed dominance of the regular party and organized labor. Within weeks, this would become the "reality" of reform politics for an important set of elite actors. It would provide militant reformers with a major asset in their attempt to reinterpret key reform guidelines; it would provide party officials with a major incentive to surrender and acquiesce.

The fine points of this conflict contained additional portents for the fate of the opposing coalitions, and thus for the course of reform politics. Or at least, the points of tension within the two grand, contending coalitions were now easy to see. The old alliance between the regular party and organized labor was as solid as ever; the newer alliance between party dissidents and the ideological and reform organizations was even more so. It was the existing ties of racial minorities to the orthodox coalition, then, and the alleged ties of women to the alternative coalition, which were strained by this conflict.

Black politicians were pulled publicly in both directions, and for some, the tension was extreme. J. Charles Evers of Mississippi was the best example. When first contacted by Hughes partisans, Evers had declined to take a public position. But continued attention had brought him over in Hughes's direction, and on the Monday night before the committee meeting, at a party at the Virginia home of Edward Kennedy, he had been quoted as indicating that he would go with Hughes. Despite that, the opposition campaign, and the demographics of the opposition candidate, continued to bother him. When the Executive Committee met on Tuesday afternoon, he skipped the meeting but instructed his proxy to go with Harris, saying afterward that "the whole black community is watching me, and I can't go against one of my own or I'll look nothing more than a fool." Finally, at the full committee session the next afternoon, Evers was dragged back across the line and voted for Harold Hughes.[44]

The Evers case was overdrawn. But it was indicative of the cross-pressures on black politicians in general from the orthodox and alternative coalitions—cross-pressures, essentially, between their mass base and their elite contacts. The black leadership would continue to wander in the course of reform politics. This tension and cross-pressure would explain its lesser role in the attempt to reinterpret demographic requirements. It would explain its limited victory, and ultimate loss, in that same struggle. (See chapter 17.)

There was far less drama in the case of female members of the National Committee. There were many more of them, and they had been present on the committee, en masse, for a much longer time than its black members. Accordingly, the demographics of the contestants and of their supporters meant little to these committee members. They voted through their attachment to the regular party or to organized reform factions; their vote was indistinguishable from that of their male colleagues. Nevertheless, within weeks,

when it came time to fight over the proper interpretation of reform requirements for demographic representation, it would be feminist organizations
which would take the lead—and secure the victory. (See chapter 17.)

The triumph of the regular party in the selection of Pat Harris, then, had
come in the context of a massive overall victory for party rules reform. If this
small triumph was the item on which outside observers focused, that did not
obscure the fact that it served almost as a consolation prize for the side which
lost the main contest. Barring truly explosive developments, party regulars had
already lost the bulk of the substantive outcomes in reform politics, in February, in the months which followed, and again in October. The small wins
which they had chalked up along the way would prove to be little more, in
essence, than pyrrhic victories of the definitional sort.

Indeed, the lingering elements of the committee meeting on the Final
Call—the press reports of its outcome, the impressions shared by outside observers—were destined to remain as influential factors in the final stage of reform politics. In that meeting, party regulars had surrendered their preferred
institutional arrangements for selecting delegates and nominating a president.
Yet within weeks, the continuing perception of that meeting was to help drive
these same party regulars to placate party reformers by going on to surrender
the interpretation and translation of these reform requirements as well.

The Re-creation of Reform: The Women's

Caucus and Demographic Representation

IN WHICH, efforts to change the interpretation of key reform provisions emerge after passage of the Final Call; the first of these is an attempt by a new organization of feminists to extract a dramatically altered interpretation of the "reasonable relationship" clause; and their striking success results in formal demographic quotas. AND IN WHICH, the process of translating reformed rules becomes the essence of reform politics; efforts at revision become so extensive as to constitute noteworthy institutional change of their own; and the successful effort on demographic representation lends a new character to the entire reform package, while adding the final groups to the alternative Democratic coalition.

THE National Committee meeting of October 12, 13, and 14 was a watershed in the politics of party reform. Most fundamentally, it marked the last, logical point for coordinated resistance by the state parties to sweeping demands for change in their internal arrangements. When that point passed without so much as the appearance of serious opposition, the success of institutional reform was guaranteed. In that sense, the October meeting was the final grand turning point in the entire reform chronicle.

The meeting marked a lesser transition within the politics of implementation as well. In the months before this meeting, the central struggle in reform politics involved the imposition of national reform directives, and the central issue was the extent of state compliance, formal and informal. In the months after, reform politics revolved instead around efforts to extract sharply different interpretations of the meaning of official rules, and the central issue was the appropriate practical translation of these abstract reform standards.

The potential for this meeting of the National Committee to become a major point of revolt by the regular party—its "last hurrah" in the politics of party reform—was never very great. The National Committee had already acted on the more important set of reform recommendations, the guidelines of the Party Structure Commission. The state parties had already begun to move, slowly but ineluctably, into compliance with those guidelines.

Still, the committee meeting had constituted the final, readily accessible means of coordinating any rebellion. When the coordinated resistance which did surface was concentrated on electing Pat Harris rather than Harold Hughes as temporary chairman of a convention committee and when the entire reform package of the Party Structure *and* Rules Commissions was adopted without so much as a discouraging word, that possibility was gone forever. In two short bursts over the next six months, the remainder of the state parties fell into line with the demands of the Final Call.

Despite this progress—despite the collapse even of individual, decentralized opposition—one last aspect of reform politics did become more problematic in the aftermath of the committee meeting. This was the attempt to influence the specific interpretation—the precise institutional translation—of reforms which were now generally acknowledged to be on their way to universal implementation. Eventually, some of these *re*interpretations were to be so substantial that they would qualify as major institutional changes in their own right. They might never have been realized without the National Committee meeting of mid-October. But they were implicit neither in its proceedings nor in its outcomes. When they were nevertheless imposed, the total package of party reforms became noticeably different from what it had been as late as October 14, 1971.

Two areas came in for special attention from would-be re-interpreters: demographics and proportionality. Attempts to revise the Call's strictures on demographic representation were initiated externally, by interested organizations, and then bargained out with the Party Structure Commission and the office of the national chairman. Attempts to revise the Call's strictures on proportional representation were generated internally, at the Party Structure Commission, and then bargained out with state party leaders. Ultimately, both attempts recorded a clear and substantial success.

The most obvious and most dramatic of these efforts began to show results within hours of the adjournment of the National Committee. This was the attempt to convert the Call's language on demographic balance into explicit numerical targets—into demographic quotas. At the heart of this effort was the National Women's Political Caucus, formed only months before passage of the Final Call, and focused on reform only weeks after that passage.

The caucus began by creating a special task force, a familiar device of reform politics, to press the national parties for an extended translation of their demographic requirements—the obvious point of entry for a new women's group. Within days, at a crucial meeting with the Democratic national chairman, the chairman of the Party Structure Commission, and the temporary Credentials chairman for the 1972 Convention, this task force succeeded in extracting its full substantive desires—in truth, its wildest dreams—for the interpretation of Guidelines A–1 and A–2.

The outcome was a historic product, even on its own terms. It became the most widely recognized reinterpretation of reform standards, because it resulted not just in an understanding, but in a public ruling, touching every state. It became the most intellectually controversial reinterpretation, because it blended two theoretically inconsistent approaches to party reform and created all the practical tensions believed to follow from that. It became the most emotionally loaded revision, because it flew in the face of explicit, contrary reassurances from every stage in the reform process—and because it flew so far. But controversy and contradiction aside, this resolution instantly acquired the full political force of the Final Call. In the process, it lent a noticeably different character to the entire reform package.

Beyond all this, the result was an important contribution to institutional change and to the circulation of elites. This result shifted the position of the national party on demographics, past opposition to discrimination, through affirmative action for selected minorities, and into an explicit requirement of numerical standards. As such, it constituted a *new* institutional change of major proportions. Moreover, the search for this result mobilized and then melded the final elements of the alternative Democratic coalition. In consequence, that search became one of the major events in the politics of implementation, in the overall politics of party reform, and perhaps, depending on the fate of its products, in American political history.

The Opportunity for Revision and the Drive for Quotas

The general, and generally acknowledged, triumph of implementation was both a major victory and a further opportunity for dedicated party reformers. It was a victory because the program obtaining widespread acquiescence was essentially their program. Its adoption might owe more to the serendipitous outcome of the 1970 elections or to the calculations of the regular party leadership than to pressure from reform activists. But its growing enactment was no less real for that, nor any less congruent with the wishes of these same reformers.

The general success of implementation was also a major opportunity. At a minimum, this final surge toward compliance was the obvious, last chance for reform advocates to see that these rules were given the institutional translation which they themselves preferred. Beyond that, if the passing of the National Committee meeting and the unchallenged acceptance of the Final Call provided the obvious temporal point at which to make one more push for "proper" interpretation, the evident success of implementation in the states gave aspiring reinterpreters a special advantage which they had never previously possessed.

For if the state parties were clearly going to comply with national reform directives, then all that was required for additional reform gains was an after-the-fact retranslation of those rules. That is, the universal move toward implementation in the aftermath of the National Committee meeting was both the last and the best chance to reopen prior compromises and drive them in the direction reformers desired. This surge, in short, constituted one final opportunity to seek through reinterpretation what these reformers had failed to secure through direct endorsement from either the Party Structure Commission or the National Committee.

The struggle for widespread compliance and the struggle for specific (re)interpretations were hardly distinct in an analytic or even a temporal sense. Negotiations between national reform actors and state party officials had always involved possible alternative translations of a single reform text. Deliberate attempts to secure reinterpretations—to overthrow the reading of the national party and to substitute the preference of a challenger—had been going on for months before the October meeting of the National Committee.[1]

Yet the committee meeting was a clear transition in the politics of implementation. The meeting evidently coincided with increased activity by a range of groups which were attempting to extract alternative translations. Indeed, the mobilization of many of these groups for the contest over a temporary Credentials chairman was the prelude to their more effective participation in attempts to reinterpret key provisions of the Final Call. Moreover, the success of these attempts was probably dependent on prior passage of that Call and on the prior triumph of implementation. While the fate of nationwide compliance hung in the balance, the chances of stiffening reform rules whose milder versions were still not meeting general acceptance were surely remote.

Only when nationwide compliance became assured could organized reformers and their associated interest groups hope to extract revised institutional translations of the underlying reform text. Yet ironically, if these groups were successful, the very tardiness of their exercise would become an asset. For they would then be organized and in place, to see that state party officials honored whatever revised rules emerged. And they would then be available and pre-pared, to see that they themselves benefited from revised party rules.

The most dramatic of the attempts to secure in translation what had not been secured in the drafting or adoption of reform guidelines, the one most clearly separate in an analytic sense from the drive for widespread compliance and the one following most closely upon the October meeting of the National Committee, came in the area of demographic representation. The peculiar lack of precision in commission pronouncements on demographic consider-ations for party reform had been remarked by friend and foe alike at nearly every turn. Through the fall of 1971, however, these provisions had managed to retain a degree of ambiguity greater than those of any other guidelines, a fact which even dedicated supporters, like Bob Nelson, recognized:

> Right from the start you could sense, you just knew, that A–2 would be the key guideline of the whole thing. Early on we began advising them that they had better go as far as they could, because this was so easily used for challenges.

Originally, there had been only one guideline on demographic representa-tion, and it had reapplied the existing prohibition on discrimination by race, color, creed, or national origin. The staff members who developed it, while hardly insensitive to problems of demographic prejudice, had been primarily concerned with *participation*, with creating an open and accessible process. They had noted the inconsistency between this approach and an attempt at guaranteeing any predetermined result; they had flatly rejected a demographic emphasis.

The commissioners as a body, in the work sessions leading up to their final meeting, had added a second guideline on demographics: A–2 (Discrimination on the Basis of Age or Sex). But they had not considered it of much impor-tance, and they had kept this new guideline at an even weaker and more horta-tory level than A–1, using it more as a statement of long-range party goals than as an institutional constraint on the process of delegate selection. They, too, had fought instead over participatory issues like proportionality, over man-dated changes in outcome like apportionment, and over their own powers and responsibilities.

At the final meeting of the commission, however, the situation had changed, and the ambiguity which would dog these guidelines for the next two years had been introduced. Guidelines A–1 and A–2 had not only gener-ated the major debate of this final session; they had colored the outcome on the other major issues debated there. The key provision—in some sense, the "kicker" in the entire report—was a demand that racial minorities, youth, and women be represented in state delegations "in reasonable relationship to their presence in the population of the state."[2] Dick Wade brought this specific language to the crucial meeting. Birch Bayh drove it through the commission proper. Fred Dutton extended it to A–2.

This provision surfaced again and again. State party officials queried its institutional meaning. Reporters inquired after its practical demands. Reformers asked whether it would be honored in the observance or only in the breach—as if anyone had ever agreed on what its observance would imply. National Committee members looked upon it askance.

The Party Structure Commission itself had provided an ostensible clarification, through a footnote at the time: "It is the understanding of the Commission that this is not to be accomplished by the mandatory imposition of quotas."[3] Chairman O'Brien and Counsel Califano amplified these reassurances in response to questions from the National Committee. Committee members, finally, were willing to go along with the total package only after they had probed this provision, accepted these assurances, and put them on the public record.

Obviously, nothing had prevented the "reasonable relationship" clause from reaching the stage of widespread implementation without having its practical meaning—its precise institutional requirements—defined. In principle, nothing prevented it from progressing through total certified compliance without achieving that definition. Yet in practice, the fact that it remained in this undefined state did provide a large and evident opportunity for anyone with a stake in securing a (re)translation.

The process of seeking a newly elaborated, sharply altered, practical definition of Guidelines A–1 and A–2 began immediately after the National Committee meeting of mid-October. Within a month, that process reached its resolution, and the result was more than just an evident break with the prior history of these provisions. This result required the adjustment of arrangements for delegate selection in every state; it sat in patent contradiction to the overwhelming thrust of the other sixteen guidelines; it lent a recognizably different character to the entire reform package.

The chain of events which led most directly to a reinterpretation of Guidelines A–1 and A–2 began in the early summer of 1971 at an informal conference in Washington, D.C. On July 10 and 11, about three hundred self-starters from at least twenty-six states came together to discuss the role of women in American politics. The primary institutional link among these participants was the National Organization of Women, itself only five years old, but the session was not conceived solely as a NOW function.[4]

After two days of discussion and numerous resolutions on topics political

465

and social, the participants found an additional consensus building in their midst. A significant number desired some means of institutionalizing this exercise, and the conference turned to the founding of a continuing operation. Doris N. Meissner, its first executive director, was among those who had not expected a new organization as the upshot of these July sessions:

> The initial set-up was just to have a kind of media event, but not to foresee the kind of support that we got. They really decided in the midst of the three-day meeting to set up some continuing organization. There ought to be an ongoing structure of some sort. Let's have an office, set up a newspaper, find some way to put some pressure on the parties.
>
> For my part, I'm not sure how naive I was about what was going on at that point. The formation of the Women's Political Caucus had to do with more than just reform of the Democratic Party. All of the rhetoric at the time had more than Democratic or Republican politics with it. The Women's movement had made some steps in the '60s, but until some serious thought about political action went on, it didn't seem that there could be much more.

One of the final acts of the conference, then, was to appoint a steering committee of twenty-five members to consider establishment of a formal structure. After much preliminary, informal discussion, these individuals reconvened in New York on September 10 and 11, as the National Women's Political Caucus.[5] Their first session, however, was devoted to the prerequisites of organizational survival—national governing arrangements, a link with the semiautonomous state chapters, a Washington office, some continuing staff, the omnipresent search for funds. Accordingly, it was not until the following month, at a second meeting on October 22 and 23 at the headquarters of the United Auto Workers in Detroit, that policy planning could be seriously considered.[6]

A heavy, early emphasis on the politics of delegate selection had been an evident option from the moment the caucus was created. Indeed, that possibility had been an added argument for constituting the group as more than a one-shot conference. Congresswoman Bella S. Abzug of New York, among others, had argued that national party conventions might be the most fruitful arena for a quick impact by this incipient arm of the women's movement.[7]

This possibility resurfaced on the evening of Friday, October 22, when the steering committee of the caucus considered a report from its Political Perspectives Committee. Many members still preferred to put off an explicit political move until a second national conference in the spring. Their problem, however, was the calendar: The politics of delegate selection was approaching fast; it would not wait for the new organization to establish itself more systematically. As a result, when the steering committee reconvened at 9:20 on Saturday morning, the question of a role in party—and presidential—politics was the first item on the agenda. Both a general call for action and a specific device to implement that call were quickly endorsed, through a formal motion in the caucus minutes:

> The first item was delegate selection. It was agreed that the Caucus needs serious goals fast, and that the number one priority is to get into existing decision-making positions in order to have the means for influencing 1972 decisions. That means having a fair proportion of convention delegates in both parties' conventions. To that end, the following resolution was passed:
> The Policy Council constitute a Task Force on Delegate Selection with a charge to the Task Force to launch, with no further delay, an NWPC delegate selection campaign. Such a campaign would have the purpose of developing and implementing a strategy to place media and organizational pressure on both political parties in as many states as possible to ensure the National Party Guidelines recommending full participation of women are carried out in good faith and, if they are not, to mount challenges to party delegations that are not in compliance. Such a Task Force must include persons with experience in politics, the law, knowledge of party rules, and knowledge of the delegate selection process. The Operating Committee is to be polled for approval of the Task Force membership. The Council accepts this as a PRIORITY campaign.[8]

Through this resolution, the caucus moved explicitly into the politics of party reform. The Operating Committee, an Executive Committee of the full body, began immediately to pull a Task Force on Delegate Selection together. Doris Meissner, its executive director, began to assemble the background material to help this task force plan its approach. Meissner queried Carol Casey at the Party Structure Commission, and Casey assembled what became the bulk of the factual information in the hands of the task force.[9] At the same time, Fred Dutton, the Party Structure commissioner, mailed an advisory memo on legal options to caucus headquarters, outlining an aggressive interpretation of Guideline A–2, and this became the guiding strategic document.[10]

Armed with this material, Meissner drafted two initial communications. The first was to Robert J. Dole, chairman of the Republican National Committee, the second to Lawrence F. O'Brien, his Democratic counterpart. Both letters requested a meeting as soon as possible. Both were destined to produce that meeting. The letter to O'Brien was fated to produce a historic product as well:

Dear Chairman O'Brien:
   The National Women's Political Caucus has set up a Task Force of women political leaders and lawyers from across the nation to make certain that women

are fairly represented at the 1972 Democratic National Convention. A delegation from the Task Force would like to meet with you in the very near future to discuss ways in which the Democratic National Committee and the office of the National Chairman can help achieve this goal.[11]

The letter continued by asserting that the "principal mandate of the reform commission" had been to require "affirmative steps" for women, youth, and minorities. It went on to "anticipate" that when O'Brien met with his aspiring presidential nominees, he would urge "reasonable relationship" standards upon them in the construction of their delegate slates. It suggested that the chairman undertake his own effort at affirmative action within the National Committee. Despite all this, the central proposal of the letter, and the obvious substantive focus for the requested meeting, was a new interpretation of Guideline A–2:

> We want to make clear our understanding of the meaning of "reasonable representation." Given the fact that women are 52.2% of the total population and are a majority in all but four states, "reasonable representation" can only mean that women constitute a majority of all but several of the state delegations. A majority cannot be made a minority without violating a fundamental and unmistakable value in a popularly based political system like ours. Failure to ensure reasonable representation will undoubtedly result in serious credentials challenges by women's groups in the various states.[12]

The following day, the caucus released both letters at a press conference publicizing formation of its Task Force on Delegate Selection.[13] The letter to Dole had gone into the mails beforehand, and he had already replied. O'Brien, however, was forced to receive his communication in conjunction with this press release. Whatever his private feelings about this treatment, O'Brien, too, agreed immediately to a session with the new task force and suggested the following Thursday, November 18. He agreed as well to bring Don Fraser, the Party Structure chairman, Pat Harris, the temporary Credentials chairman, and relevant staffers from the National Committee.[14] The task force found these arrangements fully acceptable, and the meeting was confirmed.

There remained some disagreement about the proper approach to national politics within the policy council of the women's caucus. Some members still viewed involvement with the two major parties as an inevitable corruption of their overriding goals. Others insisted that any involvement in internal party affairs at least be continually and resolutely bipartisan, to avoid subordination to one party's interests. Both groups were about to lose the argument.

Their defeat stemmed in part from the character of existing rules within the two major parties. The Republican party had few codified strictures; it had no demographic footholds at all. The Democratic party had new, extensive, reform standards, with inherently greater room for (re)interpretation; it possessed a reform movement clustered around those rules, with predictable sympathy for the goals of the women's caucus; it offered a grand, obvious, and ambiguous ruling on demographic representation, one which almost cried out for procedural elucidation. Meissner watched this provision, like a magnet, draw her Task Force on Delegate Selection:

> When we went to the Republican Chairman, there wasn't anything like A–2 to go on. We couldn't say, "It says that you must do this, and if that doesn't mean that, what does it mean?" We got a little from the Republicans on the Democratic shirttail, but that was all.

If this were not enough, the women's caucus in general and its task force in particular were heavily populated by reform Democrats. At the founding conference the preceding July, only 15 percent of those in attendance had confessed to Republican leanings.[15] At the first meeting of the policy council in September, when the members had moved to add representation of minority groups to this governing board, they had seen the need, explicitly, to include "Republicans."[16] Even within this expanded policy council, those who were most eager to get into the politics of delegate selection were uniformly Democratic women of the reform persuasion. Meissner had mixed feelings about this tendency for the nascent political organization to become so thoroughly enmeshed in Democratic party affairs. Those feelings did not blind her to the controlling influence of Democratic reformers on her governing board:

> However, what was really going on after the formation of the Caucus was, consciously or unconsciously, aimed at getting into the Democratic party. Bella [Abzug], and Gloria [Steinem], and more important, fundamental party types like Arvonne Fraser, Korynne Horbal, and LaDonna Harris, the core visible Democrats, were all reform types. They were into anti-war and all that. A lot of the arguments that we had early were parallel to the arguments that the Democrats had already been going through.

Not surprisingly, the task force assigned to pursue the issue was dominated by reform Democrats. Its formal leaders, Bella S. Abzug and Patsy T. Mink, were Democratic congresswomen. Its staff, besides Meissner who continued to experience some discomfort with this arrangement, consisted of Phyllis N. Segal, wife of Eli J. Segal, former commission counsel. Its sources of technical support were Carol Casey and Anne Wexler, current staff assistant and former staff consultant at the Party Structure Commission.

The crucial new participant was Phyllis Segal, who was not only more sympathetic than Meissner to the Democratic drift of the task force but viewed it as inevitable in any case. Segal had been the one to focus Abzug's attention on the possibilities inherent in delegate politics, through some early legal research.[17] She had then helped Meissner draw up the resolution which made delegate selection a priority issue for the women's caucus. She had come to serve as one of the most evident and critical links between the caucus and the Party Structure Commission:

> I wrote that paper in December 1970. The paper had already been written. It was put in the *Congressional Record* in April of 1971. It was because of that paper that I became involved in the first meeting of the National Women's Political Caucus. The fact that the Caucus was formed after the [Party Structure] Commission had met meant that this was a natural issue for the Caucus to act on. NWPC really had much broader goals and purposes than that, but this was an idea whose time had come.
>
> There was no script going into that first meeting. It did just evolve after that. My own interest has been at the intersection of the party reform and women's issues. I was involved in the Task Force on Delegate Selection. This was established very quickly.

The National Environment for Reinterpretation

While the meeting between the task force from the women's caucus and the delegation from the office of the national chairman was to be the central site for the reinterpretation of party rules on demographic representation, and while the task force might well have extracted the eventual result entirely on its own, the atmosphere for its meeting was conditioned by a number of external developments, none of its own making. Other organizations—some demographic, some not—had been probing the interpretation of the "reasonable relationship" clause. Other individuals, on their own, had attempted to advance the fortunes of the new women's organization. The national press, with no coordinated intent, was structuring the environment for its crucial session. Alternative solutions—varying numerical interpretations—were already in the air.

Perhaps the earliest queries about the meaning of the new party standard for demographic representation had come not from feminist groups, but from established organizations of black public officeholders. Black groups, however, were contributory but not crucial to a reinterpretation of Guidelines A–1 and A–2, because they possessed all the liabilities inherent in their assets. For example, they already possessed a nucleus of national political leaders and a far larger group of local party and public officials. Moreover, the elected officials among them even possessed an overhead organization, the National Conference of Black Elected Officials.

Yet these individuals had all been elected without the benefit of reformed rules, and they all had far more concrete policy goals than party reform. All were full-fledged political leaders, with the full range of responsibilities which that entailed. Indeed, their constituents had been uninterested in the reform movement from the beginning. If that were not enough, many of these leaders could be expected to be delegates to the Democratic convention under *un*-reformed rules. Most members of the Congressional Black Caucus, for example, had already been delegates to the 1968 Convention.[18]

To top this off, black political leaders lacked the immediate social access to national reform principals of the feminist spokesmen. In the obvious but critical case, Mayor Richard G. Hatcher of Gary, Indiana, chairman of the National Conference of Black Elected Officials, could not possibly have the access to Don Fraser, the Chairman of the Party Structure Commission, that Arvonne (Mrs. Don) Fraser of the policy council of the National Women's Political Caucus had. If the case of the Frasers seemed an extreme example, the case of the Segals, Eli and Phyllis, was little different, and those commission personnel with an interest in demographic representation were, in fact, uniformly concerned with women rather than blacks or youth.

Despite these "liabilities", black political organizations did contribute not just generally but specifically to the environment for the crucial meeting between the women's task force and national party officials. At several points during the fall of 1971, Chairman O'Brien journeyed across to Capitol Hill to sit with the Congressional Black Caucus and discuss party issues. An interpretation for newly framed standards on demographic representation was never absent from these discussions.

More pointedly, the National Conference of Black Elected Officials held its annual convention in Washington the very week of the meeting between party officials and the women's task force, and the Congressional Black Caucus offered a special panel on delegate selection, where the precise meaning of Guidelines A–1 and A–2 was an inevitable topic of conversation. During that same session, a large group of black officials from around the nation heard Mayor Hatcher report privately on previous conversations with Chairman O'Brien, although this report from Hatcher made it clear that his demand for explicit quota provisions had been mainly a bargaining ploy and did not even extend to the nonprimary states:

Richard G. Hatcher, Democratic Mayor of Gary, Ind., told the closed strategy session of a recent meeting he and other black politicians had with Lawrence F. O'Brien, chairman of the Democratic Party.

Mr. Hatcher said the 12 black political figures had made 13 requests of the Democratic leadership and that "while there has been some response, it is too early to evaluate" just what will be done.

The requests included expansion of the Democratic National Committee to reflect a minority involvement of 20 percent, creation of a minority affairs division that would receive 20 percent of the committee's annual budget, and a pledge that 20 percent of the delegate slate in Presidential primary states would "reflect black participation."[19]

Curiously, there was no counterpart contribution of any sort from recognizable youth groups. If the emerging demographic categories really were "women, youth, and minorities," to use the slogan of the day, then the middle element in that triumvirate was simply missing in efforts to secure a reinterpretation of Guidelines A–1 and A–2. At the end of August, there had, in fact, been an effort to create a national youth organization. Duane Draper, president of the Association of Student Governments, had approached David Ifshin, outgoing president of the National Student Association [NSA], with precisely this suggestion, at the annual convention of NSA.[20]

It was never clear that college students represented young people in general; in statistical terms, they clearly did not. It was not obvious that the national student organizations spoke even for college students; campus politics was a peculiar realm all its own. But even within those parameters, a simple union between the two college organizations for the narrow purpose of delegate selection proved impossible. Ifshin pointedly rebuffed Draper's overtures, noting that the "moderate politics" of the latter put him off. He was seconded by numerous opposition speakers, who echoed the charge that Draper was "trying to bring everyone into one nice big system."[21] When the two student organizations failed to create a national youth caucus, then, they eliminated even an incipient input to the reinterpretation of Guideline A–2 from self-promoted "youth."

On the other hand, demographic groups were hardly the only ones with an interest in the proper interpretation of Guidelines A–1 and A–2. The ideological and reform organizations in the alternative Democratic coalition were also concerned. Like the black groups, they took both general and specific actions which contributed to the environment for the crucial meeting between national party officials and the task force from the women's caucus. Even more than the black groups, they shifted toward demanding a precise numerical approach to demographic representation. Unlike the black groups, however, they were centrally concerned with the fate of women, rather than blacks or youth.

Among these organizations, the linchpin was the Center for Political Reform. The prime mover at the center, Ken Bode, had originally been far more interested in participation, access, and openness than in demographic guarantees. But during the spring and summer of 1971, Bode's center had become the driving force in a number of other efforts to reinterpret commission standards.[22] As the reinterpretation of Guidelines A–1 and A–2 became an increasing focus among organizations in the alternative Democratic coalition, Bode quickly added that effort to his roster of substantive targets.

The best evidence of Bode's evolving commitment, however, came not from his own center, but from the Convention Task Force of Americans for Democratic Action, which he, of course, co-chaired. At its first meeting on July 7, the ADA task force had discussed the proper interpretation of "reasonable relationship" language. The topic, however, was not a major one and its actual priority was underlined by the fact that only one of the discussants had been a woman.[23]

By the second meeting of the group on October 15, this had changed. The National Women's Political Caucus had been officially created; Bode moved forcefully to provide links with that new organization. A *Reasonable Representation Project* was created, to give the ADA task force a special, internal, institutionalized focus on Guidelines A–1 and A–2. Brenda Fasteau, of the policy council of the women's caucus, was appointed to co-chair this subcommittee, along with Joseph Gebhardt, counsel to Bode's Center. Phyllis Segal, chief staff assistant to the women's caucus, and Anne Wexler, chief staffer on the Voting Rights Project of Common Cause, were added to its roster.[24]

By the third meeting of the Convention Task Force on November 8, this Reasonable Representation Project was prepared to report. Indeed, the report of the Reasonable Representation Project was adopted by the full ADA task force on the very day that the women's caucus was writing to Chairman O'Brien to request a meeting, and its proposal—a modified quota system with clear numerical limits—became an additional, focused contribution to the environment for that meeting:

> It was decided that the Task Force would adopt a "20% deviation" formula for judging compliance with the reasonable representation guidelines. The Task Force favors representation of women, racial minorities, and young people in percentages at least as great as their exact percentage of the state population. However, it believes a delegation should be subject to challenge if these groups are not represented by a percentage which deviates below their exact proportion of the population by no more than 20% of that population. For example: Women com-

prise approximately 50% of each state's population. Therefore, a delegation that has less than 40% women would not have satisfactorily met with the reasonable representation guidelines.[25]

A number of individual actors had also attempted, during the summer and early fall of 1971, to bring the National Women's Political Caucus into direct communication with the Party Structure Commission, the obvious starting point in any effort at a formal reinterpretation of Guidelines A–1 and A–2. Moreover, each of these individuals had pressed the notion of explicit numerical targets, and these alleged goals became tighter and tighter as time passed.

Eli Segal had begun this process, when he took a draft resolution on demographic standards before the July meeting of the full commission. At that time, no less a personage than Don Fraser, eventually the key actor in the reinterpretation of Guidelines A–1 and A–2, had moved to scuttle this proposed revision. Segal had called for a maximum deviation of 40 percent from state population figures, a numerical standard, albeit a weak one, for the representation of women, youth, and minorities. Fraser had opposed any such statement, and the assembled commissioners had supported him.

One of those who had not supported the soft approach was Fred Dutton, and he became a more consequential link between the women's caucus and the national commission. Dutton had been a major supporter of "reasonable relationship" language from the beginning; indeed, he had been the major reason this language was extended to Guideline A–2. When the women's caucus was created, he rushed forward again with offers of support; in fact, he was present at the formative session of "Friends of the Caucus," a coordinate group for male sympathizers.[26]

Dutton's interest in the subject remained strong, and when the women's caucus created its Task Force on Delegate Selection, he came back with a detailed legal brief on the "proper" interpretation of A–1 and A–2. This brief became the framework for the letter from Meissner to O'Brien, the one requesting a meeting with the task force. Indeed, some of its content was transferred almost intact.[27] Finally, on November 1, two weeks before National Chairman O'Brien brought Commission Chairman Fraser and Credentials Chairman Harris to meet with this task force, Dutton wrote to Fraser, too, with additional thoughts on the proper standard for demographic representation, with a reprise of his legal brief for the women's caucus—and with the most refined set of numbers yet introduced:

> The record shows that we were clear we want no quotas. But my brief takes the position that when the commission and then the DNC voted that women shall be represented in reasonable relationship to their proportion of the popula-

tion, that means they are entitled to an absolute majority. They constitute 52.2% of the adult population of this country 18 or over, according to the 1970 census. A majority cannot be made into a minority in a popularly based political process without violating a very fundamental concept. The violation would be quite unreasonable. That argument avoids the whole quota question.

Obviously, the delegations cannot provide for women to be represented at an exact 52.2% level. But anything below 50.1% would change their majority share into a minority. It is also reasonable to expect that the Democratic Party will err as much for women as against them; and therefore as many delegations must have women above the 52.2% base as below it. Federal courts are now saying that in Congressional District reapportionment, a range of about 4% is all right in defining substantial equality. Analogizing to our delegate situation, a range from 50.1% to 54.3%—that is ranging as much above as below—allows about the same 4% variation on which many federal courts are settling in this other area.[28]

Fraser had, in fact, begun to move in this direction well before he was nudged by Dutton. In July, when the Party Structure Commission had reconvened, he was still resisting any national elaborations on Guidelines A–1 and A–2. By October, he was leading his commission toward a new interpretation of these very standards, one involving a set of affirmative activities by the state political parties.

One major influence on this shift was his wife, Arvonne S. Fraser. who was a charter member of the National Women's Political Caucus and of its original policy council. She also served as an informal connection among Washington activists concerned with feminist issues. During late summer and early fall, these individuals met occasionally to discuss responses which might turn the coming politics of delegate selection to the particular advantage of feminist groups. Phyllis Segal was one of Fraser's regular attendees; the possibility of a numerical (re)interpretation of Guideline A–2 was always part of their discussion:

> Sometime in September, there was a big meeting at Don Fraser's home in Washington. This was arranged by Arvonne Fraser, of course. At least twenty people were there, to discuss what could be done about this. Then later, maybe in October, Arvonne organized another meeting at Senator Hart's home, but he wasn't there. She was instrumental in setting up these meetings.

These sessions began to pay off. By early October, Don Fraser was prepared to reassemble the Party Structure Commission and to readdress its stand on demographic representation. Indeed, in calling this meeting of his commission to the attention of National Committee members, he paid explicit tribute to the role of his wife in propelling the demographic issue to *his* attention:

Let me just say, along the way, that my wife suggested I bring this article down. You cannot read it, but I will read the headline for you: "Norway's Women Elect Female Majorities in 50 Towns." That gives you some idea where my wife stands. (Laughter and applause.) My impression from where I stand is that that is a fairly significant portent for the future here in the United States.[29]

Fraser began to speed that future the next morning, when he presented a draft of his demographic revision to the Party Structure Commission. On Friday, October 15, a small core of the commission faithful assembled in Washington to tie up loose ends in commission business and to face one major agenda item, a detailed, four-page elaboration of the requirements of Guidelines A–1 and A–2. In considering and then endorsing this elaboration, the day after passage of the Final Call, the commission not only contributed to the largest single shift in guideline translation. It also, in effect, highlighted the shift from the long period when the extent of guideline compliance had hung in the balance to the short but crucial period in which guideline interpretation would be the essence of the politics of party reform.

The revised draft which Fraser put before his members began by tackling the alleged inconsistency between the first two guidelines, which appeared to urge a particular outcome, and the other sixteen, which clearly urged participation—and responsiveness to it. The draft then went on to make a recognizable shift toward those who preferred explicit mathematical requirements, by specifying cases where A–1 and A–2 did have quotalike implications:

> There are several points in the delegate selection process at which the political party must act affirmatively to broaden representation in accordance with Guidelines A–1 and A–2. These occur especially under slate-making procedures. They include nominating committees as well as committees working under the direction of, or in consultation with, presidential candidates.
>
> Thus, whenever an organized group meets to recommend, or nominate, or otherwise engage in procedures for the purpose of selecting delegates, it is reasonable to impose on such group the burden of seeking to achieve reasonable relationship in its recommendations.[30]

When the statement turned to concrete *steps,* however, it pulled back from the brink and offered what could more accurately be classed as a program of affirmative action, of targeted activities to guarantee the participation which would result in extensive demographic representation.[31] The commission still contained some sentiment for standing pat, for leaving these provisions as they had been left in July. But this point of view was increasingly enfeebled by low turnout, and the desertion of the commission chairman had essentially sealed its fate. George Mitchell, despite his own odyssey in reform politics, made one final, bootless attempt to endorse the option of self-restraint:

> In 1971, I went to some meetings, but I didn't go to all of them. I had some disputes over their authority to write all these letters and interpretations without consulting with more people. That was the kind of thing that was less interesting to people, though. Fraser took a much more active role and understood these rules better than McGovern ever did. I have no clear recollection of the debate on this. We had a discussion that this was changing our own rules, but we lost on it.

One other element, less obviously relevant than the public actions of the Party Structure Commission, the policy demands of interested organizations, or even the private interventions of specific individuals, powerfully conditioned the environment for this crucial session. This was the general press interpretation of the National Committee meeting on the Final Call, a journalistic consensus which ramified through the following weeks until it, too, became a critical aspect of the climate for subsequent reform negotiations.

Three points in this consensus were of particular importance. The first was that the meeting had represented a clear and convincing triumph of regulars over reformers. This interpretation had been implicit in the pattern of coverage itself. Most national reporters had focused on the Harris-Hughes dust-up, in significant detail; many had not even mentioned the *undebated acceptance of both the Party Structure and Rules Commission reports*. But an implicit consensus was hardly the end of the matter. The *New York Times* had broken its story of the coming battle with "Democratic Reformers and Old Guard Split over Filling '72 Convention Post"; *Time* had wrapped it up with "Democrats: Round 1 to the Regulars."[32]

The second point in this press consensus was that the result had been effectively orchestrated by the national chairman, putting him squarely in the regular camp. A consensus that this had indeed been a critical contest between regulars and reformers made the role of O'Brien almost automatic: He became the factional leader for one side, the side opposed to reform. *Time* went on to report that "the most powerful persuader, though, was Old Pro O'Brien"; the *New York Times* noted that the chairman had "masterminded Mrs. Harris's election while she stayed in the background."[33]

The third and final point in this press interpretation was that the instrument of O'Brien's triumph had been Patricia Harris, in contradiction to her "logical" position. In moving to this conclusion, newsmen were, of course, accepting the slogan of the day about the appropriate place of blacks in the two contending elite coalitions. Nevertheless, the *New York Times* plunged ahead and spelled out the alleged symbolic contradictions in the appointment of Harris:

> Committee members from the South found themselves, ironically, in the position of supporting a black woman. Jacob M. Arvey of Illinois, a committeeman for 21 years, said he had never expected to see this.
> Although some complained privately about what they were doing, the Southerners, always supporters of the traditionalist wing, went down the line.[34]

Yet the most severe recriminations were reserved for the period after the meeting had adjourned, the period, coincidentally, when negotiations over an interpretation for Guidelines A–1 and A–2 were coming to a head. Eli Segal offered "O'Brien vs. Hughes: Inside the Squeeze on Party Reform," garnished with a sketch of a gun-toting O'Brien athwart the corpse of a glassy-eyed Hughes.[35] Even more intense was the criticism which fell on Pat Harris, the silent candidate. At the meeting of the policy council of the women's caucus a week later, the same meeting which was to authorize creation of a Task Force on Delegate Selection, the new organization gave her the back of its hand:

> A motion to send letters of congratulation to any women appointed to a high post, and to start with Pat Roberts Harris of the Democratic Party Credentials Committee, was tabled until the next meeting.[36]

Earlier, black supporters of Harold Hughes for temporary Credentials chairman had been even more explicit:

> Georgia state representative Julian Bond called the selection of Mrs. Harris "a cynical trick." He observed that she had been dean of the Howard Law School and an Ambassador to Luxembourg, but claimed that neither job "qualified her to be head of the credentials committee." Bond charged that O'Brien thought that "politicians like myself will be reluctant to oppose Mrs. Harris, because we do not want to be called chauvinist pigs, and because she is black."[37]

A New Standard for Demographic Representation

The culmination of all this unfocused groundwork was entirely unexpected, even by those who were most delighted by the result. The Task Force on Delegate Selection, of course, looked forward to the chance to confront relevant officials from the national party over the content and meaning of Guideline A–2. But even optimistic participants envisioned this as the opening session in what might—ideally—become a continuing drive. From the other side, most of those who arrived in company with the national chairman expected less from the initial session, and did not look forward to anything like a series of confrontations.

A good deal of internal jockeying occurred within the caucus over who should be included in its delegation. This did not, however, imply serious illusions about political muscle. The letter to Chairman O'Brien had referred to a network of women's lawyers around the country, ready and waiting to mount multiple challenges based on Guideline A–2. Phyllis Segal, a part of that alleged network—and a law *student*, not a lawyer—saw no reason for the chairman and his staff to quail before that reference:

> The National Women's Political Caucus has been frequently in the position of acting far beyond its actual organization. There was no specific legal threat, but it was the threat that you need women, and women are tired of being involved in only the most meaningless ways. We would have had to say that the Women's Caucus was organized in only a small number of states. It [the meeting's outcome] fell into place much more easily than I could have expected. We didn't go in there for that. In fact, NWPC didn't even *have* much legal back-up at that time.

Congresswomen Abzug and Mink became spokesmen for the delegation; Segal and Meissner were their primary staff support. They turned to Anne Wexler for assistance in developing an internal briefing memo, and Wexler steered them to the charts in *Mandate for Reform*, especially the ones showing the presence of women in the various delegations in 1968.[38] Despite this, Meissner, too, knew that they would be whistling in the dark:

> Nothing in the name of the organization had been going on out in the states at this point. New York women may have been doing something on their own. Minnesota women might, too, but the November meeting didn't even involve them. We did collect statistics on the number of women in party posts in most places. We began to rant and rave about this.

The real programmatic goals of the negotiating team were modest. Guideline A–2 was their major point of entry. Inevitably, the delegation would begin by pressing for a strict mathematical interpretation; inevitably, it would fall back on some more limited goal. The statement from Don Fraser on affirmative action seemed the logical point of compromise. That statement contained no detailed demands for state plans on affirmative action; the team from the women's caucus could reasonably ask for a follow-up memo adding institutional detail and incorporating some of their suggestions. Beyond this, they could, ritualistically, press Chairman O'Brien to redouble his efforts for compliance. And that was about it. Phyllis Segal saw their tactical approach as determined largely by the situation:

> We were meeting with Larry O'Brien and Don Fraser. Wexler, Mink, myself, Abzug, Meissner, O'Brien, Pat Harris, and other DNC staff. NWPC didn't go into that meeting with prima facie language [see below], but just to see what these provisions do mean, and to demand that they be enforced.

The meeting took place on the evening of Thursday, November 18, at national party headquarters in the Watergate complex. Larry O'Brien, the national chairman, and his assistant, Bill Welsh; Don Fraser, the Party Structure chairman, and his assistant, Bob Nelson; Pat Harris, the temporary Credentials chairman; Mary Lou Burg, national vice chairman; and Harriet E. Cipriani, director of Democratic women's activities, faced the leadership and staff of the delegation from the caucus task force, plus Anne Wexler, who had crossed the aisle for the occasion. Meissner watched her delegation come running at these official party representatives:

> The idea was to get a commitment from the top. There was a November meeting with O'Brien. Then we met with Dole. The question of who would be the delegation was difficult. Bella, Patsy Mink, Phyllis Segal, and a few others eventually made it up. We went to see O'Brien and Fraser. The prima facie evidence provision comes directly out of this meeting. The point of the meeting was not so much to inform them that we were going whole-hog, but to get an interpretation of what A–2 meant. The burden of proof went on the party, not on the women's delegations. . . . We were pressuring all the time. We said, "You have this rule. Something must be done about it." The rhetoric was great at the time.

From the other side, Nelson experienced this barrage as little short of ferocious and believed that the character of the assault—its intensity, its hostility—had an influence all its own:

> There would simply be no other reasonable way to resolve that issue in the party except by very stringent measures. There was very strong pressure by blacks and activist women; they were the roots. I remember sitting across the table from these women; they were attempting to make you hate yourself for being a man. They took the tactics that would work best. There was a constant threat of legal actions.

Despite the memory by some participants of an extended and unpleasant evening, the break in these discussions came quickly. It was Fraser who brought matters to a head, by converting the informal, verbal assurances which were being offered around the table into formal language—in a way which took even caucus negotiators by surprise:

> The women were arguing that A–1 and A–2 were not being observed. Mink, Abzug, and Meissner, Pat Harris, myself, and O'Brien. "If the delegation was so badly unbalanced, you've got a prima facie case," I said. Patsy Mink said, "Why don't you put that in writing?"

What Fraser put in writing in a subsequent letter of transmittal was a provision creating precise demographic quotas in everything but name. Deviance from demographic percentages in a state population would constitute prima facie evidence of discrimination; the burden of proof would then be shifted to the state party, to show that neither its rules nor its procedures had been discriminatory. What this accomplished, of course, was the introduction of precise numerical standards into the delegate selection process, along with the presumption that a state which did not meet these standards was inherently discriminatory. What it implied, in turn, was a system of demographic quotas. A state which did not meet the percentage test would be asked to demonstrate that it possessed an affirmative action program sufficient to prevent discrimination on the basis of sex, age, or race—*as measured by the resulting demographic percentages.* The logical recourse for a concerned state party was to implement an institutional arrangement which could guarantee achievement of these barely implicit demographic requirements.

The result was an eye-opener for nearly everyone in attendance. Phyllis Segal watched Bill Welsh as Fraser offered his new interpretation:

> The *"prima facie,* shifting the burden of proof" concept did not come from Pat Harris. Perhaps people recall Pat Harris because it was a surprise. They were lined up on one side, with the staff behind them, and I could see the face fall on one of the staffmen when the *prima facie* idea was being enunciated.

If Welsh's jaw did truly drop, he was not alone in his surprise. Even Doris Meissner, who would bend her efforts toward seeing that every possible delegate was squeezed from this new interpretation, was astonished:

> We knew that we had gotten a major victory. We all talked of it as being a spearhead type of thing, not just for women but for all out-groups. We simply ascribed it to the fact that we had made a fairly effective show of force, far beyond what we knew that we were at that point. It was one of my first insights into political bluffing. It was based on some potential, but we didn't have nearly what they thought we did. We would have gone for 10 percent, but they gave us 50 and allowed us to make the challenges.
>
> We were going to make ferocious noises over the next eight months. If you

assume that something went wrong with the Democrats over the next year, you have to assume that this was a major ruining point. I don't imagine that the quota/numerical judgments would have been made in the Credentials Committee if we hadn't gotten this. None of the other out-groups were organized to such an extent to be able to do this. At this point, *nobody* had any idea of the difficulties in putting together the delegations. By February, nobody in his right mind would have given this kind of commitment to us.

This "commitment" had to survive two subsequent hurdles. First, it had to be endorsed by a scheduled meeting of the Party Structure Commission the next morning, so that it became official commission policy. Next, it had to be endorsed by the national chairman in the days to follow, so that it could not be honored in differential fashion by the individual state parties. Only then would the final room for maneuver, the last element of textual ambiguity, be eliminated.

The Party Structure Commission had scheduled a breakfast meeting on the morning of November 19 as a preliminary to the day's main event, the first joint gathering of the Party Structure and Rules Commissions. When the Rules Commission had completed its report, in the fall of 1971, there had been some debate over the fate of the two bodies. O'Brien had taken the view that they should tend to the implementation of their respective recommendations. The remaining task in party reform—analysis and recommendations on party structure in general, with special attention to the structure of the national party—could then be assigned to some new body, which he would appoint. Both sitting commission chairmen, however, had taken this suggestion very badly, and their willingness to go public with their displeasure had led O'Brien to agree that these two commissions should continue to meet jointly, to create an official charter for the Democratic party.[39]

Originally, then, this breakfast session of the Party Structure Commission was intended merely to review compliance progress and to address procedural issues which might have arisen since the last commission meeting. On the morning of November 19, however, the meeting received a major, new, agenda item—a revolutionary new interpretation of Guidelines A–1 and A–2. Despite the expanded significance of this agenda, simple attendance erased even the possibility of significant, new dissent.

Among the corporal's guard which actually assembled for breakfast on November 19, only Sam Beer had opposed a straightforward quota interpretation at the *original* adoption session in November of 1969—two full years, to the day, before. Accordingly, if the Fraser reinterpretation was a revolutionary change in commission policy, those who attended the subsequent breakfast were unbothered by that fact. Carol Casey saw the automatic character of their response:

By then, there was little full Commission involvement in the decision. Fraser wanted to do this, and we went along. Right from the start, many of the reformers had felt that the Commission should be in an adversary role—Segal, Wexler, and Bode, for example. The NDC felt this very strongly. There was constant agitation toward that. The Women's Caucus ult'mately got them to do this. It was ultimately a compromise. The meeting was attended by very few members; no one asked whether it was in fact a quorum. . . .

The women wanted quotas, guarantees. We had a breakfast meeting with Pat Harris, Don Fraser, several Commission members. I remember Dutton and Wexler. There was just a feeling that this type of regulation would clarify things in a way that might be helpful to the state chairmen, so that they could begin to gather their evidence in defense. Anne Wexler was representing women's views. Bill Dodds, too. Pat Harris represented the prima facie language. The women had not had specific language. Harris wanted something specific, and Fraser certainly agreed.

Beer, the one attendee who retained strong reservations both about the wisdom of this particular action and about the legitimacy of the process by which it had been accomplished, did manage to provoke some additional discussion. But he, too, saw the inevitability of the result:

I remember one of those later sessions very well. That was the one that brought home to me, more than anything I've ever read, the importance of the press, the way—and you know the theory—that the press brings the rest of the public with it when it covers something. There we were, meeting in one room, and they had put these women in the next room to us. All during our session, we could hear them talking. And clapping. And chanting, as I remember. How are you going to stand against that, when many of your own colleagues in that room, from the Commission, agree with it, too, and with no one there to *report* what you are doing, but knowing that as you leave the room, you will have to file out past those women in the next room?

The one possible gap in the closing circle of reinterpretation was Chairman O'Brien. In theory, O'Brien might still have decided, after a good night's sleep, that he had been an apparent but unwitting accomplice to the proceedings of the previous evening and that he did not want to be identified with the language which had been enunciated there. Since he had not committed himself to any of it in writing, he might, again in theory, have backed away from this provision even after it had been endorsed by the Party Structure Commission. At the very least, he might have abstained from further action of his own, thereby guaranteeing an expanded range of ambiguity for the institutional translation of these new demographic requirements.[40]

On October 15, when Fraser had begun to crack the authorized interpretation of Guidelines A–1 and A–2, with a demand for the active stimulation by state political parties of participation by selected groups, O'Brien had responded very cautiously. In fact, he had forced Fraser to circulate the commission resolution essentially on his own, with no covering letter from the national chairman and with no coordinate role in its announcement. By his self-restraint, O'Brien had managed to leave himself some additional leeway in the evaluation of state compliance. On November 19, much of the chairman's staff, including Bill Welsh, felt that Fraser had again gone much further than necessary, to placate the women's delegation—perhaps forfeiting, in the process, all the other practical and symbolic benefits associated with reform:

> I was opposed to the Fraser-O'Brien memo. Pat was involved in that to some extent. I thought that that was much tougher than it had to be; they didn't have to deal with it on that hard basis. O'Brien was at that point fishing for the Vice Presidential nomination. He was pressured fairly heavily by a meeting with the black caucus of black elected officials. NWPC was beating him over the head. O'Brien, for political purposes, went beyond what was needed at all.[41]

At this point, however, Pat Harris, Don Fraser, and the policy council of the women's caucus were to step in—sequentially, independently, but cumulatively—to shut off any apparent option. Harris moved first. Once the new language on A–1 and A–2 had been formally drafted, Harris became a solid supporter, and she, as much as anyone, prevented O'Brien from having second thoughts in public. John Stewart observed the full array of negotiations—more like unilateral communications—which led from the meeting on Thursday evening, November 18, to an eventual letter of endorsement from O'Brien on Wednesday, December 8:

> It was the same process again, the extension of those earlier things, plus the fact that O'Brien wanted to indicate that they were not out to destroy the guidelines [after the Harris-Hughes affair]. He wanted to hold the left in.
> Pat Harris and Fraser asked him to do it, and after that, he agreed to do it. Pat said, "Look, god-dammit, I've taken a lot of heat on this, and I've hung in there, and I'm asking you to do this because I don't want to have to take more of a beating on this, and I need something to use as a standard." O'Brien said, "Well, if that's what you want to do, you have my support."

Then, ten days after the meeting of the Party Structure Commission, when there had been no public response from the national chairman, Fraser bucked the whole matter to O'Brien again, directly and publicly. In an official letter of transmittal, dated November 29, the Party Structure chairman summarized the actions of his own commission and outlined what they appeared to require, not just from the state parties, but from the national chairman:

The conclusions reached by our Commission are as follows:

(a) Guidelines A–1 and A–2 require state parties to (1) take affirmative steps to encourage the widespread participation of women, minorities and young people in the political process and (2) to take affirmative steps to encourage representation of these groups on the national convention delegation in reasonable relationship to their presence in the population of the state. On October 15, 1971, our Commission elaborated on how to bring these Guidelines to general public attention in a statement which has been circulated to the party, nationwide.

(b) The *standard* to be met by state parties and slate-making bodies is *full* compliance with Guidelines A–1 and A–2 as adopted in the Call to the 1972 Convention.

(c) We believe that state parties should be on notice that whenever the proportion of women, minorities, and young people in a delegation offered for seating in Miami is less than the proportion of these groups in the total population, and the delegation is challenged on the grounds that Guidelines A–1 and A–2 were not complied with, such a challenge will constitute a *prima facie* showing of violation of the Guidelines, and the state Democratic Party along with the challenged delegation has the burden of showing that the state party took full affirmative action to achieve such representation, including an *effective* affirmative action program along the lines outlined in our policy statement adopted on October 15, 1971. This shall not, of course, be construed as lessening in any way the requirement of full compliance with the Guidelines by each state party.

We urge that you write to party officials in the United States and state this position as the official position of the National Democratic Party. We also urge you to call upon each state party to adopt immediately an affirmative action program.[42]

Finally, at the end of that week, in one more attempt to see that O'Brien did indeed "write to party officials in the United States and state this position as the official position of the National Democratic Party," the women's caucus swung into action. On Friday, the Washington staff released the letter from Fraser in its entirety, in a statement aimed at showing that "key officials of both the Republican and Democratic parties made new commitments today to work for the goal of increased representation of women at the Presidential nominating conventions next year."[43] On Saturday, at 3:30 in the afternoon, the policy council of the women's caucus held a press conference to report in greater detail on their meetings with Chairman Dole, held only the day before, and with Chairman O'Brien, held a full two weeks previously.[44]

Each of the relevant actors—Harris, Fraser, and the NWPC—were to get their wish the following Wednesday, December 8. On that date, O'Brien drafted a long covering letter, attached it to Fraser's letter of November 29, threw in the affirmative action memo from the Party Structure Commission, and sent the entire packet to every state chairman, vice chairman, National

Committee member, and governor. In the process, he alerted them in no uncertain terms to the expanded demands of Guidelines A–1 and A–2:

> The enclosed letter from Congressman Don Fraser, chairman of the Commission on Party Structure and Delegate Selection, and the October 18, 1971, memorandum represent information critically important to the Democratic leadership in the states. Many have asked how the state parties can most effectively meet their obligations under the Delegate Selection Guidelines A–1 and A–2.
>
> I want to underscore those points in Congressman Fraser's letter that emphasize the importance of each state's taking specific, affirmative actions to encourage the representation and involvement of women, minorities, and young people in the selection of delegations to the 1972 Democratic National Convention and as members of the delegations. . . .
>
> I would appreciate having a report from each state by mid-January on the affirmative action steps being taken by the state party to fulfill the provisions of Guidelines A–1 and A–2, as well as efforts to communicate the full reform effort to all groups in our party.
>
> As national chairman, I am fully committed to having women, young people and minority groups represented in the state delegations to the Convention as nearly as possible in proportion to their representation in the population.[45]

Implications

The reinterpretation of Guidelines A–1 and A–2 was a dramatic change from any perspective. It was dramatic in substance. This revision moved the national party from prohibition of discrimination, past the requirement of affirmative action, into the territory of explicit demographic quotas. It was dramatic in manner of accomplishment as well. This reinterpretation was the product of private negotiations with one, newly organized, external pressure group; it was achieved with no other intraparty consultation.

The resulting textual interpretation—the new institutional translation—had appeared in a fashion which also underlined the final shift in reform politics. That is, its arrival marked the shift from a politics of party reform in which compliance was the central concern to one in which the practical translation of *successful* reform rules was the core activity—and it marked that transition in a short, sharp, concentrated fashion. Before the National Committee had endorsed the Final Call, and before the state parties had begun to tumble into line with its provisions, there would have been no possibility of the actual resolution on Guidelines A–1 and A–2. Within weeks of those two developments, that resolution had occurred.

The National Committee would never have accepted the language of this revision. Indeed, committee members had questioned even the milder, more ambiguous version contained in the report of the Party Structure Commission. The state parties would surely have resisted compliance much more actively if it had implied this controversial arrangement. Most of those parties had never been very enthusiastic about the *un*reinterpreted package of reforms. Yet by the time Chairman O'Brien informed all these individuals of his new demographic requirements, the first major wave of new implementations in the aftermath of the National Committee meeting had already occurred. It was too late for extended state resistance; the National Committee would not meet again until the National Convention assembled.

The route to this resolution had been stunningly straightforward. The key external group, the National Women's Political Caucus, was authorized in July and created in September. It focused on delegate selection in October. It requested a meeting with the national party leadership in early November and secured that meeting—and then this monumental reinterpretation—*two weeks later.* The new organization wrapped up its institutional victory in a memo from Chairman O'Brien on December 8, making it a matter of months—or even weeks, depending on the measure—from the creation of the women's caucus to its ultimate triumph in the politics of party reform.

In truth, this resolution owed something to an accident of timing and something to a general environment which had been created, almost accidentally, by others. The accident of timing was simply described: An earlier approach to reform negotiations would have faltered in an inhospitable environment; a later approach would have been, quite simply, too late. But the new organization began with a rush. That rush fell within the period of the triumph of implementation and of the rise of several new efforts at institutional translation. And the result was another—historic, unprecedented—institutional change.

These negotiations might have proceeded exactly as they did had there been nothing more to the story than the rise, strategic focus, and archetypal bluff of the women's caucus. No other groups were directly involved in the reinterpretation of demographic reform; no other groups had such remarkable access to key decision-makers. Yet the outcome received important contributions—one cannot know how important in the absence of contrary conditions—from the activities of other noteworthy organizations and from the available solutions already in the air.

The period of the creation of the National Women's Political Caucus was also a period when numerous other organizations turned their attention to demographic representation. Black groups, like the Congressional Black Caucus and the National Conference of Black Elected Officials, and liberal organizations, like the Center for Political Reform and Americans for Democratic Action, were part of this constellation. While they were never part of the direct negotiations on demographic interpretation, they did swell the ranks of those asserting that the policy of the national party needed to be reopened. At the same time, they added definition to the argument which resulted, by asserting that any new solution should contain explicit, numerical standards.

Ken Bode was the diagnostic case. Bode had, of course, helped draft the original text on party reform, with its emphasis on participation and its *deemphasis* on demographics. By the summer of 1971, however, Bode, too, was caught up in the atmosphere surrounding formation of the women's caucus, and he moved to become another source of pressure for the advancement of women—as a demographic group—within the Democratic party. The intellectual tension between participatory rules and fixed demographic outcomes had not changed. The social milieu in which party reformers were located *had*, and that was the dominant consideration.

The status—and shift—of Bode, however, was unremarkable compared with that of Don Fraser. Fraser had been out of the room for the original vote on the "reasonable relationship" clause, at the final commission meeting in November of 1969. He had *opposed* a numerical translation when the commission reconvened in July of 1971. Yet shortly after that, he, too, was caught up in the developments—the moment, the movement, and the milieu—surrounding formation of the women's caucus, an event in which his wife, Arvonne, was a central figure. By October 15, it was Fraser who tore the commission loose from its moorings and began the move to a new interpretation of demographic requirements. On November 18, it was Fraser who enunciated the new translation, the revised interpretation, of demographic standards—of demographic quotas.

The meaning of these developments for institutional change was self-evident. A certain major outcome was demanded of every state, from every process of delegate selection. Indeed, that demand was so wide-ranging, and so inconsistent with the rest of the reform package *and* with the rest of party history, that it gave the entire reform package a new cast, just as it was reaching implementation.

On the other hand, if the total package of participatory reforms was remarkable both for its breadth and depth and for its break with the historically dominant approach to delegate selection, then perhaps the new, partially inconsistent element was still a fitting complement. Indeed, the new amendments could be made to *symbolize* the shift from a party-based to a participatory system: Once, the principal ex officio delegates at national party conventions had been regular-party officials; now, the principal ex officio delegates were to be women, youth, and racial minorities.

The arrival of this new institutional translation possessed major implications for the fate of the alternative—and even the orthodox—Democratic coalitions as well. The search for this late revision mobilized and put into place the last major elements of the alternative coalition. The search confirmed that other alleged elements would never be mobilized and placed at all. It even confirmed that the orthodox coalition would remain largely as it had been for almost forty years.

As a result, the drive for a reinterpretation of party standards on demographic representation became the final contribution to the construction of an alternative Democratic coalition. Moreover, the success of that drive, the resulting institutional change, became an institutionalized contribution to the enshrining of that coalition within the institutions, rules, and procedures of presidential politics, and that was the final, grand impact of a revised reading of Guidelines A–1 and A–2.

Originally, what became the alternative Democratic coalition had consisted of little more than the national party dissidents of 1968. In short order, however, they were joined by the established reform factions, the opposition to the regular party in the states, as their obvious, and numerically superior, allies. Numerous additional elements had been posited for this coalition—the ideological and reform organizations, for example, along with disadvantaged demographic groups of all sorts. But while spokesmen for these elements did turn up, sporadically and individually, at the public hearings of the Party Structure Commission, they were not at first organizationally in evidence.

During the national press debate over the progress of state party compliance, in the summer of 1971, the situation changed. The liberal groups and the reform organizations were effectively mobilized; they were publicly integrated in an alternative coalition; they would remain allied with it for the duration. Old-line liberal organizations like Americans for Democratic Action, new reform operations like Common Cause, and specialized entities like the Center for Political Reform all heeded the warnings of the national press and placed their organizations squarely and publicly behind party dissidents and established reform factions.

Only the "newer" demographic groups—women, youth, and racial minorities—were still missing. They continued to be adduced as obvious members of the alternative coalition. Indeed, previously mobilized members of that coalition continued to speak in their name. But an organizational presence was not yet in place.

The creation of the National Women's Political Caucus, its rapid move into Democratic reform politics, and its stunning success in reinterpreting Guidelines A–1 and A–2 changed all this. The caucus was established in September of 1971. By November, it had secured the major, focused, institutional revision in the entire politics of party reform. After that, the caucus was the obvious organizational spokesman for the feminist sector of the alternative coalition. After that, there were rules specifically benefiting this sector—and its alleged demographic allies—in presidential politics.

The status of the other, alleged, demographic members of this alternative coalition was to remain ambiguous, through 1972 and beyond, though for sharply differing reasons. For the youth component of this alternative coalition, the inability to generate a recognized organizational presence produced only a marginal relevance to continuing reform politics. For the black component, on the other hand, the varied political pressures falling upon numerous, previously successful, black political leaders prevented them from moving in any one concerted direction. At the same time, the basic social affinity of their rank-and-file for the orthodox Democratic coalition further retarded any comprehensive shift.[46]

The youth component of the alternative Democratic coalition never played a significant role in internal party affairs. There was ultimately an umbrella organization aspiring to speak for young people everywhere. It, too, managed to negotiate with national reform actors. But this organization never acquired a deliverable constituency of any sort. It never managed to speak even for those college-based activists who remained important to the next round of presidential campaigns. It never, as a consequence, undertook much more than the maintenance of a national headquarters and the production of national communications.

The black component of the alternative Democratic coalition was quite different. Where feminist political elites were clearly within the alternative Democratic coalition, and where youth elites with extended organizational ties were essentially nonexistent, black political leaders were found in both the orthodox and the alternative coalitions. Some individual leaders, in fact, shifted back and forth, now asserting identification with one, now with the other. Overall, however, black political leadership never came close to deserting its traditional political alliance.

Black political leaders already constituted a congeries of serious, recognized, constituency-based spokesmen. Moreover, they were already a recognized, major part of the orthodox Democratic coalition. The reinterpretation of Guidelines A–1 and A–2 had been the first major maneuver in party politics by the emerging leaders of feminist organizations. Black politicians, on the other hand, had long since carved out their niche within the national Democratic party, and they had prior policy successes to protect within it. They could—and would—continue to seek more from their partners in the orthodox coalition *and* from its aspiring alternative, but they could hardly be drawn off as a body to join the latter.

In fact, the needs of the mass constituencies of these black political leaders were more likely to be advanced by the orthodox than the alternative coalition. Or at least, the mass base for every other element of the alternative coalition was essentially white-collar, from the original party dissidents, to the continuing reform factions, through the ideological and reform organizations, to the active supporters of women's (or youth) politics. The mass base of the major actors in the orthodox coalition, on the other hand, was resolutely blue-collar, from the leaders of the remaining political machines, through party regulars in general, to the major voices of organized labor. Blacks, in the mass public, were overwhelmingly blue-collar, too.

These underlying distinctions among demographic groups were to remain important to an understanding of the politics of party reform. From the first, there had been good reason to believe that participatory reforms would not be kind to black Democrats in the way that they would to organized feminists—thanks largely to the demands of these reforms for education and technical skills, rather than for social solidarity. After 1972, in a sort of metaphor for the entire situation, even the quota provisions hammered out in the fall of 1971 were to confirm this distinction. Within four years, explicit quota provisions applying to women would begin to expand, to every aspect of party affairs, including membership—equal division—on the reformed National Committee. Within four years, quota provisions applying to blacks would be *dropped*, even at national party conventions.[47]

Yet these were, again, long-term developments. In the meantime, the crucial considerations were that Chairman O'Brien had promulgated a radical new interpretation of Guidelines A–1 and A–2 and that several organizations with this new interpretation as their primary focus had been created to seek advantage from it. Reform politics had moved well into its final phase. The institutional structure of party reform had achieved its final codified adjustment before the national convention. The alternative Democratic coalition had acquired its final addition to membership.

CHAPTER

18

The Re-creation of Reform: The Party

Structure Commission and Proportionality

IN WHICH, the remainder of the state parties fall into line behind the
Final Call; the commission staff and leadership seize their opportunity to
reinterpret reformed rules; and the most sweeping of their efforts, the effort
to impose formal proportionality, is dramatically displayed in the state of
Texas. AND IN WHICH, the process of translating abstract rules into
concrete institutions remains at the heart of reform politics; significant institutional change, undemanded by the full commission and unforeseen by
the National Committee, continues to occur; and the resulting institutional
matrix comes to approximate, very closely, the original desires of the alternative Democratic coalition.

THE REINTERPRETATION of Guidelines A–1 and A–2—the retranslation of national requirements for demographic representation—had been externally generated. That reinterpretation had been elicited as a response to
pressures from a new organization, the National Women's Political Caucus,
which had this change as a specific focus. The result, the coming of formal
demographic quotas, had been officially recognized and codified. Yet the bulk
of guideline revisions after passage of the Final Call possessed none of these
characteristics.

Instead, most of these revisions were internally generated, at the Party
Structure Commission. Most were secured through bargaining between the
commission entourage and the state party leadership, in response to pressures
which had been not just initiated but continually sustained by these same commission actors. The resulting revisions were then widely but only informally
recognized—and never codified at all, lest their evident deviation from the
official text be too outrageously obvious.

The outstanding example was proportional representation. The requirement of formal proportionality was another reinterpretation with great institutional reach, and another sharp break with prior party practice. Sought publicly, early, it met with substantial conflict but minimal success. Sought privately, late, its realization gained dramatic value from the fact that both the Party Structure Commission and the National Committee had been so evidently—officially—opposed.

The imposition of formal proportionality remained a private goal of the commission leadership and staff through all these official reverses. When they found themselves ultimately at the center of a general trend to implementation—indeed, when they found themselves orchestrating that trend by virtue of their right to certify state reform programs—the remaining commission entourage seized upon its opportunity and pushed the state parties toward what these reformers had come to see as the proper course of party reform, on proportionality and on numerous lesser issues.

The state providing the most stark testimony to the extent of commission efforts was Texas. Texas was the largest state to use a convention system for selecting its delegates. It was one of the last to knuckle under and conform to national guidelines—and this reflected a deliberate intent to avoid compliance. As a result, the triumph of party reform in the Lone Star State attested both to the pressure of the national drift toward compliance and to the role of national reformers in seeking reinterpretations of reform.

Along the way, Texas featured major scandals with an impact on reform politics. It endured a bruising change of leadership, with reform as both partial cause and partial effect. It offered a succession of indigenous commissions, with a proliferation of ostensible reform plans. Yet when the dust had settled, after a byzantine set of maneuvers within the state party itself, after a particularly involved set of negotiations between major state actors and national party reformers, and after the filing of *the wrong rules*—the rules which failed, not the ones which succeeded—Texas emerged with certified compliance and with formal proportionality.

This informal, national drive toward proportional representation was only the most noteworthy of a set of informal, national drives toward reinterpretation—almost re-creation—of reform. When these reforms, old and new, were finally implemented, when states like Texas accepted not just the original package but the subsequent revision, too, the triumph of party reform nationwide was assured. In fact, the package of reforms *as initially desired* by spokesmen for the alternative Democratic coalition was essentially accepted, and implemented, and awaiting the arrival of the first round of reformed presidential politics.

The Collapse of Opposition and the Rise of Reinterpretation

Two short but separable rounds of state party compliance followed passage of the Final Call. In the first, those parties which had seemed well on the way to certification by the time the National Committee met merely completed the necessary formalities and came into full conformity. In the second, the remaining parties, those whose intentions had always been ambiguous, saw the changed political environment resulting from this first round of compliance and followed their brethren into the fold.

The first wave in this final surge came between mid-October and mid-December. By the time the Party Structure Commission released its year-end report, on December 15, Fraser and Nelson were able to count twenty-five state parties in certified compliance, nineteen either in substantial compliance or with certified rules awaiting formal adoption, and only seven with a less attractive record. (See figure 18.1.a.)[1] As always, those in full compliance were preponderantly volunteer rather than organized. Those in evident noncompliance were overwhelmingly organized rather than volunteer. Those in the middle category were a mix of the two party types. Nevertheless, by December 15, 1971, the crucial consideration was that a full half of *all* the state parties were in complete and absolute certification. If any significant number of those awaiting approval moved ahead—and most had already offered precise timetables for acceptance of their reform packages—then simple numerical pressure would soon be added to the arsenal of party reformers.

Over the next three months, this numerical pressure, coupled with the usual exhortations from national reformers and even a gubernatorial election or two, combined to erase any ambiguity in the fate of party reform. Those states which were in substantial conformity but which fell short of one or two guidelines were encouraged, by this combination of factors, to overcome their focused reluctance and come into full compliance. Those states which retained an active distaste for the entire reform movement discovered that the raw calculus of reform—the likelihood that credentials proceedings at the national convention would injure them as much or more than local implementation of national rules—made it necessary to swallow hard and accept defeat. A second wave of adoptions began.

Some of these late efforts had a cliff-hanging quality. Louisiana, for example, did not even *start* its reform efforts until after the gubernatorial election of February 1. Despite that date, Edwin W. Edwards, the incoming governor, like many new governors before him, aspired to lead his state delegation to the 1972 Convention and did *not* aspire to burst upon the national scene

(a) By December 15, 1971

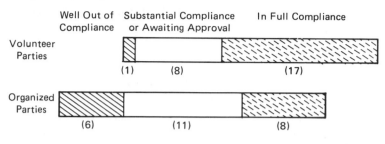

(b) By March 9, 1972

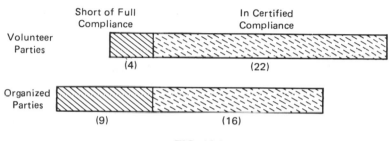

FIG. 18.1

Final Progress Toward State Party Compliance

through a credentials challenge. Before he was even inaugurated, Edwards moved to bring his state into line.[2]

By the day after the New Hampshire primary, the traditional opening of the presidential season, there were thirty-eight states in full compliance, with more to follow. (See figure 18.1.b.) Even at this advanced stage, the fundamental difference between volunteer and organized political parties remained, a testimony to the influence of basic party structure. But by this time, clear majorities of both categories were in full compliance, and that was the consequential fact.

Three more states ultimately joined these thirty-eight, bringing the certified total to forty-one. Of the remaining ten, most were characterized by a single, trivial violation. Only New York, Montana, and West Virginia, out of fifty-one original candidates for resistance, were in serious *non*compliance, one which might realistically affect delegate outcomes. The summary figures for total guideline acceptance told the same tale, even more powerfully. By the time the last delegates had been selected, the fifty states and the District of Columbia were in conformity with 905 of the 918 commission guidelines, a success rate of 98.6 percent. Only two of the nonconformities—with C–1 (Adequate Public Notice) in New York and West Virginia—were accurately classed as serious. In 94 percent of the states, or 99 percent of the guidelines, reform was essentially achieved.[3]

This extended national drift toward compliance was also a major cause—and a major support—for the shift from a focus on ultimate compliance statistics to a focus on the ultimate translation of individual reform guidelines, now clearly destined to attain general acceptance. The Task Force on Delegate Selection of the National Women's Political Caucus had blundered into this national drift, as an implicit asset in their search for a reinterpretation of Guidelines A–1 and A–2. They had been rewarded with a dramatic new (re)translation, with, in effect, demographic quotas.

The staff and leadership of the Party Structure Commission, on the other hand, were well aware of this drift as it developed. They had the richest background information; they kept the final tally. This remaining commission entourage was also far better positioned to take advantage of the drift than any outsider could be. It bargained about the details of state reform plans; it had corralled the right to certify final state compliance. Not surprisingly, then, these remaining commission actors used the trend of compliance to put direct pressure on the recalcitrant states. More surprisingly, perhaps, they also used this trend to reinterpret a far broader range of guideline provisions, and of entire guidelines. When they were finished, national reform forces had (re)gained almost everything which they had been forced to sacrifice since the initial drafting of proposed reforms.

An interest by commission personnel in possible revisions of their reform text was hardly new. Immediately after the final drafting session of the full commission, on November 19 and 20, 1969, the commission staff had gone on to alter standards for apportionment, to prohibit candidacies by favorite sons, and to enjoin state or local parties from endorsing a slate of delegates—all with nothing more than their own sense of the proper elucidation of commission pronouncements to guide them.

Yet once these guidelines were published, attempts at reinterpretation were not a primary emphasis for the commission staff or leadership. Instead, they concentrated on the establishment of their own right—and their right alone—to judge the compliance of the individual states. The failure of the National Committee to seek an immediate confrontation became the first practical contribution to this authority. Or at least, the distaste of committee members for any action on party reform, amplified by the disorganization within the committee as one chairman departed and the search for another began, guaranteed that the *committee* would not poach on commission territory.

The successful assault by commission supporters on Ad Hoc Committee No. 1 completed this process. The Ad Hoc Committee was the first organizational move by the new national chairman, Larry O'Brien, in reform politics. When it was effectively restrained, the commission had guaranteed that the *chairman*, too, would move gingerly when entering its substantive turf. In the process, in a development which was not specifically contemplated but which had the greatest of implications for the course of reform politics, the commission assured its own continuation.

After that, the details of compliance negotiations did become the main concern of commission principals. As they did, the advantages inherent in commission management of these negotiations became increasingly, self-consciously apparent. "Commission management," of course, meant direction by the commission chairman and remaining staff, not by the commission as a collectivity. The inherent advantages in this management ranged from the suggestion of alternative wording, through the coordination of state and national reform pressures, to the granting of final approval. The leeway involved in this arrangement, and the way it devolved on this handful of individuals, was not lost on Carol Casey and the others who remained at commission headquarters:

> What is somewhat interesting is that the Commission never voted on who was in compliance and who wasn't. . . . It was important that the Commission never did meet on this. The only way to insure consistency was to have one person do it.

In late 1970, the commission staff moved to capitalize on these assets explicitly, by developing a set of Model Party Rules. Staff members were not yet prepared to withhold certification from states which did not meet this advanced statement of their evolving preferences. They were, however, fully prepared to elaborate those preferences and introduce them into compliance politics. These newly elaborated institutional implications were intended to help the state parties in translating abstract recommendations into concrete institutions for delegate selection. In passing, they took any number of provisions in the commission report much farther than a majority of the commissioners would have been willing to go.

The Model Party Rules did not play this role immediately. For in early 1971, there was a forced period of marking time at the Party Structure Commission. The remaining commission entourage waited for the new Democratic governors who had been elected in late 1970 to take office. They waited, with far more anxiety, for the National Committee to address their guidelines through the Preliminary Call. But the Call passed, the governors arrived, and after that, the willingness of the commission entourage to seek informal reinterpretations grew apace.

Through the summer of 1971, the emphasis was still on gaining assurance of compliance from as many states as possible, and the severity of reform requirements was still frequently reduced in return for acquiescence with a specific timetable. By the fall of 1971, the emphasis had shifted toward securing compliance with the most aggressive attainable reading of reform guidelines. Again, an attempt to push the state parties toward more desirable institutional translations had never been absent from discussions between national party reformers and state party officials. But in late 1971 and early 1972, after the National Committee had adopted its Final Call and as it became clear that the bulk of the state parties would indeed comply, this attempt intensified.

The most dramatic, single issue in the attempt at reinterpretation by key commission actors, even at the beginning but especially at the end, was proportional representation. Early on, the commission staff had come to believe that formal proportionality was a necessary adjunct to participatory institutions of delegate selection, if perfect structural equity was to be attained and, more importantly, if insurgent movements were to escape the braking effect of regular-party rules. The draft report going forward to the full commission gave proportionality a central place in its integrated recommendations.

The commissioners had recognized in this an issue of potential consequence, and they had debated it at length whenever it surfaced. Yet they were never willing to endorse the staff proposal, and they would, in fact, have defeated it in one of their early sessions had Vice Chairman Hughes not made proportional representation the beneficiary of some imaginative parliamentary maneuvers. At their final meeting in November, however, even Hughes could not save it, and the commissioners decided to *urge,* not require, proportionality—and to note explicitly that the election of delegates by district would suffice to accomplish this goal.[4]

The commissioners had spoken so clearly that the staff did not attempt to make proportionality one of those items which it retranslated in the course of publishing the commission report. By late 1970, however, the staff was back on the case. The Model Party Rules, drafted at year's end, endorsed formal proportional representation in the suggested text for *every* institution of delegate selection and went on to urge precise mathematical systems of proportionality in their voting processes.[5]

The commission entourage eventually settled on proportionality by standing division or by roll-call vote as the ideal translation of Guideline B–6 (Adequate Representation of Minority Views). But from early 1971 on, the preference of the staff and leadership for this arrangement, and the lengths to which they would go to impose this preference, grew in proportion—in exaggeration, really—with their general shift toward insistence on compliance with an enlightened reading of the guidelines text. Casey observed the change:

> It was clearly our conception that the spirit of the guidelines was better served if the proportionality went to the lowest level. We argued that if you're going to use the Hare system or cumulative voting, it would become so complicated—you could go to straight proportionality. But if you did that, you should use it below the congressional district level, because at that level you would have already shut people out.

Reform Politics in Texas and the Drive for Proportionality

The informal but persistent staff effort to expand the interpretation of Guideline B–6 fell on any number of states. But it was Texas in which this informal pressure toward formal proportional representation received its most dramatic and most extended test. Texas had been the largest state to use the unit rule at the 1968 Convention. It possessed a classic organized party, southern style, which did not even bother to hide its contempt for reform. The state was thus resolutely majoritarian and implacably regular. It would still be resisting compliance after ten states had begun *selecting* their delegates, a scant six weeks before Texas itself had to begin delegate selection.

The major actors in the regular party in Texas had shifted considerably after the election of 1968. John B. Connally did not stand for re-election as governor, and he was succeeded by his lieutenant governor, Preston E. Smith. Simultaneously, Will D. Davis, state party chairman under Connally and erstwhile Party Structure commissioner, was replaced by Elmer C. Baum, Smith's choice to chair the State Democratic Executive Committee [SDEC].

Baum was, if anything, more dedicated than Davis in his dislike of reform and reformers. In September of 1969, as the national commission was moving toward its final session, Baum wrote to George McGovern, noting that the SDEC liked its existing rules and was not about to appoint a local commission. Again in November, a few days before the final drafting session of the Party Structure Commission, Baum wrote to McGovern, underlining his fear that the commission might recommend proportionality and urging it to concentrate instead on organizational unity and electoral victory.[6] His views did not change substantially over the next two years:

The main push for reform came from the Young Democrats, and we let them sit in and express themselves. I let the Young Democrats sit in on Executive Committee meetings. Between 1968 and 1971, there was no division on the SDEC. There were some folks—they're labelled "activists"—they wanted all kinds of changes. But they weren't on the SDEC.

There was a tranquil period between 1968 and 1971. Reform of the party wasn't too much discussed. We heard about reform. We got a lot of material. But the SDEC never did get too excited because we had a unified party, and the SDEC was functioning well.

Only the arrival of Larry O'Brien in the national chairmanship, a man with blue-ribbon, regular-party credentials and one whom Baum admired personally, led Baum to relent sufficiently to create a Texas reform committee. Even then, national reformers must have drawn little comfort from the appointment of this "Committee to Study the Guidelines of the Commission on Party Structure and Delegate Selection—Texas." For its chairman was none other than Will Davis, the outstanding dissident commissioner on the national reform body.[7]

Davis did set his membership to the task at hand. He undertook some personal research on the interaction of the Texas election code with the national commission report, and if he continued to look for the minimal steps by which Texas might satisfy national guidelines, he also prepared a report on ways to harmonize the inescapable differences. Indeed, on January 18, 1971, Davis followed through by addressing the full SDEC, where he secured endorsement of five specific legislative changes and where he promised to bring additional proposals for supplementary state rules to some subsequent meeting.[8]

And at that point, the reform process stopped completely. The next day, inauguration day for Preston Smith, what became the "Sharpstown Scandal" broke into the open. The ripples—and eventually the waves—from that scandal were to wash over not just the state legislature and the state insurance, banking, and brokerage communities, but even the Jesuit Fathers and the Apollo astronauts.[9]

Frank W. Sharp was a multiple-venture entrepreneur who had sold inflated insurance stock, financed through unsecured loans from his Sharpstown State Bank, to extract a state law creating a private insurance company for state bank deposits—all to rescue him from inquiries by the Federal Deposit Insurance Corporation and, especially, the Federal Securities and Exchange Commission. One of the early beneficiaries of these financial machinations was Chairman Baum, acting as agent for himself and for Governor Smith. Despite that, at the end of the 1970 legislative session—in the action which more than anything else qualified him as a maverick in the grand Texas tradition—Smith vetoed the bill at the heart of this rescue effort, and his veto effectively, at least by hindsight, sealed the fate of Sharp.[10]

By early 1971, the details of the Sharpstown affairs were beginning to attract attention. Calls for the resignation of Chairman Baum followed almost immediately. Yet with no resolution of the crisis, Baum was not inclined to resign. And with his name under such an ominous cloud, he was not inclined to assemble the SDEC. As a result, the state party was effectively inactive for the next nine months, from January 19 through October 7.

During this period, no resolution of the reform debate in Texas was practically possible. Two events which powerfully conditioned the ultimate outcome did, however, occur. One was passage of a state statute on party rules. This forced the SDEC to develop a state party constitution; it even imposed a timetable for achieving that goal. The other was the creation of another reform committee. This provided the framework within which reform negotiations would resume; it produced the reform package—the "losing" reform package in all but the ultimate sense—which came to govern Texas party affairs.

The original plan of indigenous party reformers was to use the legislature to demand not just the existence of written rules, but compliance with national reform directives. This approach was the brainchild of Carrin M. Patman, national committeewomen for Texas and a member of Ad Hoc Committee No. 1. Her idea was to move a bill on party rules through the Texas legislature, as an ostensible means to restore public confidence after the Sharpstown scandal.

The complete device—a statutory requirement of compliance with national reform guidelines—almost succeeded. It was one step away from the desk of the governor, at a point where the Senate-House conference committee could have approved it, when alarmed party regulars woke up and responded with restraining amendments. Reformers settled for a bill which commanded the state committees to create written party rules and which specified some of the topics these had to cover. Patman was still delighted to have a statutory goad to reform:

> I hatched the idea of using the legislature. There were no written party rules of any kind before 1972, which had been a real boon to conservative control. I felt that once they had to write rules down, we'd get some authentic reform. The deliberate tactic was to get the state committee to write those rules—the Governor's influence, a liberal State Senate, and the House desire to overcome the Sharpstown image.
> The bill passed the Senate, and got through the House on the local calendar by accident. Two Republicans did raise objections, but Bill Patman [husband of

the national committeewoman] took a deal with these guys and wrote it and sent it through. Then the Senate and the House would not agree.

Then Smith put some heat on. He was listening on the intercom. It failed in the House again. That led Mauzy to move that the Senate caucus on the House amendments. But the word had already gotten from Davis and Barnes to oppose it. The only written rules for parties were in the Texas election code. The compliance part was deleted by the Republicans. The conservatives in the conference would not give in on that.

Simultaneously, reformers on the state level pressed Chairman Baum to create a newly invigorated body to address the issue of party reform in Texas. The original operation, the Davis Committee, was in organizational limbo, and nothing in the new statute was likely to revive it. Reformers on the national level, including Chairman O'Brien, added voices to this chorus. Baum was still not prepared to reassemble the State Democratic Executive Committee. But he did possess the power to appoint a study group without SDEC approval, and as spring passed into summer, he exercised that authority.

His new Rules Committee had ten members, all drawn from the SDEC but most with a professed interest in writing a party code. It was chaired by William R. Anderson, Jr., of Corpus Christi; its most active participant, albeit ex officio, was Carrin Patman.[11] The new group assembled on August 7, 1971, and after discussing various approaches to state party regulation, the members asked Anderson to develop a draft. Anderson spent the next three weeks drawing up a highly tentative proposal and tried it out on Davis and Patman, the ranking and emerging experts on Texas party rules. Davis declined any further role in party reform. Patman, however, collected her own circle of advisers, confronted them with the Anderson draft, and went to work on an extensive revision, with the Model Party Rules from the national commission as her guiding framework.[12]

To that point, reform politics in Texas had been roughly similar to reform politics in many other states with organized political parties, although the thoroughness of local resistance made Texas an exaggerated case even there. The leadership of the regular party had remained in control—and in opposition. A local reform commission had gone its own way, with no evident relevance to internal party affairs and no serious promise of a successful reform product. National reform figures had found no means to deal themselves into local reform politics in an effective manner.

On October 7, everything changed. On that date, Elmer Baum finally resigned as chairman of the State Democratic Executive Committee. Within eight weeks, the entire configuration of party forces within Texas was altered. Within eight weeks, national party reformers had re-entered Texas reform politics as well. The new local alignment, pressed by state law from within and by the accelerating mathematics of compliance from without, was forced to confront an explicit reform package. The new national presence not only augmented the array of forces interested in local party reform but, this time, injected specific substantive proposals aimed at shaping the Texas reform program, including, most centrally, proportional representation.

Charges and recriminations would forever obscure the nuances of the struggle to succeed Baum as state chairman, but certain minimal facts were generally acknowledged. Baum resigned without advance notice. The governor lacked a candidate to succeed him and, in fact, professed a lack of interest. The nominating committee of the SDEC settled quickly on a favorite, Roy L. Orr, committeeman from suburban Dallas. Committee dissidents rallied to an alternative, John C. White, the eleven-term secretary of agriculture. White became the candidate of the governor as well. And Orr defeated White, 32 to 31, on October 20, two weeks after the resignation of Baum.[13]

These two weeks drew the lines between the core of the regular party and those who would eventually support a reform package more acceptable to national reformers. Obviously, the regulars succeeded in retaining the chairmanship, even over the opposition of a sitting governor. Curiously, the nature of their triumph both expanded the reform coalition and left the regulars weaker than they had previously been.

The two weeks between the resignation of Baum and his replacement by Orr also encompassed momentous events outside of Texas. The National Committee adopted the Final Call, essentially unchanged. Those parties still out of compliance with this official reform document began to abandon their opposition and move toward conformity. The continuing struggles between the partisans of Orr and White over reform politics inside Texas then provided the means by which national reformers could enter local party politics. The accelerating drift of other states into compliance armed these outside actors for state party battles.

Committee regulars had rallied quickly to Roy Orr, as a symbol of hardline regularity. Orr was a recorded opponent of reform in the national mode. Indeed, he had been the lone member to speak in opposition to the proposed changes from Will Davis, when Davis had presented them to the SDEC in January of 1971. Orr was a continuing opponent of mavericks within the state party as well. He had chafed under the detachment of incumbent Governor Smith; he was willing to stand against him when the chairmanship came open.[14]

On the other side, the coalition around John White was much more diverse. That coalition began with the committed state reformers, a comparative handful. But it added some regular members who were loyal to the governor, some personal supporters of White himself, and some scattered mavericks and insurgents who were reliable critics of the dominant faction. What was crucial about the battle, however, was not so much the initial diversity of this losing, opposition faction, but the way that it was welded together for subsequent politicking in the SDEC.

This fight was so central to Texas party politics that it drew the lines outside the SDEC as well. The two members of the National Committee, for example, were active—and split. Patman, the moving force in the Rules Committee, backed White and labored mightily on his behalf. Strauss, national committeeman and national treasurer, offered a public letter of support for Orr.[15] Governor Smith, of course, was the leading public official behind White, but he was joined by Bob Bullock, a former gubernatorial aide who had become secretary of state. Because much party business fell under the state election code, and because the secretary of state oversaw its administration, Bullock was, in effect, the other consequential official for conflict over party rules.

Orr took no immediate action on the reform issue. Patman rushed ahead with her reform package, in the hope that its completion would resolve the issue. On November 11, with this foreclosure in mind, Patman sent Orr an advance draft. Ten days later, Orr fired back, not with any substantive comment, but with an expansion of the Rules Committee.[16] To the ten members already in place, he added twelve new members, to head off what he regarded as an antiparty document:

> I broadened the reform commission; I could see what was going to happen. A lot of people who were very active on that were not representative of the state executive committee. They led people to believe that things had to be a certain way, but we learned that this was not so.
> Any time you forget about your elected officials, when you have to make an exception to put your own Governor or your state chairman on the delegation, you've got a problem. After all, they *have* to have a constituency.
> This other [the Davis Committee] was a study committee, an ad hoc committee. The Anderson Committee was the official committee. If I had to turn to it again, I would dismiss the whole committee. You don't have somebody as your assistant unless you have some control over them, unless they share your views.

Orr sent his new members to the Rules Committee with a general mandate to protect the regular party and with specific instructions to cancel a public hearing on the evolving Patman draft, scheduled for December 4. That hearing was indeed canceled. The balance of the full committee was effectively adjusted as well, with most original members continuing to support the original draft and all new appointees seeking to establish some distance from it.

Patman made one more attempt to foreclose the entire matter, with help from the national commission. In the short run, this attempt, too, was unsuccessful. Yet it constituted the real opening wedge for national reformers in Texas party politics. It heralded the arrival of proportional representation. And it attested, inescapably, to the presence of an informal effort to reinterpret party reform on the national level, and to enforce proportionality nationwide.

After Orr enlarged the Rules Committee, Patman went back to Bob Nelson at the Party Structure Commission with her draft rules. She presented them for analysis and comment; she sought explicit endorsement. Nelson considered these proposed rules carefully and responded with eight specific changes. Two of these were procedural elaborations pure and simple. Two beefed up the provisions on affirmative action and demographic representation. *Four,* the crucial structural revisions, added explicit proportionality to the precinct caucuses, to the county or senatorial district caucuses, and to the statewide convention, as well as to the nominating committees, if any, at each level.[17]

Perhaps the clearest indication of the change which this represented in the status—the interpretation—of proportionality is found in a comparison with the original compliance letter for the Texas Democratic party, mailed in February of 1970. In that letter, painstakingly assembled by the commission staff to include the full range of nonconformities without giving offense, Texas had been found in violation of Guidelines A–1, A–2, A–5, B–1, B–4, B–5, B–7, C–1, and C–6. It had been judged *in compliance* with Guideline B–6 (Adequate Representation of Minority Views), the very guideline which formed the basis of its compliance problems from late 1971 on.[18]

Patman weighed these suggestions carefully. She judged that full, formal, proportional representation, from top to bottom, would never succeed in the Lone Star State. But she added proportionality to the precinct caucuses, through a standing division there, and she inserted proportionality into the statewide convention, through a straw poll of delegates as they registered. Otherwise, she accepted the proposals from Nelson almost verbatim and sent her revised draft back to commission headquarters. On December 1, she secured the desired notification from Chairman Fraser himself:

> HAVE REVIEWED PROPOSED NEW PARTY RULES FOR DELE-GATE SELECTION IN TEXAS AND ARE PLEASED TO INFORM YOU THEY WOULD FULLY COMPLY. URGE FINAL ACTION BY PARTY AS SOON AS POSSIBLE.
> CONGRESSMAN DONALD M. FRASER.[19]

Patman turned this around in a letter to the chairman of the Texas Rules Committee, Bill Anderson, a letter which she released to the press:

Congratulations to you and members of your SDEC Rules Subcommittee on successfully completing a most challenging assignment: i.e., to come up with a tentative draft that 1) fully complies with the intricate new guidelines required for Texas to be seated at the '72 National Convention; 2) apparently complies with our immensely complicated state laws; and 3) yet, largely follows the traditional procedures of our Texas party, where these still fit our changing needs and goals. . . .

Again, congratulations on a difficult job well done in finishing "Party Rules: Phase I"![20]

National reform actors had never been absent from reform politics in the state of Texas. The Party Structure Commission had held a public hearing in Houston in June of 1969, and that had been one of the few such gatherings where prestigious party regulars came out to testify. Chairman O'Brien had convinced Chairman Baum to appoint the first indigenous reform committee, and had helped convince him to appoint the second. Bob Nelson, of course, had communicated with all available actors and more, trying—in a sort of momentum by memorandum—to generate some serious reform activity in Texas.

Nevertheless, it was the Fraser telegram which truly enmeshed these national figures in Texas party politics. The immediate response of the regular party in Texas, however, was not to surrender to a purportedly higher authority, but to widen the split between emerging local coalitions of regulars and reformers. Moreover, the response of the national commission to this widening split was to be a major tactical blunder, one which appeared to sacrifice the more aggressive reform program in Texas and which threatened to sacrifice the national drive for proportional representation.

The completion and certification of Patman's rules was hardly enough to resolve the reform situation in Texas, although it did lead Chairman Orr to change his mind and allow a rescheduled public hearing on party reform. It also, however, led him to make a widely publicized trip to Washington to consult with the Texas congressional delegation. Orr took along John S. Brunson, committeeman from Houston and nominal leader of the regular faction on the Rules Committee. While the state chairman was on Capitol Hill, Brunson stopped in at the Party Structure Commission for some general conversation with Bob Nelson.[21] Brunson credited that visit with opening his eyes to the reality of reform politics:

Much of our information was coming from Carrin Patman. She was on the National Committee. Some time later, we learned that she was not a clear window at all, but a distortion. Someone in Washington pulled her string—the reform commission probably.

My own interest began to quicken at this point. I was not too concerned, even then. I didn't pay much attention until we got a draft from the Anderson Committee. We had a meeting; we were presented with a draft; we were advised that it complied. The original draft went so far beyond the requirements that it addressed not just the mechanics of the delegate selection process, but the mechanics of the state party, too, which was none of the McGovern Commission's business.

What occurred to everybody was that the information we were receiving was inaccurate. That draft was an attempt to change the complexion of the Democratic Party of Texas! . . . I then drafted my own delegate selection part. It was not one that we thought would comply. I went to Washington before this to talk to Nelson. That's when I first learned the disparity between what the SDEC was being told and what the facts were.

Brunson returned to Texas and joined with Robert W. "Corky" Smith of Dallas to begin work in earnest on an alternative reform package. While their new draft was still in process, the new year arrived, and with it, on January 12, 1972, the public hearing on the original version of the Rules Committee report, the "Anderson rules." Approximately forty people testified before the Rules Committee at the Commodore Perry Building in Austin, including major party figures of all perspectives, with reform preferences to match.[22] Yet the hearing was perhaps most consequential for marking the return to reform politics of Will Davis, Party Structure commissioner and chairman of the first indigenous reform committee, with the lengthiest testimony of all.

Davis's commentary, studded with proposed changes in article and section of the Anderson draft, was enough to alarm state reformers; within days, it would be enough to deal him back into local reform negotiations.[23] Before that, however, the full Rules Committee agreed to meet and address an official draft, on Friday, January 28. That date provided partisans of the Anderson rules with a target, albeit a belated one, when they might finally hope to achieve preliminary compliance with national regulations. It provided opponents, partisans of the semisecret Brunson rules, with a date by which they had to go public, or forget the matter.

In response, Brunson and "Corky" Smith redoubled their efforts. They revised their previous draft to attain compliance—minimal compliance, to be sure, but compliance nevertheless. They took their revised rules to Washington, on January 25, for a second, more formal meeting with Nelson and Casey at the Party Structure Commission. For this, they arranged to have Strauss prepare the way and make an official introduction.[24]

That meeting produced some hard bargaining over the particular text—even the specific wording—of the Brunson rules. Formal proportionality stayed out. So did the extension of national reforms to state party business. On the other hand, the election of most delegates from specified districts was guaranteed. So was the possibility of amendment for any nominating committee report. These revisions, finally, were added on the spot. At the end of a long and tightly argued session, Nelson agreed to seek a letter from Fraser, putting the revised rules in compliance, and Casey watched Brunson and Smith depart:

> Brunson and Smith came to see Bob and me. We went over the points of difference. We did not get a positive response from them. "We'll call Bob Strauss and have him come in and talk to you folks." They were there to cut a political deal. Brunson never got a blanket letter, but he got a conditional compliance letter. But Carrin was very upset by that. Even if her rules were fairer and better, we still could not call Brunson out of compliance.
>
> It looked for a while like there would not be any rules in Texas. The Brunson people were toeing a thin line. They wanted to get something through, but they didn't want to look too liberal. We felt that any rules at all were in jeopardy, so that either they would not go for anything—but Carrin was hoping that pressure would cause them to cave in totally. At that point, *we* just wanted *something*. If Carrin could pull it out and get better rules, good, but we were willing to accept the Brunson rules.

The next day, Fraser did indeed reply with a letter of compliance, tentative and circumscribed as it was. Fraser made a point of spelling out the changes in wording which the four principals had adopted the previous day. He did, however, close by noting that "with this or similar language, this process will meet the Guidelines."[25] Brunson, in turn, did not immediately go public with his certification. Instead, he held it for a tactically appropriate time:

> I didn't act to keep everybody happy; I acted to comply with the rules and preserve the party. . . . Corky Smith and I returned to Washington with our own draft. Nelson took this draft to Fraser, and gave us a letter saying that they complied.
>
> That meeting with Nelson was the turning point, in that it gave us to understand the many ways in which these rules could be fulfilled. We didn't tell anybody we had this letter from Fraser; we just held it.
>
> We went into the Rules Committee with our own draft. Ms. Patman had a letter from Fraser saying that her rules complied; she had a telegram. She was not stating, but she was implying, that her rules, and her rules alone, complied. I stood up and circulated my draft, along with a xerox of my letter.

The surprise was destined to be only partial, because Nelson called Patman to report the result of his session with Brunson and Smith. Patman saw the potential unraveling of all her efforts and demanded some document restoring her priority. The national staff, appreciating what they suddenly saw as a tactical error of major proportions, began the process of reversing themselves. The morning of the Rules Committee meeting, Fraser telegraphed Patman again, this time with a comparison of the Anderson and Brunson rules, one centering on their largest procedural difference, the scope of proportional representation:

> You have inquired which of the proposed drafts are most responsive to the overall requirements and recommendations of the commission. The proposed rules dated on November 11 [the Anderson rules] most fully meet the overall guidelines.
>
> Specifically the Commission recommended in Guideline B–6 that minority political views be represented at every level of the process and in the delegation to the national convention. Although not mandatory, the draft of the proposed rules of November 11 fully complied with this recommendation, whereas the draft presented earlier this week does not respond to this recommendation.
>
> In other respects the November 11 draft deals more extensively with the internal structure of the state party. Those provisions are beyond our jurisdiction. The final decision on how to meet the mandate of the 1968 convention calling for "full, meaningful and timely participation" of all Democrats in the delegate selection process rests with the Texas state Democratic party. We stand ready to be of further assistance if needed.[26]

It was not enough. On the morning of January 28, John Brunson, fortified by *his* compliance letter, moved to substitute the Brunson rules for the Anderson rules. His motion passed; the Texas party had a new definition of party reform. The Lone Star State seemed on its way at last to national compliance, minimal though it might be. The national drive for proportional representation was stalled, and might be over.

The "Theft" of Party Reform

No one, however, believed that this was the end of rules politicking in Texas. Formally, the next step was clear. The State Democratic Executive Committee was to meet on March 13. Because the new state statute on party rules required official filing at least a month before delegate selection began, this meeting had to address a final plan. Informally, there were numerous incentives for continued negotiations, and these held the potential for producing a very different package for consideration by the SDEC.

Some of these incentives were internal to the SDEC itself. Both the Brunson *and* the Anderson drafts retained supporters there; these supporters could be expected to divide roughly as they had for the chairmanship in October, thereby sustaining the viability of the draft which had been rejected by the Rules Committee. Some of these incentives were external to the entire state of Texas. Indeed, in response to the events of January 28, when the Brunson draft had ambushed the Anderson draft in the Rules Committee, national reform actors moved deliberately to destabilize the Texas situation.

Patman, feeling traduced not just by the Brunson faction but by national reform staffers, appealed to these national actors for help—and mobilized major Texas officials to support her:

> Smith and Bullock and I raised cain with Fraser. He had approved the Brunson version. What was the pressure for that? Then he came back and wired that the Brunson draft was minimal. That wire was read to the SDEC.

This time, Fraser also issued a press release, containing a much stronger expression of preference between the Brunson and the Anderson drafts:

> Reports from Texas indicate growing confusion there concerning efforts of the Texas State Democratic Party to comply with this Commission's 18 guidelines for delegate selection in 1972 and about the Commission's position on the proposals for rules changes. . . .
>
> In my judgment, the Anderson Draft is the more superior set of rules, meeting not only the letter but the spirit of the guidelines. The substitute draft on the other hand must be viewed as minimal in meeting the bare requirements of the guidelines.
>
> The Anderson Draft is vastly stronger in its provisions to encourage the participation of young people, women, and minorities in the delegate selection process. Its proportional representation provision, though relatively modest, would go far in giving full voice in representation to them as well as to all Texas Democrats in the present nominating process. Moreover, the party organizational concepts set forth in the Anderson Draft are soundly conceived and consistent with the action that virtually every other state Democratic Party has taken, or is taking to open its structures.
>
> In any case, the ultimate test of compliance for any state will lie in the actual implementation of the new rules in choosing convention delegates. While the substitute draft of rules that we reviewed would technically meet minimum standards, if amended as we indicated, it is my candid view that the party would have to go to unusual lengths in the implementation process to make certain that the guidelines are fully met.[27]

By then, national actors had determined not to falter in support of their allies in Texas; after this, they followed their chosen course aggressively and without deviation. Nelson was shocked and embarrassed by their contribution to the Brunson massacre of the Patman (Anderson) draft:

> They [the Brunson rules] were very, very skillfully drafted, and didn't look bad. They were absolutely minimal compliance, a very strict interpretation, but they were not within the *spirit* of the guidelines. If we had said yes, we would have jerked the rug out from under Carrin and whatever was going on down there. We found good reasons for turning them down; we had to *look* for those reasons. We wanted to be consistent and tough at that point.

These pressures were reinforced, powerfully, by the general drift toward implementation and compliance in the national party as a whole. By early 1972, the presence of that drift was undeniable, and the commission entourage was wielding it as a huge, intangible club. In Texas, even regular-party leaders were beginning to face the possibility, undreamed of short years before, that the giant Texas delegation might be restructured on the floor of the national convention, or actually expelled. Texas newspapers had long since begun to discuss the possibility explicitly.[28]

The upshot was a gradual resumption of negotiations over a compromise reform package. Initially, these negotiations arose not between Brunson and Anderson, but between Patman and Davis. Davis had re-emerged as a central figure in state reform politics. While he talked with Patman about further compromises to avoid a bruising battle in the state committee, he tested the national commitment to the Anderson rules, in a letter to Nelson:

> Please ask Congressman Fraser whether he feels the revised Texas rules (not the Anderson rules) are equal to, superior to, or inferior to the Rules adopted by the states of Alabama, Arkansas, Hawaii, Maine, Nevada, Pennsylvania, and Utah, and any other state which has any assured proportional representation by election of delegates at units smaller than the Congressional District. If Texas is superior to these other states, why not say so? Has anything been said to the other states about "minimal compliance"?[29]

Nelson, however, was having none of it:

> Of the states you mentioned, it is our opinion that the rules adopted in Alabama, Maine, Pennsylvania, and Utah are superior to the so-called Brunson Rules, specifically because nominating procedures are clearly spelled out and explicit opportunity given for indicating a presidential preference.
>
> There is another point to consider in all this as well. Maine and Alabama were the first states to comply. We thought at the time they wrote their rules that they were exceptionally good—and they were, in comparison to the other 48 state parties. But what has happened in the ensuing period of time is that the other states have profited from those early rules and generally speaking, state party rules have gotten progressively better as we have moved along. Moreover, on the question of "minimal compliance," Mr. Brunson and Mr. Smith made no bones about their intention, which was to do as little as possible to meet the Guidelines and achieve absolute minimal compliance.[30]

By then, Davis was already engaged in talks with Patman about a compromise package. His major concern, despite his status as a Party Structure commissioner, was the intrusion of the Patman draft into *state* party business. Her intentions in that regard were equally clear. Months before, she had begun with the state legislature, as a means to compel reform activity on both national and state party business. By February of 1972, she had turned to the national commission—as a means to compel reform activity on both national and state party business again.

The solution, perhaps, was obvious. Patman ceded most of the state party arrangements to Davis. Davis accepted most of her national party arrangements, including proportional representation at the precinct level and in the statewide convention. After this, the separation of state and national party business was complete—and would not be reopened. After this, the major issue separating reformers and regulars was the presence of proportional representation—and would be until the final reform rules were filed.

While these private talks were occurring, Patman was also collecting public endorsements, from Senator Lloyd Bentsen, from Governor Smith and Secretary Bullock, and even from Ben Barnes, the lieutenant governor and gubernatorial candidate of the regular party. Bullock also refloated his charge that Roy Orr, by having become a Dallas County commissioner, was no longer entitled to hold the state chairmanship and was, in fact, in violation of state law.[31]

From the other side, Brunson was pressing Nelson and Fraser to *maintain* their endorsement of both state plans, by pressing them, like Davis, to compare the Brunson rules with certified reforms in other states. But this time, Nelson was not only doing nothing to encourage him; he was keeping Patman fully apprised of any national approaches by Brunson. His letter to Brunson himself went back on March 8:

> In response to your request, I am enclosing copies of rules from three states: Virginia, Iowa, and Vermont.
> These are convention states as is Texas, and will give you an idea of what some of the other states have done.
> I hope you will find this information useful.[32]

That same day, a copy of this letter went to Patman, with a handwritten note on the bottom:

> Carrin:
> This is the package. Not much help here for those who want minimal compliance.[33]

In this environment, the two nominal leaders, John Brunson and Bill Anderson, came back together on March 12, the day before the SDEC meeting. A meeting of the full Rules Committee was the occasion for this discussion. But that meeting was merely an opportunity for private and decentralized negotiations among the major actors. Patman hoped that her revised version of the Anderson rules would become the text for these negotiations. An amended version of the *Brunson* rules, revising them in light of stipulations from Davis, became the working document instead.

From there, Brunson and Anderson went back and forth, with frequent consultations between Anderson and his original subgroup and with an intermittent, unavailing attempt by militant reformers to introduce yet a third package into this dialog. From a wearying series of exchanges, Brunson saw a compromise emerge:

> Strauss, on the morning of March 12 comes in and meets with us—myself, Smith, Anderson, and some others—and says that we must come up with a compromise. From 9:00 A.M. that morning until 1:00 A.M. the next morning. He was the impetus to get it resolved.
>
> The Anderson group—the liberal faction—had a caucus going on. Anderson would go back and forth, for several hours. There was a purple felt-tipped version. The night before the SDEC meeting, this caucus approved, then disapproved.
>
> You're not sure, at this point, what will happen in the SDEC, because you're not sure who's coming. When you have only a one-vote majority, you can't be too cocky.
>
> The compromise version could not be reproduced. It had to be read into the record bit by bit. Purple felt-tipped copies are read from.

This confusion, exhaustion, and linguistic disorganization was reflected the following day at the meeting of the full SDEC. The members were, on the whole, relieved that a compromise package, endorsed by both Brunson and Anderson, had emerged. Many had come to believe that the balance of compliance was so overwhelming that Texas might actually be unseated at the coming national convention; most had grown tired of the continuous, involved wrangling over delegate selection reform. Whether the members fully understood the substance of their compromise, however, was quite another question, as Billie Carr, a partisan of the militant reform alternative, noted:

> First, Anderson would get up and start saying things, and Carrin Patman would shake her head, saying, "No, no, that's not right." Then Brunson would get up, and he might have some idea what was in them, but he couldn't explain it coherently, and Corky Smith would shake his head. Then Bean would chime in, and he wouldn't have any idea what he was talking about.[34]

What resulted, in any case, was a reform package, apparently resolving the major differences to date. For the governance of state party affairs, the compromise was essentially the Brunson draft. Both sides acknowledged the rescue of the regular party from national reforms, although the provision of detailed rules for state activity was still a noteworthy gain for reformers. For the governance of national delegate selection, the compromise had *removed* formal proportionality, although it guaranteed the selection of most delegates by district. Beyond that, it had moved toward the Anderson rules on the specificity of the package as a whole, and it had split some of the difference on provisions for affirmative action.

The remaining formal steps to implement this package were straightforward. The hen-tracked draft of the compromise had to be converted to a clean copy; that copy had to be filed with the secretary of state by the first week in April. The informal agreement in the aftermath of the SDEC meeting was equally simple. Anderson would create the clean copy; Brunson would sign off on it; Chairman Orr would file it with Secretary Bullock.

The actual denouement for Texas reform politics, however, was to be as convoluted and controversial as anything which preceded it. Anderson developed a version of the March 13 product and passed it along to Brunson. Brunson was flabbergasted, and saw the situation slipping rapidly from his grasp:

> Anderson was then charged with the responsibility of completing it so that it could be filed. The draft that I got from him had such disparity, for example the amendments required three-fourths rather than two-thirds. He had twelve to fifteen deviations from the compromise. I said that this wasn't what the deal was.

Brunson contacted Anderson directly and asserted that this was not at all the substance of the compromise. Anderson, in turn, contacted Patman:

> Anderson didn't know his own rules. He would let them rewrite them, send it to him, and jointly file that document with the Secretary of State. They had rewritten this with over thirty differences. At that point, Anderson says he will file our document. He files with the Secretary of State, who is an ally of ours and says these are authentic.

Anderson did not consult further with Brunson or Orr. Instead, he found five co-signatories, all of whom had been on the losing side of the struggle in the SDEC, and filed directly with the secretary of state. The document he filed was essentially the Anderson rules, as drafted by Patman, as strengthened by Nelson, and as restrained by Davis. That is, the document he filed was *not* the version which had emerged from negotiations between Anderson and Brunson before the SDEC meeting. It was *not* the version which was retyped by Anderson in the aftermath of SDEC adoption. It was an unofficial incarnation predating both revisions.

Secretary Bullock, an active supporter of the Anderson faction from the start, simply accepted these rules and promulgated them. Chairman Orr, the major external constituent of the Brunson faction, faced an impossible dilemma:

> Each side thought that the other had double-crossed them. I don't think that Bill Anderson would have done this, but some of the others would. What was entered with the Secretary of State was in direct violation of what was agreed to, of what was passed.
>
> We didn't want the bad publicity. We didn't want to destroy the party, its unity. We could have changed them back. What should have been filed was what was in the minutes of the March meeting.
>
> I don't believe that the national party should dictate to the state party. The only reason the national party exists is because it is made up of fifty states. I wanted just enough rules to get seated. That's all. But people got stampeded. People are prone not to take a chance.
>
> You have a hard enough time as chairman of a state party. Anything you do, you make half of them mad. I didn't want to be the first one not to get my party seated. If you could recap it and make everybody understand what you were doing, but the rank-and-file would never understand.

The regular party leadership, after considering their options, acquiesced in the filing of the "wrong rules." The hour was desperately late, a fact which National Committeeman Strauss, normally an ally of Orr and Brunson, stepped back in to emphasize. The response of the SDEC, if it was reassembled for the same confused and acrimonious process, was no more certain than ever. The press, however, was very likely, or so the regulars felt, to side with the Anderson faction in interpreting these events. Brunson decided to take his satisfaction from having successfully uncoupled reform of delegate selection from reform of state party affairs:

> Legally, the rules were probably never adopted. Anderson would testify that what he filed was exactly what he had agreed on. I met with Roy Orr and several others, and we decided that the smart thing would be to forget it. We'd look like crybabies.
>
> There is a March 27 letter from me to Roy Orr, saying that the rules filed by six "minority members" have been filed. This kind of high-handedness is what more responsible members have had to contend with. They had a telegram from Preston Smith saying that he fully supported the Anderson draft.
>
> Our motive was to maintain and control the mechanics of the party machinery in Texas. We felt that we would have to do something other than what our

rules said on delegate selection in order to get a compromise. We were only fighting for half, but they were fighting for the whole loaf—and didn't know it.

In a final fillip to the entire struggle—one fully in keeping with events to date—the leaders of the regular party took their time in printing and distributing the newly adopted rules. As a result, Patman and her allies became alarmed again and rushed out with a private printing:

> Orr then refused to get the rules printed up. We were worried not just about whether he would print them, but whether they would print the real rules. Orr announces that he will have them printed up at two dollars apiece for interested Democrats. I printed up 5,000 copies which I announced through the press would sell for 5 cents apiece. I sold out right away. I printed another 3,000. Orr then drops his price to fifty cents.[35]

Implications

Reform politics in Texas brought together most of the developments—the backgrounds and outlooks, the incentives and pressures—which characterized the politics of implementation in its final days. Most of the die-hard resisters were organized parties, with a recognized stake in unreformed arrangements. As an organized party, southern style, the Texas Democracy had opposed national party reforms, publicly and vocally, from the beginning. Moreover, most of the die-hard resisters had *not* been the recipients of those common but crucial developments which had changed the course of reform politics in other, initially resistant states.

Again, Texas was a leading example. Texas did not get a new governor in the general election of 1970. Instead, it got a major governmental scandal, one which essentially put the state party to sleep from January to October. Texas did acquire a state statute demanding written party rules; it did acquire the reform commission which became the framework for serious reform negotiations. But for ten months during 1971, the State Democratic Executive Committee could not even meet, and the reform process was effectively moribund.

When the state party awoke after this ten-month hiatus, the political world outside had changed. The National Committee had adopted a Preliminary Call and then a Final Call to the 1972 Convention, containing the guidelines of the Party Structure Commission, verbatim. A majority of state parties were already in full, certified compliance with those guidelines, and more were coming in daily. The simple mathematics of compliance had become a powerful, indirect pressure for local party reform.

The regular party in Texas did not surrender easily. A new state chairman, who was determinedly hostile to reform, restated official opposition and packed the relevant party committee. Yet the very battle which installed him also expanded the opposing faction. This faction became the means for national reformers to enter Texas politics. National reformers determined not only to enter and secure conformity, but to impose conformity with *reinterpreted* national reforms.

A set of intricate negotiations ensued. These involved several reform packages. They involved several local factions, multiple factional leaders, and key freelance operators, to boot. Their interaction produced two national endorsements of local reform programs, one of which was partially retracted. This eventually culminated in last-minute, pen-and-pencil trading of key reform provisions. Yet all this resulted, ultimately, in the filing of an earlier, losing, reform package.

Even under these conditions, even with a conflictual process and a dramatic outcome, Texas did not reveal the full extent of efforts by the national commission to secure reinterpretations of the official reform text. Texas did confirm the extent to which the commission entourage was willing to practice creative revision, and thus the degree to which it was willing to reject the notion of interpretive self-restraint. These national reformers developed specific, extensive, and consequential reinterpretations all their own; they used the leverage in the certification process to press—indeed to impose—these reinterpretations upon the state political parties.

What even Texas did not reveal was the manner in which national actors, having reached an informal but strong consensus on the proper way to (re)translate major reform guidelines, went on to produce a new set of *procedural standards* to govern their own approach to state certification. By late 1971, the national entourage felt a need for some general precepts in this area, to respond to the situation in which state party leaders would finally agree to go along with (reinterpreted) national reforms, only to find themselves blocked by state law or by a state party constitution.

The problem of taking party rules preferred by the national commission through a hostile state legislature had been addressed first, in an official elaboration of "all feasible efforts."[36] Here, the full commission had determined that parallel, extralegal implementation could be enough to guarantee compliance and certification. From there, it was but a short step to the staff conclusion that it was sometimes wiser to ask the state party leadership to promulgate reform rules directly, rather than to risk those rules in the legislature. Carol Casey urged this approach for states as important as California:

> Once the bill was introduced, we didn't feel that it absolutely had to be by law. We felt that the candidate could still name the [slate-making] committee, but that the committee would then follow *party* rules. Our main concern was that if they went for passage and it failed, then they would go back to their old system, having made "all feasible efforts."

An even stronger ruling about the means to compliance was generated for states with a local party rule requiring a state party convention for changes of this significance. Here, the commission staff produced a legal opinion, to the effect that when the convening of a statewide convention was difficult, as judged by local party officials and national reform actors in consort, then adoption by the incumbent state committee would suffice.[37] Minnesota actually precipitated this opinion; proportionality was, in fact, the issue around which it revolved. Evasion of a state party convention, and the circuitous route around it, left substantial bad feeling among regular Democrats in Minnesota. But it did produce formal proportionality, and it did appear, to national staffers like Casey, as the only route to that outcome:

> Minnesota was the first state in which there would be a few things that didn't get through the state constitutional convention. We came up with an interpretation on this end that a state committee could adopt the rules and make it a standing rule of the party until the convention next met. We also did this in Arizona.

Nevertheless, reform politics in Texas offered most of the standard elements in the final maneuvering for national implementation and compliance, in a version, like that of Pennsylvania, perhaps a trifle larger than life. Yet this reform politics had one other characteristic, hardly the norm but hardly atypical either, which deserves some mention: It had been a "dirty business," almost from beginning to end, with numerous private understandings, public double-crosses, and the culminating "theft" of party reform through the filing of the wrong rules package.

Despite this sardonic summary, the situation in Texas was not all that different from the situation in Pennsylvania, where a late "deal" involving not just the substance of party rules but the dispersal of patronage had greased the way to success. Indeed, the situation in Texas was not all that different from the situation in many volunteer-party states. In Minnesota, for example, a final, impromptu meeting of the state committee, without the possibility of attendance by numerous absentees who were known to oppose proportionality, appended proportional rules to a previously adopted reform package. In California, participatory rules for delegate slating could not be pried out of legislative committees at all, but were eased—sneaked—through the legislature as an amendment from the flood during the flood of bills at the end of the session.

There is a familiar demonology to popular accounts of democratic politics—there are in fact two conflicting versions—which is available to explain such happenings. In one view, individuals who become rigidly attached to a desired outcome begin to believe that the end justifies the means. They are even willing, as in this case, *to steal reform*. In the other view, there are never any true ends in politics; there are only means. The extraction of party reform, accordingly, is propelled by the same mix of drives and motives as the extraction of anything else, and if the behavior of the people behind it turns out to be not much different from the behavior of those on the other side, that should come as no surprise.

Both of these explanations should probably remain at the level of demonology. Or at least, they are more useful as hypotheses about the human condition than as institutional analyses of particular politics. What the peculiar character of the reform resolution in so many states does suggest, however, is that there may be something inherent in democratic politics—that is, in a politics with many decentralized positions of formal power which must be knit together coalitionally in order to produce any given change—which leads most actors in that politics to adopt certain styles of behavior.

This inherent dynamic of democratic politics produces theoretical ironies for the observer of party reform and practical anxieties for the analyst of institutional change. It produces irony for the observer of reform politics because one side is invariably proposing changes based on the fact that the *other* side behaves in these ways—*and then goes on to secure those changes by behaving similarly*. It produces anxiety for the analyst of institutional change because the resulting reforms are invariably instituted in the belief that these behaviors, part of the essential character of democratic politics, *should not go on—and will not under reformed rules*. Texas, Pennsylvania, Minnesota, California—and who knows how many others?—all presented forceful instances of this fundamental pattern in reform politicking, a pattern productive of such strong theoretical irony and practical anxiety, too.

More concretely, the outcome in Texas offered powerful direct implications for the fate of institutional change. The mere acquiescence of Texas, of course, was a major contribution to the realization of reform nationwide. Texas was a large state; it was a reliably Democratic state; it was an ostentatious holdout against the tide of party reform. When it fell, that tide had evidently swept almost everything in its path.

Even more portentously, the acquiescence of Texas marked the point at which the original reform package, drafted by incipient reformers a full three years before, had been almost entirely realized within the national Democratic party. The major item here, of course, the item whose extraction brought the institutional change envisioned by party reformers to its maximum implementation for 1972, was formal proportional representation. Texas, as the largest convention state, as one of those most committed to majoritarian rules, and as the symbol of die-hard, last-ditch resistance, provided the main arena for testing the ability of national reformers to impose formal proportionality, as an informal reinterpretation, essentially on their own.

The triumph—the imposition—of proportionality in Texas, then, was a grand institutional change in its own right. Moreover, that triumph merely capped a set of smaller victories, bringing proportionality to a host of other, smaller states. This had been a goal of party reformers from the beginning. It had been thwarted in the major official arenas for reform politics, the Party Structure Commission and the National Committee. It was realized unofficially, once the full commission and the full committee were out of the way, by a committed band of national reformers left behind at commission headquarters.

Yet even proportionality was only the most impressive example of the drive by these remaining commission actors to reinterpret reformed rules. Right behind it, for example, was slate making, through the drive by these same actors to enforce newly elaborated, participatory rules for the construction of delegate slates. In fact, the two efforts were crucially and practically linked. Proportionality triumphed in the convention states when it conquered Texas. It did not triumph in the primary states when it could not conquer California. Yet the California case, too, became a tribute to the ability of commission reformers to reinterpret the requirements of reform, and thus to the extent of the institutional change ultimately imposed.

National reformers had begun with an attempt to impose formal proportionality on California as well.[38] But when state party actors would not budge, commission principals turned to the one other guideline, C–6 (Slate-Making), which gave them a chance to inject opportunities for elaborated participation into the California system of delegate selection. C–6 had been left in an ambiguous state. The commission entourage determined to capitalize on this ambiguity, to extend the guideline to presidential primaries, to limit the role of the candidates in delegate slating, and to create a whole new participatory mechanism, a preliminary public caucus *within* the presidential primary, whose decisions would merely be ratified by the subsequent primary vote. Casey recalled their shift:

The California caucus arrangement was developed for Wisconsin and Florida. We had already suggested it to Massachusetts. This became the accepted method. It was our usual way to do slate-making. This was in the Model Party Rules, which were earlier than the California discussion.

California party leaders were not enthusiastic about this arrangement either, but to their fundamental desire for certification was added the growing drift toward compliance nationwide and the adamant stand of national commission actors. The result was the imposition of by far the largest participatory caucuses of candidate supporters in the entire national party. The result was also a tribute to the success of the commission entourage in reinterpreting yet another major guideline, and in altering yet another major institution of delegate selection.[39]

Indeed, the California and Texas cases confirmed the realization of almost the full panoply of institutional changes originally desired by militant party reformers. Most of those changes, of course, had gone through the Party Structure Commission itself, and into *Mandate for Reform*, and then through the National Committee, essentially unamended. Four issues, however—demographics, proportionality, apportionment, and slating—had generated extended debate within the commission and had produced a compromise position, one subsequently endorsed by the committee, too.

Yet among these issues, only apportionment, which had to be addressed through the courts, had not been reinterpreted in line with the original position of militant reformers by early 1972. The National Women's Political Caucus, with a crucial assist from Don Fraser, the commission chairman, had secured the militant position on demographic representation. The remaining commission entourage had secured the militant position on proportional representation, at least within the convention states, and had gone on to add a militant reading of the requirements for slate-making as well.

The outcome was striking. Originally, the commission staff had wanted elaborately codified rules for delegate selection in every state party. By the time delegate selection began, it had achieved that, unequivocally. The fact of this codification was a historic breakthrough. The substance of that codification magnified the achievement. In 1969, the commission staff had wanted participatory institutions of delegate selection, their most crucial policy desire, including the substitution of candidate primaries for delegate primaries and of participatory conventions for party caucuses. By 1972, it had achieved this audacious goal, the bedrock of all the others, in all but three states.

Again in 1969, the commission staff had wanted full, formal, proportional representation, to go along with these new institutions. It had lost in the commission, a loss ratified by the National Committee. Yet by 1972, it had secured formal proportionality for many convention states, and for some primary states as well. In a similar fashion, the commission staff had wanted open, binding, public assemblies to slate the delegates for conventions and primaries. It had managed, by 1972, to overcome the ambiguity of the commission text and to come close to realizing its full, original desire in this realm, too.

Finally, the commission staff had toyed, at the very beginning, with explicit demographic requirements. Although it had backed away from that notion, the commissioners had kept the possibility alive; and in late 1971, the commission chairman had come back in and had converted ambiguous guidelines—and a difficult footnote—into formal demographic quotas. At that point, the revised structure for presidential selection, conceived originally by reform partisans, was essentially in place. The alternative coalition of Democratic elites, which supported and hoped to benefit from these reformed institutions, was largely in place as well. And there was little to do except conduct nomination campaigns under reformed procedures, and see what they produced.

If these rules worked as their framers hoped, they would facilitate the extension of party reform to the rest of the national party, including the Democratic National Committee. Moreover, if these rules worked as supporters hoped, they would simultaneously bring to power and then institutionalize the alternative Democratic coalition. These reforms were already the largest coordinated change in the mechanics of presidential selection since the development of the national party convention. They stood on the brink of being the vehicle for a major change in the entire character of presidential politics.

CONCLUSION

Politics after Reform: Institutional Change

and the Circulation of Elites, 1972–1984

IN WHICH, the constriction of the official party is shown to be the critical result of sweeping change in the mechanics of presidential selection; the roots of this change are traced to habitual patterns of party decision-making, wrongly applied; and the implications of this constriction for the character of party, and presidential, politics are elaborated. AND IN WHICH, the chronicle of reform politics is extended to the present in order to extract insights on recent political history; the concepts organizing the full chronicle—reform politics, institutional change, and the circulation of elites—are recast as the means for understanding contemporary American politics; and the reader is left to apply the resulting analysis to the American political future.

IOWA DEMOCRATS opened the actual nomination contest when they began selecting their delegates to the 1972 Convention in local precinct meetings on January 24, 1972. In doing so, they reaffirmed the goal of democratically selecting a president, in a process which had been occurring quadrennially for almost two hundred years. In doing so, they inaugurated extensively reformed procedures for selecting a president, which mark the modern era in presidential, and party, politics.

The surface details of the campaign which followed have been thoroughly recorded. Its actors, their encounters, and the strategies and tactics, issues and images, incidents and events along the way have all been logged in colorful detail in numerous contemporary accounts.[1] Yet there was another, more consequential politics—the politics of party reform—entwined with this campaign. This book has been the story of that other politics—how it came to be, how it came to be the way it was, and what this implies for American political life.

What was the upshot of this concentrated reform politics, when condensed to its essence and stripped of its nuances? *What did it all come down to?* At bottom, what had happened was the constriction—and at times the absolute elimination—of the regular party in the mechanics of delegate selection and presidential nomination. A catalog of individual reforms composed this outcome. But each reform was only another means by which the regular party had been constricted—at times erased—within the process of presidential selection.

How could a series of decisions *internal to the party itself* convert the regular party into a minor actor in presidential politics? *How could this happen?* Remarkably, party officials treated these critical choices about party reform—about the institutions of delegate selection—as they had treated most party choices stretching back a hundred years: as one more, separate and co-equal arena for decision, in which the most intensely interested participants were permitted to wield the greatest influence, even though they were wielding it over rules and procedures which could affect the outcome in numerous other arenas.

What did this imply for the shape of the American political future? *What did it all mean?* The formal changes were clearly the most extensive in 140 years; they were the most extensive *planned* changes in the entire history of American parties. Not surprisingly, their practical impact could be seen everywhere. It could be seen in the character of participants at the local level, in a shift from party officeholders to independent activists and from spokesmen for a blue-collar rank and file to members of a white-collar electorate. It could be seen in the nomination campaigns which linked this rank and file to the aspiring candidates, in a shift from party-based operations with a small candidate entourage to candidate-based operations in active and extended competition with the party. It could be seen in the identity of the candidates themselves, in a shift from party careerists to political insurgents, from insiders to outsiders.

Yet it was among the collection of continuing specialists in presidential and party politics, among those who manage campaigns and then become the major political appointees in subsequent governments, that the most dramatic and consequential impact occurred. There is a continuing group, an available population, almost a "political class," of these individuals. They are the crucial connection between the party rank and file and the presidential candidate—whether they reflect the wishes of that rank and file accurately or not. Their preferences will inevitably shape priorities among public issues, and policy solutions among those priorities.

When these individuals changed over *as a group* in the aftermath of party reform, when not just their personal identities but their attachments to larger social groups changed swiftly and strongly, that change testified to—and was itself—a fundamental reshaping of American national politics. Its arrival confirmed the significance of sweeping changes in the mechanics of presidential selection. At the same time, its arrival confirmed that many of the major actors from the coalition which had controlled the dominant party in American politics for the lifetime of most Americans had actually been eliminated—had disappeared—from the political scene.

The institutional arrangements underpinning this new era have been adjusted, amended, and fine-tuned in the years since 1972, and a few words on these subsequent adjustments are a necessary part of any conclusion. Yet a short summary of developments in the interim also supports an implicit premise behind the entire preceding reform narrative: That by any reasonable standard the quadrennium between 1968 and 1972, the focus of this book, was the critical round of reform politicking. It created the entire domain of reform politics; it gave that domain its principal direction; it was responsible for the bulk of all the practical changes which resulted.

Because this is so, the reform narrative, taken as a whole, constitutes an even larger argument about the shape of American politics or, indeed, of democratic politics in general. This chronicle, as presented, has been an argument that the politics surrounding the rules of the game is often more crucial than any of the politicking which occurs within them. It has been an argument that change in these political rules, at least when broad, deep, and theoretically consistent, can alter the character of the politicking which occurs within them as well. It has been an argument, finally, that the crucial aspect of this changed character is a change in the social identity—in the backgrounds, values, and beliefs—of the major supporting actors in democratic politics.

Fundamental Results of the Politics of Party Reform

What did the concentrated reform politics of 1968–1972 produce? What was the essential character of the formal change, the change in the mechanics of delegate selection and presidential nomination, produced by reform politics in this crucial quadrennium? The answer is deceptively simple. Yet it is affirmed in reform after reform, in guideline after guideline, imposed during this period and honed during the reform periods to follow. At bottom, the result of all these reforms was *the diminution, the constriction, at times the elimination, of the regular party in the politics of presidential selection.*

This result was evident in the basic institutions for selecting delegates, the bedrock of the entire institutional matrix for presidential nominations. Within the convention states, the party had moved from traditional party caucuses, where party officeholders came together to begin the process, to participatory conventions, where any professed Democrat could come out to participate and where party officeholders might be at an active disadvantage. At a stroke, then, the regular party had been unseated. Within the primary states, the party had moved from delegate primaries, where local notables—usually party or community leaders—had been selected under their own names, to candidate primaries, where the name of the contender was the dominant consideration and where the names of the delegates were not even necessarily presented. At a stroke, again, the guaranteed role of the regular party had been discarded.[2]

But what was true of this institutional bedrock was also true of the edifice built upon it. Thus, the reforms insisted that the slating of delegates to be selected under any of these institutions be removed from the hands of party officials and even, perhaps, from the hands of the candidates, to be lodged in open meetings of self-selected participants. At the same time, the reforms provided that party leaders would not be permitted to use the numerical dominance of the orthodox Democratic coalition to reassert control of the state delegation indirectly, through rules advantaging this majority; instead, the states would be pressed to operate through formal proportional representation. Finally, in a diagnostic expression of this entire drift, the reforms abolished ex officio seats to reward party service and introduced ex officio seats to recognize demographic categories—with the expectation that these guaranteed positions would not simply go to party officials who were young, female, or black.

Sometimes, under these conditions, the disappearance of the regular party was nearly total. Other times, it was a matter of converting the regular party into one more organized interest group in the contest for control of a presidential nomination—and not always the first among equals even then. In part, this restriction (and consequent practical diminution) was an inevitable result of taking the open and participatory, rather than the organized and disciplined, definition of party reform. In another part, this restriction reflected the explicit hostility of party reformers to the regular party and its leadership. Together, in any case, these two complementary thrusts were enough to reduce the role of the regular party in presidential politics, and at times to eliminate it.

That was surely their most consequential and direct impact upon the institutions of delegate—and presidential—selection. This fact has frequently been obscured by analysts who argue that "the party" is really composed of whoever participates in the mechanics of selecting delegates. But if the party is understood as it would be understood in most other developed countries, or if it is translated as it was usually translated in the United States before reform, as *the regular party,* then the upshot of this institutional change is clear, and the extent of the practical changes which follow from it becomes less surprising.

Along the way, in a less grand development which nevertheless reaches into the present day, the initial round of reform politics may have institutionalized the politics of party reform. At a minimum, events inside the national Democratic party converted the realm of party rules—the realm of the rules of delegate selection and presidential nomination—into a new policy arena with its own substantive issues, its own specialized actors, and its own distribution of influence, an arena where the most concerned and most highly mobilized had managed to secure their policy wishes and might hope to secure them again and again. This realm of party rules was at least sufficiently institutionalized to produce a new round of reform conflict in each period between national party conventions since 1972.[3]

None of this guarantees that one round of reform politics will succeed another on into the indefinite future. Yet reform activity has been such a reliable feature of the political lives of most individuals who are concerned with party or presidential politics for such a substantial period that a contrary prediction, the demise of party reform, is surely the more risky guess. Indeed, the reaction of individual states to the further reforms of 1980–1984, the latest round of party reform, suggests that there will be enough unanticipated consequences in presidential politics to produce yet another call for a succeeding round of reform politics between 1984 and 1988.

How did the concentrated reform politics of 1968–1972 produce these sweeping reforms, this sweeping institutional change, within the national Democratic party? How could that politics result in the constriction of the regular party, especially when most—almost all—of the key decisions in reform politics had to be taken by regular-party officials, inside the party itself? Again, the answer is deceptively simple. For it lies in a continuing pattern of decision-making within the regular party, a pattern which stretches back perhaps a hundred years and which was applied—and wrongly applied—to the particular incidents in reform politics between 1968 and 1972.

The fundamental pattern, the key to this puzzle of self-liquidation, has to do with a set of associated, continuing traditions in American party politics. These include a coalitional approach to party affairs and a brokerage approach to political leadership. They imply accommodation—"cutting the deal"—whenever possible. Calculations by participants in the politics of party reform which accord with this general pattern—recall again that the key negotiations during this period were conducted almost entirely within the regular party—were everywhere.

At the very beginning, at the 1968 Convention, when the politics of recommendation was launched, the fate of the reform resolutions which inaugurated official activity on party reform was explained largely by this fundamental approach to party decision-making. The 1968 Convention was determinedly regular in its political orientation; indeed, it was the last such convention in our era. Yet its dominant participants, regular-party delegates and leaders of the Humphrey campaign as well, while they could surely have defeated the Rules minority report as they had defeated all other minority reports at the convention, did not mobilize against it. And they did not do so because they wanted to provide a sop to the losing side, in the hope that it might be brought around for the general election; because they felt that the reform realm was comparatively inconsequential, especially if they continued to control the party after the convention; and because they viewed this sort of compensation as an appropriate part of ongoing politics.

Two and a half years later, at the beginning of what became the politics of implementation, when there was a reform report calling for sweeping institutional change and when a new national chairman, Larry O'Brien, had to decide what to do about that report, the same general calculations came into play. O'Brien was not enthusiastic about the contents of this report, and he found himself in a position where he could easily emasculate, even annihilate, those contents within the National Committee, the keystone structure of the regular party. Yet he decided that this would needlessly alienate the reform minority, which cared about the fate of this report above all; he decided that the party needed some reform rules and that these would do as well (or as badly) as any; and he judged that a parceling out of available rewards—recall "personnel to the regulars, rules to the reformers"—was not just a sensible but an appropriate way to do party business. At what was potentially a turning point in the politics of party reform, then, sweeping institutional change was saved once more.

Analytic accounts of party behavior have highlighted these same tendencies for decades, not always admiringly. In these accounts, the parties are said to be remarkably open to penetration by significant, focused interests. Orthodox party leaders are described as believing that *everything* can be bargained out. Anecdotal accounts are effectively parallel, and a good deal juicier. Politely, they assert that in politics it is better to deal everyone in that to foster conflicts which may be deleterious to all. Impolitely, they say that it is worth buying opponents off, as long as the cost is not too high.[4]

Between 1968 and 1972, the particular application of this general calculus of appeasement was still strongly colored by events, like the elections of 1970, which created so many new Democratic governors with an incipient sympathy for reform. It was still strongly colored by the individuals who got to make the key decisions, like Chairman Harris and then Chairman O'Brien. But it was not an alien calculus in and of itself. Indeed, in the most general sense, regular party leaders were only acting in character, a character built up over decades, when they went along—fingers crossed, whistling in the dark—with the local implementation of national guidelines for state delegate selection, and with the most extensive planned reform of party procedures in American political history.

The intervening years have seen those reforms extended rather than re-trenched. This is clearest with the basic institutions of delegate selection, the institutional underpinnings for the entire process of presidential nomination. For 1976, the few remaining holdouts, those few states which had refused to change from the delegate primary to the candidate primary or from the party caucus to the participatory convention, were defeated and corraled. For 1980, there was nothing further to gain. The same is true, however, for most other institutional areas, like the area of the rules allocating delegates among presidential contenders. For 1976, the winner-take-all rule was outlawed completely, removing it from presidential politics within the Democratic party. For 1980, the districted rule, the one by which delegates are elected directly but by smaller districts, was outlawed as well, leaving only three states with anything other than formal proportional representation.[5]

Each of these extensions has practical impacts of its own. Yet all have essentially continued the drift of institutional change imparted between 1968 and 1972. All thus underline the essential point about the impact of the first round of party reform: that it restricted, and often removed, the regular party from the mechanics of presidential selection. Each of these subsequent developments, from 1972 through 1980, takes that central development further. If the official party was in sad straits for 1972, then, those straits became sadder for 1976, and sadder still for 1980.

The Changing Shape of American Politics

What was the contribution of reformed institutions of delegate selection to the practical character of presidential politics in the aftermath of systematic implementation and compliance? Stated differently, how have these reforms shaped contemporary American politics? The reforms at issue were wide and deep. They were based upon a particular theoretical approach to party politics—one sharply divergent from existing practice. They were centrally planned, nationally imposed, and historically unprecedented. Not surprisingly, practical impacts from such extensive change could be seen—and experienced—at every level.[6]

These impacts could be seen at the local level, at the "grass roots." Before reform, there was an American party system in which one party, the Republicans, was primarily responsive to white-collar constituencies and in which another, the Democrats, was primarily responsive to blue-collar constituencies. After reform, there were two parties each responsive to quite different white-collar coalitions, while the old blue-collar majority within the Democratic party was forced to try to squeeze back into the party once identified predominantly with its needs. The class base of the two elite coalitions contending over party reform, the orthodox and the alternative Democratic coalitions, had hinted at this. But it was the institutional structure they produced, and its impact on the rank-and-file membership of the Democratic party, which ultimately created the effect.

The implementation of thorough and complete institutional arrangements on the participatory model did mean that there were far more opportunities for mass participation. In turn, the total number of direct participants rose tremendously; the multiplication of presidential primaries alone would have guaranteed this. Yet the *opportunity* for direct participation was also a *requirement* of participation if the individual was to acquire influence. And there, the character of new political institutions ran up against the—perhaps immutable—character of continuing social life.

Turnout in primary elections has always been lower than turnout at the general election; turnout in party conventions has always been lower even than turnout in primaries. Moreover, turnout in all three forums has always been clearly and sharply related to social background—to social class, to the distinction between blue-collar and white-collar occupations and neighborhoods, outlooks and values—and it has always favored white-collar elements. When intensive participatory arrangements were imposed upon the national Democratic party—an essentially blue-collar party—the potential for redirecting that party toward the concerns of its white-collar minority was instantly created. That potential was realized within months through some of the critical contests of 1972. It has been an ever-present threat, sometimes as a shaping influence, sometimes as the decisive one, in every contest since.[7]

Similarly major but informal effects on the organization of nomination campaigns, the campaigns which link the general public with the candidates and with other elite actors in presidential politics, followed with similar rapidity.

Once the institutional structure of delegate selection had been changed so that the regular party did not have an automatic claim on the nomination process, and once regular party officials could not be courted as the logical route to a nomination, candidates were automatically encouraged to build campaign organizations of their own. Indeed, the creation of open arenas for delegate selection in almost every state, where any candidate could build a campaign in principle, meant that every candidate needed to do so in actual practice.

The possibility still existed that the candidate whose nomination campaign was constructed of the greatest share of the regular party would succeed in becoming the nominee; he might, at least, have a comparatively easier time building his campaign organization. But the possibility that most campaigns would be independently constructed and would now be competing with, rather than courting, the regular party had simultaneously been *guaranteed*, thanks to reforms which removed the official party from the mechanics of delegate selection and which then reduced the influence of the blue-collar constituencies which had long provided the social base for that party.[8]

Developments at the top of the campaign, among the contenders themselves, confirmed the sweeping impact of participatory institutions of delegate selection. For they confirmed the reach of these reformed party rules into the political characteristics even of the eventual nominees themselves. And they began to introduce the massive change in the character of the other actors in national politics associated with this impact.

Neither George McGovern, the nominee of 1972, nor Jimmy Carter, the nominee and president of 1976 and the nominee again in 1980, would—almost could—have been nominated under unreformed rules. The idea of classifying this fact as one more aspect of "the circulation of elites" may be an unfamiliar one; the events in question are all too familiar. Under an unreformed set of institutional arrangements for selecting delegates, especially given the existing preferences of party officials across the country, McGovern was an implausible selection as the Democratic nominee for president in 1972. With those same leadership preferences but under a reformed party structure, he was, of course, the nominee.

Moreover, and more crucially, had there been an unreformed set of institutional arrangements for selecting delegates in 1976, especially given the existing preferences of party officials around the country, *Jimmy Carter* was an even more unlikely selection as the Democratic standard-bearer. Under a reformed party structure, he was first a nominee, then a president. Indeed, after the extension and consolidation of party reform in the election laws of state after state, it was possible, with caution, to extend the analysis to the *Republican* party. Or at least, given the existing preferences of Republican party officials and an unreformed process of delegate selection, Ronald Reagan would almost surely have failed to mount a serious challenge to the sitting president, Gerald Ford, in 1976. That failure, in turn, would at least have made his successful run in 1980 far more problematic.[9]

So much is generally conceded. Yet this most obvious, and obviously significant, fallout from institutional reform coincides with, but partially masks, the more fundamental reconstruction in presidential politics which went on beneath it, at the level of those specialized political actors who make up nomination campaigns and then staff the presidential governments which sometimes follow. Gradually, during the politics of party reform which preceded the nomination campaigns of 1972, an alternative coalition of Democratic elites had been carpentered together. By 1972, the gap—the chasm—between this alternative coalition and an orthodox Democratic counterparty was as extreme as that gap is likely to get in situations which cannot themselves be described as revolutionary.

The alternative Democratic coalition was built on some existing dissident elements within the national party, like the established reform factions and the active participants in the losing nomination campaigns of 1968. It expanded by stripping off a few elements intermittently allied with the orthodox coalition, like the established liberal interest groups. It added some totally new elements which came to organizational life only during this period, like the new feminist and explicit reform organizations. And it emerged to face an orthodox Democratic counterpart, consisting principally of the regular party and organized labor. Racial minorities, the alleged remaining element in *both* coalitions, were somewhat divided between them, although in truth it was mostly their leadership which was divided, while the rank and file remained solidly inside the orthodox coalition.

It is worth stopping to emphasize what was, and was not, new in this. Nomination contests in which such clear-cut, extended, and mutually hostile grand coalitions oppose each other *are* a comparative rarity. Yet they do appear, and when they do, they ordinarily contain the seeds of their own resolution: The orthodox coalition will triumph, perhaps adding some elements of the alternative coalition after the nomination to prevent a recurrence of similar, extended divisions. If by some chance the *alternative* coalition triumphs, its candidate will lose the general election, and the orthodox coalition will resume the machinery of power, adding some elements from the alternative coalition and sending the rest into the political wilderness.[10]

What was different for 1972, of course, was a revolutionary change in the mechanics of delegate selection and in the process of presidential selection which followed. This meant that the normal odds on the triumph of the ortho-dox coalition had been altered, more sharply than all but the most perceptive analysts understood. It meant that the possibilities for that coalition to reassert control over the machinery of presidential selection were also far more limited than those same analysts, or than party professionals, realized. By 1972, then, the preconditions for a watershed in American party politics—an engineered watershed, no less—were clearly in existence.

And the rest, as the old saw rightfully notes, is history. The immediate result was one of the few cases falling outside the traditional pattern of nomination politics. The continuing result was nothing less than the transformation of the elite stratum in presidential politics, that collection of specialized political actors who mount campaigns and who staff the presidential administrations which follow. When George McGovern, the eventual champion of the alter-native coalition, secured the Democratic nomination for president, the more extended members of the coalition itself secured enough influence to prevent major changes in their preferred arrangements for presidential selection. When McGovern was succeeded four years later by Jimmy Carter, as the next product of reformed presidential politics, the stage was set for a far more exten-sive replacement of elite political actors in the national Democratic party and, this time, in the national government as well.

In this, it was the original distinction between orthodox and alternative Democratic coalitions which continued and which came again to the political forefront when McGovern was replaced by Carter as the standard-bearer for the national Democratic party. That distinction, in turn, was transmitted through the elite actors populating the presidential campaigns (which were now independent of the regular party) and then gaining the politically ap-pointive positions in a new presidential administration. As a result, it was ulti-mately Carter, not McGovern, who brought the alternative Democratic coali-tion into the White House, into the federal executive branch, and even, through unusual opportunities for judicial appointments, into the courts.

The precise pool of presidential activists which Jimmy Carter brought to power with him in 1976—and again, it was the *Carter campaign* which at-tested to the real change in the character of national elites within the Demo-cratic party, as it was the *Carter administration* which brought these new elites to power nationally—might not have overlapped person by person with the alternative coalition forged during 1968–1972. Yet the overlap between gen-eral populations of political actors, between the types of active individuals in the McGovern and Carter campaigns as characterized by their social back-grounds, their political experiences, and their organizational ties, was great indeed.

George Wallace, in 1976, tried to pillory Jimmy Carter by describing him as "southern-fried McGovern." That was clearly wrong. But had he focused on the major actors in the Carter campaign and had he come back to comment on the personnel decisions of the Carter administration, he could have found substantial evidence to support his comparison. For in large part, the rise of Jimmy Carter confirmed the extent of elite replacement in national politics, by testifying to the character and continuity of the national political elites associated with reform politics and institutional change. The independent activists and associated interest groups which rallied to the Carter campaign were the logical progeny, the direct descendants—some were the same individuals—of the alternative Democratic coalition which had rallied to George McGovern, albeit mixed a trifle differently, as all nomination campaigns are.[11]

This fact, too, was frequently obscured by analysts who concentrated on the differences in public ideology between McGovern and Carter. McGovern was probably the most liberal of the Democratic nominees since Franklin Roosevelt affirmed what became the orthodox Democratic coalition. Carter was probably the most conservative in that same multigenerational stretch. Clearly, it was not explicit ideology which connected the two men.

Instead, it was institutional arrangements and, especially, elite coalitions. For the Carter campaign was every bit as independent of the regular party as that of George McGovern. It was every bit as *dependent* on reformed institutional arrangements for its ultimate success. And it was every bit as reflective of the basic distinctions between elites in presidential politics which the original split over party reform had identified. It required a Carter campaign and a Carter administration to show that this basic distinction was not just a matter of surface differences from one campaign year to the next. Instead, the distinction was so fundamental that it would recur year after year. Moreover, it was so closely tied to new institutional arrangements that one side within it should triumph year after year as well, unless those arrangements themselves were changed.

Between 1968 and 1972, it was possible to believe that the essential difference between the orthodox and the alternative coalitions of Democratic elites was between liberalism and radicalism, between, as symbols, Hubert Humphrey on the one hand and George McGovern on the other. The arrival of Jimmy Carter, with the same type of campaign organization and a new sample of the same population of elite supporters as McGovern, should have disabused most observers of that notion. Indeed, the original, underlying distinction between the orthodox and the alternative Democratic coalitions should have disabused those observers from the first. That distinction was between an aggregation of blue-collar versus white-collar constituencies. The notion that blue-collar coalitions are conservative while white-collar coalitions are liberal ought, initially, to have given everyone pause.

That it did not was in part a reflection of the more subtle distinctions required at the elite level. Leading spokesmen for the groups in both coalitions, after all, were evidently white-collar. Yet when the focus was the social background of the individuals composing the *constituency* for these elites—the constituency for the regular party versus the constituency for reform factions, the constituency for organized labor versus the constituency for ideological and reform groups, the constituency for the civil rights organizations versus that for organized feminists—the difference was clear, indeed stark.

The significance of these distinctions should not be overdrawn, even in extrapolation. Both Jimmy Carter and George McGovern—and Hubert Humphrey and Lyndon Johnson, for that matter—would have seen their political agendas determined in part by events outside the control of any president. Both Carter and McGovern—and Humphrey and Johnson—would have found a need to alter those agendas further in order to address the desires of other political actors, in the Congress, in the states, in the major interest groups, and so on. The character of the elite coalitions which they brought to power with them would have modified but not eliminated these fundamental constraints of political life.

Yet day in and day out, in the myriad smaller decisions of national politics, the substitution of an alternative for an orthodox Democratic coalition, especially when these coalitions did have profound and continuing differences, was likely to have a profound and continuing effect. Indeed, the substitution of one elite coalition for the other in the national party and the national government was likely, in short order, to shape even the way external events and other political actors were perceived and handled. For these crucial intermediary elites, these links between the general public and its political institutions, had a clear set of issue concerns and beliefs about politics and social life which they brought with them when they entered party, and then public, office. And these differed sharply from the counterpart concerns and beliefs of the old, orthodox, Democratic coalition.

Some of these differences in issue concerns and political beliefs were obvious, being inherent in the organizational ties of new party and governmental appointees. Thus, a significant subset of the alternative Democratic coalition, a subset likely to be appointed to the precisely relevant substantive positions, was fundamentally concerned with feminist issues, in the same way that the counterpart subset of the orthodox Democratic coalition had been concerned with racial issues above all.

Others of these differences in concerns and beliefs were rooted more generally in the distinction between a blue-collar and a white-collar coalition. The new appointees from the alternative Democratic coalition were likely, for example, to be concerned with the quality of life in general and with the state of the natural environment in particular, in the same way that their counterpart from the orthodox Democratic coalition had been concerned with economic welfare in general and with economic progress and growth in particular.

Some of these differences were rooted more in the way the alternative and orthodox coalitions were connected to local communities. The orthodox coalition had constructed its candidacies (and governments) from the regular party and from associated community leaders; the alternative coalition staffed its campaigns (and governments) from independent activists and issue-based organizations with an explicitly national focus. Thus, the relevant subset of the alternative coalition was likely to be concerned with rights and liberties, where their counterparts from the orthodox coalition had been more concerned with public order and the control of crime.

Finally, some of these differences in issue concerns and political perceptions derived even more indirectly from a difference in social milieu. In foreign affairs, for example, the members of the alternative coalition were among those more likely to concentrate on seeing the United States live by its official values when addressing other nations, while leaving those nations free to pursue their own destinies. The members of the orthodox coalition, by contrast, had been among those demonstrably more likely to concentrate on pursuing American interests abroad and on actively opposing developments inimical to the emergence of democratic regimes.

As 1984 approaches, what can be said about the permanence or transience of all these changes in the character of national party politics? In other words, should the changes introduced by way of institutional reform during the period between 1968 and 1980 be treated as the new shape of national politics or only as an extended and consequential but ultimately diversionary interval in the underlying course of American history? These questions gain pointedness from the character of the most recent round of party reform. The two rounds after 1972, those between 1972 and 1976 and between 1976 and 1980, were clearly dominated by the same concerns, and by some of the same actors, as the initial round. They largely consolidated developments evident from that earlier period. The round between 1980 and 1984, however, has been just as clearly characterized, though hardly dominated, by a reaction to some of the resulting developments. For the first time, serious, countervailing efforts at institutional reform have appeared.

For 1984, individual states will be permitted, for example, to move away from full, formal, proportional representation and back to the direct election of delegates by district. States must still pass the appropriate legislation; as this is written, few have. Moreover, for 1984, there will be an increase in the total of ex officio delegates at the national convention, to 14 percent, with the selection of these delegates entirely from public and party officeholders. This is the change which has aroused the most controversy; it *will* be implemented as designed; it is trumpeted as a means to bring the official party back into the nomination process.

This ballyhoo is probably out of all proportion to the real effect of the change. For this new cadre of ex officio delegates has been not so much introduced into the process of presidential selection as tacked onto the end. Ex officio delegates created in this fashion are not as likely to shape the course of presidential politics as they are to affirm its outcome. Only intransigent participants would overthrow an evolving consensus on the emerging winner at the final moment; party and public officeholders are the least likely aspirants for the role of intransigent.

These emendations, of course, in no way lessen the contributions of reform politics and institutional change to the political outcomes of the years between 1968 and 1984. Those impacts were real, from top to bottom. They have long since been logged into American political life, and into political history. Moreover, these lesser adjustments—these tinkerings, really—have left the reformed structure of delegate selection basically intact. If there is to be reaction and recovery, then, it has not yet arrived. Finally, several aspects of the practical politics of presidential nomination have changed so dramatically during the intervening years that they may be incapable of restoration, even with more drastic institutional adjustments.

One tribute to the extent of the change in the character of presidential politics, an obvious but a powerful one, is the decline of the distinction between "regulars" and "reformers," among the aspirants for a presidential nomination and among the elite actors who support them. After a period in which a liberal party insurgent, George McGovern, and a conservative party insurgent, Jimmy Carter, have been party standard-bearers, "regularity" itself is a vanishing concept. Indeed, when defined by the backgrounds, incentives, and ways of looking at politics which typified party regulars in 1968, there are few serious regulars in evidence at all.

Extended consideration would surely produce additional examples of aspects of the informal politics of presidential selection which have changed so dramatically as to be incapable of restoration. Yet the summary point remains the same: The fundamental changes introduced in the original round of reform politics and fine-tuned in the interim continue essentially undisturbed. They may yet prove to have been contributors to an aberrational period in presidential politics, from 1968 to 1984. But the evidence supporting that interpretation is still to emerge.

Final Implications

The politics of party reform surrounding all this received precious little attention during the time it was unfolding, and surprisingly little in the period since. In that sense, it surely deserves to be dubbed "quiet." Yet this politics produced sweeping institutional change in the mechanics of delegate selection, and hence of presidential selection, too. And it produced, over a succession of elections, extensive circulation of political elites, that is, extensive change in the backgrounds, experiences, perceptions, and values of the major actors in presidential politics. In that sense, it is properly described as a "revolution."

In the longest run, of course, greater social changes—international conflicts, economic dislocations, demographic upheavals, technological breakthroughs, even new national ideologies—may rise and overwhelm the impact of this institutional change and this elite circulation. Such changes, at least, hold that potential. Yet the converse is equally true, and perhaps more to the point. For in the absence of social developments sufficient to revolutionize political life in the United States, this institutional change and this elite replacement are real occurrences, on a historic scale. They are increasingly likely to be the shaping factors for the course of national politics. They retain some potential even for determining the response of national political actors to other, external, social upheavals in demography, technology, economics, or foreign affairs.

A concentrated reform politics of the sort occurring between 1968 and 1972 is itself a rarity. The emergence of planned institutional change of the scope arising from that reform politics, and the appearance of alternative elite coalitions focused on that institutional change in such extended and clear-cut opposition, must be counted rarer still. When the side of systematic reform triumphs, when the proposed institutional change reaches full implementation, and when an extensive, aspiring, alternative coalition comes to power by means of this sweeping institutional reform, the hallmarks of a development of consequence are present, and the events in question almost call out for sustained inquiry.

Between 1968 and 1972, all of these rare events did occur within the national Democratic party. Moreover, if all these events are both massive and rare, it must be counted an additional, massive peculiarity that they occurred in such a quiet, unattended, almost offhand manner. Yet they did. And when they had occurred, the immediate course of presidential politics was noticeably, powerfully different. And when it was, the promise of a restructuring of national politics itself was in the air, in a way it had not been before reform.

Summary of the Official Guidelines

of the Commission on Party Structure

and Delegate Selection

A–1   Discrimination on the Basis of Race, Color, Creed, or National Origin

Requires that the six basic elements from the Special Equal Rights Committee be added to all state party rules

Requires affirmative steps to overcome past discrimination, including minority presence in the state delegation in reasonable relationship to group presence in the state as a whole

A–2   Discrimination on the Basis of Age or Sex

Requires affirmative steps to overcome past discrimination, including presence of young people (ages 18–30) and women in reasonable relationship to their presence in the state as a whole

Requires state parties to allow Democrats aged 18–30 to participate in all party affairs

A–3   Voter Registration

Urges each state party to assess the burdens of state law, custom, or practice, as outlined in the report of the Grass Roots Subcommittee, and to remove or alleviate such barriers

A–4   Costs and Fees; Petition Requirements

Urges removal of all costs and fees in the delegate selection process; requires removal of all fees over $10, of all mandatory assessments on delegates and alternates, and of all fees which would constitute a strain on the individual

Requires removal of all petition requirements in excess of 1% of the standard for measuring Democratic strength for any delegate candidacies

A–5   Existence of Party Rules

Requires state parties to adopt and make readily available rules which describe the delegate selection process with detail and clarity; lists seven specific aspects which such rules should include

Requires rules which will facilitate maximum participation

Requires explicit written rules with uniform dates and times for all meetings in the delegate selection process; exempts rural areas if dates and times are uniform within the geographic area

B–1   Proxy Voting

Requires state parties to forbid the use of proxy voting in all procedures for delegate selection

B–2   Clarity of Purpose

Requires state parties to make clear to voters how any given party process contributes to the presidential nomination

Requires state parties to designate the delegate selection process as distinct from other party business

B–3   Quorum Provisions

Requires that state parties adopt a quorum of not less than 40% for all committees involved in the delegate selection process

B–4   Selection of Alternates; Filling of Delegate and Alternate Vacancies

Requires state parties to prohibit the selection of alternates by the delegate himself or by the state chairman

Requires state parties to fill all vacancies thorough a timely and representative party committee, a reconvening of the original selection body, or the selection of the delegation itself

B–5   Unit Rule

Requires state parties to forbid the unit rule and the practice of instructing delegates to vote against their preferences at any stage of the delegate selection process

B–6   Adequate Representation of Minority Views on Presidential Candidates at Each Stage in the Delegate Selection Process

Urges each state party to provide for fair representation of minority views on presidential candidates; recommends that the 1972 Convention require such representation to the highest level of the process

543

Suggests that such representation be accomplished either by dividing delegate votes according to presidential strength or by selecting delegates from fairly apportioned districts; promises to stimulate additional discussion

B–7   Apportionment

Requires state parties to apportion delegates to the national convention on a formula giving equal weight to total population and prior Democratic vote for President

Requires convention states to select at least 75% of their delegates at the district level or below; requires convention states to apportion lower-level delegates by population and/or some measure of Democratic strength

C–1   Adequate Public Notice

Requires convention states to circulate a concise public statement of the relationship between ongoing party business and delegate selection

Requires primary states to identify the presidential preference of candidates for delegate and of candidates for any party committee which selects delegates; requires placement of "uncommitted" designation next to the names of those who do not reveal a preference

C–2   Automatic (Ex Officio) Delegates

Requires state parties to repeal rules which provide for ex officio delegates

C–3   Open and Closed Processes

Urges state parties to provide for easy access and frequent opportunity for party enrollment by unaffiliated voters and non-Democrats

C–4 Premature Delegate Selection (Timeliness)

Requires that all activities of delegate selection occur within the calendar
   year of the Convention
Requires state parties to prohibit officials elected or appointed before the
   calendar year from choosing nominating committees or proposing or endorsing a slate of delegates, even when challenge procedures exist

C–5 Committee Selection Processes

Requires state parties to publicize the delegate selection role (if any) of the
   state committee at the time of its election
Requires state parties to limit delegates chosen in this fashion to not more
   than 10% of the state total; recommends that state parties not permit any
   part of the delegation to be selected by party committees

C–6 Slate Making

Requires state parties to extend to the process of nominating delegates all
   guarantees of full and meaningful opportunity to participate which apply
   to the delegate selection process
Requires any slate-making body to observe adequate public notice, easy access to participation, and right to challenge the result, with the proviso
   that a slate bearing the name of a presidential candidate be assembled
   with due consultation with that candidate or his representatives

APPENDIX

B

Roster of Personal Interviews

Thomas P. Alder, Washington, D.C.
Sigmund Arywitz, Los Angeles, California
Richard J. Aurelio, New York, New York
Charles J. Backstrom, Minneapolis, Minnesota
Don Bailey, Greensburg, Pennsylvania
Alexander E. Barkan, Washington, D.C.
Joseph M. Barr, Pittsburgh, Pennsylvania
Elmer C. Baum, Austin, Texas
Samuel H. Beer, Cambridge, Massachusetts
Meyer Berger, Pittsburgh, Pennsylvania
Kenneth A. Bode, Washington, D.C., and Easton, Maryland
Jessie Bourneuf, New York, New York
John S. Brunson, Houston, Texas
Joseph A. Califano, Washington, D.C.
M. R. Callahan, San Francisco, California
Billy Joe Camp, Montgomery, Alabama
Collin J. Carl, Austin, Texas
Billie J. Carr, Houston, Texas
Carol F. Casey, Washington, D.C.
William L. Cavala, Berkeley, California
Joseph Cerrell, Los Angeles, California
Richard Chapman, Philadelphia, Pennsylvania
Warren M. Christopher, Los Angeles, California
William J. Connell, Washington, D.C.
Geoffrey Cowan, Los Angeles, California
Horace J. Culbertson, Lewistown, Pennsylvania

Lanny J. Davis, Washington, D.C.
Russell W. Davis, Harrisburg, Pennsylvania
William Dodds, Washington, D.C.
John Donhoff, Mill Valley, California
Joseph A. Doorley, Providence, Rhode Island
Frederick Dutton, Washington, D.C.
Henry F. Fischer, Minneapolis, Minnesota
Donald M. Fraser, New York, New York
Joseph Freitas, Jr., San Francisco, California
Verrick O. French, Washington, D.C.
JoAnn Evans Gardner, Pittsburgh, Pennsylvania
Molly Yard Garrett, Pittsburgh, Pennsylvania
Elizabeth S. Gatov, Kentfield, California
Rhoda Grant, Minneapolis, Minnesota
Stanley L. Greigg, Washington, D.C.
John Harmon, Harrisburg, Pennsylvania
Forrest J. Harris, Minneapolis, Minnesota
Robert Hauge, Houston, Texas
G. W. Holsinger, San Mateo, California
Koryne E. Horbal, St. Paul, Minnesota
Harry Hubbard, Austin, Texas
Leonid Hurwicz, Minneapolis, Minnesota
Molly Ivins, Austin, Texas
Haynes Johnson, Washington, D.C.
Michael Johnson, Philadelphia, Pennsylvania
Geraldine M. Joseph, Minneapolis, Minnesota
Michael J. Jurasinski, Reading, Pennsylvania
Max M. Kampelman, Washington, D.C.
Gerald Kaufman, Harrisburg, Pennsylvania
Thomas A. Kelm, St. Paul, Minnesota
Virginia Kerr, Philadelphia, Pennsylvania
Richard C. Leone, Trenton, New Jersey
Emma Long, Austin, Texas
Stuart M. Long, Austin, Texas
Eugene E. J. Maier, Philadelphia, Pennsylvania
AnnaMaria Malloy, Valley Forge, Pennsylvania
Charles T. Manatt, Los Angeles, California
Frank Mankiewicz, Washington, D.C.
Martin Matthews, Richardson, Texas
Oscar H. Mauzy, Austin, Texas

Alpha Maxey, Roseville, Minnesota
Anthony J. May, Canton, Ohio
George S. McGovern, Washington, D.C.
William R. McGrann, Jr., Minneapolis, Minnesota
Doris J. Meissner, Washington, D.C.
George J. Mitchell, Portland, Maine
Richard Moe, Washington, D.C.
Jerrold V. Moss, Philadelphia, Pennsylvania
Stewart R. Mott, New York, New York
Sterling Munro, Washington, D.C.
Victor S. Navasky, New York, New York
Robert W. Nelson, Washington, D.C.
Gerald A. New, Chambersburg, Pennsylvania
Donald E. Nicoll, Durham, New Hampshire
William A. Obricki, Pittsburgh, Pennsylvania
Lawrence F. O'Brien, New York, New York
James G. O'Hara, Washington, D.C.
Roy L. Orr, DeSota, Texas
Carrin M. Patman, Austin, Texas
James L. Pederson, St. Paul, Minnesota
John Perkins, Washington, D.C.
John E. Powers, Boston, Massachusetts
Joseph Quinn, Los Angeles, California
Norval D. Reece, Harrisburg, Pennsylvania
Stephen Reinhardt, Beverly Hills, California
Gerald I. Roth, Allentown, Pennsylvania
David Rowe, St. Paul, Minnesota
John N. Scales, Greensburg, Pennsylvania
Richard M. Scammon, Washington, D.C.
Eli J. Segal, New York, New York
Phyllis N. Segal, New York, New York
Marvin S. Shapiro, Los Angeles, California
William K. Shearer, Lemon Grove, California
Harlan M. Smith, Roseville, Minnesota
Margaret Smith, Roseville, Minnesota
Charles Snider, Montgomery, Alabama
Ann B. Solem, Mill Valley, California
Warren R. Spannaus, St. Paul, Minnesota
Richard G. Stearns, Boston, Massachusetts
Ronald Steiger, Houston, Texas

ROSTER OF PERSONAL INTERVIEWS

John G. Stewart, Washington, D.C.
Dennis E. Thiemann, Harrisburg, Pennsylvania
Hall E. Timanus, Houston, Texas
Terry S. Utterback, Los Angeles, California
Robert S. Vance, Birmingham, Alabama
John Vento, Penn Hills, Pennsylvania
Richard C. Wade, New York, New York
Carmen H. Warschaw, Los Angeles, California
Ben J. Wattenberg, Washington, D.C.
Jack R. Weinrauch, Harrisburg, Pennsylvania
William B. Welsh, Washington, D.C.
Kenneth S. Wendler, Austin, Texas
Jean M. Westwood, Washington, D.C.
Anne Wexler, Washington, D.C.
Wynelle W. White, Austin, Texas
Marilyn A. Young, Wyncote, Pennsylvania

Acknowledgments and Methods

THE NARRATIVE of *Quiet Revolution* begins with a meeting in West Hartford, Connecticut. But the story of that narrative begins with a drive to the San Francisco airport. One of my stray assignments during time spent as a research assistant at the University of California at Berkeley was to see that Austin Ranney, then of the University of Wisconsin at Madison but previously a Party Structure commissioner, caught his plane. En route, Austin piqued my curiosity about reform politics, an act whose consequences neither he nor I could foresee. I continued to work on a doctoral dissertation on urban political organizations, but only, in truth, until I could extract a tiny budget for travel and xerox from the Institute of Governmental Studies, courtesy of the Director, Eugene Lee. James Lengle, my fellow graduate student, and I went to Washington on the classic shoestring—cheap hotel, bad food, no taxis—and discovered a treasure chest (really thirty cardboard boxes) of artifacts from the politics of party reform.

These were the papers of the Commission on Party Structure and Delegate Selection, the McGovern-Fraser Commission. They may be among the most complete archival resources on any political operation of consequence, and for a peculiar reason: They were slated to be destroyed. The entire printed record of the commission, including not just originals and drafts of working documents but internal memoranda and personal jottings as well, was never "cleaned." Instead, it was put out for the trashman behind the Democratic National Committee, in order to conserve space for the 1972 presidential campaign. William Crotty of Northwestern University, erstwhile consultant to the reform commission, rescued these materials and hauled them for temporary accession to the National Archives. In doing so, he joined Austin Ranney as a crucial indirect influence on *Quiet Revolution*.

This material was enough to turn curiosity into obsession. Mary Walton Livingston of Presidential Libraries at the National Archives introduced me to the entire collection and led me through it in a consistently supportive fashion. Afterward, the breadth and density of this material created a snowball effect, permitting the aggregation of more and more of the printed record as numerous individuals contributed bits and pieces. The private papers of Eli Segal, Thomas Alder, and Carrin Patman are especially noteworthy in this regard; the documents collected by Kenneth Bode on the way to a book of his own (which he ultimately abandoned) were simply invaluable.

The initial density of this material permitted the interviews which followed to begin at a level of shared comprehension which might otherwise not have been achieved even in the final product. Yet despite this archival foundation, it was still, of course, the participants in the reform politicking at the heart of the story who made the compilation of that story possible—by filling in the details, and the perspectives, and the emotional overlay which completed the narrative itself. I have wondered on many occasions why so many people contributed to such an extent. Of my original long list of intended interviewees, a portion of which appears in Appendix B, precisely four people turned me down. Of those whose names appear, most talked for more than an hour; many talked for hours on end; key individuals made themselves available for several sessions.

Those who do their work by interviewing know many of the reasons people talk. They are flattered. They are concerned with their place in history. They are confident that they can structure your interpretation. Beyond that, and buttressing all these motivations, is a fundamental norm of American politics which says that one *should* talk. I believe I know why these individuals also talked at such length and with, in most cases, such frankness. Most participants—regulars as well as reformers, losers as well as winners—retained an abiding interest in the topic of party rules and party reform. Moreover, most believed, for good or ill, that they had been part of a historic moment. They were not necessarily able to place that moment in context, much less to see where it might lead, but the sense of having taken part in a turning point in American political history was widespread. I trust that the depth and detail of some of the quotations from these individuals will attest as powerfully as any word of thanks to the reliable courtesy and frequent generosity of people whose roles in the reform narrative are as diverse as the cast of characters itself.

Bearding these individuals in their geographically dispersed dens required more than receptivity by the principals; it required some direct financial support as well. A year as a graduate fellow at the Russell Sage Foundation provided almost three thousand dollars—out of a research budget with a thousand-dollar ceiling—for travel and communication. The repeated graciousness of Hugh Cline and Arnold Shore at the foundation—each time after a stern lecture—explained this mathematical feat. A string of guest rooms and pallets on the floor then constituted the necessary lodging. Ivan Lee in Long Beach,

ACKNOWLEDGMENTS AND METHODS

California; James and Patricia Lengle in Berkeley, California; Samuel and Dianne Kernell in St. Paul, Minnesota; Russell Boekenkroeger and Susan Christian in Pittsburgh, Pennsylvania; Valerie Pettis in Boston, Massachusetts; and Steven and Maygene Daniels, over and above all others, in Washington, D.C., opened their homes to a benign but distracted guest who monopolized their telephones, kept strange hours, and ignored the traditional amenities. While I did not have a network of hosts from my youth in Austin, Texas, and Montgomery, Alabama, a number of individuals there took me into their homes for shorter stretches, in what must be seen as an even more extraordinary exercise in grace.

The manuscript which resulted had a different kind of territory to traverse but acquired a set of professional guides who were every bit as generous. The first complete version of this manuscript served as a Ph.D. dissertation at the University of California at Berkeley, for a dissertation committee chaired by Nelson Polsby and rounded out by Allan Sindler and Aaron Wildavsky. Nelson, in particular, urged me on and on, always prodding, never dictating, always insisting that there must be even more. Rather than put this overwhelmingly detailed narrative of reform politics directly into print, however, I chose to use it to pursue two of my major theoretical interests, in institutional change and in the circulation of elites; to employ it as the base from which to sketch out some larger developments in American politics, like the shifting class base of that politics or the particular role of the national press; and to rely upon it to make an implicit argument about the proper *study* of American political life. In this, once more, I was encouraged by Messrs. Polsby, Sindler, and Wildavsky who, each in his own way, offered precisely that advice.

Yet it was really Robert Merton at the Russell Sage Foundation who aided, pushed, and pulled me into following the advice I claimed to honor. More than anyone else, Bob was the one asking, "What do you mean? What are the central concepts? What are their practical referents?" A Mertonian conversation is always the invitation to stretch one's intellectual horizon. The Mertonian edit—there is no adequate phrase for editorial activity on this range of levels—is a marvel which only those who have experienced it can understand. But the true character of this continuing dialog is probably best revealed by the fact that little in the manuscript was directly suggested by the senior member, while much was a direct response to questions or newly perceived contradictions and puzzles arising in conversation with him.

Others also did more than their share. Austin Ranney read substantial portions of the manuscript, as did Elaine Kamarck, James Lengle, and Samuel Beer. David Truman read the entire product twice, commenting all the way. James Coleman and David Hammack took a crack at specific pieces. Marshall Robinson restrained himself, most of the time, from asking when the evolving project would finally be finished, and thus ensured the ample and supportive resources of the Russell Sage Foundation as draft turned into draft and analysis emerged from narrative. At a crucial point when the foundation building was literally under construction, Joshua Lederberg of the Rockefeller University provided both an institutional home and the support of his three assistants, Sandra Walsh, Anne Guardello, and Mary Jane Zimmerman.

A manuscript with this complex evolution required extensive technical support. Carolyn Salisbury (subsequently Ponturo) of the Russell Sage Foundation began the typing. Randa Murphy and Jacqueline Tillman of the American Enterprise Institute continued it. Marjorie Laue of the Russell Sage Foundation resumed the effort and inherited perhaps the largest single share of typing duties; Marjorie also did the newspaper work and associated fact-hunting which carried the manuscript through its intermediary stages. Elva Marabella followed Marjorie as typing progressed. Sandra Still was the primary typist as the project reached a conclusion. Henrietta de Sterke supported both Ellie and Sandy with her usual precision and high energy and may have typed as great a share of the finished product as anyone. Although she typed only a line or two, and then under extreme duress, Miriam Feldblum provided the critical research support during all the later stages—combing the libraries of New York; perusing the newspapers of California, Pennsylvania, Minnesota, or Texas; proofreading text as it appeared, while querying far more than elisions and misspellings; and always providing a kind of moral support to which no author is entitled but which any author would gratefully accept.

At the very end, as this manuscript neared book form, one more small supporting cast entered the picture. Sylvia Newman did all the official copyediting, with a light hand and a deft touch. Judith Greissman superintended the total process of publication at Basic Books. And Priscilla Lewis at the Russell Sage Foundation offered parallel services to all of these individuals, advising on questions of style and format, monitoring the production process diligently and completely, and managing the myriad minor crises of publication which only the experienced can even imagine.

Finally, there were contributors who fit none of these categories. Hugh O'Neill provided a daily colleagueship which was no less important for the difficulty in classifying it. The completion of my personal universe, through the addition of Wanda Shafer, speeded completion of this manuscript in a fashion which neither she nor I would ever have expected. The roster of all these individuals—these supporters, these contributors—is surely grounds for appreciation. A quick look back at all these developments is equally grounds for humility. A furtive look ahead is reason to close with the hope that the resulting narrative and analysis fills the niches and serves the purposes for which it is offered.

554

NOTES

Introduction

1. This earlier peak period for institutional reform is covered in Louise Overacker, *The Presidential Primary* (New York: Macmillan, 1926), especially chap. 2, "History of the Presidential Primary Movement," pp. 11–22.

2. See "Origins of the National Convention System," in Paul T. David, Ralph M. Goldman, and Richard C. Bain, *The Politics of National Party Conventions,* rev. ed.; condensed by Kathleen Sproul (New York: Vintage Books, 1964), pp. 39–64.

3. Compare Richard D. Hupman and Robert L. Tienken, comps., *Nomination and Election of the President and Vice President of the United States* (Washington: U.S. Government Printing Office, 1968), with Commission on Party Structure and Delegate Selection, Report, "Delegate Selection in 1972: A State by State Summary" undated, Presidential Libraries, National Archives, Washington, D.C.

4. The way in which critical resources, key participants, major public issues, and the character of nominees are affected by institutional arrangements is one major theme in three standard, prereform works on American political parties: E. Pendleton Herring, *The Politics of Democracy: American Parties in Action* (New York: Norton, 1965), first published in 1940; E. E. Schattschneider, *Party Government* (New York: Holt, 1942); and V. O. Key, Jr., *Politics, Parties, and Pressure Groups* (New York: Crowell, 1966), first published in 1942.

5. The two seminal works, featuring notably different orientations toward the concept, are Vilfredo Pareto, *The Mind and Society* (New York: Harcourt, Brace, 1935), and Gaetano Mosca, *The Ruling Class* (New York: McGraw-Hill, 1939).

Chapter 1

1. William Borders, "200 M'Carthy Men Bolt in Hartford," *New York Times,* June 23, 1968, p. 1.; Jack Zaiman, "McCarthy Faction Bolts Convention; Regulars Won't Yield Extra Seat," *Hartford Courant,* June 23, 1968, pp. 1, 10, and 14.

2. All quotations from the principals in reform politics are from personal interviews unless otherwise noted. With the exception of three interviews conducted by telephone, all were conducted face to face. The median length was between one and a half and two hours, although a few were as short as forty-five minutes, and those with key staff members of the official reform commission ran as long as six hours, spread over several days. A full list of interview respondents is contained in Appendix B.

3. *Report of the National Advisory Commission on Civil Disorders* (New York: Bantam Books, 1968).

4. Commission on the Democratic Selection of Presidential Nominees and K.S. Giniger Company, Inc., contract, September 10, 1968, Presidential Libraries, National Archives, Washington, D.C.

5. This roster, along with a thumbnail partisan biography of each staff volunteer, is contained in Commission on the Democratic Selection of Presidential Nominees, memorandum to the file, July 31, 1968, Presidential Libraries, National Archives, Washington, D.C.

6. Dutton was so strongly interested in reform and change that he would eventually write a book of his own on the subject. Frederick G. Dutton, *Changing Sources of Power* (New York: McGraw-Hill, 1972).

7. Alder to Howard Morgan, July 25, 1968, Presidential Libraries, National Archives, Washington, D.C.

8. Congressional Quarterly Service, *The Presidential Nominating Conventions 1968* (Washington: Congressional Quarterly, 1968), p. 103 (hereafter cited as *Conventions 1968*).

9. For Bailey, the arrangement probably seemed harmless. Among the big-three convention committees—Platform, Credentials, and Rules—Rules was traditionally the most honorific and least substantive. In fact, the last truly major issue to come out of the Rules Committee had been the proposal to abolish the requirement of a two-thirds majority for nomination, in 1936. See "The Two Thirds Rule," in Paul T. David, Ralph M. Goldman, and Richard C. Bain, *The Politics of National Party Conventions*, rev. ed.; condensed by Kathleen Sproul (New York: Vintage Books, 1964), pp. 186–88.

10. Commission on the Democratic Selection of Presidential Nominees, press release, "Hughes to Head Commission Survey of Democratic Delegate Selection," August 4, 1968, Presidential Libraries, National Archives, Washington, D.C.

11. Morgan, Sueppel, Taylor, and Wexler to "Dear Fellow Delegate," form letter, August 6, 1968, Presidential Libraries, National Archives, Washington, D.C.

12. Geoff Cowan and Simon Lazarus III each took some rough notes on the proceedings, to inform their subsequent report, and these became the sole written record of the Winnetka meeting. Cowan, "Notes from Cowan"; Lazarus, "Winnetka Meeting: Notes from Lazarus", Presidential Libraries, National Archives, Washington, D.C.

13. Since the early 1950s, this had been a promise that the Democratic ticket would be on the ballot under the party's own name in the delegate's home state. For a lively account of one of the battles which produced this interpretation, see John Madigan, "The Reluctant Candidate," *The Reporter*, November 24, 1953, pp. 19–26.

14. Commission on the Democratic Selection of Presidential Nominees, *The Democratic Choice* (New York: Commission on the Democratic Selection of Presidential Nominees, 1968). For delegate selection and the case of Minnesota, see p. 32; for delegate allocation and the case of California, see p. 28.

15. Ibid., p. 1.

16. Ibid., p. 2.

17. Roy Reed, "Humphrey Asks Abolition of Unit Rule at Convention," *New York Times*, July 30, 1968, p. 1.

18. James C. Wright, Jr., "Rules Committee Memorandum," Presidential Libraries, National Archives, Washington, D.C., p. 1.

19. This particular chronology and most subsequent dates and times for the event of the 1968 Convention are drawn from *Conventions 1968*.

20. Majority Report of the Committee on Rules and Order of Business, as reprinted in *Conventions 1968*, p. 196.

21. Ibid.

22. Minority Report of the Committee on Rules and Order of Business, as reprinted in *Conventions 1968*, p. 198.

23. These were first conveyed to major state party figures in Richard J. Hughes, chairman, Special Equal Rights Committee, to all members of the Democratic National Committee, memorandum, untitled, July 26, 1967, with attachment, "Some Basic Elements in Enabling Voter Participation in Party Affairs," Presidential Libraries, National Archives, Washington, D.C. They then achieved evident mandatory status in John M. Bailey, chairman, Democratic National Committee, "Call for the 1968 Democratic National Convention," January 9, 1968, Presidential Libraries, National Archives, Washington, D.C.

24. Majority Report of the Committee on Credentials, as reprinted in *Conventions 1968*, pp. 199–200.

25. Final Report of the Special Equal Rights Committee of the Democratic National Committee, as reprinted in *Conventions 1968*, pp. 197–98.

26. Kampelman is also the source of the quotation from McCandless.

27. The quotation from Chancellor is as recalled by Anne Wexler.

28. *Conventions 1968*, p. 148.

29. Recorded tallies for all minority reports which went to a roll call are broken out by state in *Conventions 1968*, pp. 89, 140, and 146.

30. Geoff Cowan confirmed Segal's perception: "Nobody understood what the voting was about. Nobody. Hughes spoke for it. Don Fraser spoke for it. A Humphrey delegate introduced it. A second Humphrey delegate seconded it."

31. Theodore H. White, *The Making of the President 1968* (New York: Pocket Books, 1970), pp. 375–76.

32. Max Frankel of the *New York Times* was prescient in giving this entire chain of possibilities serious consideration. Frankel, "Delegate Fights Transform Party," *New York Times*, August 28, 1968, p. 1. The handful of others who considered the chain at all presumably saw too many links, too many weak links, to justify analyzing any possible new political universe. The *Washington Post*, for example, recorded passage of the Credentials majority and Rules minority reports in the last few paragraphs of its article on credentials challenges at the 1968 Convention, where it summarized the contents of both reports very briefly and referred to them as "delegate selection reform proposals which came from different committees and are somewhat duplicative." Richard L. Lyons, "Credentials Battle Ends; Alabama, Carolina Challenges Fail," *Washington Post*, August 28, 1968, p. A6.

Chapter 2

1. Humphrey to O'Brien, October 7, 1968, Presidential Libraries, National Archives, Washington, D.C.

National Committee, press release, "Vice President Humphrey
n to Maximize Democracy in Party Nominating Process," October
ial Libraries, National Archives, Washington, D.C.
anson, "Rebellious Democrats Establish Coalition to Seek Party Re-
rk Times, October 7, 1968, p. 40.
lerbers, "M'Carthy Resists Party Unity Move," *New York Times,* Octo-
p. 35.
ert Krim, "Rebel Democrats Set Up a Coalition," *Washington Post,* Octo-
3, p. A1; and Donald Janson, "Rebellious Democrats Establish Coalition
arty Reform," *New York Times,* October 7, 1968, p. 40.
Commission on the Democratic Selection of Presidential Nominees to Mem-
he Democratic National Committee, memorandum, "Principal Actions of the
Democratic National Convention Re: Delegate Selection and Rules Reform,"
ber, 1968, Presidential Libraries, National Archives, Washington, D.C.

7. Hughes to O'Brien, October 21, 1968, private papers of Thomas P. Alder.

8. O'Brien to Hughes, October 28, 1969, private papers of Thomas P. Alder.

9. William J. Connell, a top aide from the Humphrey campaign and a staff member from the vice presidential office, believed that the vice president was being insulated deliberately from the appointment process, but Connell ultimately shared the
problems of other interested Humphrey staffers:

> I was very involved with the O'Brien list. O'Brien was not, in my judg-
> ment, a very responsive Chairman to the Vice President. He made it a point
> to separate himself from the Vice President. He didn't freely consult to
> any degree with me, and I don't think with Humphrey. He had important
> ties to the old Kennedy group, and he got many names from them. On the
> other hand, I couldn't really have cared less about these commissions during
> the campaign.
>
> After the campaign, Humphrey's intellectual and emotional exhaustion
> was shared by me, and by many of the others. I felt that Humphrey should
> keep a grip on his friends in the National Committee, but it was a case
> where I had to find a career, too.

10. Larry O'Brien had been campaign manager for both John and Robert Kennedy
and needed no introduction to these circles. By mid-November, the *Washington Post*
was reporting that "Kennedy aides these days show more interest in the makeup of
the commissions than in the Party Chairmanship." Walter Pincus, "Humphrey Moves
to Rebuild Party," *Washington Post,* November 21, 1968, p. A1.

11. David S. Broder, "O'Brien Quits Post as Party Chairman," *Washington Post,*
January 8, 1969, p. A1; Warren Weaver, Jr., "O'Brien Quits as Democratic National
Chairman," *New York Times,* January 8, 1969, p. 28.

12. Warren Weaver, Jr., "Humphrey Said to Favor Harris for Chairmanship,"
New York Times, January 10, 1969, p. 31; Weaver, "Sanford Spurns Party Leadership," *New York Times,* January 11, 1969, p. 16; "Humphrey for Harris as Chairman
of Party," *New York Times,* January 12, 1969, p. 39; E. W. Kenworthy, "Harris Named
National Chairman by Democrats," *New York Times,* January 15, 1969, p. 22.

13. F. Grant Sawyer, National Committeeman from Nevada, offered what became
Resolution No. 12:

> *Sawyer:* The similarity of this Commission's function and that authorized
> by the Convention in adopting the Credentials Committee report is appar-

ent. Duplicating effort can be avoided by combining the two actions into one overall Committee.

THEREFORE, IT IS RESOLVED that the Chairman of the Democratic National Committee promptly appoint a Committee on Party Structure and Delegate Selection, composed of representative Democrats. The Committee, with adequate staff resources, shall begin functioning in ample time to permit States to make whatever law and rules changes as may be necessary to meet the letter and the spirit of the 1972 Call. Also, it shall report periodically to the Democratic National Committee and to the 1972 Convention and its Committees.

Democratic National Committee, "Transcript of Proceedings, January 14, 1969," Presidential Libraries, National Archives, Washington, D.C., pp. 161–62.

14. New Democratic Coalition, press release, untitled, January 19, 1969, private papers of Eli J. Segal.

15. For states which received more than one member, geographic balance was considered internally as well. California, for example, would have one northern, one central valley, and two southern commissioners on Party Structure, roughly paralleling its population. Similarly, Texas would get one Dallas–Fort Worth, one Austin–Houston, and one San Antonio member.

16. Actually, one local official, Albert A. Pena, a county commissioner, made his way onto the list *after* the Party Structure Commission had been officially announced—thanks to demands for some additional *demographic* representation. (See below.)

17. Even when it became evident that the new national chairman, Fred Harris, was unreceptive, the Iowa Freshman continued to emphasize, publicly, his desire for the Party Structure chairmanship:

> Because his proposals were adopted by the convention, Mr. Hughes, now a Senator, would have liked to head the new committee.
>
> "I would like the job," he said today. "I made this very clear to Fred (Harris) last Friday. But I understand that I'm not acceptable to some people."

E. W. Kenworthy, "McGovern to Head Panel on Convention Reform," *New York Times*, February 5, 1969, p. 28.

18. David S. Broder, "Democrats Plan to Give McGovern Reform Job," *Washington Post*, February 4, 1969, p. A1; E. W. Kenworthy, "McGovern to Head Panel on Convention Reform," *New York Times*, February 5, 1969, p. 28.

19. The notice of his intention was Bickel to Hughes, January 29, 1969. His letter back to President McGeorge Bundy of the Ford Foundation, carrying through, was Bickel to Bundy, January 29, 1969. Both are in private papers of Thomas P. Alder.

20. Alder believed that Segal's virtues were more important to the task at hand and spoke accordingly:

> Geoff said that I could not do it. Geoff proposed Sy Lazarus; Eli Segal proposed himself. Eli knew more and was more motivated for the infighting. I thought that was what was important. Sy was brighter and a better writer. Eli was very anxious for the job. However, Eli had worked for Joe Resnick, who was very anti-Kennedy. McGovern really had a hard time with that.

21. The news articles announcing appointment of this commission were all based

from the initial, uncorrected press release of February 8. David S. Broder,
⎫ Pick Units to Reform Party," *Washington Post,* February 9, 1969, p. A1;
⎫s Name 2 Reform Units," *New York Times,* February 9, 1969, p. 68. Table
⎫ver, is based on the roster of Party Structure commissioners for the initial
⎫ on March 1, and thus includes additions and changes.

Thomas P. Alder, memorandum, "Draft Outline: Topics for Presentation to
⎫ Meeting of the Committee on Party Structure and Delegate Selection, Demo-
⎫c Party," February 22, 1969, Presidential Libraries, National Archives, Washing-
⎫, D.C.

23. Rumors about the elevation of Houtchens to the national chairmanship traced
⎫ll the way back to the preconvention period, when Humphrey aides were believed
to have discussed the possibility with Governor Hearnes, in the course of corralling
Missouri's votes at the Democratic Convention. Then, when O'Brien was appointed
national chairman in the postconvention period, with the announced intention of remaining only through the general election, Governor Hearnes had publicly asserted
that Houtchens would be O'Brien's successor—an assertion which drew neither confirmation nor denial from the Humphrey camp. As the question of a new chairman began
to attract attention again, in late November, the Houtchens rumor found its way into
the national press. Walter Pincus, "Humphrey Moves to Rebuild Party," *Washington
Post,* November 21, 1968, p. A1; "Democrats Form Two New Panels," *New York
Times,* November 24, 1968, p. 51. Houtchens himself would confirm nothing more
than his willingness to do "anything he [Humphrey] asks me to do." "Houtchens Comment on Post," *New York Times,* November 24, 1968, p. 51.

24. Donald Janson, "Rebellious Democrats Establish Coalition to Seek Party Reform," *New York Times,* October 7, 1968, p. 40; Douglas E. Kneeland, "New Democratic Coalition Says It Will Seek A Wide Following," *New York Times,* November
25, 1968, p. 32; Steven R. Roberts, "Democratic Group Battling To Keep Alive 'New
Politics' of '68," *New York Times,* December 28, 1968, p. 17.

Chapter 3

1. "Democrats Name Two Reform Groups," *New York Times,* February 9, 1969,
p. 68.

2. "Remarks by Mrs. Anne Wexler, Co-Author, Minority Report of the 1968
Rules Committee," March 1, 1969; private papers of Eli J. Segal.

3. Majority Report of the Committee on Rules and Order of Business, adopted
as amended, August 27, 1968, as reprinted in Congressional Quarterly Service, *The
Presidential Nominating Conventions 1968* (Washington: Congressional Quarterly,
1968), p. 196 (hereafter cited as *Conventions 1968*).

4. Majority Report of the Committee on Credentials, adopted August 27, 1968,
as reprinted in *Conventions 1968,* pp. 199–200.

5. "Remarks by Mrs. Anne Wexler," pp. 2–3.

6. Minority Report of the Committee on Rules and Order of Business, adopted
August 27, 1968, as reprinted in *Conventions 1968,* p. 198.

7. A clear majority of all delegates to the 1968 Convention had been selected through these devices. For concise definitions, see chap. 4 or, especially, chap. 7.

8. "Remarks by Mrs. Anne Wexler," pp. 3–4.

9. Minority Report of the Committee on Rules and Order of Business, p. 198.

10. The first suggestion was probably Dutton to McGovern, memorandum, "Your Party Structure and Delegate Selection Committee," February 11, 1969, Presidential Libraries, National Archives, Washington, D.C., p. 1. Another was Alder, memorandum, "Draft Outline: Topics for Presentation to Initial Meeting of the Committee on Party Structure and Delegate Selection, Democratic Party," February 22, 1969, private papers of Thomas P. Alder.

11. Segal to McGovern, memorandum, "Your Statement on Organization of Special Committee," February 25, 1969, private papers of Kenneth A. Bode.

12. Theodore H. White, *The Making of the President 1968* (New York: Pocket Books, 1970), pp. 453–54.

13. Commission on Party Structure and Delegate Selection, "Official Summary of March 1, 1969, Meeting," Presidential Libraries, National Archives, Washington, D.C.

14. All three citations are from the comments by Hughes. Office of Senator Harold E. Hughes, press release, "Remarks by Senator Harold E. Hughes," March 1, 1969, private papers of Eli J. Segal; but see also Office of Senator George McGovern, press release, "Opening Statement," March 1, 1969, Presidential Libraries, National Archives, Washington, D.C.

15. Commission on Party Structure and Delegate Selection, partial transcript, "Commission Meeting, March 1, 1969," private papers of Kenneth A. Bode.

16. David S. Broder, "Democratic Critics Run Reform Unit," *Washington Post*, March 2, 1969, p. A1; see also E. W. Kenworthy, "McGovern Warns Party on Reform," *New York Times*, March 2, 1969, p. 41.

17. Alder to Bickel, February 26, 1969, private papers of Thomas P. Alder.

18. The evolutionary perspective on party structure and party reform appeared with the arrival of national debates about the role of political parties at the turn of the century. A leading example was Henry Jones Ford, *The Rise and Growth of American Politics* (New York: Macmillan, 1898). A successor with substantial influence was E. Pendleton Herring, *The Politics of Democracy: American Parties in Action* (New York: Norton, 1940).

The two divergent schools of thought on deliberate party reform are clearly and succinctly reviewed, both for their doctrinal content and for their attendant politics, in James W. Ceaser, *Presidential Selection: Theory and Development* (Princeton: Princeton University Press, 1979). See especially chap. 3, "Martin Van Buren and the Case for Electoral Restraint," and chap. 4, "Woodrow Wilson and the Origin of the Modern View of Presidential Selection."

Ceaser traces the disciplined party school to ex-President Van Buren and elucidates it through his *Autobiography of Martin Van Buren*, ed. John C. Fitzpatrick (Washington: Annual Report of the American Historical Society, 1918), and through his *Inquiry into the Origin and Course of Political Parties in the United States* (New York: Hurd and Houghton, 1867). Ceaser places the participatory school of party reform at the doorstep of the prepresidential political scientist, Woodrow Wilson, and extracts it carefully from *Congressional Government* (Boston: Houghton Mifflin, 1885) and *Con-*

stitutional Government in the United States (New York: Columbia University Press, 1908).

19. The three main theoretical approaches to party reform were each subsequently applied to the product and the deliberations of the Commission on Party Structure and Delegate Selection. The evolutionary perspective is used by Austin Ranney, himself a Party Structure commissioner, in *Curing the Mischiefs of Faction: Party Reform in America* (Berkeley: University of California Press, 1975). The participatory perspective is explicitly applied in William J. Crotty, *Decision for the Democrats: Reforming the Party Structure* (Baltimore: Johns Hopkins University Press, 1978). At the close of his comprehensive analysis, James W. Ceaser brings the disciplined party perspective to bear, in *Presidential Selection: Theory and Development,* pp. 260–353.

Chapter 4

1. Commission on Party Structure and Delegate Selection, memorandum, "Proposed Task Forces," March 26, 1969, Presidential Libraries, National Archives, Washington, D.C. The original membership lists for these task forces remained essentially the same, although individual members did not hesitate to shift from one to another on an ad hoc basis, when they could not make one of their assigned hearings but could attend one for a different task force. The crucial exception, the one change in task force membership which did have to be formally recorded, concerned the chairmanship of Task Force E. George McGovern had initially slated I. W. Abel for this chairmanship, but when Abel withdrew from the full Commission, McGovern had to recognize that fact by promoting Earl G. Graves to his position. Bob Nelson to Task Force E, memorandum, untitled, April 17, 1969, private papers of Kenneth A. Bode.

2. McGovern to Commission Members, form letter, April 3, 1969, Presidential Libraries, National Archives, Washington, D.C., 1 p.

3. Nelson to Regional Coordinators, memorandum, "Format for Public Hearings," April 10, 1969, Presidential Libraries, National Archives, Washington, D.C.

4. The relationship between the commission and the National Committee, on the other hand, or at least between the commission staff and the office of the national chairman was further confirmed by the staff response to these contributions:

> The only plausible argument that the McGovern Commission is "a branch or subsidiary of a national committee" springs from its acceptance of space and salaries from the DNC. These are very flimsy criteria, however, to conclude that a parent-subsidiary relationship exists. Certainly, the facts that: (1) the McGovern Commission and the DNC are committees different in origin and purpose; (2) the McGovern Commission was not even established by its parent; (3) the McGovern Commission could operate (legally) without reliance upon the DNC; and (4) a substantial portion of its operating costs comes from sources independent of the DNC, militate against the notion of a parent-subsidiary relationship. In all probability, the contributions of space and salary by the DNC to the McGovern Commission should be classified as legal "gifts."

Segal to Nelson, memorandum, "Applicability of Federal Corrupt Practices Act to Contributions and Expenditures of the McGovern Commission," July 9, 1969, Presidential Libraries, National Archives, Washington, D.C., p. 2. Nelson was to overrule Segal and file regular reports under the Act.

5. McGovern had actually attempted a fundraising press release in early April, with the goal of securing numerous small contributions, but this had been unsuccessful (Office of Senator George McGovern, press release, untitled, April 11, 1969, private papers of Kenneth A. Bode). A month later, a shift to the direct approach was slightly more productive, drawing two $1,000 donations and a few smaller amounts from personal contacts of Chairman McGovern and Vice Chairman Hughes (Commission on Party Structure and Delegate Selection, untitled financial report, for the period May 1–August 1, 1969, Presidential Libraries, National Archives, Washington, D.C., p. 2).

6. Ibid.

7. Collins to members of the Subcommittee on Party Structure, March 21, 1969, private papers of Kenneth A. Bode.

8. Eli J. Segal, "Prospectus: The Subcommittee on Model Delegate Selection of the National Committee's Commission on Party Structure and Delegate Selection," undated, "Prospectus: The Subcommittee on Party Structure of the National Committee's Commission on Party Structure and Delegate Selection," undated, "Prospectus: The Subcommittee on Grass Roots Participation of the Democratic National Committee's Commission on Party Structure and Delegate Selection," undated, Presidential Libraries, National Archives, Washington, D.C.

9. Some of the flavor of the summer intern experience came through in the remembrances of Jessie Bocurncuf, who transferred into the interns' group shortly after the initial ten had assembled:

I was a sophomore in college, and I went to work in McGovern's office for the summer. After a very little bit of that, I said, "No way. If this is what it's all about, I don't need it." McGovern then had two committees which were also his, the nutrition committee and the reform commission, and he gave me the chance to go with either, and I picked the reform commission.

We worked during the summer on the states, on researching their rules. Most of my time was spent in the Library of Congress or on the phone to the state parties. That took a lot of time. Some states, Tennessee I think, didn't even *have* any written rules.

I remember that it was always running out of money during the summer, and there were all sorts of problems with that. We were always going broke. The interns had their own intrigues, too. For example, there were two black interns who threatened to quit during the summer.

When I first went there, I worked directly for Ken Bode. But after several days of that, I shifted into research on the states, and Marcia Goodman took over. He was *so* disorganized, you couldn't do *anything* with him.

Fred Harris seemed like the enemy then. Fred has changed so much. Then he was such a slimy pol, the slimiest. He wanted to put a lid on it, we thought. It didn't help any when his secretary left and came over. I'm sure he didn't care for that.

10. Wade to McGovern, June 20, 1969, Presidential Libraries, National Archives, Washington, D.C., p. 1.

11. Their version of the new concordat was contained in Commission staff to McGovern, memorandum, "Wednesday (7/9/69) Meeting with Consultant Committee," July 8, 1969, private papers of Eli J. Segal.

12. Commission staff to McGovern, memorandum, "Compliance Report—Time-Table," July 14, 1969, private papers of Kenneth A. Bode.

13. Before the hearings were even finished, the staff had hinted at this lack of transfer, in a memo to all commissioners:

> For the most part, witnesses have offered constructive suggestions. It is unfortunate that we have neither the resources nor the mandate to explore all of the questions which they have raised. On the other hand, the failure of witnesses to raise a relevant issue should not suggest that the Commission will not pass on it.

Commission staff to Commission members, memorandum, "Task Force Hearing Themes," May 27, 1969, Presidential Libraries, National Archives, Washington, D.C., p. 3.

14. Eli J. Segal, "Model Delegate Selection," June 12, 1969, and "Subcommittee on Model Delegate Selection: Schedule of Activities," undated, Presidential Libraries, National Archives, Washington, D.C.

15. Bode to Lindheim, August 25, 1969, Presidential Libraries, National Archives, Washington, D.C.

16. This strategy—compliance reports first, followed by a general statement of principles—had guided staff thinking through the time when staff members began to narrow their substantive focus (see commission staff to McGovern, memorandum, "Wednesday (7/9/69) Meeting with Consultant Committee," Presidential Libraries, National Archives, Washington, D.C).

17. The "full, meaningful, and timely" directive had itself been pasted together by the commission staff for the inaugural meeting of the full Commission. Thereafter, Eli Segal had convinced John R. Schmidt and Wayne W. Whalen, credentials strategists for the McCarthy forces at the 1968 Convention, to draft a law review piece supporting this construction. Schmidt and Whalen, "Credentials Contests at the 1968—and 1972—Democratic National Conventions," *Harvard Law Review,* 82 (May 1969): 7, pp. 1438–90, especially pp. 1459–61. Segal, however, remained fearful that some aggressive commissioner might challenge this interpretation and limit the commission's field of inquiry. While he strove to complete the draft report, then, he sought additional, outside support for the additive interpretation of "full, meaningful, and timely." Richard Hertzog, a Washington attorney, was one of those he contacted:

> Either of these interpretations is satisfactory for our purposes, but—and this is the question which I think needs work—can it not be argued that the language of the Rules Committee Report supercedes the language of the Credentials Committee Report and that we lose the word "meaningful"?
>
> If you have any thoughts on the matter, I would like to have them within the next week or so. For obvious reasons, I would appreciate your keeping this memo confidential.

Segal to Hertzog, memorandum, untitled, August 8, 1969, private papers of Eli J. Segal.

18. Commission on the Democratic Selection of Presidential Nominees, *The Democratic Choice* (New York: Commission on the Democratic Selection of Presidential Nominees, 1968).

19. Eli J. Segal, "Model Delegate Selection," June 12, 1969; Presidential Libraries, National Archives, Washington, D.C.

20. Commission on the Democratic Selection of Presidential Nominees, *The Democratic Choice;* Eli J. Segal, "Prospectus: The Subcommittee on Model Delegate Selection of the National Committee's Commission on Party Structure and Delegate Selection"; Segal, "Model Delegate Selection."

21. The provisions establishing these institutional effects required substantial interpretation in all three documents, though more in the prospectus and report of the Model Delegate Subcommittee than in the report of the Hughes Commission. The relevant sections were Eli J. Segal, "Prospectus," pp. 4–5; Segal, "Model Delegate Selection," Parts 5, 6, and 7; Commission on the Democratic Selection of Presidential Nominees, *The Democratic Choice,* chap. 1, "Convention Delegate Selection: How States Choose," pp. 17–33.

22. Segal, "Model Delegate Selection," pt. 8, "Democratic Procedures," pp. 4–7.

23. Segal, "Model Delegate Selection," pt. 4, "Model Delegate Selection by Presidential Poll," p. 7.

24. One last procedural alternative retained some vitality through the first fall meeting of the Executive Committee. Ken Bode continued to prefer delaying publication of the general guidelines until the Commission had issued an even more general policy statement, to be heralded as a "Bill of Rights for Democrats".

> Before the Report is distributed to the general public and given a chance to stand or fall on its own merits, party leaders may join together and seriously affect the Report's effectiveness.
>
> One way to minimize this might be to adopt a set of principles with a lofty sounding name like a "Bill of Rights for Democrats," some weeks before we adopt the "full and timely" report. This Bill of Rights would contain 10 principles from which virtually the entire Report could be traced. We should sell the Bill of Rights to the press, distribute it as widely as possible, and encourage party organizations to adopt it. When the Report is completed and released, the prior existence of a widely circulated and accepted Bill of Rights will make its legitimacy much more easily justified.

Segal and Bode to McGovern, memorandum, "Agenda for Executive Committee Meeting," August 27, 1969; private papers of Kenneth A. Bode.

Shortly after Bode penned this argument, however, events caught up with this alternative, too. Once the pressure to develop the central report began to build, the notion of yet a third publication—beyond the report and the compliance letters which could follow—simply lost its charm. The possibility of publishing such a document still made it onto the agenda for the August meeting of the Executive Committee, but the committee never discussed that possibility, and the notion never surfaced again.

25. Segal and Bode to McGovern, memorandum, "Agenda for Executive Committee Meeting," p. 4.

26. Segal, "Model Delegate Selection," pt. 5, "Model Delegate Selection by Convention," p. 7.

27. Perhaps the best statement of the connection between these experiences, these policy preferences, and the reform recommendations which resulted is John S. Saloma III and Frederick H. Sontag, *Parties: The Real Opportunity for Effective Citizen Politics* (New York: Vintage Books, 1973).

28. Lindheim, Caridi, and subcommittee staff to Stevenson, memorandum, untitled and undated; Presidential Libraries, National Archives, Washington, D.C., p. 2.

29. The centrality of differential turnout by social background to the operation of political institutions, and the varying impact of this differential turnout within differing institutional frameworks, is a central finding of the survey of research on participation in Lester W. Millbrath, *Political Participation: How and Why Do People Get Involved in Politics?* (Chicago: Rand McNally, 1977). See especially chap. 4, "Political Participation as a Function of Social Position." An analysis of the–powerful–effects of variation in turnout by social background which is focused specifically on the institutions of delegate selection in 1968 and 1972 is James I. Lengle, *Representation and Presidential Primaries: The Democratic Party in the Post-Reform Era* (Westport, Conn.: Greenwood Press, 1981). See especially chap. 2, "Demographic Representation in Presidential Primaries."

30. The geographic distribution of reform and regular factions within the Democratic party was a major finding in the classic work on the difference between these factions, James Q. Wilson, *The Amateur Democrat: Club Politics in Three Cities,* especially chap. 9, "The Class Basis of Amateur Democrats" (Chicago: University of Chicago Press, 1962). For a detailed case of this geographic distribution and its impact in the reform politics of 1968–72, see chap. 12 below, "The Politics of Implementation Writ Small: Pennsylvania Accepts Reform."

31. Perhaps the best statement of the connection between the appearance of a potential constituency for party reform, the practical advantages—and needs—of that constituency, and the character of the reform recommendations appropriate to those advantages and needs came from an actual Party Structure commissioner, Frederick G. Dutton, in *Changing Sources of Power: American Politics in the 1970s* (New York: McGraw-Hill, 1971).

Chapter 5

1. Segal and Bode to McGovern, memorandum, "Agenda for Executive Committee Meeting, August 28, 1969," August 27, 1969, private papers of Kenneth A. Bode.

2. Segal and Bode had, in fact, committed these fears to paper when it became clear that Fred Harris, the national chairman, would have to be present at this session of the Executive Committee. The commission was again in financial distress, the National Committee was the logical starting point in a hunt for funds, and Harris was inevitably invited to the August 28 meeting. Nevertheless, Segal and Bode closed their planning memo with the exhortation that Chairman McGovern limit Harris's presence to those items on which it was absolutely unavoidable:

Miscellaneous information and suggestions: Especially since we are trying to preserve our independence from the Democratic National Committee, it would be setting a dangerous precedent if the Chairman of the DNC were allowed to attend any portion of our meeting beyond item 3 of the agenda. Fred Harris may not be able to make the beginning of the meeting (he expects to arrive about 11:00 A.M.), in which case we suggest that Bob Nelson's talk about finances be postponed. When Senator Harris arrives, we can suspend discussion of whatever matter is on the floor, Bob Nelson can address himself to finances, and Senator Harris can respond. At the completion of that exercise, Senator Harris's presence at the meeting is no longer required.

Segal and Bode to McGovern, "Agenda for the Executive Committee Meeting, August 28, 1969," p. 4.

3. Executive Committee of the Commission on Party Structure and Delegate Selection, "Draft Transcript of Proceedings, August 28, 1969," Presidential Libraries, National Archives, Washington, D.C., p. 1.

4. Ibid., p. 4.

5. Ibid., p. 8.

6. Ibid., pp. 9–10.

7. Ibid., p. 10.

8. Staff to Executive Committee, Commission on Party Structure and Delegate Selection, memorandum, "Proposed Guidelines, 'Full, Meaningful, and Timely' Opportunity to Participate in the Delegate Selection Process," undated, Presidential Libraries, National Archives, Washington, D.C.

9. Collins did not formally spell out his definitions until the meeting of the full commission on September 23, when a challenge from the other side—from those who counseled even greater care in asserting commission powers—forced him to define his terms:

When the term "call upon" is used herein, it is meant to carry the full authority of the Commission to obtain the accomplishment of the stated purpose. When the Commission does not have the authority to mandate the desired changes, the term will be construed to call upon all those having such authority to use all feasible efforts to accomplish the change.

Transcription of tapes, "Meeting of the Commission on Party Structure and Delegate Selection, September 23 and 24, 1969," private papers of Kenneth A. Bode.

10. Participants remember the production of a full transcript of the September 11 meeting of the Executive Committee, but that transcript was not available at the National Archives or in the private papers of major staff members. As a result, this account of the second meeting of the Executive Committee was based on extended interviews with the participants, on official documents entering and leaving the meeting, and on comparison with other recorded events in this sequence, without the additional testing against an official transcript which was possible for other meetings.

11. Compare Staff to Executive Committee, Commission on Party Structure and Delegate Selection, memorandum, "Proposed Guidelines, 'Full, Meaningful, and Timely' Opportunity," with Commission on Party Structure and Delegate Selection, "Proposed Guidelines," September 23, 1969, Presidential Libraries, National Archives, Washington, D.C.

12. Bode and Segal to McGovern, memorandum, untitled and undated but surely September 22, 1969, private papers of Kenneth A. Bode.

13. "Opening Statement of Senator George McGovern, Chairman, Democratic Commission on Party Structure and Delegate Selection, Tuesday, September 23, 1969," Presidential Libraries, National Archives, Washington, D.C., p. 1.

14. McGovern to Commission Members, memorandum, "Proposed Guidelines, 'Full, Meaningful, and Timely Opportunity to Participate' in the Delegate Selection Process," dated only as September, 1969, Presidential Libraries, National Archives, Washington, D.C.

15. Compare the texts in Commission on Party Structure and Delegate Selection, "Proposed Guidelines," September 23, 1969, with those in McGovern to Dear Friend, with attachments, October 3, 1969, Presidential Libraries, National Archives, Washington, D.C. For quorum requirements, compare pp. 8–9 with p. 6, respectively; for uniform dates and places, compare p. 7 with p. 5.

16. Voting yes were Commissioners Beer, Dodds, Graves, Henry, Hughes, Knox, Mixner, and Pena. Voting no were Collins, Davis, Dutton, English, Mitchell, Peden, Rampton, and Stevenson. Commissioners Bayh, Fraser, and McGovern were temporarily absent. Transcription of tapes, "Meeting of the Commission on Party Structure and Delegate Selection, September 23 and 24, 1969," private papers of Kenneth A. Bode.

17. This resolution was unofficially confirmed in Howard G. Gamser to James G. O'Hara, memorandum, "Breakfast Meeting This Date," September 15, 1969, private papers of Eli J. Segal. The differing positions going into this breakfast meeting were summarized in Segal to McGovern, memorandum, "Overlapping Jurisdiction of Mc-Govern and O'Hara Commissions," August 18, 1969, and Howard G. Gamser, "Memorandum: Jurisdiction over State-by-State Delegate Apportionment Formula," undated, Presidential Libraries, National Archives, Washington, D.C.

18. McGovern to Dear Friend, cited October 3, 1969, and attached document, untitled hereafter cited as Commission on Party Structure and Delegate Selection, memorandum, "Proposed Guidelines for Public Review," October 3, 1969, Presidential Libraries, National Archives, Washington, D.C. The two supplemental papers went out under a second McGovern to Dear Friend, October 20, 1969, and included Alexander M. Bickel, "Fair Representation of Minority Political Views," and Richard C. Wade, "Apportionment," Presidential Libraries, National Archives, Washington, D.C.

19. These four memos are, respectively: Commission Staff to Commission members, memorandum, "Responses to Proposed Guidelines," November 12, 1969; " 'Requires'—'Urges'—'Recommends'—'All Feasible Efforts,' " November 12, 1969; "Commission Action on Apportionment and the Fair Representation of Minority Political Views," November 12, 1969; "Clarifying Language and Suggested Substantive Changes," November 13, 1969, Presidential Libraries, National Archives, Washington, D.C.

20. Ibid.

21. The *New York Times* and the *Washington Post* offered pieces on each day's events. The *Atlanta Constitution* offered the Associated Press summary for the first day but not the second. The *Dallas Morning News,* the *Cleveland Plain Dealer,* and the *San Francisco Chronicle* included news service accounts for the second day but

not the first. The *Denver Post*, the *Chicago Tribune*, the *Los Angeles Times*, the *Houston Post*, and the *St. Louis Post-Dispatch* did not report on either day. Among these, see Warren Weaver, Jr., "Democrats Split on Party Reform," *New York Times*, September 24, 1969, p. 16; Weaver, "Democratic Reform Commission Asks Full Party Participation for Youths from 18 to 20," *New York Times*, September 25, 1969, p. 27; William Greider, "McGovern Unit Divided Over Delegate Issue," *Washington Post*, September 24, 1969, p. A2; "Democrats Urged to Accept 18-Year-Olds," *Washington Post*, September 25, 1969, p. A6.

22. Two hearings captured the range of these confrontations. The first was the one scheduled for New Orleans on May 22, 1969. J. Marshall Brown, national committeeman for Louisiana, led a public attack on the proposed session, an attack which was privately supported by many other party and public officeholders. Brown asserted that the Party Structure Commission had not only ignored protocol in "invading" Louisiana, but had provided late and limited notice of its hearing to the regular party and early and extensive notice to party dissidents. His protests were so vehement that the hearing was transferred to Jackson, Mississippi. Brown to Harris, May 13, 1969, and J. Marshall Brown, press release, untitled, June 5, 1969, Presidential Libraries, National Archives, Washington, D.C. Brown then clashed directly with commission personnel at a rescheduled hearing in New Orleans on July 19. "Demos Favor Open Method of Selection," *New Orleans Times-Picayune*, July 20, 1969, pp. 1 and 8.

The contrasting example was in Chicago, on June 7, 1969. There, Mayor Richard J. Daley appeared with his own lengthy and detailed proposals for delegate selection reform. Chairman McGovern, however, having taken charge of the task force for this particular hearing, ignored Daley's substance and instead used the occasion to urge him to drop charges against dissidents arrested during the 1968 Convention. Daley and McGovern traded angry words over the suggestion. Arthur Siddon, "Plea for 'Soft-Stand' by McGovern Is Refused by Daley," *Chicago Tribune*, June 8, 1969, p. 1; James Campbell, "McGovern and Daley Reopen Old Wounds," *Washington Post*, June 8, 1969, p. A1.

23. On the fate of the New Democratic Coalition, see Steven V. Roberts, "For Former Supporters of McCarthy and Kennedy, New Politics Is a Many-Splintered Thing," *New York Times*, October 5, 1969, p. 68; Paul R. Wieck, "What Happened to the New Politics?" *The New Republic*, February 28, 1970, pp. 12–13; and "The Middle Class Meanders," in Stephen C. Schlesinger, *The New Reformers* (Boston: Houghton Mifflin, 1975), pp. 109–36.

Chapter 6

1. Commission Staff to Commission Members, memorandum, " 'Requires'—'Urges'—'Recommends'—'All Feasible Efforts,' " November 12, 1969, Presidential Libraries, National Archives, Washington, D.C.

2. Commission Staff to McGovern, memorandum, "Items to be Discussed At Breakfast Meeting," November 3, 1969, Presidential Libraries, National Archives, Washington, D.C., p. 2.

3. Commission on Party Structure and Delegate Selection, memorandum, "Proposed Guidelines for Public Review," October 3, 1969, Presidential Libraries, National Archives, Washington, D.C., p. 3.

4. Author's transcription of tapes, "Meeting of the Commission on Party Structure and Delegate Selection, November 19–20, 1969," files of the Democratic National Committee, Washington, D.C. In this chapter, all direct quotations which begin with the name of the speaker italicized, are from the author's transcription of this complete set of tapes for the November 19–20 meeting. Individual footnotes are omitted for these quotations. When short comments transcribed from these tapes are introduced directly into the text, those quotations are still footnoted. Normal conventions of footnoting continue for all other citations, and direct quotations from personal interviews continue to be presented in the form used in preceding chapters.

5. Ibid.

6. Ibid.

7. Commission on Party Structure and Delegate Selection, memorandum, "Proposed Guidelines for Public Review," p. 3.

8. Commission on Party Structure and Delegate Selection, *Mandate for Reform* (Washington: Democratic National Committee, 1970), p. 40.

9. Each guideline had gone through three systematic revisions on its way to the November meetings. These were: Staff to Executive Committee, Commission on Party Structure and Delegate Selection, memorandum, "Proposed Guidelines, 'Full, Meaningful, and Timely' Opportunity to Participate in the Delegate Selection Process," undated; Commission on Party Structure and Delegate Selection, "Proposed Guidelines," September 23, 1969; and Commission on Party Structure and Delegate Selection, memorandum, "Proposed Guidelines for Public Review," October 3, 1969. The guidelines were then recast unofficially by the staff during the weeks leading up to the November meetings, in Commission Staff to Commission Members, memorandum, "Clarifying Language and Suggested Substantive Changes," November 13, 1969. The textual analysis in this chapter is based on these four documents—all in Presidential Libraries, National Archives, Washington, D.C.

10. *Mandate for Reform,* p. 44.

11. Alexander M. Bickel, "Fair Representation of Minority Political Views," undated but mailed under a covering letter, McGovern to Dear Friend, October 20, 1969, Presidential Libraries, National Archives, Washington, D.C.

12. Richard C. Wade, "Apportionment," undated but mailed under a covering letter, McGovern to Dear Friend, October 20, 1969, Presidential Libraries, National Archives, Washington, D.C.

13. It was during this series of exchanges, when several side conversations were in progress but when no real motion was in evidence, that the telephone in the Senate Caucus Room began to ring. Mitchell looked at his colleagues and announced, "It's Nixon calling. He says we're doing great." "Meeting of the Commission on Party Structure and Delegate Selection, November 19–20, 1969."

14. *Mandate for Reform,* p. 45.

15. "Meeting of the Commission on Party Structure and Delegate Selection, November 19–20, 1969."

16. *Mandate for Reform,* p. 45.

17. Commission Staff to Commission Members, memorandum, "Clarifying Language and Suggested Substantive Changes," p. 7.

18.   *Mandate for Reform,* p. 47.

19.   Minority Report of the Committee on Rules and Order of Business, adopted August 27, 1968, as reprinted in Congressional Quarterly Service, *The Presidential Nominating Conventions 1968* (Washington: Congressional Quarterly Service, 1968), p. 198.

20.   One other, even less tangible contribution to the product of this final meeting—and again, one which contributed to the side of militant reform—was the character of the rhetoric used in public argument over the draft guidelines. If those who were most critical of staff proposals suffered from insufficient numbers, a lack of formal leadership, and the total absence of staff, they were also frequently on the unpleasant end of a style of public discourse in which they themselves did not engage. Mixner, Dutton, and Hughes, among the commissioners, and even Bode, Segal, and Wexler, among the staff, turned intermittently to an extremely forceful, morally loaded, pointedly ad hominem rhetoric. Austin Ranney was one who found this particularly frustrating:

> I would guess that Fred Dutton took up about 75 percent of the Commission's time, and now that I think about it, Dave Mixner took the other 75 percent. Mixner was always reliving 1968 at the top of his lungs, and anyone who dared disagree with him was consummately evil.
>
> Yeah, but Fred Dutton was the one who got me most of all. He'd look at me and say, "Well, Professor, I guess the question is, 'Do you want to be for democracy or not?', 'Are you for or against blacks?' " and so on. I've always hated that "well, Professor" business. I always wanted to grab him by the throat and say, "Well, Lawyer, how simple-minded can you be?"

Chapter 7

1.   This time, most major newspapers did offer at least the wire service account of the two-day session. This is contained, for example, in the *Louisville Courier-Journal,* the *Dallas Morning News,* the *Atlanta Constitution,* the *Cleveland Plain Dealer,* the *Denver Post,* the *Chicago Tribune,* and the *Philadelphia Inquirer.* Among those who offered accounts from their own reporters, see especially, R. W. Apple, Jr., "Democrats Bar Delegate Order," *New York Times,* November 20, 1969, p. 21; Apple, "Democrats Widen Urban Influence," *New York Times,* November 21, 1969, p. 21; William Greider, "Democrats Reform Delegate Selection," *Washington Post,* November 21, 1969, p. A2.

2.   The more limited injunction to *have* written rules, along with the seven minimum inclusions, were contained in Guideline A–5 (Existence of Party Rules). Commission on Party Structure and Delegate Selection, *Mandate for Reform* (Washington: Democratic National Committee, 1970), pp. 41–42. But in a very real sense, the larger break with American political practice was contributed not by any one guideline but by the commission report as a whole.

3.   The records of the Party Structure Commission, subsequently transferred to the National Archives, were a highly useful compilation of state party rules and practices in delegate selection. These were most comprehensively summarized in the "state-books" which the commission used during its fall meetings on the draft guide-

lines; they were also carefully excerpted for the detailed compliance letters which eventually went out to all state chairmen. The most comprehensive survey of state party rules and procedures in the immediate postwar period was in Paul T. David, Malcolm C. Moos, and Ralph M. Goldman, *Presidential Nominating Politics in 1952*, vols. 1–4 (Baltimore: Johns Hopkins University Press, 1954). A similarly useful survey for the 1930s was in Ralph L. Baldridge, comp., *Manner of Selecting Delegates to National Political Conventions With Information on States Holding Presidential Primaries* (Washington: U.S. Government Printing Office, 1939).

4.   The interaction of three separate guidelines was necessary to dispatch the party caucus. C–4 (Timeliness) forbade sitting party officials from convening for the purpose of delegate selection. B–2 (Clarity of Purpose) required that even when these officials were selected concurrently, they had to be chosen outside a separable, and specially marked, process of delegate selection. A–5 (Existence of Party Rules) finished the prohibition by demanding that any Democrat be permitted to participate in this explicitly restructured procedure (*Mandate for Reform*, pp. 47, 43, and 41–42, respectively).

5.   Guideline C–1 (Adequate Public Notice) produced the ban on the delegate primary through a single phrase requiring "information on the ballot as to the presidential preference of (1) candidates or slates for delegate. . . ." (*Mandate for Reform*, p. 46). An ironic look at the intentions of the commissioners in the aftermath of this prohibition on party caucusesand delegate primaries was first recorded by Commissioner Austin Ranney, in "The Line of the Peas: The Impact of the McGovern-Fraser Commission's Reforms," a paper presented to the Annual Meeting of the American Political Science Association in 1972, subsequently revised for Ranney, "Changing the Rules of the Nominating Game," in James D. Barber, ed., *Choosing the President* (Englewood Cliffs, N.J.: Prentice-Hall, 1974), pp. 73–74.

6.   Guideline C–5 (Committee Selection Processes) contained the 10 percent ceiling and required that any committee which availed itself of this narrowed privilege be constructed in accordance with the other seventeen guidelines, as applicable (*Mandate for Reform*, pp. 47–48).

7.   Guideline B–6, formally and fully titled "Adequate Representation of Minority Views on Presidential Candidates at Each Stage in the Delegate Selection Process," contributed these strictures (*Mandate for Reform*, pp. 44–45).

8.   Guideline B–7 (Apportionment) accomplished this (*Mandate for Reform*, p. 45).

9.   This extension, in all its ambiguity, was contained in the final Guideline, C–6 (Slate-Making) (*Mandate for Reform*, p. 48).

10.   Guidelines A–1 (Discrimination on the Basis of Race, Color, Creed, or National Origin) and A–2 (Discrimination on the Basis of Age or Sex) offered the provisions in question. The footnote which elaborated upon, without necessarily clarifying, the intent of the commissioners was below A–2 on the printed page but was referenced to both guidelines (*Mandate for Reform*, pp. 39–40).

11.   The text of Guideline C–2 obviously removed these lesser figures from their previously reserved positions, but the staff managed to word the title to suggest that the National Committee might be included in this removal. Or at least the title as published referred the reader directly to the other guideline, C–4 (Premature Delegate Selection), which was the basis for dispossessing the National Committee. The pub-

lished title read "C–2, Automatic (Ex Officio) Delegates (see also C–4)" (*Mandate for Reform*, p. 46).

12. The "B" guidelines in particular were aimed at insulating the choice of a presidential nominee from influence by party officialdom. Guideline B–1 (Proxy Voting) had been adopted after a debate which featured this insulation as an explicit argument. B–2 (Clarity of Purpose) had gone on to rule that party officials could not blend the mechanics of delegate selection with other, normal, party business. B–3 (Quorum Provisions) had prevented the regular party from meeting at all under some circumstances. And B–4 (Selection of Alternates/Filling of Vacancies) had guaranteed that the regular party, stripped of most activities in delegate selection, would not come back in at the replacement stage.

Even after the commissioners adjourned, this move to separate the regular party from the process of delegate selection continued, through some additional *staff* initiatives. In Guideline C–4, for example, the staff added a provision that no party officials who were not elected in accordance with these regulations could either propose *or endorse* a slate of delegates (*Mandate for Reform*, p. 47). In such a provision, the attempted abasement of the regular party was at its zenith, since it was *only* the official party—not interest groups, not issue coalitions, and not candidate campaigns—which was ordered to abide by this restriction.

13. For a comprehensive review of the impact of these structural changes, see James W. Ceasar, *Reforming the Reforms: A Critical Analysis of the Presidential Selection Process* (Cambridge, Mass.: Ballinger, 1982); Nelson W. Polsby, *Consequences of Party Reform* (New York: Basic Books, 1983); and "The Reform of Political Institutions," in William J. Crotty, *Political Reform & the American Experiment* (New York: Crowell, 1977), pp. 193–264. These three examinations of the impact of reform differ profoundly in their view of its ultimate virtues. None, however, discovers any need to refer to delegate apportionment in the course of their analyses.

14. Author's transcription of tapes, "Meeting of the Commission on Party Structure and Delegate Selection, November 19–20, 1969," files of the Democratic National Committee, Washington, D.C. Another example of this criterion of concrete impact, again from the debate on apportionment, involved John English and Will Davis, and highlighted both the role of personal experience and the conflict between a philosophy of open and participatory parties and one of organized and disciplined counterparts:

> *English:* We're adding a provision here for enrollment. Now in my state, I'll tell you what will happen. The City of New York, which will control the state, will now apportion on the basis of enrollment, and the City of New York has the enrollment. It will dominate the delegates; they will choose about 70 percent of the delegates to the national convention. . . .
> *Davis* (interrupts): Then use another method.
> *English:* We allow this, and they'll adopt it.

15. Guideline B–7 (Apportionment), required that 75 percent of a state delegation be selected below the statewide level and extended the new apportionment formula to the grass-roots level as well. Guideline B–5 (Unit Rule) created the ban on favorite sons, via footnote 4. Guideline C–4 (Premature Delegate Selection) prohibited endorsement of any delegate slate by the regular party (*Mandate for Reform*, pp. 45, 44, and 47, respectively).

16. This continuing difference was a source of persistent tension between the two leadership figures. Or at least, the no-holds-barred attitude of Hughes was a continual irritant to McGovern:

> I came to distrust Hughes very strongly through getting to know him as Vice Chairman. He was so blunt and inflexible, and had a bad sense for timing. I felt that if Hughes had been Chairman, he would have driven us right into the ditch. Sometimes Hughes would come to me himself with something that "just had to be done," but I would try to finesse him and wait him out. You often had to finesse things in that Commission, or it would have flown apart.

Chapter 8

1. Recalled in personal interview.

2. Author's transcription of tapes, "Meeting of the Commission on Party Structure and Delegate Selection, November 19–20, 1969," files of the Democratic National Committee, Washington, D.C.

3. Eli Segal did go on to collect some formal propositions supporting the claim that the guidelines were already party law. Segal, "Delegate Selection Standards: The Democratic Party's Experience," *George Washington Law Review,* 38 (July 1970). 5, pp. 873–91. Even his advisers on this article, however, John R. Schmidt and Wayne W. Whalen, who had written an earlier law review piece to support aggressive action by the commission, did not believe that formal assertions were worth much in the face of the practical politics in this realm. Schmidt and Whalen to Segal, August 26, 1969, private papers of Eli J. Segal.

4. The largest share of this work became the responsibility of Carol Casey, former intern and eventual staff assistant:

> Our earlier state reports were based on hearsay, conversations with reporters and state chairmen, etc., and that was good enough for the Commission. But then the compliance letters had to be based on state law and actual party rules.

5. McGovern to National Committeemen and Committeewomen, December 9, 1969, Presidential Libraries, National Archives, Washington, D.C.

6. This went to the chairman on December 16, along with a page of tactical suggestions:

> We think it best for you to sign the cover letter and let the report stand as a staff analysis, so that you personally won't be implicated in any errors that occur in our compliance report at this time.
>
> You may want the report accompanying the cover letter entitled something like "The (Michigan) Delegate Selection Process: A Staff (or, "A Preliminary Staff") Analysis." We believe the word "compliance" or its equivalent should not be used in the title or in the text of the analysis.

Staff to McGovern, memorandum, "Compliance Letters," December 16, 1969, Presidential Libraries, National Archives, Washington, D.C., p. 1.

7. McGovern to Thomas Z. Minehart, February 27, 1970, Presidential Libraries, National Archives, Washington, D.C.

8. These figures were drawn from "Party Record of Compliance, 1968–1972," final table in Commission on Party Structure and Delegate Selection, draft report, untitled and undated, Presidential Libraries, National Archives, Washington, D.C., p. 35. This draft was prepared by the commission staff in preparation for the 1972 Convention.

9. This mailing was Commission on Party Structure and Delegate Selection, memorandum, "Proposed Guidelines for Public Review," October 3, 1969, Presidential Libraries, National Archives, Washington, D.C. Returns were summarized in Commission Staff to Commission Members, memorandum, "Responses to Proposed Guidelines," November 12, 1969, Presidential Libraries, National Archives, Washington, D.C.

While the mailing of guidelines for public review was an obvious opportunity for unhappy outsiders to respond, they would probably have had to do so in some way other than merely answering this formal query in order to have had much serious impact. For the cataloguing of formal responses became, in fact, one more opportunity for the *staff* to reconstruct these in the most useful way—useful, that is, for channeling the commissioners in its preferred direction.

10. Bode and Segal to McGovern, memorandum, "Commission Report," January 26, 1970, Presidential Libraries, National Archives, Washington, D.C., plus attachment.

11. Richard G. Stearns, "The Presidential Nominating Process in the United States: The Constitution of the Democratic National Convention" (thesis, Balliol College, Oxford University, June, 1971).

12. Commission Staff to Commission Members, memorandum, "Commission Report," January 30, 1970, Presidential Libraries, National Archives, Washington, D.C.

13. Bode and Segal to McGovern, memorandum, "Commission Report," p. 1.

14. R. W. Apple, Jr., "Harris Quits Post as Democrats' Chief," *New York Times*, February 7, 1970, p. 1; William Greider, "Harris Quits Top Party Job," *Washington Post*, February 7, 1970, p. A1.

15. Commission on Party Structure and Delegate Selection, *Mandate for Reform* (Washington: Democratic National Committee, 1970).

16. Ibid., p. 7.

17. Ibid., p. 6.

18. Ibid., p. 9. The law review article by Eli Segal, published three months later, went even further with the same construction, by removing the ellipse and the asterisk:

> The Convention resolution directing the appointment of the Commission indicated that the Commission would be responsible for aiding the states in meeting the requirement of the 1972 Call that all party members have a "full, meaningful, and timely opportunity" to participate.

Segal, "Delegate Selection Standards" pp. 881–82.

19. *Mandate for Reform*, p. 36.

20. Ibid., p. 49.

21. R. W. Apple, Jr., "Democrats Press for Party Reform," *New York Times*, April 29, 1970, p. 1.

22. Ibid.

23. The absence of minority reports in the published report of the commission—the failure of internal critics to produce and append their internal criticism—surely worked in the same fashion. That is, the absence of minority reports also reduced apparent conflict, while permitting the commission staff to continue to operate in an untrammeled fashion.

Chapter 9

1. See, for example, "O'Brien is Expected to Head Democrats," *New York Times,* February 18, 1970, p. 18; "Humphrey Is Seeking O'Brien as Chairman," *New York Times,* February 24, 1970, p. 34; "HHH Asks O'Brien to Take Party Post," *Washington Post,* February 24, 1970, p. 2.

2. James M. Naughton, "O'Brien Turns Down Chairmanship of Democrats," *New York Times,* February 27, 1970, p. 23.
It was not merely outsiders who were caught short by O'Brien's withdrawal:
> No one was more surprised or upset than former Vice-President Hubert
> H. Humphrey, who as titular leader of the out-of-power party had searched
> for a new chairman that all factions could accept.
> Humphrey offered the post to O'Brien in a meeting last Friday and was
> so certain he would accept that personal letters from Humphrey were pre-
> pared for mailing today to the 108 national committeemembers telling
> them that O'Brien was the consensus choice.

William Greider, "O'Brien Rejects Party Post," *Washington Post,* February 27, 1970, p. 1.

3. Christopher Lydon, "Fight to Lead Democrats Breaks Out in Committee," *New York Times,* March 2, 1970, p. 1.

4. The quotations from Arvey are, respectively, from R. W. Apple, Jr., "Democrats Back O'Brien for Post," *New York Times,* March 3, 1970, p. 21; and William Chapman, "O'Brien Gets 2d Party Bid," *Washington Post,* March 3, 1970, p. 1.

5. R. W. Apple, Jr., "O'Brien Accepts Democrats' Call," *New York Times,* March 4, 1970, p. 1; and William Chapman, "O'Brien Accepts Offer to Become Party Chief," *Washington Post,* March 4, 1970, p. 1.

6. William Chapman, "Victory Seen for O'Brien Despite Rivals," *Washington Post,* March 5, 1970, p. 2.

7. R. W. Apple, Jr., "O'Brien Elected Party Chairman," *New York Times,* March 6, 1970, p. 1.; William Chapman, "Democrats Make Choice of O'Brien Unanimous," *Washington Post,* March 6, 1970, p. 2.

8. Lawrence F. O'Brien, *No Final Victories: A Life in Politics—From John F. Kennedy to Watergate* (Garden City, N.Y.: Doubleday, 1974), p. 273.

9. Immediately after O'Brien's first rejection of the chairmanship, for example, George McGovern issued a statement urging that subsequent recruiting efforts be carried out in a different manner, one which would "keep faith with the commitment" of the 1968 Convention. James M. Naughton, "O'Brien Turns Down Chairmanship of Democrats," *New York Times,* February 27, 1970, p. 23. Immediately after O'Brien

relented and agreed to return as chairman, another group of self-conscious dissident Democrats, including David Mixner of the Party Structure Commission and Julian Bond of the old Hughes Commission, issued a statement asserting that "the lessons of 1968 have been neglected". R. W. Apple, Jr., "Group of Left-Wing Democrats Assails Methods Used in Selecting National Chairman," *New York Times*, March 5, 1970, p. 25.

10.   For the rumors—and rumblings—of discontent from these various sources, see James M. Naughton, "O'Brien Turns Down Chairmanship of Democrats," *New York Times*, February 27, 1970, p. 23; William Greider, "O'Brien Rejects Party Post," *Washington Post*, February 27, 1970, p. 1; R. W. Apple, Jr., "Democrats Back O'Brien for Post," *New York Times*, March 3, 1970, p. 21; William Chapman, "O'Brien Gets 2d Party Bid," *Washington Post*, March 3, 1970, p. 1. The appointment of McNair, completing this slate of national officers, is noted in "Democrats Name McNair," *New York Times*, April 5, 1970, p. 52.

11.   Califano to O'Brien, memorandum, "Status of Guidelines Issued by Commission on Party Structure and Delegate Selection," May 18, 1970, Presidential Libraries, National Archives, Washington, D.C., p. 1.

12.   Ibid., p. 3.

13.   Ibid., p. 4.

14.   Ibid.

15.   Democratic National Committee, "Transcript of Proceedings, May 22, 1970," Presidential Libraries, National Archives, Washington, D.C., p. 36.

16.   The Chairman of Ad Hoc Committee No. 1 was Geraldine M. Joseph, vice chairman of the Democratic National Committee. Its members were George J. Mitchell, national committeeman from Maine and member of the Party Structure Commission; Carrin M. Patman, national committeewoman from Texas; F. Grant Sawyer, national committeeman from Nevada; and Richard B. Stoner, national committeeman from Indiana.

17.   O'Brien to McGovern, May 23, 1970, Presidential Libraries, National Archives, Washington, D.C., p. 2.

18.   O'Brien to Members of the Commission on Party Structure and Delegate Selection, May 25, 1970, Presidential Libraries, National Archives, Washington, D.C.

19.   Indeed, a decision to withdraw from open party conflict by one principal actor, Hubert Humphrey, was also central to both selections. The fact that Humphrey retreated from politics in the aftermath of the 1968 election was crucial to the arrival of Harris at the national chairmanship. The fact that Humphrey was unprepared to drive his preference to a conflicted vote in the aftermath of Harris's resignation was crucial to the return of O'Brien as national chairman.

20.   This long-run implication was necessarily hidden even to the most perceptive observers; the short-run perception—that O'Brien was freer to choose his own course on party reform than he would otherwise have been—was available to the more incisive, like R. W. Apple, Jr.:

> The problem with Mr. Humphrey's defense, in the view of many Democrats, is that the impression had already been created, rightly or wrongly, that the 1968 Presidential candidate has lost his clout. Power in America is a fragile thing, which flows away from those who are believed by their peers to have lost it. Nothing fails, in other words, like the appearance of

failure. "The important thing," said one pro-Humphrey Governor today, "is that he failed to put across his choice, period."

That, too, is partly unfair. Mr. O'Brien did turn the former Vice President down. But Mr. Welsh would have been elected had Mr. Humphrey wanted to turn the screws. He had at least 6 of the 10 votes on the executive committee and probably would have had one or two more in a showdown. A majority of the full 108-member committee could certainly have been mobilized for him. But Mr. Humphrey chose not to push his titular leadership of the party that far.

The result is that Mr. O'Brien has been elected owing little to anyone. He will be able to preach unity more convincingly than if he had been Mr. Humphrey's man, but he will also become a rival power center within the party, like it or not.

R. W. Apple, Jr., "Dilemma of Hubert Humphrey," *New York Times,* March 7, 1970, p. 15.

Chapter 10

1. At first, their Executive Committee gave some signs of maintaining a larger commission presence. Thus, the committee did reassemble in McGovern's Senate office on the morning of July 7, to show the flag and to discuss future projects. But there was little at this stage for the committee to do, and the members adjourned until their next session—presumably in the fall, actually a full twelve months later.

In the same fashion, interested commissioners did constitute themselves as a Subcommittee on Youth Participation during the summer of 1970 and actually held a public hearing on the morning of July 29. Yet once that event had passed—once it had gained some of the desired press coverage—the subcommittee, too, disappeared from sight.

2. This reluctance to intervene was not for lack of exhortation from the staff. On July 17, for example, Bob Nelson requested all commission members to search out states where their intervention might be effective and to undertake it. Robert Nelson, Staff Director, to All Commission Members and Consultants, memorandum, "Status of Progress in States and Territories," July 17, 1970, Presidential Libraries, National Archives, Washington, D.C.

Nevertheless, this was fated to be an unproductive source of pressure for reform. Most commissioners had been selected for their *disconnection* from state party structures. Most of those for whom this was not so were either *opposed* to significant provisions in the commission report or were drawn off into other political activities, like pursuit of a presidential nomination.

3. Their advice was contained in Bode and Segal to McGovern, memorandum, undated but surely within the week of May 23–30, 1970, private papers of Kenneth A. Bode. The upshot was a joint letter from McGovern and O'Brien to all the state chairmen, endorsing the need for immediate action on reform (McGovern and O'Brien to Democratic State Chairmen, July 20, 1970, Presidential Libraries, National Archives, Washington, D.C.).

4. For the interaction of these two men and their supporters in 1968, see "Crossroads, 1968," in Albert M. Eisele, *Almost to the Presidency: A Biography of Two American Politicans* (Blue Earth, Minn.: Piper Company, 1972), pp. 283–92. For a more personal view of politics in Minnesota in that year, one which gives a strong sense of its organizational and emotional disarray, see David Lebedoff, *Ward Number Six* (New York: Scribner, 1972).

5. The reform commission was the DFL Advisory Committee on Constitutional Revision. Its report was "1968 DFL State Constitution with Proposed Changes," undated, Presidential Libraries, National Archives, Washington, D.C. Adoption came at a special constitutional convention in St. Paul, on September 20–21, 1969. The resulting revision was *Constitution of the Democratic-Farmer-Labor Party of Minnesota* (Minneapolis: The DFL State Central Committee, 1969).

6. Koryne Horbal and Warren R. Spannaus to Senator George McGovern, March 18, 1969, Presidential Libraries, National Archives, Washington, D.C.

7. The Pennsylvania story is recounted in chap. 12, "The Politics of Implementation Writ Small: Pennsylvania Accepts Reform."

8. For accounts of the California primary campaign, the assassination of Robert Kennedy on its final night, and the fallout from these events, see Theodore H. White, *The Making of the President 1968* (New York: Atheneum, 1969); and Lewis Chester, Godfrey Hodgson, and Bruce Page, *An American Melodrama: The Presidential Campaign of 1968* (New York: Viking Press, 1969).

9. The first of these communications from the national staff was, of course, the official compliance letter. McGovern to Boas, February 27, 1970, and attachment; Presidential Libraries, National Archives, Washington, D.C.. The California commission was announced in two releases in the spring California Democratic Party, press release, untitled, April 14, 1970; California Democratic Party, press release, "California Commission on Democratic Party Reform," June 15, 1970, Presidential Libraries, National Archives, Washington, D.C.

10. California Democratic Party, press release, untitled, April 14, 1970, p. 2.

11. The Texas story is recounted in chap. 18, "The Re-creation of Reform Standards: The Commission Staff and Proportionality."

12. These basic notions were systematically assembled and used to analytic advantage in James Q. Wilson, *The Amateur Democrat: Club Politics in Three Cities* (Chicago: University of Chicago Press, 1962). Wilson returned to them in a more abstract fashion in *Political Organizations* (New York: Basic Books, 1973).

13. There is no evident, single source on the distribution of volunteer and organized parties for the period from 1970 through 1972. Figure 10.1 was constructed by applying the definitions used throughout this chapter to three general sources on party behavior. In this, the manner in which nomination and election campaigns were constructed within a state was given special note.

The most detailed and comprehensive source was the specialized news weeklies, *National Journal* and, especially, *Congressional Quarterly*, for the period from January of 1966 through November of 1974. *Congressional Quarterly*, in particular, offered numerous individual state reports during these years, as well as at least one preprimary review and one systematic summary before the general elections for all the states as a group. For the 1970 elections, for example, *Congressional Quarterly Weekly Report* published eight special issues: "Election 1970: A Pre-Primary Supplement," February

20, 1970; "Election 1970: A Political Supplement," July 24, 1970; "Election 1970: The East," October 2, 1970; "Election 1970: The West," October 9, 1970; "Election 1970: The Midwest," October 16, 1970; "Election 1970: The South," October 23, 1970; "Election 1970: A Special Political Report," October 28, 1970; and "The 1970 Election: Results and Analyses," November 6, 1970.

A second source on the incidence of state party types was a set of collected commentaries on political life in the fifty states. Of particular use here was Daniel J. Elazar, *American Federalism: A View from the States* (New York: Crowell, 1966). Elazar's components of state "political culture" have a clear overlap with the elements which distinguish volunteer from organized state parties, and his "geology" (his mapping) of the appearance of these political cultures bears a clear resemblance to the mapping of state party types in Figure 10.1. See especially his chap. 4, "The States and the Political Setting," pp. 79–116.

A mammoth collection of reports on individual states, far more anecdotal but containing numerous instructive details, is the nine-volume corpus from Neal R. Peirce, *The Megastates of America* (1972); *The Pacific States of America* (1972); *The Mountain States of America* (1972); *The Great Plains States of America* (1973); *The Deep South States of America* (1974); *The Border South States* (1975); *The New England States* (1976); *The Mid-Atlantic States of America* (1977), co-authored with Michael Barone; and *The Great Lakes States of America* (1980), co-authored with John Keefe (New York: Norton, 1972–80).

The classification resulting from these two sources of data was then checked against a third source, the personal impressions of key participants in reform politics during this period. Partial impressions from many relevant figures are scattered throughout the text. But two individuals central to the progress of the party reform were questioned about the state parties in more systematic fashion. Lawrence F. O'Brien, Democratic national chairman, and Robert W. Nelson, staff director for the Party Structure Commission, each offered numerous comments in passing about the structure of party politics within various states; both were asked more specifically to describe those parties in these general terms; both graciously consented to do so. The outcome of this combined data set is Figure 10.1.

14.   Some explanations for this decline are summarized succinctly in "Local Politics: Old-Time Machines and Modern Variants," in Fred I. Greenstein, *The American Party System and the American People*, 2d ed. (Englewood Cliffs, N.J.: Prentice-Hall, 1970). Both the mix in existing patterns of party structure and, especially, the reasons for the persistence of organized parties are discussed theoretically in Raymond E. Wolfinger, "Why Political Machines Have not Withered and Other Revisionist Thoughts," *Journal of Politics*, 34 (May 1972): 365–98.

15.   The best example of this sort of analysis applied to a set of American parties remains V. O. Key, Jr., *Southern Politics in State and Nation* (New York: Vintage Books, 1949).

16.   Figure 10.2 was developed by combining two commission synopses: Commission on Party Structure and Delegate Selection, report, "Party Reform One Year Later: A Summary of Developments in State Democratic Parties," March 1970, and Robert W. Nelson, memorandum to the file, untitled, June 12, 1970, Presidential Libraries, National Archives, Washington, D.C.

In these and all subsequent figures on the progress of compliance, the "state parties" include those in the fifty states and the District of Columbia, but not those in the four territories. The status of the latter was difficult even for the commission staff to monitor, and they were rarely included in commission summaries.

17. Figure 10.3 was developed from Robert W. Nelson, Staff Director, to Executive Committee Members, memorandum, "Response of State Parties to Date," July 6, 1970, Presidential Libraries, National Archives, Washington, D.C.

Chapter 11

1. Numerous articles about the 1970 midterm elections characterize them as a referendum on the fledging Nixon administration. See, for example, David S. Broder, "GOP Senate Gains, House Standoff Seen," *Washington Post*, October 11, 1970, pp. A1 and 18; "Gains Seen For Both Parties," *Washington Post*, October 12, 1970, pp. A1 and 2; "Nixon Unlikely to Get a GOP Senate," *Washington Post*, November 1, 1970, p. B1. See also, Max Frankel, "A Trendless Election," *New York Times*, October 13, 1970, p. 38; Tom Wicker, "Mr. Nixon at Half-Time," *New York Times*, November 5, 1970, p. 47; R. W. Apple, Jr., "Election: What Vote Meant—Nixon Must Change to Survive," *New York Times*, November 8, 1970, Part IV, p. 1.

2. These prefatory comments were actually contained on page two of the note transferring the draft report of the subcommittee to the national chairman. The note itself was McGovern to O'Brien, September 24, 1970; the attached draft was Commission on Party Structure and Delegate Selection, report, "Youth Participation Subcommittee Report," Presidential Libraries, National Archives, Washington, D.C.

3. Hughes, like McGovern, was out on the hustings in the fall of 1970, supporting local Democratic candidates, and creating the possibility of reciprocal support at some later date; for example, Robert H. Phelps, "Senator Hughes Quietly Pushes 1972 Presidential Bid," *New York Times*, October 29, 1970, p. 48.

4. Democratic National Committee, press release, "O'Brien Names Rep. Fraser to Head Reform Panel," January 7, 1971, Presidential Libraries, National Archives, Washington, D.C.

5. Figure 11.1 was developed from Richard M. Scammon, comp. and ed., *America Votes*, vol. 9, 1970 (Washington, D.C.: Governmental Affairs Institute, 1972).

6. The classic overview of these differences in institutional perspective is V. O. Key, Jr., *American State Politics: An Introduction* (New York: Knopf, 1956). Useful analyses of these two contrasting institutions, the governorship and the state chairmanship, based upon data and impressions from the period between 1968 and 1972 are in Thad L. Beyle and J. Oliver Williams, eds., *The American Governor in Behavioral Perspective* (New York: Harper & Row, 1972); Robert J. Huckshorn, *Party Leadership in the States* (Amherst: University of Massachusetts Press, 1976).

7. Figure 11.2 was developed from Congressman Donald M. Fraser, commission chairman, to Democratic Party Chairmen, memorandum, "Report on the Status of the States," January 7, 1971, and Commission on Party Structure and Delegate Selection, memorandum to the file, "Report on Status of State Parties," December 15, 1971, Presidential Libraries, National Archives, Washington, D.C.

8. Bob Nelson watched the internal opposition to reform in Georgia, buttressed by party rules which concentrated formal power in the hands of the incumbent governor, Lester G. Maddox, crumble rapidly with the advent of the self-proclaimed reformer, Jimmy Carter:

> They were the farthest out of compliance of any state. There had never been in their entire history an *elected* official of the state party. There was no party structure beyond the Governor. Theoretically, if they had had a Republican Governor, *he* would have appointed their party officials.
>
> Their State Chairman and National Committee people were part of the Maddox machine. Marge Thurman, their National Committeewoman, wanted to do some things. When Carter came in, he laid down a mandate for the first constitutional convention ever. They had to begin by writing some sets of rules; we sent out a model set of rules. We took what was a political system and put it into a quasi-judicial system. In March, 1971, Carter gave them the mandate; once he laid down the mandate, that was it.

9. Analyses of gubernatorial races by *Congressional Quarterly, Newsweek, Time,* and the *Washington Post* all make reference to this larger subset of explicit "progressives." "Election 1970: A Special Political Report," *Congressional Quarterly Weekly Report,* October 28, 1970; "The 1970 Election: Results and Analyses," *Congressional Quarterly Weekly Report,* November 6, 1970; "How the Races Look in the Homestretch," *Newsweek,* November 2, 1970, pp. 26–27; "Governors: A Democratic Blitz," *Newsweek,* November 16, 1970, pp. 44–45; "New Crop of Governors," *Time,* November 23, 1970, pp. 31–32; David S. Broder, "Republicans Lose Governorship Edge," *Washington Post,* November 4, 1970, p. A1; and William Chapman, "GOP Margin in Governors Wiped Out," *Washington Post,* November 4, 1970, p. A10.

10. Two sharply different analyses which nevertheless agree on these associated virtues of reform are William J. Crotty, *Reform and the American Experiment* (New York: Crowell, 1977); and Samuel P. Huntington, *American Politics: The Promise of Disharmony* (Cambridge, Mass.: Belknap Press, 1981).

11. A general formulation for this sort of comparison is Harold D. Lasswell, *Politics: Who Gets What, When, How* (New York: Meridian Books, 1958), first published in 1936. A specific application to the presidential politics of 1972 is Jeane J. Kirkpatrick, *The New Presidential Elite: Men and Women in National Politics* (New York: Russell Sage Foundation, 1976).

12. Eventually, there would indeed be a professional literature defending the regular party in presidential politics and criticizing participatory reforms. Three main works in this literature are Austin Ranney, *Curing the Mischiefs of Faction: Party Reform in America* (Berkeley: University of California Press, 1975); James W. Ceaser, *Presidential Selection: Theory and Development* (Princeton: Princeton University Press, 1979); and Nelson W. Polsby, *Consequences of Party Reform* (New York: Basic Books, 1983). The key fact about such works for the defense of party regularity in 1970, of course, was that they were still all prospective.

13. Donald M. Fraser, M.C., Chairman, to All State Democratic Parties and Reform Commissions, memorandum and report, "Model of Party Rules," undated but

mailed in early March 1971, Presidential Libraries, National Archives, Washington, D.C.

14. Each of these facets—elaboration, detail, precise alternatives, and resulting constriction of choice—is visible, for example, in the staff's rendering of Guideline B–7 (Apportionment) in "Model of Party Rules," pp. 17, 5, and 6 (in that order).

15. O'Brien's own account of these developments is in his autobiography, *No Final Victories: A Life in Politics—From John F. Kennedy to Watergate* (Garden City, N.Y.: Doubleday, 1974), pp. 313–16. A more comprehensive account—with a less sanitized version of O'Brien's response—is Theodore H. White, *The Making of the President 1972* (New York: Bantam Books, 1973), pp. 249–55.

Chapter 12

1. Useful, short, summary analyses of both the primary and general election contests are "Political Notes: Pa. Primary Outlook," *Congressional Quarterly Weekly Report*, May 6, 1966, pp. 931–32; and "Eastern States Outlook: Pennsylvania," *Congressional Quarterly Weekly Report*, September 30, 1966, pp. 2280–81.

2. For the April 23 primary results, see, for example, Ben A. Franklin, "Pennsylvania Vote Favors McCarthy and Senator Clark," *New York Times*, April 24, 1968, p. 29; "McCarthy Takes 10 to 1 Lead in Pa.," *Washington Post*, April 24, 1968, p. 1. Also see, "Tate Says Humphrey Had Edge Among Penna Delegates," *Philadelphia Inquirer*, May 24, 1968, p. 10, for the outcome of the state committee meeting.

3. For the record, this first reform commission was authorized by the state committee on May 23, 1968. The commission was appointed by Chairman Minehart on February 17, 1969. Its lone public hearing was held on July 17, 1969. Culbertson, its chairman, was not sorry to see it go:

> I don't think there was much sentiment for rules change in the State Committee. Minehart appointed me because he knew I could handle dirty problems, although I was not a Minehart supporter. I had felt that, since Shapp had won the nomination against the organization, he should be able to name his own man. The organization was in the hands of the Casey group, though, and they went for Minehart.
>
> The Rules Reform Committee met maybe twice in 1969. Usually, State Committee meetings were at one in the afternoon. Our meeting would be at ten in the morning, so that we could make a report to them.

4. Kline to McGovern, October 22, 1969, Presidential Libraries, National Archives, Washington, D.C., pp. 1–2.

5. The most ambitious of these was a single-spaced analysis of Pennsylvania rules and reform options in the late summer of 1970. Stephen Paul Mahinka, Majority Staff, To Whom It May Concern, memorandum, "McGovern Commission," August, 1970, Presidential Libraries, National Archives, Washington, D.C.

6. The reports in *Congressional Quarterly* on the primary and general election are again a short and useful summary; see "May 19 Pennsylvania Governor's Race is

Rerun of 1966," *Congressional Quarterly Weekly Report,* May 8, 1970, pp. 1232–33; "Eastern States Outlook: Pennsylvania," *Congressional Quarterly Weekly Report,* October 2, 1970, pp. 2375–76.

7. Fraser to Scales, undated but mailed January 22, 1971, Presidential Libraries, National Archives, Washington, D.C.

8. McGovern to Minehart, February 27, 1970, and attached "Analysis of the Delegate Selection Process," Presidential Libraries, National Archives, Washington, D.C.

9. Shapp to O'Brien, January 21, 1971, Presidential Libraries, National Archives, Washington, D.C.

10. Apparently, only the first fifteen pages of this draft document remain. Kenneth A. Bode, Center for Political Reform, to Pennsylvania Committees on Democratic Party Reform, memorandum, untitled and undated; private papers of Kenneth A. Bode.

11. New to Dear County Chairman, June 14, 1971, New to Dear Rules Reform Commission Member, June 14, 1971, New to O'Brien, June 15, 1971, Presidential Libraries, National Archives, Washington, D.C.

12. Russell W. Davis, state committee member from Cumberland County in rural central Pennsylvania, was one of those who attended instead, in order to vote no:

> At that time, there was just general confusion. The people from Delaware, Chester, and Bucks [counties in southeastern Pennsylvania] were leading that. Len Pevar was raising some hell. General confusion, plus the natural antipathy to being told how to run your own house. That was enough to kill off that report.

13. Maier quickly perceived the lack of consistency in national advice: "We were constantly hit by groups coming in and claiming to be 'authoritative,' from the National Committee. They *never* had any credentials."

14. Because reporters were excluded from the central events, newspaper accounts of this session are characterized by an awareness that something with surface drama was occurring but by a concurrent inability to give that "something" practical detail. See, for example, Cliff Linedecker, "Phone Call by Shapp Salvages Delegate Reform Bill," *Philadelphia Inquirer,* September 26, 1971, p. 4.

15. The reformers could be taken to task for being piously insincere, in adopting the very behaviors which had led them to attack the regular party. The regulars were following stereotyped form, to the point of trading the rules of the game for a few more jobs on the turnpike and a seat on the Turnpike Commission.

Of more consequence than this theoretically inappropriate debate was the fact that the Pennsylvania resolution was one more stereotypical version of the frequent solution at the national level—rules to the reformers, perquisites under them to the regulars. Even at the time, while they would not have used this precise formulation to describe the outcome, Pennsylvania observers, like AnnaMaria Malloy, saw the arrangement in quite similar terms:

> Scales was the product of a deal. Scales became Chairman if he would appoint a rules reform commission. Scales was a good compromise. We knew he had made a deal with the regulars not to disrupt their arrangements. It never occurred to the regulars that such a thing as rules reform would occur. Patronage was their focus, and they had made a deal with Shapp on that.

Chapter 13

1.   This very analysis had guided some of the principals at the Party Structure Commission in their original decision to bypass the National Committee and seek some initial successes in the states. Fred Dutton reflected on the danger to the reform drive represented by an attempt to address the National Committee directly, in early 1970, instead of waiting to accumulate some successes and then addressing it in early 1971:

> In a vague, subjective way, you had to be for "reform," and the only way to be for reform was to go with what the Commission had produced. On the other hand, if you pressed too hard too early, you might have forced exactly the wrong result. You might get knocked down, and then your momentum would be over. I felt that the staff was much too eager to join battle when things were running in our favor. You've got to protect your main position. If Bode had sucked us in, they would have jeopardized the main things.

2.   Methods of electing members of the National Committee are briefly summarized in the official book of the 1972 Convention, *Democrats in Convention 1972* (Washington, D.C.: Democratic National Committee, 1972), pp. 185–241.

3.   Cornelius P. Cotter and Bernard C. Hennessy, *Politics Without Power: The National Party Committees* (New York: Atherton Press, 1964), p. 3.

4.   Figure 13.1 was developed from Congressman Donald M. Fraser, Commission Chairman, to Democratic Party Chairmen, memorandum, "Report on the Status of the States," January 7, 1971; Presidential Libraries, National Archives, Washington, D.C.

5.   Navasky had put these ruminations on the public record at the time:

> My own view is that O'Brien, the son of Irish immigrant parents, is more than a power broker specializing in political hedge funds. He is something of a transition figure, combining traditional skills with untraditional experience and sophistication.
>
> At 51, O'Brien is a little old to serve as an instrument of the so-called New Politics, yet ironically that could prove to be his role . . .

Victor S. Navasky, "The Nomination, as Seen and Directed by the Best Politician in the Country," *New York Times Sunday Magazine*, September 8, 1968, pp. 32, 134–40.

6.   The draft text *before* amendment by the Executive Committee does not seem to have survived in either the National Archives or the records of the National Committee. Nevertheless, its substantive peregrinations are easily deciphered. The initial text for the rules of delegate selection was "The Official Guidelines of the Commission," in Commission on Party Structure and Delegate Selection, *Mandate for Reform* (Washington, D.C.; Democratic National Committee, 1970), pp. 38–48. The two major proposals on convention operations are covered in newspaper accounts of the Rules Commission. R. W. Apple, Jr., "Delegate Reform: A Democratic Showdown," *New York Times*, February 17, 1971, p. 14; David S. Broder, "Democrats Back Delegate Plan," *Washington Post*, February 17, 1971, p. A2. The final product after addition of O'Brien's proposed amendments was, of course, the Preliminary Call itself.

Democratic National Committee, "Preliminary Call for the 1972 Democratic National Convention," February 19, 1971; Presidential Libraries, National Archives, Washington, D.C..

7. Precise estimates of the size of these four blocs within the National Committee are difficult to derive, especially since the assignment of individual members to the various blocs was, in this case, made in the course of lobbying them about subsequent support. Most observers would have put the committed reform bloc at about a quarter of the membership, as did Jean Westwood of Utah, one of its most loyal adherents:

> There was a straw vote on Albert Rains early in this period. On that test vote, we got about thirty out of one hundred [and ten] members. This was all we could ever get as a liberal bloc. We knew that we could get that, but it was all.

8. Geri Joseph believed that this bloc was effectively the largest one, when classified for these purposes, within the National Committee:

> I think there was a tremendous uncertainty at the time. They couldn't see what would be the result of this stuff. They also knew that there had to be some changes. So if they had questions in their minds, a lot of them held back for that reason.

9. Barr of Pennsylvania was one of these members: "I'd bring up from time to time the question, 'Why aren't the Republicans doing any of this if it's so attractive?' "

10. Fraser was also responsible for providing Califano with the material which Califano—and O'Brien—would use in defending the guidelines substantively, a task he could undertake with a good deal more enthusiasm than O'Hara, since O'Brien was supporting Fraser's commission in its entirety—and challenging O'Hara's commission in its entirety as well. O'Brien to Fraser, February 5, 1971; Fraser to O'Brien, February 11, 1971, with attachments; Presidential Libraries, National Archives, Washington, D.C.

11. Bode's letter to an old nemesis, Carmen Warschaw, Party Structure commissioner and national committeewoman from California, was typical:

> I have learned that there is a move on to get the O'Hara Commission formula changed. . . . Our preliminary calculations indicate that this would be the kind of formula that would seriously penalize the larger states. Compared to the present O'Hara Commission formula, California would lose 23 delegates, New York 24, Pennsylvania 14, Michigan 8, Ohio 19, New Jersey 6, and so forth.

Bode to Warschaw, February 11, 1971; private papers of Kenneth A. Bode.

12. The best single source on the state party chairmen during this period is Robert J. Huckshorn, *Party Leadership in the States* (Amherst: University of Massachusetts Press, 1976).

13. Actually, there had been one informal meeting of state chairmen in 1969 and another in 1970, but it was not until the spring of 1971 that the "association" obtained office space and secretarial support, and not until the fall that it obtained an executive director. See "The Association of State Democratic Chairmen," in Robert J. Huckshorn, *Party Leadership in the States,* pp. 179–81.

14. For other events on the COPE calendar during this period, see Damon Stetson, "Democratic Hopefuls Woo Labor Council," New York *Times,* February 17, 1971, p. 15; "Labor Maps Plans for '72 Vote Drive," New York *Times,* February 18,

1971, p. 23. John Perkins, Barkan's chief lieutenant at COPE, experienced the same frustration with the way events unfolded:

> For February, 1971, Barkan had said, "Don't be too hasty." We couldn't even get Humphrey to deliver the Minnesota people. Al had called a number of people and asked them to lay it on the line. We got to Humphrey and Muskie, but they didn't follow through. Barkan was in Florida for the Executive Committee meeting, so he didn't have time to get into it. We took a short vacation after that, and then that meeting was on us. We asked Humphrey and Muskie and Jackson to talk to their people, to say that this was too complex. "Give us *time* to mobilize against it."

15. This proposal was later to receive serious consideration in joint meetings of the Rules and Party Structure commissions. "Democratic Reform Panels to Conduct Joint Study," *New York Times*, November 14, 1971, p. 66. The proposal was eventually endorsed as a reform for consideration by the 1972 Convention. Warren Weaver, Jr., "Democrats Urge Parley to Guide Party Standards," *New York Times*, May 20, 1972, p. 14; William Chapman, "Off-Year Democratic Convention Eyed," *Washington Post*, May 20, 1972, p. A2.

Chapter 14

1. This meeting was reported to the public in R. W. Apple, Jr., "Democratic Rivals Agree Not to Feud in Presidential Bid," *New York Times*, February 11, 1971, pp. 1 and 20.

2. Executive Committee of the Democratic National Committee, "Transcript of Proceedings, February 17, 1971," Presidential Libraries, National Archives, Washington, D.C., p. 49.

3. Ibid., p. 136.

4. Ibid., pp. 30–31.

5. William Chapman, "Democrats Vote Plan for Delegate Split," *Washington Post*, February 18, 1971, p. A4.

6. R. W. Apple, Jr., "Democrats Alter Reform Formula," *New York Times*, February 18, 1971, p. 17.

7. Democratic National Committee, "Transcript of Proceedings, February 19, 1971," Presidential Libraries, National Archives, Washington, D.C., p. 2.

8. Ibid., p. 6.

9. Ibid., p. 54.

10. Ibid., pp. 60–61.

11. Ibid., p. 73.

12. Ibid., pp. 87–88.

13. Ibid., pp. 89–90.

14. This final ballot is on p. 164 of Democratic National Committee, "Transcript of Proceedings, February 19, 1971." Preceding votes are recorded on pages 115–63. The threat by English, that this might not be the final word on interstate apportionment, is reported in R. W. Apple, Jr., "Democrats Reform Rules on Convention Delegates," *New York Times*, February 20, 1971, pp. 1 and 12

15. Democratic National Committee, "Transcript of Proceedings, February 19, 1971," pp. 168–69.

16. These institutions themselves are more thoroughly defined, and the impact of the guidelines on their fate is more completely elucidated, in chap. 7, "The Meaning of the Mandate: Formal Rules and Practical Effects."

17. This clause was officially presented in the section on "Legal Status of the Guidelines" in Commission on Party Structure and Delegate Selection, *Mandate for Reform* (Washington, D.C.: Democratic National Committee, 1970), p. 36.

18. Joseph A. Califano, Jr., *A Presidential Nation* (New York: Norton, 1975), pp. 147–48.

19. This impact was evident within twenty-four hours of the speech itself. For the critical response and some complaints from other nomination hopefuls, see David E. Rosenbaum, "Muskie's 'Stature' Called Factor Behind TV Reply," *New York Times,* November 4, 1970, p. 22.

20. R. W. Apple, Jr., "The Democrats Reform Rules on Convention Delegates," *New York Times,* February 20, 1971, p. 12. Most major newspapers did cover the National Committee meeting. Most, accordingly, did not fail to acknowledge this chapter in reform politics, although many centered almost exclusively on the fight over interstate apportionment. Other extended accounts include William Chapman, "Democrats Vote Convention Reforms," *Washington Post,* February 20, 1971, p. A5; Jules Witcover, "Democrats OK Plan for Convention Delegates," *Los Angeles Times,* February 20, 1971, p. A5; Loye Miller, Jr., "Democrats Seek to be More Democratic," *Philadelphia Inquirer,* February 20, 1971, pp. 1 and 3.

21. Steve Reinhardt, a committed reformer who had begun this meeting with a printed statement criticizing O'Brien's attitude toward reform, did not really differ from Stewart in his analysis:

> When the DNC finally came to consider them formally in early 1971, the only change they made was to add DNC members to the delegations. We couldn't believe it at the time. Afterwards, now, I believe that it happened for a number of reasons. Most reformers wanted the rules; most moderates, including O'Brien, didn't believe that they would mean much. O'Brien very much wanted to avoid the kind of bloodletting which characterized 1968, and he was sure that many reformers were ready for this again, so he talked to the more intelligent conservatives. The smart conservatives are open to argument, and the dumber ones are disciplined. He convinced them that not much would change, so they went along. Also, I don't think you should underestimate the tremendous symbolic attraction of reform.

Chapter 15

1. The Pennsylvania case, where a local reform commission—the second such body since 1968—simply ceased to meet after the governor and the state chairman became serious about party reform, was as good an example as any.

2. The animus behind this view arose from a fear that an old order might indeed

be passing—and from a perception of the ties between state size, large and small; state party structure, organized and volunteer; state receptivity to national exhortations for reform; and state contribution to the Democratic vote for president. The suspicion was clear: Small states, volunteer parties, responsiveness to reform, and lack of a Democratic vote all went together; so did large states, organized parties, hostility to reform, and Democratic support at the polls.

Neither Barr nor those who shared his implicit perception were likely to resort to statistical presentations to unpack their beliefs. The varying inclination to that sort of argument was, after all, one of the defining social differences between committed party regulars and committed party reformers. Yet had these regulars possessed the motivation, there were indeed statistics to support their view. Or at least, organized parties, those most likely to resist reform, were the usual home of the Democratic electoral vote. (See below.) No one collected these numbers, however, and statistical arguments continued to be the province of the other side.

Over- and Underrepresentation of:

	Volunteer Parties	Organized Parties
In the Democratic Electoral Vote – 1968	(26%)	(74%)
In the Democratic Electoral Vote – 1960	(27%)	(73%)
Within the General Population	(42%)	(58%)
On the Democratic National Committee	(51%)	(49%)

3. "Democrats Warned of '72 Seating Fights," *New York Times*, May 30, 1971, p. 33.

4. Examples of both tendencies by the news weeklies, of the tendency to cover reform only as an afterward to something else or only in conjunction with coverage of the National Committee, include "Ed Muskie—And the Pack," *Newsweek*, November 16, 1970, pp. 33–37; and "Political Notes: Unconventional Reform," *Time*, March 1, 1971, p. 12. The clearest exception among reporters generally was R. W. Apple, Jr., who not only followed the specific events in reform politics for their own sake—albeit still at the *national* level—but even recapitulated on occasion, as with "Democrats: 'Trauma' of 1968 Curbs Role of Leaders and Bosses," *New York Times*, February 21, 1971, p. 2. A rare exception to the overwhelming tendency of national media to focus on national events was Paul R. Wieck, "Defying the Bosses in Illinois and Texas," *New Republic*, March 1, 1971, p. 12.

5. Andrew J. Glass and Jonathan Cottin, "Democratic Reform Drive Falters as Spotlight Shifts to Presidential Race," *National Journal*, June 19, 1971, p. 1293.

6. Ibid.

7. Ibid, p. 1300.

8. Ken Bode, "Turning Sour: Democratic Party Reform," *The New Republic,* July 10, 1971, pp. 19–20.

9. Ibid., p. 23.

10. R. W. Apple, Jr., "Democrats Press '72 Guidelines," *New York Times,* July 17, 1971, p. 24.

11. In this, Apple was almost prescient, for the tensions which he observed between the majority of participatory guidelines and those few which attempted to mandate a certain result would eventually produce a quiet but dramatic battle over guideline interpretation, one with far-reaching consequences for the impact of party reform:

> Washington, July 26—The Democratic Party's reform movement, which grew out of the divisive and uproarious 1968 convention in Chicago, may yet succeed in averting similar hostilities in 1972. Or, ironically, it may create new tensions.
>
> . . . [A]lthough many professionals resented the reforms, they were approved by the national committee. Slowly, however, some of the professionals have concluded that the guidelines in some cases push them toward contradictory goals.
>
> Maximum public participation is called for on the one hand, for example, while on the other, state parties are told that their convention delegations must include blacks, women, and young people in rough proportions to their numbers in the electorate. If women run for delegate in primaries and lose to men, can the state party be said to have defied the reform guidelines?

R. W. Apple, Jr., "Reform of Democrats," *New York Times,* July 27, 1971, p. 20.

12. Apple, "Reform of Democrats."

13. Andrew J. Glass, Jr., "Are the Democrats Serious About Reform?" *The Progressive,* October 1971, p. 14.

14. Ibid., p. 16.

15. Donald M. Fraser, "A Communication," *The New Republic,* August 21 and 28, 1971, p. 31.

16. Marvin L. Madeson, "Correspondence: Democratic Party Reform," *The New Republic,* October 2, 1971, p. 32.

17. Bode to Madeson, September 14, 1971, private papers of Kenneth A. Bode.

18. Ranney to Nelson, September 16, 1971; Presidential Libraries, National Archives, Washington D.C., p. 1.

19. Austin Ranney, "The People's Forum: Recommends Democratic Reform," *The Progressive,* November 1971, p. 48.

20. These statistics were drawn from Commission Chairman Donald Fraser and Staff to Commission on Party Structure and Delegate Selection of the Democratic National Committee, memorandum, "A Report," July 16, 1971; Presidential Libraries, National Archives, Washington, D.C.

21. Apple, "Reform of Democrats."

22. Such norms are examined explicitly, both in prescription and in practice, in Michael J. Robinson and Margaret A. Sheehan, *Over the Wire and on TV: CBS and UPI in Campaign '80* (New York: Russell Sage Foundation, 1983).

23. A marketing survey of subscribers to *The New Republic,* conducted in 1981, gave detail to these impressions and confirmed them as a continuing phenomenon.

In social background, for example, 85 percent of subscribers held a college degree, and 71 percent were in professional or managerial occupations, a statistic which understates the white-collar character of this readership. In politics, by the same token, over 80 percent of those surveyed claimed to have undertaken explicitly political activities during the previous year. (Mark Clements Research, Inc., "New Republic Subscriber Survey," April, 1981, tables 52, 57, and 15, respectively).

24. Easily the most comprehensive source on Common Cause, though it has, unfortunately, remained in manuscript form, is Andrew J. McFarland's "Common Cause: The Reform Machine."

25. Richard Halloran, "Vote Drive Begun by Common Cause," *New York Times*, February 9, 1971, p. 9.

26. The Voting Rights Project would not only remain involved with the drive to secure full implementation; it would also attempt to stimulate efforts by members of Common Cause to take full advantage of these newly participatory rules. See, for example, the series of "Time to Act" bulletins developed for each of the states in 1972 and issued under the signature of John Gardner himself. Along the way, Anne Wexler would join the special units of several other organizations with parallel goals—the Convention Task Force of Americans for Democratic Action, the Delegate Selection Task Force of the National Women's Political Caucus—and would thus serve as an additional, personal link among these new reform units.

27. A short biography from the period is Richard L. Madden, "Freshman Lowenstein Is Unconventional Member of Congress," *New York Times*, October 19, 1969, p. 77. Ascension to the top spot at ADA is covered in "Lowenstein Named A.D.A. Chairman," *New York Times*, May 2, 1971, p. 47.

28. Dana Adams Schmidt, "A.D.A. to Oversee Conventions in '72 for Fair Process," *New York Times*, June 20, 1971, p. 23.

29. Americans for Democratic Action, "Minutes, ADA 1972 Convention Task Force Meeting," July 7, 1971; private papers of Kenneth A. Bode.

30. Congressman Donald M. Fraser, Chairman, Commission on Party Structure and Delegate Selection, press release, untitled, June 14, 1971; Presidential Libraries, National Archives, Washington, D.C.

31. Commission on Party Structure and Delegate Selection, "Agenda for Executive Committee Luncheon," June 20, 1971; Presidential Libraries, National Archives, Washington, D.C.

32. Fraser to State Chairmen, June 29, 1971; Presidential Libraries, National Archives, Washington, D.C., pp. 1–2.

33. Figure 15.1 was developed from Commission Chairman Donald Fraser and Staff to Commission on Party Structure and Delegate Selection of the Democratic National Committee, memorandum, "A Report," July 16, 1971; Presidential Libraries, National Archives, Washington, D.C.

34. O'Brien to Commission Members, July 15, 1971, Presidential Libraries, National Archives, Washington, D.C. O'Brien also took the opportunity to respond to the charge that he was "starving out" reform:

> While we have limited resources with which to work, the Democratic National Committee to date has expanded over $292,000 in direct support of the two reform Commissions established by the Convention. This is only one measure of how important we believe these efforts to be.

35. Commission on Party Structure and Delegate Selection, "Agenda for Meet-

ing," July 16, 1971, with appended roster of attendees; Presidential Libraries, National Archives, Washington, D.C.

36. Kenneth A. Bode, resolution, "Commission Policy on Challenges to Delegations," July 16, 1971; private papers of Kenneth A. Bode.

37. Commission on Party Structure and Delegate Selection, resolution, "Commission Policy on Challenges to Delegations," July 16, 1971; Presidential Libraries, National Archives, Washington, D.C.

38. In carrying out this policy the Commission shall make certain that its actions and involvement in no way abridge the prerogatives and jurisdictions of the Credentials Committee and are wholly consistent with the credentials certification process as provided in the Preliminary Call to the 1972 Convention. Such involvement will also be contingent upon approval by the Commission.

Commission on Party Structure and Delegate Selection, resolution, "Commission Policy on Litigation Involving Guidelines," July 16, 1971; Presidential Libraries, National Archives, Washington, D.C.

39. Commission on Party Structure and Delegate Selection, resolution, "Resolution on National Committee Action," July 16, 1971; Presidential Libraries, National Archives, Washington, D.C.

40. The text of this resolution is no longer available either from the files of the National Archives or from the private papers of its author, but Segal recalls the 40 percent figure quite clearly, and others present at the meeting recall addressing the resolution.

41. Americans for Democratic Action, "Minutes, ADA 1972 Convention Task Force Meeting," July 7, 1971, p. 4.

42. Commission on Party Structure and Delegate Selection, "Commission Statement on 'All Feasible Efforts,'" July 16, 1971; Presidential Libraries, National Archives, Washington, D.C., pp. 2–3.

43. Fraser to O'Brien, July 20, 1971; Presidential Libraries, National Archives, Washington, D.C., p. 1.

44. Donald M. Fraser, Commission Chairman, to State Democratic Party Chairmen Where Legislation Is Required to Meet the Guidelines, memorandum, "All Feasible Efforts," August 9, 1971; Presidential Libraries, National Archives, Washington, D.C., pp. 1–2.

Chapter 16

1. Figure 16.1 was developed from Commission on Party Structure and Delegate Selection, "State by State Synopsis," October 12, 1971; and from Commission on Party Structure and Delegate Selection, untitled report, October 14, 1971; Presidential Libraries, National Archives, Washington, D.C.

2. Even after the October meeting on the Final Call, Eli Segal believed that this remained the crucial question in reform politics:

Procedural changes often alter the patterns of power, but more often they merely force the people involved to use the power that they have. The new rituals can be followed and the old people still favored, but not without plenty of jockeying and stiff-arming in the wings.

Eli Segal, "O'Brien vs. Hughes: Inside the Squeeze on Party Reform," *Washington Monthly,* December 1971, p. 55.

George Mitchell, who eventually worked actively for Harold Hughes, heard the same general possibility being discussed on the other side: "Larry was saying to Barkan, I heard, that the rules will be in, but things will be much the same."

3. The final meeting of the Rules Commission took place on July 30, 1971. Tim O'Brien, "Democrats Finish Efforts on Reform," *Washington Post,* July 31, 1971, p. A4; Warren Weaver, Jr., "Democrats Vote Rule on Loyalty," *New York Times,* July 31, 1971, p. 12.

4. R. W. Apple, Jr., "Hughes Quits as Presidential Aspirant," *New York Times,* July 16, 1971, p. 9.

5. Eli Segal to Senator, memorandum, "Chairmanship of Credentials Committee," September 14, 1971; private papers of Eli J. Segal.

6. A short biographical sketch is "Credentials Chairman: Patricia Roberts Harris," *New York Times,* October 14, 1971, p. 25.

7. "Democrats: Round 1 to the Regulars," *Time,* October 25, 1971, p. 13.

8. Eli Segal, "O'Brien vs. Hughes," p. 48.

9. The notion did resurface one more time, on Tuesday, October 12, the day of the Executive Committee meeting, when Coretta Scott King, widow of Dr. Martin Luther King, Jr., publicly wired Larry O'Brien, Ed Muskie, and Hubert Humphrey to place Westwood's suggestion directly before them. King to O'Brien, Muskie, and Humphrey, telegram, October 12, 1971; private papers of Eli J. Segal.

10. R. W. Apple, Jr., "Muskie May Back Reform Bloc in Key Preconvention Dispute," *New York Times,* October 9, 1971, p. 13.

11. R. W. Apple, Jr., "Struggle for Democratic Credentials Post is Tight," *New York Times,* October 12, 1971, p. 26.

12. The endorsement from Harris is contained in Apple, "Muskie May Back Reform Bloc in Key Preconvention Dispute," p. 13. The endorsement from McCarthy is in William Greider, "Sen. Hughes Hopes for Long-Shot Win in Democratic Test," *Washington Post,* October 12, 1971, p. A2.

13. McGovern's standing with Democratic voters is included in "Kennedy and Muskie Share Lead in a Gallup Survey of Democrats," *New York Times,* August 1, 1971, p. 28.

14. The role of Kennedy is mentioned in R. W. Apple, Jr., "Democrats Back Mrs. Harris, 9–3," *New York Times,* October 13, 1971, p. 23; and earlier in Apple, "Muskie May Back Reform Bloc," p. 13.

15. Apple, "Muskie May Back Reform Bloc."

16. R. W. Apple, Jr., "Democratic Reformers and Old Guard Split Over Filling '72 Convention Post," *New York Times,* October 8, 1971, p. 22.

17. Apple, "Muskie May Back Reform Bloc in Key Preconvention Dispute," p. 1.

18. Apple, "Struggle for Democratic Credentials Post."

19. Ibid.

20. These projections are contained in Greider, "Sen. Hughes Hopes for Long-Shot"; Apple, "Democrats Back Mrs. Harris, 9–3"; and William Chapman, "O'Brien Wins First Round in Party Fight," *Washington Post,* October 13, 1971, p. A10.

21. Apple, "Democratic Reformers and Old Guard Split Over Filling '72 Convention Post," p. 22.

22. Executive Committee of the Democratic National Committee, "Transcript of Proceedings, October 12, 1971," Presidential Libraries, National Archives, Washington, D.C., pp. 67–68.

23. Ibid., pp. 70–71.

24. Ibid., pp. 71–72.

25. Ibid., p. 88. Voting for Harris were Arvey of Illinois; Barr of Pennsylvania; Broderick of Maine, as a proxy for Evers of Mississippi, the member at large; Brown of Louisiana; Joseph, the vice chairman; O'Brien, the chairman; Owens of Alabama; Rosenthal of Connecticut; Strauss, the national treasurer, who was otherwise proxied to Banks of Colorado for most of the meeting. Voting for Hughes were Jeffrey of Michigan; Reinhardt of California; and Westwood of Utah.

26. Apple, "Democrats Back Mrs. Harris."

27. See, for example, Chapman, "O'Brien Wins First Round in Party Fight."

28. The quotation from Humphrey is in "Democrats: Round 1 to the Regulars"; the quotation from Muskie is in R. W. Apple, Jr., "Mrs. Harris Wins Democratic Post," *New York Times,* October 14, 1971, p. 25.

29. Judith H. Parris, *The Convention Problem: Issues in Reform of Presidential Nominating Procedures* (Washington, D.C.: Brookings Institution, 1972), pp. 88–89 and 178–79.

30. Democratic National Committee, "Transcript of Proceedings, October 13, 1971"; Presidential Libraries, National Archives, Washington, D.C., pp. 50–68.

31. Ibid., p. 79.

32. Ibid., p. 83.

33. Ibid.

34. Commission on Party Structure and Delegate Selection, Congressman Donald M. Fraser, Chairman to State Democratic Party Leaders, memorandum, "Guidelines A–1 and A–2," October 18, 1971; Presidential Libraries, National Archives, Washington, D.C.

35. Democratic National Committee, "Transcript of Proceedings," p. 87.

36. Ibid., pp. 88–89.

37. Ibid., p. 97.

38. Ibid., pp. 113–30.

39. Of the members in attendance from volunteer-party states 72 percent went for the Joseph amendment (excising the Powers amendment), while of the members from organized-party states 60 percent did so. More revealing was the division between representatives from states with approved party rules versus those from states featuring delay or inaction. Of those whose states were in potential conformity 78 percent endorsed the Joseph amendment; of those without even potential conformity 56 percent *opposed* that amendment. The difference, however, was not sufficient to defeat the proposal.

40. Democratic National Committee, "Transcript of Proceedings," p. 131–32.

41. At the individual level, the actual number of votes shifted from their normal

moorings by all this preballot activity was perhaps 6, out of 110. One Hughes vote had been driven over to Harris in Alaska, allegedly because of COPE pressure there. One Harris vote had gone to Hughes in Massachusetts, through some arm-twisting by Teddy Kennedy. One evident Harris loyalist had felt pressed to abstain in Nevada. Another Harris vote had been converted to an abstention in New Jersey, when a proxy holder contradicted the wishes of the official member. Two Hughes partisans ended by abstaining, against their announced bill, in North Dakota. These six votes, of course, netted out to zero.

42. Anne Wexler, one of the most active lobbyists for Harold Hughes, also agreed: "I felt that Pat Harris was a good choice, but it became a fight between liberals and conservatives, and the candidates got pulled in. . . . It became a symbolic thing, but it was the wrong battle."

43. Apple, "Mrs. Harris Wins Democratic Post," p. 1; and "Mrs. Harris Vows to Fight Mistrust," *New York Times*, October 15, 1971, p. 19; "All in the Family," *Newsweek*, October 25, 1971, p. 49.

44. The migration of Charles Evers is chronicled, in passing, in Apple, "Democrats Back Mrs. Harris," and "Mrs. Harris Wins Democratic Post."

Chapter 17

1. The most clear-cut of these attempts were a pair of court cases aimed at overturning the national formula for delegate apportionment. The first was brought by Lester G. Maddox, governor of Georgia, in conjunction with assorted Georgia state officials and on behalf of the southern states generally. It was resolved in October of 1971, when the Supreme Court refused an appeal from lower court decisions against the suit (92 S. Ct. 109). The second was brought by Kenneth A. Bode, in conjunction with the National Committee members for California and New York and on behalf of the larger states generally. It was resolved three months later, in January of 1972, when the Supreme Court again refused to hear an appeal from an unfriendly decision (92 S. Ct. 684).

2. Commission on Party Structure and Delegate Selection, *Mandate for Reform* (Washington, D.C.: Democratic National Committee, 1970), p. 40.

3. Ibid.

4. Eileen Shanahan, "Women Organize for Political Power," *New York Times*, July 11, 1971, pp. 1 and 22; Tim O'Brien, "Women Organize for More Power," *Washington Post*, July 11, 1971, pp. A1 and A10.

5. National Women's Political Caucus, "Minutes—National Policy Council Meeting," September 10–11, 1971; files of the National Women's Political Caucus, Washington, D.C.

6. National Women's Political Caucus, "Minutes," October 22–23, 1971; files of the National Women's Political Caucus, Washington, D.C.

7. The conference, in turn, had put her advice in an official resolution:
Reform of existing politics of the Democratic and Republican parties, "which have excluded women." Specifically, the women demand that females "comprise 50 percent of the delegates to both parties' 1972 national

conventions and that women be represented on every convention committee and party committee."
Tim O'Brien, "Women's Caucus Seeks U.S. Ban on Sex Bias," *Washington Post,* July 13, 1971, p. A2.

8.   National Women's Political Caucus, "Minutes," October 22–23, 1971, p. 4.

9.   Casey to National Women's Political Caucus, memorandum, "Compliance Status of State Parties," October 21, 1971, Presidential Libraries, National Archives, Washington, D.C.

10.   The legal memorandum itself has survived neither in the files of the National Women's Political Caucus nor in those of the National Archives. A reprise on the memorandum, however, is in Dutton to Fraser, November 1, 1971, Presidential Libraries, National Archives, Washington, D.C.

11.   Abzug, (Fannie Lou) Hamer, (Liz) Carpenter, and (Mildred) Jeffrey to O'Brien, November 8, 1971, private papers of Kenneth A. Bode.

12.   Ibid.

13.   Eileen Shanahan, "Caucus to Seek Equal Number of Women Convention Delegates," *New York Times,* November 10, 1971, p. 36.

14.   O'Brien to Abzug, Hamer, Carpenter, and Jeffrey, November 8, 1971; Presidential Libraries, National Archives, Washington, D.C.

15.   Eileen Shanahan, "Women Organize for Political Power," p. 22.

16.   National Women's Political Caucus, "Minutes," September 10–11, 1971, p. 3.

17.   Phyllis N. Segal, "Women and Political Parties: The Legal Dimensions of Discrimination," 117 *Congressional Record* 895, April 6, 1971, Extension of Remarks by Rep. Griffiths, pp. E2773–E77.

18.   John Conyers (D-Mich.), Charles Diggs (D-Mich.), Robert Nix (D-Penna.), and William Dawson (D-Ill.) had all been delegates. Augustus Hawkins (D-Calif.) was slated as a delegate, but had failed to be elected when the stand-in slate for Hubert Humphrey was defeated in the California primary. Only Adam Clayton Powell (D-N.Y.) had not been slated. *Congressional Quarterly's Guide to Congress* 2nd ed., [Washington, D.C.: Congressional Quarterly, 1976], pp. 527–28 and 617–18.

19.   Thomas A. Johnson, "Black Caucus Calls National Political Convention," *New York Times,* November 21, 1971, p. 68.

20.   Anthony Ripley, "First Woman President Heads National Student Association," *New York Times,* August 29, 1971, p. 48.

21.   Ibid.

22.   Foremost among these efforts was the attempt to reinterpret national requirements for delegate allocation among, and potentially within, the states. The key case, *Bode* v. *National Democratic Party,* actually bore his name. See note 1 above.

23.   Americans For Democratic Action, "Minutes, ADA 1971 Convention Task Force Meeting, July 7, 1971," private papers of Kenneth A. Bode.

24.   These assignments are contained in Ken Bode, Co-Chairman to Members of ADA Convention Task Force, memorandum, "Task Force Assignments," October 19, 1971; private papers of Kenneth A. Bode.

25.   ADA 1972 Convention Task Force, "Minutes, November 8, 1971," private papers of Kenneth A. Bode.

26.   Enid Nemy, "Betty Friedan Says a Woman Should Run Against Celler," *New*

York Times, August 26, 1971, p. 42; also, "Friends of The Caucus," *Washington Post,* August 26, 1971, p. C2.

27. Compare, for example, the assertion by Dutton that "a majority cannot be made into a minority in a popularly based political process without violating a very fundamental concept" with the translation by Meissner as "a majority cannot be made a minority without violating a fundamental and unmistakable value in a popularly based political system," Dutton to Fraser, November 1, 1971, p. 1.; and Abzug el al. to O'Brien, November 8, 1971, pp. 1–2; respectively.

28. Dutton to Fraser, November 1, 1971.

29. Democratic National Committee, "Transcript of Proceedings, October 13, 1971;" Presidential Libraries, National Archives, Washington, D.C., p. 84.

30. Commission on Party Structure and Delegate Selection, Congressman Donald M. Fraser, Chairman to State Democratic Party Leaders, memorandum, "Guidelines A–1 and A–2," October 18, 1971, Presidential Libraries, National Archives, Washington, D.C., p. 2.

31. Ibid.

32. R. W. Apple, Jr., "Democratic Reformers and Old Guard Split Over Filling '72 Convention Post," *New York Times,* October 8, 1971, p. 22; and "Democrats: Round I to the Regulars," *Time,* October 28, 1971, p. 13.

33. "Democrats: Round I," p. 13; and R. W. Apple, Jr., "Mrs. Harris Vows to Fight Mistrust," *New York Times,* October 15, 1971, p. 19.

34. R. W. Apple, Jr., "Mrs. Harris Wins Democratic Post," *New York Times,* October 14, 1971, p. 25.

35. Eli Segal, "O'Brien vs. Hughes: Inside the Squeeze on Party Reform," *Washington Monthly,* December 1971, pp. 49–50.

36. National Women's Political Caucus, "Minutes," October 22–23, 1971, p. 6.

37. William Chapman, "Democratic Reform Vowed by Mrs. Harris," *Washington Post,* October 15, 1971, p. 2.

38. *Mandate for Reform,* p. 28.

39. R. W. Apple, Jr., "Radical Reshaping of Democratic Party Is Urged by Heads of 2 Reform Panels," *New York Times,* March 26, 1972, p. 56; David S. Broder, "The Democratic Party," *Washington Post,* May 16, 1972, p. A19; "Democratic Reform Panels to Conduct Joint Study," *New York Times,* November 14, 1971, p. 66.

40. Four months later, when the National Welfare Rights Organization pressed O'Brien about demographic guarantees for the poor, he responded in precisely this way, by emphasizing the supremacy of participation in the reform canon:

> So that the various presidential candidates may be aware of the NWRO's interest in becoming involved in the presidential nominating process of our party, I am providing a copy of your letter to each of them, as well as to every State Democratic Party chairman. As you know, however, it is vital that everyone understand that since virtually all delegates to the 1972 Democratic National Convention must be elected by either a primary or open convention process, that it is necessary that they run as candidates for delegate. That is one of the basic thrusts of the reform Guidelines, and one of the principal purposes of the state brochures is to inform people, as widely as possible, how the process works.

O'Brien to (George) Wiley, Executive Director, National Welfare Rights Organization, February 1, 1972; Presidential Libraries, National Archives, Washington, D.C., p. 1.

41. Rumors about O'Brien's interest in a vice-presidential nomination were commonplace, both before and during the 1972 Convention. Welsh was reporting his perceptions before the convention. Vick French, former aid to Chairman Harris and subsequent principal in the McGovern campaign, reported his perceptions at the convention itself: "McGovern was consciously using O'Brien's interest in being V.P. Or if McGovern wasn't, the McGovern *campaign* certainly was. We dangled that quite deliberately in order to try to influence O'Brien's rulings at the Convention."

42. Fraser to O'Brien, November 29, 1971, Presidential Libraries, National Archives, Washington, D.C., pp. 1–2.

43. "Party Aides Widen Commitment on Women Delegates Next Year," *New York Times*, December 4, 1971, p. 18.

44. National Women's Political Caucus, "Minutes," December 4–5, 1971; files of the National Women's Political Caucus, Washington, D.C., p. 1.

45. Democratic National Committee, Lawrence F. O'Brien, National Chairman to Democratic State Chairmen, Democratic Vice Chairmen, Members of the Democratic National Committee, Democratic Governors, memorandum, "Delegate Selection Guidelines and State Party Action," December 8, 1971, Presidential Libraries, National Archives, Washington, D.C., pp. 1–2.

46. In the immediate aftermath of the victory of the Women's Caucus on Guidelines A–1 and A–2, a formal representation of the alleged practical relationship among these three demographic groups—women, youth, and minorities—did appear. On January 7, 1972, with full-page ads in ten major newspapers under the leading question "WHO'S GOING TO CHOOSE OUR NEXT PRESIDENT? A FEW PARTY BOSSES, OR WE, THE PEOPLE?", Stewart R. Mott, millionaire philanthropist, launched "People Politics," a holding company of the National Youth Caucus, the National Black Caucus, and Women's Education for Delegate Selection, with a special subvention to the Center for Political Reform. Mott's own summary of the fate of these organizations—substantial impact for WEDS, marginal impact for NYC, little or no impact for NBC—is as good as any:

> I saw that a young, black, and female convention would be the key to whomever I preferred. I became very impressed with Ken Bode's grasp of the situation. I had met Bode at a lunch hosted by Bronfman. Marty Peretz had financed much of his operation, but he withdrew, and I then had long talks with Bode. I bankrolled the whole thing from then on.
>
> I also saw the need for a youth caucus, a black caucus, and a women's caucus. We did all of this through the Methodist Church. I made a substantial grant to the Methodist Church, which was divided up among the black, women's, and youth groups.
>
> The best organized and most functional among these was WEDS. The black group never got organized. The director wanted a fully cushioned payroll, but I wouldn't buy that. The youth groups did some for very little money. They were fighting the O'Brien quota figure, which was based on total population.

47. The establishment of equal division for women was contained in the new charter for the Democratic party in Article III. Section 3 and Article X. Section 6, of the

Charter and the By-Laws of the Democratic Party of the United States (Washington: Democratic National Committee, undated), pp.5 and 10, respectively. The abolition of demographic quotas for blacks at the National Convention came about through the rules of delegate selection for 1976, in Section 18, Affirmative Action, of Commission on Delegate Selection and Party Structure, *Democrats All* (Washington, D.C.: Democratic National Committee, 1973), pp. 21–22.

Chapter 18

1.   The first part of Figure 18.1 was developed from Commission on Party Structure and Delegate Selection, "Report on Status of State Parties," December 15, 1971, the second part from Commission on Party Structure and Delegate Selection, untitled summary, March 9, 1972. Presidential Libraries, National Archives, Washington, D.C.

2.   For a summary of the extent of the problem, see Nelson to O'Brien, memorandum, "Louisiana Action on Guidelines," December 22, 1971; Presidential Libraries, National Archives, Washington, D.C. By March 9, the problem had nevertheless been resolved, see Commission on Party Structure and Delegate Selection, untitled summary, March 9, 1972.

3.   These figures were derived from Commission on Party Structure and Delegate Selection, "Status of the States in Meeting Guidelines," April 27, 1972, and from Congressman Donald M. Fraser, Chairman, Commission on Party Structure and Delegate Selection, Democratic National Committee, untitled press release, April 28, 1972. Presidential Libraries, National Archives, Washington, D.C.

4.   Guideline B–6 (Adequate Representation of Minority Views on Presidential Candidates at Each Stage in the Delegate Selection Process) in Commission on Party Structure and Delegate Selection, *Mandate for Reform* (Washington, D.C.: Democratic National Committee, 1970), pp. 44–45.

5.   Guideline B–6 in Commission on Party Structure and Delegate Selection, "Model of Party Rules," undated, Presidential Libraries, National Archives, Washington, D.C., pp. 14–17.

6.   Baum to McGovern, September 8, 1969, and Baum to McGovern, November 17, 1969, Presidential Libraries, National Archives, Washington, D.C.

7.   The appointment came in "Minutes of the Meeting of the State Democratic Executive Committee, Austin, Texas, June 20, 1970," pp. 2–3; membership was listed in "Minutes of the Organizational Meeting of the Committee to Study the Guidelines of the Commission on Party Structure and Delegate Selection—Texas," p. 1; Presidential Libraries, National Archives, Washington, D.C.

8.   Part of the research by Davis is Davis to Nelson, October 19, 1970, and Nelson to Davis, October 28, 1970. The response of the SDEC is in "Minutes of the Meeting of the State Democratic Executive Committee Held in Austin, Texas, January 18, 1971," pp. 2–3; Presidential Libraries, National Archives, Washington, D.C.

9.   The story broke with multiple reports in most major newspapers in Texas. See especially Anne James, "SEC Suit Names Sharp, Others; Alleges Improper Stock Dealings," *Houston Post*, January 19, 1971, pp. 1 and 2, along with three front-page pieces

the next day. See also Tom Johnson, "Dr. Baum Tells of Stock Profits," *Dallas Morning News*, January 20, 1971, p. 1; and John Geddie, "Governor Says His Partner Handled Stock Transaction," *Dallas Morning News*, January 29, 1971, p. 5.

10.   A useful and inclusive summary, stretching all the way to the Jesuits and the astronauts, is Martin Waldron, "The Frank Sharp Affair: Vast Scandal Stuns Democrats in Texas," *New York Times*, August 1, 1971, p. 50.

11.   Because the SDEC was not meeting, there was no formal record of the appointment of this new Rules Committee, although it was officially in existence by July 19, when Baum wrote to Fraser and mentioned it in passing. Baum to Fraser, July 19, 1971; Presidential Libraries, National Archives, Washington, D.C.

12.   The first draft of what became the "Anderson Rules" was William R. Anderson, Jr., "Rules of the Democratic Party of Texas," private papers of Carrin M. Patman. This draft went to Patman and Davis on August 24. Anderson to Patman and Anderson to Davis, August 24, 1971; Presidential Libraries, National Archives, Washington, D.C.

13.   Useful reports include Sam Kinch, Jr., "Dr. Baum Resigns as State Democratic Chairman," *Dallas Morning News*, October 12, 1971, p. A1; Stewart Davis, "SDEC Panel Selects Orr Party Head," *Dallas Morning News*, October 19, 1971, p. 1; Sam Kinch, Jr., "White Claims Party Job," *Dallas Morning News*, October 20, 1971, p. 1A; Tom Johnson, "Democrats Elect Orr as Chairman," *Dallas Morning News*, October 21, 1971, p. 1A. Baum's resignation was given on October 7, but did not become public until October 11, thereby explaining the discrepancy in dates between actual resignation and published reports.

14.   Orr went into the position in full awareness of the costs imposed by his strategy:

> I challenged Smith; my people challenged his recommendation. That's not an easy thing. Then after you win, you don't have the support of the Governor, like you'd like to have. After Connally went off the scene, we didn't have a state leader that was interested, that was strong.

15.   (Robert S.) Strauss to (Mrs. Ralph S.) O'Connor, October 19, 1971; Presidential Libraries, National Archives, Washington, D.C.

16.   This rules package, the essence of the "Anderson Rules" for the duration of reform politicking, was SDEC Subcommittee on Rules, "Rules of the Democratic Party of Texas," November 11, 1971; private papers of Carrin M. Patman. The expansion of the Subcommittee on Rules; in response, was contained in Orr to Anderson, November 20, 1971, as cited in George Kuempel, "Orr Accused of Blocking Party Reform," *Austin American*, December 12, 1971, pp. I and 6A.

17.   Nelson to Patman, November 29, 1971; Presidential Libraries, National Archives, Washington, D.C.

18.   McGovern to Baum, February 27, 1970, and attached "Analysis of the Delegate Selection Process," Presidential Libraries, National Archives, Washington, D.C.

19.   Fraser to Patman, telegram, December 1, 1971; private papers of Carrin M. Patman.

20.   Patman to Anderson, December 3, 1971, for release December 5, 1971; private papers of Carrin M. Patman.

21.   For example, Bo Byers, "Orr in Washington for Talk with Texas Democrats," *Houston Chronicle*, December 15, 1971, p. 4.

22. Sam Kinch, Jr., "Democratic Rule Reformers Warned Challenges Possible," *Dallas Morning News*, January 13, 1972, p. 24a; Art Wiese, "Democrats Spar Over Reform Rules," *Houston Post*, January 13, 1972, p. 16A.

23. "Analysis of All Specific Recommendations Contained in the Transcript of Will Davis' Testimony at the Public Hearing on Democratic Party Rules, January 12, 1972, in Austin, Texas," private papers of Carrin M. Patman.

24. Their rules package, the core of what became the "Brunson rules," was John S. Brunson and Robert W. Smith, "Rules of the Democratic Party of Texas," undated but completed somewhere between January 12 and January 24, 1972; private papers of Carrin M. Patman.

25. Fraser to Brunson and Smith, January 26, 1972; Presidential Libraries, National Archives, Washington, D.C.

26. Fraser to Patman and (Governor Preston) Smith, telegram, January 28, 1972; private papers of Carrin M. Patman.

27. Congressman Donald M. Fraser, Chairman, Commission on Party Structure and Delegate Selection, press release, untitled, February 10, 1972, pp. 1–2; Presidential Libraries, National Archives, Washington, D.C.

28. Press discussions of this possibility surfaced after Patman had released her telegram from Fraser, saying that the Anderson rules complied, and as Orr was preparing to leave for Washington, to consult the Texas congressional delegation. See, for example, Bo Byers, "Orr in Washington to Talk with Texas Democrats," and Patricia Martinets, "New Demo Rules Revealed Amid Dissent," *Fort Worth Star-Telegram*, December 17, 1971, p. 15A. The topic never disappeared from state political discussion after that.

29. Davis to Nelson, February 23, 1972; Presidential Libraries, National Archives, Washington, D.C.

30. Nelson to Davis, March 3, 1972; Presidential Libraries, National Archives, Washington, D.C., pp. 1–2.

31. Patman was outraged:

> We were bushwhacked. They came up with a draft which no one had seen before, which they didn't even have enough copies of. Corky Smith wrote this draft. I think that Davis may have been behind it.
>
> I went looking for endorsements after the hearing. Preston Smith endorsed, so did [Senator Lloyd] Bentsen, so did [Lieutenant Governor Ben] Barnes. Only [Dolph] Briscoe didn't, and Brunson was one of his men. . . .
>
> Bob Bullock, the Secretary of State, says that Roy Orr cannot legally be both Dallas County Commissioner and Chairman of the SDEC. This was in March of 1972.

32. Nelson to Brunson, March 8, 1972; Presidential Libraries, National Archives, Washington, D.C.

33. Nelson to Brunson, addendum to Patman, March 8, 1972; Presidential Libraries, National Archives, Washington, D.C.

34. Carr, along with W. V. Ballew, Jr., was the architect of the third aspiring reform package in Texas. This was the product of indigenous, militant reformers and went forward as the "Bean Rules," for Woodrow W. Bean of El Paso. Their major external advisor was Ken Bode, at the Center for Political Reform.

35. The Patman packet was "Rules of the Democratic Party of Texas, Made Available Courtesy of Carrin M. Patman, Democratic National Committeewoman for Texas," undated but published in early April, 1972; private papers of Carrin M. Patman. In short order, there was an identical booklet, differing only in that its listed author and publisher was the State Democratic Executive Committee of Texas.

36. Commission on Party Structure and Delegate Selection, "Commission Statement on 'All Feasible Efforts,'" July 16, 1971; Presidential Libraries, National Archives, Washington, D.C.

37. The legal opinion itself does not appear to have survived into the National Archives, but both Nelson and Casey recall its creation—and its utility.

38. The most persistent effort to impose proportionality on Texas, and the one which first alerted California party leaders to the fact that they might not be in compliance with national rules, was launched, not by the commission entourage, but by Ken Bode. Terry S. Utterback, chief aide to Charles T. Manatt, the state chairman, recalled Bode's arrival:

> In late January, Manatt was elected. In early February, Bode came to California, and met with Manatt, myself, Les River, Warschaw, Reinhardt, and some legislative leaders. Bode came out with his buckskin suit, with fringes, with hair down his back. That set everyone's teeth on edge.
>
> This was a three-hour argument with Bode. "We'll challenge your ass," he said. "We'll challenge this. We'll challenge that. Your rules stink." I remember him saying that.
>
> We certainly didn't want any more meetings like that. But Manatt said, "If these guys are going to challenge us and the challenge might be viable, we'd better take another look." After that, we corresponded furiously with Nelson.

39. Even then, the result hung in the balance through the final days of the legislative session, the last session which could possibly change the state primary law. Because many of the California primary provisions were in the state election code, the legislature had to be brought along with the ultimate compromise. But state legislators were not interested in the caucus arrangement, and rank-and-file members would not vote the bill out of committee. It was passed eventually through legislative sleight of hand, on the last day of the session, as an amendment on the floor, bypassing the relevant committees. Even then, even after being slipped through the legislature, its fate hung in the balance for three weeks until Governor Ronald W. Reagan, a Republican, signed the bill.

Conclusion

1. The best known of the contemporary accounts of the full campaign is Theodore H. White, *The Making of the President 1972* (New York: Atheneum, 1973). But see also Ernest R. May and Janet Fraser, eds., *Campaign '72: The Managers Speak* (Cambridge, Mass.: Harvard University Press, 1973); Gary W. Hart, *Right from the Start: A Chronicle of the McGovern Campaign* (New York: Quadrangle Books, 1973);

and Lanny J. Davis, *The Emerging Democratic Majority: Lessons and Legacies from the New Politics* (New York: Stein and Day, 1974), especially pt. 3, "Muskie vs. McGovern: The Fight for Leadership."

2. This argument is elaborated in Byron E. Shafer, "Anti-Party Politics," *The Public Interest* 63 (Spring 1981): 95–110.

3. The three subsequent reform texts, the successors to *Mandate for Reform,* are Commission on Delegate Selection and Party Structure, *Democrats All* (Washington: Democratic National Committee, 1973); Commission on Presidential Nomination and Party Structure, *Openness, Participation and Party Building: Reforms for a Stronger Democratic Party* (Washington: Democratic National Committee, 1978); and *Report of the Commission on Presidential Nomination* (Washington, D.C.: Democratic National Committee, 1982).

4. Perhaps the leading critical view by a professional analyst is E. E. Schattschneider, *Party Government* (New York: Holt, 1942); more charitable is Herbert Agar, *The Price of Union* (Boston: Houghton, 1950). The classic of anecdotal accounts, though considerably earlier than these, is William L. Riordan, comp., *Plunkitt of Tammany Hall* (New York: McClure, Phillips, 1905). That the underlying viewpoint did not change substantially over time is suggested by Milton Rakove, *Don't Make No Waves—Don't Back No Losers: An Insider's Analysis of the Daley Machine* (Bloomington: Indiana University Press, 1975).

5. Tables 3–1, 3–2, and 3–3 in James W. Ceaser, *Reforming the Reforms: A Critical Analysis of the Presidential Selection Process* (Cambridge, Mass.: Ballinger, 1982), provide the summary documentation for these institutional developments.

6. A careful and detailed account of reform politics within the Democratic party between 1968 and 1972 is hardly the complete base for an analysis of the impact of reform after implementation, and this caveat becomes more pressing as one moves farther out from reform politicking itself and farther into the character of the resulting practical developments. Yet a full and careful analysis of this reform politics does provide a more secure understanding both of the character of the institutional changes which proceeded from that politics and of the social forces, the groups and individuals, which were coming to prominence in party affairs during this period. If these are added to the more global, and generally acknowledged, developments in presidential politics during the interim, the possibility for useful—or at least thought-provoking—speculations would appear to increase, and this final section is an attempt at such extensions and projections. While it is informed by a historical narrative previously missing from such analysis, it is also elaborated far beyond what the facts of that narrative will directly sustain. These speculations cannot benefit from the density of argument or the preponderance of evidence of the previous eighteen chapters. They must be presented—and addressed—in a very different spirit.

7. The multiplication of presidential primaries is detailed in table 3–1 of Ceaser, *Reforming the Reforms.* The most thorough summary of research on turnout is Lester W. Milbrath and M. L. Goel, *Political Participation: How and Why People Get Involved in Politics,* 2nd ed. (Chicago: Rand McNally, 1977), especially chap. 4, "Political Participation as a Function of Social Position." The California primary of 1972—the winner-take-all primary which sealed the McGovern nomination—was one of the most dramatic cases where differential turnout by social class determined the outcome. See "The Effect of Unrepresentativeness: The 1972 California Presidential

Primary," chap. 4 in James I. Lengle, *Representation and Presidential Primaries: The Democratic Party in the Post-Reform Era* (Westport, Conn.: Greenwood Press, 1981).

8. The independence of nomination campaigns from the official party is now consensual lore among students of the organization of campaigns, but campaign organization itself remains an understudied topic. Useful summary thoughts are contained in Nelson W. Polsby, *Consequences of Party Reform* (New York: Oxford University Press, 1983), especially in pt. 2, "Consequences for Political Parties," p. 72, where the author notes:

> The mounting of a presidential campaign has come more and more to resemble the production of a Broadway show. . . . Rather than depending upon alliances with and commitments from state party organizations or interest groups allied to factions within state party organizations, candidates for the Presidency are increasingly obliged to mount their search for delegates by building their own personal organizations, state by state.

A joint conference of the Democratic and Republican National Committees at Harvard University in December of 1981 produced similar observations from both sides of the partisan aisle. See John F. Bibby, "The Role of Political Parties in the Nomination Process," and Everett Carll Ladd, "The Proper Role of Parties in Presidential Nominee Selection," reprinted in *Commonsense* 4 (No. 2), 21–32 and 33–39, respectively.

9. Early in each presidential year, the Gallup organization does a report on the preferences of county chairmen across the country for each party, and this ordinarily becomes the most systematic information available on official party attitudes. For a prediction about 1972 which heeded these preferences of party officials and which ignored reformed arrangements for delegate selection, see "The Making of a Front Runner," *Newsweek*, January 10, 1972, pp. 13–16, profiling Edmund Muskie. For a set of complex and interrelated predictions about 1976, one which did not credit the preferences of party officials as heavily but which nevertheless dismissed the prospects of Jimmy Carter in a few scattered paragraphs, see Arthur T. Hadley, *The Invisible Primary* (Englewood Cliffs, N.J.: Prentice-Hall, 1976).

10. The various and diverse patterns on the way to a nomination, the mix of candidates and supporters found in presidential selections since 1936, are featured in William R. Keech and Donald R. Matthews, *The Party's Choice* (Washington, D.C.: Brookings Institution, 1976). The most concise and powerful way to summarize the outcomes is Angus Campbell, "A Classification of Presidential Elections," chap. 4 in Angus Campbell et al., *Elections and the Political Order* (New York: Wiley, 1966). A fuller and more integrated analysis, emphasizing the character of the electoral coalitions possible at a given time, is John Kessel, *Presidential Campaign Politics: Coalition Strategies and Citizen Responses* (Homewood, Ill.: Dorsey Press, 1980).

11. A highly suggestive piece in this regard is Linda E. Demkovic, " 'Outsiders' Comfortable on the Inside," *National Journal*, November 25, 1978, pp. 1892–98. The appointment of cabinet secretaries themselves is a less precise indicator of the same trend, but see also Nelson W. Polsby, "Presidential Cabinet Making: Lessons for the Political System," *Political Science Quarterly* 93 (Spring 1978); 15–25. But perhaps the most accessible way to keep track of appointments within this elite stratum is the "People" section at the end of each *National Journal*.

Index

Quiet Revolution provides the first definitive account of this struggle for reform, an account that is at once modern political history and an illuminating analysis of contemporary American politics. Based on candid interviews with numerous key participants and on extensive archival material, this compelling narrative offers the fascination of political maneuvers closely observed, the drama of momentous events unfolding, and the challenge of a new politics newly interpreted.

A preliminary version of this study was awarded the 1980 E. E. Schattschneider Prize of the American Political Science Association.

✳   ✳   ✳

BYRON E. SHAFER is a Resident Scholar at the Russell Sage Foundation.